WEBSTER'S DICTIONARY OF THE ENGLISH LANGUAGE

WEBSTER'S DICTIONARY OF THE ENGLISH LANGUAGE

CREATED IN COOPERATION WITH THE EDITORS OF

MERRIAM-WEBSTER

Dalmatian Press

This 2011 Edition published by arrangement with Federal Street Press, a division of Merriam-Webster, Incorporated

Distributed by: **Dalmatian Press**
118 Seaboard Lane, Franklin, TN 37067
CE11585/1110

ISBN 1-40377-641-9

Printed in Fort Wayne, IN, USA
11 12 13 14 CLI 5 4 3 2 1

Preface

This new dictionary is unique in many respects. While small in size, it contains more than 19,000 words that represent the very core of the language. It is intended to serve as a quick reference for spelling, hyphenation, and meaning of the words in everyday use. Conciseness of presentation necessarily requires special treatment of entries, and this book has a number of special features all its own.

Entry words appear in **boldface type** with raised periods to indicate where they can be hyphenated at the end of a line in writing. Words that begin an entry paragraph are **main entry words** and are followed by definitions or cross-references to related entries.

> **aard·vark** . . . : ant-eating African mammal
> **abroad** . . . **1:** over a wide area **2 :** outside one's country
> **ate** *past of* EAT

Variant spellings of bold words are shown following a comma.

> **blond, blonde** . . . **1 :** fair in complexion

Labels indicating a word's grammatical function in the sentence **(part of speech)** are shown as abbreviations in italics after the bold word.

> **cam·era** *n* **:** box with a lens for taking pictures . . .
> **cam·ou·flage** *vb* **:** hide by disguising . . .
> **can·did** *adj* **1 :** frank **2 :** not posed . . .
> — **can·did·ly** *adv* . . .

Within an entry paragraph, derived words with the same spelling but a different part of speech are represented by a **swung dash** and are provided with their own definitions.

> **di·rect** *vb* **1 :** address **2 :** cause to move or to follow a certain course . . .
> ~ *adj* **1 :** leading to or coming from a point without deviation or interruption . . .

Derived words are run on undefined at the end of the entry when their meanings are self-evident from the definitions preceding. This treatment allows for the saving of space to permit many more words to be entered and at the same time shows word relationships.

> **ex·haust** *vb* **1 :** draw out or develop completely **2 :** use up . . .
> ~ *n* **:** waste steam or gas from an engine . . . — **ex·haus·tion** *n*
> — **ex·haus·tive** *adj*

Main entries with the same spelling but not derived from one another are entered separately, marked with a superscript numeral.

> **¹file** *n* **:** tool for smoothing or sharpening . . .
> **²file** *vb* **1 :** arrange in order **2 :** enter or record officially . . .
> **³file** *n* **:** row of persons or things one behind the other

Plurals of nouns, principal parts of verbs, and comparative and superlative forms of adjectives (and adverbs) are know as **inflected forms.** Those formed by the regular addition of a suffix (such as *-s, -ed, -ing, -er, -est*) are well-known regular formations and are not shown in this dictionary. Inflections formed by an internal change in the spelling of the word (or no change) are shown inside parentheses. For nouns, the forms shown will be plurals (*pl*); for verbs, the forms shown will be past tense (*past*) and past participle (*past part*). The past and past participle are separated by a semicolon. If variant spellings are shown for any inflected form, that spelling is set off by a slash (/).

> **grow** *vb* **grew; grown 1 :** come into existence and develop to maturity
> **knife** *n* **knives :** sharp blade with a handle . . .
> [1]**lie** *vb* **lay; lain 1 :** be in, rest in, or assume a horizontal position . . .
> **moose** *n* **moose :** large heavy-antlered deer
> **prove** *vb* **proved; proved/prov·en 1 :** test by experiment or by a standard . . .

When a particular sense of a word is used in a special way, such as used only in the plural form, that information is indicated after the sense number.

> **re·fresh·ment** *n* **1 :** act of refreshing **2** *pl* **:** light meal

If at a particular sense the form of the inflection is unique or not regularly formed, that information is also provided.

> **an·ten·na** *n* **1** *pl* **an·ten·nae :** one of the long slender paired sensory organs on the head of an arthropod **2** *pl* **an·ten·nas :** metallic device for sending or receiving radio waves
> **young** *adj* **1 :** being in the first or an early stage of life . . . ~ *n* **young :** persons or animals that are young
> **up** *adv* **1 :** in or to a higher position or level . . . ~ *vb* **1 up; upped :** act abruptly **2 upped; upped :** move or cause to move upward . . .

In the first example, the form of the plural is different for each of the two noun senses and is therefore shown. In the second example, the plural form for the noun sense is unchanged. In the third example, the verb inflections for the past tense are different for each of these two verb senses.

To show the range of entries on a page, **guide words** appear at the top, indicating the first main entry word and the last main entry word on that page.

Common **abbreviations**, including those used in this book, are shown in a separate section immediately following the dictionary proper.

Abbreviations

Most of these abbreviations are shown in one form only. Variation in use of periods, in kind of type, and in capitalization is frequent and widespread (as mph, MPH, m.p.h., Mph)

abbr abbreviation
AD in the year of our Lord
adj adjective
adv adverb
AK Alaska
AL, Ala Alabama
alt alternate, altitude
a.m., A.M. before noon
Am, Amer America, American
amt amount
anon anonymous
ans answer
Apr April
AR Arkansas
Ariz Arizona
Ark Arkansas
assn association
asst assistant
atty attorney
Aug August
ave avenue
AZ Arizona

BC before Christ
bet between
bldg building
blvd boulevard
Br, Brit Britain, British
bro brother
bros brothers
bu bushel

c carat, cent, centimeter, century, chapter, cup
C Celsius, centigrade
CA, Cal, Calif California
Can, Canad Canada, Canadian
cap capital, capitalize, capitalized
Capt captain
ch chapter, church
cm centimeter
co company, county
CO Colorado
COD cash on delivery, collect on delivery
col column
Col colonel, Colorado
Colo Colorado
conj conjunction
Conn Connecticut
cpu central processing unit
ct cent, court
CT Connecticut
cu cubic
CZ Canal Zone

d penny
DC District of Columbia
DDS doctor of dental surgery
DE Delaware
Dec December
Del Delaware
dept department
DMD doctor of dental medicine
doz dozen
Dr doctor
DST daylight saving time

E east, eastern, excellent
ea each
e.g. for example
Eng England, English
esp especially
etc et cetera

f false, female, forte
F Fahrenheit
FBI Federal Bureau of Investigation
Feb February
fem feminine
FL, Fla Florida
fr father, from
Fri Friday
ft feet, foot, fort

g gram
G good
Ga, GA Georgia
gal gallon
GB gigabyte
gen general
geog geographic, geographical, geography
gm gram
gov governor
govt government
gt great
GU Guam

HI Hawaii
hr hour
HS high school
ht height
Ia, IA Iowa
ID Idaho
i.e. that is
IL, Ill Illinois
in inch
IN Indiana
inc incorporated
Ind Indian, Indiana
interj interjection
intrans intransitive

Jan January
jr, jun junior

Kan, Kans Kansas
KB kilobyte
kg kilogram
km kilometer
KS Kansas
Ky, KY Kentucky

l left, liter
La, LA Louisiana
lb pound
Lt lieutenant
ltd limited

m male, meter, mile
MA Massachusetts
Maj major
Mar March
masc masculine
Mass Massachusetts
MB megabyte

Md Maryland
MD doctor of medicine, Maryland
Me, ME Maine
Mex Mexican, Mexico
mg milligram
MI, Mich Michigan
min minute
Minn Minnesota
Miss Mississippi
ml milliliter
mm millimeter
MN Minnesota
mo month
Mo, MO Missouri
Mon Monday
Mont Montana
mpg miles per gallon
mph miles per hour
MS Mississippi
mt mount, mountain
MT Montana

n noun
N north, northern
NC North Carolina
ND, N Dak North Dakota
NE Nebraska, northeast
Neb, Nebr Nebraska
Nev Nevada
NH New Hampshire
NJ New Jersey
NM, N Mex New Mexico
no north, number
Nov November
NV Nevada
NW northwest
NY New York

O Ohio
obj object, objective
Oct October
off office
OH Ohio
OK, Okla Oklahoma
OR, Ore, Oreg Oregon
oz ounce, ounces

p page
Pa, PA Pennsylvania
part participle
pat patent
Penn, Penna Pennsylvania
pg page
pk park, peck
pkg package
pl plural
p.m., P.M. afternoon
PO post office
poss possessive
pp pages
pr pair
PR Puerto Rico
prep preposition
pres present, president
prof professor
pron pronoun
PS postscript, public school
pt pint, point
PTA Parent-Teacher Association
PTO Parent-Teacher Organization

qt quart

r right
rd road, rod
recd received
reg region, regular
res residence
Rev reverend
RFD rural free delivery
RI Rhode Island
rpm revolutions per minute
RR railroad
RSVP please reply
rt right
rte route

S south, southern
Sat Saturday
SC South Carolina
sci science
Scot Scotland, Scottish
SD, S Dak South Dakota
SE southeast
sec second
Sept September
SI International System of Units
sing singular
so south
sq square
sr senior
Sr sister
SS steamship
st state, street
St saint
Sun Sunday
SW southwest

t true
tbs, tbsp tablespoon
TD touchdown
Tenn Tennessee
Tex Texas
Thurs, Thu Thursday
TN Tennessee
trans transitive
tsp teaspoon
Tues, Tue Tuesday
TX Texas

UN United Nations
US United States
USA United States of America
USSR Union of Soviet Socialist Republics
usu usual, usually
UT Utah

v verb
Va, VA Virginia
var variant
vb verb
VG very good
vi verb intransitive
VI Virgin Islands
vol volume
VP vice president
vs versus
vt verb transitive
Vt, VT Vermont

W west, western
WA, Wash Washington
Wed Wednesday
WI, Wis, Wisc Wisconsin
wk week
wt weight
WV, W Va West Virginia
WWW World Wide Web
WY, Wyo Wyoming

yd yard
yr year

A

[1]a *n* **:** 1st letter of the alphabet
[2]a *indefinite article* **:** one or some — used to indicate an unspecified or unidentified individual
aard•vark *n* **:** ant-eating African mammal
aback *adv* **:** by surprise
ab•a•lo•ne *n* **:** large edible shellfish
aban•don *vb* **:** give up without intent to reclaim — **aban•don** *n* — **aban•doned** *adj* — **aban•don•ment** *n*
abase *vb* **:** lower in dignity — **abase•ment** *n*
abate *vb* **:** decrease or lessen — **abate•ment** *n*
ab•bess *n* **:** head of a convent
ab•bey *n* **:** monastery or convent
ab•bot *n* **:** head of a monastery
ab•bre•vi•ate *vb* **:** shorten — **ab•bre•vi•a•tion** *n*
ab•di•cate *vb* **:** renounce — **ab•di•ca•tion** *n*
ab•do•men *n* **1 :** body area between chest and pelvis **2 :** hindmost part of an insect — **ab•dom•i•nal** *adj* — **ab•dom•i•nal•ly** *adv*
ab•er•ra•tion *n* **:** deviation or distortion — **ab•er•rant** *adj*
abet *vb* **:** incite or encourage — **abet•tor, abet•ter** *n*
abey•ance *n* **:** state of inactivity
ab•hor *vb* **:** hate — **ab•hor•rence** *n* — **ab•hor•rent** *adj*
abide *vb* **1 :** endure **2 :** remain, last, or reside
abil•i•ty *n* **1 :** competence **2:** natural aptitude
ab•ject *adj* **:** low in spirit or hope — **ab•jec•tion** *n* — **ab•ject•ly** *adv* — **ab•ject•ness** *n*
ablaze *adj or adv* **:** on fire
able *adj* **1 :** having sufficient power, skill, or resources **2 :** skilled or efficient — **ably** *adv*
ab•lu•tion *n* **:** washing of one's body
ab•nor•mal *adj* **:** deviating from the normal or average — **ab•nor•mal•i•ty** *n* — **ab•nor•mal•ly** *adv*
aboard *adv* **:** on, onto, or within a car, ship, or aircraft ~ *prep* **:** on or within
abode *n* **:** residence
abol•ish *vb* **:** do away with — **ab•o•li•tion** *n*
abom•i•na•ble *adj* **:** thoroughly unpleasant or revolting
abom•i•nate *vb* **:** hate — **abom•i•na•tion** *n*
ab•orig•i•nal *adj* **1 :** original **2 :** primitive
ab•orig•i•ne *n* **:** original inhabitant
abort *vb* **:** terminate prematurely — **abor•tion** *n* — **abor•tive** *adj*
abound *vb* **:** be plentiful
about *adv* **:** around ~ *prep* **1 :** on every side of **2 :** on the verge of **3 :** having as a subject
above *adv* **:** in or to a higher place ~ *prep* **1 :** in or to a higher place than **2 :** more than
above•board *adv or adj* **:** without deception
abrade *vb* **:** wear away by rubbing — **abra•sion** *n* — **abra•sive** *adj* — **abra•sive•ly** *adv*
abreast *adv or adj* **1 :** side by side **2 :** up to a standard or level
abridge *vb* **:** shorten or condense — **abridg•ment, abridge•ment** *n*
abroad *adv or adj* **1 :** over a wide area **2 :** outside one's country
abrupt *adj* **1 :** sudden **2 :** so quick as to seem rude — **abrupt•ly** *adv*
ab•scess *n* **:** collection of pus surrounded by inflamed tissue — **ab•scessed** *adj*
ab•scond *vb* **:** run away and hide
ab•sent *adj* **:** not present ~ **ab•sent** *vb* **:** keep oneself away — **ab•sence** *n* — **absen•tee** *n*
ab•sent•mind•ed *adj* **:** unaware of one's surroundings or action — **ab•sent•mind•ed•ly** *adv* — **ab•sent•mind•ed•ness** *n*
ab•so•lute *adj* **1 :** pure **2 :** free from restriction **3 :** definite — **ab•so•lute•ly** *adv*
ab•so•lu•tion *n* **:** remission of sins
ab•solve *vb* **:** set free of the consequences of guilt
ab•sorb *vb* **1 :** suck up or take in as a sponge does **2 :** engage (one's attention) — **ab•sor•ben•cy** *n* — **ab•sor•bent** *adj or n* — **ab•sorb•ing** *adj* — **ab•sorp•tion** *n* — **ab•sorp•tive** *adj*
ab•stain *vb* **:** refrain from doing something — **ab•stain•er** *n* — **ab•sten•tion** *n* — **ab•sti•nence** *n*
ab•ste•mi•ous *adj* **:** sparing in use of food or drink — **ab•ste•mi•ous•ly** *adv* — **ab•ste•mi•ous•ness** *n*
ab•stract *adj* **1 :** expressing a quality apart from an object **2 :** not representing something specific ~ *n* **:** summary ~ *vb* **1 :** remove or separate **2 :** make an abstract of — **ab•stract•ly** *adv* — **ab•stract•ness** *n* — **ab•strac•tion** *n*

ab•surd *adj* : ridiculous or unreasonable — **ab•sur•di•ty** *n* — **ab•surd•ly** *adv*
abun•dant *adj* : more than enough — **abun•dance** *n* — **abun•dant•ly** *adv*
abuse *vb* **1** : misuse **2** : mistreat **3** : attack with words ~ *n* **1** : corrupt practice **2** : improper use **3** : mistreatment **4** : coarse and insulting speech — **abus•er** *n* — **abu•sive** *adj* — **abu•sive•ly** *adv* — **abu•sive•ness** *n*
abut *vb* : touch along a border — **abut•ter** *n* — **abut•ment** *n*
abys•mal *adj* **1** : immeasurably deep **2** : wretched — **abys•mal•ly** *adv*
abyss *n* : immeasurably deep gulf
acad•e•my *n* **1** : private high school **2** : society of scholars or artists — **ac•a•dem•ic** *adj or n* — **ac•a•dem•i•cal•ly** *adv*
ac•cede *vb* **1** : become a party to an agreement **2** : express approval **3** : enter upon an office
ac•cel•er•ate *vb* **1** : bring about earlier **2** : speed up — **ac•cel•er•a•tion** *n* — **ac•cel•er•a•tor** *n*
ac•cent *n* **1** : distinctive manner of pronunciation **2** : prominence given to one syllable of a word **3** : mark (as ´, `, ˆ) over a vowel in writing or printing to indicate pronunciation ~ *vb* : emphasize — **ac•cen•tu•al** *adj* — **ac•cen•tu•ate** *vb* — **ac•cen•tu•a•tion** *n*
ac•cept *vb* **1** : receive willingly **2** : agree to — **ac•cept•abil•i•ty** *n* — **ac•cept•able** *adj* — **ac•cep•tance** *n*
ac•cess *n* : capability or way of approaching — **ac•ces•si•bil•i•ty** *n* — **ac•ces•si•ble** *adj*
ac•ces•so•ry *n* **1** : nonessential addition **2** : one guilty of aiding a criminal — **ac•ces•so•ry** *adj*
ac•ci•dent *n* **1** : event occurring by chance or unintentionally **2** : chance — **ac•ci•den•tal** *adj* — **ac•ci•den•tal•ly** *adv*
ac•claim *vb or n* : praise — **ac•cla•ma•tion** *n*
ac•cli•mate *vb* : acclimatize — **ac•cli•ma•tion** *n*
ac•cli•ma•tize *vb* : accustom to a new climate or situation — **ac•cli•ma•ti•za•tion** *n*
ac•co•lade *n* : expression of praise
ac•com•mo•date *vb* **1** : adapt **2** : provide with something needed **3** : hold without crowding — **ac•com•mo•da•tion** *n*
ac•com•pa•ny *vb* **1** : go or occur with **2** : play supporting music — **ac•com•pa•ni•ment** *n* — **ac•com•pa•nist** *n*
ac•com•plice *n* : associate in crime
ac•com•plish *vb* : do, fulfill, or bring about — **ac•com•plished** *adj* — **ac•com•plish•er** *n* — **ac•com•plish•ment** *n*
ac•cord *vb* **1** : grant **2** : agree ~ *n* **1** : agreement **2** : willingness to act — **ac•cor•dance** *n* — **ac•cor•dant** *adj*
ac•cord•ing•ly *adv* : consequently
according to *prep* **1** : in conformity with **2** : as stated by
ac•cor•di•on *n* : keyboard instrument with a bellows and reeds ~ *adj* : folding like an accordion bellows — **ac•cor•di•on•ist** *n*
ac•cost *vb* : approach and speak to esp. aggressively
ac•count *n* **1** : statement of business transactions **2** : credit arrangement with a vendor **3** : report **4** : worth **5** : sum deposited in a bank ~ *vb* : give an explanation — **ac•count•able** *adj* — **ac•count•abil•i•ty** *n* — **ac•coun•tant** *n*
ac•cou•tre•ment, ac•cou•ter•ment *n* **1** : accessory item — usu. pl. **2** : identifying characteristic
ac•cred•it *vb* **1** : approve officially **2** : attribute — **ac•cred•i•ta•tion** *n*
ac•crue *vb* : be added by periodic growth — **ac•cru•al** *n*
ac•cu•mu•late *vb* : collect or pile up — **ac•cu•mu•la•tion** *n*
ac•cu•rate *adj* : free from error — **ac•cu•ra•cy** *n* — **ac•cu•rate•ly** *adv* — **ac•cu•rate•ness** *n*
ac•cursed, ac•curst *adj* **1** : being under a curse **2** : damnable
ac•cuse *vb* : charge with an offense — **ac•cu•sa•tion** *n* — **ac•cused** *n* — **ac•cus•er** *n*
ac•cus•tom *vb* : make familiar through use or experience
ace *n* : one that excels
acer•bic *adj* : sour or biting in temper, mood, or tone
acet•amin•o•phen *n* : pain reliever
ac•e•tate *n* : fabric or plastic derived from acetic acid
ace•tic acid *n* : acid found in vinegar
ache *vb* **1** : suffer a dull persistent pain **2** : yearn — **ache** *n*
achieve *vb* : gain by work or effort — **achieve•ment** *n* — **achiev•er** *n*
ac•id *adj* **1** : sour or biting to the taste **2** : sharp in manner **3** : of or relating to an acid ~ *n* : sour water-soluble chemical compound that reacts with a base to form a salt — **acid•ic** *adj* — **acid•i•fy** *vb* — **acid•i•ty** *n* — **ac•id•ly** *adv*

ac•knowl•edge *vb* **1 :** admit as true **2 :** admit the authority of **3 :** express thanks for — **ac•knowl•edg•ment** *n*
ac•me *n* **:** highest point
ac•ne *n* **:** skin disorder marked esp. by pimples
acorn *n* **:** nut of the oak
acous•tic *adj* **:** relating to hearing or sound — **acous•ti•cal** *adj* — **acous•ti•cal•ly** *adv*
acous•tics *n sing or pl* **1 :** science of sound **2 :** qualities in a room that affect how sound is heard
ac•quaint *vb* **1 :** inform **2 :** make familiar — **ac•quain•tance** *n* — **ac•quain•tance•ship** *n*
ac•qui•esce *vb* **:** consent or submit — **ac•qui•es•cence** *n* — **ac•qui•es•cent** *adj* — **ac•qui•es•cent•ly** *adv*
ac•quire *vb* **:** gain — **ac•qui•sition** *n* — **ac•qui•si•tive** *adj*
ac•quit *vb* **1 :** pronounce not guilty **2 :** conduct (oneself) usu. well — **ac•quit•tal** *n*
acre *n* **1** *pl* **:** lands **2 :** 4840 square yards — **acre•age** *n*
ac•rid *adj* **:** sharp and biting — **acrid•i•ty** *n* — **ac•rid•ly** *adv* — **ac•rid•ness** *n*
ac•ri•mo•ny *n* **:** harshness of language or feeling — **ac•ri•mo•ni•ous** *adj* — **ac•ri•mo•ni•ous•ly** *adv*
ac•ro•bat *n* **:** performer of tumbling feats — **ac•ro•bat•ic** *adj*
across *adv* **:** to or on the opposite side ∼ *prep* **1 :** to or on the opposite side of **2 :** on so as to cross
acryl•ic *n* **1 :** plastic used for molded parts or in paints **2 :** synthetic textile fiber
act *n* **1 :** thing done **2 :** law **3 :** main division of a play ∼ *vb* **1 :** perform in a play **2 :** conduct oneself **3 :** operate **4 :** produce an effect — **ac•tive** *adj or n* — **ac•tive•ly** *adv* — **ac•tor** *n* — **ac•tress** *n*
ac•tion *n* **1 :** legal proceeding **2 :** manner or method of performing **3 :** activity **4 :** thing done over a period of time or in stages **5 :** combat **6 :** events of a literary plot **7 :** operating mechanism
ac•ti•vate *vb* **:** make active or reactive — **ac•ti•va•tion** *n*
ac•tiv•i•ty *n* **1 :** quality or state of being active **2 :** what one is actively doing
ac•tu•al *adj* **:** really existing — **ac•tu•al•i•ty** *n* — **ac•tu•al•iza•tion** *n* — **ac•tu•al•ize** *vb* — **ac•tu•al•ly** *adv*
ac•tu•ary *n* **:** one who calculates insurance risks and premiums — **ac•tu•ar•i•al** *adj*
acu•men *n* **:** mental keenness
acu•punc•ture *n* **:** treatment by puncturing the body with needles — **acu•punc•tur•ist** *n*
acute *adj* **1 :** sharp **2 :** containing less than 90 degrees **3 :** mentally alert **4 :** severe — **acute•ly** *adv* — **acute•ness** *n*
ad *n* **:** advertisement
ad•age *n* **:** old familiar saying
ad•a•mant *adj* **:** insistent — **ad•a•mant•ly** *adv*
adapt *vb* **:** adjust to be suitable for a new use or condition — **adapt•abil•i•ty** *n* — **adapt•able** *adj* — **ad•ap•ta•tion** *n* — **adap•ter** *n* — **adap•tive** *adj*
add *vb* **1 :** join to something else so as to increase in amount **2 :** say further **3 :** find a sum — **ad•di•tion** *n* — **ad•di•tion•al** *adj*
ad•der *n* **1 :** poisonous European snake **2 :** No. American snake
ad•dict *n* **:** one who is psychologically or physiologically dependent (as on a drug) ∼ *vb* **:** cause to become an addict — **ad•dic•tion** *n* — **ad•dic•tive** *adj*
ad•di•tive *n* **:** substance added to another
ad•dle *vb* **:** confuse
ad•dress *vb* **1 :** direct one's remarks to **2 :** mark an address on ∼ *n* **1 :** formal speech **2 :** place where a person may be reached or mail may be delivered
adept *adj* **:** highly skilled — **adept•ly** *adv* — **adept•ness** *n*
ad•e•quate *adj* **:** good or plentiful enough — **ad•e•qua•cy** *n* — **ad•e•quate•ly** *adv*
ad•here *vb* **1 :** remain loyal **2 :** stick fast — **ad•her•ence** *n* — **ad•her•ent** *adj or n*
ad•he•sion *n* **:** act or state of adhering
ad•he•sive *adj* **:** tending to adhere ∼ *n* **:** adhesive substance
adieu *n* **:** farewell
ad•ja•cent *adj* **:** situated near or next
ad•jec•tive *n* **:** word that serves as a modifier of a noun — **ad•jec•ti•val** *adj* — **ad•jec•ti•val•ly** *adv*
ad•join *vb* **:** be next to
ad•journ *vb* **:** end a meeting — **ad•journ•ment** *n*
ad•ju•di•cate *vb* **:** settle judicially — **ad•ju•di•ca•tion** *n*
ad•junct *n* **:** something joined or added but not essential
ad•just *vb* **:** fix, adapt, or set right — **ad•just•able** *adj* — **ad•just•er, ad•jus•tor** *n* — **ad•just•ment** *n*

ad–lib *vb* : speak without preparation — **ad–lib** *n or adj*
ad•min•is•ter *vb* **1** : manage **2** : give out esp. in doses — **ad•min•is•tra•ble** *adj*
ad•min•is•tra•tion *n* **1** : process of managing **2** : persons responsible for managing — **ad•min•is•tra•tive** *adj* — **ad•min•is•tra•tive•ly** *adv* — **ad•min•is•tra•tor** *n*
ad•mi•ra•ble *adj* : worthy of admiration — **ad•mi•ra•bly** *adv*
ad•mi•ral *n* : commissioned officer in the navy ranking next below a fleet admiral
ad•mire *vb* : have high regard for — **ad•mi•ra•tion** *n* — **ad•mir•er** *n* — **ad•mir•ing•ly** *adv*
ad•mis•si•ble *adj* : that can be permitted — **ad•mis•si•bil•i•ty** *n*
ad•mis•sion *n* **1** : act of admitting **2** : admittance or a fee paid for this **3** : acknowledgment of a fact
ad•mit *vb* **1** : allow to enter **2** : permit **3** : recognize as genuine — **ad•mit•ted•ly** *adv* — **ad•mit•tance** *n*
ad•mix•ture *n* **1** : thing added in mixing **2** : mixture
ad•mon•ish *vb* : rebuke — **ad•mon•ish•ment** *n* — **ad•mo•ni•tion** *n* — **ad•mon•i•to•ry** *adj*
ado *n* **1** : fuss **2** : trouble
ado•be *n* : sun-dried building brick
ad•o•les•cence *n* : period of growth between childhood and maturity — **ad•o•les•cent** *adj or n*
adopt *vb* **1** : take (a child of other parents) as one's own child **2** : take up and practice as one's own — **adop•tion** *n*
adore *vb* **1** : worship **2** : be extremely fond of — **ador•able** *adj* — **ador•ably** *adv* — **ad•o•ra•tion** *n*
adorn *vb* : decorate with ornaments — **adorn•ment** *n*
adrift *adv or adj* **1** : afloat without motive power or moorings **2** : without guidance or purpose
adroit *adj* : dexterous or shrewd — **adroit•ly** *adv* — **adroit•ness** *n*
adult *adj* : fully developed and mature ~ *n* : grown-up person — **adult•hood** *n*
adul•ter•ate *vb* : make impure by mixture — **adul•ter•a•tion** *n*
adul•tery *n* : sexual unfaithfulness of a married person — **adul•ter•er** *n* — **adul•ter•ess** *n* — **adul•ter•ous** *adj*
ad•vance *vb* **1** : bring or move forward **2** : promote **3** : lend ~ *n* **1** : forward movement **2** : improvement **3** : offer ~ *adj* : being ahead of time — **ad•vance•ment** *n*
ad•van•tage *n* **1** : superiority of position **2** : benefit or gain — **ad•van•ta•geous** *adj* — **ad•van•ta•geous•ly** *adv*
ad•vent *n* **1** *cap* : period before Christmas **2** : a coming into being or use
ad•ven•ture *n* **1** : risky undertaking **2** : exciting experience — **ad•ven•tur•er** *n* — **ad•ven•ture•some** *adj* — **ad•ven•tur•ous** *adj*
ad•verb *n* : word that modifies a verb, an adjective, or another adverb — **ad•ver•bi•al** *adj* — **ad•ver•bi•al•ly** *adv*
ad•ver•sary *n* : enemy or rival — **ad•ver•sary** *adj*
ad•verse *adj* : opposing or unfavorable — **ad•verse•ly** *adv* — **ad•ver•si•ty** *n*
ad•ver•tise *vb* : call public attention to — **ad•ver•tise•ment** *n* — **ad•ver•tis•er** *n* — **ad•ver•tis•ing** *n*
ad•vice *n* : recommendation with regard to a course of action
ad•vis•able *adj* : wise or prudent — **ad•vis•abil•i•ty** *n*
ad•vise *vb* : give advice to — **ad•vis•abil•i•ty** *n* — **ad•vis•able** *adj* — **ad•vis•er, ad•vis•or** *n* — **ad•vise•ment** *n*
ad•vi•so•ry *adj* : having power to advise
ad•vo•cate *n* : one who argues or pleads for a cause or proposal ~ *vb* : recommend — **ad•vo•ca•cy** *n*
ae•gis *n* : protection or sponsorship
aer•ate *vb* : supply or impregnate with air — **aer•a•tion** *n* — **aer•a•tor** *n*
ae•ri•al *adj* : inhabiting, occurring in, or done in the air ~ *n* : antenna
aer•o•bic *adj* : using or needing oxygen
aer•o•bics *n sing or pl* : exercises that produce a marked increase in respiration and heart rate
aero•dy•nam•ics *n* : science of bodies in motion in a gas — **aero•dy•nam•ic** *adj* — **aero•dy•nam•i•cal•ly** *adv*
aero•nau•tics *n* : science dealing with aircraft — **aero•nau•ti•cal** *adj*
aero•sol *n* **1** : liquid or solid particles suspended in a gas **2** : substance sprayed as an aerosol
aero•space *n* : earth's atmosphere and the space beyond — **aero•space** *adj*
aes•thet•ic *adj* : relating to beauty — **aes•thet•i•cal•ly** *adv* — **aes•thet•ics** *n*
af•fa•ble *adj* : easy to talk to — **af•fa•bil•i•ty** *n* — **af•fa•bly** *adv*

af·fair *n* : something that relates to or involves one

[1]af·fect *vb* : assume for effect — **af·fec·ta·tion** *n*

[2]affect *vb* : produce an effect on

af·fect·ed *adj* **1 :** pretending to some trait **2 :** artificially assumed to impress — **af·fect·ed·ly** *adv*

af·fect·ing *adj* : arousing pity or sorrow — **af·fect·ing·ly** *adv*

af·fec·tion *n* : kind or loving feeling — **af·fec·tion·ate** *adj* — **af·fec·tion·ate·ly** *adv*

af·fi·da·vit *n* : sworn statement

af·fil·i·ate *vb* : become a member or branch — **af·fil·i·ate** *n* — **af·fil·i·a·tion** *n*

af·fin·i·ty *n* : close attraction or relationship

af·firm *vb* : assert positively — **af·fir·ma·tion** *n*

af·fir·ma·tive *adj* : asserting the truth or existence of something ∼ *n* : statement of affirmation or agreement

af·flict *vb* : cause pain and distress to — **af·flic·tion** *n*

af·flu·ence *n* : wealth — **af·flu·ent** *adj*

af·ford *vb* **1 :** manage to bear the cost of **2 :** provide

af·front *vb or n* : insult

af·ghan *n* : crocheted or knitted blanket

aflame *adj or adv* : flaming

afloat *adj or adv* : floating

afoot *adv or adj* **1 :** on foot **2 :** in progress

afraid *adj* : filled with fear

afresh *adv* : anew

af·ter *adv* : at a later time ∼ *prep* **1 :** behind in place or time **2 :** in pursuit of ∼ *conj* : following the time when ∼ *adj* **1 :** later **2 :** located toward the back

af·ter·life *n* : existence after death

af·ter·math *n* : results

af·ter·noon *n* : time between noon and evening

af·ter·thought *n* : later thought

af·ter·ward, af·ter·wards *adv* : at a later time

again *adv* **1 :** once more **2 :** on the other hand **3 :** in addition

against *prep* **1 :** directly opposite to **2 :** in opposition to **3 :** so as to touch or strike

ag·ate *n* : quartz with bands or masses of various colors

age *n* **1 :** length of time of life or existence **2 :** particular time in life (as majority or the latter part) **3 :** quality of being old **4 :** long time **5 :** period in history ∼ *vb* : become old or mature — **age·less** *adj*

aged *adj* **1 :** old **2 :** allowed to mature

agen·da *n* : list of things to be done

agent *n* **1 :** means **2 :** person acting or doing business for another — **agen·cy** *n*

ag·gra·vate *vb* **1 :** make more severe **2 :** irritate — **ag·gra·va·tion** *n*

ag·gre·gate *adj* : formed into a mass ∼ *vb* : collect into a mass ∼ *n* **1 :** mass **2 :** whole amount

ag·gres·sion *n* **1 :** unprovoked attack **2 :** hostile behavior — **ag·gres·sor** *n* — **ag·gres·sive** *adj* — **ag·gres·sive·ly** *adv* — **ag·gres·sive·ness** *n*

ag·grieve *vb* **1 :** cause grief to **2 :** inflict injury on

ag·ile *adj* : able to move quickly and easily — **agil·i·ty** *n*

ag·i·tate *vb* **1 :** shake or stir back and forth **2 :** excite or trouble the mind of **3 :** try to arouse public feeling — **ag·i·ta·tion** *n* — **ag·i·ta·tor** *n*

ag·nos·tic *n* : one who doubts the existence of God

ago *adj or adv* : earlier than the present

agog *adj* : full of excitement

ag·o·nize *vb* : suffer mental agony — **ag·o·niz·ing·ly** *adv* — **ag·o·ny** *n*

agree *vb* **1 :** be of the same opinion **2 :** express willingness **3 :** get along together **4 :** be similar **5 :** be appropriate, suitable, or healthful — **agree·able** *adj* — **agree·able·ness** *n* — **agree·ably** *adv* — **agree·ment** *n*

ag·ri·cul·ture *n* : farming — **ag·ri·cul·tur·al** *adj* — **ag·ri·cul·tur·ist, ag·ri·cul·tur·al·ist** *n*

aground *adv or adj* : on or onto the bottom or shore

ahead *adv or adj* **1 :** in or toward the front **2 :** into or for the future **3 :** in a more advantageous position

ahead of *prep* **1 :** in front or advance of **2 :** in excess of

aid *vb* : provide help or support ∼ *n* : help

aide *n* : helper

AIDS *n* : serious disease of the human immune system

ail *vb* **1 :** trouble **2 :** be ill — **ail·ment** *n*

aim *vb* **1 :** point or direct (as a weapon) **2 :** direct one's efforts ∼ *n* **1 :** an aiming or the direction of aiming **2 :** object or purpose — **aim·less** *adj* — **aim·less·ly** *adv* — **aim·less·ness** *n*

air *n* **1 :** mixture of gases surrounding the earth **2 :** melody **3 :** outward appearance **4 :** artificial manner **5 :** compressed air **6 :** travel by or use of aircraft **7 :** medium of transmission of radio waves ~ *vb* **1 :** expose to the air **2 :** broadcast — **air•borne** *adj*

air–condition *vb* **:** equip with an apparatus (**air conditioner**) for filtering and cooling the air

air•craft *n* (**air•craft**) **:** craft that flies

air force *n* **:** military organization for conducting warfare by air

air•lift *n* **:** a transporting of esp. emergency supplies by aircraft — **air•lift** *vb*

air•line *n* **:** air transportation system — **air•lin•er** *n*

air•mail *n* **:** system of transporting mail by airplane — **air•mail** *vb*

air•plane *n* **:** fixed-wing aircraft heavier than air

air•port *n* **:** place for landing aircraft and usu. for receiving passengers

air•tight *adj* **:** tightly sealed to prevent flow of air

air•waves *n pl* **:** medium of transmission of radio waves

airy *adj* **1 :** delicate **2 :** breezy

aisle *n* **:** passage between sections or rows

ajar *adj or adv* **:** partly open

akin *adj* **1 :** related by blood **2 :** similar in kind

al•a•bas•ter *n* **:** white or translucent mineral

alac•ri•ty *n* **:** cheerful readiness

alarm *n* **1 :** warning signal or device **2 :** fear at sudden danger ~ *vb* **1 :** warn **2 :** frighten

alas *interj* — used to express unhappiness, pity, or concern

al•be•it *conj* **:** even though

al•bum *n* **1 :** book for displaying a collection (as of photographs) **2 :** collection of recordings

al•bu•men *n* **1 :** white of an egg **2 :** albumin

al•bu•min *n* **:** protein found in blood, milk, egg white, and tissues

al•co•hol *n* **1 :** intoxicating agent in liquor **2 :** liquor — **al•co•hol•ic** *adj or n* — **al•co•hol•ism** *n*

al•cove *n* **:** recess in a room or wall

al•der•man *n* **:** city official

ale *n* **:** beerlike beverage — **ale•house** *n*

alert *adj* **1 :** watchful **2 :** quick to perceive and act ~ *n* **:** alarm ~ *vb* **:** warn — **alert•ly** *adv* — **alert•ness** *n*

al•fal•fa *n* **:** cloverlike forage plant

al•ga *n* **:** any of a group of lower plants that includes seaweed — **al•gal** *adj*

al•ge•bra *n* **:** branch of mathematics — **al•ge•bra•ic** *adj* — **al•ge•bra•i•cal•ly** *adv*

alias *adv* **:** otherwise called ~ *n* **:** assumed name

al•i•bi *n* **1 :** defense of having been elsewhere when a crime was committed **2 :** justification ~ *vb* **:** offer an excuse

alien *adj* **:** foreign ~ *n* **1 :** foreign-born resident **2 :** extraterrestrial

alien•ate *vb* **:** cause to be no longer friendly — **alien•ation** *n*

align *vb* **:** bring into line — **align•er** *n* — **align•ment** *n*

alike *adj* **:** identical or very similar ~ *adv* **:** equally

al•i•men•ta•ry *adj* **:** relating to or functioning in nutrition

al•i•mo•ny *n* **:** money paid to a separated or divorced spouse

alive *adj* **1 :** having life **2 :** lively or animated

al•ka•li *n* **:** strong chemical base — **al•ka•line** *adj* — **al•ka•lin•i•ty** *n*

all *adj* **1 :** the whole of **2 :** greatest possible **3 :** every one of ~ *adv* **1 :** wholly **2 :** so much **3 :** for each side ~ *pron* **1 :** whole number or amount **2 :** everything or everyone

Al•lah *n* **:** God of Islam

al•lay *vb* **1 :** alleviate **2 :** calm

al•lege *vb* **:** assert without proof — **al•le•ga•tion** *n* — **al•leg•ed•ly** *adv*

al•le•giance *n* **:** loyalty

al•le•go•ry *n* **:** story in which figures and actions are symbols of general truths — **al•le•gor•i•cal** *adj*

al•ler•gen *n* **:** something that causes allergy — **al•ler•gen•ic** *adj*

al•ler•gy *n* **:** abnormal reaction to a substance — **al•ler•gic** *adj* — **al•ler•gist** *n*

al•le•vi•ate *vb* **:** relieve or lessen — **al•le•vi•a•tion** *n*

al•ley *n* **1 :** place for bowling **2 :** narrow passage between buildings

al•li•ance *n* **:** association

al•li•ga•tor *n* **:** large aquatic reptile related to the crocodiles

al•lit•er•a•tion *n* **:** repetition of initial sounds of words — **al•lit•er•a•tive** *adj*

al•lo•cate *vb* **:** assign — **al•lo•ca•tion** *n*

al•lot *vb* **:** distribute as a share — **al•lot•ment** *n*

al•low *vb* **1 :** admit or concede **2 :** permit — **al•low•able** *adj*

al·low·ance *n* **1 :** allotted share **2 :** money given regularly for expenses
al·loy *n* **:** metals melted together — **al·loy** *vb*
all right *adv or adj* **1 :** satisfactorily **2 :** yes **3 :** certainly
al·lude *vb* **:** refer indirectly — **al·lu·sion** *n* — **al·lu·sive** *adj*
al·lure *vb* **:** entice ∼ *n* **:** attractive power
al·ly *vb* **:** enter into an alliance — **al·ly** *n*
al·ma·nac *n* **:** annual information book
al·mighty *adj* **:** having absolute power
al·most *adv* **:** very nearly
alms *n* **:** charitable gift
aloft *adv* **:** high in the air
alone *adj* **1 :** separated from others **2 :** not including anyone or anything else — **alone** *adv*
along *prep* **1 :** in line with the direction of **2 :** at a point on or during ∼ *adv* **1 :** forward **2 :** as a companion
along·side *adv or prep* **:** along or by the side
alongside of *prep* **:** alongside
aloud *adv* **:** so as to be heard
al·pha·bet *n* **:** ordered set of letters of a language — **al·pha·bet·i·cal, al·pha·bet·ic** *adj* — **al·pha·bet·i·cal·ly** *adv*
al·pha·bet·ize *vb* **:** arrange in alphabetical order — **al·pha·bet·iz·er** *n*
al·ready *adv* **:** by a given time
al·so *adv* **:** in addition
al·tar *n* **:** structure for rituals
al·ter *vb* **:** make different — **alter·a·tion** *n*
al·ter·ca·tion *n* **:** dispute
al·ter·nate *adj* **1 :** arranged or succeeding by turns **2 :** every other ∼ *vb* **:** occur or cause to occur by turns ∼ *n* **:** substitute — **al·ter·nate·ly** *adv* — **al·ter·na·tion** *n*
al·ter·na·tive *adj* **:** offering a choice — **al·ter·na·tive** *n* — **al·ter·na·tive·ly** *adv*
al·though *conj* **:** even though
al·ti·tude *n* **1 :** distance up from the ground **2 :** angular distance above the horizon
al·to *n* **:** lower female choral voice
al·to·geth·er *adv* **1 :** wholly **2 :** on the whole
al·tru·ism *n* **:** concern for others — **al·tru·ist** *n* — **al·tru·is·tic** *adj* — **al·tru·is·ti·cal·ly** *adv*
alu·mi·num *n* **:** silver-white malleable ductile light metallic element
al·ways *adv* **1 :** at all times **2 :** forever
am *pres 1st sing of* BE
amal·gam *n* **1 :** mercury alloy **2 :** mixture
amass *vb* **:** gather
am·a·teur *n* **1 :** person who does something for pleasure rather than for pay **2 :** person who is not expert — **am·a·teur·ish** *adj* — **ama·teur·ism** *n*
am·a·to·ry *adj* **:** of or expressing sexual love
amaze *vb* **:** fill with wonder — **amaze·ment** *n* — **amaz·ing·ly** *adv*
am·a·zon *n* **:** tall strong woman — **am·a·zo·ni·an** *adj*
am·bas·sa·dor *n* **:** representative esp. of a government — **am·bas·sa·do·ri·al** *adj* — **am·bas·sa·dor·ship** *n*
am·ber *n* **:** yellowish fossil resin or its color
am·bi·dex·trous *adj* **:** equally skilled with both hands — **am·bi·dex·trous·ly** *adv*
am·bi·ence, am·bi·ance *n* **:** pervading atmosphere
am·big·u·ous *adj* **:** having more than one interpretation — **am·bi·gu·i·ty** *n*
am·bi·tion *n* **:** eager desire for success or power — **am·bi·tious** *adj* — **am·bi·tious·ly** *adv*
am·ble *vb* **:** go at a leisurely gait — **am·ble** *n*
am·bu·lance *n* **:** vehicle for carrying injured or sick persons
am·bu·la·to·ry *adj* **1 :** relating to or adapted to walking **2 :** able to walk about
am·bush *n* **:** trap by which a surprise attack is made from a place of hiding — **am·bush** *vb*
amen *interj* — used for affirmation esp. at the end of prayers
ame·na·ble *adj* **:** ready to yield or be influenced
amend *vb* **1 :** improve **2 :** alter in writing — **amend·ment** *n*
amends *n sing or pl* **:** compensation for injury or loss
ame·ni·ty *n* **1 :** agreeableness **2** *pl* **:** social conventions **3 :** something serving to comfort or accommodate
ami·a·ble *adj* **:** easy to get along with — **ami·a·bil·i·ty** *n* — **ami·a·bly** *adv*
am·i·ca·ble *adj* **:** friendly — **am·i·ca·bly** *adv*
amino acid *n* **:** nitrogen-containing acid
am·mo·nia *n* **1 :** colorless gaseous compound of nitrogen and hydrogen **2 :** solution of ammonia in water
am·mu·ni·tion *n* **1 :** projectiles fired from guns **2 :** explosive items used in war
am·ne·sia *n* **:** sudden loss of memory — **am·ne·si·ac, am·ne·sic** *adj or n*
am·nes·ty *n* **:** a pardon for a group — **am·nes·ty** *vb*
amoe·ba *n* **:** tiny one-celled animal that occurs esp. in water — **amoe·bic** *adj*
amok *adv* **:** in a violent or uncontrolled way

among *prep* **1 :** in or through **2 :** in the number or class of **3 :** in shares to each of

am•o•rous *adj* **1 :** inclined to love **2 :** being in love **3 :** indicative of love — **am•o•rous•ly** *adv* — **am•o•rous•ness** *n*

am•or•tize *vb* **:** get rid of (as a debt) gradually with periodic payments — **amor•ti•za•tion** *n*

amount *vb* **1 :** be equivalent **2 :** reach a total ∼ *n* **:** total number or quantity

am•per•sand *n* **:** character & used for the word *and*

am•phib•i•ous *adj* **1 :** able to live both on land and in water **2 :** adapted for both land and water — **am•phib•i•an** *n*

am•phi•the•ater *n* **:** oval or circular structure with rising tiers of seats around an arena

am•ple *adj* **1 :** large **2 :** sufficient — **am•ply** *adv*

am•pli•fy *vb* **:** make louder, stronger, or more thorough — **am•pli•fi•ca•tion** *n* — **am•pli•fi•er** *n*

am•pli•tude *n* **1 :** fullness **2 :** extent of a vibratory movement

am•pu•tate *vb* **:** cut off (a body part) — **am•pu•ta•tion** *n* — **am•pu•tee** *n*

am•u•let *n* **:** ornament worn as a charm against evil

amuse *vb* **1 :** engage the attention of in an interesting and pleasant way **2 :** make laugh — **amuse•ment** *n*

an *indefinite article* **:** a — used before words beginning with a vowel sound

anach•ro•nism *n* **:** one that is chronologically out of place — **anach•ro•nis•tic** *adj*

ana•gram *n* **:** word or phrase made by transposing the letters of another word or phrase

anal *adj* **:** relating to the anus

an•al•ge•sic *n* **:** pain reliever

anal•o•gy *n* **1 :** similarity between unlike things **2 :** example of something similar — **an•a•log•i•cal** *adj* — **an•a•log•i•cal•ly** *adv* — **anal•o•gous** *adj*

anal•y•sis *n* **1 :** examination of a thing to determine its parts **2 :** a method of treatment of psychological problems — **an•a•lyst** *n* — **an•a•lyt•ic, an•a•lyt•i•cal** *adj* — **an•a•lyt•i•cal•ly** *adv*

an•a•lyze *vb* **:** make an analysis of

an•ar•chism *n* **:** theory that all government is undesirable — **an•ar•chist** *n or adj* — **an•ar•chis•tic** *adj*

an•ar•chy *n* **:** lack of government or order — **an•ar•chic** *adj* — **an•ar•chi•cal•ly** *adv* — **an•ar•chism** *n* — **an•ar•chist** *n or adj* — **an•ar•chis•tic** *adj*

anath•e•ma *n* **1 :** solemn curse **2 :** person or thing accursed or intensely disliked

anat•o•my *n* **:** science dealing with the structure of organisms — **an•a•tom•ic, an•a•tom•i•cal** *adj* — **an•a•tom•i•cal•ly** *adv* — **anat•o•mist** *n*

an•ces•tor *n* **:** one from whom an individual is descended

an•ces•try *n* **1 :** line of descent **2 :** ancestors — **an•ces•tral** *adj*

an•chor *n* **1 :** heavy device that catches in the sea bottom to hold a ship in place **2 :** anchorperson ∼ *vb* **:** hold or become held in place by or as if by an anchor — **an•chor•age** *n*

an•chor•per•son *n* **:** news broadcast coordinator

an•cho•vy *n* **:** small herringlike fish

an•cient *adj* **1 :** having existed for many years **2 :** belonging to times long past — **an•cient** *n*

and *conj* — used to indicate connection or addition

an•drog•y•nous *adj* **1 :** having characteristics of both male and female **2 :** suitable for either sex

an•ec•dote *n* **:** brief story — **an•ec•dot•al** *adj*

ane•mia *n* **:** blood deficiency — **ane•mic** *adj*

an•es•the•sia *n* **:** loss of bodily sensation

an•es•thet•ic *n* **:** agent that produces anesthesia — **an•es•thet•ic** *adj* — **anes•the•tist** *n* — **anes•the•tize** *vb*

an•eu•rysm, an•eu•rism blood-filled bulge of a blood vessel

anew *adv* **:** over again

an•gel *n* **:** spiritual being superior to humans — **an•gel•ic, an•gel•i•cal** *adj* — **an•gel•i•cal•ly** *adv*

an•ger *n* **:** strong feeling of displeasure ∼ *vb* **:** make angry

an•gi•na *n* **:** painful disorder of heart muscles — **an•gi•nal** *adj*

[1]an•gle *n* **1 :** figure formed by the meeting of 2 lines in a point **2 :** sharp corner **3 :** point of view ∼ *vb* **:** turn or direct at an angle

[2]angle *vb* **:** fish with a hook and line — **an•gler** *n* — **an•gle•worm** *n* — **an•gling** *n*

an•go•ra *n* **:** yarn or cloth made from the hair of an Angora goat or rabbit

an•gry *adj* **:** feeling or showing anger — **an•gri•ly** *adv*

an•guish *n* **:** extreme pain or distress of mind — **an•guished** *adj*

an•gu•lar *adj* **1 :** having many or sharp angles **2 :** thin and bony — **an•gu•lar•i•ty** *n*

an•i•mal *n* **1 :** living being capable of feeling and voluntary motion **2 :** lower animal as distinguished from humans

an•i•mate *adj* **:** having life ~ *vb* **1 :** give life or vigor to **2 :** make appear to move — **an•i•mat•ed** *adj*

an•i•ma•tion *n* **1 :** liveliness **2 :** animated cartoon

an•i•ma•tron•ic : relating to an electrically animated mechanical figure

an•i•mus *n* **:** deep-seated hostility — **an•i•mos•i•ty** *n*

an•ise *n* **:** herb related to the carrot with aromatic seeds (**ani•seed**) used in flavoring

an•kle *n* **:** joint or region between the foot and the leg — **an•kle•bone** *n*

an•nals *n pl* **:** chronological record of history — **an•nal•ist** *n*

an•nex *vb* **:** assume political control over (a territory) ~ *n* **:** added building — **an•nex•a•tion** *n*

an•ni•hi•late *vb* **:** destroy — **an•ni•hi•la•tion** *n*

an•ni•ver•sa•ry *n* **:** annual return of the date of a notable event or its celebration

an•no•tate *vb* **:** furnish with notes — **an•no•ta•tion** *n* — **an•no•ta•tor** *n*

an•nounce *vb* **:** make known publicly — **an•nounce•ment** *n* — **an•nounc•er** *n*

an•noy *vb* **:** disturb or irritate — **an•noy•ance** *n* — **an•noy•ing•ly** *adv*

an•nu•al *adj* **1 :** occurring once a year **2 :** living only one year — **an•nu•al** *n* — **an•nu•al•ly** *adv*

an•nu•i•ty *n* **:** amount payable annually or the right to such a payment

an•nul *vb* **:** make legally void — **an•nul•ment** *n*

anom•a•ly *n* **:** something abnormal or unusual — **anom•a•lous** *adj*

anon•y•mous *adj* **:** of unknown origin — **an•o•nym•i•ty** *n* — **anon•y•mous•ly** *adv*

an•oth•er *adj* **1 :** any or some other **2 :** one more ~ *pron* **1 :** one more **2 :** one different

an•swer *n* **1 :** something spoken or written in reply to a question **2 :** solution to a problem ~ *vb* **1 :** reply to **2 :** be responsible **3 :** be adequate — **an•swer•er** *n* — **an•swer•able** *adj*

ant *n* **:** small social insect — **ant•hill** *n*

ant•ac•id : agent that counteracts acidity

an•tag•o•nize *vb* **:** cause to be hostile — **an•tag•o•nism** *n* — **an•tag•o•nist** *n* — **an•tag•o•nis•tic** *adj*

ant•arc•tic *adj, often cap* **:** relating to the region near the south pole

an•te•ced•ent *n* **:** one that comes before — **an•te•ced•ent** *adj*

an•te•lope *n* **:** deerlike mammal related to the ox

an•ten•na *n* **1** *pl* **an•ten•nae :** one of the long slender paired sensory organs on the head of an arthropod **2** *pl* **an•ten•nas :** metallic device for sending or receiving radio waves

an•them *n* **:** song or hymn of praise or gladness

an•thol•o•gy *n* **:** literary collection

an•thro•poid *n* **:** large ape — **an•thro•poid** *adj*

an•thro•pol•o•gy *n* **:** science dealing with humans — **an•thro•po•log•i•cal** *adj* — **an•thro•pol•o•gist** *n*

an•ti•bi•ot•ic *n* **:** substance that inhibits harmful microorganisms — **an•ti•bi•ot•ic** *adj*

an•ti•body *n* **:** bodily substance that counteracts the effects of a foreign substance or organism

an•tic *n* **:** playful act ~ *adj* **:** playful

an•tic•i•pate *vb* **1 :** be prepared for **2 :** look forward to — **an•tic•i•pa•tion** *n* — **an•tic•i•pa•to•ry** *adj*

an•ti•dote *n* **:** remedy for poison

an•ti•his•ta•mine : drug for treating allergies and colds

an•tip•a•thy *n* **:** strong dislike

an•ti•quat•ed *adj* **:** out-of-date — **an•ti•quar•i•an** *n*

an•tique *adj* **:** very old or out-of-date — **an•tique** *n*

an•tiq•ui•ty *n* **1 :** ancient times **2** *pl* **:** relics of ancient times

an•ti•sep•tic *adj* **:** killing or checking the growth of germs — **an•ti•sep•tic** *n* — **an•ti•sep•ti•cal•ly** *adv*

ant•ler *n* **:** solid branched horn of a deer — **ant•lered** *adj*

ant•onym *n* **:** word of opposite meaning

anus *n* **:** the rear opening of the alimentary canal

an•vil *n* **:** heavy iron block on which metal is shaped

anx•ious *adj* **1 :** uneasy **2 :** earnestly wishing — **anx•ious•ly** *adv* — **anx•i•ety** *n*

any *adj* **1 :** one chosen at random **2 :** of whatever number or quantity ~ *pron* **1 :** any one or ones **2 :** any amount ~ *adv* **:** to any extent or degree

any•body *pron* **:** anyone
any•how *adv* **1 :** in any way **2 :** nevertheless
any•more *adv* **:** at the present time
any•one *pron* **:** any person
any•place *adv* **:** anywhere
any•thing *pron* **:** any thing whatever
any•time *adv* **:** at any time whatever
any•way *adv* **:** anyhow
any•where *adv* **:** in or to any place
aor•ta *n* **:** main artery from the heart — **aor•tic** *adj*
apart *adv* **1 :** separately in place or time **2 :** aside **3 :** to pieces
apart•ment *n* **:** set of usu. rented rooms
ap•a•thy *n* **:** lack of emotion or interest — **ap•a•thet•ic** *adj* — **ap•a•thet•i•cal•ly** *adv*
ape *n* **:** large tailless primate ∼ *vb* **:** imitate
apex *n* **:** highest point
aphid *n* **:** small insect that sucks plant juices
aph•ro•di•si•ac *n* **:** substance that excites sexual desire
apiece *adv* **:** for each one
apol•o•gize *vb* **:** make an apology — **apol•o•get•ic** *adj* — **apol•o•get•i•cal•ly** *adv* — **apol•o•gist** *n*
apol•o•gy *n* **1 :** formal justification **2 :** expression of regret for a wrong
apos•tle *n* **:** disciple or advocate — **apos•tle•ship** *n* — **ap•os•tolic** *adj*
apos•tro•phe *n* **:** punctuation mark ' to indicate the possessive case or the omission of a letter or figure
apoth•e•cary *n* **:** druggist
ap•pall *vb* **:** fill with horror or dismay
ap•pa•ra•tus *n* **1 :** equipment **2 :** complex machine or device
ap•par•el *n* **:** clothing
ap•par•ent *adj* **1 :** visible **2 :** obvious **3 :** having the appearance of being — **ap•par•ent•ly** *adv*
ap•peal *vb* **1 :** try to have a court case reheard **2 :** ask earnestly **3 :** have an attraction — **ap•peal** *n*
ap•pear *vb* **1 :** become visible or evident **2 :** come into the presence of someone **3 :** seem — **ap•pear•ance** *n*
ap•pease *vb* **:** pacify with concessions — **ap•pease•ment** *n*
ap•pen•dec•to•my *n* **:** surgical removal of the appendix
ap•pen•di•ci•tis *n* **:** inflammation of the appendix
ap•pen•dix *n* **1 :** supplementary matter **2 :** narrow closed tube extending from lower right intestine
ap•pe•tite *n* **1 :** natural desire esp. for food **2 :** preference
ap•pe•tiz•er *n* **:** food or drink to stimulate the appetite — **ap•pe•tiz•ing** *adj* — **ap•pe•tiz•ing•ly** *adv*
ap•plaud *vb* **:** show approval esp. by clapping
ap•plause *n* **:** a clapping in approval
ap•ple *n* **:** rounded fruit with firm white flesh
ap•pli•ance *n* **:** household machine or device
ap•ply *vb* **1 :** place in contact **2 :** put to practical use **3 :** devote (one's) attention or efforts to something **4 :** submit a request **5 :** have reference or a connection — **ap•pli•ca•ble** *adj* — **ap•pli•ca•bil•i•ty** *n* — **ap•pli•cant** *n* — **ap•pli•ca•tion** *n* — **ap•pli•ca•tor** *n*
ap•point *vb* **1 :** set or assign officially **2 :** equip or furnish — **ap•poin•tee** *n* — **ap•point•ment** *n*
ap•praise *vb* **:** set value on — **ap•prais•al** *n* — **ap•prais•er** *n*
ap•pre•ci•ate *vb* **1 :** value justly **2 :** be grateful for **3 :** increase in value — **ap•pre•cia•ble** *adj* — **ap•pre•cia•bly** *adv* — **ap•pre•cia•tion** *n* — **ap•pre•cia•tive** *adj*
ap•pre•hen•sive *adj* **:** fearful — **ap•pre•hen•sive•ly** *adv* — **ap•pre•hen•sive•ness** *n*
ap•pren•tice *n* **:** person learning a craft ∼ *vb* **:** employ or work as an apprentice — **ap•pren•tice•ship** *n*
ap•proach *vb* **1 :** move nearer or be close to **2 :** make initial advances or efforts toward — **ap•proach** *n* — **ap•proach•able** *adj*
ap•pro•pri•ate *vb* **1 :** take possession of **2 :** set apart for a particular use ∼ *adj* **:** suitable — **ap•pro•pri•ate•ly** *adv* — **ap•pro•pri•ate•ness** *n* — **ap•pro•pria•tion** *n*
ap•prove *vb* **:** accept as satisfactory — **ap•prov•al** *n*
ap•prox•i•mate *adj* **:** nearly correct or exact ∼ *vb* **:** come near — **ap•prox•i•mate•ly** *adv* — **ap•prox•i•ma•tion** *n*
April *n* **:** 4th month of the year having 30 days
apron *n* **:** protective garment
apropos of *prep* **:** with regard to
apt *adj* **1 :** suitable **2 :** likely **3 :** quick to learn — **apt•ly** *adv* — **apt•ness** *n*
ap•ti•tude *n* **1 :** capacity for learning **2 :** natural ability
aquar•i•um *n* **:** glass container for aquatic animals and plants

aquat•ic *adj* : of or relating to water — **aquatic** *n*

aq•ue•duct *n* : conduit for carrying running water

ar•bi•trary *adj* **1** : selected at random **2** : autocratic — **ar•bi•trari•ly** *adv* — **ar•bi•trari•ness** *n*

ar•bi•trate *vb* : settle a dispute as arbitrator — **ar•bi•tra•tion** *n*

ar•bi•tra•tor *n* : one chosen to settle a dispute

ar•bor *n* : shelter under branches or vines — **ar•bo•re•al** *adj*

arc *n* **1** : part of a circle **2** : bright sustained electrical discharge ~ *vb* : form an arc

ar•cade *n* : arched passageway between shops

¹arch *n* : curved structure spanning an opening ~ *vb* : cover with or form into an arch

²arch *adj* **1** : chief — usu. in combination **2** : mischievous — **arch•ly** *adv* — **arch•ness** *n*

ar•chae•ol•o•gy, ar•che•ol•o•gy *n* : study of past human life — **ar•chae•o•log•i•cal** *adj* — **ar•chae•ol•o•gist** *n*

ar•cha•ic *adj* : belonging to an earlier time — **ar•cha•i•cal•ly** *adv*

arch•an•gel *n* : angel of high rank

arch•bish•op *n* : chief bishop — **arch•bish•op•ric** *n*

arch•di•o•cese *n* : diocese of an archbishop

ar•chery *n* : shooting with bow and arrows — **ar•cher** *n*

ar•chi•pel•a•go *n* : group of islands

ar•chi•tec•ture *n* **1** : building design **2** : style of building **3** : manner of organizing elements — **ar•chi•tect** *n* — **ar•chi•tec•tur•al** *adj* — **ar•chi•tec•tur•al•ly** *adv*

ar•chives *n pl* : public records or their storage place — **archi•vist** *n*

arch•way *n* : passageway under an arch

arc•tic *adj* **1** : relating to the region near the north pole **2** : frigid

ar•dent *adj* : characterized by warmth of feeling — **ar•dent•ly** *adv*

ar•dor *n* : warmth of feeling

ar•du•ous *adj* : difficult — **ar•du•ous•ly** *adv* — **ar•du•ous•ness** *n*

are *pres 2d sing or pres pl of* BE

ar•ea *n* **1** : space for something **2** : amount of surface included **3** : region **4** : range covered by a thing or concept

area code *n* : 3-digit area-identifying telephone number

are•na *n* **1** : enclosed exhibition area **2** : sphere of activity

ar•gue *vb* **1** : give reasons for or against something **2** : disagree in words — **argu•able** *adj* — **ar•gu•ment** *n* — **ar•gu•men•ta•tive** *adj*

ar•id *adj* : very dry — **arid•i•ty** *n*

arise *vb* **arose; aris•en 1** : get up **2** : originate

ar•is•toc•ra•cy *n* : upper class — **aris•to•crat** *n* — **aris•to•crat•ic** *adj*

arith•me•tic *n* : mathematics that deals with numbers — **ar•ith•met•ic, ar•ith•met•i•cal** *adj*

ark *n* : big boat

¹arm *n* **1** : upper limb **2** : branch — **armed** *adj* — **arm•less** *adj*

²arm *vb* : furnish with weapons ~ *n* **1** : weapon **2** : branch of the military forces **3** *pl* : family's heraldic designs

armed forces *n pl* : military

ar•mor *n* : protective covering — **ar•mored** *adj*

ar•mory *n* : factory or storehouse for arms

arm•pit *n* : hollow under the junction of the arm and shoulder

ar•my *n* **1** : body of men organized for war esp. on land **2** : great number

aro•ma *n* : usu. pleasing odor — **ar•o•mat•ic** *adj*

around *adv* **1** : in or along a circuit **2** : on all sides **3** : near **4** : in an opposite direction ~ *prep* **1** : surrounding **2** : along the circuit of **3** : to or on the other side of **4** : near

arouse *vb* **1** : awaken from sleep **2** : stir up — **arous•al** *n*

ar•raign *vb* **1** : call before a court to answer to an indictment **2** : accuse — **ar•raign•ment** *n*

ar•range *vb* **1** : put in order **2** : settle or agree on **3** : adapt (a musical composition) for voices or instruments — **ar•range•ment** *n* — **ar•rang•er** *n*

ar•ray *vb* **1** : arrange in order **2** : dress esp. splendidly ~ *n* **1** : arrangement **2** : rich clothing **3** : imposing group

ar•rest *vb* **1** : stop **2** : take into legal custody — **ar•rest** *n*

ar•rive *vb* **1** : reach a destination, point, or stage **2** : come near in time — **ar•riv•al** *n*

ar•ro•gant *adj* : showing an offensive sense of superiority — **ar•ro•gance** *n* — **ar•ro•gant•ly** *adv*

ar•ro•gate *vb* : to claim without justification

ar•row *n* : slender missile shot from a bow — **ar•row•head** *n*

ar•se•nic *n* : solid grayish poisonous chemical element

ar•son *n* : willful or malicious burning of property — **ar•son•ist** *n*
art *n* **1** : skill **2** : branch of learning **3** : creation of things of beauty or works so produced **4** : ingenuity — **art•ful** *adj* — **art•ful•ly** *adv* — **art•ful•ness** *n* — **art•less** *adj* — **art•less•ly** *adv* — **art•less•ness** *n* — **art•ist** *n* — **ar•tis•tic** *adj* — **ar•tis•ti•cal•ly** *adv* — **ar•tis•try** *n*
ar•te•rio•scle•ro•sis *n* : hardening of the arteries — **ar•te•rio•scle•rot•ic** *adj or n*
ar•tery *n* **1** : tubular vessel carrying blood from the heart **2** : thoroughfare — **ar•te•ri•al** *adj*
ar•thri•tis *n* : inflammation of the joints — **ar•thrit•ic** *adj or n*
ar•ti•cle *n* **1** : distinct part of a written document **2** : nonfictional published piece of writing **3** : word (as *an, the*) used to limit a noun **4** : item or piece
ar•tic•u•late *adj* : able to speak effectively ~ *vb* **1** : utter distinctly **2** : unite by joints — **ar•tic•u•late•ly** *adv* — **ar•tic•u•late•ness** *n* — **ar•tic•u•la•tion** *n*
ar•ti•fi•cial *adj* **1** : man-made **2** : not genuine — **ar•ti•fi•ci•al•i•ty** *n* — **ar•ti•fi•cial•ly** *adv* — **ar•ti•fi•cial•ness** *n*
ar•til•lery *n* : large-caliber firearms
ar•ti•san *n* : skilled craftsman
arty *adj* : pretentiously artistic — **art•i•ly** *adv* — **art•i•ness** *n*
as *adv* **1** : to the same degree **2** : for example ~ *conj* **1** : in the same way or degree as **2** : while **3** : because **4** : though ~ *pron* — used after *same* or *such* ~ *prep* : in the capacity of
as•bes•tos *n* : fibrous incombustible mineral
as•cen•dant *n* : dominant position ~ *adj* **1** : moving upward **2** : dominant — **as•cen•dan•cy** *n*
as•cent *n* **1** : act of moving upward **2** : degree of upward slope
as•cribe *vb* : attribute — **as•crib•able** *adj* — **as•crip•tion** *n*
[1]**ash** *n* : tree related to the olives
[2]**ash** *n* : matter left when something is burned — **ash•tray** *n*
ashamed *adj* : feeling shame — **asham•ed•ly** *adv*
ash•en *adj* : deadly pale
ashore *adv* : on or to the shore
aside *adv* **1** : toward the side **2** : out of the way
aside from *prep* **1** : besides **2** : except for
as•i•nine *adj* : foolish — **as•i•nin•i•ty** *n*
ask *vb* **1** : call on for an answer or help **2** : utter (a question or request) **3** : invite
askance *adv* **1** : with a side glance **2** : with lack of trust
askew *adv or adj* : out of line
asleep *adv or adj* **1** : sleeping **2** : numbed **3** : inactive
as of *prep* : from the time of
as•par•a•gus *n* : tall herb related to the lilies or its edible stalks
as•pect *n* **1** : way something looks to the eye or mind **2** : phase
as•phalt *n* : dark tarlike substance used in paving
as•phyx•i•ate *vb* : suffocate — **as•phyx•ia** *n* — **as•phyx•i•a•tion** *n*
as•pire *vb* : have an ambition — **as•pir•ant** *n* — **as•pi•ra•tion** *n*
as•pi•rin *n* : pain reliever
ass *n* **1** : long-eared animal related to the horse **2** : stupid person
as•sail *vb* : attack violently — **as•sail•able** *adj* — **as•sail•ant** *n*
as•sas•si•nate *vb* : murder esp. for political reasons — **as•sas•sin** *n* — **as•sas•si•na•tion** *n*
as•sault *n or vb* : attack
as•say *n* : analysis (as of an ore) to determine quality or properties — **as•say** *vb*
as•sem•ble *vb* **1** : collect into one place **2** : fit together the parts of
as•sem•bly *n* **1** : meeting **2** *cap* : legislative body **3** : a fitting together of parts — **as•sem•bly•man** *n* — **as•sem•bly•wom•an** *n*
as•sent *vb or n* : consent
as•sert *vb* **1** : declare **2** : defend — **as•ser•tion** *n* — **as•sert•ive** *adj* — **as•sert•ive•ness** *n*
as•sess *vb* **1** : impose (as a tax) **2** : evaluate for taxation — **as•sess•ment** *n* — **as•ses•sor** *n*
as•set *n* **1** *pl* : individually owned property **2** : advantage or resource
as•sid•u•ous *adj* : diligent — **as•si•du•i•ty** *n* — **as•sid•u•ous•ly** *adv* — **as•sid•u•ous•ness** *n*
as•sign *vb* **1** : transfer to another **2** : appoint to a duty **3** : designate as a task **4** : attribute — **as•sign•able** *adj* — **as•sign•ment** *n*
as•sist *vb* : help — **as•sist** *n* — **as•sis•tance** *n* — **as•sis•tant** *n*

as•so•ci•ate *vb* **1 :** join in companionship or partnership **2 :** connect in thought — **as•so•ci•ate** *n* — **as•so•ci•a•tion** *n*
as•sort•ed *adj* **:** consisting of various kinds
as•sort•ment *n* **:** assorted collection
as•sume *vb* **1 :** take upon oneself **2 :** pretend to have or be **3 :** take as true — **as•sump•tion** *n*
as•sure *vb* **1 :** give confidence or conviction to **2 :** guarantee — **as•sur•ance** *n*
as•ter•isk *n* **:** a character * used as a reference mark or as an indication of omission of words
as•ter•oid *n* **:** small planet between Mars and Jupiter
asth•ma *n* **:** disorder marked by difficulty in breathing — **asth•mat•ic** *adj or n*
astig•ma•tism *n* **:** visual defect — **as•tig•mat•ic** *adj*
as•ton•ish *vb* **:** amaze — **as•ton•ish•ing•ly** *adv* — **as•ton•ish•ment** *n*
as•tound *vb* **:** fill with confused wonder — **as•tound•ing•ly** *adv*
astray *adv or adj* **:** off the right path
astride *adv* **:** with legs apart or one on each side ∼ *prep* **:** with one leg on each side of
as•trin•gent *adj* **:** causing shrinking or puckering of tissues — **as•trin•gen•cy** *n* — **as•trin•gent** *n*
as•trol•o•gy *n* **:** prediction of events by the stars — **as•trol•o•ger** *n* — **as•tro•log•i•cal** *adj*
as•tro•nau•tics *n* **:** construction and operation of spacecraft — **as•tro•naut** *n* — **as•tro•nau•tic, as•tro•nau•ti•cal** *adj*
as•tro•nom•i•cal *adj* **1 :** relating to astronomy **2 :** extremely large
as•tron•o•my *n* **:** study of the celestial bodies — **as•tron•o•mer** *n*
as•tute *adj* **:** shrewd — **as•tute•ly** *adv* — **as•tute•ness** *n*
asy•lum *n* **1 :** refuge **2 :** institution for care esp. of the insane
at *prep* **1** — used to indicate a point in time or space **2** — used to indicate a goal **3** — used to indicate condition, means, cause, or manner
ate *past of* EAT
athe•ist *n* **:** one who denies the existence of God — **athe•ism** *n* — **athe•is•tic** *adj*
ath•lete *n* **:** one trained to compete in athletics
ath•let•ics *n sing or pl* **:** exercises and games requiring physical skill — **ath•let•ic** *adj*
atlas *n* **:** book of maps
ATM *n* **:** computerized machine for performing basic bank functions
at•mo•sphere *n* **1 :** mass of air surrounding the earth **2 :** surrounding influence — **at•mo•spher•ic** *adj* — **at•mo•spher•i•cal•ly** *adv*
at•om *n* **1 :** tiny bit **2 :** smallest particle of a chemical element that can exist alone or in combination
atom•ic *adj* **1 :** relating to atoms **2 :** nuclear
at•om•iz•er *n* **:** device for dispersing a liquid as a very fine spray
atone *vb* **:** make amends — **atone•ment** *n*
atop *prep* **:** on top of ∼ *adv or adj* **:** on, to, or at the top
atri•um *n* **1 :** open central room or court **2 :** heart chamber that receives blood from the veins
atro•cious *adj* **:** appalling or abominable — **atro•cious•ly** *adv* — **atro•cious•ness** *n* — **atroc•i•ty** *n*
at•ro•phy *n* **:** wasting away of a bodily part or tissue — **at•ro•phy** *vb*
at•tach *vb* **1 :** seize legally **2 :** bind by personalities **3 :** join — **at•tach•ment** *n*
at•ta•ché *n* **:** technical expert on a diplomatic staff
at•tack *vb* **1 :** try to hurt or destroy with violence or words **2 :** set to work on ∼ *n* **1 :** act of attacking **2 :** fit of sickness
at•tain *vb* **1 :** achieve or accomplish **2 :** reach — **at•tain•abil•i•ty** *n* — **at•tain•able** *adj* — **at•tain•ment** *n*
at•tempt *vb* **:** make an effort toward — **attempt** *n*
at•tend *vb* **1 :** handle or provide for the care of something **2 :** accompany **3 :** be present at **4 :** pay attention — **at•ten•dance** *n* — **at•ten•dant** *adj or n*
at•ten•tion *n* **1 :** concentration of the mind on something **2 :** notice or awareness — **at•ten•tive** *adj* — **at•ten•tive•ly** *adv* — **at•ten•tive•ness** *n*
at•test *vb* **:** certify or bear witness — **at•tes•ta•tion** *n*
at•tic *n* **:** space just below the roof
at•tire *vb* **:** dress — **at•tire** *n*
at•ti•tude *n* **1 :** posture or relative position **2 :** feeling, opinion, or mood
at•tor•ney *n* **:** legal agent
at•tract *vb* **1 :** draw to oneself **2 :** have emotional or aesthetic appeal for — **at•trac•tion** *n* — **at•trac•tive** *adj* — **at•trac•tive•ly** *adv* — **at•trac•tive•ness** *n*
at•tri•bute *n* **:** inherent characteristic ∼ *vb* **1 :** regard as having a specific cause or origin **2**

: regard as a characteristic — **at•trib•ut•able** *adj* — **at•tri•bu•tion** *n*
auc•tion *n* : public sale of property to the highest bidder — **auc•tion** *vb* — **auc•tion•eer** *n*
au•dac•i•ty *n* : boldness or insolence — **au•da•cious** *adj*
au•di•ble *adj* : capable of being heard — **au•di•bly** *adv*
au•di•ence *n* **1** : formal interview **2** : group of listeners or spectators
au•dio *adj* : relating to sound or its reproduction ~ *n* : television sound — **au•dio•vi•su•al** *adj*
au•dit *vb* : examine financial accounts — **au•dit** *n* — **au•di•tor** *n*
au•di•tion *n* : tryout performance — **au•di•tion** *vb*
au•di•to•ri•um *n* : room or building used for public performances
au•di•to•ry *adj* : relating to hearing
au•ger *n* : tool for boring
aug•ment *vb* : enlarge or increase — **aug•men•ta•tion** *n*
au•gur *n* : prophet ~ *vb* : predict — **au•gu•ry** *n*
Au•gust *n* : 8th month of the year having 31 days
aunt *n* **1** : sister of one's father or mother **2** : wife of one's uncle
au•ra *n* **1** : distinctive atmosphere **2** : luminous radiation
au•ral *adj* : relating to the ear or to hearing
au•ro•ra bo•re•al•is *n* : display of light in the night sky of northern latitudes
aus•pic•es *n pl* : patronage and protection
aus•pi•cious *adj* : favorable
aus•tere *adj* : severe — **aus•tere•ly** *adv* — **aus•ter•i•ty** *n*
au•then•tic *adj* : genuine — **au•then•ti•cal•ly** *adv* — **au•then•tic•i•ty** *n*
au•then•ti•cate *vb* : prove genuine — **au•then•ti•ca•tion** *n*
au•thor *n* **1** : writer **2** : creator — **au•thor•ship** *n*
au•thor•i•tar•i•an *adj* : marked by blind obedience to authority
au•thor•i•ta•tive *adj* : being an authority — **au•thor•i•ta•tive•ly** *adv* — **au•thor•i•ta•tive•ness** *n*
au•thor•i•ty *n* **1** : expert **2** : right, responsibility, or power to influence **3** *pl* : persons in official positions
au•tho•rize *vb* : permit or give official approval for — **au•tho•ri•za•tion** *n*
au•tism *n* : mental disorder marked by impaired ability to communicate and form social relationships and by repetitive behavior patterns
au•to *n* : automobile
au•to•bi•og•ra•phy *n* : writer's own life story — **au•to•bi•og•ra•pher** *n* — **au•to•bio•graph•i•cal** *adj*
au•toc•ra•cy *n* : government by one person having unlimited power — **au•to•crat** *n* — **au•to•crat•ic** *adj* — **au•to•crat•i•cal•ly** *adv*
au•to•graph *n* : signature ~ *vb* : write one's name on
au•to•mate *vb* : make automatic — **au•to•ma•tion** *n*
au•to•mat•ic *adj* **1** : involuntary **2** : designed to function without human intervention ~ *n* : automatic device (as a firearm) — **au•to•mat•i•cal•ly** *adv*
au•to•mo•bile *n* : 4-wheeled passenger vehicle with its own power source
au•to•mo•tive *adj* : relating to automobiles
au•ton•o•mous *adj* : having independent existence or function — **au•ton•o•mous•ly** *adv* — **au•ton•o•my** *n*
au•top•sy *n* : medical examination of a corpse
au•tumn *n* : season between summer and winter — **au•tum•nal** *adj*
aux•il•ia•ry *adj* **1** : being a supplement or reserve **2** : accompanying a main verb form to express person, number, mood, or tense — **aux•il•ia•ry** *n*
avail•able *adj* **1** : usable **2** : accessible — **avail•abil•i•ty** *n*
av•a•lanche *n* : mass of sliding or falling snow or rock
avenge *vb* : take vengeance for — **aveng•er** *n*
av•e•nue *n* **1** : way of approach **2** : broad street
av•er•age *adj* **1** : being about midway between extremes **2** : ordinary ~ *vb* **1** : be usually **2** : find the mean of ~ *n* : mean
averse *adj* : feeling dislike or reluctance — **aver•sion** *n*
avert *vb* : turn away
avi•a•tion *n* : operation or manufacture of airplanes — **avi•a•tor** *n*
av•id *adj* **1** : greedy **2** : enthusiastic — **avid•i•ty** *n* — **av•id•ly** *adv*
av•o•ca•do *n* : tropical fruit with green pulp
av•o•ca•tion *n* : hobby

avoid *vb* **1 :** keep away from **2 :** prevent the occurrence of **3 :** refrain from — **avoid•able** *adj* — **avoid•ance** *n*
av•oir•du•pois *n* **:** system of weight based on the pound of 16 ounces
await *vb* **:** wait for
awake *vb* (**awoke; awok•en**) **:** wake up — **awake** *adj*
awak•en *vb* **:** wake up
award *vb* **:** give (something won or deserved) ∼ *n* **1 :** judgment **2 :** prize
aware *adj* **:** having realization or consciousness — **aware•ness** *n*
away *adv* **1 :** from this or that place or time **2 :** out of the way **3 :** in another direction **4 :** from one's possession ∼ *adj* **1 :** absent **2 :** distant
awe *n* **:** respectful fear or wonder ∼ *vb* **:** fill with awe — **awe•some** *adj* — **awe•struck** *adj*
aw•ful *adj* **1 :** inspiring awe **2 :** extremely disagreeable **3 :** very great — **aw•ful•ly** *adv*
awk•ward *adj* **1 :** clumsy **2 :** embarrassing — **awk•ward•ly** *adv* — **awk•ward•ness** *n*
awl *n* **:** hole-making tool
aw•ning *n* **:** window cover
ax, axe *n* **:** chopping tool
ax•i•om *n* **:** generally accepted truth — **ax•i•om•at•ic** *adj*
ax•is *n* **:** center of rotation — **ax•i•al** *adj* — **ax•i•al•ly** *adv*
ax•le *n* **:** shaft on which a wheel revolves
aye *adv* **:** yes ∼ *n* **:** a vote of yes
aza•lea *n* **:** rhododendron with funnel-shaped blossoms
az•i•muth *n* **:** horizontal direction expressed as an angle
azure *n* **:** blue of the sky — **azure** *adj*

B

b *n* **:** 2d letter of the alphabet
bab•ble *vb* **1 :** utter meaningless sounds **2 :** talk foolishly or too much — **babble** *n* — **bab•bler** *n*
ba•bel *n* **:** noisy confusion
ba•boon *n* **:** large Asian or African ape with a doglike muzzle
ba•by *n* **:** very young child ∼ *vb* **:** pamper — **baby** *adj* — **ba•by•hood** *n* — **ba•by•ish** *adj*
ba•by–sit *vb* **:** care for children while parents are away — **baby–sit•ter** *n*
became *past of* BECOME
bac•ca•lau•re•ate *n* **:** bachelor's degree
bach•e•lor *n* **1 :** holder of lowest 4-year college degree **2 :** unmarried man — **bach•e•lor•hood** *n*
ba•cil•lus *n* **:** rod-shaped bacterium — **bac•il•lary** *adj*
back *n* **1 :** part of a human or animal body nearest the spine **2 :** part opposite the front **3 :** player farthest from the opponent's goal ∼ *adv* **1 :** to or at the back **2 :** ago **3 :** to or in a former place or state **4 :** in reply ∼ *adj* **1 :** located at the back **2 :** not paid on time **3 :** moving or working backward **4 :** not current ∼ *vb* **1 :** support **2 :** go or cause to go back **3 :** form the back of — **back•ache** *n* — **back•er** *n* — **back•ing** *n* — **back•less** *adj* — **back•rest** *n*
back•bone *n* **1 :** bony column in the back that encloses the spinal cord **2 :** firm character
back•drop *n* **:** painted cloth hung across the rear of a stage
back•gam•mon *n* **:** board game
back•ground *n* **1 :** scenery behind something **2 :** sum of a person's experience or training
back•hand *n* **:** stroke (as in tennis) made with the back of the hand turned forward — **back•hand** *adj or vb* — **back•hand•ed** *adj*
back•lash *n* **:** adverse reaction
back•log *n* **:** accumulation of things to be done — **backlog** *vb*
back•pack *n* **:** camping pack carried on the back ∼ *vb* **:** hike with a backpack — **back•pack•er** *n*
back•slide *vb* **:** lapse in morals or religious practice — **back•slid•er** *n*
back•up *n* **:** substitute
back•ward, back•wards *adv* **1 :** toward the back **2 :** with the back foremost **3 :** in a reverse direction **4 :** toward an earlier or worse state ∼ *adj* **1 :** directed, turned, or done backward **2 :** retarded in development — **back•ward•ness** *n*
back•woods *n pl* **:** remote or isolated place
ba•con *n* **:** salted and smoked meat from a pig
bac•te•ri•um *n* (**bac•te•ria**) **:** microscopic plant — **bac•te•ri•al** *adj* — **bac•te•ri•o•log•ic,**

bac•te•ri•o•log•i•cal *adj* — **bac•te•ri•ol•o•gist** *n* — **bac•te•ri•ol•o•gy** *n*

bad *adj* **worse; worst 1 :** not good **2 :** naughty **3 :** faulty **4 :** spoiled — **bad** *n or adv* — **bad•ly** *adv* — **bad•ness** *n*

bade *past of* BID

badge *n* **:** symbol of status

bad•ger *n* **:** burrowing mammal ~ *vb* **:** harass

bad•min•ton *n* **:** tennislike game played with a shuttlecock

baf•fle *vb* **:** perplex ~ *n* **:** device to alter flow (as of liquid or sound) — **baf•fle•ment** *n*

bag *n* **:** flexible usu. closable container ~ *vb* **1 :** bulge out **2 :** put in a bag **3 :** catch in hunting

ba•gel *n* **:** hard doughnut-shaped roll

bag•gage *n* **:** traveler's bags and belongings

bag•gy *adj* **:** puffed out like a bag — **bag•gi•ness** *n*

bag•pipe *n* **:** musical instrument with a bag, a tube with valves, and sounding pipes — often pl.

[1]**bail** *n* **:** container for scooping water out of a boat — **bail** *vb* — **bail•er** *n*

[2]**bail** *n* **1 :** security given to guarantee a prisoner's appearance in court **2 :** release secured by bail ~ *vb* **:** bring about the release of by giving bail

bai•liff *n* **1 :** British sheriff's aide **2 :** minor officer of a U.S. court

bail•out *n* **:** rescue from financial distress

bait *vb* **1 :** harass with dogs usu. for sport **2 :** furnish (a hook or trap) with bait ~ *n* **:** lure esp. for catching animals

bake *vb* **:** cook in dry heat esp. in an oven ~ *n* **:** party featuring baked food — **bak•er** *n* — **bak•ery** *n* — **bake•shop** *n*

bal•ance *n* **1 :** weighing device **2 :** counteracting weight, force, or influence **3 :** equilibrium **4 :** that which remains ~ *vb* **1 :** compute the balance **2 :** equalize **3 :** bring into harmony or proportion — **bal•anced** *adj*

bal•co•ny *n* **:** platform projecting from a wall

bald *adj* **1 :** lacking a natural or usual covering (as of hair) **2 :** plain — **bald•ing** *adj* — **bald•ly** *adv* — **bald•ness** *n*

bale *n* **:** large bundle ~ *vb* **:** pack in a bale — **bal•er** *n*

bale•ful *adj* **1 :** deadly **2 :** ominous

[1]**ball** *n* **1 :** rounded mass **2 :** game played with a ball ~ *vb* **:** form into a ball

[2]**ball** *n* **:** large formal dance — **ball•room** *n*

bal•lad *n* **1 :** narrative poem **2 :** slow romantic song — **bal•lad•eer** *n*

bal•last *n* **:** heavy material to steady a ship or balloon ~ *vb* **:** provide with ballast

bal•le•ri•na *n* **:** female ballet dancer

bal•let *n* **:** theatrical dancing

bal•loon *n* **:** inflated bag ~ *vb* **1 :** travel in a balloon **2 :** swell out — **bal•loon•ist** *n*

bal•lot *n* **1 :** paper used to cast a vote **2 :** system of voting ~ *vb* **:** vote

balmy *adj* **:** gently soothing — **balm•i•ness** *n*

ba•lo•ney *n* **:** nonsense

bal•sam *n* **1 :** aromatic resinous plant substance **2 :** balsam-yielding plant — **bal•sam•ic** *adj*

bam•boo *n* **:** tall tropical grass with strong hollow stems

ban *vb* **:** prohibit ~ *n* **:** legal prohibition

ba•nal *adj* **:** ordinary and uninteresting — **ba•nal•ity** *n*

ba•nana *n* **:** elongated fruit of a treelike tropical plant

[1]**band** *n* **1 :** something that ties or binds **2 :** strip or stripe different (as in color) from nearby matter **3 :** range of radio wavelengths ~ *vb* **1 :** enclose with a band **2 :** unite for a common end — **band•ed** *adj* — **band•er** *n*

[2]**band** *n* **1 :** group **2 :** musicians playing together — **band•stand** *n*

ban•dage *n* **:** material used esp. in dressing wounds ~ *vb* **:** dress or cover with a bandage

ban•dan•na, ban•dana *n* **:** large colored figured handkerchief

ban•dit *n* **:** outlaw or robber — **ban•dit•ry** *n*

band•wag•on *n* **:** candidate, side, or movement gaining support

[1]**bang** *vb* **:** strike, thrust, or move usu. with a loud noise ~ *n* **1 :** blow **2 :** sudden loud noise ~ *adv* **:** directly

[2]**bang** *n* **:** fringe of short hair over the forehead — usu. pl. ~ *vb* **:** cut in bangs

ban•gle *n* **:** bracelet

ban•ish *vb* **1 :** force by authority to leave a country **2 :** expel — **ban•ish•ment** *n*

ban•is•ter *n* **1 :** upright support for a rail **2 :** handrail

ban•jo *n* **:** stringed instrument with a drumlike body — **banjo•ist** *n*

[1]**bank** *n* **1 :** piled-up mass **2 :** rising ground along a body of water **3 :** sideways slope along a curve ~ *vb* **1 :** form a bank **2 :** cover (as a fire) to keep inactive **3 :** incline (an airplane) laterally

[2]**bank** *n* : tier of objects
[3]**bank** *n* **1** : money institution **2** : reserve supply ~ *vb* : conduct business in a bank — **bank•book** *n* — **bank•er** *n* — **bank•ing** *n*
bank•rupt *n* : one required by law to forfeit assets to pay off debts ~ *adj* **1** : legally a bankrupt **2** : lacking something essential — **bankrupt** *vb* — **bank•rupt•cy** *n*
ban•ner *n* : flag ~ *adj* : excellent
ban•quet *n* : ceremonial dinner — **banquet** *vb*
ban•shee *n* : wailing female spirit that foretells death
ban•tam *n* : miniature domestic fowl
ban•ter *n* : good-natured joking — **banter** *vb*
bap•tize *vb* : administer baptism to — **baptism** *n* — **bap•tis•mal** *adj*
bar *n* **1** : long narrow object used esp. as a lever, fastening, or support **2** : barrier **3** : body of practicing lawyers **4** : wide stripe **5** : food counter **6** : place where liquor is served **7** : vertical line across the musical staff ~ *vb* **1** : obstruct with a bar **2** : shut out **3** : prohibit ~ *prep* : excluding — **barred** *adj* — **barroom** *n* — **bar•tend•er** *n*
barb *n* : sharp projection pointing backward — **barbed** *adj*
bar•bar•ian *adj* **1** : relating to people considered backward **2** : not refined — **barbarian** *n* — **bar•bar•ic** *adj*
bar•ba•rous *adj* **1** : lacking refinement **2** : mercilessly cruel — **bar•bar•ism** *n* — **bar•bar•i•ty** *n* — **bar•ba•rous•ly** *adv*
bar•be•cue *n* : gathering at which barbecued food is served ~ *vb* : cook over hot coals or on a spit often with a highly seasoned sauce
bar•ber *n* : one who cuts hair
bare *adj* **1** : naked **2** : not concealed **3** : empty **4** : leaving nothing to spare **5** : plain ~ *vb* : make or lay bare — **bare•foot, bare•foot•ed** *adv or adj* — **bare–hand•ed** *adv or adj* — **bare•head•ed** *adv or adj* — **bare•ly** *adv* — **bare•ness** *n*
bare•back, bare•backed *adv or adj* : without a saddle
bare•faced *adj* : open and esp. brazen
bar•gain *n* **1** : agreement **2** : something bought for less than its value ~ *vb* **1** : negotiate **2** : barter
barge *n* : broad flat-bottomed boat ~ *vb* : move rudely or clumsily — **barge•man** *n*
bari•tone *n* : male voice between bass and tenor
[1]**bark** *vb* **1** : make the sound of a dog **2** : speak in a loud curt tone ~ *n* : sound of a barking dog
[2]**bark** *n* : tough corky outer covering of a woody stem or root ~ *vb* : remove bark or skin from
bark•er *n* : one who calls out to attract people to a show
barn *n* : building for keeping hay or livestock — **barn•yard** *n*
barn•storm *vb* : tour through rural districts giving performances
ba•rom•e•ter *n* : instrument for measuring atmospheric pressure — **baro•met•ric** *adj*
bar•racks *n sing or pl* : soldiers' housing
bar•rel *n* **1** : closed cylindrical container **2** : amount held by a barrel **3** : cylindrical part ~ *vb* **1** : pack in a barrel **2** : move at high speed
bar•ren *adj* **1** : unproductive of life **2** : uninteresting — **bar•ren•ness** *n*
bar•rette *n* : clasp for a woman's hair
bar•ri•cade *n* : barrier — **barricade** *vb*
bar•ri•er *n* : something that separates or obstructs
bar•ter *vb* : trade by exchange of goods — **barter** *n*
[1]**base** *n* **1** : bottom **2** : fundamental part **3** : beginning point **4** : supply source of a force **5** : compound that reacts with an acid to form a salt ~ *vb* : establish — **base•less** *adj*
[2]**base** *adj* **1** : inferior **2** : contemptible — **base•ly** *adv* — **base•ness** *n*
base•ball *n* : game played with a bat and ball by 2 teams
base•ment *n* : part of a building below ground level
bash *vb* : strike violently ~ *n* : heavy blow
bash•ful *adj* : self-conscious — **bash•ful•ness** *n*
ba•sic *adj* **1** : relating to or forming the base or essence **2** : relating to a chemical base — **ba•si•cal•ly** *adv* — **ba•sic•i•ty** *n*
ba•sin *n* **1** : large bowl or pan **2** : region drained by a river
ba•sis *n* **1** : something that supports **2** : fundamental principle
bask *vb* : enjoy pleasant warmth
bas•ket *n* : woven container — **bas•ket•ful** *n*
bas•ket•ball *n* : game played with a ball on a court by 2 teams
[1]**bass** *n* : spiny-finned sport and food fish
[2]**bass** *n* **1** : deep tone **2** : lowest choral voice
bas•set hound *n* : short-legged dog with long ears

bas•soon *n* : low-pitched wind instrument
bas•tard *n* **1 :** illegitimate child **2 :** offensive person ~ *adj* **1 :** illegitimate **2 :** inferior — **bas•tard•ize** *vb* — **bas•tardy** *n*
¹baste *vb* : sew temporarily with long stitches
²baste *vb* : moisten at intervals while cooking
¹bat *n* **1 :** stick or club **2 :** sharp blow ~ *vb* : hit with a bat
²bat *n* : small flying mammal
³bat *vb* : wink or blink
batch *n* : quantity used or produced at one time
bath *n* **1 :** a washing of the body **2 :** water for washing the body **3 :** liquid in which something is immersed **4 :** bathroom **5 :** large financial loss — **bath•robe** *n* — **bath•room** *n* — **bath•tub** *n*
bathe *vb* **1 :** wash in liquid **2 :** flow against so as to wet **3 :** shine light over **4 :** take a bath or a swim — **bath•er** *n*
bat•tal•ion *n* : military unit composed of a headquarters and two or more companies
¹bat•ter *vb* : beat or damage with repeated blows
²batter *n* : mixture of flour and liquid
³batter *n* : player who bats
bat•tery *n* **1 :** illegal beating of a person **2 :** group of artillery guns **3 :** group of electric cells
bat•ting *n* : layers of cotton or wool for stuffing
bat•tle *n* : military fighting ~ *vb* : engage in battle — **bat•tle•field** *n*
bat•tle•ship *n* : heavily armed ship of war
bau•ble *n* : a small ornament
bawdy *adj* : obscene or lewd — **bawd•i•ly** *adv* — **bawd•i•ness** *n*
bawl *vb* : cry loudly ~ *n* : long loud cry
¹bay *adj* : reddish brown ~ *n* : bay-colored animal
²bay *n* : European laurel
³bay *n* **1 :** compartment **2 :** area projecting out from a building and containing a window (**bay window**)
⁴bay *vb* : bark with deep long tones ~ *n* **1 :** position of one unable to escape danger **2 :** baying of dogs
⁵bay *n* : body of water smaller than a gulf and nearly surrounded by land
bay•ou *n* : creek flowing through marshy land
ba•zaar *n* **1 :** market **2 :** fair for charity
BB *n* : small shot pellet
be *vb* **was; were; been; am; is; are 1 :** equal **2 :** exist **3 :** occupy a certain place **4 :** occur ~ *verbal auxiliary* — used to show continuous action or to form the passive voice
beach *n* : sandy shore of a sea, lake, or river ~ *vb* : drive ashore — **beach•comb•er** *n*
bea•con *n* : guiding or warning light or signal
bead *n* : small round body esp. strung on a thread ~ *vb* : form into a bead — **bead•ing** *n* — **beady** *adj*
bea•gle *n* : small short-legged hound
beak *n* : bill of a bird — **beaked** *adj*
bea•ker *n* **1 :** large drinking cup **2 :** laboratory vessel
beam *n* **1 :** large long piece of timber or metal **2 :** ray of light **3 :** directed radio signals for the guidance of pilots ~ *vb* **1 :** send out light **2 :** smile **3 :** aim a radio broadcast
bean *n* : edible plant seed borne in pods
¹bear *n* **1 :** large heavy mammal with shaggy hair **2 :** gruff or sullen person — **bear•ish** *adj*
²bear *vb* (**bore; borne**) **1 :** carry **2 :** give birth to or produce **3 :** endure **4 :** press **5 :** go in an indicated direction — **bear•able** *adj* — **bear•er** *n*
beard *n* **1 :** facial hair on a man **2 :** tuft like a beard ~ *vb* : confront boldly — **beard•ed** *adj* — **beard•less** *adj*
bear•ing *n* **1 :** way of carrying oneself **2 :** supporting object or purpose **3 :** significance **4 :** machine part in which another part turns **5 :** direction with respect esp. to compass points
beast *n* **1 :** animal **2 :** brutal person — **beast•li•ness** *n* — **beast•ly** *adj*
beat *vb* (**beat; beat•en/beat**) **1 :** strike repeatedly **2 :** defeat **3 :** act or arrive before **4 :** throb ~ *n* **1 :** single stroke or pulsation **2 :** rhythmic stress in poetry or music ~ *adj* : exhausted — **beat•er** *n*
be•at•i•fy *vb* : make happy or blessed — **be•atif•ic** *adj* — **be•at•i•fi•ca•tion** *n*
be•at•i•tude *n* : saying in the Sermon on the Mount (Matthew 5:3-12) beginning "Blessed are"
beau•ty *n* : qualities that please the senses or mind — **beau•te•ous** *adj* — **beau•te•ously** *adv* — **beau•ti•fi•ca•tion** *n* — **beau•ti•fi•er** *n* — **beau•ti•ful** *adj* — **beau•ti•ful•ly** *adv* — **beau•ti•fy** *vb*
bea•ver *n* : large fur-bearing rodent
be•cause *conj* : for the reason that
because of *prep* : by reason of
beck•on *vb* : summon esp. by a nod or gesture
be•come *vb* **became; become 1 :** come to be **2 :** be suitable — **be•com•ing** *adj* — **be•com•ing•ly** *adv*
bed *n* **1 :** piece of furniture to sleep on **2 :** flat

or level surface ~ *vb* : put or go to bed — **bed•room** *n* — **bed•spread** *n*
bed•bug *n* : wingless bloodsucking insect
bed•ding *n* **1 :** sheets and blankets for a bed **2 :** soft material (as hay) for an animal's bed
bed•rid•den *adj* : kept in bed by illness
bed•rock *n* : solid subsurface rock — **bedrock** *adj*
[1]bee *n* : 4-winged honey-producing insect — **bee•hive** *n* — **bee•keep•er** *n* — **bees•wax** *n*
[2]bee *n* : neighborly work session
beech *n* : tree with smooth gray bark and edible nuts (**beech•nuts**) — **beech•en** *adj*
beef *n* : flesh of a steer, cow, or bull ~ *vb* : strengthen — used with *up* — **beef•steak** *n*
bee•line *n* : straight course
been *past part of* BE
beep *n* : short usu. high-pitched warning sound — **beep** *vb* — **beep•er** *n*
beer *n* : alcoholic drink brewed from malt and hops — **beery** *adj*
beet *n* : garden root vegetable
bee•tle *n* : 4-winged insect
be•fore *adv* **1 :** in front **2 :** earlier ~ *prep* **1 :** in front of **2 :** earlier than ~ *conj* : earlier than
be•fore•hand *adv or adj* : in advance
be•fud•dle *vb* : confuse
beg *vb* : ask earnestly
beg•gar *n* : one that begs ~ *vb* : make poor — **beg•gar•ly** *adj* — **beg•gary** *n*
be•gin *vb* **be•gan; be•gun 1 :** start **2 :** come into being — **be•gin•ner** *n*
be•grudge *vb* **1 :** concede reluctantly **2 :** look upon disapprovingly
be•guile *vb* **1 :** deceive **2 :** amuse
be•half *n* : benefit
be•have *vb* : act in a certain way
be•hav•ior *n* : way of behaving — **be•hav•ior•al** *adj*
be•head *vb* : cut off the head of
be•hind *adv* : at the back ~ *prep* **1 :** in back of **2 :** less than **3 :** supporting
be•hold *vb* : see — **be•hold•er** *n*
beige *n* : yellowish brown — **beige** *adj*
be•ing *n* **1 :** existence **2 :** living thing
be•lat•ed *adj* : delayed
belch *vb* **1 :** expel stomach gas orally **2 :** emit forcefully — **belch** *n*
be•lea•guer *vb* **1 :** besiege **2 :** harass
bel•fry *n* : bell tower
be•lief *n* **1 :** trust **2 :** something believed
be•lieve *vb* **1 :** trust in **2 :** accept as true **3 :** hold as an opinion — **be•liev•able** *adj* — **be•liev•ably** *adv* — **be•liev•er** *n*
be•lit•tle *vb* **1 :** disparage **2 :** make seem less
bell *n* : hollow metallic device that rings when struck ~ *vb* : provide with a bell
belle *n* : beautiful woman
bel•lig•er•ent *adj* **1 :** waging war **2 :** aggressively asserting one's own will — **bel•lig•er•ence** *n* — **bel•lig•er•en•cy** *n* — **belligerent** *n*
bel•low *vb* : make a loud deep roar or shout — **bellow** *n*
bel•lows *n sing or pl* : device with sides that can be compressed to expel air
bel•ly *n* : abdomen ~ *vb* : bulge
be•long *vb* **1 :** be suitable **2 :** be owned **3 :** be a part of
be•long•ings *n pl* : possessions
be•loved *adj* : dearly loved — **beloved** *n*
be•low *adv* : in or to a lower place ~ *prep* : lower than
belt *n* **1 :** strip (as of leather) worn about the waist **2 :** endless band to impart motion **3 :** distinct region ~ *vb* **1 :** put a belt around **2 :** beat soundly
be•muse *vb* : confuse
bench *n* **1 :** long seat **2 :** judge's seat **3 :** court
bend *vb* (**bent; bent**) **1 :** curve or cause a change of shape in **2 :** turn in a certain direction ~ *n* **1 :** act of bending **2 :** curve
be•neath *adv or prep* : below
bene•dic•tion *n* : closing blessing
bene•fac•tor *n* : one who gives esp. charitable aid
ben•e•fit *n* **1 :** something that does good **2 :** help **3 :** fund-raising event — **benefit** *vb* — **ben•e•fi•cial** *adj* — **ben•e•fi•cial•ly** *adv* — **ben•e•fi•cia•ry** *n*
be•nev•o•lence *n* **1 :** charitable nature **2 :** act of kindness — **be•nev•o•lent** *adj* — **be•nev•o•lent•ly** *adv*
be•nign *adj* **1 :** gentle or kindly **2 :** not malignant — **be•nig•ni•ty** *n*
bent *n* : aptitude or interest
be•numb *vb* : make numb esp. by cold
be•queath *vb* **1 :** give by will **2 :** hand down — **be•quest** *n*
be•rate *vb* : scold harshly
be•reaved *adj* : suffering the death of a loved one ~ *n pl* **bereaved :** one who is bereaved — **be•reave•ment** *n*
be•ret *n* : round soft visorless cap

ber•ry *n* **:** small pulpy fruit

ber•serk *adj* **:** acting out of control or insane — **berserk** *adv*

berth *n* **1 :** place where a ship is anchored **2 :** place to sit or sleep esp. on a ship **3 :** job ~ *vb* **:** to bring or come into a berth

be•seech *vb* **:** entreat

be•side *prep* **1 :** by the side of **2 :** besides

be•sides *adv* **1 :** in addition **2 :** further to what has been said ~ *prep* **1 :** other than **2 :** in addition to

be•siege *vb* **:** lay siege to — **be•sieg•er** *n*

best *adj, superlative of* GOOD **1 :** excelling all others **2 :** most productive **3 :** largest ~ *adv superlative of* WELL **1 :** in the best way **2 :** most ~ *n* **:** one that is best ~ *vb* **:** outdo

bes•tial *adj* **1 :** relating to beasts **2 :** brutish — **bes•ti•al•i•ty** *n*

best man *n* **:** chief male attendant at a wedding

be•stow *vb* **:** give — **be•stow•al** *n*

bet *n* **1 :** something risked or pledged on the outcome of a contest **2 :** the making of a bet ~ *vb* **bet; bet 1 :** risk (as money) on an outcome **2 :** make a bet with

be•tray *vb* **1 :** seduce **2 :** report or reveal to an enemy by treachery **3 :** abandon **4 :** prove unfaithful to **5 :** reveal unintentionally — **be•tray•al** *n* — **be•tray•er** *n*

be•troth *vb* **:** promise to marry — **be•troth•al** *n* — **be•trothed** *n*

bet•ter *adj, comparative of* GOOD **1 :** more than half **2 :** improved in health **3 :** of higher quality ~ *adv comparative of* WELL **1 :** in a superior manner **2 :** more ~ *n* **1 :** one that is better **2 :** advantage ~ *vb* **1 :** improve **2 :** surpass — **bet•ter•ment** *n*

bet•tor, bet•ter *n* **:** one who bets

be•tween *prep* **1** — used to show two things considered together **2 :** in the space separating **3** — used to indicate a comparison or choice ~ *adv* **:** in an intervening space or interval

bev•el *n* **:** slant on an edge ~ *vb* **1 :** cut or shape to a bevel **2 :** incline

bev•er•age *n* **:** drink

be•ware *vb* **:** be cautious

be•wil•der *vb* **:** confuse — **be•wil•der•ment** *n*

be•witch *vb* **1 :** affect by witchcraft **2 :** charm — **be•witch•ment** *n*

be•yond *adv* **1 :** farther **2 :** besides ~ *prep* **1 :** on or to the farther side of **2 :** out of the reach of **3 :** besides

bi•an•nu•al *adj* **:** occurring twice a year — **bi•an•nu•al•ly** *adv*

bi•as *n* **1 :** line diagonal to the grain of a fabric **2 :** prejudice ~ *vb* **:** prejudice

bib *n* **:** shield tied under the chin to protect the clothes while eating

Bi•ble *n* **1 :** sacred scriptures of Christians **2 :** sacred scriptures of Judaism or another religion — **bib•li•cal** *adj*

bib•li•og•ra•phy *n* **:** list of writings on a subject or of an author — **bib•li•og•ra•pher** *n* — **bib•li•o•graph•ic** *adj*

bi•cen•ten•ni•al *n* **:** 200th anniversary — **bicentennial** *adj*

bi•ceps *n* **:** large muscle of the upper arm

bick•er *vb or n* **:** squabble

bi•cus•pid *n* **:** double-pointed tooth

bi•cy•cle *n* **:** 2-wheeled vehicle moved by pedaling ~ *vb* **:** ride a bicycle — **bi•cy•cler** *n* — **bi•cy•clist** *n*

bid *vb* **bade/bid; bid•den/bid 1 :** order **2 :** invite **3 :** express **4 :** make a bid ~ *n* **1 :** act of bidding **2 :** buyer's proposed price — **bid•da•ble** *adj* — **bid•der** *n*

bide *vb* **1 :** wait **2 :** dwell

bi•en•ni•al *adj* **1 :** occurring once in 2 years **2 :** lasting 2 years — **biennial** *n* — **bi•en•ni•al•ly** *adv*

bifocals *n pl* **:** eyeglasses that correct for near and distant vision

big *adj* **:** large in size, amount, or scope — **bigness** *n*

big•a•my *n* **:** marrying one person while still married to another — **big•a•mist** *n* — **big•a•mous** *adj*

big•ot *n* **:** one who is intolerant of others — **big•ot•ed** *adj* — **big•ot•ry** *n*

big shot *n* **:** important person

big•wig *n* **:** big shot

bike *n* **:** bicycle or motorcycle

bi•ki•ni *n* **:** woman's brief 2-piece bathing suit

bile *n* **1 :** greenish liver secretion that aids digestion **2 :** bad temper

bi•lin•gual *adj* **:** using 2 languages

bilk *vb* **:** cheat

[1]**bill** *n* **:** jaws of a bird together with their horny covering ~ *vb* **:** caress fondly — **billed** *adj*

[2]**bill** *n* **1 :** draft of a law **2 :** list of things to be paid for **3 :** printed advertisement **4 :** piece of paper money ~ *vb* **:** submit a bill or account to

bill•board *n* **:** surface for displaying advertising bills

bill•fold *n* **:** wallet

bil•liards *n* : game of driving balls into one another or into pockets on a table
bil•lion *n* : 1000 millions — **billion** *adj* — **billionth** *adj or n*
bil•low *n* **1** : great wave **2** : rolling mass ~ *vb* : swell out — **bil•lowy** *adj*
billy goat *n* : male goat
bin *n* : storage box
bi•na•ry *adj* : consisting of 2 things — **binary** *n*
bind *vb* **1** : tie **2** : obligate **3** : unite into a mass **4** : bandage — **bind•er** *n* — **binding** *n*
binge *n* : excessive indulgence
bin•go *n* : game of covering numbers on a card
bin•oc•u•lar *adj* : of or relating to both eyes ~ *n* : binocular optical instrument — *usu. pl.*
bio•chem•is•try *n* : chemistry dealing with organisms — **bio•chemi•cal** *adj or n* — **bio•chem•ist** *n*
bio•de•grad•able *adj* : able to be reduced to harmless products by organisms — **bio•de•grad•abil•i•ty** *n* — **bio•deg•ra•da•tion** *n* — **bio•de•grade** *vb*
bi•og•ra•phy *n* : written history of a person's life — **bi•og•ra•pher** *n* — **bi•o•graph•i•cal** *adj*
bi•ol•o•gy *n* : science of living beings and life processes — **bi•o•log•ic, bi•o•log•i•cal** *adj* — **bi•ol•o•gist** *n*
bi•on•ic *adj* : having normal biological capabilities enhanced by electronic or mechanical devices
bio•phys•ics *n* : application of physics to biological problems — **bio•phys•i•cal** *adj* — **bio•phys•i•cist** *n*
bi•op•sy *n* : removal of live bodily tissue for examination
bi•par•ti•san *adj* : involving members of 2 parties
bi•ped *n* : 2-footed animal
birch *n* : deciduous tree with close-grained wood — **birch, birch•en** *adj*
bird *n* : warm-blooded egg-laying vertebrate with wings and feathers — **bird•bath** *n* — **bird•house** *n* — **bird•seed** *n*
bird's–eye *adj* **1** : seen from above **2** : of a general or superficial nature
birth *n* **1** : act or fact of being born or of producing young **2** : origin — **birth•day** *n* — **birth•mark** *n* — **birth•place** *n* — **birth•rate** *n* — **birth•right** *n*
bis•cuit *n* : small bread made with leavening other than yeast
bi•sect *vb* : divide into 2 parts — **bi•sec•tion** *n* — **bi•sec•tor** *n*
bish•op *n* : clergy member higher than a priest
bish•op•ric *n* **1** : diocese **2** : office of bishop
bi•son *n pl* **bison** : large shaggy wild ox of central U.S.
bis•tro *n* : small restaurant or bar
[1]bit *n* **1** : part of a bridle that goes in a horse's mouth **2** : drilling tool
[2]bit *n* **1** : small piece or quantity **2** : small degree
bitch *n* : female dog ~ *vb* : complain
bite *vb* **bit; bit•ten** **1** : to grip or cut with teeth or jaws **2** : dig in or grab and hold **3** : sting **4** : take bait ~ *n* **1** : act of biting **2** : bit of food **3** : wound made by biting — **bit•ing** *adj*
bit•ten *past part of* BITE
bit•ter *adj* **1** : having an acrid lingering taste **2** : intense or severe **3** : extremely harsh or resentful — **bit•ter•ly** *adv* — **bit•ter•ness** *n*
bi•valve *n* : animal (as a clam) with a shell of 2 parts — **bivalve** *adj*
bi•zarre *adj* : very strange — **bi•zarre•ly** *adv*
blab *vb* : talk too much
black *adj* **1** : of the color black **2** : having dark skin **3** : soiled **4** : lacking light **5** : wicked or evil **6** : gloomy ~ *n* **1** : black pigment or dye **2** : something black **3** : color of least lightness **4** : person of a dark-skinned race ~ *vb* : blacken — **black•ing** *n* — **black•ish** *adj* — **black•ly** *adv* — **black•ness** *n*
black–and–blue *adj* : darkly discolored from bruising
black•ball *vb* **1** : ostracize **2** : boycott — **blackball** *n*
black•ber•ry *n* : black or purple fruit of a bramble
black•board *n* : dark surface for writing on with chalk
black•en *vb* **1** : make or become black **2** : harm the reputation of
black•head *n* : small dark oily mass plugging the outlet of a skin gland
black hole *n* : invisible extremely massive celestial object
black•jack *n* **1** : flexible leather-covered club **2** : card game ~ *vb* : hit with a blackjack
black•list *n* : list of persons to be punished or boycotted — **blacklist** *vb*
black•mail *n* **1** : extortion by threat of exposure **2** : something extorted by blackmail — **blackmail** *vb* — **black•mail•er** *n*

black·out *n* **1 :** darkness due to electrical failure **2 :** brief fainting spell — **black out** *vb*
black·smith *n* **:** one who forges iron
black·top *n* **:** dark tarry material for surfacing roads — **blacktop** *vb*
blad·der *n* **:** sac into which urine passes from the kidneys
blade *n* **1 :** leaf esp. of grass **2 :** something resembling the flat part of a leaf **3 :** cutting part of an instrument or tool — **blad·ed** *adj*
blame *vb* **1 :** find fault with **2 :** hold responsible or responsible for — **blam·able** *adj* — **blame** *n* — **blame·less** *adj* — **blame·less·ly** *adv* — **blame·worthy** *adj*
bland *adj* **1 :** smooth in manner **2 :** soothing **3 :** tasteless — **bland·ly** *adv* — **bland·ness** *n*
blank *adj* **1 :** showing or causing a dazed look **2 :** lacking expression **3 :** empty **4 :** free from writing **5 :** downright ~ *n* **1 :** an empty space **2 :** form with spaces to write in **3 :** unfinished form (as of a key) **4 :** cartridge with no bullet ~ *vb* **:** cover or close up — **blank·ly** *adv* — **blank·ness** *n*
blan·ket *n* **1 :** heavy covering for a bed **2 :** covering layer ~ *vb* **:** cover ~ *adj* **:** applying to a group
blare *vb* **:** make a loud harsh sound — **blare** *n*
bla·sé *adj* **:** indifferent to pleasure or excitement
blas·pheme *vb* **:** speak blasphemy — **blas·phem·er** *n* — **blas·phe·mous** *adj* — **blas·phe·my** *n*
blast *n* **1 :** violent gust of wind **2 :** explosion ~ *vb* **:** shatter by or as if by explosive — **blast off** *vb* **:** take off esp. in a rocket
bla·tant *adj* **:** offensively showy — **bla·tan·cy** *n* — **bla·tant·ly** *adv*
¹blaze *n* **1 :** fire **2 :** intense direct light **3 :** strong display ~ *vb* **:** burn or shine brightly
²blaze *n* **1 :** white stripe on an animal's face **2 :** trail marker esp. on a tree ~ *vb* **:** mark with blazes
bleach *vb* **:** whiten — **bleach** *n*
bleach·ers *n sing or pl* **:** spectator stand without a roof
bleak *adj* **1 :** desolately barren **2 :** lacking cheering qualities — **bleak·ish** *adj* — **bleak·ly** *adv* — **bleak·ness** *n*
bleary *adj* **:** dull or dimmed esp. from fatigue
bleat *n* **:** cry of a sheep or goat or a sound like it — **bleat** *vb*
bleed *vb* **1 :** lose or shed blood **2 :** feel distress **3 :** flow from a wound **4 :** draw fluid from **5 :** extort money from — **bleed·er** *n*
blem·ish *vb* **:** spoil by a flaw ~ *n* **:** noticeable flaw
¹blench *vb* **:** flinch
²blench *vb* **:** grow or make pale
blend *vb* **1 :** mix thoroughly **2 :** combine into an integrated whole — **blend** *n* — **blend·er** *n*
bless *vb* **1 :** consecrate by religious rite **2 :** invoke divine care for **3 :** make happy — **bless·ed, blest** *adj* — **bless·ed·ly** *adv* — **bless·ed·ness** *n* — **bless·ing** *n*
blew *past of* BLOW
blight *n* **1 :** plant disorder marked by withering or an organism causing it **2 :** harmful influence **3 :** deteriorated condition ~ *vb* **:** affect with or suffer from blight
blimp *n* **:** airship holding form by pressure of contained gas
blind *adj* **1 :** lacking or quite deficient in ability to see **2 :** not intelligently controlled **3 :** having no way out ~ *vb* **1 :** to make blind **2 :** dazzle ~ *n* **1 :** something to conceal or darken **2 :** place of concealment — **blind·ly** *adv* — **blind·ness** *n*
blind·fold *vb* **:** cover the eyes of — **blindfold** *n*
blink *vb* **1 :** wink **2 :** shine intermittently ~ *n* **:** wink
bliss *n* **1 :** complete happiness **2 :** heaven or paradise — **bliss·ful** *adj* — **bliss·ful·ly** *adv*
blis·ter *n* **1 :** raised area of skin containing watery fluid **2 :** raised or swollen spot ~ *vb* **:** develop or cause blisters
blithe *adj* **:** cheerful — **blithe·ly** *adv* — **blithe·some** *adj*
blitz *n* **1 :** series of air raids **2 :** fast intensive campaign — **blitz** *vb*
bliz·zard *n* **:** severe snowstorm
bloat *vb* **:** swell
blob *n* **:** small lump or drop
bloc *n* **:** group working together
block *n* **1 :** solid piece **2 :** frame enclosing a pulley **3 :** quantity considered together **4 :** large building divided into separate units **5 :** a city square or the distance along one of its sides **6 :** obstruction **7 :** interruption of a bodily or mental function ~ *vb* **:** obstruct or hinder
block·ade *n* **:** isolation of a place usu. by troops or ships — **block·ade** *vb* — **block·ad·er** *n*
block·head *n* **:** stupid person

blond, blonde *adj* **1 :** fair in complexion **2 :** of a light color — **blond, blonde** *n*
blood *n* **1 :** red liquid that circulates in the heart, arteries, and veins of animals **2 :** lifeblood **3 :** line of descent from common ancestors — **blood•ed** *adj* — **blood•less** *adj* — **blood•stain** *n* — **blood•stained** *adj* — **blood•suck•er** *n* — **blood•suck•ing** *n* — **bloody** *adj*
blood•hound *n* **:** large hound with a keen sense of smell
blood•mo•bile *n* **:** truck for collecting blood from donors
blood•shed *n* **:** slaughter
blood•shot *adj* **:** inflamed to redness
blood•thirsty *adj* **:** eager to shed blood — **blood•thirst•i•ly** *adv* — **blood•thirst•i•ness** *n*
bloom *n* **1 :** flower **2 :** period of flowering **3 :** fresh or healthy look ~ *vb* **1 :** yield flowers **2 :** mature — **bloomy** *adj*
bloop•er *n* **:** public blunder
blos•som *n or vb* **:** flower
blot *n* **1 :** stain **2 :** blemish ~ *vb* **1 :** spot **2 :** dry with absorbent paper — **blot•ter** *n*
blotch *n* **:** large spot — **blotch** *vb* — **blotchy** *adj*
blouse *n* **:** loose garment reaching from the neck to the waist
[1]**blow** *vb* **blew; blown 1 :** move forcibly **2 :** send forth a current of air **3 :** sound **4 :** shape by blowing **5 :** explode **6 :** bungle ~ *n* **1 :** gale **2 :** act of blowing — **blow•er** *n* — **blowy** *adj*
[2]**blow** *n* **1 :** forcible stroke **2** *pl* **:** fighting **3 :** calamity
blow•out *n* **:** bursting of a tire
blow•torch *n* **:** small torch that uses a blast of air
[1]**blub•ber** *n* **:** fat of whales
[2]**blubber** *vb* **:** cry noisily
blud•geon *n* **:** short club ~ *vb* **:** hit with a bludgeon
blue *adj* **1 :** of the color blue **2 :** melancholy ~ *n* **:** color of the clear sky — **blu•ish** *adj*
blue•ber•ry *n* **:** edible blue or blackish berry
blue•bird *n* **:** small bluish songbird
blue jay *n* **:** American crested jay
blues *n pl* **1 :** depression **2 :** music in a melancholy style
[1]**bluff** *adj* **1 :** rising steeply with a broad flat front **2 :** frank ~ *n* **:** cliff
[2]**bluff** *vb* **:** deceive by pretense ~ *n* **:** act of bluffing — **bluff•er** *n*
blun•der *vb* **1 :** move clumsily **2 :** make a stupid mistake ~ *n* **:** bad mistake
blunt *adj* **1 :** not sharp **2 :** tactless ~ *vb* **:** make dull — **blunt•ly** *adv* — **blunt•ness** *n*
blur *n* **1 :** smear **2 :** something perceived indistinctly ~ *vb* **:** cloud or obscure — **blur•ry** *adj*
blurb *n* **:** short publicity notice
blurt *vb* **:** utter suddenly
blush *n* **:** reddening of the face — **blush** *vb* — **blush•ful** *adj*
blus•ter *vb* **1 :** blow violently **2 :** talk or act with boasts or threats — **blus•ter** *n* — **blus•tery** *adj*
boa *n* **1 :** a large snake (as the **boa con•stric•tor**) that crushes its prey **2 :** fluffy scarf
boar *n* **:** male swine
board *n* **1 :** long thin piece of sawed lumber **2 :** flat thin sheet esp. for games **3 :** daily meals furnished for pay **4 :** official body ~ *vb* **1 :** go aboard **2 :** cover with boards **3 :** supply meals to — **board•er** *n*
board•walk *n* **:** wooden walk along a beach
boast *vb* **:** praise oneself or one's possessions — **boast** *n* — **boast•er** *n* — **boast•ful** *adj* — **boast•ful•ly** *adv*
boat *n* **:** small vessel for traveling on water — **boat** *vb* — **boat•man** *n*
[1]**bob** *vb* **1 :** move up and down **2 :** appear suddenly
[2]**bob** *n* **1 :** float **2 :** woman's short haircut ~ *vb* **:** cut hair in a bob
bob•bin *n* **:** spindle for holding thread
bob•ble *vb* **:** fumble — **bobble** *n*
bob•cat *n* **:** small American lynx
bob•sled *n* **:** racing sled — **bobsled** *vb*
bob•white *n* **:** quail
[1]**bode** *vb* **:** indicate by signs
[2]**bode** *past of* BIDE
bod•ice *n* **:** close-fitting top of dress
bodi•ly *adj* **:** relating to the body ~ *adv* **1 :** in the flesh **2 :** as a whole
body *n* **1 :** the physical whole of an organism **2 :** human being **3 :** main part **4 :** mass of matter **5 :** group — **bod•ied** *adj* — **bodi•less** *adj* — **body•guard** *n*
bog *n* **:** swamp ~ *vb* **:** sink in or as if in a bog — **bog•gy** *adj*
bo•gey *n* **:** someone or something frightening
bog•gle *vb* **:** overwhelm with amazement
bo•gus *adj* **:** fake

[1]**boil** *n* **:** inflamed swelling
[2]**boil** *vb* **1 :** heat to a temperature (**boiling point**) at which vapor forms **2 :** cook in boiling liquid **3 :** be agitated — **boil** *n*
boil•er *n* **:** tank holding hot water or steam
bois•ter•ous *adj* **:** noisily turbulent — **bois•ter•ous•ly** *adv*
bold *adj* **1 :** courageous **2 :** insolent **3 :** daring — **bold•ly** *adv* — **bold•ness** *n*
boll *n* **:** seed pod
boll weevil *n* **:** small grayish weevil that infests the cotton plant
bo•lo•gna *n* **:** large smoked sausage
bol•ster *n* **:** long pillow ~ *vb* **:** support
bolt *n* **1 :** flash of lightning **2 :** sliding bar used to fasten a door **3 :** roll of cloth **4 :** threaded pin used with a nut ~ *vb* **1 :** move suddenly **2 :** fasten with a bolt **3 :** swallow hastily
bomb *n* **:** explosive device ~ *vb* **:** attack with bombs — **bomb•er** *n* — **bomb•proof** *adj*
bom•bard *vb* **:** attack with or as if with artillery — **bom•bard•ment** *n*
bom•bast *n* **:** pretentious language — **bom•bas•tic** *adj*
bomb•shell *n* **1 :** bomb **2 :** great surprise
bona fide *adj* **1 :** made in good faith **2 :** genuine
bo•nan•za *n* **:** something yielding a rich return
bon•bon *n* **:** piece of candy
bond *n* **1** *pl* **:** something that restrains **2 :** uniting force **3 :** obligation made binding by money **4 :** interest-bearing certificate ~ *vb* **1 :** insure **2 :** cause to adhere — **bond•hold•er** *n*
bond•age *n* **:** slavery
bonds•man *n* **:** slave
bone *n* **:** skeletal material ~ *vb* **:** to free from bones — **bone•less** *adj* — **bony** *adj*
bon•er *n* **:** blunder
bon•fire *n* **:** outdoor fire
bon•net *n* **:** hat for a woman or infant
bo•nus *n* **:** extra payment
boo *n* **:** shout of disapproval — **boo** *vb*
book *n* **1 :** paper sheets bound into a volume **2 :** long literary work or a subdivision of one ~ *vb* **:** reserve — **book•case** *n* — **book•ish** *adj* — **book•let** *n* — **book•mark** *n* — **book•sell•er** *n* — **book•shelf** *n*
book•ie *n* **:** bookmaker
book•keep•er *n* **:** one who keeps business accounts — **book•keep•ing** *n*
book•mak•er *n* **:** one who takes bets — **book•mak•ing** *n*
[1]**boom** *n* **1 :** long spar to extend the bottom of a sail **2 :** beam projecting from the pole of a derrick
[2]**boom** *vb* **1 :** make a deep hollow sound **2 :** grow rapidly esp. in value ~ *n* **1 :** booming sound **2 :** rapid growth
boo•mer•ang *n* **:** angular club that returns to the thrower
boon *n* **:** benefit
boor *n* **:** rude person — **boor•ish** *adj*
boost *vb* **1 :** raise **2 :** promote — **boost** *n* — **boost•er** *n*
boot *n* **1 :** covering for the foot and leg **2 :** kick ~ *vb* **:** kick
boo•tee, boo•tie *n* **:** infant's knitted sock
booth *n* **:** small enclosed stall or seating area
boot•leg *vb* **:** make or sell liquor illegally — **bootleg** *adj or n* — **boot•leg•ger** *n*
boo•ty *n* **:** plunder
booze *vb* **:** drink liquor to excess ~ *n* **:** liquor — **booz•er** *n* — **boozy** *adj*
bor•der *n* **1 :** edge **2 :** boundary ~ *vb* **1 :** put a border on **2 :** be close
[1]**bore** *vb* **1 :** pierce **2 :** make by piercing ~ *n* **:** cylindrical hole or its diameter — **bor•er** *n*
[2]**bore** *past of* BEAR
[3]**bore** *n* **:** one that is dull ~ *vb* **:** tire with dullness — **bore•dom** *n*
born *adj* **1 :** brought into life **2 :** being such by birth
borne *past part of* BEAR
bor•ough *n* **:** incorporated town or village
bor•row *vb* **1 :** take as a loan **2 :** take into use
bo•som *n* **:** breast ~ *adj* **:** intimate — **bo•somed** *adj*
boss *n* **:** employer or supervisor ~ *vb* **:** supervise — **bossy** *adj*
bot•a•ny *n* **:** plant biology — **bo•tan•i•cal** *adj* — **bot•a•nist** *n* — **bot•a•nize** *vb*
botch *vb* **:** do clumsily — **botch** *n*
both *adj or pron* **:** the one and the other ~ *conj* — used to show each of two is included
both•er *vb* **1 :** annoy or worry **2 :** take the trouble — **bother** *n* — **both•er•some** *adj*
bot•tle *n* **:** container with a narrow neck and no handles ~ *vb* **:** put into a bottle
bot•tle•neck *n* **:** place or cause of congestion
bot•tom *n* **1 :** supporting surface **2 :** lowest part or place — **bottom** *adj* — **bot•tom•less** *adj*
bot•u•lism *n* **:** acute food poisoning
bough *n* **:** large tree branch
bought *past of* BUY

boul•der *n* : large rounded rock — **boul•dered** *adj*

bou•le•vard *n* : broad thoroughfare

bounce *vb* **1 :** spring back **2 :** make bounce — **bounce** *n* — **bouncy** *adj*

[1]**bound** *adj* : intending to go

[2]**bound** *n* : limit or boundary ~ *vb* : be a boundary of — **bound•less** *adj* — **bound•less•ness** *n*

[3]**bound** *adj* **1 :** obliged **2 :** having a binding **3 :** determined **4 :** incapable of failing

[4]**bound** *n* : leap ~ *vb* : move by springing

bound•ary *n* : line marking extent or separation

boun•ty *n* **1 :** generosity **2 :** reward — **boun•te•ous** *adj* — **boun•te•ous•ly** *adv* — **boun•ti•ful** *adj* — **boun•ti•ful•ly** *adv*

bou•quet *n* **1 :** bunch of flowers **2 :** fragrance

bout *n* **1 :** contest **2 :** outbreak

bou•tique *n* : specialty shop

bo•vine *adj* : relating to cattle — **bovine** *n*

[1]**bow** *vb* **1 :** submit **2 :** bend the head or body ~ *n* : act of bowing

[2]**bow** *n* **1 :** bend or arch **2 :** weapon for shooting arrows **3 :** knot with loops **4 :** rod with stretched horsehairs for playing a stringed instrument ~ *vb* : curve or bend — **bow•man** *n* — **bow•string** *n*

[3]**bow** *n* : forward part of a ship — **bow** *adj*

bow•els *n pl* **1 :** intestines **2 :** inmost parts

[1]**bowl** *n* : concave vessel or part — **bowl•ful** *n*

[2]**bowl** *n* : round ball for bowling ~ *vb* : roll a ball in bowling — **bowl•er** *n*

bowl•ing *n* : game in which balls are rolled to knock down pins

[1]**box** *n* : evergreen shrub — **box•wood** *n*

[2]**box** *n* **1 :** container usu. with 4 sides and a cover **2 :** small compartment ~ *vb* : put in a box

[3]**box** *n* : slap ~ *vb* **1 :** slap **2 :** fight with the fists — **box•er** *n* — **box•ing** *n*

box•car *n* : roofed freight car

box office *n* : theater ticket office

boy *n* : male child — **boy•hood** *n* — **boy•ish** *adj* — **boy•ish•ly** *adv* — **boy•ish•ness** *n*

boy•cott *vb* : refrain from dealing with — **boy•cott** *n*

boy•friend *n* **1 :** male friend **2 :** woman's regular male companion

brace *n* **1 :** crank for turning a bit **2 :** something that resists weight or supports **3 :** punctuation mark { or } ~ *vb* **1 :** make taut or steady **2 :** invigorate **3 :** strengthen

brace•let *n* : ornamental band for the wrist or arm

brack•et *n* **1 :** projecting support **2 :** punctuation mark [or] **3 :** class ~ *vb* **1 :** furnish or fasten with brackets **2 :** place within brackets **3 :** group

brag *vb* : boast — **brag** *n*

brag•gart *n* : boaster

braid *vb* : weave together ~ *n* : something braided

braille *n* : system of writing for the blind using raised dots

brain *n* **1 :** organ of thought and nervous coordination enclosed in the skull **2 :** intelligence ~ *vb* : smash the skull of — **brained** *adj* — **brain•less** *adj* — **brainy** *adj*

braise *vb* : cook (meat) slowly in a covered dish

brake *n* : device for slowing or stopping ~ *vb* : slow or stop by a brake

bram•ble *n* : prickly shrub

bran *n* : edible cracked grain husks

branch *n* **1 :** division of a plant stem **2 :** part ~ *vb* **1 :** develop branches **2 :** diverge — **branched** *adj*

brand *n* **1 :** identifying mark made by burning **2 :** mark of disgrace **3 :** distinctive kind (as of goods from one firm) ~ *vb* : mark with a brand

brand–new *adj* : unused

bran•dy *n* : liquor distilled from wine

brash *adj* **1 :** impulsive **2 :** aggressively self-assertive

brass *n* **1 :** alloy of copper and zinc **2 :** outrageous confidence in oneself **3 :** high-ranking military officers — **brassy** *adj*

bras•siere *n* : woman's undergarment to support the breasts

brat *n* : ill-behaved child — **brat•ti•ness** *n* — **brat•ty** *adj*

bra•va•do *n* : false bravery

brave *adj* : showing courage ~ *vb* : face with courage — **brave•ly** *adv* — **brav•ery** *n*

brawl *n* : noisy quarrel or violent fight — **brawl** *vb* — **brawl•er** *n*

brawn *n* : muscular strength — **brawny** *adj* — **brawn•i•ness** *n*

bra•zen *adj* **1 :** made of brass **2 :** bold — **bra•zen•ly** *adv* — **bra•zen•ness** *n*

bra•zier *n* : charcoal grill

breach *n* **1 :** breaking of a law, obligation, or standard **2 :** gap ~ *vb* : make a breach in

bread *n* : baked food made of flour ~ *vb* : cover with bread crumbs

breadth *n* : width

bread•win•ner *n* : wage earner

break *vb* **broke; bro•ken 1** : knock into pieces **2** : fail to fulfill or respect **3** : force a way into or out of **4** : exceed **5** : interrupt **6** : fail ~ *n* **1** : act or result of breaking **2** : stroke of good luck — **break•able** *adj or n* — **break•age** *n* — **break•er** *n* — **break in** *vb* **1** : enter by force **2** : interrupt **3** : train — **break out** *vb* **1** : erupt with force **2** : develop a rash

break•down *n* : physical or mental failure — **break down** *vb*

break•fast *n* : first meal of the day — **breakfast** *vb*

breast *n* **1** : milk-producing gland esp. of a woman **2** : front part of the chest

breast•bone *n* : bone connecting the ribs in front

breath *n* **1** : slight breeze **2** : air breathed in or out — **breath•less** *adj* — **breath•less•ly** *adv* — **breath•less•ness** *n* — **breathy** *adj*

breathe *vb* **1** : draw air into the lungs and expel it **2** : live **3** : utter

breath•tak•ing *adj* : exciting

breech•es *n pl* : trousers ending near the knee

breed *vb* **1** : give birth to **2** : propagate **3** : raise ~ *n* **1** : kind of plant or animal usu. developed by humans **2** : class — **breed•er** *n*

breeze *n* : light wind ~ *vb* : move fast — **breezy** *adj*

brev•i•ty *n* : shortness or conciseness

brew *vb* : make by fermenting or steeping — **brew** *n* — **brew•er** *n* — **brew•ery** *n*

bri•ar *var of* BRIER

bribe *vb* : corrupt or influence by gifts ~ *n* : something offered or given in bribing — **brib•able** *adj* — **brib•ery** *n*

bric–a–brac *n pl* : small ornamental articles

brick *n* : building block of baked clay — **brick** *vb* — **brick•lay•er** *n* — **brick•lay•ing** *n*

bride *n* : woman just married or about to be married — **brid•al** *adj*

bride•groom *n* : man just married or about to be married

brides•maid *n* : woman who attends a bride at her wedding

[1]**bridge** *n* **1** : structure built for passage over a depression or obstacle **2** : upper part of the nose **3** : compartment from which a ship is navigated **4** : artificial replacement for missing teeth ~ *vb* : build a bridge over — **bridge•able** *adj*

[2]**bridge** *n* : card game for 4 players

bri•dle *n* : headgear to control a horse ~ *vb* **1** : put a bridle on **2** : restrain **3** : show hostility or scorn

brief *adj* : short or concise ~ *n* : concise summary (as of a legal case) ~ *vb* : give final instructions or essential information to — **briefly** *adv* — **brief•ness** *n*

brief•case *n* : case for papers

[1]**bri•er** *n* : thorny plant

[2]**brier** *n* : heath of southern Europe

bri•gade *n* **1** : large military unit **2** : group organized for a special activity

bright *adj* **1** : radiating or reflecting light **2** : cheerful **3** : intelligent — **bright•en** *vb* — **bright•en•er** *n* — **bright•ly** *adv* — **brightness** *n*

bril•liant *adj* **1** : very bright **2** : splendid **3** : very intelligent — **bril•liance** *n* — **bril•lian•cy** *n* — **bril•liant•ly** *adv*

brim *n* : edge or rim ~ *vb* : be or become full — **brim•ful** *adj* — **brim•less** *adj* — **brimmed** *adj*

brin•dled *adj* : gray or tawny with dark streaks or flecks

brine *n* **1** : salt water **2** : ocean — **brin•i•ness** *n* — **briny** *adj*

bring *vb* (**brought; brought**) **1** : cause to come with one **2** : persuade **3** : produce **4** : sell for — **bring•er** *n* — **bring about** *vb* : make happen — **bring up** *vb* **1** : care for and educate **2** : cause to be noticed

brink *n* : edge

bri•quette, bri•quet *n* : pressed mass (as of charcoal)

brisk *adj* **1** : lively **2** : invigorating — **briskly** *adv* — **brisk•ness** *n*

bris•ket *n* : breast or lower chest of a quadruped

bris•tle *n* : short stiff hair ~ *vb* **1** : stand erect **2** : show angry defiance **3** : appear as if covered with bristles — **bris•tly** *adj*

brit•tle *adj* : easily broken — **brit•tle•ness** *n*

broach *n* : pointed tool (as for opening casks) ~ *vb* **1** : pierce (as a cask) to open **2** : introduce for discussion

broad *adj* **1** : wide **2** : spacious **3** : clear or open **4** : obvious **5** : tolerant in outlook **6** : widely applicable **7** : dealing with essential points — **broad•en** *vb* — **broad•ly** *adv* — **broad•ness** *n*

broad•cast *n* **1 :** transmission by radio waves **2 :** radio or television program ~ *vb* **1 :** scatter or sow in all directions **2 :** make widely known **3 :** send out on a broadcast — **broad•cast•er** *n*
broad–mind•ed *adj* **:** tolerant of varied opinions — **broad–mind•ed•ly** *adv* — **broad–mind•ed•ness** *n*
broad•side *n* **1 :** simultaneous firing of all guns on one side of a ship **2 :** verbal attack
broc•co•li *n* **:** green vegetable akin to cauliflower
bro•chure *n* **:** pamphlet
broil *vb* **:** cook by radiant heat — **broil** *n*
broil•er *n* **1 :** utensil for broiling **2 :** chicken fit for broiling
[1]**broke** *past of* BREAK
[2]**broke** *adj* **:** out of money
bro•ken *adj* **:** imperfectly spoken — **bro•ken•ly** *adv*
bro•ken•heart•ed *adj* **:** overcome by grief or despair
bro•ker *n* **:** agent who buys and sells for a fee — **broker** *vb* — **bro•ker•age** *n*
bron•chus *n* **:** division of the windpipe leading to a lung — **bron•chi•al** *adj*
bronze *vb* **:** make bronze in color ~ *n* **1 :** alloy of copper and tin **2 :** yellowish brown — **bronzy** *adj*
brooch *n* **:** ornamental clasp or pin
brood *n* **:** family of young ~ *vb* **1 :** sit on eggs to hatch them **2 :** ponder ~ *adj* **:** kept for breeding — **brood•er** *n* — **brood•ing•ly** *adv*
[1]**brook** *vb* **:** tolerate
[2]**brook** *n* **:** small stream
broom *n* **1 :** flowering shrub **2 :** implement for sweeping — **broom•stick** *n*
broth *n* **:** liquid in which meat has been cooked
broth•el *n* **:** house of prostitutes
broth•er *n* **1 :** male sharing one or both parents with another person **2 :** kinsman — **broth•er•hood** *n* — **broth•er•li•ness** *n* — **broth•er•ly** *adj*
broth•er–in–law *n* **brothers–in–law :** brother of one's spouse or husband of one's sister or of one's spouse's sister
brought *past of* BRING
brow *n* **1 :** eyebrow **2 :** forehead **3 :** edge of a steep place
brow•beat *vb* **:** intimidate
brown *adj* **1 :** of the color brown **2 :** of dark or tanned complexion ~ *n* **:** a color like that of coffee ~ *vb* **:** make or become brown — **brown•ish** *adj*
browse *vb* **1 :** graze **2 :** look over casually — **brows•er** *n*
brows•er *n* **:** computer program for accessing Web sites
bruise *vb* **1 :** make a bruise on **2 :** become bruised ~ *n* **:** surface injury to flesh
brunch *n* **:** late breakfast, early lunch, or combination of both
bru•net, bru•nette *adj* **:** having dark hair and usu. dark skin — **bru•net, brunette** *n*
[1]**brush** *n* **1 :** small cut branches **2 :** coarse shrubby vegetation
[2]**brush** *n* **1 :** bristles set in a handle used esp. for cleaning or painting **2 :** light touch ~ *vb* **1 :** apply a brush to **2 :** remove with or as if with a brush **3 :** dismiss in an offhand way **4 :** touch lightly — **brush up** *vb* **:** renew one's skill
brush–off *n* **:** curt dismissal
brusque *adj* **:** curt or blunt in manner — **brusque•ly** *adv*
bru•tal *adj* **:** like a brute and esp. cruel — **bru•tal•i•ty** *n* — **bru•tal•ize** *vb* — **bru•tal•ly** *adv*
brute *adj* **1 :** relating to beasts **2 :** unreasoning **3 :** purely physical ~ *n* **1 :** beast **2 :** brutal person — **brut•ish** *adj*
bub•ble *vb* **:** form, rise in, or give off bubbles ~ *n* **:** globule of gas in or covered with a liquid — **bub•bly** *adj*
buc•ca•neer *n* **:** pirate
buck *n* **1 :** male animal (as a deer) **2 :** dollar ~ *vb* **1 :** jerk forward **2 :** oppose
buck•et *n* **:** pail — **buck•et•ful** *n*
buck•le *n* **1 :** clasp (as on a belt) for two loose ends **2 :** bend or fold ~ *vb* **1 :** fasten with a buckle **2 :** apply oneself **3 :** bend or crumple
buck•skin *n* **:** soft leather (as from the skin of a buck) — **buckskin** *adj*
buck•tooth *n* **:** large projecting front tooth — **buck–toothed** *adj*
buck•wheat *n* **:** herb whose seeds are used as a cereal grain or the seeds themselves
bud *n* **1 :** undeveloped plant shoot **2 :** partly opened flower ~ *vb* **1 :** form or put forth buds **2 :** be or develop like a bud
Bud•dhism *n* **:** religion of eastern and central Asia — **Bud•dhist** *n or adj*
bud•dy *n* **:** friend
budge *vb* **:** move from a place
bud•get *n* **1 :** estimate of income and expenses **2 :** plan for coordinating income and expenses

3 : money available for a particular use — **budget** *vb or adj* — **bud•get•ary** *adj*
buff *n* **1** : yellow to orange yellow color **2** : enthusiast ~ *adj* : of the color buff ~ *vb* : polish
buf•fa•lo *n* : wild ox (as a bison)
[1]buff•er *n* : shield or protector
[2]buffer *n* : one that buffs
[1]buf•fet *n* : blow or slap ~ *vb* : hit esp. repeatedly
[2]buf•fet *n* : meal at which people serve themselves
buf•foon *n* : clown — **buf•foon•ery** *n*
bug *n* **1** : small usu. obnoxious crawling creature **2** : 4-winged sucking insect **3** : unexpected imperfection **4** : disease-producing germ **5** : hidden microphone ~ *vb* **1** : pester **2** : conceal a microphone in
bug•gy *n* : light carriage
bu•gle *n* : trumpetlike brass instrument — **bugler** *n*
build *vb* (**built; built**) **1** : put together **2** : establish **3** : increase ~ *n* : physique — **build•er** *n*
build•ing *n* **1** : roofed and walled structure **2** : art or business of constructing buildings
bulb *n* **1** : large underground plant bud **2** : rounded or pear-shaped object — **bul•bous** *adj*
bulge *n* : swelling projecting part ~ *vb* : swell out
bulk *n* **1** : magnitude **2** : indigestible food material **3** : large mass **4** : major portion ~ *vb* : cause to swell or bulge — **bulky** *adj*
bull *n* : large adult male animal (as of cattle) ~ *adj* : male
bull•dog *n* : compact short-haired dog
bull•doze *vb* **1** : move or level with a tractor (**bull•doz•er**) having a broad blade **2** : force
bul•let *n* : missile to be shot from a gun — **bullet•proof** *adj*
bul•le•tin *n* **1** : brief public report **2** : periodical
bull•fight *n* : sport of taunting and killing bulls — **bull•fight•er** *n*
bull•frog *n* : large deep-voiced frog
bul•lion *n* : gold or silver esp. in bars
bull's–eye *n* : center of a target
bul•ly *n* : one who hurts or intimidates others ~ *vb* : act like a bully toward
bul•rush *n* : tall coarse rush or sedge
bul•wark *n* **1** : wall-like defense **2** : strong support or protection
bum *vb* **1** : wander as a tramp **2** : get by begging ~ *n* : idle worthless person ~ *adj* : bad
bum•ble•bee *n* : large hairy bee
bump *vb* : strike or knock forcibly ~ *n* **1** : sudden blow **2** : small bulge or swelling — **bumpy** *adj*
[1]bum•per *adj* : unusually large
[2]bump•er *n* : shock-absorbing bar at either end of a car
bump•kin *n* : awkward country person
bun *n* : sweet biscuit or roll
bunch *n* : group ~ *vb* : form into a group — **bunchy** *adj*
bun•dle *n* **1** : several items bunched together **2** : something wrapped for carrying **3** : large amount ~ *vb* : gather into a bundle
bun•ga•low *n* : one-story house
bun•gle *vb* : do badly — **bungle** *n* — **bungler** *n*
bun•ion *n* : inflamed swelling of the first joint of the big toe
[1]bunk *n* : built-in bed that is often one of a tier ~ *vb* : sleep
[2]bunk *n* : nonsense
bun•ker *n* **1** : storage compartment **2** : protective embankment
bun•ny *n* : rabbit
[1]bun•ting *n* : small finch
[2]bunting *n* : flag material
buoy *n* : floating marker anchored in water ~ *vb* **1** : keep afloat **2** : raise the spirits of — **buoy•an•cy** *n* — **buoy•ant** *adj*
bur, burr *n* : rough or prickly covering of a fruit — **bur•ry** *adj*
bur•den *n* **1** : something carried **2** : something oppressive **3** : cargo ~ *vb* : load or oppress — **bur•den•some** *adj*
bu•reau *n* **1** : chest of drawers **2** : administrative unit **3** : business office
bu•reau•cra•cy *n* **1** : body of government officials **2** : unwieldy administrative system — **bu•reau•crat** *n* — **bu•reau•crat•ic** *adj*
bur•geon *vb* : grow
bur•glary *n* : forcible entry into a building to steal — **bur•glar** *n* — **bur•glar•ize** *vb*
Bur•gun•dy *n* : kind of table wine
buri•al *n* : act of burying
bur•lap *n* : coarse fabric usu. of jute or hemp
bur•lesque *n* **1** : witty or derisive imitation **2** : broadly humorous variety show ~ *vb* : mock
bur•ly *adj* : strongly and heavily built

burn *vb* **1 :** be on fire **2 :** feel or look as if on fire **3 :** alter or become altered by or as if by fire or heat **4 :** cause or make by fire ~ *n* **:** injury or effect produced by burning — **burn•er** *n*

bur•nish *vb* **:** polish

burp *n or vb* **:** belch

bur•ro *n* **:** small donkey

bur•row *n* **:** hole in the ground made by an animal ~ *vb* **:** make a burrow — **bur•row•er** *n*

bur•si•tis *n* **:** inflammation of a sac (**bur•sa**) in a joint

burst *vb* **1 :** fly apart or into pieces **2 :** enter or emerge suddenly ~ *n* **:** sudden outbreak or effort

bury *vb* **1 :** deposit in the earth **2 :** hide

bus *n* **:** large motor-driven passenger vehicle ~ *vb* **:** travel or transport by bus

bus•boy *n* **:** waiter's helper

bush *n* **1 :** shrub **2 :** rough uncleared country **3 :** a thick tuft or mat — **bushy** *adj*

bush•el *n* **:** 4 pecks

bush•ing *n* **:** metal lining used as a guide or bearing

busi•ness *n* **1 :** vocation **2 :** commercial or industrial enterprise **3 :** personal concerns — **busi•ness•man** *n* — **busi•ness•wom•an** *n*

[1]**bust** *n* **1 :** sculpture of the head and upper torso **2 :** breasts of a woman

[2]**bust** *vb* **1 :** burst or break **2 :** tame ~ *n* **1 :** punch **2 :** failure

bus•tle *vb* **:** move or work briskly ~ *n* **:** energetic activity

busy *adj* **1 :** engaged in action **2 :** being in use **3 :** full of activity ~ *vb* **:** make or keep busy — **busi•ly** *adv*

busy•body *n* **:** meddler

but *conj* **1 :** if not for the fact **2 :** that **3 :** without the certainty that **4 :** rather **5 :** yet ~ *prep* **:** other than

butch•er *n* **1 :** one who slaughters animals or dresses their flesh **2 :** brutal killer **3 :** bungler — **butcher** *vb* — **butch•ery** *n*

but•ler *n* **:** chief male household servant

[1]**butt** *vb* **:** strike with a butt ~ *n* **:** blow with the head or horns

[2]**butt** *n* **1 :** target **2 :** victim

[3]**butt** *vb* **:** join edge to edge

[4]**butt** *n* **:** large end or bottom

butte *n* **:** isolated steep hill

but•ter *n* **:** solid edible fat churned from cream ~ *vb* **:** spread with butter — **but•ter•fat** *n* — **but•ter•milk** *n* — **but•tery** *adj*

but•ter•cup *n* **:** yellow-flowered herb

but•ter•fly *n* **:** insect with 4 broad wings

but•ter•nut *n* **:** edible nut of a tree related to the walnut or this tree

but•ter•scotch *n* **:** candy made from sugar, corn syrup, and water

but•tocks *n pl* **:** rear part of the hips

but•ton *n* **1 :** small knob for fastening clothing **2 :** buttonlike object ~ *vb* **:** fasten with buttons

but•ton•hole *n* **:** hole or slit for a button ~ *vb* **:** hold in talk

but•tress *n* **1 :** projecting structure to support a wall **2 :** support — **buttress** *vb*

bux•om *adj* **:** having a large bosom

buy *vb* (**bought; bought**) **:** purchase ~ *n* **:** bargain — **buy•er** *n*

buzz *vb* **:** make a low humming sound ~ *n* **:** act or sound of buzzing

buz•zard *n* **:** large bird of prey

buzz•er *n* **:** signaling device that buzzes

buzz•word *n* **:** word or phrase in current popular use

by *prep* **1 :** near **2 :** through **3 :** beyond **4 :** throughout **5 :** no later than ~ *adv* **1 :** near **2 :** farther

by•gone *adj* **:** past — **bygone** *n*

by•law, bye•law *n* **:** organization's rule

by–line *n* **:** writer's name on an article

by•pass *n* **:** alternate route ~ *vb* **:** go around

by–prod•uct *n* **:** product in addition to the main product

by•stand•er *n* **:** spectator

by•way *n* **:** side road

by•word *n* **:** proverb

C

c *n* **:** 3d letter of the alphabet

cab *n* **1 :** light closed horse-drawn carriage **2 :** taxi **3 :** compartment for a driver — **cab•bie, cab•by** *n* — **cab•stand** *n*

ca•bana *n* **:** shelter at a beach or pool

cab•bage *n* **:** vegetable with a dense head of leaves

cab•in *n* **1 :** private room on a ship **2 :** small house **3 :** airplane compartment

cab•i•net *n* **1 :** display case or cupboard **2**

: advisory council of a head of state — **cab•i•net•mak•er** *n* — **cab•i•net•mak•ing** *n* — **cab•i•net•work** *n*

ca•ble *n* **1** : strong rope, wire, or chain **2** : telegram sent through a cable under the sea **3** : bundle of electrical wires ~ *vb* : send a cablegram to

ca•cao *n* : So. American tree whose seeds (**cacao beans**) yield cocoa and chocolate

cack•le *vb* : make a cry or laugh like the sound of a hen — **cackle** *n* — **cack•ler** *n*

cac•tus *n* : drought-resistant flowering plant with scales or prickles

ca•dav•er *n* : dead body — **ca•dav•er•ous** *adj*

cad•die, cad•dy *n* : golfer's helper — **caddie, caddy** *vb*

ca•det *n* : student in a military academy

ca•fé *n* : restaurant

caf•e•te•ria *n* : self-service restaurant

cage *n* : box of wire or bars for confining an animal ~ *vb* : put or keep in a cage

cake *n* **1** : food of baked or fried usu. sweet batter **2** : compacted mass ~ *vb* **1** : form into a cake **2** : encrust

ca•lam•i•ty *n* : disaster — **ca•lam•i•tous** *adj* — **ca•lam•i•tous•ly** *adv*

cal•cu•late *vb* **1** : determine by mathematical processes **2** : judge — **cal•cu•la•ble** *adj* — **cal•cu•la•tion** *n* — **cal•cu•la•tor** *n*

cal•cu•lat•ing *adj* : shrewd

cal•en•dar *n* : list of days, weeks, and months

[1]**calf** *n* **calves** : young cow or related mammal — **calf•skin** *n*

[2]**calf** *n* **calves** : back part of the leg below the knee

cal•i•brate *vb* : adjust precisely — **cal•i•bra•tion** *n*

cal•is•then•ics *n sing or pl* : stretching and jumping exercises — **cal•is•then•ic** *adj*

call *vb* **1** : shout **2** : summon **3** : demand **4** : telephone **5** : make a visit **6** : name — **call** *n* — **call•er** *n* — **call down** *vb* : reprimand — **call off** *vb* : cancel

call•ing *n* : vocation

cal•li•ope *n* : musical instrument of steam whistles

cal•lous *adj* **1** : thickened and hardened **2** : without apparent feelings ~ *vb* : make callous — **cal•los•i•ty** *n* — **cal•lous•ly** *adv* — **cal•lous•ness** *n*

cal•lus *n* : callous area on skin or bark ~ *vb* : form a callus

calm *n* **1** : period or condition of peacefulness or stillness ~ *adj* : still or tranquil ~ *vb* : make calm — **calm•ly** *adv* — **calm•ness** *n*

cal•o•rie *n* : unit for measuring heat and energy value of food

calves *pl of* CALF

cam *n* : machine part that slides or rotates irregularly to transmit linear motion

came *past of* COME

cam•el *n* : large hoofed mammal of desert areas

cam•eo *n* : gem carved in relief

cam•era *n* : box with a lens for taking pictures — **cam•era•man** *n*

cam•ou•flage *vb* : hide by disguising — **camouflage** *n*

camp *n* **1** : place to stay temporarily esp. in a tent **2** : group living in a camp ~ *vb* : make or live in a camp — **camp•er** *n* — **campground** *n* — **camp•site** *n*

cam•paign *n* : series of military operations or of activities meant to gain a result — **campaign** *vb*

cam•pus *n* : grounds and buildings of a college or school

[1]**can** *vb,* (*past* **could**) **1** : be able to **2** : be permitted to by conscience or feeling **3** : have permission or liberty to

[2]**can** *n* : metal container ~ *vb* : preserve by sealing in airtight cans or jars — **can•ner** *n* — **can•nery** *n*

ca•nal *n* **1** : tubular passage in the body **2** : channel filled with water

ca•nary *n* : yellow or greenish finch often kept as a pet

can•cel *vb* **1** : cross out **2** : destroy, neutralize, or match the force or effect of — **cancel** *n* — **can•cel•la•tion** *n* — **can•cel•er, can•cel•ler** *n*

can•cer *n* **1** : malignant tumor that tends to spread **2** : slowly destructive evil — **can•cer•ous** *adj* — **can•cer•ous•ly** *adv*

can•did *adj* **1** : frank **2** : not posed — **can•did•ly** *adv* — **can•did•ness** *n*

can•di•date *n* : one who seeks an office or membership — **can•di•da•cy** *n*

can•dle *n* : tallow or wax molded around a wick and burned to give light — **can•dle•light** *n* — **can•dle•stick** *n*

can•dy *n* : food made from sugar ~ *vb* : encrust in sugar

cane *n* **1** : slender plant stem **2** : a tall woody grass or reed **3** : stick for walking or beating ~ *vb* **1** : beat with a cane **2** : weave or make with cane — **can•er** *n*

ca•nine *adj* : relating to dogs ~ *n* **1** : pointed tooth next to the incisors **2** : dog
can•is•ter *n* : cylindrical container
can•ker *n* : mouth ulcer — **can•ker•ous** *adj*
can•ni•bal *n* : human or animal that eats its own kind — **can•ni•bal•ism** *n* — **can•ni•bal•is•tic** *adj* — **can•ni•bal•ize** *vb*
can•non *n* : large heavy gun — **can•non•ball** *n* — **can•non•eer** *n*
can•not : can not — **cannot but** : be bound to
ca•noe *n* : narrow sharp-ended boat propelled by paddles — **canoe** *vb* — **ca•noe•ist** *n*
[1]**can•on** *n* **1** : regulation governing a church **2** : authoritative list **3** : an accepted principle
[2]**canon** *n* : clergy member in a cathedral — **ca•non•i•cal** *adj* — **ca•non•i•cal•ly** *adv*
can•on•ize *vb* : recognize as a saint — **can•on•iza•tion** *n*
can•o•py *n* : overhanging cover — **canopy** *vb*
can't : can not
can•ta•loupe *n* : muskmelon with orange flesh
can•teen *n* **1** : place of recreation for service personnel **2** : water container
can•tor *n* : synagogue official who sings liturgical music
can•vas *n* **1** : strong cloth orig. used for making tents and sails **2** : set of sails **3** : oil painting
can•vass *vb* : solicit votes, orders, or opinions from ~ *n* : act of canvassing — **can•vass•er** *n*
can•yon *n* : deep valley with steep sides
cap *n* **1** : covering for the head **2** : top or cover like a cap **3** : upper limit ~ *vb* **1** : provide or protect with a cap **2** : climax — **cap•ful** *n*
ca•pa•ble *adj* : able to do something — **ca•pa•bil•i•ty** *n* — **ca•pa•bly** *adv*
ca•pac•i•ty *n* **1** : ability to contain **2** : volume **3** : ability **4** : role or job ~ *adj* : equaling maximum capacity
[1]**cape** *n* : point of land jutting out into water
[2]**cape** *n* : garment that drapes over the shoulders
cap•il•lary *adj* **1** : resembling a hair **2** : having a very small bore ~ *n* : tiny thin-walled blood vessel
[1]**cap•i•tal** *adj* **1** : punishable by death **2** : being in the series A, B, C rather than a, b, c **3** : relating to capital **4** : excellent ~ *n* **1** : capital letter **2** : seat of government **3** : wealth **4** : total face value of a company's stock **5** : investors as a group — **cap•i•tal•ize** *vb* — **cap•i•tal•i•za•tion** *n*
[2]**capital** *n* : top part of a column
cap•i•tal•ism *n* : economic system of private ownership of capital — **cap•i•tal•ist** *n or adj* — **cap•i•tal•is•tic** *adj*
cap•i•tol *n* : building in which a legislature sits
cap•size *vb* : overturn
cap•sule *n* **1** : enveloping cover (as for medicine) **2** : small pressurized compartment for astronauts ~ *adj* : very brief or compact — **cap•su•lar** *adj* — **cap•su•lat•ed** *adj*
cap•tain *n* **1** : commander of a body of troops **2** : officer in charge of a ship **3** : commissioned officer in the navy ranking next below a rear admiral or a commodore **4** : commissioned officer (as in the army) ranking next below a major **5** : leader ~ *vb* : be captain of — **cap•tain•cy** *n*
cap•tion *n* **1** : title **2** : explanation with an illustration — **caption** *vb*
cap•ti•vate *vb* : attract and charm — **cap•ti•va•tion** *n* — **cap•ti•va•tor** *n*
cap•tive *adj* **1** : made prisoner **2** : confined or under control — **captive** *n* — **cap•tiv•i•ty** *n*
cap•tor *n* : one that captures
cap•ture *n* : seizure by force or trickery ~ *vb* : take captive
car *n* **1** : vehicle moved on wheels **2** : cage of an elevator
car•a•mel *n* **1** : burnt sugar used for flavoring and coloring **2** : firm chewy candy
car•bo•hy•drate *n* : compound of carbon, hydrogen, and oxygen
car•bon *n* **1** : chemical element occurring in nature esp. as diamond and graphite **2** : piece of carbon paper or a copy made with it
car•bon•ate *vb* : impregnate with carbon dioxide — **car•bon•ation** *n*
car•cin•o•gen *n* : agent causing cancer — **car•ci•no•gen•ic** *adj*
card *n* **1** : playing card **2** *pl* : game played with playing cards **3** : small flat piece of paper
card•board *n* : stiff material like paper
car•di•ac *adj* : relating to the heart
car•di•nal *n* **1** : official of the Roman Catholic Church **2** : bright red songbird
cardinal number *n* : number (as 1, 82, 357) used in counting
car•di•ol•o•gy *n* : study of the heart — **car•di•ol•o•gist** *n*
care *n* **1** : anxiety **2** : watchful attention **3** : supervision ~ *vb* **1** : feel anxiety or concern **2** : like **3** : provide care — **care•free** *adj* — **care•ful** *adj* — **care•ful•ly** *adv* — **care•ful-**

ness *n* — **care•giv•er** *n* — **care•less** *adj* — **care•less•ly** *adv* — **care•less•ness** *n*

ca•reer *n* **:** vocation ~ *vb* **:** go at top speed

ca•ress *n* **:** tender touch ~ *vb* **:** touch lovingly or tenderly

car•go *n* **:** transported goods

car•i•ca•ture *n* **:** distorted representation for humor or ridicule — **caricature** *vb* — **car•i•ca•tur•ist** *n*

car•na•tion *n* **:** showy flower

car•ni•val *n* **1 :** festival **2 :** traveling enterprise offering amusements

car•ni•vore *n* **:** flesh-eating animal — **car•niv•o•rous** *adj* — **car•niv•o•rous•ly** *adv* — **car•niv•o•rous•ness** *n*

car•ol *n* **:** song of joy — **carol** *vb* — **car•ol•er, car•ol•ler** *n*

car•ou•sel, car•rou•sel *n* **:** merry-go-round

car•pen•ter *n* **:** one who builds with wood — **carpenter** *vb* — **car•pen•try** *n*

car•pet *n* **:** fabric floor covering ~ *vb* **:** cover with a carpet — **car•pet•ing** *n*

car•riage *n* **1 :** conveyance **2 :** manner of holding oneself **3 :** wheeled vehicle

car•rot *n* **:** orange root vegetable

car•ry *vb* **1 :** move while supporting **2 :** hold (oneself) in a specified way **3 :** support **4 :** keep in stock **5 :** reach to a distance **6 :** win — **car•ri•er** *n* — **carry on** *vb* **1 :** conduct **2 :** behave excitedly — **carry out** *vb* **:** put into effect

cart *n* **:** wheeled vehicle ~ *vb* **:** carry in a cart — **cart•age** *n* — **cart•er** *n*

car•ti•lage *n* **:** elastic skeletal tissue — **car•ti•lag•i•nous** *adj*

car•ton *n* **:** cardboard box

car•toon *n* **1 :** humorous drawing **2 :** comic strip — **cartoon** *vb* — **car•toon•ist** *n*

car•tridge *n* **1 :** tube containing powder and a bullet or shot for a firearm **2 :** container of material for insertion into an apparatus

carve *vb* **1 :** cut with care **2 :** cut into pieces or slices — **carv•er** *n*

cas•cade *n* **:** small steep waterfall ~ *vb* **:** fall in a cascade

[1]**case** *n* **1 :** particular instance **2 :** convincing argument **3 :** inflectional form esp. of a noun or pronoun **4 :** fact **5 :** lawsuit **6 :** instance of disease — **in case :** as a precaution — **in case of :** in the event of

[2]**case** *n* **1 :** box **2 :** outer covering ~ *vb* **1 :** enclose **2 :** inspect

cash *n pl* **cash 1 :** ready money **2 :** money paid at the time of purchase ~ *vb* **:** give or get cash for

ca•shew *n* **:** tropical American tree or its nut

cash•ier *n* **:** person who receives and records payments

cash•mere *n* **:** fine goat's wool or a fabric of this

ca•si•no *n* **:** place for gambling

cas•ket *n* **:** coffin

cas•se•role *n* **:** baking dish or the food cooked in this

cas•sette *n* **:** case containing magnetic tape

cast *vb* (**cast; cast**) **1 :** throw **2 :** deposit (a ballot) **3 :** assign parts in a play **4 :** mold ~ *n* **1 :** throw **2 :** appearance **3 :** rigid surgical dressing **4 :** actors in a play

cast•er *n* **:** small wheel on furniture

cas•tle *n* **:** fortified building

ca•su•al *adj* **1 :** happening by chance **2 :** showing little concern **3 :** informal — **ca•su•al•ly** *adv* — **ca•su•al•ness** *n*

ca•su•al•ty *n* **1 :** serious or fatal accident **2 :** one injured, lost, or destroyed

cat *n* **1 :** small domestic mammal **2 :** related animal (as a lion) — **cat•like** *adj*

cat•a•log, cat•a•logue *n* **1 :** list **2 :** book containing a description of items ~ *vb* **1 :** make a catalog of **2 :** enter in a catalog — **cat•a•log•er, cat•a•logu•er** *n*

cat•a•pult *n* **:** device for hurling or launching — **catapult** *vb*

ca•tas•tro•phe *n* **1 :** great disaster or misfortune **2 :** utter failure — **cat•a•stroph•ic** *adj* — **cat•a•stroph•i•cal•ly** *adv*

catch *vb* **caught; caught 1 :** capture esp. after pursuit **2 :** trap **3 :** detect esp. by surprise **4 :** grasp **5 :** get entangled **6 :** become affected with or by **7 :** seize and hold firmly ~ *n* **1 :** act of catching **2 :** something caught **3 :** something that fastens **4 :** hidden difficulty — **catch•er** *n*

catch•ing *adj* **:** infectious

catchy *adj* **:** likely to catch interest

cat•e•chism *n* **:** set of questions and answers esp. to teach religious doctrine

cat•e•go•ry *n* **:** group or class — **cat•e•go•ri•za•tion** *n* — **cat•e•go•rize** *vb*

ca•ter *vb* **1 :** provide food for **2 :** supply what is wanted — **ca•ter•er** *n*

cat•er•cor•ner, cat•er–cor•nered *adv or adj* **:** in a diagonal position

cat•er•pil•lar *n* **:** butterfly or moth larva

ca•the•dral *n* **:** principal church of a diocese

Cath·o·lic *n* **:** member of the Roman Catholic Church — **Ca·thol·i·cism** *n*

cat·tle *n pl* **:** domestic bovines — **cat·tle·man** *n*

cat·ty *adj* **:** mean or spiteful — **cat·ti·ly** *adv* — **cat·ti·ness** *n*

Cau·ca·sian *adj* **:** relating to the white race — **Caucasian** *n*

caught *past of* CATCH

cau·li·flow·er *n* **:** vegetable having a compact head of usu. white undeveloped flowers

caulk *vb* **:** make seams watertight — **caulk** *n* — **caulk·er** *n*

cause *n* **1 :** something that brings about a result **2 :** reason **3 :** lawsuit **4 :** principle or movement to support ~ *vb* **:** be the cause of — **caus·al** *adj* — **cau·sal·i·ty** *n* — **caus·al·ly** *adv* — **cau·sa·tion** *n* — **caus·ative** *adj* — **cause·less** *adj* — **caus·er** *n*

caus·tic *adj* **1 :** corrosive **2 :** sharp or biting — **caustic** *n*

cau·tion *n* **1 :** warning **2 :** care or prudence ~ *vb* **:** warn — **cau·tion·ary** *adj*

cau·tious *adj* **:** taking caution — **cau·tious·ly** *adv* — **cau·tious·ness** *n*

cave *n* **:** natural underground chamber — **cave in** *vb* **:** collapse

cav·ern *n* **:** large cave — **cav·ern·ous** *adj* — **cav·ern·ous·ly** *adv*

cav·i·ar, cav·i·are *n* **:** salted fish roe

cav·i·ty *n* **1 :** unfilled place within a mass **2 :** decay in a tooth

CD *n* **:** compact disc

cease *vb* **:** stop — **cease·less** *adj*

ce·dar *n* **:** cone-bearing tree with fragrant durable wood

ceil·ing *n* **1 :** overhead surface of a room **2 :** upper limit

cel·e·brate *vb* **1 :** perform with appropriate rites **2 :** honor with ceremonies **3 :** praise highly — **cel·e·brant** *n* — **cel·e·bra·tion** *n* — **cel·e·bra·tor** *n*

cel·e·brat·ed *adj* **:** renowned

ce·leb·ri·ty *n* **1 :** renown **2 :** well-known person

cel·ery *n* **:** herb grown for crisp edible stalks

ce·les·tial *adj* **1 :** relating to the sky **2 :** heavenly

cell *n* **1 :** small room **2 :** tiny mass of protoplasm that forms the fundamental unit of living matter **3 :** container holding an electrolyte for generating electricity — **celled** *adj*

cel·lar *n* **:** room or area below ground

cel·lo *n* **:** bass member of the violin family — **cel·list** *n*

cell phone *n* **:** portable cordless telephone

cel·lu·lar *adj* **:** relating to or consisting of cells

Cel·sius *adj* **:** relating to a thermometer scale on which the freezing point of water is 0° and the boiling point is 100°

ce·ment *n* **1 :** powdery mixture of clay and limestone that hardens when wetted **2 :** binding agent ~ *vb* **:** unite or cover with cement

cem·e·tery *n* **:** burial ground

cen·sor *n* **:** one with power to suppress anything objectionable (as in printed matter) ~ *vb* **:** be a censor of — **cen·so·ri·al** *adj* — **cen·sor·ship** *n*

cen·sure *n* **:** official reprimand ~ *vb* **:** find blameworthy — **cen·sur·able** *adj*

cen·sus *n* **:** periodic population count — **census** *vb*

cent *n* **:** monetary unit equal to $\frac{1}{100}$ of a basic unit of value

cen·ten·ni·al *n* **:** 100th anniversary — **centennial** *adj*

cen·ter *n* **1 :** middle point **2 :** point of origin or greatest concentration **3 :** region of concentrated population **4 :** player near the middle of the team ~ *vb* **1 :** place, fix, or concentrate at or around a center **2 :** have a center — **cen·ter·piece** *n*

cen·ti·grade *adj* **:** Celsius

cen·ti·me·ter *n* **:** $\frac{1}{100}$ meter

cen·ti·pede *n* **:** long flat many-legged arthropod

cen·tral *adj* **1 :** constituting or being near a center **2 :** essential or principal — **cen·tral·ly** *adv*

cen·tral·ize *vb* **:** bring to a central point or under central control — **cen·tral·i·za·tion** *n* — **cen·tral·iz·er** *n*

cen·tri·fuge *n* **:** machine that separates substances by spinning

cen·tu·ry *n* **:** 100 years

ce·ram·ic *n* **1** *pl* **:** art or process of shaping and hardening articles from clay **2 :** product of ceramics — **ceramic** *adj*

ce·re·al *adj* **:** made of or relating to grain or to the plants that produce it ~ *n* **1 :** grass yielding edible grain **2 :** food prepared from a cereal grain

cer·e·bel·lum *n* **:** part of the brain controlling muscular coordination — **cer·e·bel·lar** *adj*

ce·re·bral *adj* **1 :** relating to the brain, intellect, or cerebrum **2 :** appealing to the intellect

ce•re•brum *n* **:** part of the brain that contains the higher nervous centers

cer•e•mo•ny *n* **1 :** formal act prescribed by law, ritual, or convention **2 :** prescribed procedures — **cer•e•mo•ni•al** *adj or n* — **cer•e•mo•ni•ous** *adj*

cer•tain *adj* **1 :** settled **2 :** true **3 :** specific but not named **4 :** bound **5 :** assured ~ *pron* **:** certain ones — **cer•tain•ly** *adv* — **cer•tain•ty** *n*

cer•tif•i•cate *n* **:** document establishing truth or fulfillment

cer•ti•fy *vb* **1 :** verify **2 :** endorse — **cer•ti•fi•able** *adj* — **cer•ti•fi•ably** *adv* — **cer•ti•fi•ca•tion** *n* — **cer•ti•fi•er** *n*

chafe *vb* **1 :** fret **2 :** make sore by rubbing

chain *n* **1 :** flexible series of connected links **2** *pl* **:** something that restrains **3 :** linked series ~ *vb* **:** bind or connect with a chain

chair *n* **1 :** seat with a back **2 :** position of authority or dignity **3 :** presiding officer ~ *vb* **:** act as presiding officer of — **chair•man** *n* — **chair•man•ship** *n* — **chair•wom•an** *n*

chalk *n* **1 :** soft limestone **2 :** chalky material used as a crayon ~ *vb* **:** mark with chalk — **chalky** *adj* — **chalk up** *vb* **1 :** credit **2 :** achieve

chalk•board *n* **:** blackboard

chal•lenge *vb* **1 :** dispute **2 :** invite or dare to act or compete — **challenge** *n* — **chal•leng•er** *n*

cham•ber *n* **1 :** room **2 :** enclosed space **3 :** legislative meeting place or body **4** *pl* **:** judge's consultation room — **cham•bered** *adj*

champ *n* **:** champion

cham•pagne *n* **:** sparkling white wine

cham•pi•on *n* **1 :** advocate or defender **2 :** winning contestant ~ *vb* **:** protect or fight for — **cham•pi•on•ship** *n*

chance *n* **1 :** element of existence that cannot be predicted **2 :** opportunity **3 :** probability **4 :** risk **5 :** raffle ticket ~ *vb* **1 :** happen **2 :** encounter unexpectedly **3 :** risk — **chance** *adj*

chan•de•lier *n* **:** hanging lighting fixture

change *vb* **1 :** make or become different **2 :** exchange **3 :** give or receive change for ~ *n* **1 :** a changing **2 :** excess from a payment **3 :** money in smaller denominations **4 :** coins — **change•able** *adj* — **change•less** *adj* — **chang•er** *n*

chan•nel *n* **1 :** deeper part of a waterway **2 :** means of passage or communication **3 :** strait **4 :** broadcast frequency ~ *vb* **:** make or direct through a channel

chant *vb* **:** sing or speak in one tone — **chant** *n* — **chant•er** *n*

Cha•nu•kah *var of* HANUKKAH

cha•os *n* **:** complete disorder — **cha•ot•ic** *adj* — **cha•ot•i•cal•ly** *adv*

[1]**chap** *n* **:** fellow

[2]**chap** *vb* **:** dry and crack open usu. from wind and cold

cha•pel *n* **:** private or small place of worship

chap•er•on, chap•er•one : older person who accompanies young people at a social gathering ~ *vb* **:** act as chaperon at or for — **chap•er•on•age** *n*

chap•lain *n* **:** clergy member in a military unit or a prison — **chap•lain•cy** *n*

chap•ter *n* **1 :** main book division **2 :** branch of a society

char•ac•ter *n* **1 :** letter or graphic mark **2 :** trait or distinctive combination of traits **3 :** peculiar person **4 :** fictional person — **char•ac•ter•i•za•tion** *n* — **char•ac•ter•ize** *vb*

char•ac•ter•is•tic *adj* **:** typical ~ *n* **:** distinguishing quality — **char•ac•ter•is•ti•cal•ly** *adv*

char•coal *n* **:** porous carbon prepared by partial combustion

charge *vb* **1 :** give an electric charge to **2 :** impose a task or responsibility on **3 :** command **4 :** accuse **5 :** rush forward in assault **6 :** assume a debt for **7 :** fix as a price ~ *n* **1 :** excess or deficiency of electrons in a body **2 :** tax **3 :** responsibility **4 :** accusation **5 :** cost **6 :** attack — **charge•able** *adj*

char•i•ot *n* **:** ancient 2-wheeled vehicle — **char•i•o•teer** *n*

cha•ris•ma *n* **:** special ability to lead — **char•is•mat•ic** *adj*

char•i•ty *n* **1 :** love for mankind **2 :** generosity or leniency **3 :** alms **4 :** institution for relief of the needy — **char•i•ta•ble** *adj* — **char•i•ta•ble•ness** *n* — **char•i•ta•bly** *adv*

charm *n* **1 :** something with magic power **2 :** appealing trait **3 :** small ornament ~ *vb* **:** fascinate — **charm•er** *n* — **charm•ing** *adj* — **charm•ing•ly** *adv*

chart *n* **1 :** map **2 :** diagram ~ *vb* **1 :** make a chart of **2 :** plan

char•ter *n* **1 :** document granting rights **2 :** constitution ~ *vb* **1 :** establish by charter **2 :** rent — **char•ter•er** *n*

chase *vb* **1 :** follow trying to catch **2 :** drive away — **chase** *n* — **chas•er** *n*
chasm *n* **:** gorge
chaste *adj* **1 :** abstaining from all or unlawful sexual relations **2 :** modest or decent **3 :** severely simple — **chaste•ly** *adv* — **chaste-ness** *n* — **chas•ti•ty** *n*
chas•tise *vb* **1 :** punish **2 :** censure — **chas-tise•ment** *n*
chat *n* **:** informal talk — **chat** *vb* — **chat•ty** *adj*
chat•ter *vb* **1 :** utter rapidly succeeding sounds **2 :** talk fast or too much — **chatter** *n* — **chat-ter•er** *n*
chauf•feur *n* **:** hired car driver ~ *vb* **:** work as a chauffeur
cheap *adj* **1 :** not expensive **2 :** shoddy — **cheap** *adv* — **cheap•en** *vb* — **cheap•ly** *adv* — **cheap•ness** *n*
cheap•skate *n* **:** stingy person
cheat *n* **1 :** act of deceiving **2 :** one that cheats ~ *vb* **1 :** deprive through fraud or deceit **2 :** violate rules dishonestly — **cheat•er** *n*
check *n* **1 :** sudden stoppage **2 :** restraint **3 :** test or standard for testing **4 :** written order to a bank to pay money **5 :** ticket showing ownership **6 :** slip showing an amount due **7 :** pattern in squares or fabric in such a pattern **8 :** mark placed beside an item noted ~ *vb* **1 :** slow down or stop **2 :** restrain **3 :** compare or correspond with a source or original **4 :** inspect or test for condition **5 :** mark with a check **6 :** leave or accept for safekeeping or shipment **7 :** checker — **check in** *vb* **:** report one's arrival — **check out** *vb* **:** settle one's account and leave
[1]**check•er** *n* **:** piece in checkers ~ *vb* **:** mark with different colors or into squares
[2]**checker** *n* **:** one that checks
check•ers *n* **:** game for 2 played on a checkerboard — **check•er•board** *n*
check•mate *vb* **:** thwart completely — **check-mate** *n*
check•up *n* **:** physical examination
ched•dar *n* **:** hard smooth cheese
cheek *n* **1 :** fleshy side part of the face **2 :** impudence — **cheeked** *adj* — **cheeky** *adj*
cheer *n* **1 :** good spirits **2 :** food and drink for a feast **3 :** shout of applause or encouragement ~ *vb* **1 :** give hope or courage to **2 :** make or become glad **3 :** urge on or applaud with shouts — **cheer•er** *n* — **cheer•ful** *adj* — **cheer•ful•ly** *adv* — **cheer•ful•ness** *n* — **cheer•lead•er** *n* — **cheer•less** *adj* — **cheer-less•ly** *adv* — **cheer•less•ness** *n*
cheery *adj* **:** cheerful — **cheer•i•ly** *adv* — **cheer•i•ness** *n*
cheese *n* **:** curd of milk usu. pressed and cured — **cheesy** *adj*
chef *n* **:** chief cook
chem•i•cal *adj* **1 :** relating to chemistry **2 :** working or produced by chemicals ~ *n* **:** substance obtained by chemistry — **chem•i-cal•ly** *adv*
chem•ist *n* **:** one trained in chemistry
chem•is•try *n* **:** science that deals with the composition and properties of substances
che•mo•ther•a•py *n* **:** use of chemicals in the treatment of disease — **che•mo•ther•a•peu-tic** *adj*
cher•ish *vb* **:** hold dear
cher•ry *n* **:** small fleshy fruit of a tree related to the roses or the tree or its wood
cher•ub *n* **1** *pl* **cher•u•bim :** angel **2** *pl* **cher-ubs :** chubby child — **che•ru•bic** *adj*
chess *n* **:** game for 2 played on a checkerboard — **chess•board** *n* — **chess•man** *n*
chest *n* **1 :** boxlike container **2 :** part of the body enclosed by the ribs and breastbone — **chest•ed** *adj*
chest•nut *n* **:** nut of a tree related to the beech or the tree
chew *vb* **:** crush or grind with the teeth ~ *n* **:** something to chew — **chew•able** *adj* — **chew•er** *n* — **chewy** *adj*
chic *n* **:** smart elegance of dress or manner ~ *adj* **1 :** stylish **2 :** currently fashionable
chick *n* **:** young chicken or bird
chick•a•dee *n* **:** small grayish American bird
chick•en *n* **1 :** common domestic fowl or its flesh used as food **2 :** coward
chief *n* **:** leader ~ *adj* **1 :** highest in rank **2 :** most important — **chief•dom** *n* — **chief•ly** *adv*
child *n* **chil•dren 1 :** unborn or recently born person **2 :** son or daughter — **child•bear•ing** *n or adj* — **child•birth** *n* — **child•hood** *n* — **child•ish** *adj* — **child•ish•ly** *adv* — **child-ish•ness** *n* — **child•less** *adj* — **child•less-ness** *n* — **child•like** *adj* — **child•proof** *adj*
chili, chile, chil•li *n* **1 :** hot pepper **2 :** spicy stew of ground beef, chilies, and beans
chill *vb* **:** make or become cold or chilly ~ *adj* **:** moderately cold ~ *n* **1 :** feeling of coldness with shivering **2 :** moderate coldness
chilly *adj* **:** noticeably cold — **chill•i•ness** *n*

chime *n* **:** set of tuned bells or their sound ~ *vb* **:** make bell-like sounds — **chime in** *vb* **:** break into or join in a conversation
chim•ney *n* **1 :** passage for smoke **2 :** glass tube around a lamp flame
chimp *n* **:** chimpanzee
chim•pan•zee *n* **:** small ape
chin *n* **:** part of the face below the mouth — **chin•less** *adj*
chi•na *n* **1 :** porcelain ware **2 :** domestic pottery
chip *n* **1 :** small thin flat piece cut or broken off **2 :** thin crisp morsel of food **3 :** counter used in games **4 :** flaw where a chip came off **5 :** small slice of semiconductor containing electronic circuits ~ *vb* **:** cut or break chips from — **chip in** *vb* **:** contribute
chip•munk *n* **:** small striped ground-dwelling rodent
chip•per *adj* **:** lively and cheerful
chi•ro•prac•tic *n* **:** system of healing based esp. on manipulation of body structures — **chi•ro•prac•tor** *n*
chirp *n* **:** short sharp sound like that of a bird or cricket — **chirp** *vb*
chis•el *n* **:** sharp-edged metal tool ~ *vb* **1 :** work with a chisel **2 :** cheat — **chis•el•er** *n*
chit•chat *n* **:** casual conversation — **chitchat** *vb*
chiv•al•ry *n* **1 :** system or practices of knighthood **2 :** spirit or character of the ideal knight — **chi•val•ric** *adj* — **chiv•al•rous** *adj* — **chiv•al•rous•ly** *adv* — **chiv•al•rous•ness** *n*
chive *n* **:** herb related to the onion
chlo•rine *n* **:** chemical element that is a heavy strong-smelling greenish yellow irritating gas
chlo•ro•phyll *n* **:** green coloring matter of plants
chock *n* **:** wedge for blocking the movement of a wheel — **chock** *vb*
chock–full *adj* **:** full to the limit
choc•o•late *n* **1 :** ground roasted cacao beans or a beverage made from them **2 :** candy made of or with chocolate **3 :** dark brown
choice *n* **1 :** act or power of choosing **2 :** one selected **3 :** variety offered for selection ~ *adj* **1 :** worthy of being chosen **2 :** selected with care **3 :** of high quality
choir *n* **:** group of singers esp. in church — **choir•boy** *n* — **choir•mas•ter** *n*
choke *vb* **1 :** hinder breathing **2 :** clog or obstruct ~ *n* **1 :** a choking or sound of choking **2 :** valve for controlling air intake in a gasoline engine
cho•les•ter•ol *n* **:** waxy substance in animal tissues
choose *vb* (**chose; cho•sen**) **1 :** select after consideration **2 :** decide **3 :** prefer — **choos•er** *n* — **choosy** *adj*
chop *vb* **1 :** cut by repeated blows **2 :** cut into small pieces ~ *n* **1 :** sharp downward blow **2 :** small cut of meat often with part of a rib — **chop•per** *n*
chop•py *adj* **1 :** rough with small waves **2 :** jerky or disconnected — **chop•pi•ly** *adv* — **chop•pi•ness** *n*
cho•ral *adj* **:** relating to or sung by a choir or chorus or in chorus — **cho•ral•ly** *adv*
cho•rale *n* **1 :** hymn tune or harmonization of a traditional melody **2 :** chorus or choir
[1]**chord** *n* **:** harmonious tones sounded together
chore *n* **1** *pl* **:** daily household or farm work **2 :** routine or disagreeable task
cho•re•og•ra•phy *n* **:** art of composing and arranging dances — **cho•reo•graph** *vb* — **cho•re•og•ra•pher** *n* — **cho•reo•graph•ic** *adj*
cho•rus *n* **1 :** group of singers or dancers **2 :** part of a song repeated at intervals **3 :** composition for a chorus ~ *vb* **:** sing or utter together
chose *past of* CHOOSE
cho•sen *adj* **:** favored
[1]**chow** *n* **:** food
[2]**chow** *n* **:** thick-coated muscular dog
chow•der *n* **:** thick soup usu. of seafood and milk
chris•ten *vb* **1 :** baptize **2 :** name — **chris•ten•ing** *n*
Chris•tian *n* **:** adherent of Christianity ~ *adj* **:** relating to or professing a belief in Christianity or Jesus Christ — **Chris•tian•ize** *vb*
Chris•ti•an•i•ty *n* **:** religion derived from the teachings of Jesus Christ
Christ•mas *n* **:** December 25 celebrated as the birthday of Christ
chro•mo•some *n* **:** part of a cell nucleus that contains the genes — **chro•mo•som•al** *adj*
chron•ic *adj* **:** frequent or persistent — **chron•i•cal•ly** *adv*
chron•i•cle *n* **:** history ~ *vb* **:** record — **chron•i•cler** *n*
chro•nol•o•gy *n* **:** list of events in order of their occurrence — **chron•o•log•i•cal** *adj* — **chron•o•log•i•cal•ly** *adv*
chub•by *adj* **:** fat — **chub•bi•ness** *n*

[1]**chuck** *vb* **1 :** tap **2 :** toss ∼ *n* **1 :** light pat under the chin **2 :** toss
[2]**chuck** *n* **1 :** cut of beef **2 :** machine part that holds work or another part
chuck•le *vb* **:** laugh quietly — **chuckle** *n*
chum *n* **:** close friend ∼ *vb* **:** be chums — **chum•my** *adj*
chump *n* **:** fool
chunk *n* **1 :** short thick piece **2 :** sizable amount
chunky *adj* **1 :** thickly built **2 :** containing chunks
church *n* **1 :** building esp. for Christian public worship **2 :** whole body of Christians **3 :** denomination **4 :** congregation — **church•go•er** *n* — **church•go•ing** *adj or n* — **church•yard** *n*
churn *n* **:** container in which butter is made ∼ *vb* **1 :** agitate in a churn **2 :** shake violently
chute *n* **:** trough or passage
chutz•pah *n* **:** nerve or insolence
ci•der *n* **:** apple juice
ci•gar *n* **:** roll of leaf tobacco for smoking
cig•a•rette *n* **:** cut tobacco rolled in paper for smoking
cinch *n* **1 :** strap holding a saddle or pack in place **2 :** sure thing — **cinch** *vb*
cin•der *n* **1** *pl* **:** ashes **2 :** piece of partly burned wood or coal
cin•e•ma *n* **:** movies or a movie theater — **cin•e•mat•ic** *adj*
cin•na•mon *n* **:** spice from an aromatic tree bark
ci•pher *n* **1 :** zero **2 :** code
cir•cle *n* **1 :** closed symmetrical curve **2 :** cycle **3 :** group with a common tie ∼ *vb* **1 :** enclose in a circle **2 :** move or revolve around
cir•cuit *n* **1 :** boundary **2 :** regular tour of a territory **3 :** complete path of an electric current **4 :** group of electronic components — **cir•cuit•ry** *n*
cir•cu•lar *adj* **1 :** round **2 :** moving in a circle ∼ *n* **:** advertising leaflet — **cir•cu•lar•i•ty** *n*
cir•cu•late *vb* **:** move or cause to move in a circle or from place to place or person to person — **cir•cu•la•tion** *n* — **cir•cu•la•to•ry** *adj*
cir•cum•cise *vb* **:** cut off the foreskin of — **cir•cum•ci•sion** *n*
cir•cum•fer•ence *n* **:** perimeter of a circle
cir•cum•stance *n* **1 :** fact or event **2** *pl* **:** surrounding conditions **3** *pl* **:** financial situation — **cir•cum•stan•tial** *adj*
cir•cum•vent *vb* **:** get around esp. by trickery — **cir•cum•ven•tion** *n*
cir•cus *n* **:** show with feats of skill, animal acts, and clowns
cite *vb* **1 :** summon before a court **2 :** quote **3 :** refer to esp. in commendation — **ci•ta•tion** *n*
cit•i•zen *n* **:** member of a country — **cit•i•zen•ry** *n* — **cit•i•zen•ship** *n*
cit•rus *n* **:** evergreen tree or shrub grown for its fruit (as the orange or lemon)
city *n* **:** place larger or more important than a town
civ•ics *n* **:** study of citizenship — **civ•ic** *adj*
civ•il *adj* **1 :** relating to citizens **2 :** polite **3 :** relating to or being a lawsuit — **civ•il•ly** *adv*
ci•vil•ian *n* **:** person not in a military, police, or fire-fighting force
ci•vil•i•ty *n* **:** courtesy
civ•i•lize *vb* **:** raise from a primitive stage of cultural development — **civ•i•li•za•tion** *n* — **civ•i•lized** *adj*
civil war *n* **:** war among citizens of one country
clad *adj* **:** being covered
claim *vb* **1 :** demand or take as the rightful owner **2 :** maintain ∼ *n* **1 :** demand of right or ownership **2 :** declaration **3 :** something claimed — **claim•ant** *n*
clair•voy•ant *adj* **:** able to perceive things beyond the senses — **clair•voy•ance** *n* — **clair•voy•ant** *n*
clam *n* **:** bivalve mollusk
clam•my *adj* **:** being damp, soft, and usu. cool — **clam•mi•ness** *n*
clam•or *n* **1 :** uproar **2 :** protest — **clamor** *vb* — **clam•or•ous** *adj*
clamp *n* **:** device for holding things together — **clamp** *vb*
clan *n* **:** group of related families — **clan•nish** *adj* — **clan•nish•ness** *n*
clan•des•tine *adj* **:** secret
clang *n* **:** loud metallic ringing — **clang** *vb*
clank *n* **:** brief sound of struck metal — **clank** *vb*
clap *vb* **1 :** strike noisily **2 :** applaud ∼ *n* **1 :** loud crash **2 :** noise made by clapping the hands
clap•per *n* **:** tongue of a bell
clar•i•fy *vb* **:** make or become clear — **clar•i•fi•ca•tion** *n*
clar•i•net *n* **:** woodwind instrument shaped like a tube — **clar•i•net•ist, clar•i•net•tist** *n*
clar•i•ty *n* **:** the quality of being clear
clash *vb* **1 :** make or cause a clash **2 :** be in

opposition or disharmony ~ *n* **1 :** crashing sound **2 :** hostile encounter

clasp *n* **1 :** device for holding things together **2 :** embrace or grasp ~ *vb* **1 :** fasten **2 :** embrace or grasp

class *n* **1 :** group of the same status or nature **2 :** social rank **3 :** course of instruction **4 :** group of students ~ *vb* **:** classify — **class·less** *adj* — **class·mate** *n* — **class·room** *n*

clas·sic *adj* **1 :** serving as a standard of excellence **2 :** classical ~ *n* **:** work of enduring excellence and esp. of ancient Greece or Rome — **clas·si·cal** *adj* — **clas·si·cal·ly** *adv* — **clas·si·cism** *n* — **clas·si·cist** *n*

clas·si·fied *adj* **:** restricted for security reasons

clas·si·fy *vb* **:** arrange in or assign to classes — **clas·si·fi·ca·tion** *n* — **clas·si·fi·er** *n*

clat·ter *n* **:** rattling sound — **clat·ter** *vb*

clause *n* **1 :** separate part of a document **2 :** part of a sentence with a subject and predicate

claus·tro·pho·bia *n* **:** fear of closed or narrow spaces — **claus·tro·pho·bic** *adj*

claw *n* **:** sharp curved nail or naillike part of an animal ~ *vb* **:** scratch or dig — **clawed** *adj*

clay *n* **:** plastic earthy material — **clay·ey** *adj*

clean *adj* **1 :** free from dirt or disease **2 :** pure or honorable **3 :** thorough ~ *vb* **:** make or become clean — **clean** *adv* — **clean·er** *n* — **clean·li·ness** *n* — **clean·ly** *adv* — **clean·ness** *n*

cleanse *vb* **:** make clean — **cleans·er** *n*

clear *adj* **1 :** bright **2 :** free from clouds **3 :** transparent **4 :** easily heard, seen or understood **5 :** free from doubt **6 :** free from restriction or obstruction ~ *vb* **1 :** make or become clear **2 :** go away **3 :** free from accusation or blame **4 :** explain or settle **5 :** net **6 :** jump or pass without touching ~ *n* **:** clear space or part — **clear** *adv* — **clear·ance** *n* — **clear·ly** *adv*

clear·ing *n* **:** land cleared of wood

[1]**cleave** *vb* **:** adhere

[2]**cleave** *vb* **:** split apart — **cleav·er** *n*

clef *n* **:** sign on the staff in music to show pitch

cleft *n* **:** crack

clench *vb* **1 :** hold fast **2 :** close tightly

cler·gy *n* **:** body of religious officials — **cler·gy·man** *n*

cler·ic *n* **:** member of the clergy

cler·i·cal *adj* **1 :** relating to the clergy **2 :** relating to a clerk or office worker

clerk *n* **1 :** official responsible for record-keeping **2 :** person doing general office work **3 :** salesperson in a store — **clerk** *vb* — **clerk·ship** *n*

clev·er *adj* **1 :** resourceful **2 :** marked by wit or ingenuity — **clev·er·ly** *adv* — **clev·er·ness** *n*

cli·ché *n* **:** trite phrase — **cli·chéd** *adj*

click *n* **:** slight sharp noise ~ *vb* **:** make or cause to make a click

cli·ent *n* **1 :** person who engages professional services **2 :** customer

cli·en·tele *n* **:** body of customers

cliff *n* **:** high steep face of rock

cli·mate *n* **:** average weather conditions over a period of years — **cli·mat·ic** *adj*

cli·max *n* **:** the highest point ~ *vb* **:** come to a climax — **cli·mac·tic** *adj*

climb *vb* **1 :** go up or down by use of hands and feet **2 :** rise ~ *n* **:** a climbing — **climb·er** *n*

clinch *vb* **1 :** fasten securely **2 :** settle **3 :** hold fast or firmly — **clinch** *n* — **clinch·er** *n*

cling *vb* (**clung; clung**) **1 :** adhere firmly **2 :** hold on tightly

clin·ic *n* **:** facility for diagnosis and treatment of outpatients — **clin·i·cal** *adj* — **clin·i·cal·ly** *adv*

clink *vb* **:** make a slight metallic sound — **clink** *n*

[1]**clip** *vb* **:** fasten with a clip ~ *n* **:** device to hold things together

[2]**clip** *vb* **1 :** cut or cut off **2 :** hit ~ *n* **1 :** clippers **2 :** sharp blow **3 :** rapid pace

clip·per *n* **1** *pl* **:** implement for clipping **2 :** fast sailing ship

clique *n* **:** small exclusive group of people

cloak *n* **1 :** loose outer garment **2 :** something that conceals ~ *vb* **:** cover or hide with a cloak

clob·ber *vb* **:** hit hard

clock *n* **:** timepiece not carried on the person ~ *vb* **:** record the time of

clock·wise *adv or adj* **:** in the same direction as a clock's hands move

clod *n* **1 :** lump esp. of earth **2 :** dull insensitive person

clog *n* **1 :** restraining weight **2 :** thick-soled shoe ~ *vb* **1 :** impede with a clog **2 :** obstruct passage through **3 :** become plugged up

clone *n* **1 :** offspring produced from a single organism **2 :** copy

[1]**close** *vb* **1 :** shut **2 :** cease operation **3 :** terminate **4 :** bring or come together ~ *n* **:** conclusion or end

[2]**close** *adj* **1 :** confining **2 :** secretive **3 :** strict

4 : stuffy **5 :** having little space between items **6 :** fitting tightly **7 :** near **8 :** intimate **9 :** accurate **10 :** nearly even — **close** *adv* — **close•ly** *adv* — **close•ness** *n*
clos•et *n* **:** small compartment for household utensils or clothing
clo•sure *n* **1 :** act of closing **2 :** something that closes
clot *n* **:** dried mass of a liquid — **clot** *vb*
cloth *n* **1 :** fabric **2 :** tablecloth
clothe *vb* **:** dress
clothes *n pl* **:** clothing
cloth•ing *n* **:** covering for the human body
cloud *n* **1 :** visible mass of particles in the air **2 :** something that darkens, hides, or threatens ~ *vb* **:** darken or hide — **cloud•burst** *n* — **cloud•i•ness** *n* — **cloud•less** *adj* — **cloudy** *adj*
clout *n* **1 :** blow **2 :** influence ~ *vb* **:** hit forcefully
clove *n* **:** dried flower bud of an East Indian tree used as a spice
clo•ver *n* **:** leguminous herb with usu. 3-part leaves
clown *n* **:** funny costumed entertainer esp. in a circus ~ *vb* **:** act like a clown — **clown•ish** *adj* — **clown•ish•ly** *adv* — **clown•ish•ness** *n*
cloy *vb* **:** disgust with excess — **cloy•ing•ly** *adv*
club *n* **1 :** heavy wooden stick **2 :** playing card of a suit marked with a black figure like a clover leaf **3 :** group associated for a common purpose ~ *vb* **:** hit with a club
cluck *n* **:** sound made by a hen — **cluck** *vb*
clue *n* **:** piece of evidence that helps solve a problem ~ *vb* **:** provide with a clue
clump *n* **1 :** cluster **2 :** heavy tramping sound ~ *vb* **:** tread heavily
clum•sy *adj* **1 :** lacking dexterity, nimbleness, or grace **2 :** tactless — **clum•si•ly** *adv* — **clum•si•ness** *n*
clung *past of* CLING
clus•ter *n* **:** group ~ *vb* **:** grow or gather in a cluster
clutch *vb* **:** grasp ~ *n* **1 :** grasping hand or claws **2 :** control or power **3 :** coupling for connecting two working parts in machinery
clut•ter *vb* **:** fill with things that get in the way — **clutter** *n*
coach *n* **1 :** closed 2-door 4-wheeled carriage **2 :** railroad passenger car **3 :** bus **4 :** 2d-class air travel **5 :** one who instructs or trains performers ~ *vb* **:** instruct or direct as a coach
coal *n* **1 :** glowing fragment from a fire **2 :** black solid mineral used as fuel — **coal•field** *n*
co•ali•tion *n* **:** temporary alliance
coarse *adj* **1 :** composed of large particles **2 :** rough or crude — **coarse•ly** *adv* — **coars•en** *vb* — **coarse•ness** *n*
coast *n* **:** seashore ~ *vb* **:** move without effort — **coast•al** *adj* — **coast•line** *n*
coast•er *n* **1 :** one that coasts **2 :** plate or mat to protect a surface
coast guard *n* **:** military force that guards or patrols a coast — **coast•guards•man** *n*
coat *n* **1 :** outer garment for the upper body **2 :** external growth of fur or feathers **3 :** covering layer ~ *vb* **:** cover with a coat — **coat•ed** *adj* — **coat•ing** *n*
coax *vb* **:** move to action or achieve by gentle urging or flattery
cob•bler *n* **1 :** shoemaker **2 :** deep-dish fruit pie
cob•web *n* **:** network spun by a spider or a similar filament
cock *n* **1 :** male fowl **2 :** valve or faucet ~ *vb* **1 :** draw back the hammer of a firearm **2 :** tilt to one side — **cock•fight** *n*
cock•eyed *adj* **1 :** tilted to one side **2 :** slightly crazy
cock•pit *n* **:** place for a pilot, driver, or helmsman
cock•roach *n* **:** nocturnal insect often infesting houses
cock•tail *n* **1 :** iced drink of liquor and flavorings **2 :** appetizer
cocky *adj* **:** too confident in oneself — **cock•i•ly** *adv* — **cock•i•ness** *n*
co•coa *n* **1 :** cacao **2 :** powdered chocolate or a drink made from this
co•co•nut *n* **:** large nutlike fruit of a tropical palm (**coconut palm**)
co•coon *n* **:** case protecting an insect pupa
cod *n pl* **cod :** food fish of the No. Atlantic
cod•dle *vb* **:** pamper
code *n* **1 :** system of laws or rules **2 :** system of signals
co•ed *n* **:** female student in a coeducational institution — **coed** *adj*
co•ed•u•ca•tion *n* **:** education of the sexes together — **co•ed•u•ca•tion•al** *adj*
co•erce *vb* **:** force — **co•er•cion** *n* — **co•er•cive** *adj*

cof•fee *n* : drink made from the roasted and ground seeds (**coffee beans**) of a tropical shrub — **cof•fee•house** *n* — **cof•fee•pot** *n*
cof•fin *n* : box for burial
cog *n* : tooth on the rim of a gear — **cogged** *adj* — **cog•wheel** *n*
cog•ni•zance *n* : notice or awareness — **cog•ni•zant** *adj*
co•hab•it *vb* : live together as husband and wife — **co•hab•i•ta•tion** *n*
co•here *vb* : stick together — **co•he•sion** *n* — **co•he•sive** *adj* — **co•he•sive•ly** *adv* — **co•he•sive•ness** *n*
co•her•ent *adj* **1** : able to stick together **2** : logically consistent — **co•her•ence** *n* — **co•her•ent•ly** *adv*
coil *vb* : wind in a spiral ~ *n* : series of loops (as of rope)
coin *n* : piece of metal used as money ~ *vb* **1** : make (a coin) by stamping **2** : create — **coin•age** *n* — **coin•er** *n*
co•in•cide *vb* **1** : be in the same place **2** : happen at the same time **3** : be alike — **co•in•ci•dence** *n* — **co•in•ci•dent** *adj* — **co•in•ci•den•tal** *adj*
co•la *n* : carbonated soft drink
col•an•der *n* : perforated utensil for draining food
cold *adj* **1** : having a low or below normal temperature **2** : lacking warmth of feeling **3** : suffering from lack of warmth ~ *n* **1** : low temperature **2** : minor respiratory illness — **cold•ly** *adv* — **cold•ness** *n* — **in cold blood** : with premeditation
cold–blood•ed *adj* **1** : cruel or merciless **2** : having a body temperature that varies with the temperature of the environment
cole•slaw *n* : cabbage salad
col•ic *n* : sharp abdominal pain — **col•icky** *adj*
col•i•se•um *n* : arena
col•lab•o•rate *vb* **1** : work jointly with others **2** : help the enemy — **col•lab•o•ra•tion** *n* — **col•lab•o•ra•tor** *n*
col•lapse *vb* **1** : fall in **2** : break down physically or mentally **3** : fold down ~ *n* : breakdown — **col•laps•ible** *adj*
col•lar *n* : part of a garment around the neck ~ *vb* **1** : seize by the collar **2** : grab — **col•lar•less** *adj*
col•lar•bone *n* : bone joining the breastbone and the shoulder blade
col•league *n* : associate
col•lect *vb* **1** : bring, come, or gather together **2** : receive payment of ~ *adv or adj* : to be paid for by the receiver — **col•lect•ible, col•lect•able** *adj* — **col•lec•tive** *adj* — **col•lec•tive•ly** *adv* — **col•lec•tion** *n* — **col•lec•tor** *n*
col•lege *n* : institution of higher learning granting a bachelor's degree — **col•le•gian** *n* — **col•le•giate** *adj*
col•lide *vb* : strike together — **col•li•sion** *n*
col•lie *n* : large long-haired dog
col•lu•sion *n* : secret cooperation for deceit — **col•lu•sive** *adj*
co•logne *n* : perfumed liquid
[1]co•lon *n* : lower part of the large intestine — **co•lon•ic** *adj*
[2]colon *n* : punctuation mark : used esp. to direct attention to following matter
col•o•nel *n* : commissioned officer (as in the army) ranking below a general
col•o•nize *vb* **1** : establish a colony in **2** : settle — **col•o•ni•za•tion** *n* — **col•o•niz•er** *n*
col•o•ny *n* **1** : people who inhabit a new territory or the territory itself **2** : animals of one kind (as bees) living together — **co•lo•nial** *adj or n* — **col•o•nist** *n*
col•or *n* **1** : quality of visible things distinct from shape that results from light reflection **2** *pl* : flag **3** : liveliness ~ *vb* **1** : give color to **2** : blush — **col•or•fast** *adj* — **col•or•ful** *adj* — **col•or•less** *adj*
col•or–blind *adj* : unable to distinguish colors — **color blindness** *n*
col•ored *adj* **1** : having color **2** : of a race other than the white ~ *n* : colored person
co•los•sus *n* : something of great size or scope — **co•los•sal** *adj*
colt *n* : young male horse — **colt•ish** *adj*
col•umn *n* **1** : vertical section of a printed page **2** : regular feature article (as in a newspaper) **3** : pillar **4** : row (as of soldiers) — **co•lum•nar** *adj* — **col•um•nist** *n*
co•ma *n* : deep prolonged unconsciousness — **co•ma•tose** *adj*
comb *n* **1** : toothed instrument for arranging the hair **2** : crest on a fowl's head — **comb** *vb* — **combed** *adj*
com•bat *vb* : fight — **com•bat** *n* — **com•bat•ant** *n* — **com•bat•ive** *adj*
com•bine *vb* : join together ~ *n* **1** : association for business or political advantage **2** : harvesting machine — **com•bi•na•tion** *n*
com•bust *vb* : to catch fire — **com•bus•ti•bil•i•ty** *n* — **com•bus•ti•ble** *adj or n* — **com•bus•tion** *n*

come *vb* **came; come 1 :** move toward or arrive at something **2 :** reach a state **3 :** originate or exist **4 :** amount — **come clean** *vb* **:** confess — **come into** *vb* **:** acquire, achieve — **come off** *vb* **:** succeed — **come to** *vb* **:** regain consciousness — **come to pass :** happen — **come to terms :** reach an agreement

come•back *n* **1 :** retort **2 :** return to a former position — **come back** *vb*

co•me•di•an *n* **1 :** comic actor **2 :** funny person **3 :** entertainer specializing in comedy

co•me•di•enne *n* **:** a woman who is a comedian

com•e•dy *n* **1 :** an amusing play **2 :** humorous entertainment

com•et *n* **:** small bright celestial body having a tail

com•fort *n* **1 :** consolation **2 :** well-being or something that gives it ~ *vb* **1 :** give hope to **2 :** console — **com•fort•able** *adj* — **com•fort•ably** *adv*

com•fort•er *n* **1 :** one that comforts **2 :** quilt

com•ic *adj* **1 :** relating to comedy **2 :** funny ~ *n* **1 :** comedian **2 :** sequence of cartoons — **com•i•cal** *adj*

com•ing *adj* **:** next

com•ma *n* **:** punctuation mark, used esp. to separate sentence parts

com•mand *vb* **1 :** order **2 :** control ~ *n* **1 :** act of commanding **2 :** an order given **3 :** mastery **4 :** troops under a commander — **com•man•dant** *n*

com•man•deer *vb* **:** seize by force

com•mand•er *n* **1 :** officer commanding an army or subdivision of an army **2 :** commissioned officer in the navy ranking below a captain

com•mand•ment *n* **:** order

com•mem•o•rate *vb* **:** celebrate or honor — **com•mem•o•ra•tion** *n* — **com•mem•o•ra•tive** *adj*

com•mence *vb* **:** start

com•mence•ment *n* **1 :** beginning **2 :** graduation ceremony

com•mend *vb* **1 :** entrust **2 :** recommend **3 :** praise — **com•mend•able** *adj* — **com•men•da•tion** *n*

com•ment *n* **:** statement of opinion or remark — **comment** *vb*

com•men•tary *n* **:** series of comments

com•men•ta•tor *n* **:** one who discusses news

com•merce *n* **:** business

com•mer•cial *adj* **:** designed for profit or for mass appeal ~ *n* **:** broadcast advertisement — **com•mer•cial•ize** *vb* — **com•mer•cial•ly** *adv*

com•mis•sary *n* **:** store esp. for military personnel

com•mis•sion *n* **1 :** order granting power or rank **2 :** panel to judge, approve, or act **3 :** the doing of an act **4 :** agent's fee ~ *vb* **1 :** confer rank or authority to or for **2 :** request something be done

com•mis•sion•er *n* **1 :** member of a commission **2 :** head of a government department

com•mit *vb* **1 :** turn over to someone for safekeeping or confinement **2 :** perform or do **3 :** pledge — **com•mit•ment** *n*

com•mit•tee *n* **:** panel that examines or acts on something

com•mod•i•ty *n* **:** article for sale

com•mon *adj* **1 :** public **2 :** shared by several **3 :** widely known, found, or observed **4 :** ordinary ~ *n* **:** community land — **com•mon•ly** *adv* — **in common :** shared together

com•mon•place *n* **:** cliché ~ *adj* **:** ordinary

com•mon•wealth *n* **:** state

com•mo•tion *n* **:** disturbance

com•mu•ni•cate *vb* **1 :** make known **2 :** transmit **3 :** exchange information or opinions — **com•mu•ni•ca•ble** *adj* — **com•mu•ni•ca•tion** *n* — **com•mu•ni•ca•tive** *adj*

Com•mu•nion *n* **:** Christian sacrament of partaking of bread and wine

com•mu•nism *n* **1 :** social organization in which goods are held in common **2** *cap* **:** political doctrine based on revolutionary Marxist socialism — **com•mu•nist** *n or adj, often cap* — **com•mu•nis•tic** *adj, often cap*

com•mu•ni•ty *n* **:** body of people living in the same place under the same laws

com•mute *vb* **1 :** reduce (a punishment) **2 :** travel back and forth regularly ~ *n* **:** trip made in commuting — **com•mu•ta•tion** *n* — **com•mut•er** *n*

[1]**com•pact** *adj* **1 :** hard **2 :** small or brief ~ *vb* **:** pack together ~ *n* **1 :** cosmetics case **2 :** small car — **com•pact•ly** *adv* — **com•pact•ness** *n*

[2]**com•pact** *n* **:** agreement

compact disc *n* **:** plastic-coated disc with laser-readable recorded music

com•pan•ion *n* **1 :** close friend **2 :** one of a pair — **com•pan•ion•able** *adj* — **com•pan•ion•ship** *n*

com•pa•ny *n* **1 :** business organization **2**

: group of performers **3 :** guests **4 :** infantry unit

com•pare *vb* **1 :** represent as similar **2 :** check for likenesses or differences ~ *n* **:** comparison — **com•pa•ra•ble** *adj* — **com•par•a•tive** *adj or n* — **com•par•a•tive•ly** *adv* — **com•par•i•son** *n*

com•part•ment *n* **:** section or room

com•pass *n* **1 :** scope **2 :** device for drawing circles **3 :** device for determining direction

com•pas•sion *n* **:** pity — **com•pas•sion•ate** *adj*

com•pat•i•ble *adj* **:** harmonious — **com•pat•i•bil•i•ty** *n*

com•pel *vb* **:** cause through necessity

com•pen•sate *vb* **1 :** offset or balance **2 :** repay — **com•pen•sa•tion** *n* — **com•pen•sa•to•ry** *adj*

com•pete *vb* **:** strive to win — **com•pe•ti•tion** *n* — **com•pet•i•tive** *adj* — **com•pet•i•tive•ness** *n* — **com•pet•i•tor** *n*

com•pe•tent *adj* **:** capable — **com•pe•tence** *n* — **com•pe•ten•cy** *n*

com•pile *vb* **:** collect or compose from several sources — **com•pi•la•tion** *n* — **com•pil•er** *n*

com•pla•cen•cy *n* **:** unusual satisfaction with oneself — **com•pla•cent** *adj*

com•plain *vb* **1 :** express grief, pain, or discontent **2 :** make an accusation — **com•plain•ant** *n* — **com•plain•er** *n* — **com•plaint** *n*

com•ple•ment *n* **1 :** something that completes **2 :** full number or amount ~ *vb* **:** complete — **com•ple•men•ta•ry** *adj*

com•plete *adj* **1 :** having all parts **2 :** finished **3 :** total ~ *vb* **1 :** make whole **2 :** finish — **com•plete•ly** *adv* — **com•plete•ness** *n* — **com•ple•tion** *n*

com•plex *adj* **1 :** having many parts **2 :** intricate ~ *n* **:** psychological problem — **com•plex•i•ty** *n*

com•plex•ion *n* **:** hue or appearance of the skin esp. of the face — **com•plex•ioned** *adj*

com•pli•cate *vb* **:** make complex or hard to understand — **com•pli•cat•ed** *adj* — **com•pli•ca•tion** *n*

com•pli•ment *n* **1 :** flattering remark **2** *pl* **:** greeting ~ *vb* **:** pay a compliment to

com•pli•men•ta•ry *adj* **1 :** praising **2 :** free

com•ply *vb* **:** conform or yield — **com•pli•ance** *n* — **com•pli•ant** *n*

com•po•nent *n* **:** part of something larger ~ *adj* **:** serving as a component

com•pose *vb* **1 :** create (as by writing) or put together **2 :** calm **3 :** set type — **com•pos•er** *n* — **com•po•si•tion** *n*

com•pos•ite *adj* **:** made up of diverse parts — **composite** *n*

com•post *n* **:** decayed organic fertilizing material

com•po•sure *n* **:** calmness

[1]**com•pound** *vb* **1 :** combine or add **2 :** pay (interest) on principal and accrued interest ~ *adj* **:** made up of 2 or more parts ~ *n* **:** something that is compound

[2]**com•pound** *n* **:** enclosure

com•pre•hend *vb* **1 :** understand **2 :** include — **com•pre•hen•si•ble** *adj* — **com•pre•hen•sion** *n* — **com•pre•hen•sive** *adj*

com•press *vb* **:** squeeze together ~ *n* **:** pad for pressing on a wound — **com•pres•sion** *n* — **com•pres•sor** *n*

com•prise *vb* **1 :** contain or cover **2 :** be made up of

com•pro•mise *vb* **:** settle differences by mutual concessions — **com•pro•mise** *n*

com•pul•sion *n* **1 :** coercion **2 :** irresistible impulse — **com•pul•sive** *adj* — **com•pul•so•ry** *adj*

com•pute *vb* **:** calculate — **com•pu•ta•tion** *n*

com•put•er *n* **:** electronic data processing machine — **com•put•er•i•za•tion** *n* — **com•put•er•ize** *vb*

com•rade *n* **:** companion — **com•rade•ship** *n*

con•cave *adj* **:** curved like the inside of a sphere — **con•cav•i•ty** *n*

con•ceal *vb* **:** hide — **con•ceal•ment** *n*

con•cede *vb* **:** grant

con•ceit *n* **:** excessively high opinion of oneself — **con•ceit•ed** *adj*

con•ceive *vb* **1 :** become pregnant **2 :** think of — **con•ceiv•able** *adj* — **con•ceiv•ably** *adv*

con•cen•trate *vb* **1 :** gather together **2 :** make stronger **3 :** fix one's attention ~ *n* **:** something concentrated — **con•cen•tra•tion** *n*

con•cen•tric *adj* **:** having a common center

con•cept *n* **:** thought or idea

con•cep•tion *n* **1 :** act of conceiving **2 :** idea

con•cern *vb* **1 :** relate to **2 :** involve ~ *n* **1 :** affair **2 :** worry **3 :** business — **con•cerned** *adj* — **con•cern•ing** *prep*

con•cert *n* **1 :** agreement or joint action **2 :** public performance of music — **con•cert•ed** *adj*

con•cer•to *n* **:** orchestral work with solo instruments

con•ces•sion *n* **1 :** act of conceding **2 :** something conceded **3 :** right to do business on a property

con•cil•ia•to•ry *adj* **:** doing what's necessary to gain goodwill

con•cise *adj* **:** said in few words — **con•cise•ly** *adv* — **con•cise•ness** *n* — **con•ci•sion** *n*

con•clude *vb* **1 :** end **2 :** decide — **con•clu•sion** *n* — **con•clu•sive** *adj* — **con•clu•sive•ly** *adv*

con•coct *vb* **:** prepare or devise — **con•coc•tion** *n*

con•cord *n* **:** agreement

con•cor•dance *n* **1 :** agreement **2 :** index of words — **con•cor•dant** *adj*

con•course *n* **:** open space where crowds gather

con•crete *adj* **1 :** naming something real **2 :** actual or substantial **3 :** made of concrete ~ *n* **:** hard building material made of cement, sand, gravel, and water

con•cur *vb* **:** agree — **con•cur•rence** *n*

con•cur•rent *adj* **:** happening at the same time

con•cus•sion *n* **1 :** shock **2 :** brain injury from a blow

con•demn *vb* **1 :** declare to be wrong, guilty, or unfit for use **2 :** sentence — **con•dem•na•tion** *n*

con•dense *vb* **1 :** make or become more compact **2 :** change from vapor to liquid — **con•den•sa•tion** *n* — **con•dens•er** *n*

con•de•scend *vb* **1 :** lower oneself **2 :** act haughtily — **con•de•scen•sion** *n*

con•di•ment *n* **:** pungent seasoning

con•di•tion *n* **1 :** necessary situation or stipulation **2** *pl* **:** state of affairs **3 :** state of being ~ *vb* **:** put into proper condition — **con•di•tion•al** *adj* — **con•di•tion•al•ly** *adv*

con•do•lence *n* **:** expression of sympathy — usu. pl.

con•do•min•i•um *n* **:** individually owned apartment

con•done *vb* **:** overlook or forgive

con•du•cive *adj* **:** tending to help or promote

con•duct *n* **1 :** management **2 :** behavior ~ *vb* **1 :** guide **2 :** manage or direct **3 :** be a channel for **4 :** behave — **con•duc•tion** *n* — **con•duc•tive** *adj* — **con•duc•tiv•i•ty** *n* — **con•duc•tor** *n*

cone *n* **1 :** scaly fruit of pine and related trees **2 :** solid figure having a circular base and tapering sides

con•fec•tion *n* **:** sweet dish or candy — **con•fec•tion•er** *n*

con•fed•er•ate *adj* **1 :** united in a league **2** *cap* **:** relating to the 11 southern states that seceded from the U.S. in 1860 and 1861 ~ *n* **1 :** ally **2** *cap* **:** adherent of the Confederacy ~ *vb* **:** unite — **con•fed•er•a•cy** *n* — **con•fed•er•a•tion** *n*

con•fer *vb* **1 :** give **2 :** meet to exchange views — **con•fer•ee** *n* — **con•fer•ence** *n*

con•fess *vb* **1 :** acknowledge or disclose one's misdeed, fault, or sin **2 :** declare faith in — **con•fes•sion** *n* — **con•fes•sion•al** *n or adj*

con•fes•sor *n* **1 :** one who confesses **2 :** priest who hears confessions

con•fet•ti *n* **:** bits of paper or ribbon thrown in celebration

con•fide *vb* **1 :** share private thoughts **2 :** reveal in confidence — **con•fi•dant** *n*

con•fi•dence *n* **1 :** trust **2 :** certainty of one's nature or ability **3 :** something confided — **con•fi•dent** *adj* — **con•fi•den•tial** *adj* — **con•fi•den•tial•ly** *adv* — **con•fi•dent•ly** *adv*

con•fig•u•ra•tion *n* **:** arrangement

con•fine *vb* **1 :** restrain or restrict to a limited area **2 :** imprison — **con•fine•ment** *n* — **con•fin•er** *n* — **con•fines** *n pl*

con•firm *vb* **1 :** ratify **2 :** verify **3 :** admit as a full member of a church or synagogue — **con•fir•ma•tion** *n*

con•fis•cate *vb* **:** take by authority — **con•fis•ca•tion** *n* — **con•fis•ca•to•ry** *adj*

con•flict *n* **1 :** war **2 :** clash of ideas ~ *vb* **:** clash

con•form *vb* **1 :** make or be like **2 :** obey — **con•for•mi•ty** *n*

con•front *vb* **:** oppose or face — **con•fron•ta•tion** *n*

con•fuse *vb* **1 :** make mentally uncertain **2 :** jumble — **con•fu•sion** *n*

con•geal *vb* **1 :** freeze **2 :** become thick and solid

con•ge•nial *adj* **:** kindred or agreeable — **con•ge•ni•al•i•ty** *n*

con•gest *vb* **:** overcrowd or overfill — **con•ges•tion** *n* — **con•ges•tive** *adj*

con•glom•er•ate *adj* **:** made up of diverse parts ~ *vb* **:** form into a mass ~ *n* **:** diversified corporation — **con•glom•er•a•tion** *n*

con•grat•u•late *vb* **:** express pleasure to for good fortune — **con•grat•u•la•tion** *n* — **con•grat•u•la•to•ry** *adj*

con•gre•gate *vb* : assemble — **con•gre•ga•tion** *n* — **con•gre•ga•tion•al** *adj*

con•gress *n* : assembly of delegates or of senators and representatives — **con•gres•sio•nal** *adj* — **con•gress•man** *n* — **con•gress•wom•an** *n*

co•ni•fer *n* : cone-bearing tree — **co•nif•er•ous** *adj*

con•ju•gate *vb* : give the inflected forms of (a verb) — **con•ju•ga•tion** *n*

con•junc•tion *n* **1** : combination **2** : occurrence at the same time **3** : a word that joins other words together — **con•junc•tive** *adj*

con•jure *vb* **1** : summon by sorcery **2** : practice sleight of hand **3** : entreat — **con•jur•er, con•ju•ror** *n*

con•nect *vb* : join or associate — **con•nect•able** *adj* — **con•nec•tion** *n* — **con•nec•tive** *n or adj* — **con•nec•tor** *n*

con•nive *vb* **1** : pretend ignorance of wrongdoing **2** : cooperate secretly — **con•niv•ance** *n*

con•nois•seur *n* : expert judge esp. of art

con•quer *vb* : defeat or overcome — **con•quer•or** *n*

con•quest *n* **1** : act of conquering **2** : something conquered

con•science *n* : awareness of right and wrong

con•sci•en•tious *adj* : honest and hard-working — **con•sci•en•tious•ly** *adv*

con•scious *adj* **1** : aware **2** : mentally awake or alert **3** : intentional — **con•scious•ly** *adv* — **con•scious•ness** *n*

con•se•crate *vb* **1** : declare sacred **2** : devote to a solemn purpose — **con•se•cra•tion** *n*

con•sec•u•tive *adj* : following in order — **con•sec•u•tive•ly** *adv*

con•sen•sus *n* **1** : agreement in opinion **2** : collective opinion

con•sent *vb* : give permission or approval — **consent** *n*

con•se•quence *n* **1** : result or effect **2** : importance — **con•se•quent** *adj* — **con•se•quen•tial** *adj* — **con•se•quent•ly** *adv*

con•ser•va•tive *adj* **1** : disposed to maintain the status quo **2** : cautious — **con•ser•va•tism** *n* — **con•ser•va•tive** *n* — **con•ser•va•tive•ly** *adv*

con•ser•va•to•ry *n* : school for art or music

con•serve *vb* : keep from wasting ~ *n* : candied fruit or fruit preserves — **con•ser•va•tion** *n* — **con•ser•va•tion•ist** *n*

con•sid•er *vb* **1** : think about **2** : give thoughtful attention to **3** : think that — **con•sid•er•ate** *adj* — **con•sid•er•ation** *n*

con•sid•er•able *adj* **1** : significant **2** : noticeably large — **con•sid•er•a•bly** *adv*

con•sign *vb* **1** : transfer **2** : send to an agent for sale — **con•sign•ee** *n* — **con•sign•ment** *n* — **con•sign•or** *n*

con•sist *vb* **1** : be inherent — used with *in* **2** : be made up — used with *of*

con•sis•ten•cy *n* **1** : degree of thickness or firmness **2** : quality of being consistent

con•sis•tent *adj* : being steady and regular — **con•sis•tent•ly** *adv*

[1]con•sole *vb* : soothe the grief of — **con•so•la•tion** *n*

[2]con•sole *n* : cabinet or part with controls

con•sol•i•date *vb* : unite or compact — **con•sol•i•da•tion** *n*

con•so•nant *n* **1** : speech sound marked by constriction or closure in the breath channel **2** : letter other than *a, e, i, o,* and *u* — **con•so•nan•tal** *adj*

con•spic•u•ous *adj* : very noticeable — **con•spic•u•ous•ly** *adv*

con•spire *vb* : secretly plan an unlawful act — **con•spir•a•cy** *n* — **con•spir•a•tor** *n* — **con•spir•a•to•ri•al** *adj*

con•sta•ble *n* : police officer

con•stant *adj* **1** : steadfast or faithful **2** : not varying **3** : continually recurring ~ *n* : something unchanging — **con•stan•cy** *n* — **con•stant•ly** *adv*

con•stel•la•tion *n* : group of stars

con•sti•pa•tion *n* : difficulty of defecation — **con•sti•pate** *vb*

con•stit•u•ent *adj* **1** : component **2** : having power to elect ~ *n* **1** : component part **2** : one who may vote for a representative — **con•stit•u•en•cy** *n*

con•sti•tute *vb* **1** : establish **2** : be all or a basic part of

con•sti•tu•tion *n* **1** : physical composition or structure **2** : the basic law of an organized body or the document containing it — **con•sti•tu•tion•al** *adj* — **con•sti•tu•tion•al•i•ty** *n*

con•strain *vb* **1** : compel **2** : confine **3** : restrain — **con•straint** *n*

con•strict *vb* : draw or squeeze together — **con•stric•tion** *n* — **con•stric•tive** *adj*

con•struct *vb* : build or make — **con•struc•tion** *n* — **con•struc•tive** *adj*

con•strue *vb* : explain or interpret

con•sul *n* **1** : Roman magistrate **2** : government commercial official in a foreign country — **con•sul•ar** *adj* — **con•sul•ate** *n*

con•sult *vb* **1 :** ask the advice or opinion of **2 :** confer — **con•sul•tant** *n* — **con•sul•ta•tion** *n*

con•sume *vb* **:** eat or use up — **con•sum•able** *adj* — **con•sum•er** *n*

con•sump•tion *n* **1 :** act of consuming **2 :** use of goods

con•tact *n* **1 :** a touching **2 :** association or relationship **3 :** connection or communication ~ *vb* **1 :** come or bring into contact **2 :** communicate with

con•ta•gion *n* **1 :** spread of disease by contact **2 :** disease spread by contact — **con•ta•gious** *adj*

con•tain *vb* **1 :** enclose or include **2 :** have or hold within **3 :** restrain — **con•tain•er** *n* — **con•tain•ment** *n*

con•tam•i•nate *vb* **:** soil or infect by contact or association — **con•tam•i•na•tion** *n*

con•tem•plate *vb* **:** view or consider thoughtfully — **con•tem•pla•tion** *n* — **con•tem•pla•tive** *adj*

con•tem•po•ra•ne•ous *adj* **:** contemporary

con•tem•po•rary *adj* **1 :** occurring or existing at the same time **2 :** of the same age — **con•tem•po•rary** *n*

con•tempt *n* **1 :** feeling of scorn **2 :** state of being despised **3 :** disobedience to a court or legislature — **con•tempt•ible** *adj*

con•temp•tu•ous *adj* **:** feeling or expressing contempt — **con•temp•tu•ous•ly** *adv*

con•tend *vb* **1 :** strive against rivals or difficulties **2 :** argue **3 :** maintain or claim — **con•tend•er** *n*

[1]**con•tent** *adj* **:** satisfied ~ *vb* **:** satisfy ~ *n* **:** ease of mind — **con•tent•ed** *adj* — **con•tent•ed•ly** *adv* — **con•tent•ed•ness** *n* — **con•tent•ment** *n*

[2]**con•tent** *n* **1** *pl* **:** something contained **2** *pl* **:** subject matter (as of a book) **3 :** essential meaning **4 :** proportion contained

con•ten•tion *n* **:** state of contending — **con•ten•tious** *adj* — **con•ten•tious•ly** *adv*

con•test *vb* **:** dispute or challenge ~ *n* **1 :** struggle **2 :** game — **con•test•able** *adj* — **con•tes•tant** *n*

con•text *n* **:** words surrounding a word or phrase

con•ti•nent *n* **:** great division of land on the globe — **con•ti•nen•tal** *adj*

con•tin•gen•cy *n* **:** possible event

con•tin•gent *adj* **:** dependent on something else ~ *n* **:** a quota from an area or group

con•tin•u•al *adj* **1 :** continuous **2 :** steadily recurring — **con•tin•u•al•ly** *adv*

con•tin•ue *vb* **1 :** remain in a place or condition **2 :** endure **3 :** resume after an intermission **4 :** extend — **con•tin•u•ance** *n* — **con•tin•u•ation** *n*

con•tin•u•ous *adj* **:** continuing without interruption — **con•ti•nu•ity** *n* — **con•tin•u•ous•ly** *adv*

con•tort *vb* **:** twist out of shape — **con•tor•tion** *n*

con•tour *n* **1 :** outline **2** *pl* **:** shape

con•tra•band *n* **:** illegal goods

con•tract *n* **:** binding agreement ~ *vb* **1 :** establish or undertake by contract **2 :** become ill with **3 :** make shorter — **con•trac•tion** *n* — **con•trac•tor** *n* — **con•trac•tu•al** *adj* — **con•trac•tu•al•ly** *adv*

con•tra•dict *vb* **:** state the contrary of — **con•tra•dic•tion** *n* — **con•tra•dic•to•ry** *adj*

con•trap•tion *n* **:** device or contrivance

con•trary *adj* **1 :** opposite in character, nature, or position **2 :** mutually opposed **3 :** unfavorable **4 :** uncooperative or stubborn — **con•trari•ly** *adv* — **con•trari•wise** *adv* — **con•trary** *n*

con•trast *n* **1 :** unlikeness shown by comparing **2 :** unlike color or tone of adjacent parts ~ *vb* **1 :** show differences **2 :** compare so as to show differences

con•tra•vene *vb* **:** go or act contrary to

con•trib•ute *vb* **:** give or help along with others — **con•tri•bu•tion** *n* — **con•trib•u•tor** *n* — **con•trib•u•to•ry** *adj*

con•trite *adj* **:** repentant — **con•tri•tion** *n*

con•trive *vb* **1 :** devise or make with ingenuity **2 :** bring about — **con•triv•ance** *n* — **con•triv•er** *n*

con•trol *vb* **1 :** exercise power over **2 :** dominate or rule ~ *n* **1 :** power to direct or regulate **2 :** restraint **3 :** regulating device — **con•trol•la•ble** *adj* — **con•trol•ler** *n*

con•tro•ver•sy *n* **:** clash of opposing views — **con•tro•ver•sial** *adj*

con•va•lesce *vb* **:** gradually recover health — **con•va•les•cence** *n* — **con•va•les•cent** *adj or n*

con•vec•tion *n* **:** circulation in fluids due to warmer portions rising and colder ones sinking — **con•vec•tion•al** *adj* — **con•vec•tive** *adj*

con•vene *vb* : assemble or meet
con•ve•nience *n* **1 :** personal comfort or ease **2 :** device that saves work — **con•ve•nient** *adj* — **con•ve•nient•ly** *adv*
con•vent *n* : community of nuns
con•ven•tion *n* **1 :** agreement esp. between nations **2 :** large meeting **3 :** body of delegates **4 :** accepted usage or way of behaving — **con•ven•tion•al** *adj* — **con•ven•tion•al•ly** *adv*
con•ver•sa•tion *n* : an informal talking together — **con•ver•sa•tion•al** *adj*
[1]**con•verse** *vb* : engage in conversation — **con-verse** *n*
[2]**con•verse** *adj* : opposite — **con•verse** *n* — **con•verse•ly** *adv*
con•vert *vb* **1 :** turn from one belief or party to another **2 :** change ~ *n* : one who has adopted a religion — **con•ver•sion** *n* — **con•vert•er, con•ver•tor** *n* — **con•vert•ible** *adj*
con•vert•ible *n* : automobile with a removable top
con•vex *adj* : curved or rounded like the outside of a sphere — **con•vex•i•ty** *n*
con•vey *vb* : transport or transmit — **con•vey•ance** *n* — **con•vey•or** *n*
con•vict *vb* : find guilty ~ *n* : person in prison
con•vic•tion *n* **1 :** act of convicting **2 :** strong belief
con•vince *vb* : cause to believe — **con•vinc•ing•ly** *adv*
con•viv•ial *adj* : cheerful or festive — **con•viv•i•al•i•ty** *n*
con•vo•lut•ed *adj* **1 :** intricately folded **2 :** intricate
con•vo•lu•tion *n* : convoluted structure
con•voy *vb* : accompany for protection ~ *n* : group of vehicles or ships moving together
con•vul•sion *n* : violent involuntary muscle contraction — **con•vulse** *vb* — **con•vul•sive** *adj*
coo *n* : sound of a pigeon — **coo** *vb*
cook *n* : one who prepares food ~ *vb* : prepare food — **cook•book** *n* — **cook•er** *n* — **cook•ery** *n* — **cook•ware** *n*
cook•ie, cooky *n* : small sweet flat cake
cool *adj* **1 :** moderately cold **2 :** not excited **3 :** unfriendly ~ *vb* : make or become cool ~ *n* **1 :** cool time or place **2 :** composure — **cool•ant** *n* — **cool•er** *n* — **cool•ly** *adv* — **cool•ness** *n*
coop *n* : enclosure usu. for poultry ~ *vb* : confine in or as if in a coop
co–op *n* : cooperative
co•op•er•ate *vb* : act jointly — **co•op•er•a•tion** *n* — **co•op•er•a•tive** *adj or n*
co•or•di•nate *adj* : equal esp. in rank ~ *n* : any of a set of numbers used in specifying the location of a point on a surface or in space ~ *vb* **1 :** make or become coordinate **2 :** work or act together harmoniously — **co•or•di•nate•ly** *adv* — **co•or•di•na•tion** *n* — **co•or•di•na•tor** *n*
cop *n* : police officer
cope *vb* : deal with difficulties
co•pi•lot *n* : assistant airplane pilot
cop•ing *n* : top layer of a wall
co•pi•ous *adj* : very abundant — **co•pi•ous•ly** *adv* — **co•pi•ous•ness** *n*
cop•per *n* **1 :** malleable reddish metallic chemical element **2 :** penny — **cop•pery** *adj*
copy *n* **1 :** imitation or reproduction of an original **2 :** writing to be set for printing ~ *vb* **1 :** make a copy of **2 :** imitate — **copi•er** *n* — **copyist** *n*
copy•right *n* : sole right to a literary or artistic work ~ *vb* : get a copyright on
cor•al *n* **1 :** skeletal material of colonies of tiny sea polyps **2 :** deep pink — **coral** *adj*
cord *n* **1 :** usu. heavy string **2 :** long slender anatomical structure **3 :** measure of firewood equal to 128 cu. ft. **4 :** small electrical cable ~ *vb* **1 :** tie or furnish with a cord **2 :** pile (wood) in cords
cor•dial *adj* : warmly welcoming — **cor•di•al•i•ty** *n* — **cor•dial•ly** *adv*
cor•du•roy *n* **1 :** heavy ribbed fabric **2** *pl* : trousers of corduroy
core *n* **1 :** central part of some fruits **2 :** inmost part ~ *vb* : take out the core of — **cor•er** *n*
cork *n* **1 :** tough elastic bark of a European oak (**cork oak**) **2 :** stopper of cork ~ *vb* : stop up with a cork — **corky** *adj*
[1]**corn** *n* : cereal grass (as Indian corn) or its seeds ~ *vb* : cure or preserve in brine — **corn•cob** *n* — **corn•meal** *n* — **corn•stalk** *n* — **corn•starch** *n*
[2]**corn** *n* : local hardening and thickening of skin
cor•nea *n* : transparent part of the coat of the eyeball — **cor•ne•al** *adj*
cor•ner *n* **1 :** point or angle formed by the meeting of lines or sides **2 :** place where two streets meet **3 :** inescapable position **4 :** control of the supply of something ~ *vb* **1 :** drive

into a corner **2 :** get a corner on **3 :** turn a corner

cor•ner•stone *n* **1 :** stone at a corner of a wall **2 :** something basic

cor•net *n* **:** trumpetlike instrument

cor•o•nary *adj* **:** relating to the heart or its blood vessels ~ *n* **1 :** thrombosis of an artery supplying the heart **2 :** heart attack

cor•o•na•tion *n* **:** crowning of a monarch

cor•o•ner *n* **:** public official who investigates causes of suspicious deaths

[1]**cor•po•ral** *adj* **:** bodily

[2]**corporal** *n* **:** noncommissioned officer ranking below a sergeant

cor•po•ra•tion *n* **:** legal creation with the rights and liabilities of a person — **cor•po•rate** *adj*

cor•po•re•al *adj* **:** physical or material — **cor•po•re•al•ly** *adv*

corps *n* **1 :** subdivision of a military force **2 :** working group

corpse *n* **:** dead body

cor•pus•cle *n* **:** blood cell

cor•ral *n* **:** enclosure for animals — **cor•ral** *vb*

cor•rect *vb* **1 :** make right **2 :** chastise ~ *adj* **1 :** true or factual **2 :** conforming to a standard — **cor•rec•tion** *n* — **cor•rec•tive** *adj* — **cor•rect•ly** *adv* — **cor•rect•ness** *n*

cor•re•late *vb* **:** show a connection between — **cor•re•late** *n* — **cor•re•la•tion** *n* — **cor•rel•a•tive** *n or adj*

cor•re•spond *vb* **1 :** match **2 :** communicate by letter — **cor•re•spon•dence** *n* — **cor•re•spond•ing•ly** *adv*

cor•re•spon•dent *n* **1 :** person one writes to **2 :** reporter

cor•ri•dor *n* **:** passageway connecting rooms

cor•rode *vb* **:** wear away by chemical action — **cor•ro•sion** *n* — **cor•ro•sive** *adj or n*

cor•rupt *vb* **1 :** change from good to bad **2 :** bribe ~ *adj* **:** morally debased — **cor•rupt•ible** *adj* — **cor•rup•tion** *n*

cor•sage *n* **:** bouquet worn by a woman

cos•met•ic *n* **:** beautifying preparation ~ *adj* **:** relating to beautifying

cos•mic *adj* **1 :** relating to the universe **2 :** vast or grand

cos•mo•naut *n* **:** Soviet or Russian astronaut

cos•mo•pol•i•tan *adj* **:** belonging to all the world — **cos•mo•pol•i•tan** *n*

cos•mos *n* **:** universe

cost *n* **1 :** amount paid for something **2 :** loss or penalty ~ *vb* **cost; cost 1 :** require so much in payment **2 :** cause to pay, suffer, or lose — **cost•li•ness** *n* — **cost•ly** *adj*

cos•tume *n* **:** clothing

co•sy *var of* COZY

cot *n* **:** small bed

cote *n* **:** small shed or coop

cot•tage *n* **:** small house

cot•ton *n* **:** soft fibrous plant substance or thread or cloth made of it — **cot•ton•seed** *n* — **cot•tony** *adj*

cot•ton•mouth *n* **:** poisonous snake

couch *vb* **1 :** lie or place on a couch **2 :** phrase ~ *n* **:** bed or sofa

couch potato *n* **:** one who spends a great deal of time watching television

cou•gar *n* **:** large tawny wild American cat

cough *vb* **:** force air from the lungs with short sharp noises — **cough** *n*

could *past of* CAN

couldn't : could not

coun•cil *n* **1 :** assembly or meeting **2 :** body of lawmakers — **coun•cil•lor, coun•cil•or** *n* — **coun•cil•man** *n* — **coun•cil•wom•an** *n*

coun•sel *n* **1 :** advice **2 :** deliberation together **3** *pl* **coun•sel :** lawyer ~ *vb* **1 :** advise **2 :** consult together — **coun•sel•or, coun•sel•lor** *n*

[1]**count** *vb* **1 :** name or indicate one by one to find the total number **2 :** recite numbers in order **3 :** rely **4 :** be of value or account ~ *n* **1 :** act of counting or the total obtained by counting **2 :** charge in an indictment — **count•able** *adj* — **count•less** *adj*

[2]**count** *n* **:** European nobleman

coun•te•nance *n* **:** face or facial expression ~ *vb* **:** allow or encourage

[1]**count•er** *n* **1 :** piece for reckoning or games **2 :** surface over which business is transacted

[2]**count•er** *n* **:** one that counts

[3]**coun•ter** *vb* **:** oppose ~ *adv* **:** in an opposite direction ~ *n* **:** offsetting force or move ~ *adj* **:** contrary

coun•ter•act *vb* **:** lessen the force of — **coun•ter•ac•tive** *adj*

coun•ter•bal•ance *n* **:** balancing influence or weight ~ *vb* **:** oppose or balance

coun•ter•clock•wise *adv or adj* **:** opposite to the way a clock's hands move

coun•ter•feit *vb* **1 :** copy in order to deceive **2 :** pretend ~ *adj* **:** not genuine ~ *n* **:** fraudulent copy — **coun•ter•feit•er** *n*

coun•ter•part *n* **:** one that is similar or corresponds

coun·ter·sign *n* : secret signal ~ *vb* : add a confirming signature to
count·ess *n* : wife or widow of a count or an earl or a woman holding that rank in her own right
coun·try *n* **1** : nation **2** : rural area ~ *adj* : rural — **coun·try·man** *n*
coun·try·side *n* : rural area or its people
coun·ty *n* : local government division esp. of a state
coup *n* **1** : brilliant sudden action or plan **2** : sudden overthrow of a government
coupe *n* : 2-door automobile with an enclosed body
cou·ple *vb* : link together ~ *n* **1** : pair **2** : two persons closely associated or married
cou·pling *n* : connecting device
cou·pon *n* : certificate redeemable for goods or a cash discount
cour·age *n* : ability to conquer fear or despair — **cou·ra·geous** *adj*
course *n* **1** : progress **2** : ground over which something moves **3** : part of a meal served at one time **4** : method of procedure **5** : subject taught in a series of classes ~ *vb* **1** : hunt with dogs **2** : run speedily — **of course** : as might be expected
court *n* **1** : residence of a sovereign **2** : sovereign and his or her officials and advisers **3** : area enclosed by a building **4** : space marked for playing a game **5** : place where justice is administered ~ *vb* : seek to win the affections of — **court·house** *n* — **court·room** *n* — **court·ship** *n*
cour·te·ous *adj* : showing politeness and respect for others — **cour·te·ous·ly** *adv*
cour·te·sy *n* : courteous behavior
court–mar·tial *n* **courts–mar·tial** : military trial court — **court–martial** *vb*
court·yard *n* : enclosure open to the sky that is attached to a house
cous·in *n* : child of one's uncle or aunt
cove *n* : sheltered inlet or bay
cov·e·nant *n* : binding agreement — **cov·e·nant** *vb*
cov·er *vb* **1** : place something over or upon **2** : protect or hide **3** : include or deal with ~ *n* : something that covers — **cov·er·age** *n*
co·vert *adj* : secret ~ *n* : thicket that shelters animals
cov·et *vb* : desire enviously — **cov·et·ous** *adj*
[1]**cow** *n* : large adult female animal (as of cattle) — **cow·hide** *n*
[2]**cow** *vb* : intimidate
cow·ard *n* : one who lacks courage — **cow·ard·ice** *n* — **cow·ard·ly** *adv or adj*
cow·boy *n* : a mounted ranch hand who tends cattle
cow·er *vb* : shrink from fear or cold
cow·girl *n* : woman ranch hand who tends cattle
coy *adj* : shy or pretending shyness
coy·ote *n* : small No. American wolf
co·zy *adj* : snug
crab *n* : short broad shellfish with pincers
crab·by *adj* : cross
[1]**crack** *vb* **1** : break with a sharp sound **2** : fail in tone **3** : break without completely separating ~ *n* **1** : sudden sharp noise **2** : witty remark **3** : narrow break **4** : sharp blow **5** : try
[2]**crack** *adj* : extremely proficient
crack·down *n* : disciplinary action — **crack down** *vb*
crack·er *n* : thin crisp bakery product
crack·le *vb* **1** : make snapping noises **2** : develop fine cracks in a surface — **crack·le** *n*
crack–up *n* : crash
cra·dle *n* : baby's bed ~ *vb* **1** : place in a cradle **2** : hold securely
craft *n* **1** : occupation requiring special skill **2** : craftiness **3** *pl usu* **craft** : structure designed to provide transportation **4** *pl usu* **craft** : small boat — **crafts·man** *n* — **crafts·man·ship** *n*
crafty *adj* : sly — **craft·i·ness** *n*
crag *n* : steep cliff — **crag·gy** *adj*
cram *vb* **1** : eat greedily **2** : pack in tight **3** : study intensely for a test
cramp *n* **1** : sudden painful contraction of muscle **2** *pl* : sharp abdominal pains ~ *vb* **1** : affect with cramp **2** : restrain
cran·ber·ry *n* : red acid berry of a trailing plant
crane *n* **1** : tall wading bird **2** : machine for lifting heavy objects ~ *vb* : stretch one's neck to see
crank *n* **1** : bent lever turned to operate a machine **2** : eccentric ~ *vb* : start or operate by turning a crank
cranky *adj* : irritable
crash *vb* **1** : break noisily **2** : fall and hit something with noise and damage ~ *n* **1** : loud sound **2** : action of crashing **3** : failure
crate *n* : wooden shipping container — **crate** *vb*
cra·ter *n* : volcanic depression

crave *vb* : long for — **crav•ing** *n*
crawl *vb* **1 :** move slowly (as by drawing the body along the ground) **2 :** swarm with creeping things ~ *n* : very slow pace
cray•on *n* : stick of chalk or wax used for drawing or coloring — **crayon** *vb*
craze *vb* : make or become insane ~ *n* : fad
cra•zy *adj* **1 :** mentally disordered **2 :** wildly impractical — **cra•zi•ly** *adv* — **cra•zi•ness** *n*
creak *vb or n* : squeak — **creaky** *adj*
cream *n* **1 :** yellowish fat-rich part of milk **2 :** thick smooth sauce, confection, or cosmetic **3 :** choicest part ~ *vb* : beat into creamy consistency — **creamy** *adj*
cream•ery *n* : place where butter and cheese are made
crease *n* : line made by folding — **crease** *vb*
cre•ate *vb* : bring into being — **cre•ation** *n* — **cre•ative** *adj* — **cre•ativ•i•ty** *n* — **cre•a•tor** *n*
crea•ture *n* : lower animal or human being
cre•den•tials *n pl* : evidence of qualifications or authority
cred•i•ble *adj* : believable — **cred•i•bil•i•ty** *n*
cred•it *n* **1 :** balance in a person's favor **2 :** time given to pay for goods **3 :** belief **4 :** esteem **5 :** source of honor ~ *vb* **1 :** believe **2 :** give credit to — **cred•it•able** *adj* — **cred•it•ably** *adv*
credit card *n* : a card authorizing purchases on credit
cred•i•tor *n* : person to whom money is owed
creed *n* : statement of essential beliefs
creek *n* : small stream
creep *vb* **(crept; crept) 1 :** crawl **2 :** grow over a surface like ivy — **creep** *n* — **creep•er** *n*
cre•mate *vb* : burn up (a corpse) — **cre•ma•tion** *n* — **cre•ma•to•ry** *n*
cre•scen•do *adv or adj* : growing louder — **crescendo** *n*
cres•cent *n* : shape of the moon between new moon and first quarter
crest *n* **1 :** tuft on a bird's head **2 :** top of a hill or wave **3 :** part of a coat of arms ~ *vb* : rise to a crest — **crest•ed** *adj*
cre•vasse *n* : deep fissure esp. in a glacier
crev•ice *n* : narrow fissure
crew *n* : body of workers (as on a ship) — **crew•man** *n*
crib *n* **1 :** grain storage bin **2 :** baby's bed ~ *vb* : put in a crib
crick•et *n* : insect noted for the chirping of the male
crime *n* : serious violation of law — **crim•i•nal** *n or adj*
crin•kle *vb* : wrinkle — **crinkle** *n* — **crin•kly** *adj*
crip•ple *n* : disabled person ~ *vb* : disable
cri•sis *n* : decisive or critical moment
crisp *adj* **1 :** easily crumbled **2 :** firm and fresh **3 :** lively **4 :** invigorating — **crisp** *vb* — **crisp•ly** *adv* — **crisp•ness** *n* — **crispy** *adj*
criss•cross *n* : pattern of crossed lines ~ *vb* : mark with or follow a crisscross
cri•te•ri•on *n* : standard
crit•ic *n* **1:** judge of literary or artistic works **2:** one who criticizes — **crit•i•cal** *adj* — **crit•i•cal•ly** *adv*
crit•i•cize *vb* **1 :** judge as a critic **2 :** find fault — **crit•i•cism** *n*
croak *n* : hoarse cry (as of a frog) — **croak** *vb*
crock *n* : thick earthenware pot or jar — **crock•ery** *n*
croc•o•dile *n* : large reptile of tropical waters
cro•cus *n* : herb with spring flowers
crook *n* **1 :** bent or curved tool or part **2 :** thief ~ *vb* : curve sharply
crook•ed *adj* **1 :** bent **2 :** dishonest — **crook•ed•ness** *n*
crop *n* **1 :** pouch in the throat of a bird or insect **2 :** short riding whip **3 :** something that can be harvested ~ *vb* **1 :** trim **2 :** appear unexpectedly — used with *up*
cro•quet *n* : lawn game of driving balls through wickets
cross *n* **1 :** figure or structure consisting of an upright and a cross piece **2 :** interbreeding of unlike strains ~ *vb* **1 :** intersect **2 :** cancel **3 :** go or extend across **4 :** interbreed ~ *adj* **1 :** going across **2 :** contrary **3 :** marked by bad temper — **cross•ing** *n* — **cross•ly** *adv*
cross–ex•am•ine *vb* : question about earlier testimony — **cross–ex•am•i•na•tion** *n*
cross–eyed *adj* : having the eye turned toward the nose
cross–re•fer *vb* : refer to another place (as in a book) — **cross–ref•er•ence** *n*
cross•roads *n* : place where two roads cross
cross section *n* : representative portion
cross•walk *n* : path for pedestrians crossing a street
crotch *n* : angle formed by the parting of 2 legs or branches
crouch *vb* : stoop over — **crouch** *n*
[1]crow *n* : large glossy black bird

[2]crow *vb* **1 :** make the loud sound of the cock **2 :** gloat ~ *n* **:** cry of the cock
crowd *vb* **:** collect or cram together ~ *n* **:** large number of people
crown *n* **1 :** wreath of honor or victory **2 :** royal headdress **3 :** top or highest part ~ *vb* **1 :** place a crown on **2 :** honor — **crowned** *adj*
cru•cial *adj* **:** vitally important
cru•ci•fix *n* **:** representation of Christ on the cross
cru•ci•fix•ion *n* **:** act of crucifying
cru•ci•fy *vb* **1 :** put to death on a cross **2 :** persecute
crude *adj* **1 :** not refined **2 :** lacking grace or elegance ~ *n* **:** unrefined petroleum — **crude•ly** *adv* — **cru•di•ty** *n*
cru•el *adj* **:** causing suffering to others — **cru•el•ly** *adv* — **cru•el•ty** *n*
cruise *vb* **1 :** sail to several ports **2 :** travel at the most efficient speed — **cruise** *n*
cruis•er *n* **1 :** ship of war **2 :** police car
crumb *n* **:** small fragment
crum•ble *vb* **:** break into small pieces — **crum•bly** *adj*
crum•ple *vb* **1 :** crush together **2 :** collapse
crunch *vb* **:** chew or press with a crushing noise ~ *n* **:** crunching sound — **crunchy** *adj*
cru•sade *n* **1** *cap* **:** medieval Christian expedition to the Holy Land **2 :** reform movement — **crusade** *vb* — **cru•sad•er** *n*
crush *vb* **1 :** squeeze out of shape **2 :** grind or pound to bits **3 :** suppress ~ *n* **1 :** severe crowding **2 :** infatuation
crust *n* **1 :** hard outer part of bread or a pie **2 :** hard surface layer — **crust•al** *adj* — **crusty** *adj*
crutch *n* **:** support for use by the disabled in walking
cry *vb* **1 :** call out **2 :** weep ~ *n* **1 :** shout **2 :** fit of weeping **3 :** characteristic sound of an animal
cryp•tic *adj* **:** enigmatic
cryp•tog•ra•phy *n* **:** coding and decoding of messages — **cryp•tog•ra•pher** *n*
crys•tal *n* **1 :** transparent quartz **2 :** something (as glass) like crystal **3 :** body formed by solidification that has a regular repeating atomic arrangement — **crys•tal•line** *adj*
crys•tal•lize *vb* **:** form crystals or a definite shape — **crys•tal•li•za•tion** *n*
cub *n* **:** young animal
cube *n* **1 :** solid having 6 equal square sides **2 :** product obtained by taking a number 3 times as a factor ~ *vb* **1 :** raise to the 3d power **2 :** form into a cube **3 :** cut into cubes — **cu•bic** *adj*
cu•bi•cle *n* **:** small room
cuck•oo *n* **:** brown European bird ~ *adj* **:** silly
cu•cum•ber *n* **:** fleshy fruit related to the gourds
cud•dle *vb* **:** lie close
[1]cue *n* **:** signal — **cue** *vb*
[2]cue *n* **:** stick used in pool
[1]cuff *n* **1 :** part of a sleeve encircling the wrist **2 :** folded trouser hem
[2]cuff *vb or n* **:** slap
cu•li•nary *adj* **:** of or relating to cookery
cull *vb* **:** select
cul•pa•ble *adj* **:** deserving blame
cul•prit *n* **:** guilty person
cult *n* **1 :** religious system **2 :** faddish devotion — **cult•ist** *n*
cul•ti•vate *vb* **1 :** prepare for crops **2 :** foster the growth of **3 :** refine — **cul•ti•va•tion** *n*
cul•ture *n* **1 :** cultivation **2 :** refinement of intellectual and artistic taste **3 :** particular form or stage of civilization — **cul•tur•al** *adj* — **cul•tured** *adj*
cum•ber•some *adj* **:** awkward to handle due to bulk
cun•ning *adj* **1 :** crafty **2 :** clever **3 :** appealing ~ *n* **1 :** skill **2 :** craftiness
cup *n* **1 :** small drinking vessel **2 :** contents of a cup **3 :** a half pint ~ *vb* **:** shape like a cup — **cup•ful** *n*
cup•board *n* **:** small storage closet
cup•cake *n* **:** small cake
cu•ra•tor *n* **:** one in charge of a museum or zoo
curb *n* **1 :** restraint **2 :** raised edging along a street ~ *vb* **:** hold back
curd *n* **:** coagulated milk
cur•dle *vb* **1 :** form curds **2 :** sour
cure *n* **1 :** recovery from disease **2 :** remedy ~ *vb* **1 :** restore to health **2 :** process for storage or use — **cur•able** *adj*
cur•few *n* **:** requirement to be off the streets at a set hour
cu•ri•ous *adj* **1 :** eager to learn **2 :** strange — **cu•ri•os•i•ty** *n* — **cu•ri•ous•ly** *adv* — **cu•ri•ous•ness** *n*
curl *vb* **1 :** form into ringlets **2 :** curve ~ *n* **1 :** ringlet of hair **2 :** something with a spiral form — **curl•er** *n* — **curly** *adj*
cur•ren•cy *n* **1 :** general use or acceptance **2 :** money

cur•rent *adj* : occurring in or belonging to the present ∼ *n* **1** : swiftest part of a stream **2** : flow of electricity
cur•ric•u•lum *n* : course of study
curse *n* **1** : a calling down of evil or harm upon one **2** : affliction ∼ *vb* **1** : call down injury upon **2** : swear at **3** : afflict
cur•sor *n* : indicator on a computer screen
curt *adj* : rudely abrupt — **curt•ly** *adv* — **curt•ness** *n*
cur•tail *vb* : shorten — **cur•tail•ment** *n*
cur•tain *n* : hanging screen that can be drawn back or raised — **cur•tain** *vb*
curt•sy, curt•sey *n* : courteous bow made by bending the knees — **curt•sy, curt•sey** *vb*
cur•va•ture *n* : amount or state of curving
curve *vb* : bend from a straight line or course ∼ *n* **1** : a bending without angles **2** : something curved
cush•ion *n* **1** : soft pillow **2** : something that eases or protects ∼ *vb* **1** : provide with a cushion **2** : soften the force of
cus•tard *n* : sweetened cooked mixture of milk and eggs
cus•to•dy *n* : immediate care or charge — **cus•to•di•al** *adj* — **cus•to•di•an** *n*
cus•tom *n* **1** : habitual course of action **2** *pl* : import taxes ∼ *adj* : made to personal order — **cus•tom•ar•i•ly** *adv* — **cus•tom•ary** *adj* — **custom–built** *adj* — **cus•tom–made** *adj*
cus•tom•er *n* : buyer
cut *vb* (**cut; cut**) **1** : penetrate or divide with a sharp edge **2** : experience the growth of (a tooth) through the gum **3** : shorten **4** : remove by severing **5** : intersect ∼ *n* **1** : something separated by cutting **2** : reduction — **cut•ter** *n* — **cut in** *vb* : thrust oneself between others
cute *adj* : pretty
cut•lery *n* : cutting utensils
cut•let *n* : slice of meat
cut•throat *n* : murderer ∼ *adj* : ruthless
cy•ber•space *n* : online world of the Internet
cy•cle *n* **1** : period of time for a series of repeated events **2** : recurring round of events **3** : long period of time **4** : bicycle or motorcycle ∼ *vb* : ride a cycle — **cy•clic, cy•cli•cal** *adj* — **cy•clist** *n*
cy•clone *n* : tornado — **cy•clon•ic** *adj*
cyl•in•der *n* **1** : long round body or figure **2** : rotating chamber in a revolver **3** : piston chamber in an engine — **cy•lin•dri•cal** *adj*
cyn•ic *n* : one who attributes all actions to selfish motives — **cyn•i•cal** *adj* — **cyn•i•cism** *n*
cyst *n* : abnormal bodily sac — **cys•tic** *adj*
czar *n* : ruler of Russia until 1917 — **czar•ist** *n or adj*

D

d *n* : 4th letter of the alphabet
[1]**dab** *n* : gentle touch or stroke ∼ *vb* : touch or apply lightly
[2]**dab** *n* : small amount
dab•ble *vb* **1** : splash **2** : work without serious effort — **dab•bler** *n*
dad *n* : father
dad•dy *n* : father
daf•fo•dil *n* : narcissus with trumpetlike flowers
dag•ger *n* : knife for stabbing
dai•ly *adj* **1** : occurring, done, or used every day or every weekday **2** : computed in terms of one day ∼ *n* : daily newspaper — **daily** *adv*
dain•ty *n* : something delicious ∼ *adj* : delicately pretty — **dain•ti•ly** *adv* — **dain•ti•ness** *n*
dairy *n* : farm that produces or company that processes milk — **dairy•maid** *n* — **dairy•man** *n*
dai•sy *n* : tall leafy-stemmed plant bearing showy flowers
dal•ly *vb* **1** : flirt **2** : dawdle — **dal•li•ance** *n*
[1]**dam** *n* : female parent of a domestic animal
[2]**dam** *n* : barrier to hold back water — **dam** *vb*
dam•age *n* **1** : loss or harm due to injury **2** *pl* : compensation for loss or injury ∼ *vb* : do damage to
dame *n* : woman of rank or authority
damn *vb* **1** : condemn to hell **2** : curse — **dam•na•ble** *adj* — **dam•na•tion** *n* — **damned** *adj*
damp *n* : moisture ∼ *vb* **1** : reduce the draft in **2** : restrain **3** : moisten ∼ *adj* : moist — **damp•en** *vb* — **damp•ness** *n*
damp•er *n* : movable plate to regulate a flue draft
dam•sel *n* : young woman
dance *vb* : move rhythmically to music ∼ *n*

: act of dancing or a gathering for dancing — **danc•er** *n*

dan•de•li•on *n* **:** common yellow-flowered herb

dan•druff *n* **:** whitish thin dry scales of skin on the scalp

dan•dy *n* **1 :** man too concerned with clothes **2 :** something excellent ∼ *adj* **:** very good

dan•ger *n* **1 :** exposure to injury or evil **2 :** something that may cause injury — **dan•ger•ous** *adj*

dan•gle *vb* **1 :** hang and swing freely **2 :** be left without support or connection **3 :** allow or cause to hang **4 :** offer as an inducement

dap•per *adj* **:** neat and stylishly dressed

dap•ple *vb* **:** mark with colored spots

dare *vb* **1 :** have sufficient courage **2 :** urge or provoke to contend — **dare** *n* — **dar•ing** *n or adj*

dare•dev•il *n* **:** recklessly bold person

dark *adj* **1 :** having little or no light **2 :** not light in color **3 :** gloomy ∼ *n* **:** absence of light — **dark•en** *vb* — **dark•ly** *adv* — **dark•ness** *n*

dar•ling *n* **1 :** beloved **2 :** favorite ∼ *adj* **1 :** dearly loved **2 :** very pleasing

dart *n* **1 :** small pointed missile **2** *pl* **:** game of throwing darts at a target **3 :** tapering fold in a garment **4 :** quick movement ∼ *vb* **:** move suddenly or rapidly

dash *vb* **1 :** smash **2 :** knock or hurl violently **3 :** ruin **4 :** perform or finish hastily **5 :** move quickly ∼ *n* **1 :** sudden burst, splash, or stroke **2 :** punctuation mark — **3 :** tiny amount **4 :** showiness or liveliness **5 :** sudden rush **6 :** short race **7 :** dashboard

dash•board *n* **:** instrument panel

da•ta *n sing or pl* **:** factual information

da•ta•base *n* **:** data organized for computer search

[1]**date** *n* **:** edible fruit of a palm

[2]**date** *n* **1 :** day, month, or year when something is done or made **2 :** historical time period **3 :** social engagement or the person one goes out with ∼ *vb* **1 :** determine or record the date of **2 :** have a date with **3 :** originate — **to date :** up to now

dat•ed *adj* **:** old-fashioned

daub *vb* **:** smear ∼ *n* **:** something daubed on — **daub•er** *n*

daugh•ter *n* **:** human female offspring

daugh•ter–in–law *n* (**daughters–in–law**) **:** wife of one's son

daw•dle *vb* **1 :** waste time **2 :** loiter

dawn *vb* **1 :** grow light as the sun rises **2 :** begin to appear, develop, or be understood ∼ *n* **:** first appearance (as of daylight)

day *n* **1 :** period of light between one night and the next **2 :** 24 hours **3 :** specified date **4 :** particular time or age **5 :** period of work for a day — **day•break** *n* — **day•light** *n* — **day•time** *n*

day•dream *n* **:** fantasy of wish fulfillment — **daydream** *vb*

daze *vb* **1 :** stun by a blow **2 :** dazzle — **daze** *n*

daz•zle *vb* **1 :** overpower with light **2 :** impress greatly — **dazzle** *n*

dead *adj* **1 :** lifeless **2 :** unresponsive or inactive **3 :** exhausted **4 :** obsolete **5 :** precise ∼ *n* **dead 1 :** one that is dead — usu. with *the* **2 :** most lifeless time ∼ *adv* **1 :** completely **2 :** directly — **dead•en** *vb*

dead•beat *n* **:** one who will not pay debts

dead heat *n* **:** tie in a contest

dead•line *n* **:** time by which something must be finished

dead•lock *n* **:** struggle that neither side can win — **deadlock** *vb*

dead•ly *adj* **1 :** capable of causing death **2 :** very accurate **3 :** fatal to spiritual progress **4 :** suggestive of death **5 :** very great ∼ *adv* **:** extremely — **dead•li•ness** *n*

dead•pan *adj* **:** showing no expression — **dead•pan** *n or vb or adv*

deaf *adj* **:** unable or unwilling to hear — **deaf•en** *vb* — **deaf•ness** *n*

deaf–mute *n* **:** deaf person unable to speak

deal *n* **1 :** indefinite quantity **2 :** distribution of playing cards **3 :** negotiation or agreement **4 :** treatment received **5 :** bargain ∼ *vb* **dealt; dealt 1 :** distribute playing cards **2 :** be concerned with **3 :** administer or deliver **4 :** take action **5 :** sell **6 :** reach a state of acceptance — **deal•er** *n* — **deal•ing** *n*

dean *n* **1 :** head of a group of clergy members **2 :** university or school administrator **3 :** senior member

dear *adj* **1 :** highly valued or loved **2 :** expensive ∼ *n* **:** loved one — **dear•ly** *adv* — **dear•ness** *n*

death *n* **1 :** end of life **2 :** cause of loss of life **3 :** state of being dead **4 :** destruction or extinction — **death•less** *adj* — **death•ly** *adj or adv*

de•base *vb* **:** hurt the value or dignity of

de•bate *vb* **:** discuss a question by argument — **de•bat•able** *adj* — **debate** *n* — **de•bat•er** *n*
de•bil•i•tate *vb* **:** make ill or weak — **de•bil•i•ty** *n*
deb•it *n* **:** account entry of a payment or debt ~ *vb* **:** record as a debit
de•bris *n* **:** remains of something destroyed
debt *n* **1 :** sin **2 :** something owed **3 :** state of owing — **debt•or** *n*
de•but *n* **1 :** first public appearance **2 :** formal entrance into society — **debut** *vb* — **deb•u•tante** *n*
de•cade *n* **:** 10 years
dec•a•dence *n* **:** deterioration — **dec•a•dent** *adj or n*
de•cal *n* **:** picture or design for transfer from prepared paper
de•cap•i•tate *vb* **:** behead — **de•cap•i•ta•tion** *n*
de•cay *vb* **1 :** decline in condition **2 :** decompose — **decay** *n*
de•cease *n* **:** death — **decease** *vb*
de•ceit *n* **1 :** deception **2 :** dishonesty — **de•ceit•ful** *adj* — **de•ceit•ful•ly** *adv* — **de•ceit•ful•ness** *n*
de•ceive *vb* **:** trick or mislead — **de•ceiv•er** *n*
de•cel•er•ate *vb* **:** slow down
De•cem•ber *n* **:** 12th month of the year having 31 days
de•cent *adj* **1 :** good, right, or just **2 :** wearing clothes **3 :** not obscene **4 :** fairly good — **de•cen•cy** *n* — **de•cent•ly** *adv*
de•cep•tion *n* **1 :** act or fact of deceiving **2 :** fraud — **de•cep•tive** *adj* — **de•cep•tive•ly** *adv* — **de•cep•tive•ness** *n*
de•cide *vb* **1 :** make a choice or judgment **2 :** bring to a conclusion **3 :** cause to decide
de•cid•ed *adj* **1 :** beyond doubt or question **2 :** resolute — **de•cid•ed•ly** *adv*
dec•i•mal *n* **:** fraction in which the denominator is a power of 10 expressed by a point (**decimal point**) placed at the left — **decimal** *adj*
de•ci•pher *vb* **:** make out the meaning of — **de•ci•pher•able** *adj*
de•ci•sion *n* **1 :** act or result of deciding **2 :** determination
de•ci•sive *adj* **1 :** having the power to decide **2 :** conclusive **3 :** showing determination — **de•ci•sive•ly** *adv* — **de•ci•sive•ness** *n*
deck *n* **1 :** floor of a ship **2 :** pack of playing cards ~ *vb* **1 :** array or dress up **2 :** knock down
de•clare *vb* **1 :** make known formally **2 :** state emphatically — **dec•la•ra•tion** *n* — **de•clar•a•tive** *adj* — **de•clar•a•to•ry** *adj* — **de•clar•er** *n*
de•cline *vb* **1 :** turn or slope downward **2 :** wane **3 :** refuse to accept ~ *n* **1 :** gradual wasting away **2 :** change to a lower state or level **3 :** a descending slope — **dec•li•na•tion** *n*
de•code *vb* **:** decipher (a coded message) — **de•cod•er** *n*
de•com•pose *vb* **1 :** separate into parts **2 :** decay — **de•com•po•si•tion** *n*
de•con•ges•tant *n* **:** agent that relieves congestion
de•cor, dé•cor *n* **:** room design or decoration
dec•o•rate *vb* **1 :** add something attractive to **2 :** honor with a medal — **dec•o•ra•tion** *n* — **dec•o•ra•tive** *adj* — **dec•o•ra•tor** *n*
de•coy *n* **:** something that tempts or draws attention from another ~ *vb* **:** tempt
de•crease *vb* **:** grow or cause to grow less — **decrease** *n*
de•cree *n* **:** official order — **de•cree** *vb*
de•cre•scen•do *adv or adj* **:** with a decrease in volume
ded•i•cate *vb* **1 :** set apart for a purpose (as honor or worship) **2 :** address to someone as a compliment — **ded•i•ca•tion** *n* — **ded•i•ca•to•ry** *adj*
de•duce *vb* **:** derive by reasoning — **de•duc•ible** *adj*
de•duct *vb* **:** subtract — **de•duct•ible** *adj* — **de•duc•tion** *n* — **de•duc•tive** *adj*
deed *n* **1 :** exploit **2 :** document showing ownership ~ *vb* **:** convey by deed
deep *adj* **1 :** extending far or a specified distance down, back, within, or outward **2 :** occupied **3 :** dark and rich in color **4 :** low in tone ~ *adv* **1 :** deeply **2 :** far along in time ~ *n* **:** deep place — **deep•en** *vb* — **deep•ly** *adv*
deep–seat•ed *adj* **:** firmly established
deer *n* (**deer**) **:** ruminant mammal with antlers in the male — **deer•skin** *n*
de•fault *n* **:** failure in a duty — **default** *vb* — **de•fault•er** *n*
de•feat *vb* **1 :** frustrate **2 :** win victory over ~ *n* **:** loss of a battle or contest
def•e•cate *vb* **:** discharge feces from the bowels — **def•e•ca•tion** *n*
de•fect *n* **:** imperfection ~ *vb* **:** desert — **de•fec•tion** *n* — **de•fec•tive** *adj* — **de•fec•tor** *n*

de•fend *vb* **1 :** protect from danger or harm **2 :** take the side of — **de•fend•er** *n*

de•fen•dant *n* **:** person charged or sued in a court

de•fense *n* **1 :** act of defending **2 :** something that defends **3 :** party, group, or team that opposes another — **de•fense•less** *adj* — **de•fen•si•ble** *adj* — **de•fen•sive** *adj or n*

de•fer *vb* **:** postpone — **de•fer•ment** *n* — **de•fer•ra•ble** *adj*

de•fi•ance *n* **:** disposition to resist — **de•fi•ant** *adj*

de•fi•cient *adj* **1 :** lacking something necessary **2 :** not up to standard — **de•fi•cien•cy** *n*

def•i•cit *n* **:** shortage esp. in money

de•fine *vb* **1 :** fix or mark the limits of **2 :** clarify in outline **3 :** set forth the meaning of — **de•fin•able** *adj* — **de•fin•ably** *adv* — **de•fin•er** *n* — **def•i•ni•tion** *n*

def•i•nite *adj* **1 :** having distinct limits **2 :** clear in meaning, intent, or identity **3 :** typically designating an identified or immediately identifiable person or thing — **def•i•nite•ly** *adv*

de•fin•i•tive *adj* **1 :** conclusive **2 :** authoritative

de•flate *vb* **1 :** release air or gas from **2 :** reduce — **de•fla•tion** *n*

de•flect *vb* **:** turn aside — **de•flec•tion** *n*

de•form *vb* **1 :** distort **2 :** disfigure — **de•for•ma•tion** *n* — **de•for•mi•ty** *n*

de•fraud *vb* **:** cheat

de•frost *vb* **1 :** thaw out **2 :** free from ice — **de•frost•er** *n*

de•funct *adj* **:** dead

de•fy *vb* **1 :** challenge **2 :** boldly refuse to obey

de•gen•er•ate *adj* **:** degraded or corrupt ~ *n* **:** degenerate person ~ *vb* **:** become degenerate — **de•gen•er•a•cy** *n* — **de•gen•er•a•tion** *n* — **de•gen•er•a•tive** *adj*

de•grade *vb* **1 :** reduce from a higher to a lower rank or degree **2 :** debase **3 :** decompose — **de•grad•able** *adj* — **deg•ra•da•tion** *n*

de•gree *n* **1 :** step in a series **2 :** extent, intensity, or scope **3 :** title given to a college graduate **4 :** a 360th part of the circumference of a circle **5 :** unit for measuring temperature

de•hy•drate *vb* **1 :** remove water from **2 :** lose liquid — **de•hy•dra•tion** *n*

de•i•fy *vb* **:** make a god of — **de•i•fi•ca•tion** *n*

de•i•ty *n* **1** *cap* **:** God **2 :** a god or goddess

de•ject•ed *adj* **:** sad — **de•jec•tion** *n*

de•lay *n* **:** a putting off of something ~ *vb* **1 :** postpone **2 :** stop or hinder for a time

de•lec•ta•ble *adj* **:** delicious

del•e•gate *n* **:** representative ~ *vb* **1 :** entrust to another **2 :** appoint as one's delegate — **del•e•ga•tion** *n*

de•lete *vb* **:** eliminate something written — **de•le•tion** *n*

deli *n* **:** a delicatessen

de•lib•er•ate *adj* **1 :** determined after careful thought **2 :** intentional **3 :** not hurried ~ *vb* **:** consider carefully — **de•lib•er•ate•ly** *adv* — **de•lib•er•ate•ness** *n* — **de•lib•er•a•tion** *n* — **de•lib•er•a•tive** *adj*

del•i•ca•cy *n* **1 :** something special and pleasing to eat **2 :** fineness **3 :** frailty

del•i•cate *adj* **1 :** subtly pleasing to the senses **2 :** dainty and charming **3 :** sensitive or fragile **4 :** requiring fine skill or tact — **del•i•cate•ly** *adv*

del•i•ca•tes•sen *n* **:** store that sells ready-to-eat food

de•li•cious *adj* **:** very pleasing esp. in taste or aroma — **de•li•cious•ly** *adv* — **de•li•cious•ness** *n*

de•light *n* **1 :** great pleasure **2 :** source of great pleasure ~ *vb* **1 :** take great pleasure **2 :** satisfy greatly — **de•light•ful** *adj* — **de•light•ful•ly** *adv*

de•lin•quent *n* **:** delinquent person ~ *adj* **1 :** violating duty or law **2 :** overdue in payment — **de•lin•quen•cy** *n*

de•liv•er *vb* **1 :** set free **2 :** hand over **3 :** assist in birth **4 :** say or speak **5 :** send to an intended destination — **de•liv•er•ance** *n* — **de•liv•er•er** *n* — **de•liv•ery** *n*

del•ta *n* **:** triangle of land at the mouth of a river

de•lude *vb* **:** mislead or deceive — **de•lu•sion** *n*

de•luxe *adj* **:** very luxurious or elegant

de•mand *n* **1 :** act of demanding **2 :** something claimed as due **3 :** ability and desire to buy **4 :** urgent need ~ *vb* **1 :** ask for with authority **2 :** require

de•mean *vb* **:** degrade

de•mean•or *n* **:** behavior

de•ment•ed *adj* **:** crazy

de•mer•it *n* **:** mark given an offender

de•mise *n* **1 :** death **2 :** loss of status

de•moc•ra•cy *n* **1 :** government in which the supreme power is held by the people **2 :** political unit with democratic government — **dem-**

o•crat *n* — **dem•o•crat•ic** *adj* — **dem•o•crat•i•cal•ly** *adv* — **de•moc•ra•tize** *vb*
de•mol•ish *vb* **1 :** tear down or smash **2 :** put an end to — **de•mo•li•tion** *n*
de•mon *n* **:** evil spirit — **de•mon•ic** *adj*
dem•on•strate *vb* **1 :** show clearly or publicly **2 :** prove **3 :** explain — **de•mon•stra•ble** *adj* — **de•mon•stra•bly** *adv* — **dem•on•stra•tion** *n* — **de•mon•stra•tive** *adj or n* — **dem•on•stra•tor** *n*
de•mote *vb* **:** reduce to a lower rank — **de•mo•tion** *n*
den *n* **1 :** animal's shelter **2 :** hiding place **3 :** cozy private little room
de•ni•al *n* **:** rejection of a request or of the validity of a statement
den•im *n* **1 :** durable twilled cotton fabric **2** *pl* **:** pants of denim
de•nom•i•na•tion *n* **1 :** religious body **2 :** value or size in a series — **de•nom•i•na•tion•al** *adj*
de•nom•i•na•tor *n* **:** part of a fraction below the line
de•nounce *vb* **1 :** pronounce blameworthy or evil **2 :** inform against — **de•nun•ci•a•tion** *n*
dense *adj* **1 :** thick, compact, or crowded **2 :** stupid — **dense•ly** *adv* — **dense•ness** *n* — **den•si•ty** *n*
dent *n* **:** small depression — **dent** *vb*
den•tal *adj* **:** relating to teeth or dentistry
den•tist *n* **:** one who cares for and replaces teeth — **den•tist•ry** *n*
den•ture *n* **:** artificial teeth
de•ny *vb* **1 :** declare untrue **2 :** deny validity of **3 :** refuse to grant
de•odor•ant *n* **:** preparation to prevent unpleasant odors — **de•odor•ize** *vb*
de•part *vb* **1 :** go away or away from **2 :** die — **de•par•ture** *n*
de•part•ment *n* **1 :** area of responsibility or interest **2 :** functional division — **de•part•men•tal** *adj*
de•pend *vb* **1 :** rely for support **2 :** be determined by or based on something else — **de•pend•abil•i•ty** *n* — **de•pend•able** *adj* — **de•pen•dence** *n* — **de•pen•den•cy** *n* — **de•pen•dent** *adj or n*
de•pict *vb* **:** show by or as if by a picture — **de•pic•tion** *n*
de•plete *vb* **:** use up resources of — **de•ple•tion** *n*
de•plore *vb* **:** regret strongly — **de•plor•able** *adj*
de•port *vb* **1 :** behave **2 :** send out of the country — **de•por•ta•tion** *n* — **de•port•ment** *n*
de•pos•it *vb* **:** place esp. for safekeeping **~** *n* **1 :** state of being deposited **2 :** something deposited **3 :** act of depositing **4 :** natural accumulation — **de•pos•i•tor** *n*
de•pos•i•to•ry *n* **:** place for deposit
de•pot *n* **1 :** place for storage **2 :** bus or railroad station
de•prave *vb* **:** corrupt morally — **de•praved** *adj* — **de•prav•i•ty** *n*
de•pre•ci•ate *vb* **1 :** lessen in value **2 :** belittle — **de•pre•ci•a•tion** *n*
de•press *vb* **1 :** press down **2 :** lessen the activity or force of **3 :** discourage **4 :** decrease the market value of — **de•pres•sant** *n or adj* — **de•pressed** *adj* — **de•pres•sive** *adj or n* — **de•pres•sor** *n*
de•pres•sion *n* **1 :** act of depressing or state of being depressed **2 :** depressed place **3 :** period of low economic activity
de•prive *vb* **:** take or keep something away from — **de•pri•va•tion** *n*
depth *n* **1 :** something that is deep **2 :** distance down from a surface **3 :** distance from front to back **4 :** quality of being deep
dep•u•ty *n* **:** person appointed to act for another — **dep•u•tize** *vb*
de•rail *vb* **:** leave the rails — **de•rail•ment** *n*
de•range *vb* **1 :** upset an arrangement of **2 :** make insane — **de•range•ment** *n*
der•by *n* **1 :** horse race **2 :** stiff felt hat with dome-shaped crown
de•reg•u•late *vb* **:** remove restrictions on — **de•reg•u•la•tion** *n*
der•e•lict *adj* **1 :** abandoned **2 :** negligent **~** *n* **1 :** something abandoned **2 :** bum — **der•e•lic•tion** *n*
de•ride *vb* **:** make fun of — **de•ri•sion** *n* — **de•ri•sive** *adj* — **de•ri•sive•ly** *adv* — **de•ri•sive•ness** *n*
de•rive *vb* **1 :** obtain from a source or parent **2 :** come from a certain source **3 :** infer or deduce — **der•i•va•tion** *n* — **de•riv•a•tive** *adj or n*
der•ma•tol•o•gy *n* **:** study of the skin and its disorders — **der•ma•tol•o•gist** *n*
de•rog•a•to•ry *adj* **:** intended to lower the reputation
de•scend *vb* **1 :** move or climb down **2 :** derive **3 :** extend downward **4 :** appear suddenly (as in an attack) — **de•scen•dant, de•scen•dent** *adj or n* — **de•scent** *n*

de•scribe *vb* **:** represent in words — **de•scrib•able** *adj* — **de•scrip•tion** *n* — **de•scrip•tive** *adj*

des•e•crate *vb* **:** treat (something sacred) with disrespect — **des•e•cra•tion** *n*

de•seg•re•gate *vb* **:** eliminate esp. racial segregation in — **de•seg•re•ga•tion** *n*

[1]**des•ert** *n* **:** dry barren region — **desert** *adj*

[2]**de•sert** *n* **:** what one deserves

[3]**de•sert** *vb* **:** abandon — **de•sert•er** *n* — **de•ser•tion** *n*

de•serve *vb* **:** be worthy of

de•sign *vb* **1 :** create and work out the details of **2 :** make a pattern or sketch of ~ *n* **1 :** mental project or plan **2 :** purpose **3 :** preliminary sketch **4 :** underlying arrangement of elements **5 :** decorative pattern — **de•sign•er** *n*

des•ig•nate *vb* **1 :** indicate, specify, or name **2 :** appoint — **des•ig•na•tion** *n*

de•sire *vb* **1 :** feel desire for **2 :** request ~ *n* **1 :** strong conscious impulse to have, be, or do something **2 :** something desired — **de•sir•abil•i•ty** *n* — **de•sir•able** *adj* — **de•sir•able•ness** *n* — **de•sir•ous** *adj*

de•sist *vb* **:** stop

desk *n* **:** table esp. for writing and reading

des•o•late *adj* **1 :** lifeless **2 :** hopelessly sad ~ *vb* **:** lay waste — **des•o•la•tion** *n*

de•spair *vb* **:** lose all hope ~ *n* **:** loss of hope

des•per•ate *adj* **1 :** hopeless **2 :** rash **3 :** extremely intense — **des•per•ate•ly** *adv* — **des•per•a•tion** *n*

de•spise *vb* **:** feel contempt for — **de•spi•ca•ble** *adj*

de•spite *prep* **:** in spite of

de•spon•den•cy *n* **:** dejection — **de•spon•dent** *adj*

des•sert *n* **:** sweet food, fruit, or cheese ending a meal

des•ti•na•tion *n* **:** place where something or someone is going

des•tine *vb* **1 :** designate, assign, or determine in advance **2 :** direct

des•ti•ny *n* **:** that which is to happen in the future

des•ti•tute *adj* **1 :** lacking something **2 :** very poor — **des•ti•tu•tion** *n*

de•stroy *vb* **:** kill or put an end to — **de•stroy•er** *n* — **de•struc•ti•bil•i•ty** *n* — **de•struc•ti•ble** *adj* — **de•struc•tive** *adj* — **de•struc•tion** *n*

de•tach *vb* **:** separate — **de•tached** *adj* — **de•tach•ment** *n*

de•tail *n* **:** small item or part ~ *vb* **:** give details of

de•tain *vb* **1 :** hold in custody **2 :** delay

de•tect *vb* **:** discover — **detect•able** *adj* — **de•tec•tion** *n* — **de•tec•tor** *n*

de•tec•tive *n* **:** one who investigates crime

de•ten•tion *n* **:** confinement

de•ter *vb* **:** discourage or prevent — **de•ter•rence** *n* — **de•ter•rent** *adj or n*

de•ter•gent *n* **:** cleansing agent

de•te•ri•o•rate *vb* **:** make or become worse — **de•te•ri•o•ra•tion** *n*

de•ter•mine *vb* **1 :** decide on, establish, or settle **2 :** find out **3 :** bring about as a result — **de•ter•mi•na•tion** *n*

de•test *vb* **:** hate — **de•test•able** *adj* — **de•tes•ta•tion** *n*

det•o•nate *vb* **:** explode — **det•o•na•tion** *n* — **det•o•na•tor** *n*

de•tour *n* **:** temporary indirect route — **detour** *vb*

de•tract *vb* **:** take away — **de•trac•tion** *n* — **de•trac•tor** *n*

det•ri•ment *n* **:** damage — **det•ri•men•tal** *adj* — **det•ri•men•tal•ly** *adv*

deuce *n* **1 :** 2 in cards or dice **2 :** tie in tennis **3 :** devil — used as an oath

de•val•ue *vb* **:** reduce the value of — **de•val•u•a•tion** *n*

dev•as•tate *vb* **:** ruin — **dev•as•ta•tion** *n*

de•vel•op *vb* **1 :** grow, increase, or evolve gradually **2 :** cause to grow, increase, or reach full potential — **de•vel•op•er** *n* — **de•vel•op•ment** *n* — **de•vel•op•men•tal** *adj*

de•vi•ate *vb* **:** change esp. from a course or standard — **de•vi•ant** *adj or n* — **de•vi•ate** *n* — **de•vi•a•tion** *n*

de•vice *n* **1 :** specialized piece of equipment or tool **2 :** design

dev•il *n* **1 :** personified supreme spirit of evil **2 :** demon **3 :** wicked person ~ *vb* **1 :** season highly **2 :** pester — **dev•il•ish** *adj* — **dev•il•ry, dev•il•try** *n*

de•vi•ous *adj* **:** tricky

de•vise *vb* **1 :** invent **2 :** plot **3 :** give by will

de•vote *vb* **:** set apart for a special purpose — **de•vot•ed** *adj*

dev•o•tee *n* **:** ardent follower

de•vo•tion *n* **1 :** prayer — *usu. pl.* **2 :** loyalty and dedication — **de•vo•tion•al** *adj*

de•vour *vb* : consume ravenously — **de•vour•er** *n*
de•vout *adj* **1 :** devoted to religion **2 :** serious — **de•vout•ly** *adv* — **de•vout•ness** *n*
dew *n* : moisture condensed at night — **dew•drop** *n* — **dewy** *adj*
dex•ter•ous *adj* : skillful with the hands — **dex•ter•i•ty** *n* — **dex•ter•ous•ly** *adv*
di•a•be•tes *n* : disorder in which the body has too little insulin and too much sugar — **di•a•bet•ic** *adj or n*
di•ag•no•sis *n* : identifying of a disease from its symptoms — **di•ag•nose** *vb* — **di•ag•nos•tic** *adj*
di•ag•o•nal *adj* : extending from one corner to the opposite corner ~ *n* : diagonal line, direction, or arrangement — **di•ag•o•nal•ly** *adv*
di•a•gram *n* : explanatory drawing or plan ~ *vb* : represent by a diagram — **di•a•gram•mat•ic** *adj*
di•al *n* **1 :** face of a clock, meter, or gauge **2 :** control knob or wheel ~ *vb* : turn a dial to call, operate, or select
di•a•lect *n* : variety of language confined to a region or group
di•a•logue *n* : conversation
di•am•e•ter *n* **1 :** straight line through the center of a circle **2 :** thickness
di•a•mond *n* **1 :** hard brilliant mineral that consists of crystalline carbon **2 :** flat figure having 4 equal sides, 2 acute angles, and 2 obtuse angles **3 :** playing card of a suit marked with a red diamond **4 :** baseball field
di•a•per *n* : baby's garment for receiving bodily wastes ~ *vb* : put a diaper on
di•a•phragm *n* **1 :** sheet of muscle between the chest and abdominal cavity **2 :** contraceptive device
di•ar•rhea *n* : abnormally watery discharge from bowels
di•a•ry *n* : daily record of personal experiences — **di•a•rist** *n*
dice *n* **dice :** die or a game played with dice ~ *vb* : cut into small cubes
dic•tate *vb* **1 :** speak for a person or a machine to record **2 :** command ~ *n* : order — **dic•ta•tion** *n*
dic•ta•tor *n* : person ruling absolutely and often brutally — **dic•ta•to•ri•al** *adj* — **dic•ta•tor•ship** *n*
dic•tio•nary *n* : reference book of words with information about their meanings
did *past of* DO
didn't : did not
¹die *vb* **1 :** stop living **2 :** pass out of existence **3 :** stop or become less active **4 :** long
²die *n* **1** *pl* **dice :** small marked cube used in gambling **2** *pl* **dies :** form for stamping or cutting
die•sel *n* : engine in which high compression causes ignition of the fuel
di•et *n* : food and drink regularly consumed (as by a person) ~ *vb* : eat less or according to certain rules — **di•etary** *adj or n* — **di•et•er** *n*
dif•fer *vb* **1 :** be unlike **2 :** vary **3 :** disagree — **dif•fer•ence** *n* — **dif•fer•ent** *adj* — **dif•fer•ent•ly** *adv*
dif•fer•en•ti•ate *vb* **1 :** make or become different **2 :** attain a specialized adult form during development **3 :** distinguish — **dif•fer•en•ti•a•tion** *n*
dif•fi•cul•ty *n* **1 :** difficult nature **2 :** great effort **3 :** something hard to do, understand, or deal with — **dif•fi•cult** *adj*
dif•fuse *adj* **1 :** wordy **2 :** not concentrated ~ *vb* : pour out or spread widely — **dif•fu•sion** *n*
dig *vb* **1 :** turn up soil **2 :** hollow out or form by removing earth **3 :** uncover by turning up earth ~ *n* **1 :** thrust **2 :** cutting remark — **dig in** *vb* **1 :** establish a defensive position **2 :** begin working or eating — **dig up** *vb* : discover
¹di•gest *n* : body of information in shortened form
²di•gest *vb* **1 :** think over **2 :** convert (food) into a form that can be absorbed **3 :** summarize — **di•gest•ible** *adj* — **di•ges•tion** *n* — **di•ges•tive** *adj*
dig•it *n* **1 :** any of the figures 1 to 9 inclusive and usu. the symbol 0 **2 :** finger or toe
dig•i•tal *adj* : providing information in numerical digits — **dig•i•tal•ly** *adv*
digital camera *n* : camera that records images as digital data instead of on film
dig•ni•fy *vb* : give dignity or attention to
dig•ni•tary *n* : person of high position
dig•ni•ty *n* **1 :** quality or state of being worthy or honored **2 :** formal reserve (as of manner)
dike *n* : earth bank or dam
di•lap•i•dat•ed *adj* : fallen into partial ruin — **di•lap•i•da•tion** *n*
di•late *vb* : swell or expand — **dil•a•ta•tion** *n* — **di•la•tion** *n*
di•lem•ma *n* **1 :** undesirable choice **2 :** predicament

dil•i•gent *adj* : attentive and busy — **dil•i•gence** *n* — **dil•i•gent•ly** *adv*
dill *n* : herb with aromatic leaves and seeds
dil•ly•dal•ly *vb* : waste time by delay
di•lute *vb* : lessen the consistency or strength of by mixing with something else ~ *adj* : weak — **di•lu•tion** *n*
dim *adj* **1** : not bright or distinct **2** : having no luster **3** : not seeing or understanding clearly — **dim** *vb* — **dim•ly** *adv* — **dim•mer** *n* — **dim•ness** *n*
dime *n* : U.S. coin worth ten cents
di•men•sion *n* **1** : measurement of extension (as in length, height, or breadth) **2** : extent — **di•men•sion•al** *adj*
di•min•ish *vb* **1** : make less or cause to appear less **2** : dwindle
dim•ple *n* : small depression esp. in the cheek or chin
dine *vb* : eat dinner
din•er *n* **1** : person eating dinner **2** : railroad dining car or restaurant resembling one
din•ghy *n* : small boat
din•gy *adj* **1** : dirty **2** : shabby — **din•gi•ness** *n*
din•ner *n* : main daily meal
di•no•saur *n* : extinct often huge reptile
di•o•cese *n* : territorial jurisdiction of a bishop — **di•oc•e•san** *adj or n*
dip *vb* **1** : plunge into a liquid **2** : take out with a ladle **3** : lower and quickly raise again **4** : sink or slope downward suddenly ~ *n* **1** : plunge into water for sport **2** : sudden downward movement or incline — **dip•per** *n*
di•plo•ma *n* : record of graduation from a school
di•plo•ma•cy *n* **1** : business of conducting negotiations between nations **2** : tact — **dip•lo•mat** *n* — **dip•lo•mat•ic** *adj*
dire *adj* **1** : very horrible **2** : extreme
di•rect *vb* **1** : address **2** : cause to move or to follow a certain course **3** : show (someone) the way **4** : regulate the activities or course of **5** : request with authority ~ *adj* **1** : leading to or coming from a point without deviation or interruption **2** : frank — **direct** *adv* — **di•rect•ly** *adv* — **di•rect•ness** *n* — **di•rec•tor** *n*
direct current *n* : electric current flowing in one direction only
di•rec•tion *n* **1** : supervision **2** : order **3** : course along which something moves — **di•rec•tion•al** *adj*
di•rec•tive *n* : order
di•rec•to•ry *n* : alphabetical list of names and addresses
dirt *n* **1** : mud, dust, or grime that makes something unclean **2** : soil
dirty *adj* **1** : not clean **2** : unfair **3** : extremely improper or offensive ~ *vb* : make or become dirty — **dirt•i•ness** *n*
dis•able *vb* : make unable to function — **dis•abil•i•ty** *n*
dis•ad•van•tage *n* : something that hinders success — **dis•ad•van•ta•geous** *adj*
dis•agree *vb* **1** : fail to agree **2** : differ in opinion — **dis•agree•ment** *n*
dis•agree•able *adj* : unpleasant
dis•al•low *vb* : refuse to admit or recognize
dis•ap•pear *vb* **1** : pass out of sight **2** : cease to be — **dis•ap•pear•ance** *n*
dis•ap•point *vb* : fail to fulfill the expectation or hope of — **dis•ap•point•ment** *n*
dis•ap•prove *vb* **1** : condemn or reject **2** : feel or express dislike or rejection — **dis•ap•prov•al** *n* — **dis•ap•prov•ing•ly** *adv*
dis•arm *vb* **1** : take weapons from **2** : reduce armed forces **3** : make harmless or friendly — **dis•ar•ma•ment** *n*
di•sas•ter *n* : sudden great misfortune — **di•sas•trous** *adj*
dis•be•lieve *vb* : hold not worthy of belief — **dis•be•lief** *n*
disc *var of* DISK
dis•card *vb* : get rid of as unwanted — **dis•card** *n*
dis•cern *vb* : discover with the eyes or the mind — **dis•cern•ible** *adj* — **dis•cern•ment** *n*
dis•charge *vb* **1** : unload **2** : shoot **3** : set free **4** : dismiss from service **5** : let go or let off **6** : give forth fluid ~ *n* **1** : act of discharging **2** : a flowing out (as of blood) **3** : dismissal
dis•ci•ple *n* : one who helps spread another's teachings
dis•ci•pline *n* **1** : field of study **2** : training that corrects, molds, or perfects **3** : punishment **4** : control gained by obedience or training ~ *vb* **1** : punish **2** : train in self-control — **dis•ci•pli•nar•i•an** *n* — **dis•ci•plin•ary** *adj*
dis•close *vb* : reveal — **dis•clo•sure** *n*
dis•col•or *vb* : change the color of esp. for the worse — **dis•col•or•ation** *n*
dis•com•fort *n* : uneasiness
dis•con•nect *vb* : undo the connection of
dis•con•tent *n* : uneasiness of mind — **dis•con•tent•ed** *adj*
dis•con•tin•ue *vb* : end — **dis•con•tin•u•ance**

n — **dis·con·ti·nu·i·ty** *n* — **dis·con·tin·u·ous** *adj*
dis·cord *n* : lack of harmony — **dis·cor·dant** *adj* — **dis·cor·dant·ly** *adv*
dis·count *n* : reduction from a regular price ~ *vb* **1** : reduce the amount of **2** : disregard — **discount** *adj* — **dis·count·er** *n*
dis·cour·age *vb* **1** : deprive of courage, confidence, or enthusiasm **2** : dissuade — **dis·cour·age·ment** *n*
dis·cour·te·ous *adj* : lacking courtesy — **dis·cour·te·ous·ly** *adv* — **dis·cour·te·sy** *n*
dis·cov·er *vb* **1** : make known **2** : obtain the first sight or knowledge of **3** : find out — **dis·cov·er·er** *n* — **dis·cov·ery** *n*
dis·cred·it *vb* **1** : disbelieve **2** : destroy confidence in ~ *n* **1** : loss of reputation **2** : disbelief — **dis·cred·it·able** *adj*
dis·creet *adj* : capable of keeping a secret — **dis·creet·ly** *adv*
dis·crep·an·cy *n* : difference or disagreement
dis·crete *adj* : individually distinct
dis·cre·tion *n* **1** : discreet quality **2** : power of decision or choice — **dis·cre·tion·ary** *adj*
dis·crim·i·nate *vb* **1** : distinguish **2** : show favor or disfavor unjustly — **dis·crim·i·na·tion** *n* — **dis·crim·i·na·to·ry** *adj*
dis·cus *n* : disk hurled for distance in a contest
dis·cuss *vb* : talk about or present — **dis·cus·sion** *n*
dis·dain *n* : feeling of contempt ~ *vb* : look upon or reject with disdain — **dis·dain·ful** *adj* — **dis·dain·ful·ly** *adv*
dis·ease *n* : condition of a body that impairs its functioning — **dis·eased** *adj*
dis·en·chant *vb* : to free from illusion — **dis·en·chant·ment** *n*
dis·en·chant·ed *adj* : disappointed
dis·en·gage *vb* : release — **dis·en·gage·ment** *n*
dis·en·tan·gle *vb* : free from entanglement
dis·fa·vor *n* : disapproval
dis·fig·ure *vb* : spoil the appearance of — **dis·fig·ure·ment** *n*
dis·grace *vb* : bring disgrace to ~ *n* **1** : shame **2** : cause of shame — **dis·grace·ful** *adj* — **dis·grace·ful·ly** *adv*
dis·guise *vb* : hide the true identity or nature of ~ *n* : something that conceals
dis·gust *n* : strong aversion ~ *vb* : provoke disgust in — **dis·gust·ed·ly** *adv* — **dis·gust·ing·ly** *adv*
dish *n* **1** : vessel for serving food or the food it holds **2** : food prepared in a particular way ~ *vb* : put in a dish — **dish·cloth** *n* — **dish·rag** *n* — **dish·wash·er** *n* — **dish·wa·ter** *n*
dis·har·mo·ny *n* : lack of harmony — **dis·har·mo·ni·ous** *adj*
dis·heart·en *vb* : discourage
di·shev·el *vb* : throw into disorder — **di·shev·eled, di·shev·elled** *adj*
dis·hon·est *adj* : not honest — **dis·hon·est·ly** *adv* — **dis·hon·es·ty** *n*
dis·hon·or *n or vb* : disgrace — **dis·hon·or·able** *adj* — **dis·hon·or·ably** *adv*
dis·il·lu·sion *vb* : to free from illusion — **dis·il·lu·sion·ment** *n*
dis·in·fect *vb* : destroy disease germs in or on — **dis·in·fec·tant** *adj or n* — **dis·in·fec·tion** *n*
dis·in·te·grate *vb* : break into parts or small bits — **dis·in·te·gra·tion** *n*
dis·in·ter·est·ed *adj* **1** : not interested **2** : not prejudiced — **dis·in·ter·est·ed·ness** *n*
disk *n* : something round and flat
dis·like *n* : feeling that something is unpleasant and to be avoided ~ *vb* : regard with dislike
dis·lo·cate *vb* : move out of the usual or proper place — **dis·lo·ca·tion** *n*
dis·lodge *vb* : force out of a place
dis·loy·al *adj* : not loyal — **dis·loy·al·ty** *n*
dis·mal *adj* : showing or causing gloom — **dis·mal·ly** *adv*
dis·man·tle *vb* : take apart
dis·may *vb* : discourage — **dismay** *n*
dis·mem·ber *vb* : cut into pieces — **dis·mem·ber·ment** *n*
dis·miss *vb* **1** : send away **2** : remove from service **3** : put aside or out of mind — **dis·miss·al** *n*
dis·mount *vb* **1** : get down from something **2** : take apart
dis·obey *vb* : refuse to obey — **dis·obe·di·ence** *n* — **dis·obe·di·ent** *adj*
dis·or·der *n* **1** : lack of order **2** : breach of public order **3** : abnormal state of body or mind — **disorder** *vb* — **dis·or·der·li·ness** *n* — **dis·or·der·ly** *adj*
dis·or·ga·nize *vb* : throw into disorder — **dis·or·ga·ni·za·tion** *n*
dis·own *vb* : reject as not valid or not one's own
dis·par·age *vb* : say bad things about — **dis·par·age·ment** *n*
dis·patch *vb* **1** : send **2** : kill **3** : attend to rapidly **4** : defeat ~ *n* **1** : message **2** : news

item from a correspondent **3 :** promptness and efficiency — **dis•patch•er** *n*

dis•pense *vb* **1 :** portion out **2 :** make up and give out (remedies) — **dis•pen•sa•tion** *n* — **dis•pens•er** *n* — **dispense with :** do without

dis•perse *vb* **:** scatter — **dis•per•sal** *n* — **dis•per•sion** *n*

dis•place *vb* **1 :** expel or force to flee from home or native land **2 :** take the place of — **dis•place•ment** *n*

dis•play *vb* **:** present to view — **display** *n*

dis•please *vb* **:** arouse the dislike of — **dis•plea•sure** *n*

dis•pose *vb* **1 :** give a tendency to **2 :** settle — **dis•pos•able** *adj* — **dis•pos•al** *n* — **dis•pos•er** *n* — **dispose of 1 :** determine the fate, condition, or use of **2 :** get rid of

dis•po•si•tion *n* **1 :** act or power of disposing of **2 :** arrangement **3 :** natural attitude

dis•pro•por•tion *n* **:** lack of proportion — **dis•pro•por•tion•ate** *adj*

dis•prove *vb* **:** prove false

dis•pute *vb* **1 :** argue **2 :** deny the truth or rightness of **3 :** struggle against or over ~ *n* **:** debate or quarrel — **dis•put•able** *adj* — **dis•pu•ta•tion** *n*

dis•qual•i•fy *vb* **:** make ineligible — **dis•qual•i•fi•ca•tion** *n*

dis•re•gard *vb* **:** pay no attention to ~ *n* **:** neglect

dis•rep•u•ta•ble *adj* **:** having a bad reputation — **dis•re•pute** *n*

dis•re•spect *n* **:** lack of respect — **dis•re•spect•ful** *adj*

dis•rupt *vb* **:** throw into disorder — **dis•rup•tion** *n* — **dis•rup•tive** *adj*

dis•sat•is•fac•tion *n* **:** lack of satisfaction

dis•sat•is•fy *vb* **:** fail to satisfy

dis•sect *vb* **:** cut into parts esp. to examine — **dis•sec•tion** *n*

dis•sen•sion *n* **:** discord

dis•sent *vb* **:** object or disagree ~ *n* **:** difference of opinion — **dis•sent•er** *n*

dis•ser•vice *n* **:** injury

dis•sim•i•lar *adj* **:** different — **dis•sim•i•lar•i•ty** *n*

dis•si•pate *vb* **1 :** break up and drive off **2 :** waste or lose through neglect — **dis•si•pa•tion** *n*

dis•solve *vb* **1 :** break up or bring to an end **2 :** pass or cause to pass into solution — **dis•so•lu•tion** *n*

dis•so•nance *n* **:** discord — **dis•so•nant** *adj*

dis•suade *vb* **:** persuade not to do something — **dis•sua•sion** *n*

dis•tance *n* **1 :** measure of separation in space or time **2 :** reserve

dis•tant *adj* **1 :** separate in space **2 :** remote in time, space, or relationship **3 :** reserved — **dis•tant•ly** *adv*

dis•taste *n* **:** dislike — **dis•taste•ful** *adj*

dis•till *vb* **:** obtain by distillation — **dis•til•late** *n* — **dis•till•er** *n* — **dis•till•ery** *n*

dis•til•la•tion *n* **:** purification of liquid by evaporating then condensing

dis•tinct *adj* **1 :** distinguishable from others **2 :** readily discerned — **dis•tinc•tion** *n* — **dis•tinc•tive** *adj* — **dis•tinc•tive•ly** *adv* — **dis•tinc•tive•ness** *n* — **dis•tinct•ly** *adv* — **dis•tinct•ness** *n*

dis•tin•guish *vb* **1 :** perceive as different **2 :** set apart **3 :** discern **4 :** make outstanding — **dis•tin•guish•able** *adj* — **dis•tin•guished** *adj*

dis•tort *vb* **:** twist out of shape, condition, or true meaning — **dis•tor•tion** *n*

dis•tract *vb* **:** divert the mind or attention of — **dis•trac•tion** *n*

dis•tress *n* **1 :** suffering **2 :** misfortune **3 :** state of danger or great need ~ *vb* **:** subject to strain or distress — **dis•tress•ful** *adj*

dis•trib•ute *vb* **1 :** divide among many **2 :** spread or hand out — **dis•tri•bu•tion** *n* — **dis•trib•u•tive** *adj* — **dis•trib•u•tor** *n*

dis•trict *n* **:** territorial division

dis•trust *vb* **:** show lack of trust — **dis•trust** *n* — **dis•trust•ful** *adj*

dis•turb *vb* **1 :** interfere with **2 :** destroy the peace, composure, or order of — **dis•tur•bance** *n* — **dis•turb•er** *n*

ditch *n* **:** trench ~ *vb* **1 :** dig a ditch in **2 :** get rid of

dit•to *n* **:** more of the same

dive *vb* **1 :** plunge into water headfirst **2 :** go or put underwater **3 :** descend quickly ~ *n* **1 :** act of diving **2 :** sharp decline — **div•er** *n*

di•verge *vb* **1 :** move in different directions **2 :** differ — **di•ver•gence** *n* — **di•ver•gent** *adj*

di•verse *adj* **:** involving different forms — **di•ver•si•fi•ca•tion** *n* — **di•ver•si•fy** *vb* — **di•ver•si•ty** *n*

di•vert *vb* **1 :** turn from a course or purpose **2 :** distract **3 :** amuse — **di•ver•sion** *n*

di•vide *vb* **1 :** separate **2 :** distribute **3 :** share **4 :** subject to mathematical division — **di•vid•er** *n*

div•i•dend *n* **1 :** individual share **2 :** bonus **3 :** number to be divided

di•vine *adj* **1 :** relating to or being God or a god **2 :** supremely good ~ *n* **:** clergy member ~ *vb* **1 :** infer **2 :** predict — **di•vine•ly** *adv* — **di•vin•er** *n* — **di•vin•i•ty** *n*

di•vis•i•ble *adj* **:** capable of being divided — **di•vis•i•bil•i•ty** *n*

di•vi•sion *n* **1 :** distribution **2 :** part of a whole **3 :** disagreement **4 :** process of finding out how many times one number is contained in another

di•vi•sor *n* **:** number by which a dividend is divided

di•vorce *n* **:** legal breaking up of a marriage — **di•vorce** *vb*

di•vor•cée *n* **:** divorced woman

di•vulge *vb* **:** reveal

diz•zy *adj* **1 :** having a sensation of whirling **2 :** causing or caused by giddiness — **diz•zi•ly** *adv* — **diz•zi•ness** *n*

DNA *n* **:** compound in cell nuclei that is the basis of heredity

do *vb* **did; done 1 :** work to accomplish (an action or task) **2 :** behave **3 :** prepare or fix up **4 :** fare **5 :** finish **6 :** serve the needs or purpose of **7** — used as an auxiliary verb — **do•er** *n* — **do away with 1 :** get rid of **2 :** destroy — **do by :** deal with — **do in** *vb* **1 :** ruin **2 :** kill

doc•ile *adj* **:** easily managed — **do•cil•i•ty** *n*

[1]**dock** *vb* **1 :** shorten **2 :** reduce

[2]**dock** *n* **1 :** berth between 2 piers to receive ships **2 :** loading wharf or platform ~ *vb* **:** bring or come into dock — **dock•work•er** *n*

doc•tor *n* **1 :** person holding one of the highest academic degrees **2 :** one (as a surgeon) skilled in healing arts ~ *vb* **1 :** give medical treatment to **2 :** repair or alter — **doc•tor•al** *adj*

doc•trine *n* **:** something taught — **doc•tri•nal** *adj*

doc•u•ment *n* **:** paper that furnishes information or legal proof — **doc•u•ment** *vb* — **doc•u•men•ta•tion** *n* — **doc•u•ment•er** *n*

doc•u•men•ta•ry *adj* **1 :** of or relating to documents **2 :** giving a factual presentation — **doc•u•men•ta•ry** *n*

dodge *vb* **1 :** move quickly aside or out of the way of **2 :** evade — **dodge** *n*

doe *n* **:** adult female deer — **doe•skin** *n*

does *pres 3d sing of* DO

doesn't : does not

dog *n* **:** flesh-eating domestic mammal ~ *vb* **1 :** hunt down or track like a hound **2 :** harass — **dog•catch•er** *n* — **dog•gy** *n or adj* — **dog•house** *n*

dog–ear *n* **:** turned-down corner of a page — **dog–ear** *vb* — **dog–eared** *adj*

dog•ma *n* **:** tenet or code of tenets

dog•ma•tism *n* **:** unwarranted stubbornness of opinion — **dog•ma•tic** *adj*

do•ings *n pl* **:** events

dol•drums *n pl* **:** spell of listlessness, despondency, or stagnation

dole *n* **:** distribution esp. of money to the needy or unemployed — **dole out** *vb* **:** give out esp. in small portions

dole•ful *adj* **:** sad — **dole•ful•ly** *adv*

doll *n* **:** small figure of a person used esp. as a child's toy

dol•lar *n* **:** any of various basic monetary units (as in the U.S. and Canada)

dol•ly *n* **:** small cart or wheeled platform

dol•phin *n* **1 :** sea mammal related to the whales **2 :** saltwater food fish

do•main *n* **1 :** territory over which someone reigns **2 :** sphere of activity or knowledge

dome *n* **1 :** large hemispherical roof **2 :** roofed stadium

do•mes•tic *adj* **1 :** relating to the household or family **2 :** relating and limited to one's own country **3 :** tame ~ *n* **:** household servant — **do•mes•ti•cal•ly** *adv*

do•mes•ti•cate *vb* **:** tame — **do•mes•ti•ca•tion** *n*

dom•i•nance *n* **:** control — **dom•i•nant** *adj*

dom•i•nate *vb* **1 :** have control over **2 :** rise high above — **dom•i•na•tion** *n*

dom•i•neer *vb* **:** exercise arbitrary control

do•min•ion *n* **1 :** supreme authority **2 :** governed territory

dom•i•no *n* **:** flat rectangular block used as a piece in a game (**dominoes**)

do•nate *vb* **:** make a gift of — **do•na•tion** *n*

[1]**done** *past part of* DO

[2]**done** *adj* **1 :** finished or ended **2 :** cooked sufficiently

don•key *n* **:** sturdy domestic ass

do•nor *n* **:** one that gives

don't: do not

doo•dle *vb* **:** draw or scribble aimlessly — **doodle** *n*

doom *n* **1 :** judgment **2 :** fate **3 :** ruin — **doom** *vb*

door *n* **:** passage for entrance or a movable bar-

rier that can open or close such a passage — **door·jamb** *n* — **door·knob** *n* — **door·mat** *n* — **door·step** *n* — **door·way** *n*
dope 1 : narcotic preparation **2 :** stupid person **3 :** information ∼ *vb* **:** drug
dor·mant *adj* **:** not actively growing or functioning — **dor·man·cy** *n*
dor·mi·to·ry *n* **:** residence hall (as at a college)
dose *n* **:** quantity (as of medicine) taken at one time ∼ *vb* **:** give medicine to — **dos·age** *n*
dot *n* **1 :** small spot **2 :** small round mark made with or as if with a pen ∼ *vb* **:** mark with dots
dote *vb* **1 :** act feebleminded **2 :** be foolishly fond
dou·ble *adj* **1 :** consisting of 2 members or parts **2 :** being twice as great or as many **3 :** folded in two ∼ *n* **1 :** something twice another **2 :** one that resembles another ∼ *adv* **:** doubly ∼ *vb* **1 :** make or become twice as great **2 :** fold or bend **3 :** clench
dou·ble–cross *vb* **:** deceive by trickery — **dou·ble–cross·er** *n*
dou·bly *adv* **:** to twice the degree
doubt *vb* **1 :** be uncertain about **2 :** show lack of trust **3 :** consider unlikely ∼ *n* **1 :** uncertainty **2 :** lack of trust **3 :** inclination not to believe — **doubt·ful** *adj* — **doubt·ful·ly** *adv* — **doubt·less** *adv*
dough *n* **:** stiff mixture of flour and liquid — **doughy** *adj*
dough·nut *n* **:** small fried ring-shaped cake
douse *vb* **1 :** plunge into or drench with water **2 :** extinguish
[1]**dove** *n* **:** small wild pigeon
[2]**dove** *past of* DIVE
dove·tail *vb* **:** fit together neatly
dow·el *n* **1 :** peg used for fastening two pieces **2 :** wooden rod
[1]**down** *adv* **1 :** toward or in a lower position or state **2 :** to a lying or sitting position **3 :** as a cash deposit **4 :** on paper ∼ *adj* **1 :** lying on the ground **2 :** directed or going downward **3 :** being at a low level ∼ *prep* **:** toward the bottom of ∼ *vb* **1 :** cause to go down **2 :** defeat
[2]**down** *n* **:** fluffy feathers
down·cast *adj* **1 :** sad **2 :** directed down
down·fall *n* **:** ruin or cause of ruin
down·grade *n* **:** downward slope ∼ *vb* **:** lower in grade or position
down·heart·ed *adj* **:** sad
down·pour *n* **:** heavy rain
down·right *adv* **:** thoroughly ∼ *adj* **:** absolute or thorough
down·size *vb* **:** reduce in size
down·stairs *adv* **:** on or to a lower floor and esp. the main floor — **downstairs** *adj or n*
down–to–earth *adj* **:** practical
down·town *adv* **:** to, toward, or in the business center of a town — **downtown** *n or adj*
down·ward, down·wards *adv* **:** to a lower place or condition — **downward** *adj*
down·wind *adv or adj* **:** in the direction the wind is blowing
downy *adj* **:** resembling or covered with down
dow·ry *n* **:** property a woman gives her husband in marriage
dox·ol·o·gy *n* **:** hymn of praise to God
doze *vb* **:** sleep lightly — **doze** *n*
doz·en *n* **:** group of 12 — **doz·enth** *adj*
drab *adj* **:** dull — **drab·ly** *adv* — **drab·ness** *n*
draft *n* **1 :** act of drawing or hauling **2 :** act of drinking **3 :** amount drunk at once **4 :** preliminary outline or rough sketch **5 :** selection from a pool or the selection process **6 :** order for the payment of money **7 :** air current ∼ *vb* **1 :** select usu. on a compulsory basis **2 :** make a preliminary sketch, version, or plan of ∼ *adj* **:** drawn from a container — **draft·ee** *n* — **drafty** *adj*
drag *n* **1 :** something dragged over a surface or through water **2 :** something that hinders progress or is boring **3 :** act or an instance of dragging ∼ *vb* **1 :** haul **2 :** move or work with difficulty **3 :** pass slowly **4 :** search or fish with a drag — **drag·ger** *n*
dra·gon *n* **:** fabled winged serpent
drag·on·fly *n* **:** large 4-winged insect
drain *vb* **1 :** draw off or flow off gradually or completely **2 :** exhaust ∼ *n* **:** means or act of draining — **drain·age** *n* — **drain·er** *n* — **drain·pipe** *n*
dra·ma *n* **1 :** composition for theatrical presentation esp. on a serious subject **2 :** series of events involving conflicting forces — **dra·mat·ic** *adj* — **dra·mat·i·cal·ly** *adv* — **dram·a·tist** *n* — **dram·a·ti·za·tion** *n* — **dra·ma·tize** *vb*
drank *past of* DRINK
drape *vb* **1 :** cover or adorn with folds of cloth **2 :** cause to hang in flowing lines or folds ∼ *n* **:** curtain

drap•ery *n* **:** decorative fabric hung esp. as a heavy curtain

dras•tic *adj* **:** extreme or harsh — **dras•ti•cal•ly** *adj*

draw *vb* **drew; drawn 1 :** move or cause to move (as by pulling) **2 :** attract or provoke **3 :** extract **4 :** take or receive (as money) **5 :** bend a bow in preparation for shooting **6 :** leave a contest undecided **7 :** sketch **8 :** write out **9 :** deduce ~ *n* **1 :** act, process, or result of drawing **2 :** tie — **draw out :** cause to speak candidly — **draw up 1 :** write out **2 :** pull oneself erect **3 :** bring or come to a stop

draw•back *n* **:** disadvantage

draw•bridge *n* **:** bridge that can be raised

draw•er *n* **1 :** one that draws **2 :** sliding boxlike compartment **3** *pl* **:** underpants

draw•ing *n* **1 :** occasion of choosing by lot **2 :** act or art of making a figure, plan, or sketch with lines **3 :** something drawn

drawl *vb* **:** speak slowly — **drawl** *n*

dread *vb* **:** feel extreme fear or reluctance ~ *n* **:** great fear ~ *adj* **:** causing dread — **dread•ful** *adj* — **dread•ful•ly** *adv*

dream *n* **1 :** series of thoughts or visions during sleep **2 :** dreamlike vision **3 :** something notable **4 :** ideal ~ *vb* **1 :** have a dream **2 :** imagine — **dream•er** *n* — **dream•like** *adj* — **dreamy** *adj*

drea•ry *adj* **:** dismal — **drea•ri•ly** *adv*

drench *vb* **:** wet thoroughly

dress *vb* **1 :** put clothes on **2 :** decorate **3 :** prepare (as a carcass) for use **4 :** apply dressings, remedies, or fertilizer to ~ *n* **1 :** apparel **2 :** single garment of bodice and skirt ~ *adj* **:** suitable for a formal event — **dress•mak•er** *n* — **dress•mak•ing** *n*

dress•er *n* **:** bureau with a mirror

dress•ing *n* **1 :** act or process of dressing **2 :** sauce or a seasoned mixture **3 :** material to cover an injury

dressy *adj* **1 :** showy in dress **2 :** stylish

drew *past of* DRAW

drib•ble *vb* **1 :** fall or flow in drops **2 :** drool — **dribble** *n*

drier *comparative of* DRY

driest *superlative of* DRY

drift *n* **1 :** motion or course of something drifting **2 :** mass piled up by wind **3 :** general intention or meaning ~ *vb* **1 :** float or be driven along (as by a current) **2 :** wander without purpose **3 :** pile up under force — **drift•er** *n* — **drift•wood** *n*

drill *vb* **1 :** bore with a drill **2 :** instruct by repetition ~ *n* **1 :** tool for boring holes **2 :** regularly practiced exercise — **drill•er** *n*

drily *var of* DRYLY

drink *vb* **drank; drunk 1 :** swallow liquid **2 :** absorb **3 :** drink alcoholic beverages esp. to excess ~ *n* **1 :** beverage **2 :** alcoholic liquor — **drink•able** *adj* — **drink•er** *n*

drip *vb* **:** fall or let fall in drops ~ *n* **1 :** a dripping **2 :** sound of falling drops

drive *vb* **drove; driv•en 1 :** urge or force onward **2 :** direct the movement or course of **3 :** compel **4 :** cause to become **5 :** propel forcefully ~ *n* **1 :** trip in a vehicle **2 :** intensive campaign **3 :** aggressive or dynamic quality **4 :** basic need — **driv•er** *n*

drive–in *adj* **:** accommodating patrons in cars — **drive–in** *n*

driv•el *vb* **1 :** drool **2 :** talk stupidly ~ *n* **:** nonsense

drive•way *n* **:** usu. short private road from the street to a house

driz•zle *n* **:** fine misty rain — **drizzle** *vb*

drone *n* **1 :** male honeybee **2 :** deep hum or buzz ~ *vb* **:** make a dull monotonous sound

drool *vb* **:** let liquid run from the mouth

droop *vb* **1 :** hang or incline downward **2 :** lose strength or spirit — **droop** *n* — **droopy** *adj*

drop *n* **1 :** quantity of fluid in one spherical mass **2** *pl* **:** medicine used by drops **3 :** decline or fall **4 :** distance something drops ~ *vb* **1 :** fall in drops **2 :** let fall **3 :** convey **4 :** go lower or become less strong or less active — **drop•let** *n* — **drop•per** *n* — **drop back** *vb* **:** move toward the rear — **drop behind :** fail to keep up — **drop in** *vb* **:** pay an unexpected visit

drought *n* **:** long dry spell

drove *past of* DRIVE

drown *vb* **1 :** suffocate in water **2 :** overpower or become overpowered

drowsy *adj* **:** sleepy — **drows•i•ly** *adv* — **drows•i•ness** *n*

drug *n* **1 :** substance used as or in medicine **2 :** narcotic ~ *vb* **:** affect with drugs — **drug•gist** *n* — **drug•store** *n*

drum *n* **1 :** musical instrument that is a skin-covered cylinder beaten usu. with sticks **2 :** drum-shaped object (as a container) ~ *vb* **1**

: beat a drum **2 :** drive, force, or bring about by steady effort — **drum•beat** *n* — **drum•mer** *n*

drum•stick *n* **1 :** stick for beating a drum **2 :** lower part of a fowl's leg

drunk *adj* **:** having the faculties impaired by alcohol ~ *n* **:** one who is drunk — **drunk•ard** *n* — **drunk•en** *adj* — **drunk•en•ly** *adv* — **drunk•en•ness** *n*

dry *adj* **1 :** lacking water or moisture **2 :** thirsty **3 :** marked by the absence of alcoholic beverages **4 :** uninteresting **5 :** not sweet ~ *vb* **:** make or become dry — **dry•ly** *adv* — **dry•ness** *n*

dry–clean *vb* **:** clean (fabrics) chiefly with solvents other than water — **dry cleaning** *n*

dry•er *n* **:** device for drying

du•al *adj* **:** twofold — **du•al•ism** *n* — **du•al•i•ty** *n*

dub *vb* **:** name

du•bi•ous *adj* **1 :** uncertain **2 :** questionable — **du•bi•ous•ly** *adv* — **du•bi•ous•ness** *n*

duch•ess *n* **1 :** wife of a duke **2 :** woman holding a ducal title

[1]**duck** *n* **:** swimming bird related to the goose and swan ~ *vb* **1 :** thrust or plunge under water **2 :** lower the head or body suddenly **3 :** evade — **duck•ling** *n*

[2]**duck** *n* **:** cotton fabric

duct *n* **:** canal for conveying a fluid — **duct•less** *adj*

dude *n* **1 :** dandy **2 :** guy

due *adj* **1 :** owed **2 :** appropriate **3 :** attributable **4 :** scheduled ~ *n* **1 :** something due **2** *pl* **:** fee ~ *adv* **:** directly

du•el *n* **:** combat between 2 persons — **du•el** *vb* — **du•el•ist** *n*

du•et *n* **:** musical composition for 2 performers

dug *past of* DIG

dug•out *n* **1 :** boat made by hollowing out a log **2 :** shelter made by digging

duke *n* **:** nobleman of the highest rank — **duke•dom** *n*

dull *adj* **1 :** mentally slow **2 :** blunt **3 :** not brilliant or interesting — **dull** *vb* — **dul•lard** *n* — **dull•ness** *n* — **dul•ly** *adv*

du•ly *adv* **:** in a due manner or time

dumb *adj* **1 :** mute **2 :** stupid — **dumb•ly** *adv*

dumb•bell *n* **1 :** short bar with weights on the ends used for exercise **2 :** stupid person

dumb•found, dum•found *vb* **:** amaze

dum•my *n* **1 :** stupid person **2 :** imitative substitute

dump *vb* **:** let fall in a pile ~ *n* **:** place for dumping something (as refuse) — **in the dumps :** sad

dump•ling *n* **:** small mass of boiled or steamed dough

dumpy *adj* **:** short and thick in build

[1]**dun** *adj* **:** brownish gray

[2]**dun** *vb* **:** hound for payment of a debt

dunce *n* **:** stupid person

dune *n* **:** hill of sand

dung *n* **:** manure

dun•ga•ree *n* **1 :** blue denim **2** *pl* **:** work clothes made of dungaree

dun•geon *n* **:** underground prison

dunk *vb* **:** dip temporarily into liquid

duo *n* **:** pair

dupe *n* **:** one easily deceived or cheated — **dupe** *vb*

du•plex *adj* **:** double ~ *n* **:** 2-family house

du•pli•cate *adj* **1 :** consisting of 2 identical items **2 :** being just like another ~ *n* **:** exact copy ~ *vb* **1 :** make an exact copy of **2 :** repeat or equal — **du•pli•ca•tion** *n* — **du•pli•ca•tor** *n*

du•ra•ble *adj* **:** lasting a long time — **du•ra•bil•i•ty** *n*

du•ra•tion *n* **:** length of time something lasts

du•ress *n* **:** coercion

dur•ing *prep* **1 :** throughout **2 :** at some point in

dusk *n* **:** twilight — **dusky** *adj*

dust *n* **:** powdered matter ~ *vb* **1 :** remove dust from **2 :** sprinkle with fine particles — **dust•er** *n* — **dust•pan** *n* — **dusty** *adj*

du•ty *n* **1 :** action required by one's occupation or position **2 :** moral or legal obligation **3 :** tax — **du•te•ous** *adj* — **du•ti•able** *adj* — **du•ti•ful** *adj*

DVD *n* **:** digital video disk

dwarf *n* **:** one that is much below normal size ~ *vb* **1 :** stunt **2 :** cause to seem smaller — **dwarf•ish** *adj*

dwell *vb* **1 :** reside **2 :** keep the attention directed — **dwell•er** *n* — **dwell•ing** *n*

dwin•dle *vb* **:** become steadily less

dye *n* **:** coloring material ~ *vb* **:** give a new color to

dying *pres part of* DIE

dyke *var of* DIKE
dy•nam•ic *adj* **1 :** relating to physical force producing motion **2 :** energetic or forceful
dy•na•mite *n* **:** explosive made of nitroglycerin — **dynamite** *vb*
dy•na•mo *n* **:** electrical generator
dy•nas•ty *n* **:** succession of rulers of the same family — **dy•nas•tic** *adj*
dys•lex•ia *n* **:** disturbance of the ability to read — **dys•lex•ic** *adj*
dys•tro•phy *n* **:** disorder involving nervous and muscular tissue

E

e *n* **:** 5th letter of the alphabet
each *adj* **:** being one of the class named ~ *pron* **:** every individual one ~ *adv* **:** apiece
ea•ger *adj* **:** enthusiastic or anxious — **ea•ger•ly** *adv* — **ea•ger•ness** *n*
ea•gle *n* **:** large bird of prey
[1]**ear** *n* **:** organ of hearing or the outer part of this — **ear•ache** *n* — **ear•drum** *n* — **eared** *adj* — **ear•lobe** *n* — **ear•phone** *n* — **ear•ring** *n*
[2]**ear** *n* **:** fruiting head of a cereal
earl *n* **:** British nobleman — **earl•dom** *n*
ear•ly *adj* **1 :** relating to or occurring near the beginning or before the usual time **2 :** ancient — **early** *adv*
earn *vb* **1 :** receive as a return for service **2 :** deserve
ear•nest *n* **:** serious state of mind — **earnest** *adj* — **ear•nest•ly** *adv* — **ear•nest•ness** *n*
earn•ings *n pl* **:** something earned
ear•shot *n* **:** range of hearing
earth *n* **1 :** soil or land **2 :** planet inhabited by man — **earth•li•ness** *n* — **earth•ly** *adj* — **earth•ward** *adv*
earth•quake *n* **:** shaking or trembling of the earth
earth•worm *n* **:** long segmented worm
earthy *adj* **1 :** relating to or consisting of earth **2 :** practical **3 :** coarse — **earth•i•ness** *n*
ease *n* **1 :** comfort **2 :** naturalness of manner **3 :** freedom from difficulty ~ *vb* **1 :** relieve from distress **2 :** lessen the tension of **3 :** make easier
ea•sel *n* **:** frame to hold a painter's canvas
east *adv* **:** to or toward the east ~ *adj* **:** situated toward or at or coming from the east ~ *n* **1 :** direction of sunrise **2** *cap* **:** regions to the east — **east•er•ly** *adv or adj* — **east•ward** *adv or adj* — **east•wards** *adv*
Eas•ter *n* **:** church feast celebrating Christ's resurrection
east•ern *adj* **1** *cap* **:** relating to a region designated East **2 :** lying toward or coming from the east — **East•ern•er** *n*
easy *adj* **1 :** marked by ease **2 :** lenient — **eas•i•ly** *adv* — **eas•i•ness** *n*
easy•go•ing *adj* **:** relaxed and casual
eat *vb* (**ate; eat•en**) **1 :** take in as food **2 :** use up or corrode — **eat•able** *adj or n* — **eat•er** *n*
eaves•drop *vb* **:** listen secretly — **eaves•drop•per** *n*
ebb *n* **1 :** outward flow of the tide **2 :** decline ~ *vb* **1 :** recede from the flood state **2 :** wane
ec•cen•tric *adj* **1 :** odd in behavior **2 :** being off center — **eccentric** *n* — **ec•cen•tri•cal•ly** *adv* — **ec•cen•tric•i•ty** *n*
ec•cle•si•as•ti•cal, ecclesiastic *adj* **:** relating to a church — **ec•cle•si•as•ti•cal•ly** *adv*
echo *n* **:** repetition of a sound caused by a reflection of the sound waves — **echo** *vb*
éclair *n* **:** custard-filled pastry
eclec•tic *adj* **:** drawing or drawn from varied sources
eclipse *n* **:** total or partial obscuring of one celestial body by another — **eclipse** *vb*
ecol•o•gy *n* **:** science concerned with the interaction of organisms and their environment — **eco•log•i•cal** *adj* — **eco•log•i•cal•ly** *adv* — **ecol•o•gist** *n*
eco•nom•ics *n* **:** branch of knowledge dealing with goods and services — **econ•o•mist** *n*
econ•o•my *n* **1 :** thrifty use of resources **2 :** economic system — **eco•nom•ic** *adj* — **eco•nom•i•cal** *adj* — **ec•o•nom•i•cal•ly** *adv* — **econ•o•mize** *vb* — **econ•o•miz•er** *n* — **econ•o•my** *adj*
ec•sta•sy *n* **:** extreme emotional excitement — **ec•stat•ic** *adj* — **ec•stat•i•cal•ly** *adv*
ec•u•men•i•cal *adj* **:** promoting worldwide Christian unity
ed•dy *n* **:** whirlpool — **eddy** *vb*
Eden *n* **:** paradise
edge *n* **1 :** cutting side of a blade **2 :** line where something begins or ends ~ *vb* **1 :** give or form an edge **2 :** move gradually **3 :** narrowly defeat — **edg•er** *n*
edge•wise *adv* **:** sideways

edgy *adj* **:** nervous — **edg•i•ness** *n*
ed•i•ble *adj* **:** fit or safe to be eaten — **ed•i•bil•i•ty** *n* — **edible** *n*
ed•it *vb* **1 :** revise and prepare for publication **2 :** delete — **ed•i•tor** *n* — **ed•i•tor•ship** *n*
edi•tion *n* **1 :** form in which a text is published **2 :** total number published at one time
ed•i•to•ri•al *adj* **1 :** relating to an editor or editing **2 :** expressing opinion ~ *n* **:** article (as in a newspaper) expressing the views of an editor — **ed•i•to•ri•al•ize** *vb* — **ed•i•to•ri•al•ly** *adv*
ed•u•cate *vb* **1 :** give instruction to **2 :** develop mentally and morally **3 :** provide with information — **ed•u•ca•ble** *adj* — **ed•u•ca•tion** *n* — **ed•u•ca•tion•al** *adj* — **ed•u•ca•tor** *n*
eel *n* **:** snakelike fish
ee•rie *adj* **:** weird — **ee•ri•ly** *adv*
ef•fect *n* **1 :** result **2 :** meaning **3 :** influence **4** *pl* **:** goods or possessions ~ *vb* **:** cause to happen — **in effect :** in substance
ef•fec•tive *adj* **1 :** producing a strong or desired effect **2 :** being in operation — **ef•fec•tive•ly** *adv* — **ef•fec•tive•ness** *n*
ef•fec•tu•al *adj* **:** producing an intended effect — **ef•fec•tu•al•ly** *adv* — **ef•fec•tu•al•ness** *n*
ef•fem•i•nate *adj* **:** having qualities more typical of women than men — **ef•fem•i•na•cy** *n*
ef•fer•vesce *vb* **1 :** bubble and hiss as gas escapes **2 :** show exhilaration — **ef•fer•ves•cence** *n* — **ef•fer•ves•cent** *adj* — **ef•fer•ves•cent•ly** *adv*
ef•fi•cient *adj* **:** working well with little waste — **ef•fi•cien•cy** *n* — **ef•fi•cient•ly** *adv*
ef•fort *n* **1 :** a putting forth of strength **2 :** use of resources toward a goal **3 :** product of effort — **ef•fort•less** *adj* — **ef•fort•less•ly** *adv*
¹egg *vb* **:** urge to action
²egg *n* **1 :** rounded usu. hard-shelled reproductive body esp. of birds and reptiles from which the young hatches **2 :** a female reproductive cell — **egg•shell** *n*
egg•plant *n* **:** edible purplish fruit of a plant related to the potato
ego *n* **:** self-esteem
ego•cen•tric *adj* **:** concerned only with one's own desires or interests
ego•tism *n* **:** exaggerated sense of self-importance — **ego•tist** *n* — **ego•tis•tic, ego•tis•ti•cal** *adj* — **ego•tis•ti•cal•ly** *adv*
egre•gious *adj* **:** notably bad — **egre•gious•ly** *adv*
ei•der•down *n* **:** soft down obtained from a northern sea duck (**eider**)
eight *n* **1 :** one more than 7 **2 :** 8th in a set or series **3 :** something having 8 units — **eight** *adj or pron* — **eighth** *adj or adv or n*
eigh•teen *n* **:** one more than 17 — **eigh•teen** *adj or pron* — **eigh•teenth** *adj or n*
eighty *n* **:** 8 times 10 — **eight•i•eth** *adj or n* — **eighty** *adj or pron*
ei•ther *adj* **1 :** both **2 :** being the one or the other of two ~ *pron* **:** one of two or more ~ *conj* **:** one or the other
ejac•u•late *vb* **1 :** say suddenly **2 :** eject a fluid (as semen) — **ejac•u•la•tion** *n*
eject *vb* **:** drive or throw out — **ejec•tion** *n*
eke *vb* **:** barely gain with effort — usu. with *out*
elab•o•rate *adj* **1 :** planned in detail **2 :** complex and ornate ~ *vb* **:** work out in detail — **elab•o•rate•ly** *adv* — **elab•o•rate•ness** *n* — **elab•o•ra•tion** *n*
elapse *vb* **:** slip by
elas•tic *adj* **1 :** springy **2 :** flexible ~ *n* **1 :** elastic material **2 :** rubber band — **elas•tic•i•ty** *n*
elate *vb* **:** fill with joy — **ela•tion** *n*
el•bow *n* **1 :** joint of the arm **2 :** elbow-shaped bend or joint ~ *vb* **:** push aside with the elbow
el•der *adj* **:** older ~ *n* **1 :** one who is older **2 :** church officer
el•der•ly *adj* **:** past middle age
el•dest *adj* **:** oldest
elect *vb* **:** choose esp. by vote ~ *adj* **:** elected but not yet in office ~ *n* **elect** *pl* **:** exclusive group — **elec•tion** *n* — **elec•tive** *n or adj* — **elec•tor** *n* — **elec•tor•al** *adj*
elec•tric *adj* **1** *or* **elec•tri•cal :** relating to or run by electricity **2 :** thrilling — **elec•tri•cal•ly** *adv*
elec•tri•cian *n* **:** person who installs or repairs electrical equipment
elec•tric•i•ty *n* **1 :** fundamental form of energy occurring naturally (as in lightning) or produced artificially **2 :** electric current
elec•tri•fy *vb* **1 :** charge with electricity **2 :** equip for use of electric power **3 :** thrill — **elec•tri•fi•ca•tion** *n*
elec•tro•cute *vb* **:** kill by an electric shock — **elec•tro•cu•tion** *n*
elec•tro•mag•net *n* **:** magnet made using electric current
elec•tro•mag•ne•tism *n* **:** natural force responsible for interactions between charged parti-

cles — **elec•tro•mag•net•ic** *adj* — **elec•tro•mag•net•i•cal•ly** *adv*
elec•tron *n* : negatively charged particle within the atom
elec•tron•ic *adj* : relating to electrons or electronics — **elec•tron•i•cal•ly** *adv*
elec•tron•ics *n* : physics of electrons and their use esp. in devices
el•e•gance *n* : refined gracefulness — **el•e•gant** *adj* — **el•e•gant•ly** *adv*
el•e•ment *n* **1** *pl* : weather conditions **2** : natural environment **3** : constituent part **4** *pl* : simplest principles **5** : substance that has atoms of only one kind — **el•e•men•tal** *adj*
el•e•men•ta•ry *adj* **1** : simple **2** : relating to the basic subjects of education
el•e•phant *n* : huge mammal with a trunk and 2 ivory tusks
el•e•vate *vb* **1** : lift up **2** : exalt
el•e•va•tion *n* : height or a high place
el•e•va•tor *n* **1** : cage or platform for raising or lowering something **2** : grain storehouse
elev•en *n* **1** : one more than 10 **2** : 11th in a set or series **3** : something having 11 units — **eleven** *adj or pron* — **elev•enth** *adj or n*
elf *n* **elves** : mischievous fairy — **elf•in** *adj* — **elf•ish** *adj*
elic•it *vb* : draw forth
el•i•gi•ble *adj* : qualified to participate or to be chosen — **el•i•gi•bil•i•ty** *n*
elim•i•nate *vb* : get rid of — **elim•i•na•tion** *n*
elite *n* : choice or select group
elk *n* : large deer
el•lipse *n* : oval
el•lip•sis *n* **1** : omission of a word **2** : marks (as . . .) to show omission
el•lip•ti•cal, el•lip•tic *adj* **1** : relating to or shaped like an ellipse **2** : relating to or marked by ellipsis
elm *n* : tall shade tree
elon•gate *vb* : make or grow longer — **elon•ga•tion** *n*
elope *vb* : run away esp. to be married — **elope•ment** *n* — **elop•er** *n*
else *adv* **1** : in a different way, time, or place **2** : otherwise ~ *adj* **1** : other **2** : more
else•where *adv* : in or to another place
elude *vb* : evade — **elu•sive** *adj* — **elu•sive•ly** *adv* — **elu•sive•ness** *n*
elves *pl of* ELF
e–mail *n* : message sent or received via computers
em•bank•ment *n* : protective barrier of earth
em•bar•go *n* : ban on trade — **embargo** *vb*
em•bark *vb* **1** : go on board a ship or airplane **2** : make a start — **em•bar•ka•tion** *n*
em•bar•rass *vb* : cause distress and self-consciousness — **em•bar•rass•ment** *n*
em•bas•sy *n* : residence and offices of an ambassador
em•bel•lish *vb* : decorate — **em•bel•lish•ment** *n*
em•bez•zle *vb* : steal (money) by falsifying records — **em•bez•zle•ment** *n* — **em•bez•zler** *n*
em•blem *n* : symbol — **em•blem•at•ic** *adj*
em•body *vb* : give definite form or expression to — **em•bodi•ment** *n*
em•brace *vb* **1** : clasp in the arms **2** : welcome **3** : include — **embrace** *n*
em•broi•der *vb* : ornament with or do needlework — **em•broi•dery** *n*
em•bryo *n* : living being in its earliest stages of development — **em•bry•on•ic** *adj*
em•er•ald *n* : green gem ~ *adj* : bright green
emerge *vb* : rise, come forth, or appear — **emer•gence** *n* — **emer•gent** *adj*
emer•gen•cy *n* : condition requiring prompt action
em•i•grate *vb* : leave a country to settle elsewhere — **em•i•grant** *n* — **em•i•gra•tion** *n*
em•i•nence *n* **1** : prominence or superiority **2** : person of high rank
em•i•nent *adj* : prominent — **em•i•nent•ly** *adv*
emis•sion *n* : substance discharged into the air
emit *vb* : give off or out
emo•tion *n* : intense feeling — **emo•tion•al** *adj* — **emo•tion•al•ly** *adv*
em•per•or *n* : ruler of an empire
em•pha•sis *n* : stress
em•pha•size *vb* : stress
em•phat•ic *adj* : uttered with emphasis — **em•phat•i•cal•ly** *adv*
em•pire *n* : large state or a group of states
em•ploy *vb* **1** : use **2** : occupy ~ *n* : paid occupation — **em•ploy•ee, em•ploye** *n* — **em•ploy•er** *n* — **em•ploy•ment** *n*
em•pow•er *vb* : give power to — **em•pow•er•ment** *n*
em•press *n* **1** : wife of an emperor **2** : woman emperor
emp•ty *adj* **1** : containing nothing **2** : not occupied **3** : lacking value, sense, or purpose ~ *vb* : make or become empty — **emp•ti•ness** *n*
em•u•late *vb* : try to equal or excel — **em•u•la•tion** *n*

emul•sion *n* **1 :** mixture of mutually insoluble liquids **2 :** light-sensitive coating on photographic film
en•able *vb* **:** give power, capacity, or ability to
en•act *vb* **1 :** make into law **2 :** act out — **en•act•ment** *n*
enam•el *n* **1 :** glasslike substance used to coat metal or pottery **2 :** hard outer layer of a tooth **3 :** glossy paint — **enamel** *vb*
en•chant *vb* **1 :** bewitch **2 :** fascinate — **en•chant•er** *n* — **en•chant•ment** *n* — **en•chant•ress** *n*
en•cir•cle *vb* **:** surround
en•close *vb* **1 :** shut up or surround **2 :** include — **en•clo•sure** *n*
en•com•pass *vb* **:** surround or include
en•core *n* **:** further performance
en•coun•ter *vb* **1 :** fight **2 :** meet unexpectedly — **encounter** *n*
en•cour•age *vb* **1 :** inspire with courage and hope **2 :** foster — **en•cour•age•ment** *n*
en•crust *vb* **:** coat or cover with or as if with a crust
en•cy•clo•pe•dia *n* **:** reference work on many subjects — **en•cy•clo•pe•dic** *adj*
end *n* **1 :** point at which something stops or no longer exists **2 :** process or act of stopping **3 :** purpose ~ *vb* **1 :** stop or finish **2 :** be at the end of — **end•less** *adj* — **end•less•ly** *adv*
en•dan•ger *vb* **:** bring into danger
en•dear *vb* **:** make dear — **en•dear•ment** *n*
en•deav•or *vb or n* **:** attempt
end•ing *n* **:** end
en•do•crine *adj* **:** producing secretions distributed by the bloodstream
en•dorse *vb* **1 :** sign one's name to **2 :** approve — **en•dorse•ment** *n*
en•dow *vb* **1 :** furnish with funds **2 :** furnish naturally — **en•dow•ment** *n*
en•dure *vb* **1 :** last **2 :** suffer patiently **3 :** tolerate — **en•dur•able** *adj* — **en•dur•ance** *n*
en•e•my *n* **:** one that attacks or tries to harm another
en•er•get•ic *adj* **:** full of energy or activity — **en•er•get•i•cal•ly** *adv*
en•er•gize *vb* **:** give energy to
en•er•gy *n* **1 :** capacity for action **2 :** vigorous action **3 :** capacity for doing work
en•er•vate *vb* **:** make weak or listless — **en•er•va•tion** *n*
en•force *vb* **1 :** compel **2 :** carry out — **en•force•able** *adj* — **en•force•ment** *n*
en•fran•chise *vb* **:** grant voting rights to — **en•fran•chise•ment** *n*
en•gage *vb* **1 :** participate or cause to participate **2 :** bring or come into working contact **3 :** bind by a pledge to marry **4 :** hire **5 :** bring or enter into conflict — **en•gage•ment** *n*
en•gag•ing *adj* **:** attractive
en•gine *n* **1 :** machine that converts energy into mechanical motion **2 :** locomotive
en•gi•neer *n* **1 :** one trained in engineering **2 :** engine operator ~ *vb* **:** lay out or manage as an engineer
en•gi•neer•ing *n* **:** practical application of science and mathematics
en•grave *vb* **:** cut into a surface — **en•grav•er** *n* — **en•grav•ing** *n*
en•gross *vb* **:** occupy fully
en•gulf *vb* **:** swallow up
en•hance *vb* **:** improve in value — **en•hance•ment** *n*
enig•ma *n* **:** puzzle or mystery — **enig•mat•ic** *adj* — **enig•mat•i•cal•ly** *adv*
en•joy *vb* **:** take pleasure in — **en•joy•able** *adj* — **en•joy•ment** *n*
en•large *vb* **:** make or grow larger — **en•large•ment** *n* — **en•larg•er** *n*
en•light•en *vb* **:** give knowledge or spiritual insight to — **en•light•en•ment** *n*
en•list *vb* **1 :** join the armed forces **2 :** get the aid of — **en•list•ee** *n* — **en•list•ment** *n*
en•liv•en *vb* **:** give life or spirit to
enor•mi•ty *n* **1 :** great wickedness **2 :** huge size
enor•mous *adj* **:** great in size, number, or degree — **enor•mous•ly** *adv* — **enor•mous•ness** *n*
enough *adj* **:** adequate ~ *adv* **1 :** in an adequate manner **2 :** in a tolerable degree ~ *pron* **:** adequate number, quantity, or amount
en•quire, en•qui•ry *var of* INQUIRE, INQUIRY
en•rage *vb* **:** fill with rage
en•rich *vb* **:** make rich — **en•rich•ment** *n*
en•roll, en•rol *vb* **1 :** enter on a list **2 :** become enrolled — **en•roll•ment** *n*
en route *adv or adj* **:** on or along the way
en•sem•ble *n* **1 :** small group **2 :** complete costume
en•shrine *vb* **1 :** put in a shrine **2 :** cherish
en•sign *n* **1 :** flag **2 :** lowest ranking commissioned officer in the navy
en•slave *vb* **:** make a slave of — **en•slave•ment** *n*
en•sure *vb* **:** guarantee

en•tail *vb* **:** involve as a necessary result
en•tan•gle *vb* **:** tangle — **en•tan•gle•ment** *n*
en•ter *vb* **1 :** go or come in or into **2 :** start **3 :** set down (as in a list)
en•ter•prise *n* **1 :** an undertaking **2 :** business organization **3 :** initiative
en•ter•pris•ing *adj* **:** showing initiative
en•ter•tain *vb* **1 :** treat or receive as a guest **2 :** hold in mind **3 :** amuse — **en•ter•tain•er** *n* — **en•ter•tain•ment** *n*
en•thrall, en•thral *vb* **:** hold spellbound
en•thu•si•asm *n* **:** strong excitement of feeling or its cause — **en•thu•si•ast** *n* — **en•thu•si•as•tic** *adj* — **en•thu•si•as•ti•cal•ly** *adv*
en•tice *vb* **:** tempt — **en•tice•ment** *n*
en•tire *adj* **:** complete or whole — **en•tire•ly** *adv* — **en•tire•ty** *n*
en•ti•tle *vb* **1 :** name **2 :** give a right to
en•ti•ty *n* **:** something with separate existence
en•tou•rage *n* **:** group of attendants
en•trails *n pl* **:** intestines
[1]**en•trance** *n* **1 :** act of entering **2 :** means or place of entering — **en•trant** *n*
[2]**en•trance** *vb* **:** fascinate or delight
en•trap *vb* **:** trap — **en•trap•ment** *n*
en•treat *vb* **:** ask urgently — **en•treaty** *n*
en•trée, en•tree *n* **:** principal dish of the meal
en•tre•pre•neur *n* **:** organizer or promoter of an enterprise
en•trust *vb* **:** commit to another with confidence
en•try *n* **1 :** entrance **2 :** an entering in a record or an item so entered
enu•mer•ate *vb* **1 :** count **2 :** list — **enu•mer•a•tion** *n*
en•vel•op *vb* **:** surround — **en•vel•op•ment** *n*
en•ve•lope *n* **:** paper container for a letter
en•vi•ron•ment *n* **:** surroundings — **en•vi•ron•men•tal** *adj*
en•vi•ron•men•tal•ist *n* **:** person concerned about the environment
en•vi•rons *n pl* **:** vicinity
en•vi•sion *vb* **:** picture to oneself
en•vy *n* **1 :** resentful awareness of another's advantage **2 :** object of envy ~ *vb* **:** feel envy toward or on account of — **en•vi•able** *adj* — **en•vi•ous** *adj* — **en•vi•ous•ly** *adv*
en•zyme *n* **:** biological catalyst
eon *n* **:** indefinitely long time
ep•ic *n* **:** long poem about a hero — **epic** *adj*
ep•i•dem•ic *adj* **:** affecting many persons at one time — **epidemic** *n*
epi•der•mis *n* **:** outer layer of skin
ep•i•lep•sy *n* **:** nervous disorder marked by convulsive attacks — **ep•i•lep•tic** *adj or n*
epis•co•pal *adj* **:** governed by bishops
ep•i•sode *n* **:** occurrence — **ep•i•sod•ic** *adj*
ep•i•taph *n* **:** inscription in memory of a dead person
ep•i•thet *n* **:** characterizing often abusive word or phrase
epit•o•me *n* **1 :** summary **2 :** ideal example — **epit•o•mize** *vb*
ep•och *n* **:** extended period — **ep•och•al** *adj*
ep•oxy *n* **:** synthetic resin used esp. in adhesives ~ *vb* **:** glue with epoxy
equal *adj* **:** of the same quantity, value, quality, number, or status as another ~ *n* **:** one that is equal ~ *vb* **:** be or become equal to — **equal•i•ty** *n* — **equal•ize** *vb* — **equal•ly** *adv*
equate *vb* **:** treat or regard as equal
equa•tion *n* **:** mathematical statement that two things are equal
equa•tor *n* **:** imaginary circle that separates the northern and southern hemispheres — **equa•to•ri•al** *adj*
equi•lib•ri•um *n* **:** state of balance
equi•nox *n* **:** time when day and night are everywhere of equal length
equip *vb* **:** furnish with needed resources — **equip•ment** *n*
eq•ui•ta•ble *adj* **:** fair
eq•ui•ty *n* **1 :** justice **2 :** value of a property less debt
equiv•a•lent *adj* **:** equal — **equiv•a•lence** *n* — **equivalent** *n*
equiv•o•cate *vb* **1 :** use misleading language **2 :** avoid answering definitely — **equiv•o•cal** *adj* — **equiv•o•ca•tion** *n*
era *n* **:** period of time associated with something
erad•i•cate *vb* **:** do away with
erase *vb* **:** rub or scratch out — **eras•er** *n* — **era•sure** *n*
erect *adj* **:** not leaning or lying down ~ *vb* **1 :** build **2 :** bring to an upright position — **erec•tion** *n*
erode *vb* **:** wear away gradually
ero•sion *n* **:** process of eroding
erot•ic *adj* **:** sexually arousing — **erot•i•cal•ly** *adv* — **erot•i•cism** *n*
err *vb* **:** be or do wrong
er•rand *n* **:** short trip taken to do something often for another
er•rat•ic *adj* **1 :** eccentric **2 :** not consistent — **er•rat•i•cal•ly** *adv*

er•ro•ne•ous *adj* : wrong — **er•ro•ne•ous•ly** *adv*

er•ror *n* **1** : something that is not accurate **2** : state of being wrong

erupt *vb* : burst forth esp. suddenly and violently — **erup•tion** *n* — **erup•tive** *adj*

es•ca•late *vb* : become quickly larger or greater — **es•ca•la•tion** *n*

es•ca•la•tor *n* : moving stairs

es•ca•pade *n* : mischievous adventure

es•cape *vb* : get away or get away from ~ *n* **1** : flight from or avoidance of something unpleasant **2** : leakage **3** : means of escape ~ *adj* : providing means of escape — **es•cap•ee** *n*

es•cort *n* : one accompanying another — **escort** *vb*

esoph•a•gus *n* : muscular tube connecting the mouth and stomach

es•pe•cial•ly *adv* : particularly or notably

es•pi•o•nage *n* : practice of spying

espres•so *n* : strong steam-brewed coffee

es•quire *n* — used as a title of courtesy

es•say *n* : literary composition ~ *vb* : attempt — **es•say•ist** *n*

es•sence *n* **1** : fundamental nature or quality **2** : extract **3** : perfume

es•sen•tial *adj* : basic or necessary — **essential** *n* — **es•sen•tial•ly** *adv*

es•tab•lish *vb* **1** : bring into existence **2** : put on a firm basis **3** : cause to be recognized — **es•tab•lish•ment** *n*

es•tate *n* **1** : one's possessions **2** : large piece of land with a house

es•teem *n or vb* : regard

es•ti•mate *vb* : judge the approximate value, size, or cost ~ *n* **1** : rough or approximate calculation **2** : statement of the cost of a job — **es•ti•ma•tion** *n* — **es•ti•ma•tor** *n*

es•trange *vb* : make hostile — **es•trange•ment** *n*

et cet•era : and others esp. of the same kind

etch *vb* : produce by corroding parts of a surface with acid — **etch•er** *n* — **etch•ing** *n*

eter•nal *adj* : lasting forever — **eter•nal•ly** *adv*

eter•ni•ty *n* : infinite duration

eth•a•nol *n* : alcohol

eth•i•cal *adj* **1** : relating to ethics **2** : honorable — **eth•i•cal•ly** *adv*

eth•ics *n sing or pl* **1** : study of good and evil and moral duty **2** : moral principles or practice

eth•nic *adj* : relating to races or groups of people with common customs ~ *n* : member of a minority ethnic group

et•i•quette *n* : good manners

Eu•cha•rist *n* : Communion — **eu•cha•ris•tic** *adj*

eu•lo•gy *n* : speech in praise — **eu•lo•gis•tic** *adj* — **eu•lo•gize** *vb*

eu•phe•mism *n* : substitution of a pleasant expression for an unpleasant or offensive one — **eu•phe•mis•tic** *adj*

eu•pho•ria *n* : elation — **eu•phor•ic** *adj*

eu•ro *n* : common monetary unit of most of the European Union

eu•tha•na•sia *n* : mercy killing

evac•u•ate *vb* **1** : discharge wastes from the body **2** : remove or withdraw from — **evac•u•a•tion** *n*

evade *vb* : manage to avoid — **eva•sion** *n* — **eva•sive** *adj* — **eva•sive•ness** *n*

eval•u•ate *vb* : appraise — **eval•u•a•tion** *n*

evan•ge•lism *n* : the winning or revival of personal commitments to Christ — **evan•gel•i•cal** *adj* — **evan•ge•list** *n* — **evan•ge•lis•tic** *adj*

evap•o•rate *vb* **1** : pass off in or convert into vapor **2** : disappear quickly — **evap•o•ra•tion** *n* — **evap•ora•tor** *n*

even *adj* **1** : smooth **2** : equal or fair **3** : fully revenged **4** : divisible by 2 ~ *adv* **1** : already **2** — used for emphasis ~ *vb* : make or become even — **even•ly** *adv* — **even•ness** *n*

eve•ning *n* : early part of the night

event *n* **1** : occurrence **2** : noteworthy happening **3** : eventuality — **event•ful** *adj*

even•tu•al *adj* : later — **even•tu•al•ly** *adv*

even•tu•al•i•ty *n* : possible occurrence or outcome

ev•er *adv* **1** : always **2** : at any time **3** : in any case

ev•er•green *adj* : having foliage that remains green — **evergreen** *n*

ev•er•last•ing *adj* : lasting forever

ev•ery *adj* **1** : being each one of a group **2** : all possible

ev•ery•body *pron* : every person

ev•ery•day *adj* : ordinary

ev•ery•one *pron* : every person

ev•ery•thing *pron* : all that exists

ev•ery•where *adv* : in every place or part

evict *vb* : force (a person) to move from a property — **evic•tion** *n*

ev•i•dence *n* **1** : outward sign **2** : proof or testimony

ev•i•dent *adj* : clear or obvious — **ev•i•dent•ly** *adv*
evil *adj* : wicked ~ *n* **1** : sin **2** : source of sorrow or distress — **evil•do•er** *n* — **evil•ly** *adv*
evoke *vb* : call forth or up — **evo•ca•tion** *n* — **evoc•a•tive** *adj*
evo•lu•tion *n* : process of change by degrees — **evo•lu•tion•ary** *adj*
evolve *vb* : develop or change by degrees
ewe *n* : female sheep
ex•act *vb* : compel to furnish ~ *adj* : precisely correct — **ex•act•ing** *adj* — **ex•ac•ti•tude** *n* — **ex•act•ly** *adv* — **ex•act•ness** *n*
ex•ag•ger•ate *vb* : say more than is true — **ex•ag•ger•at•ed•ly** *adv* — **ex•ag•ger•a•tion** *n* — **ex•ag•ger•a•tor** *n*
ex•alt *vb* : glorify — **ex•al•ta•tion** *n*
ex•am *n* : examination
ex•am•ine *vb* **1** : inspect closely **2** : test by questioning — **ex•am•i•na•tion** *n*
ex•am•ple *n* **1** : representative sample **2** : model **3** : problem to be solved for teaching purposes
ex•as•per•ate *vb* : thoroughly annoy — **ex•as•per•a•tion** *n*
ex•ca•vate *vb* : dig or hollow out — **ex•ca•va•tion** *n* — **ex•ca•va•tor** *n*
ex•ceed *vb* **1** : go or be beyond the limit of **2** : do better than
ex•ceed•ing•ly *adv* : extremely
ex•cel *vb* : do extremely well or far better than
ex•cel•len•cy *n* — used as a title of honor
ex•cel•lent *adj* : very good — **ex•cel•lence** *n* — **ex•cel•lent•ly** *adv*
ex•cept *vb* : omit ~ *prep* : excluding ~ *conj* : but — **ex•cep•tion** *n*
ex•cep•tion•al *adj* : superior — **ex•cep•tion•al•ly** *adv*
ex•cerpt *n* : brief passage ~ *vb* : select an excerpt
ex•cess *n* : amount left over — **excess** *adj* — **ex•ces•sive** *adj* — **ex•ces•sive•ly** *adv*
ex•change *n* **1** : the giving or taking of one thing in return for another **2** : marketplace esp. for securities ~ *vb* : transfer in return for some equivalent — **ex•change•able** *adj*
ex•cise *n* : tax
ex•cite *vb* **1** : stir up **2** : kindle the emotions of — **ex•cit•abil•i•ty** *n* — **ex•cit•able** *adj* — **ex•ci•ta•tion** *n* — **ex•cit•ed•ly** *adv* — **ex•cite•ment** *n*
ex•claim *vb* : cry out esp. in delight — **ex•cla•ma•tion** *n* — **ex•clam•a•to•ry** *adj*
exclamation point *n* : punctuation mark ! used esp. after an interjection or exclamation
ex•clude *vb* : leave out — **ex•clu•sion** *n*
ex•clu•sive *adj* **1** : reserved for particular persons **2** : stylish **3** : sole — **exclusive** *n* — **ex•clu•sive•ly** *adv* — **ex•clu•sive•ness** *n*
ex•crete *vb* : eliminate wastes from the body — **ex•cre•ment** *n* — **ex•cre•tion** *n* — **ex•cre•to•ry** *adj*
ex•cru•ci•at•ing *adj* : intensely painful — **ex•cru•ci•at•ing•ly** *adv*
ex•cur•sion *n* : pleasure trip
ex•cuse *vb* **1** : pardon **2** : release from an obligation **3** : justify ~ *n* **1** : justification **2** : apology
ex•e•cute *vb* **1** : carry out fully **2** : enforce **3** : put to death — **ex•e•cu•tion** *n* — **ex•e•cu•tion•er** *n*
ex•ec•u•tive *adj* : relating to the carrying out of decisions, plans, or laws ~ *n* **1** : branch of government with executive duties **2** : administrator
ex•ec•u•tor *n* : person named in a will to execute it
ex•ec•u•trix *n* : woman executor
ex•em•pla•ry *adj* : so commendable as to serve as a model
ex•em•pli•fy *vb* : serve as an example of — **ex•em•pli•fi•ca•tion** *n*
ex•empt *adj* : being free from some liability ~ *vb* : make exempt — **ex•emp•tion** *n*
ex•er•cise *n* **1** : a putting into action **2** : exertion to develop endurance or a skill **3** *pl* : public ceremony ~ *vb* **1** : exert **2** : engage in exercise — **ex•er•cis•er** *n*
ex•ert *vb* : put into action — **ex•er•tion** *n*
ex•hale *vb* : breathe out — **ex•ha•la•tion** *n*
ex•haust *vb* **1** : draw out or develop completely **2** : use up **3** : tire or wear out ~ *n* : waste steam or gas from an engine or a system for removing it — **ex•haus•tion** *n* — **ex•haus•tive** *adj*
ex•hib•it *vb* : display esp. publicly ~ *n* **1** : act of exhibiting **2** : something exhibited — **ex•hi•bi•tion** *n* — **ex•hib•i•tor** *n*
ex•hil•a•rate *vb* : thrill — **ex•hil•a•ra•tion** *n*
ex•ile *n* **1** : banishment **2** : person banished from his or her country — **exile** *vb*
ex•ist *vb* **1** : have real or actual being **2** : live — **ex•is•tence** *n* — **ex•is•tent** *adj*
ex•it *n* **1** : departure **2** : way out of an enclosed space **3** : way off an expressway — **exit** *vb*
ex•o•dus *n* : mass departure

ex•on•er•ate *vb* : free from blame — **ex•on•er•a•tion** *n*
ex•or•bi•tant *adj* : exceeding what is usual or proper
ex•or•cise *vb* : drive out (as an evil spirit) — **ex•or•cism** *n* — **ex•or•cist** *n*
ex•ot•ic *adj* : foreign or strange — **exotic** *n* — **ex•ot•i•cal•ly** *adv*
ex•pand *vb* : enlarge — **ex•pan•sion** *n* — **ex•pan•sive** *adj* — **ex•pan•sive•ly** *adv* — **ex•pan•sive•ness** *n*
ex•panse *n* : very large area
ex•pa•tri•ate *n* : exile — **ex•pa•tri•ate** *adj or vb*
ex•pect *vb* **1** : look forward to **2** : consider probable or one's due — **ex•pec•tan•cy** *n* — **ex•pec•tant** *adj* — **ex•pec•tant•ly** *adv* — **ex•pec•ta•tion** *n*
ex•pe•di•ent *adj* : convenient or advantageous rather than right or just ∼ *n* : convenient often makeshift means to an end
ex•pe•dite *vb* : carry out or handle promptly — **ex•pe•dit•er** *n* — **ex•pe•di•tious** *adj*
ex•pe•di•tion *n* : long journey for work or research or the people making this
ex•pel *vb* : force out
ex•pend *vb* **1** : pay out **2** : use up — **ex•pend•able** *adj* — **ex•pen•di•ture** *n*
ex•pense *n* : cost — **ex•pen•sive** *adj* — **ex•pen•sive•ly** *adv*
ex•pe•ri•ence *n* **1** : a participating in or living through an event **2** : an event that affects one **3** : knowledge from doing ∼ *vb* : undergo
ex•per•i•ment *n* : test to discover something ∼ *vb* : make experiments — **ex•per•i•men•tal** *adj* — **ex•per•i•men•ta•tion** *n* — **ex•per•i•men•ter** *n*
ex•pert *adj* : thoroughly skilled ∼ *n* : person with special skill — **ex•pert•ly** *adv* — **ex•pert•ness** *n*
ex•per•tise *n* : skill
ex•pire *vb* **1** : breathe out **2** : die **3** : end — **ex•pi•ra•tion** *n*
ex•plain *vb* **1** : make clear **2** : give the reason for — **ex•plain•able** *adj* — **ex•pla•na•tion** *n* — **ex•plan•a•to•ry** *adj*
ex•ple•tive *n* : usu. profane exclamation
ex•plic•it *adj* : absolutely clear or precise — **ex•plic•it•ly** *adv* — **ex•plic•it•ness** *n*
ex•plode *vb* **1** : discredit **2** : burst or cause to burst violently **3** : increase rapidly — **ex•plo•sion** *n* — **ex•plo•sive** *adj* — **ex•plo•sive•ly** *adv*
ex•ploit *n* : heroic act ∼ *vb* **1** : utilize **2** : use unfairly — **ex•ploi•ta•tion** *n*
ex•plore *vb* : examine or range over thoroughly — **ex•plo•ra•tion** *n* — **ex•plor•ato•ry** *adj* — **ex•plor•er** *n*
ex•po•nent *n* **1** : mathematical symbol showing how many times a number is to be repeated as a factor **2** : advocate — **ex•po•nen•tial** *adj* — **ex•po•nen•tial•ly** *adv*
ex•port *vb* : send to foreign countries — **ex•port** *n* — **ex•por•ta•tion** *n* — **ex•port•er** *n*
ex•pose *vb* **1** : deprive of shelter or protection **2** : subject (film) to light **3** : make known — **ex•po•sure** *n*
ex•po•sé, ex•po•se *n* : exposure of something discreditable
ex•po•si•tion *n* : public exhibition
[1]**ex•press** *adj* **1** : clear **2** : specific **3** : traveling at high speed with few stops — **express** *adv or n* — **ex•press•ly** *adv*
[2]**express** *vb* **1** : make known in words or appearance **2** : press out (as juice)
ex•pres•sion *n* **1** : utterance **2** : mathematical symbol **3** : significant word or phrase **4** : look on one's face — **ex•pres•sive** *adj* — **ex•pres•sive•ness** *n*
ex•press•way *n* : high-speed divided highway with limited access
ex•pul•sion *n* : an expelling or being expelled
ex•qui•site *adj* **1** : flawlessly beautiful and delicate **2** : keenly discriminating
ex•tend *vb* **1** : stretch forth or out **2** : prolong **3** : enlarge — **ex•tend•able** *adj* — **ex•ten•sion** *n* — **ex•ten•sive** *adj* — **ex•ten•sive•ly** *adv*
ex•tent *n* : range, space, or degree to which something extends
ex•ten•u•ate *vb* : lessen the seriousness of — **ex•ten•u•a•tion** *n*
ex•te•ri•or *adj* : external ∼ *n* : external part or surface
ex•ter•mi•nate *vb* : destroy utterly — **ex•ter•mi•na•tion** *n* — **ex•ter•mi•na•tor** *n*
ex•ter•nal *adj* : relating to or on the outside — **ex•ter•nal•ly** *adv*
ex•tinct *adj* : no longer existing — **ex•tinc•tion** *n*
ex•tin•guish *vb* : cause to stop burning — **ex•tin•guish•able** *adj* — **ex•tin•guish•er** *n*
ex•tort *vb* : obtain by force or improper pressure — **ex•tor•tion** *n* — **ex•tor•tion•er** *n* — **ex•tor•tion•ist** *n*
ex•tra *adj* **1** : additional **2** : superior — **extra** *n or adv*
ex•tract *vb* **1** : pull out forcibly **2** : withdraw

(as a juice) ~ *n* **1 :** excerpt **2 :** product (as a juice) obtained by extracting — **ex·tract·able** *adj* — **ex·trac·tion** *n* — **ex·trac·tor** *n*

ex·tra·cur·ric·u·lar *adj* **:** lying outside the regular curriculum

ex·tra·dite *vb* **:** bring or deliver a suspect to a different jurisdiction for trial — **ex·tra·di·tion** *n*

ex·tra·mar·i·tal *adj* **:** relating to sexual relations of a married person outside of the marriage

ex·tra·ne·ous *adj* **:** not essential or relevant — **ex·tra·ne·ous·ly** *adv*

ex·traor·di·nary *adj* **:** notably unusual or exceptional — **ex·traor·di·nari·ly** *adv*

ex·tra·sen·so·ry *adj* **:** outside the ordinary senses

ex·tra·ter·res·tri·al *n* **:** one existing or coming from outside the earth ~ *adj* **:** relating to an extraterrestrial

ex·trav·a·gant *adj* **:** wildly excessive, lavish, or costly — **ex·trav·a·gance** *n* — **ex·trav·a·gant·ly** *adv*

ex·trav·a·gan·za *n* **:** spectacular event

ex·treme *adj* **1 :** very great or intense **2 :** very severe **3 :** not moderate **4 :** most remote ~ *n* **1 :** extreme state **2 :** something located at one end or the other of a range — **ex·treme·ly** *adv*

ex·trem·i·ty *n* **1 :** most remote part **2 :** human hand or foot **3 :** extreme degree or state (as of need)

ex·tro·vert *n* **:** gregarious person — **ex·tro·ver·sion** *n* — **ex·tro·vert·ed** *adj*

ex·u·ber·ant *adj* **:** joyously free from restraint — **ex·u·ber·ance** *n* — **ex·u·ber·ant·ly** *adv*

ex·ult *vb* **:** rejoice — **ex·ul·tant** *adj* — **ex·ul·tant·ly** *adv* — **ex·ul·ta·tion** *n*

eye *n* **1 :** organ of sight consisting of a globular structure (**eye·ball**) in a socket of the skull with thin movable covers (**eye·lids**) bordered with hairs (**eye·lash·es**) **2 :** vision **3 :** judgment **4 :** something suggesting an eye ~ *vb* **:** look at — **eye·brow** *n* — **eyed** *adj* — **eye·drop·per** *n* — **eye·glass·es** *n pl* — **eye·sight** *n* — **eye·strain** *n*

eye·let *n* **:** hole (as in cloth) for a lacing or rope

eye–open·er *n* **:** something startling — **eye–open·ing** *adj*

eye·piece *n* **:** lens at the eye end of an optical instrument

eye·sore *n* **:** unpleasant sight

eye·tooth *n* **:** upper canine tooth

eye·wit·ness *n* **:** person who actually sees something happen

F

f *n* **:** 6th letter of the alphabet

fa·ble *n* **1 :** legendary story **2 :** story that teaches a lesson — **fa·bled** *adj*

fab·ric *n* **1 :** structure **2 :** material made usu. by weaving or knitting fibers

fab·ri·cate *vb* **1 :** construct **2 :** invent — **fab·ri·cation** *n*

fab·u·lous *adj* **1 :** like, told in, or based on fable **2 :** incredible or marvelous — **fab·u·lous·ly** *adv*

fa·cade *n* **1 :** principal face of a building **2 :** false or superficial appearance

face *n* **1 :** front or principal surface (as of the head) **2 :** presence **3 :** facial expression **4 :** grimace **5 :** outward appearance ~ *vb* **1 :** challenge or resist firmly or brazenly **2 :** cover with different material **3 :** sit or stand with the face toward **4 :** have the front oriented toward — **faced** *adj* — **face·less** *adj* — **fa·cial** *adj or n*

face–lift *n* **1 :** cosmetic surgery on the face **2 :** modernization

fa·ce·tious *adj* **:** seeking to produce laughter — **fa·ce·tious·ly** *adv* — **fa·ce·tious·ness** *n*

fa·cil·i·tate *vb* **:** make easier

fa·cil·i·ty *n* **1 :** ease in doing or using **2 :** something built or installed to serve a purpose or facilitate an activity

fac·ing *n* **:** lining or covering or material for this

fac·sim·i·le *n* **:** exact copy

fact *n* **1 :** act or action **2 :** something that exists or is real **3 :** piece of information — **fac·tu·al** *adj* — **fac·tu·al·ly** *adv*

fac·tion *n* **:** part of a larger group — **fac·tion·al·ism** *n*

fac·tor *n* **1 :** something that has an effect **2 :** gene **3 :** number used in multiplying

fac·to·ry *n* **:** place for manufacturing

fac·ul·ty *n* **1 :** ability to act **2 :** power of the mind or body **3 :** body of teachers or department of instruction

fad *n* **:** briefly popular practice or interest — **fad·dish** *adj* — **fad·dist** *n*

fade *vb* **1 :** wither **2 :** lose or cause to lose freshness or brilliance **3 :** grow dim **4 :** vanish

Fahr·en·heit *adj* **:** relating to a thermometer scale with the boiling point at 212 degrees and the freezing point at 32 degrees

fail *vb* **1 :** decline in health **2 :** die away **3 :** stop functioning **4 :** fail to be successful **5 :** become bankrupt **6 :** disappoint **7 :** neglect ~ *n* **:** act of failing

fail·ing *n* **:** slight defect in character or conduct ~ *prep* **:** in the absence or lack of

fail·ure *n* **1 :** absence of expected action or performance **2 :** bankruptcy **3 :** deficiency **4 :** one that has failed

faint *adj* **1 :** cowardly or spiritless **2 :** weak and dizzy **3 :** lacking vigor **4 :** indistinct ~ *vb* **:** lose consciousness ~ *n* **:** act or condition of fainting — **faint·heart·ed** *adj* — **faint·ly** *adv* — **faint·ness** *n*

¹fair *adj* **1 :** pleasing in appearance **2 :** not stormy or cloudy **3 :** just or honest **4 :** conforming with the rules **5 :** open to legitimate pursuit or attack **6 :** light in color **7 :** adequate — **fair·ness** *n*

²fair *n* **:** exhibition for judging or selling — **fair-ground** *n*

fair·ly *adv* **1 :** in a manner of speaking **2 :** without bias **3 :** somewhat

fairy *n* **:** usu. small imaginary being — **fairy tale** *n*

fairy·land *n* **1 :** land of fairies **2 :** beautiful or charming place

faith *n* **1 :** allegiance **2 :** belief and trust in God **3 :** confidence **4 :** system of religious beliefs — **faith·ful** *adj* — **faith·ful·ly** *adv* — **faith·ful·ness** *n* — **faith·less** *adj* — **faith·less·ly** *adv* — **faith·less·ness** *n*

fake *vb* **1 :** falsify **2 :** counterfeit ~ *n* **:** copy, fraud, or impostor ~ *adj* **:** not genuine — **fak·er** *n*

fal·con *n* **:** small long-winged hawk used esp. for hunting — **fal·con·ry** *n*

fall *vb* **fell; fall·en 1 :** go down by gravity **2 :** hang freely **3 :** go lower **4 :** be defeated or ruined **5 :** commit a sin **6 :** happen at a certain time ~ *n* **1 :** act of falling **2 :** autumn **3 :** downfall **4** *pl* **:** waterfall **5 :** distance something falls

fal·la·cy *n* **1 :** false idea **2 :** false reasoning — **fal·la·cious** *adj*

fal·li·ble *adj* **:** capable of making a mistake — **fal·li·bly** *adv*

fall·out *n* **1 :** radioactive particles from a nuclear explosion **2 :** secondary effects

false *adj* **1 :** not genuine, true, faithful, or permanent **2 :** misleading — **false·ly** *adv* — **false·ness** *n* — **fal·si·fi·ca·tion** *n* — **fal·si·fy** *vb* — **fal·si·ty** *n*

false·hood *n* **:** lie

fal·ter *vb* **1 :** move unsteadily **2 :** hesitate — **fal·ter·ing·ly** *adv*

fame *n* **:** public reputation — **famed** *adj*

¹fa·mil·iar *n* **1 :** companion **2 :** guardian spirit

²fa·mil·iar *adj* **1 :** closely acquainted **2 :** forward **3 :** frequently seen or experienced — **fa·mil·iar·i·ty** *n* — **fa·mil·iar·ize** *vb* — **fa·mil·iar·ly** *adv*

fam·i·ly *n* **1 :** persons of common ancestry **2 :** group living together **3 :** parents and children **4 :** group of related individuals

fam·ine *n* **:** extreme scarcity of food

fa·mous *adj* **:** widely known or celebrated

fa·mous·ly *adv* **:** very well

¹fan *n* **:** device for producing a current of air ~ *vb* **1 :** move air with a fan **2 :** direct a current of air upon **3 :** stir to activity

²fan *n* **:** enthusiastic follower or admirer

fa·nat·ic, fa·nat·i·cal *adj* **:** excessively enthusiastic or devoted — **fanatic** *n* — **fa·nat·i·cism** *n*

fan·ci·er *n* **:** one devoted to raising a particular plant or animal

fan·cy *n* **1 :** liking **2 :** whim **3 :** imagination ~ *vb* **1 :** like **2 :** imagine ~ *adj* **1 :** not plain **2 :** of superior quality — **fan·ci·ful** *adj* — **fan·ci·ful·ly** *adv* — **fan·ci·ly** *adv*

fan·fare *n* **1 :** a sounding of trumpets **2 :** showy display

fan·tas·tic *adj* **1 :** imaginary or unrealistic **2 :** exceedingly or unbelievably great — **fan·tas·ti·cal·ly** *adv*

fan·ta·sy *n* **1 :** imagination **2 :** product of the imagination — **fan·ta·size** *vb*

FAQ *abbr* frequently asked questions

far *adv* **1 :** at or to a distance **2 :** much **3 :** to a degree **4 :** to an advanced point or extent ~ *adj* **1 :** remote **2 :** long **3 :** being more distant

farce *n* **1 :** satirical comedy with an improbable plot **2 :** ridiculous display — **far·ci·cal** *adj*

¹fare *vb* **:** get along

²fare *n* **1 :** price of transportation **2 :** range of food

fare·well *n* **1 :** wish of welfare at parting **2 :** departure — **fare·well** *adj*

far–fetched *adj* : improbable

farm *n* : place where something is raised for food ~ *vb* **1** : use (land) as a farm **2** : raise plants or animals for food — **farm•er** *n* — **farm•hand** *n* — **farm•house** *n* — **farm•ing** *n* — **farm•land** *n* — **farm•yard** *n*

far•sight•ed *adj* **1** : better able to see distant things than near **2** : judicious or shrewd — **far•sight•ed•ness** *n*

far•ther *adv* **1** : at or to a greater distance or more advanced point **2** : to a greater degree or extent ~ *adj* : more distant

far•thest *adj* : most distant ~ *adv* **1** : to or at the greatest distance **2** : to the most advanced point **3** : by the greatest extent

fas•ci•nate *vb* : transfix and hold spellbound — **fas•ci•na•tion** *n*

fash•ion *n* **1** : manner **2** : prevailing custom or style ~ *vb* : form or construct — **fash•ion•able** *adj* — **fash•ion•ably** *adv*

[1]**fast** *adj* **1** : firmly fixed, bound, or shut **2** : faithful **3** : moving or acting quickly **4** : indicating ahead of the correct time **5** : deep and undisturbed **6** : permanently dyed **7** : wild or promiscuous ~ *adv* **1** : so as to be secure or bound **2** : soundly or deeply **3** : swiftly

[2]**fast** *vb* : abstain from food or eat sparingly ~ *n* : act or time of fasting

fas•ten *vb* : attach esp. by pinning or tying — **fas•ten•er** *n* — **fas•ten•ing** *n*

fat *adj* **1** : having much fat **2** : thick ~ *n* : animal tissue rich in greasy or oily matter — **fat•ness** *n* — **fat•ten** *vb* — **fat•ty** *adj or n*

fa•tal *adj* : causing death or ruin — **fa•tal•ism** *n* — **fa•tal•ist** *n* — **fa•tal•is•tic** *adj* — **fa•tal•is•ti•cal•ly** *adv* — **fa•tal•i•ty** *n* — **fa•tal•ly** *adv*

fate *n* **1** : principle, cause, or will held to determine events **2** : end or outcome — **fat•ed** *adj* — **fate•ful** *adj* — **fate•ful•ly** *adv*

fa•ther *n* **1** : male parent **2** *cap* : God **3** : originator — **father** *vb* — **fa•ther•hood** *n* — **fa•ther•land** *n* — **fa•ther•less** *adj* — **fa•ther•ly** *adj*

father–in–law *n* (**fa•thers–in–law**) : father of one's spouse

fa•tigue *n* **1** : weariness from labor or use **2** : tendency to break under repeated stress ~ *vb* : tire out

fau•cet *n* : fixture for drawing off a liquid

fault *n* **1** : weakness in character **2** : something wrong or imperfect **3** : responsibility for something wrong **4** : fracture in the earth's crust ~ *vb* : find fault in or with — **fault•find•er** *n* — **fault•find•ing** *n* — **fault•i•ly** *adv* — **fault•less** *adj* — **fault•less•ly** *adv* — **faulty** *adj*

fau•na *n* : animals or animal life esp. of a region — **fau•nal** *adj*

fa•vor *n* **1** : approval **2** : partiality **3** : act of kindness ~ *vb* : regard or treat with favor — **fa•vor•able** *adj* — **fa•vor•ably** *adv*

fa•vor•ite *n* : one favored — **favorite** *adj* — **fa•vor•it•ism** *n*

fawn *n* : young deer

faze *vb* : disturb the composure of

fear *n* : unpleasant emotion caused by expectation or awareness of danger ~ *vb* : be afraid of — **fear•ful** *adj* — **fear•ful•ly** *adv* — **fear•less** *adj* — **fear•less•ly** *adv* — **fear•less•ness** *n* — **fear•some** *adj*

fea•si•ble *adj* : capable of being done — **fea•si•bil•i•ty** *n* — **fea•si•bly** *adv*

feast *n* **1** : large or fancy meal **2** : religious festival ~ *vb* : eat plentifully

feat *n* : notable deed

feath•er *n* : one of the light horny outgrowths that form the external covering of a bird's body — **feather** *vb* — **feath•ered** *adj* — **feath•er•less** *adj* — **feath•ery** *adj*

fea•ture *n* **1** : shape or appearance of the face **2** : part of the face **3** : prominent characteristic **4** : special attraction ~ *vb* : give prominence to — **fea•ture•less** *adj*

Feb•ru•ary *n* : 2d month of the year having 28 and in leap years 29 days

fed•er•al *adj* : of or constituting a government with power distributed between a central authority and constituent units — **fed•er•al•ism** *n* — **fed•er•al•ist** *n or adj* — **fed•er•al•ly** *adv*

fed•er•ate *vb* : join in a union of organizations — **fed•er•a•tion** *n*

fee *n* : fixed charge

fee•ble *adj* : weak or ineffective — **fee•ble•mind•ed** *adj* — **fee•ble•mind•ed•ness** *n* — **fee•ble•ness** *n* — **fee•bly** *adv*

feed *vb* **1** : give food to **2** : eat **3** : furnish ~ *n* : food for livestock — **feed•er** *n*

feel *vb* **felt; felt** **1** : perceive or examine through physical contact **2** : think or believe **3** : be conscious of **4** : seem **5** : have sympathy ~ *n* **1** : sense of touch **2** : quality of a thing imparted through touch — **feel•er** *n*

feel•ing *n* **1** : sense of touch **2** : state of mind **3** *pl* : sensibilities **4** : opinion

feet *pl of* FOOT

feign *vb* : pretend

fe•lic•i•tate *vb* : congratulate — **fe•lic•i•ta•tion** *n*
fe•line *adj* : relating to cats — **feline** *n*
fell *past of* FALL
fel•low *n* **1 :** companion or associate **2 :** man or boy — **fel•low•ship** *n*
fel•low•man *n* : kindred human being
fel•on *n* : one who has committed a felony
fel•o•ny *n* : serious crime — **fe•lo•ni•ous** *adj*
[1]felt *n* : cloth made of pressed wool and fur
[2]felt *past of* FEEL
fe•male *adj* : relating to or being the sex that bears young — **female** *n*
fem•i•nine *adj* : relating to the female sex — **fem•i•nin•i•ty** *n* — **fem•i•nism** *n* — **fem•i•nist** *n or adj*
fence *n* : enclosing barrier esp. of wood or wire ~ *vb* **1 :** enclose with a fence **2 :** practice fencing — **fenc•er** *n*
fenc•ing *n* **1 :** combat with swords for sport **2 :** material for building fences
fend•er *n* : guard over an automobile wheel
fer•ment *vb* : cause or undergo chemical decomposition ~ *n* : agitation — **fer•men•ta•tion** *n*
fern *n* : flowerless seedless green plant
fe•ro•cious *adj* : fierce or savage — **fe•ro•cious•ly** *adv* — **fe•ro•cious•ness** *n* — **fe•roc•i•ty** *n*
fer•ry *vb* : carry by boat over water ~ *n* : boat used in ferrying — **fer•ry•boat** *n*
fer•tile *adj* **1 :** producing plentifully **2 :** capable of developing or reproducing — **fer•til•i•ty** *n*
fer•til•ize *vb* : make fertile — **fer•til•iza•tion** *n* — **fer•til•iz•er** *n*
fes•ti•val *n* : time of celebration
fes•tive *adj* : joyous or happy — **fes•tive•ly** *adv* — **fes•tiv•i•ty** *n*
fe•tal *adj* : of, relating to, or being a fetus
fetch *vb* **1 :** go or come after and bring or take back **2 :** sell for
fetch•ing *adj* : attractive — **fetch•ing•ly** *adv*
fête *n* : lavish party ~ *vb* : honor or commemorate with a fête
fe•tish *n* **1 :** object believed to have magical powers **2 :** object of unreasoning devotion or concern
fe•tus *n* : vertebrate not yet born or hatched
feud *n* : prolonged quarrel — **feud** *vb*
feu•dal•ism *n* : medieval political order in which land is granted in return for service — **feu•dal** *adj* — **feu•dal•is•tic** *adj*
fe•ver *n* **1 :** abnormal rise in body temperature **2 :** state of heightened emotion — **fe•ver•ish** *adj* — **fe•ver•ish•ly** *adv*
few *pron* : not many ~ *adj* : some but not many — often with *a* ~ *n* : small number — often with *a*
few•er *pron* : smaller number of things
fi•an•cé *n* : man one is engaged to
fi•an•cée *n* : woman one is engaged to
fi•as•co *n* : ridiculous failure
fib *n* : trivial lie — **fib** *vb* — **fib•ber** *n*
fi•ber, fi•bre *n* **1 :** threadlike substance or structure (as a muscle cell or fine root) **2 :** indigestible material in food **3 :** element that gives texture or substance — **fi•brous** *adj*
fi•ber•glass *n* : glass in fibrous form in various products (as insulation)
fick•le *adj* : unpredictably changeable — **fick•le•ness** *n*
fic•tion *n* : a made-up story or literature consisting of these — **fic•tion•al** *adj*
fic•ti•tious *adj* : made up or pretended
fid•dle *n* : violin ~ *vb* **1 :** play on the fiddle **2 :** move the hands restlessly — **fid•dler** *n*
fi•del•i•ty *n* **1 :** quality or state of being faithful **2 :** quality of reproduction
fid•get *n* **1** *pl* : restlessness **2 :** one that fidgets ~ *vb* : move restlessly — **fid•gety** *adj*
field *n* **1 :** open country **2 :** cleared land **3 :** land yielding some special product **4 :** sphere of activity **5 :** area for sports **6 :** region or space in which a given effect (as magnetism) exists ~ *vb* : put into the field — **field** *adj* — **field•er** *n*
fiend *n* **1 :** devil **2 :** extremely wicked person — **fiend•ish** *adj* — **fiend•ish•ly** *adv*
fierce *adj* **1 :** violently hostile or aggressive **2 :** intense **3 :** menacing looking — **fierce•ly** *adv* — **fierce•ness** *n*
fi•ery *adj* **1 :** burning **2 :** hot or passionate — **fi•eri•ness** *n*
fi•es•ta *n* : festival
fif•teen *n* : one more than 14 — **fifteen** *adj or pron* — **fif•teenth** *adj or n*
fifth *n* **1 :** one that is number 5 in a countable series **2 :** one of 5 equal parts of something — **fifth** *adj or adv*
fif•ty *n* : 5 times 10 — **fif•ti•eth** *adj or n* — **fifty** *adj or pron*
fif•ty–fif•ty *adv or adj* : shared equally
fig *n* : pear-shaped edible fruit
fight *vb* **fought; fought** **1 :** contend against another in battle **2 :** box **3 :** struggle ~ *n* **1**

: hostile encounter **2** : boxing match **3** : verbal disagreement — **fight•er** *n*

fig•ment *n* : something imagined or made up

fig•u•ra•tive *adj* : metaphorical — **fig•u•ra•tive•ly** *adv*

fig•ure *n* **1** : symbol representing a number **2** *pl* : arithmetical calculations **3** : price **4** : shape or outline **5** : illustration **6** : pattern or design **7** : prominent person ∼ *vb* **1** : be important **2** : calculate — **fig•ured** *adj*

[1]**file** *n* : tool for smoothing or sharpening ∼ *vb* : rub or smooth with a file

[2]**file** *vb* **1** : arrange in order **2** : enter or record officially ∼ *n* : device for keeping papers in order

[3]**file** *n* : row of persons or things one behind the other ∼ *vb* : march in file

fil•i•bus•ter *n* : long speeches to delay a legislative vote — **filibuster** *vb* — **fil•i•bus•ter•er** *n*

fill *vb* **1** : make or become full **2** : stop up **3** : feed **4** : satisfy **5** : occupy fully **6** : spread through ∼ *n* **1** : full supply **2** : material for filling — **fill•er** *n* — **fill•ing** *n* — **fill in** *vb* **1** : provide information to or for **2** : substitute

fil•let *n* : piece of boneless meat or fish ∼ *vb* : cut into fillets

fil•ly *n* : young female horse

film *n* **1** : thin skin or membrane **2** : thin coating or layer **3** : strip of material used in taking pictures **4** : movie ∼ *vb* : make a movie of — **filmy** *adj*

fil•ter *n* **1** : device for separating matter from a fluid **2** : device (as on a camera lens) that absorbs light ∼ *vb* **1** : pass through a filter **2** : remove by means of a filter — **fil•ter•able** *adj* — **fil•tra•tion** *n*

filth *n* : repulsive dirt or refuse — **filth•i•ness** *n* — **filthy** *adj*

fin *n* **1** : thin external process controlling movement in an aquatic animal **2** : fin-shaped part (as on an airplane) — **finned** *adj*

fi•nal *adj* **1** : not to be changed **2** : ultimate **3** : coming at the end — **final** *n* — **fi•nal•ist** *n* — **fi•nal•i•ty** *n* — **fi•nal•ize** *vb* — **fi•nal•ly** *adv*

fi•na•le *n* : last or climactic part

fi•nance *n* **1** *pl* : money resources **2** : management of money affairs ∼ *vb* **1** : raise funds for **2** : give necessary funds to **3** : sell on credit — **fi•nan•cier** *n*

fi•nan•cial *adj* : relating to finance — **fi•nan•cial•ly** *adv*

finch *n* : songbird (as a sparrow or linnet) with a strong bill

find *vb* **1** : discover or encounter **2** : obtain by effort **3** : experience or feel **4** : gain or regain the use of **5** : decide on (a verdict) ∼ *n* **1** : act or instance of finding **2** : something found — **find•er** *n* — **find•ing** *n* — **find out** *vb* : learn, discover, or verify something

fine *n* : money paid as a penalty ∼ *vb* : impose a fine on ∼ *adj* **1** : free from impurity **2** : small or thin **3** : not coarse **4** : superior in quality or appearance ∼ *adv* : finely — **fine•ly** *adv* — **fine•ness** *n*

fin•ery *n* : showy clothing and jewels

fi•nesse *n* **1** : delicate skill **2** : craftiness — **finesse** *vb*

fin•ger *n* **1** : one of the 5 divisions at the end of the hand and esp. one other than the thumb **2** : something like a finger **3** : part of a glove for a finger ∼ *vb* **1** : touch with the fingers **2** : identify as if by pointing — **fin•gered** *adj* — **fin•ger•nail** *n* — **fin•ger•print** *n or vb* — **fin•ger•tip** *n*

fin•icky *adj* : excessively particular in taste or standards

fin•ish *vb* **1** : come or bring to an end **2** : use or dispose of entirely **3** : put a final coat or surface on ∼ *n* **1** : end **2** : final treatment given a surface — **fin•ish•er** *n*

fi•nite *adj* : having definite limits

fiord *var of* FJORD

fir *n* : evergreen tree or its wood

fire *n* **1** : light or heat and esp. the flame of something burning **2** : destructive burning (as of a house) **3** : enthusiasm **4** : the shooting of weapons ∼ *vb* **1** : kindle **2** : stir up or enliven **3** : dismiss from employment **4** : shoot **5** : bake — **fire•bomb** *n or vb* — **fire•fight-er** *n* — **fire•less** *adj* — **fire•proof** *adj or vb* — **fire•wood** *n*

fire•arm *n* : weapon (as a rifle) that works by an explosion of gunpowder

fire•ball *n* **1** : ball of fire **2** : brilliant meteor

fire•crack•er *n* : small firework that makes noise

fire•fight•er *n* : a person who fights fires

fire•fly *n* : night-flying beetle that produces a soft light

fire•place *n* : opening made in a chimney to hold an open fire

fire•side *n* **1** : place near the fire or hearth **2** : home ∼ *adj* : having an informal quality

fire•trap *n* : place apt to catch on fire

fire•work *n* : device that explodes to produce noise or a display of light

[1]**firm** *adj* **1 :** securely fixed in place **2 :** strong or vigorous **3 :** not subject to change **4 :** resolute ~ *vb* **:** make or become firm — **firm•ly** *adv* — **firm•ness** *n*
[2]**firm** *n* **:** business enterprise
first *adj* **1 :** being number one **2 :** foremost ~ *adv* **1 :** before any other **2 :** for the first time ~ *n* **1 :** number one **2 :** one that is first — **first class** *n* — **first–class** *adj or adv* — **first•ly** *adv* — **first–rate** *adj or adv*
first aid *n* **:** emergency care
fis•cal *adj* **:** relating to money — **fis•cal•ly** *adv*
fish *n* **fish :** water animal with fins, gills, and usu. scales ~ *vb* **1 :** try to catch fish **2 :** grope — **fish•er** *n* — **fish•er•man** *n* — **fish-hook** *n* — **fish•ing** *n*
fish•ery *n* **:** fishing business or a place for this
fishy *adj* **1 :** relating to or like fish **2 :** questionable
fis•sion *n* **:** splitting of an atomic nucleus — **fis•sion•able** *adj*
fist *n* **:** hand doubled up — **fist•ed** *adj* — **fist-ful** *n*
[1]**fit** *n* **:** sudden attack of illness or emotion
[2]**fit** *adj* **1 :** suitable **2 :** qualified **3 :** sound in body ~ *vb* **1 :** be suitable to **2 :** insert or adjust correctly **3 :** make room for **4 :** supply or equip **5 :** belong ~ *n* **:** state of fitting or being fitted — **fit•ly** *adv* — **fit•ness** *n* — **fit•ter** *n*
fit•ful *adj* **:** restless — **fit•ful•ly** *adv*
fit•ting *adj* **:** suitable ~ *n* **:** a small part
five *n* **1 :** one more than 4 **2 :** 5th in a set or series **3 :** something having 5 units — **five** *adj or pron*
fix *vb* **1 :** attach **2 :** establish **3 :** make right **4 :** prepare **5 :** improperly influence ~ *n* **1 :** predicament **2 :** determination of location — **fixed** *adj* — **fixed•ly** *adv* — **fixed•ness** *n* — **fix•er** *n*
fix•a•tion *n* **:** obsessive attachment — **fix•ate** *vb*
fix•ture *n* **:** permanent part of something
fizz *vb* **:** make a hissing sound ~ *n* **:** effervescence
fiz•zle *vb* **1 :** fizz **2 :** fail ~ *n* **:** failure
fjord *n* **:** inlet of the sea between cliffs
flab *n* **:** flabby flesh
flab•by *adj* **:** not firm — **flab•bi•ness** *n*
[1]**flag** *n* **1 :** fabric that is a symbol (as of a country) **2 :** something used to signal ~ *vb* **:** signal with a flag — **flag•pole** *n* — **flag•staff** *n*
[2]**flag** *vb* **:** lose strength or spirit
flag•el•late *vb* **:** whip — **flag•el•la•tion** *n*
flag•on *n* **:** container for liquids
fla•grant *adj* **:** conspicuously bad — **fla•grant-ly** *adv*
flair *n* **:** natural aptitude
flake *n* **:** small flat piece ~ *vb* **:** separate or form into flakes
flam•boy•ant *adj* **:** showy — **flam•boy•ance** *n* — **flam•boy•ant•ly** *adv*
flame *n* **1 :** glowing part of a fire **2 :** state of combustion **3 :** burning passion — **flame** *vb* — **flam•ing** *adj*
flam•ma•ble *adj* **:** easily ignited
flank *n* **:** side of something ~ *vb* **1 :** attack or go around the side of **2 :** be at the side of
flan•nel *n* **:** soft napped fabric
flap *n* **1 :** slap **2 :** something flat that hangs loose ~ *vb* **1 :** move (wings) up and down **2 :** swing back and forth noisily
flap•jack *n* **:** pancake
flare *vb* **:** become suddenly bright or excited ~ *n* **:** blaze of light
flash *vb* **1 :** give off a sudden flame or burst of light **2 :** appear or pass suddenly ~ *n* **1 :** sudden burst of light or inspiration **2 :** instant ~ *adj* **:** coming suddenly
flash•light *n* **:** small battery-operated light
flashy *adj* **:** showy — **flash•i•ly** *adv* — **flash•i-ness** *n*
flat *adj* **1 :** smooth **2 :** broad and thin **3 :** definite **4 :** uninteresting **5 :** deflated **6 :** below the true pitch ~ *n* **1 :** level surface of land **2 :** flat note in music **3 :** apartment **4 :** having lost air ~ *adv* **1 :** exactly **2 :** below the true pitch ~ *vb* **:** make flat — **flat•ly** *adv* — **flat-ness** *n* — **flat•ten** *vb*
flat•foot *n* **flat•feet :** foot condition in which the arch is flattened — **flat–foot•ed** *adj*
flat–out *adj* **1 :** being maximum effort or speed **2 :** downright
flat•ter *vb* **1 :** praise insincerely **2 :** judge or represent too favorably — **flat•ter•er** *n* — **flat-tery** *n*
flat•u•lent *adj* **:** full of gas — **flat•u•lence** *n*
flaunt *vb* **:** display ostentatiously — **flaunt** *n*
fla•vor *n* **1 :** quality that affects the sense of taste **2 :** something that adds flavor ~ *vb* **:** give flavor to — **fla•vor•ful** *adj* — **fla•vor-ing** *n* — **fla•vor•less** *adj*
flaw *n* **:** fault — **flaw•less** *adj* — **flaw•less•ly** *adv* — **flaw•less•ness** *n*
flea *n* **:** leaping bloodsucking insect
fleck *vb or n* **:** streak or spot
flee *vb* **:** run away

fleece *n* : sheep's wool ~ *vb* **1** : shear **2** : get money from dishonestly — **fleecy** *adj*

[1]fleet *vb* : pass rapidly ~ *adj* : swift — **fleet·ing** *adj* — **fleet·ness** *n*

[2]fleet *n* : group of ships

flesh *n* **1** : soft parts of an animal's body **2** : soft plant tissue (as fruit pulp) — **fleshed** *adj* — **fleshy** *adj* — **flesh out** *vb* : make fuller

flew *past of* FLY

flex *vb* : bend

flex·i·ble *adj* **1** : capable of being flexed **2** : adaptable — **flex·i·bil·i·ty** *n* — **flex·i·bly** *adv*

flick *n* : light jerky stroke ~ *vb* **1** : strike lightly **2** : flutter

flick·er *vb* **1** : waver **2** : burn unsteadily ~ *n* **1** : sudden movement **2** : wavering light

fli·er *n* **1** : aviator **2** : advertising circular

[1]flight *n* **1** : act or instance of flying **2** : ability to fly **3** : a passing through air or space **4** : series of stairs — **flight·less** *adj*

[2]flight *n* : act or instance of running away

flighty *adj* : capricious or silly — **flight·i·ness** *n*

flim·sy *adj* **1** : not strong or well made **2** : not believable — **flim·si·ly** *adv* — **flim·si·ness** *n*

flinch *vb* : shrink from pain

fling *vb* **1** : move brusquely **2** : throw ~ *n* **1** : act or instance of flinging **2** : attempt **3** : period of self-indulgence

flip *vb* **1** : cause to turn over quickly or many times **2** : move with a quick push ~ *adj* : insolent — **flip** *n*

flip·pant *adj* : not serious enough — **flip·pan·cy** *n*

flirt *vb* **1** : be playfully romantic **2** : show casual interest ~ *n* : one who flirts — **flir·ta·tion** *n* — **flir·ta·tious** *adj*

flit *vb* : dart

float *n* **1** : something that floats **2** : vehicle carrying an exhibit ~ *vb* **1** : rest on or in a fluid without sinking **2** : wander **3** : finance by issuing stock or bonds — **float·er** *n*

flock *n* : group of animals (as birds) or people ~ *vb* : gather or move as a group

flood *n* **1** : great flow of water over the land **2** : overwhelming volume ~ *vb* : cover or fill esp. with water — **flood·wa·ter** *n*

floor *n* **1** : bottom of a room on which one stands **2** : story of a building **3** : lower limit ~ *vb* **1** : furnish with a floor **2** : knock down **3** : amaze — **floor·board** *n* — **floor·ing** *n*

flop *vb* **1** : flap **2** : slump heavily **3** : fail — **flop** *n*

flop·py *adj* : soft and flexible

flo·ra *n* : plants or plant life of a region

flo·ral *adj* : relating to flowers

flo·rist *n* : flower dealer

floss *n* **1** : soft thread for embroidery **2** : thread used to clean between teeth — **floss** *vb*

flo·ta·tion *n* : process or instance of floating

[1]floun·der *n* **flounder** : a flattened fish with both eyes on the upper side

[2]flounder *vb* **1** : struggle for footing **2** : proceed clumsily

flour *n* : finely ground meal ~ *vb* : coat with flour — **floury** *adj*

flour·ish *vb* **1** : thrive **2** : wave threateningly ~ *n* **1** : embellishment **2** : fanfare **3** : wave **4** : showiness of action

flout *vb* : treat with disdain

flow *vb* **1** : move in a stream **2** : proceed smoothly and readily ~ *n* : uninterrupted stream

flow·er *n* **1** : showy plant shoot that bears seeds **2** : state of flourishing ~ *vb* **1** : produce flowers **2** : flourish — **flow·ered** *adj* — **flow·er·less** *adj* — **flow·er·pot** *n* — **flow·ery** *adj*

flown *past part of* FLY

flu *n* : acute very contagious virus disease

flub *vb* : bungle — **flub** *n*

fluc·tu·ate *vb* : change rapidly esp. up and down — **fluc·tu·a·tion** *n*

flue *n* : smoke duct

flu·ent *adj* : speaking with ease — **flu·en·cy** *n* — **flu·ent·ly** *adv*

fluff *n* **1** : something soft and light **2** : blunder ~ *vb* **1** : make fluffy **2** : make a mistake — **fluffy** *adj*

flu·id *adj* : flowing ~ *n* : substance that can flow — **flu·id·i·ty** *n* — **flu·id·ly** *adv*

fluke *n* : stroke of luck

flung *past of* FLING

flunk *vb* : fail in school work

flu·o·res·cence *n* : emission of light after initial absorption — **flu·o·resce** *vb* — **flu·o·res·cent** *adj*

flur·ry *n* **1** : light snowfall **2** : bustle **3** : brief burst of activity — **flurry** *vb*

[1]flush *vb* : cause (a bird) to fly from cover

[2]flush *n* **1** : sudden flow (as of water) **2** : sudden increase of emotion **3** : blush ~ *vb* **1** : blush **2** : wash out with a rush of liquid ~

adj **1 :** filled to overflowing **2 :** of a reddish healthy color **3 :** smooth or level **4 :** abutting — **flush** *adv*

flus•ter *vb* **:** upset — **fluster** *n*

flute *n* **1 :** pipelike musical instrument **2 :** groove — **flut•ed** *adj* — **flut•ing** *n* — **flut•ist** *n*

flut•ter *vb* **1 :** flap the wings rapidly **2 :** move with quick wavering or flapping motions **3 :** behave in an agitated manner ~ *n* **1 :** a fluttering **2 :** state of confusion — **flut•tery** *adj*

flux *n* **:** state of continuous change

[1]**fly** *vb* (**flew; flown**) **1 :** move through the air with wings **2 :** float or soar **3 :** flee **4 :** move or pass swiftly **5 :** operate an airplane

[2]**fly** *n* **:** garment closure

[3]**fly** *n* **:** winged insect

fly•er *var of* FLIER

foam *n* **1 :** mass of bubbles on top of a liquid **2 :** material of cellular form ~ *vb* **:** form foam — **foamy** *adj*

fo•cus *n* **1 :** point at which reflected or refracted rays meet **2 :** adjustment (as of eyeglasses) for clear vision **3 :** central point ~ *vb* **:** bring to a focus — **fo•cal** *adj* — **fo•cal•ly** *adv*

foe *n* **:** enemy

fog *n* **1 :** fine particles of water suspended near the ground **2 :** mental confusion ~ *vb* **:** obscure or be obscured with fog — **fog•gy** *adj* — **fog•horn** *n*

foil *n* **1 :** thin sheet of metal **2 :** one that sets off another by contrast

[1]**fold** *n* **1 :** enclosure for sheep **2 :** group with a common interest

[2]**fold** *vb* **1 :** lay one part over another **2 :** embrace ~ *n* **:** part folded

fold•er *n* **1 :** one that folds **2 :** circular **3 :** folded cover or envelope for papers

fo•liage *n* **:** plant leaves

folk *n* **1 :** people in general **2** *pl* **:** one's family ~ *adj* **:** relating to the common people

folk•lore *n* **:** customs and traditions of a people — **folk•lor•ist** *n*

folksy *adj* **:** friendly and informal

fol•low *vb* **1 :** go or come after **2 :** pursue **3 :** obey **4 :** proceed along **5 :** keep one's attention fixed on **6 :** result from — **fol•low•er** *n* — **fol•low•ing** *adj or prep*

fol•ly *n* **:** foolishness

fond *adj* **1 :** strongly attracted **2 :** affectionate **3 :** dear — **fond•ly** *adv* — **fond•ness** *n*

fon•dle *vb* **:** touch lovingly

food *n* **:** material eaten to sustain life

fool *n* **1 :** stupid person **2 :** jester ~ *vb* **1 :** waste time **2 :** meddle **3 :** deceive — **fool•ery** *n* — **fool•ish** *adj* — **fool•ish•ly** *adv* — **fool•ish•ness** *n* — **fool•proof** *adj*

fool•har•dy *adj* **:** rash — **fool•har•di•ness** *n*

foot *n* (**feet**) **1 :** end part of a leg **2 :** unit of length equal to ⅓ yard **3 :** unit of verse meter **4 :** bottom — **foot•ed** *adj* — **foot•path** *n* — **foot•print** *n* — **foot•race** *n* — **foot•rest** *n* — **foot•step** *n* — **foot•wear** *n*

foot•age *n* **:** size expressed in feet

foot•ball *n* **:** ball game played by 2 teams on a rectangular field

foot•hill *n* **:** hill at the foot of higher hills

foot•hold *n* **:** support for the feet

foot•ing *n* **1 :** foothold **2 :** basis

foot•lock•er *n* **:** small trunk

foot•loose *adj* **:** having no ties

foot•note *n* **:** note at the bottom of a page

foot•stool *n* **:** stool to support the feet

for *prep* **1** — used to show preparation or purpose **2 :** because of **3** — used to show a recipient **4 :** in support of **5 :** so as to support or help cure **6 :** so as to be equal to **7 :** concerning **8 :** through the period of ~ *conj* **:** because

for•bear *vb* **1 :** refrain from **2 :** be patient — **for•bear•ance** *n*

for•bid *vb* **1 :** prohibit **2 :** order not to do something

for•bid•ding *adj* **:** tending to discourage

force *n* **1 :** exceptional strength or energy **2 :** military strength **3 :** body (as of persons) available for a purpose **4 :** violence **5 :** influence (as a push or pull) that causes motion ~ *vb* **1 :** compel **2 :** gain against resistance **3 :** break open — **force•ful** *adj* — **force•ful•ly** *adv* — **in force 1 :** in great numbers **2 :** valid

forc•ible *adj* **1 :** done by force **2 :** showing force — **forc•i•bly** *adv*

ford *n* **:** place to wade across a stream ~ *vb* **:** wade across

fore *adv* **:** in or toward the front ~ *adj* **:** being or coming before in time, place, or order ~ *n* **:** front

fore•arm *n* **:** part of the arm between the elbow and the wrist

fore•bear *n* **:** ancestor

fore•bod•ing *n* **:** premonition of disaster — **fore•bod•ing** *adj*

fore•cast *vb* **:** predict — **forecast** *n* — **fore•cast•er** *n*

fore•close *vb* **:** take legal measures to terminate a mortgage — **fore•clo•sure** *n*

fore•fa•ther *n* **:** ancestor

fore•fin•ger *n* **:** finger next to the thumb

fore•foot *n* **:** front foot of a quadruped

fore•go *vb* **:** precede — **fore•go•ing** *n*

fore•gone *adj* **:** determined in advance

fore•ground *n* **:** part of a scene nearest the viewer

fore•hand *n* **:** stroke (as in tennis) made with the palm of the hand turned forward — **forehand** *adj*

fore•head *n* **:** part of the face above the eyes

for•eign *adj* **1 :** situated outside a place or country and esp. one's own country **2 :** belonging to a different place or country **3 :** not pertinent **4 :** related to or dealing with other nations — **for•eign•er** *n*

fore•leg *n* **:** front leg

fore•man *n* **1 :** person who speaks for a jury **2 :** workman in charge

fore•most *adj* **:** first in time, place, or order — **foremost** *adv*

fo•ren•sics *n pl* **:** art or study of speaking or debating — **fo•ren•sic** *adj*

fore•run•ner *n* **:** one that goes before

fore•see *vb* **:** see or realize beforehand — **fore•see•able** *adj*

fore•shad•ow *vb* **:** hint or suggest beforehand

fore•sight *n* **:** care or provision for the future — **fore•sight•ed** *adj* — **fore•sight•ed•ness** *n*

for•est *n* **:** large thick growth of trees and underbrush — **for•est•ed** *adj* — **for•est•er** *n* — **for•est•land** *n* — **for•est•ry** *n*

fore•stall *vb* **:** prevent by acting in advance

fore•taste *n* **:** advance indication or notion ~ *vb* **:** anticipate

fore•tell *vb* **:** predict

for•ev•er *adv* **1 :** for a limitless time **2 :** always

for•ev•er•more *adv* **:** forever

fore•warn *vb* **:** warn beforehand

for•feit *vb* **:** lose or lose the right to by an error or crime ~ *n* **:** something forfeited — **for•feiture** *n*

[1]forge *vb* **:** workshop for shaping metal ~ *vb* **1 :** form (metal) by heating and hammering **2 :** imitate falsely esp. to defraud — **forg•er** *n* — **forg•ery** *n*

[2]forge *vb* **:** move ahead steadily

for•get *vb* **1 :** be unable to think of or recall **2 :** fail to think of at the proper time — **for•get•ta•ble** *adj* — **for•get•ful** *adj* — **for•get•ful•ly** *adv*

for•give *vb* **:** pardon — **for•giv•able** *adj* — **for•give•ness** *n*

for•giv•ing *adj* **1 :** able to forgive **2 :** allowing room for error or weakness

for•go, fore•go *vb* **:** do without

fork *n* **1 :** implement with prongs for lifting, holding, or digging **2 :** forked part **3 :** a dividing into branches or a place where something branches ~ *vb* **1 :** divide into branches **2 :** move with a fork — **forked** *adj*

for•lorn *adj* **1 :** deserted **2 :** wretched — **for•lorn•ly** *adv*

form *n* **1 :** shape **2 :** set way of doing or saying something **3 :** document with blanks to be filled in **4 :** manner of performing with respect to what is expected **5 :** mold **6 :** kind or variety **7 :** one of the ways in which a word is changed to show difference in use ~ *vb* **1 :** give form or shape to **2 :** train **3 :** develop **4 :** constitute — **for•ma•tive** *adj* — **form•less** *adj*

for•mal *adj* **:** following established custom ~ *n* **:** formal social event — **for•mal•i•ty** *n* — **for•mal•ize** *vb* — **for•mal•ly** *adv*

for•mat *n* **:** general style or arrangement of something — **format** *vb*

for•ma•tion *n* **1 :** a giving form to something **2 :** something formed **3 :** arrangement

for•mer *adj* **:** coming before in time — **for•mer•ly** *adv*

for•mi•da•ble *adj* **1 :** causing fear or dread **2 :** very difficult — **for•mi•da•bly** *adv*

for•mu•la *n* **1 :** set form of words for ceremonial use **2 :** recipe **3 :** milk mixture for a baby **4 :** group of symbols or figures briefly expressing information **5 :** set form or method

for•mu•late *vb* **:** design, devise — **for•mu•la•tion** *n*

for•sake *vb* **:** renounce completely

for•swear *vb* **1 :** renounce under oath **2 :** perjure

for•syth•ia *n* **:** shrub grown for its yellow flowers

fort *n* **1 :** fortified place **2 :** permanent army post

forte *n* **:** something at which a person excels

forth *adv* **:** forward

forth•com•ing *adj* **1 :** coming or available soon **2 :** open and direct

forth•right *adj* **:** direct — **forth•right•ly** *adv* — **forth•right•ness** *n*

for•ti•fy *vb* **:** make strong — **for•ti•fi•ca•tion** *n*
for•ti•tude *n* **:** ability to endure
fort•night *n* **:** 2 weeks — **fort•night•ly** *adj or adv*
for•tress *n* **:** strong fort
for•tu•nate *adj* **1 :** coming by good luck **2 :** lucky — **for•tu•nate•ly** *adv*
for•tune *n* **1 :** prosperity attained partly through luck **2 :** good or bad luck **3 :** destiny **4 :** wealth
for•tune–tel•ler *n* **:** one who foretells a person's future — **for•tune–tell•ing** *n or adj*
for•ty *n* **:** 4 times 10 — **for•ti•eth** *adj or n* — **for•ty** *adj or pron*
fo•rum *n* **1 :** Roman marketplace **2 :** medium for open discussion
for•ward *adj* **1 :** being near or at or belonging to the front **2 :** brash ~ *adv* **:** toward what is in front ~ *n* **:** player near the front of his team ~ *vb* **1 :** help onward **2 :** send on — **for•ward•er** *n* — **for•ward•ness** *n*
for•wards *adv* **:** forward
fos•sil *n* **:** preserved trace of an ancient plant or animal ~ *adj* **:** being or originating from a fossil — **fos•sil•ize** *vb*
fos•ter *adj* **:** being, having, or relating to substitute parents ~ *vb* **:** help to grow or develop
fought *past of* FIGHT
foul *adj* **1 :** offensive **2 :** clogged with dirt **3 :** abusive **4 :** wet and stormy **5 :** unfair ~ *n* **:** a breaking of the rules in a game ~ *adv* **:** foully ~ *vb* **1 :** make or become foul or filthy **2 :** tangle — **foul•ly** *adv* — **foul-mouthed** *adj* — **foul•ness** *n*
foul–up *n* **:** error or state of confusion — **foul up** *vb* **:** bungle
found *vb* **:** establish — **found•er** *n*
foun•da•tion *n* **1 :** act of founding **2 :** basis for something **3 :** endowed institution **4 :** supporting structure — **foun•da•tion•al** *adj*
foun•der *vb* **:** sink
found•ry *n* **:** place where metal is cast
foun•tain *n* **1 :** spring of water **2 :** source **3 :** artificial jet of water
four *n* **1 :** one more than 3 **2 :** 4th in a set or series **3 :** something having 4 units — **four** *adj or pron*
four•score *adj* **:** eighty
four•some *n* **:** group of 4
four•teen *n* **:** one more than 13 — **four•teen** *adj or pron* — **four•teenth** *adj or n*
fourth *n* **1 :** one that is 4th **2 :** one of 4 equal parts of something — **fourth** *adj or adv*
fowl *n* (**fowl**) **1 :** bird **2 :** chicken
fox *n* **1 :** small mammal related to wolves **2 :** clever person ~ *vb* **:** trick — **foxy** *adj*
foy•er *n* **:** entrance hallway
frac•tion *n* **1 :** number indicating one or more equal parts of a whole **2 :** portion — **frac•tion•al** *adj* — **frac•tion•al•ly** *adv*
frac•ture *n* **:** a breaking of something — **fracture** *vb*
frag•ile *adj* **:** easily broken — **fra•gil•i•ty** *n*
frag•ment *n* **:** part broken off ~ *vb* **:** break into parts — **frag•men•tary** *adj* — **frag•men•ta•tion** *n*
fra•grant *adj* **:** having a sweet smell — **fra•grance** *n* — **fra•grant•ly** *adv*
frail *adj* **:** weak or delicate — **frail•ty** *n*
frame *vb* **1 :** plan **2 :** formulate **3 :** construct or arrange **4 :** enclose in a frame **5 :** make appear guilty ~ *n* **1 :** makeup of the body **2 :** supporting or enclosing structure **3 :** state or disposition (as of mind) — **frame•work** *n*
fran•chise *n* **1 :** special privilege **2 :** the right to vote — **fran•chi•see** *n*
frank *adj* **:** direct and sincere — **frank•ly** *adv* — **frank•ness** *n*
frank•furt•er, frank•furt *n* **:** cooked sausage
frank•in•cense *n* **:** incense resin
fran•tic *adj* **:** wildly excited — **fran•ti•cal•ly** *adv*
fra•ter•nal *adj* **1 :** brotherly **2 :** of a fraternity — **fra•ter•nal•ly** *adv*
fra•ter•ni•ty *n* **:** men's student social group
frat•er•nize *vb* **1 :** mingle as friends **2 :** associate with members of a hostile group — **frat•er•ni•za•tion** *n*
fraud *n* **:** trickery — **fraud•u•lent** *adj* — **fraud•u•lent•ly** *adv*
fray *vb* **1 :** wear by rubbing **2 :** separate the threads of **3 :** irritate
fraz•zle *vb* **:** wear out ~ *n* **:** exhaustion
freak *n* **1 :** something abnormal or unusual **2 :** enthusiast — **freak•ish** *adj* — **freak out** *vb* **1 :** experience nightmarish hallucinations from drugs **2 :** distress or become distressed
freck•le *n* **:** brown spot on the skin — **freckle** *vb*
free *adj* **1 :** having liberty or independence **2 :** not taxed **3 :** given without charge **4 :** voluntary **5 :** not in use **6 :** not fastened ~ *adv* **:** without charge ~ *vb* **:** set free — **free** *adv* — **free•born** *adj* — **free•dom** *n* — **free•ly** *adv*
free•boo•ter *n* **:** pirate

free•load *vb* : live off another's generosity — **free•load•er** *n*
free•way *n* : expressway
freeze *vb* **froze; fro•zen 1** : harden into ice **2** : become chilled **3** : damage by frost **4** : stick fast **5** : become motionless **6** : fix at one stage or level ~ *n* **1** : very cold weather **2** : state of being frozen — **freez•er** *n*
freeze–dry *vb* : preserve by freezing then drying — **freeze–dried** *adj*
freight *n* **1** : carrying of goods or payment for this **2** : shipped goods ~ *vb* : load or ship goods — **freigh•ter** *n*
french fry *vb* : fry in deep fat — **french fry** *n*
fre•net•ic *adj* : frantic — **fre•net•i•cal•ly** *adv*
fren•zy *n* : violent agitation — **fren•zied** *adj*
fre•quen•cy *n* **1** : frequent or regular occurrence **2** : number of cycles or sound waves per second
fre•quent *adj* : happening often ~ *vb* : go to habitually — **fre•quent•er** *n* — **fre•quent•ly** *adv*
fresh *adj* **1** : not salt **2** : pure **3** : not preserved **4** : not stale **5** : like new **6** : insolent — **fres•hen** *vb* — **fresh•ly** *adv* — **fresh•ness** *n*
fresh•man *n* : first-year student
fret *vb* **1** : worry or become irritated **2** : fray **3** : agitate ~ *n* **1** : worn spot **2** : irritation — **fret•ful** *adj* — **fret•ful•ly** *adv*
fric•tion *n* **1** : a rubbing between 2 surfaces **2** : clash of opinions — **fric•tion•al** *adj*
Fri•day *n* : 6th day of the week
friend *n* : person one likes — **friend•less** *adj* — **friend•li•ness** *n* — **friend•ly** *adj* — **friend•ship** *n*
fright *n* : sudden fear — **frigh•ten** *vb* — **fright•ful** *adj* — **fright•ful•ly** *adv* — **fright•ful•ness** *n*
frig•id *adj* : intensely cold — **fri•gid•i•ty** *n*
frill *n* **1** : ruffle **2** : pleasing but nonessential addition — **frilly** *adj*
fringe *n* **1** : ornamental border of short hanging threads or strips **2** : edge — **fringe** *vb*
frisk *vb* **1** : leap about **2** : search (a person) esp. for weapons
frisky *adj* : playful — **frisk•i•ly** *adv* — **frisk•i•ness** *n*
friv•o•lous *adj* : not important or serious — **fri•vol•i•ty** *n* — **friv•o•lous•ly** *adv*
frizz *vb* : curl tightly — **frizz** *n* — **frizzy** *adj*
frock *n* **1** : loose outer garment **2** : dress
frog *n* **1** : leaping amphibian **2** : hoarseness **3** : ornamental braid fastener **4** : small holder for flowers
frol•ic *vb* : romp ~ *n* : fun — **frol•ic•some** *adj*
from *prep* — used to show a starting point
front *n* **1** : face **2** : behavior **3** : main side of a building **4** : forward part **5** : boundary between air masses ~ *vb* **1** : have the main side adjacent to something **2** : serve as a front — **fron•tal** *adj*
front•age *n* : length of boundary line on a street
fron•tier *n* : outer edge of settled territory — **fron•tiers•man** *n*
frost *n* **1** : freezing temperature **2** : ice crystals on a surface ~ *vb* **1** : cover with frost **2** : put icing on (a cake) — **frosty** *adj*
frost•bite *n* : partial freezing of part of the body — **frost•bit•ten** *adj*
frost•ing *n* : icing
froth *n* : bubbles on a liquid — **frothy** *adj*
frown *vb or n* : scowl
frow•sy, frow•zy *adj* : untidy
froze *past of* FREEZE
frozen *past part of* FREEZE
fru•gal *adj* : thrifty — **fru•gal•i•ty** *n* — **fru•gal•ly** *adv*
fruit *n* **1** : usu. edible and sweet part of a seed plant **2** : result ~ *vb* : bear fruit — **fruit•cake** *n* — **fruit•ed** *adj* — **fruit•ful** *adj* — **fruit•ful•ness** *n* — **fruit•less** *adj* — **fruit•less•ly** *adv* — **fruity** *adj*
fru•ition *n* : completion
frus•trate *vb* **1** : block **2** : cause to fail — **frus•trat•ing•ly** *adv* — **frus•tra•tion** *n*
¹fry *vb* **1** : cook esp. with fat or oil **2** : be cooked by frying ~ *n* **1** : something fried **2** : social gathering with fried food
²fry *n* **fry** : recently hatched fish
fud•dy–dud•dy *n* : one who is old-fashioned or unimaginative
fudge *vb* : cheat or exaggerate ~ *n* : creamy candy
fu•el *n* : material burned to produce heat or power ~ *vb* : provide with or take in fuel
fu•gi•tive *adj* **1** : running away or trying to escape **2** : not lasting — **fu•gi•tive** *n*
ful•fill, ful•fil *vb* **1** : perform **2** : satisfy — **ful•fill•ment** *n*
full *adj* **1** : filled **2** : complete **3** : rounded **4** : having an abundance of something ~ *adv* : entirely ~ *n* : utmost degree — **full•ness** *n* — **ful•ly** *adv*
full–fledged *adj* : fully developed

fum•ble *vb* **:** fail to hold something properly — **fumble** *n*

fume *n* **:** irritating gas ∼ *vb* **1 :** give off fumes **2 :** show annoyance

fu•mi•gate *vb* **:** treat with pest-killing fumes — **fu•mi•gant** *n* — **fu•mi•ga•tion** *n*

fun *n* **1 :** something providing amusement or enjoyment **2 :** enjoyment ∼ *adj* **:** full of fun

func•tion *n* **1 :** special purpose **2 :** formal ceremony or social affair ∼ *vb* **:** have or carry on a function — **func•tion•al** *adj* — **func•tion•al•ly** *adv*

func•tion•ary *n* **:** official

fund *n* **1 :** store **2 :** sum of money intended for a special purpose **3** *pl* **:** available money ∼ *vb* **:** provide funds for

fun•da•men•tal *adj* **1 :** basic **2 :** of central importance or necessity — **fun•da•men•tal** *n* — **fun•da•men•tal•ly** *adv*

fu•ner•al *n* **:** ceremony for a dead person — **fu•ner•al** *adj* — **fu•ne•re•al** *adj*

fun•gus *n* **fun•gi :** lower plant that lacks chlorophyll — **fun•gal** *adj* — **fun•gous** *adj*

funk *n* **:** state of depression

funky *adj* **:** unconventional and unsophisticated

fun•nel *n* **1 :** cone-shaped utensil with a tube for directing the flow of a liquid **2 :** ship's smokestack ∼ *vb* **:** move to a central point or into a central channel

fun•nies *n pl* **:** section of comic strips

fun•ny *adj* **1 :** amusing **2 :** strange

fur *n* **1 :** hairy coat of a mammal **2 :** article of clothing made with fur — **fur** *adj* — **furred** *adj* — **fur•ry** *adj*

fu•ri•ous *adj* **:** fierce or angry — **fu•ri•ous•ly** *adv*

fur•nace *n* **:** enclosed structure in which heat is produced

fur•nish *vb* **1 :** provide with what is needed **2 :** make available for use

fur•nish•ings *n pl* **1 :** articles or accessories of dress **2 :** furniture

fur•ni•ture *n* **:** movable articles for a room

fur•row *n* **1 :** trench made by a plow **2 :** wrinkle or groove — **fur•row** *vb*

fur•ther *adv* **1 :** at or to a more advanced point **2 :** more ∼ *adj* **:** additional ∼ *vb* **:** promote — **fur•ther•ance** *n*

fur•ther•more *adv* **:** in addition

fur•thest *adv or adj* **:** farthest

fur•tive *adj* **:** slyly or secretly done — **fur•tive•ly** *adv* — **fur•tive•ness** *n*

fu•ry *n* **1 :** intense rage **2 :** violence

[1]fuse *n* **1 :** cord lighted to transmit fire to an explosive **2** *usu* **fuze :** device for exploding a charge ∼ *or* **fuze** *vb* **:** equip with a fuse

[2]fuse *vb* **1 :** melt and run together **2 :** unite ∼ *n* **:** electrical safety device — **fus•ible** *adj*

fu•sion *n* **1 :** process of merging by melting **2 :** union of atomic nuclei

fuss *n* **1 :** needless bustle or excitement **2 :** show of attention **3 :** objection or protest ∼ *vb* **:** make a fuss

fuss•bud•get *n* **:** one who fusses or is fussy about trifles

fussy *adj* **1 :** irritable **2 :** paying very close attention to details — **fuss•i•ly** *adv* — **fuss•i•ness** *n*

fu•tile *adj* **:** useless or vain — **fu•til•i•ty** *n*

fu•ton *n* **:** a cotton-filled mattress

fu•ture *adj* **:** coming after the present ∼ *n* **1 :** time yet to come **2 :** what will happen — **fu•tur•is•tic** *adj*

fuze *var of* FUSE

fuzz *n* **:** fine particles or fluff

fuzzy *adj* **1 :** covered with or like fuzz **2 :** indistinct — **fuzz•i•ness** *n*

G

g *n* **1 :** 7th letter of the alphabet **2 :** unit of gravitational force

gab *vb* **:** chatter — **gab** *n* — **gab•by** *adj*

ga•ble *n* **:** triangular part of the end of a building — **ga•bled** *adj*

gad•get *n* **:** device — **gad•get•ry** *n*

gaff *n* **:** metal hook for lifting fish — **gaff** *vb*

gaffe *n* **:** social blunder

gag *vb* **1 :** prevent from speaking or crying out by stopping up the mouth **2 :** retch or cause to retch ∼ *n* **1 :** something that stops up the mouth **2 :** laugh-provoking remark or act

gag•gle *n* **:** flock of geese

gai•ety *n* **:** high spirits

gai•ly *adv* **:** in a gay manner

gain *n* **1 :** profit **2 :** obtaining of profit or possessions **3 :** increase ∼ *vb* **1 :** get possession of **2 :** win **3 :** arrive at **4 :** increase or increase in **5 :** profit — **gain•er** *n* — **gain•ful** *adj* — **gain•ful•ly** *adv*

gait *n* : manner of walking or running — **gait·ed** *adj*

gal *n* : girl

ga·la *n* : festive celebration — **gala** *adj*

gal·axy *n* : very large group of stars — **ga·lac·tic** *adj*

gale *n* **1 :** strong wind **2 :** outburst

¹gall *n* **1 :** bile **2 :** insolence

²gall *n* **1 :** skin sore caused by chafing **2 :** swelling of plant tissue caused by parasites ∼ *vb* **1 :** chafe **2 :** irritate or vex

gal·lant *n* : man very attentive to women ∼ *adj* **1 :** splendid **2 :** brave **3 :** polite and attentive to women — **gal·lant·ly** *adv* — **gal·lant·ry** *n*

gall·blad·der *n* : pouch attached to the liver in which bile is stored

gal·lery *n* **1 :** outdoor balcony **2 :** long narrow passage or hall **3 :** room or building for exhibiting art **4 :** spectators — **gal·ler·ied** *adj*

gal·ley *n* **1 :** old ship propelled esp. by oars **2 :** kitchen of a ship or airplane

gal·lon *n* : unit of liquid measure equal to 4 quarts

gal·lop *n* : fast 3-beat gait of a horse — **gallop** *vb* — **gal·lop·er** *n*

gall·stone *n* : abnormal concretion in the gallbladder or bile passages

ga·lore *adj* : in abundance

ga·losh *n* : overshoe — usu. pl.

gal·va·nize *vb* **1 :** shock into action **2 :** coat (iron or steel) with zinc — **gal·va·ni·za·tion** *n* — **gal·va·niz·er** *n*

gam·ble *vb* **1 :** play a game for stakes **2 :** bet **3 :** take a chance ∼ *n* : risky undertaking — **gam·bler** *n*

game *n* **1 :** playing activity **2 :** competition according to rules **3 :** animals hunted for sport or food ∼ *vb* : gamble ∼ *adj* **1 :** plucky **2 :** lame — **game·ly** *adv* — **game·ness** *n*

game·keep·er *n* : person in charge of game animals or birds

gamy *or* **gam·ey** *adj* : having the flavor of game esp. when slightly tainted — **gam·i·ness** *n*

¹gan·der *n* : male goose

²gander *n* : glance

gang *n* **1 :** group of persons working together **2 :** group of criminals ∼ *vb* : attack in a gang — with *up*

gan·gling *adj* : lanky

gang·ster *n* : member of criminal gang

gap *n* **1 :** break in a barrier **2 :** mountain pass **3 :** empty space

gape *vb* **1 :** open widely **2 :** stare with mouth open — **gape** *n*

ga·rage *n* : shelter or repair shop for automobiles ∼ *vb* : put or keep in a garage

garb *n* : clothing ∼ *vb* : dress

gar·bage *n* **1 :** food waste **2 :** trash — **gar·bage·man** *n*

gar·ble *vb* : distort the meaning of

gar·den *n* **1 :** plot for growing fruits, flowers, or vegetables **2 :** public recreation area ∼ *vb* : work in a garden — **gar·den·er** *n*

gar·de·nia *n* : tree or shrub with fragrant white or yellow flowers or the flower

gar·gan·tuan *adj* : having tremendous size or volume

gar·gle *vb* : rinse the throat with liquid — **gar·gle** *n*

gar·ish *adj* : offensively bright or gaudy

gar·lic *n* : herb with pungent bulbs used in cooking — **gar·licky** *adj*

gar·ment *n* : article of clothing

gar·nish *vb* : add decoration to (as food) — **gar·nish** *n*

gar·ru·lous *adj* : talkative — **gar·ru·li·ty** *n* — **gar·ru·lous·ly** *adv* — **gar·ru·lous·ness** *n*

gar·ter *n* : band to hold up a stocking or sock

gas *n* **1 :** fluid (as hydrogen or air) that tends to expand indefinitely **2 :** gasoline ∼ *vb* **1 :** treat with gas **2 :** fill with gasoline — used with *up* — **gas·eous** *adj*

gash *n* : deep long cut — **gash** *vb*

gas·ket *n* : material or a part used to seal a joint

gas·light *n* : light of burning illuminating gas

gas·o·line *n* : flammable liquid from petroleum

gasp *vb* **1 :** catch the breath audibly **2 :** breathe laboriously — **gasp** *n*

gas·tric *adj* : relating to or located near the stomach

gate *n* : an opening for passage in a wall or fence — **gate·keep·er** *n* — **gate·post** *n*

gath·er *vb* **1 :** bring or come together **2 :** harvest **3 :** pick up little by little **4 :** deduce — **gath·er·er** *n* — **gath·er·ing** *n*

gaudy *adj* : tastelessly showy — **gaud·i·ly** *adv* — **gaud·i·ness** *n*

gauge *n* : instrument for measuring ∼ *vb* : measure

gauze *n* : thin often transparent fabric — **gauzy** *adj*

gave *past of* GIVE

gav•el *n* : mallet of a presiding officer, auctioneer, or judge
gawk *vb* : stare stupidly
gay *adj* **1** : merry **2** : bright and lively **3** : oriented toward one's own sex — **gay** *n*
gaze *vb* : fix the eyes in a steady intent look — **gaze** *n* — **gaz•er** *n*
ga•zette *n* : newspaper
gaz•et•teer *n* : geographical dictionary
gear *n* **1** : clothing **2** : equipment **3** : toothed wheel — **gear** *vb* — **gear•shift** *n*
geek *n* : socially inept person
geese *pl of* GOOSE
gei•sha *n* : Japanese girl or woman trained to entertain men
gel•a•tin *n* : sticky substance obtained from animal tissues by boiling — **ge•lat•i•nous** *adj*
gem *n* : cut and polished valuable stone — **gem•stone** *n*
gen•der *n* **1** : sex **2** : division of a class of words (as nouns) that determines agreement of other words
gene *n* : segment of DNA that controls inheritance of a trait
ge•ne•al•o•gy *n* : study of family pedigrees — **ge•ne•a•log•i•cal** *adj* — **ge•ne•a•log•i•cal•ly** *adv* — **ge•ne•al•o•gist** *n*
gen•er•al *adj* **1** : relating to the whole **2** : applicable to all of a group **3** : common or widespread ~ *n* **1** : something that involves or is applicable to the whole **2** : commissioned officer of the highest rank in the army, air force, or marine corps — **gen•er•al•ly** *adv* — **in general** : for the most part
gen•er•al•i•ty *n* : general statement
gen•er•al•ize *vb* : reach a general conclusion esp. on the basis of particular instances — **gen•er•al•iza•tion** *n*
gen•er•ate *vb* : create or produce
gen•er•a•tion *n* **1** : living beings constituting a single step in a line of descent **2** : production — **gen•er•a•tive** *adj*
gen•er•a•tor *n* **1** : one that generates **2** : machine that turns mechanical into electrical energy
ge•ner•ic *adj* **1** : general **2** : not protected by a trademark **3** : relating to a genus — **generic** *n*
gen•er•ous *adj* : freely giving or sharing — **gen•er•os•i•ty** *n* — **gen•er•ous•ly** *adv* — **gen•er•ous•ness** *n*
ge•net•ics *n* : biology dealing with heredity and variation — **ge•net•ic** *adj* — **ge•net•i•cal•ly** *adv* — **ge•net•i•cist** *n*
ge•nial *adj* : cheerful — **ge•nial•i•ty** *n* — **ge•nial•ly** *adv*
gen•i•tal *adj* : concerned with reproduction — **gen•i•ta•lia** *n pl* — **gen•i•tal•ly** *adv* — **gen•i•tals** *n pl*
ge•nius *n* **1** : single strongly marked capacity **2** : extraordinary intellectual power or a person having such power
geno•cide *n* : systematic destruction of a racial or cultural group
gen•teel *adj* : polite or refined
gen•tile *n* : person who is not Jewish — **gentile** *adj*
gen•til•i•ty *n* **1** : good birth and family **2** : good manners
gen•tle *adj* **1** : of a family of high social station **2** : not harsh, stern, or violent **3** : soft or delicate ~ *vb* : make gentle — **gen•tle•ness** *n* — **gen•tly** *adv*
gen•tle•man *n* : man of good family or manners — **gen•tle•man•ly** *adv*
gen•try *n* **1** : people of good birth or breeding **2** : people of a certain class
gen•u•flect *vb* : bend the knee in worship — **gen•u•flec•tion** *n*
gen•u•ine *adj* : being the same in fact as in appearance — **gen•u•ine•ly** *adv* — **gen•u•ine•ness** *n*
ge•nus *n* (**gen•era**) : category of biological classification
ge•og•ra•phy *n* **1** : study of the earth and its climate, products, and inhabitants **2** : natural features of a region — **ge•og•ra•pher** *n* — **geo•graph•ic, geo•graph•i•cal** *adj* — **geo•graph•i•cal•ly** *adv*
ge•ol•o•gy *n* : study of the history of the earth and its life esp. as recorded in rocks — **geo•log•ic, geo•log•i•cal** *adj* — **geo•log•i•cal•ly** *adv* — **ge•ol•o•gist** *n*
ge•om•e•try *n* : mathematics of the relations, properties, and measurements of solids, surfaces, lines, and angles — **geo•met•ric, geo•met•ri•cal** *adj*
ge•ra•ni•um *n* : garden plant with clusters of white, pink, or scarlet flowers
ger•bil *n* : a small Old World burrowing desert rodent
ge•ri•at•ric *adj* **1** : relating to aging or the aged **2** : old

germ *n* **1 :** microorganism **2 :** source or rudiment

ger•mi•cide *n* **:** agent that destroys germs — **ger•mi•cid•al** *adj*

ger•mi•nate *vb* **:** begin to develop — **ger•mi•na•tion** *n*

ger•und *n* **:** word having the characteristics of both verb and noun

ges•ture *n* **1 :** movement of the body or limbs that expresses something **2 :** something said or done for its effect on the attitudes of others — **ges•tur•al** *adj* — **gesture** *vb*

ge•sund•heit *interj* — used to wish good health to one who has just sneezed

get *vb* (**got; got/got•ten**) **1 :** gain or be in possession of **2 :** succeed in coming or going **3 :** cause to come or go or to be in a certain condition or position **4 :** become **5 :** be subjected to **6 :** understand **7 :** be obliged — **get along** *vb* **1 :** get by **2 :** be on friendly terms — **get by** *vb* **:** meet one's needs

get•away *n* **1 :** escape **2 :** a starting or getting under way

gey•ser *n* **:** spring that intermittently shoots up hot water and steam

ghast•ly *adj* **:** horrible or shocking

gher•kin *n* **:** small pickle

ghet•to *n* **:** part of a city in which members of a minority group live

ghost *n* **:** disembodied soul — **ghost•ly** *adv*

ghoul *n* **:** legendary evil being that feeds on corpses — **ghoul•ish** *adj*

GI *n* **:** member of the U.S. armed forces

gi•ant *n* **1 :** huge legendary being **2 :** something very large or very powerful — **giant** *adj*

gib•ber•ish *n* **:** unintelligible speech or language

gibe *vb* **:** jeer at — **gibe** *n*

gib•lets *n pl* **:** edible fowl viscera

gid•dy *adj* **1 :** silly **2 :** dizzy — **gid•di•ness** *n*

gift *n* **1 :** something given **2 :** talent — **gift•ed** *adj*

gi•gan•tic *adj* **:** very big

gig•gle *vb* **:** laugh in a silly manner — **giggle** *n* — **gig•gly** *adj*

gild *vb* **:** cover with or as if with gold

gill *n* **:** organ of a fish for obtaining oxygen from water

gilt *adj* **:** gold in color **∼** *n* **:** gold or goldlike substance on the surface of an object

gim•mick *n* **:** new and ingenious scheme, feature, or device — **gim•mick•ry** *n* — **gim•micky** *adj*

gin•ger *n* **:** pungent aromatic spice from a tropical plant — **gin•ger•bread** *n*

gin•ger•ly *adv* **:** very cautiously

gin•seng *n* **:** aromatic root of a Chinese herb

gi•raffe *n* **:** African mammal with a very long neck

gird•er *n* **:** horizontal supporting beam

gir•dle *n* **:** woman's supporting undergarment **∼** *vb* **:** surround

girl *n* **1 :** female child **2 :** young woman **3 :** sweetheart — **girl•hood** *n* — **girl•ish** *adj*

girl•friend *n* **:** frequent or regular female companion of a boy or man

gist *n* **:** main point or part

give *vb* (**gave; giv•en**) **1 :** put into the possession or keeping of another **2 :** pay **3 :** perform **4 :** contribute or donate **5 :** produce **6 :** utter **7 :** yield to force, strain, or pressure **∼** *n* **:** capacity or tendency to yield to force or strain — **give in** *vb* **:** surrender — **give out** *vb* **:** become used up or exhausted — **give up** *vb* **1 :** let out of one's control **2 :** cease from trying, doing, or hoping

give•away *n* **1 :** unintentional betrayal **2 :** something given free

giv•en *adj* **1 :** prone or disposed **2 :** having been specified

gla•cial *adj* **1 :** relating to glaciers **2 :** very slow — **gla•cial•ly** *adv*

gla•cier *n* **:** large body of ice moving slowly

glad *adj* **1 :** experiencing or causing pleasure, joy, or delight **2 :** very willing — **glad•den** *vb* — **glad•ly** *adv* — **glad•ness** *n*

glad•i•a•tor *n* **:** one who fought to the death for the entertainment of ancient Romans — **glad•i•a•to•ri•al** *adj*

glad•i•o•lus *n* **:** plant related to the irises

glam•our, glam•or *n* **:** romantic or exciting attractiveness — **glam•or•ize** *vb* — **glam•or•ous** *adj*

glance *vb* **1 :** strike and fly off to one side **2 :** give a quick look **∼** *n* **:** quick look

gland *n* **:** group of cells that secretes a substance — **glan•du•lar** *adj*

glare *vb* **1 :** shine with a harsh dazzling light **2 :** stare angrily **∼** *n* **1 :** harsh dazzling light **2 :** angry stare

glar•ing *adj* **:** painfully obvious — **glar•ing•ly** *adv*

glass *n* **1 :** hard usu. transparent material made by melting sand and other materials **2 :** something made of glass **3** *pl* **:** lenses used to correct defects of vision — **glass** *adj* —

glass•blow•er *n* — **glass•blow•ing** *n* — **glass•ful** *n* — **glass•ware** *n* — **glassy** *adj*
glau•co•ma *n* **:** state of increased pressure within the eyeball
glaze *vb* **1 :** furnish with glass **2 :** apply glaze to ~ *n* **:** glassy surface or coating
gleam *n* **1 :** transient or partly obscured light **2 :** faint trace ~ *vb* **:** send out gleams
glean *vb* **:** collect little by little — **glean•able** *adj* — **glean•er** *n*
glee *n* **:** joy — **glee•ful** *adj*
glen *n* **:** narrow hidden valley
glib *adj* **:** speaking or spoken with ease — **glib-ly** *adv*
glide *vb* **:** move or descend smoothly and effortlessly — **glide** *n*
glid•er *n* **1 :** winged aircraft having no engine **2 :** swinging porch seat
glim•mer *vb* **:** shine faintly or unsteadily ~ *n* **1 :** faint light **2 :** small amount
glimpse *vb* **:** take a brief look at — **glimpse** *n*
glint *vb* **:** gleam or sparkle — **glint** *n*
glis•ten *vb* **:** shine or sparkle by reflection — **glisten** *n*
glit•ter *vb* **:** shine with brilliant or metallic luster ~ *n* **:** small glittering ornaments — **glit-tery** *adj*
glitz *n* **:** extravagant showiness — **glitzy** *adj*
gloat *vb* **:** think of something with triumphant delight
glob *n* **:** large rounded lump
glob•al *adj* **:** worldwide — **glob•al•ly** *adv*
globe *n* **1 :** sphere **2 :** the earth or a model of it
glob•u•lar *adj* **1 :** round **2 :** made up of globules
gloom *n* **1 :** darkness **2 :** sadness — **gloom•i-ly** *adv* — **gloom•i•ness** *n* — **gloomy** *adj*
glo•ry *n* **1 :** praise or honor offered in worship **2 :** cause for praise or renown **3 :** magnificence **4 :** heavenly bliss ~ *vb* **:** rejoice proudly — **glo•ri•fi•ca•tion** *n* — **glo•ri•fy** *vb* — **glo•ri•ous** *adj* — **glo•ri•ous•ly** *adv*
gloss *n* **:** luster — **gloss•i•ly** *adv* — **gloss•i-ness** *n* — **glossy** *adj* — **gloss over** *vb* **1 :** mask the true nature of **2 :** deal with only superficially
glos•sa•ry *n* **:** dictionary — **glos•sar•i•al** *adj*
glove *n* **:** hand covering with sections for each finger
glow *vb* **1 :** shine with or as if with intense heat **2 :** show exuberance ~ *n* **:** brightness or warmth of color or feeling
glow•er *vb* **:** stare angrily — **glower** *n*
glue *n* **:** substance used for sticking things together — **glue** *vb* — **glu•ey** *adj*
glum *adj* **1 :** sullen **2 :** dismal
glut *vb* **:** fill to excess — **glut** *n*
glu•ten *n* **:** gluey protein substance in flour
glut•ton *n* **:** one who eats to excess — **glut-ton•ous** *adj* — **glut•tony** *n*
gnarled *adj* **1 :** knotty **2 :** gloomy or sullen
gnat *n* **:** small biting fly
gnaw *vb* **:** bite or chew on
go *vb* (**went; gone**) **1 :** move, proceed, run, or pass **2 :** leave **3 :** extend or lead **4 :** sell or amount — with *for* **5 :** happen **6** — used in present participle to show intent or imminent action **7 :** become **8 :** fit or harmonize **9 :** belong ~ *n* **1 :** act or manner of going **2 :** vigor **3 :** attempt — **go back on :** betray — **go by the board :** be discarded — **go for :** favor — **go off :** explode — **go one better :** outdo — **go over 1 :** examine **2 :** study — **go to town :** be very successful — **on the go :** constantly active
goad *n* **:** something that urges — **goad** *vb*
goal *n* **1 :** mark to reach in a race **2 :** purpose **3 :** object in a game through which a ball is propelled
goal•ie *n* **:** player who defends the goal
goal•keep•er *n* **:** goalie
goat *n* **:** horned ruminant mammal related to the sheep — **goat•skin** *n*
[1]**gob•ble** *vb* **:** eat greedily
[2]**gob•ble** *vb* **:** make the noise of a turkey (**gob-bler**)
gob•lin *n* **:** ugly mischievous sprite
god *n* **1** *cap* **:** supreme being **2 :** being with supernatural powers — **god•less** *adj* — **god-less•ness** *n* — **god•like** *adj* — **god•ly** *adj*
god•child *n* **:** person one sponsors at baptism — **god•daugh•ter** *n* — **god•son** *n*
god•dess *n* **:** female god
god•par•ent *n* **:** sponsor at baptism — **god•fa-ther** *n* — **god•moth•er** *n*
goes *pres 3d sing of* GO
gog•gle *vb* **:** stare wide-eyed
gog•gles *n pl* **:** protective glasses
gold *n* **:** malleable yellow metallic chemical element — **gold•smith** *n*
gold•en *adj* **1 :** made of, containing, or relating to gold **2 :** having the color of gold **3 :** precious or favorable
gold•fish *n* **:** small usu. orange or golden carp
golf *n* **:** game played by hitting a small ball

(**golf ball**) with clubs (**golf clubs**) into holes placed in a field (**golf course**) — **golf** *vb* — **golf•er** *n*

gon•do•la *n* **1 :** long narrow boat used on the canals of Venice **2 :** car suspended from a cable

gon•do•lier *n* **:** person who propels a gondola

gone *adj* **1 :** past **2 :** involved

gon•er *n* **:** hopeless case

gong *n* **:** metallic disk that makes a deep sound when struck

goo *n* **:** thick or sticky substance — **goo•ey** *adj*

good *adj* (**bet•ter; best**) **1 :** satisfactory **2 :** producing a beneficial effect **3 :** considerable **4 :** desirable **5 :** well-behaved, kind, or virtuous ~ *n* **1 :** something good **2 :** benefit **3** *pl* **:** personal property **4** *pl* **:** wares ~ *adv* **:** well — **good–heart•ed** *adj* — **good–looking** *adj* — **good–na•tured** *adj* — **goodness** *n* — **for good :** forever

good–bye, good–by *n* **:** parting remark

Good Friday *n* **:** Friday before Easter observed as the anniversary of the crucifixion of Christ

good•ly *adj* **:** considerable

good•will *n* **1 :** good intention **2 :** kindly feeling

goody *n* **:** something that is good esp. to eat

goody–goody *adj* **:** affectedly or annoyingly sweet or self-righteous — **goody–goody** *n*

goof *vb* **1 :** blunder **2 :** waste time — usu. with *off* or *around* — **goof** *n* — **goof–off** *n*

goofy *adj* **:** crazy — **goof•i•ness** *n*

goose *n* (**geese**) **:** large bird with webbed feet

goose bumps *n pl* **:** roughening of the skin caused by fear, excitement, or cold

goose•flesh *n* **:** goose bumps

goose pimples *n pl* **:** goose bumps

go•pher *n* **:** burrowing rodent

¹gore *n* **:** blood — **gory** *adj*

²gore *vb* **:** pierce or wound with a horn or tusk

¹gorge *n* **:** narrow ravine

²gorge *vb* **:** eat greedily

gor•geous *adj* **:** supremely beautiful

go•ril•la *n* **:** African manlike ape

gos•pel *n* **1 :** teachings of Christ and the apostles **2 :** something accepted as infallible truth — **gos•pel** *adj*

gos•sip *n* **1 :** person who reveals personal information **2 :** rumor or report of an intimate nature ~ *vb* **:** spread gossip — **gos•sipy** *adj*

got *past of* GET

gotten *past part of* GET

gouge *n* **1 :** rounded chisel **2 :** cavity or groove scooped out ~ *vb* **1 :** cut or scratch a groove in **2 :** to charge too much

gourd *n* **1 :** any of a group of vines including the cucumber, squash, and melon **2 :** inedible hard-shelled fruit of a gourd

gour•met *n* **:** connoisseur of food and drink

gov•ern *vb* **1 :** control and direct policy in **2 :** guide or influence strongly **3 :** restrain — **gov•ern•ment** *n* — **gov•ern•men•tal** *adj*

gov•ern•ess *n* **:** female teacher in a private home

gov•er•nor *n* **1 :** head of a political unit **2 :** automatic speed-control device — **gov•er•nor•ship** *n*

gown *n* **1 :** loose flowing outer garment **2 :** woman's formal evening dress — **gown** *vb*

grab *vb* **:** take by sudden grasp — **grab** *n*

grace *n* **1 :** unmerited divine assistance **2 :** short prayer before or after a meal **3 :** temporary relief **4 :** ease of movement or bearing ~ *vb* **1 :** honor **2 :** adorn — **graceful** *adj* — **grace•ful•ly** *adv* — **grace•ful•ness** *n* — **grace•less** *adj*

gra•cious *adj* **:** marked by kindness and courtesy or charm and taste — **gra•cious•ly** *adv* — **gra•cious•ness** *n*

grack•le *n* **:** American blackbird

grade *n* **1 :** stage in a series, order, or ranking **2 :** division of school representing one year's work **3 :** mark of accomplishment in school **4 :** degree of slope ~ *vb* **1 :** arrange in grades **2 :** make level or evenly sloping **3 :** give a grade to — **grad•er** *n* — **gra•da•tion** *n*

grade school *n* **:** school including the first six or the first eight grades

gra•di•ent *n* **:** slope

grad•u•al *adj* **:** going by steps or degrees — **grad•u•al•ly** *adv*

grad•u•ate *n* **:** holder of a diploma ~ *adj* **:** of or relating to studies beyond the bachelor's degree ~ *vb* **1 :** grant or receive a diploma **2 :** mark with degrees of measurement — **grad•u•a•tion** *n*

graf•fi•ti *n pl* **:** inscriptions on a wall

graft *vb* **:** join one thing to another so that they grow together ~ *n* **1 :** grafted plant **2 :** the getting of money dishonestly or the money so gained — **graft•er** *n*

grain *n* **1 :** seeds or fruits of cereal grasses **2 :** small hard particle **3 :** arrangement of fibers in wood — **grained** *adj* — **grainy** *adj*

gram *n* **:** metric unit of weight equal to $\frac{1}{1000}$ kilogram

gram•mar *n* **:** study of words and their functions and relations in the sentence — **gram•mar•i•an** *n* — **gram•mat•i•cal** *adj* — **gram•mat•i•cal•ly** *adv*

grammar school *n* **:** grade school

grand *adj* **1 :** large or striking in size or scope **2 :** fine and imposing **3 :** very good — **grand•ly** *adv* — **grand•ness** *n*

grand•child *n* **:** child of one's son or daughter — **grand•daugh•ter** *n* — **grand•son** *n*

grand•par•ent *n* **:** parent of one's father or mother — **grand•fa•ther** *n* — **grand•moth•er** *n*

grand•stand *n* **:** usu. roofed stand for spectators

grant *vb* **1 :** consent to **2 :** give **3 :** admit as true ~ *n* **1 :** act of granting **2 :** something granted — **grant•ee** *n* — **grant•er** *n* — **grant•or** *n*

gran•u•late *vb* **:** form into grains or crystals — **gran•u•la•tion** *n*

gran•ule *n* **:** small particle — **gran•u•lar** *adj* — **gran•u•lar•i•ty** *n*

grape *n* **:** smooth juicy edible berry of a woody vine (**grape•vine**)

grape•fruit *n* **:** large edible yellow-skinned citrus fruit

graph *n* **:** diagram that shows relationships between things — **graph** *vb*

graph•ic *adj* **1 :** vividly described **2 :** relating to the arts (**graphic arts**) of representation and printing on flat surfaces ~ *n* **1 :** picture used for illustration **2** *pl* **:** computer screen display — **graph•i•cal•ly** *adv*

graph•ite *n* **:** soft carbon used for lead pencils and lubricants

grasp *vb* **1 :** take or seize firmly **2 :** understand ~ *n* **1 :** one's hold or control **2 :** one's reach **3 :** comprehension

grass *n* **:** plant with jointed stem and narrow leaves — **grass•land** *n* — **grassy** *adj*

grass•hop•per *n* **:** leaping plant-eating insect

¹grate *n* **1 :** grating **2 :** frame of iron bars to hold burning fuel

²grate *vb* **1 :** pulverize by rubbing against something rough **2 :** irritate — **grat•er** *n* — **grat•ing•ly** *adv*

grate•ful *adj* **:** thankful or appreciative — **grate•ful•ly** *adv* — **grate•ful•ness** *n*

grat•i•fy *vb* **:** give pleasure to — **grat•i•fi•ca•tion** *n*

grat•ing *n* **:** framework with bars across it

grat•i•tude *n* **:** state of being grateful

gra•tu•i•tous *adj* **1 :** free **2 :** uncalled-for

gra•tu•ity *n* **:** tip

¹grave *n* **:** place of burial — **grave•stone** *n* — **grave•yard** *n*

²grave *adj* **1 :** threatening great harm or danger **2 :** solemn — **grave•ly** *adv* — **grave•ness** *n*

grav•el *n* **:** loose rounded fragments of rock — **grav•el•ly** *adj*

grav•i•ta•tion *n* **:** natural force of attraction that tends to draw bodies together — **grav•i•ta•tion•al** *adj*

grav•i•ty *n* **1 :** serious importance **2 :** gravitation

gra•vy *n* **:** sauce made from thickened juices of cooked meat

gray *adj* **1 :** of the color gray **2 :** having gray hair ~ *n* **:** neutral color between black and white ~ *vb* **:** make or become gray — **gray•ish** *adj* — **gray•ness** *n*

¹graze *vb* **:** feed on herbage or pasture — **graz•er** *n*

²graze *vb* **:** touch lightly in passing

grease *n* **:** thick oily material or fat ~ *vb* **:** smear or lubricate with grease — **greasy** *adj*

great *adj* **1 :** large in size or number **2 :** larger than usual — **great•ly** *adv* — **great•ness** *n*

greed *n* **:** selfish desire beyond reason — **greed•i•ly** *adv* — **greed•i•ness** *n* — **greedy** *adj*

green *adj* **1 :** of the color green **2 :** not yet ripe **3 :** not having experience ~ *vb* **:** become green ~ *n* **1 :** color between blue and yellow **2** *pl* **:** leafy parts of plants — **green•ish** *adj* — **green•ness** *n*

green•ery *n* **:** green foliage or plants

green•house *n* **:** glass structure for the growing of plants

greet *vb* **1 :** address with expressions of kind wishes **2 :** react to — **greet•er** *n*

greet•ing *n* **1 :** friendly address on meeting **2** *pl* **:** best wishes

gre•gar•i•ous *adj* **:** social or companionable — **gre•gar•i•ous•ly** *adv* — **gre•gar•i•ous•ness** *n*

gre•nade *n* **:** small missile filled with explosive or chemicals

grew *past of* GROW

grey *var of* GRAY

grey•hound *n* **:** tall slender dog noted for speed

grid *n* **1 :** grating **2 :** evenly spaced horizontal and vertical lines (as on a map)

grid•dle *n* **:** flat metal surface for cooking

grid•iron *n* **1 :** grate for broiling **2 :** football field

grief *n* **1 :** emotional suffering caused by or as if by bereavement **2 :** disaster
griev•ance *n* **:** complaint
grieve *vb* **:** feel or cause to feel grief or sorrow
griev•ous *adj* **1 :** oppressive **2 :** causing grief or sorrow — **griev•ous•ly** *adv*
grill *vb* **1 :** cook on a grill **2 :** question intensely ~ *n* **1 :** griddle **2 :** informal restaurant
grille, grill *n* **:** grating forming a barrier or screen — **grill•work** *n*
grim *adj* **1 :** harsh and forbidding in appearance **2 :** relentless — **grim•ly** *adv* — **grimness** *n*
gri•mace *n* **:** facial expression of disgust — **grimace** *vb*
grime *n* **:** embedded or accumulated dirt — **grimy** *adj*
grin *vb* **:** smile so as to show the teeth — **grin** *n*
grind *vb* (**ground; ground**) **1 :** reduce to powder **2 :** wear down or sharpen by friction **3 :** operate or produce by turning a crank ~ *n* **:** monotonous labor or routine — **grind•er** *n* — **grind•stone** *n*
grip *vb* **:** seize or hold firmly ~ *n* **1 :** grasp **2 :** control **3 :** device for holding
gripe *vb* **1 :** cause pains in the bowels **2 :** complain — **gripe** *n*
gris•ly *adj* **:** horrible or gruesome
grist *n* **:** grain to be ground or already ground — **grist•mill** *n*
gris•tle *n* **:** cartilage — **gris•tly** *adj*
grit *n* **1 :** hard sharp granule **2 :** material composed of granules **3 :** steadfast courage ~ *vb* **:** press with a grating noise — **grit•ty** *adj*
groan *vb* **1 :** moan **2 :** creak under a strain — **groan** *n*
gro•cery *n* **1 :** food store **2** *pl* **:** food and commodities sold in a grocery — **gro•cer** *n*
grog•gy *adj* **:** dazed and unsteady on the feet — **grog•gi•ly** *adv* — **grog•gi•ness** *n*
groin *n* **:** juncture of the lower abdomen and inner thigh
groom *n* **1 :** one who cares for horses **2 :** bridegroom ~ *vb* **1 :** clean and care for (as a horse) **2 :** make neat or attractive **3 :** prepare
groove *n* **1 :** long narrow channel **2 :** fixed routine — **groove** *vb*
grope *vb* **:** search for by feeling
[1]**gross** *adj* **1 :** glaringly noticeable **2 :** bulky **3 :** consisting of an overall total exclusive of deductions **4 :** vulgar ~ *n* **:** the whole before any deductions ~ *vb* **:** earn as a total — **gross•ly** *adv* — **gross•ness** *n*
[2]**gross** *n* **:** 12 dozen
grouch *n* **:** complaining person — **grouch** *vb* — **grouchy** *adj*
[1]**ground** *n* **1 :** bottom of a body of water **2** *pl* **:** sediment **3 :** basis for something **4 :** surface of the earth **5 :** conductor that makes electrical connection with the earth or a framework ~ *vb* **1 :** force or bring down to the ground **2 :** give basic knowledge to **3 :** connect with an electrical ground — **ground•less** *adj*
[2]**ground** *past of* GRIND
ground•hog *n* **:** thick-bodied short-legged burrowing rodent
group *n* **:** number of associated individuals ~ *vb* **:** gather or collect into groups
grove *n* **:** small group of trees
grow *vb* (**grew; grown**) **1 :** come into existence and develop to maturity **2 :** be able to grow **3 :** advance or increase **4 :** become **5 :** cultivate — **grow•er** *n*
growl *vb* **:** utter a deep threatening sound — **growl** *n*
grown–up *n* **:** adult — **grown–up** *adj*
growth *n* **1 :** stage in growing **2 :** process of growing **3 :** result of something growing
grub *vb* **1 :** root out by digging **2 :** search about ~ *n* **1 :** thick wormlike larva **2 :** food
grub•by *adj* **:** dirty — **grub•bi•ness** *n*
grudge *vb* **:** be reluctant to give ~ *n* **:** feeling of ill will
gru•el•ing, gru•el•ling *adj* **:** requiring extreme effort
grue•some *adj* **:** horribly repulsive
gruff *adj* **:** rough in speech or manner — **gruffly** *adv*
grum•ble *vb* **:** mutter in discontent — **grumbler** *n*
grumpy *adj* **:** cross — **grump•i•ly** *adv* — **grump•i•ness** *n*
grunge *n* **1 :** something shabby, tattered, or dirty **2 :** rock music expressing alienation and discontent — **grun•gy** *adj*
grunt *n* **:** deep guttural sound — **grunt** *vb*
guar•an•tee *n* **1 :** assurance of the fulfillment of a condition **2 :** something given or held as a security ~ *vb* **1 :** promise to be responsible for **2 :** state with certainty — **guar•an•tor** *n*
guar•an•ty *n* **1 :** promise to answer for another's failure to pay a debt **2 :** guarantee **3 :** pledge ~ *vb* **:** guarantee
guard *n* **1 :** defensive position **2 :** act of pro-

tecting **3 :** an individual or group that guards against danger **4 :** protective or safety device ~ *vb* **1 :** protect or watch over **2 :** take precautions — **guard•house** *n* — **guard•room** *n*

guard•ian *n* **:** one who has responsibility for the care of the person or property of another — **guard•ian•ship** *n*

guer•ril•la, gue•ril•la *n* **:** soldier engaged in small-scale harassing tactics

guess *vb* **1 :** form an opinion from little evidence **2 :** state correctly solely by chance **3 :** think or believe — **guess** *n*

guest *n* **1 :** person to whom hospitality (as of a house) is extended **2 :** patron of a commercial establishment (as a hotel) **3 :** person not a regular cast member who appears on a program

guide *n* **1 :** one that leads or gives direction to another **2 :** device on a machine to direct motion ~ *vb* **1 :** show the way to **2 :** direct — **guid•able** *adj* — **guid•ance** *n* — **guide•book** *n*

guide•line *n* **:** summary of procedures regarding policy or conduct

guild *n* **:** association

guile *n* **:** craftiness — **guile•ful** *adj* — **guile•less** *adj* — **guile•less•ness** *n*

guilt *n* **1 :** fact of having committed an offense **2 :** feeling of responsibility for offenses — **guilt•i•ly** *adv* — **guilt•i•ness** *n* — **guilty** *adj*

guinea pig *n* **:** small So. American rodent

guise *n* **:** external appearance

gui•tar *n* **:** 6-stringed musical instrument played by plucking

gulf *n* **1 :** extension of an ocean or a sea into the land **2 :** wide gap

[1]**gull** *n* **:** seabird with webbed feet

[2]**gull** *vb* **:** make a dupe of ~ *n* **:** dupe — **gull•ible** *adj*

gul•ly *n* **:** trench worn by running water

gulp *vb* **:** swallow hurriedly or greedily — **gulp** *n*

[1]**gum** *n* **:** tissue along the jaw at the base of the teeth

[2]**gum** *n* **1 :** sticky plant substance **2 :** gum usu. of sweetened chicle prepared for chewing — **gum•my** *adj*

gum•drop *n* **:** gumlike candy

gun *n* **1 :** cannon **2 :** portable firearm **3 :** discharge of a gun **4 :** something like a gun ~ *vb* **:** hunt with a gun — **gun•ner** *n* — **gun•fight** *n* — **gun•fight•er** *n* — **gun•fire** *n* — **gun•man** *n* — **gun•pow•der** *n* — **gun•shot** *n* — **gun•smith** *n*

gun•wale *n* **:** upper edge of a boat's side

gup•py *n* **:** tiny tropical fish

gur•gle *vb* **:** make a sound like that of a flowing and gently splashing liquid — **gur•gle** *n*

gu•ru *n* **1 :** personal religious teacher in Hinduism **2 :** expert

gush *vb* **:** pour forth violently or enthusiastically — **gush•er** *n*

gust *n* **1 :** sudden brief rush of wind **2 :** sudden outburst — **gust** *vb* — **gusty** *adj*

gus•to *n* **:** zest

gut *n* **1** *pl* **:** intestines **2 :** digestive canal **3** *pl* **:** courage ~ *vb* **:** remove the intestines of

gut•ter *n* **:** channel for carrying off rainwater

[1]**guy** *n* **:** rope, chain, or rod attached to something to steady it — **guy** *vb*

[2]**guy** *n* **:** person

guz•zle *vb* **:** drink greedily

gym *n* **:** gymnasium

gym•na•si•um *n* **:** place for indoor sports

gym•nas•tics *n* **:** physical exercises performed in a gymnasium — **gym•nast** *n* — **gym•nas•tic** *adj*

gyp *n* **1 :** cheat **2 :** trickery — **gyp** *vb*

gy•rate *vb* **:** revolve around a center — **gy•ra•tion** *n*

gy•ro•scope *n* **:** wheel mounted to spin rapidly about an axis that is free to turn in various directions

H

h *n* **:** 8th letter of the alphabet

hab•it *n* **1 :** monk's or nun's clothing **2 :** usual behavior **3 :** addiction — **hab•it–form•ing** *adj* — **ha•bit•u•al** *adj* — **ha•bit•u•al•ly** *adv*

hab•i•tat *n* **:** place where a plant or animal naturally occurs

hab•i•ta•tion *n* **1 :** occupancy **2 :** dwelling place

hab•it•able *adj* **:** capable of being lived in

[1]**hack** *vb* **1 :** cut with repeated irregular blows **2 :** cough in a short dry manner **3 :** manage successfully — **hack** *n* — **hack•er** *n*

²hack *n* **1 :** horse or vehicle for hire **2 :** saddle horse **3 :** writer for hire — **hack** *adj* — **hack·man** *n*
hack·saw *n* **:** saw for metal
had *past of* HAVE
hag *n* **1 :** witch **2 :** ugly old woman
hag·gard *adj* **:** worn or emaciated — **hag·gard·ly** *adv*
hag·gle *vb* **:** argue in bargaining — **hag·gler** *n*
¹hail *n* **1 :** precipitation in small lumps of ice **2 :** something like a rain of hail ~ *vb* **:** rain hail — **hail·stone** *n* — **hail·storm** *n*
²hail *vb* **1 :** greet or salute **2 :** summon ~ *n* **:** expression of greeting or praise — often used as an interjection
hair *n* **:** threadlike growth from the skin — **hair·brush** *n* — **hair·cut** *n* — **hair·dress·er** *n* — **haired** *adj* — **hair·i·ness** *n* — **hair·less** *adj* — **hair·line** *n* — **hair·pin** *n* — **hair·style** *n* — **hair·styl·ing** *n* — **hair·styl·ist** *n* — **hairy** *adj*
hair·breadth, hairs·breadth *n* **:** tiny distance or margin
hair·do *n* **:** style of wearing hair
hair–rais·ing *adj* **:** causing terror or astonishment
hale *adj* **:** healthy or robust
half *n* (**halves**) **:** either of 2 equal parts ~ *adj* **1 :** being a half or nearly a half **2 :** partial — **half** *adv*
half brother *n* **:** brother related through one parent only
half·heart·ed *adj* **:** without enthusiasm — **half·heart·ed·ly** *adv*
half–life *n* **:** time for half of something to undergo a process
half sister *n* **:** sister related through one parent only
half·way *adj* **:** midway between 2 points — **half·way** *adv*
half–wit *n* **:** foolish person — **half–wit·ted** *adj*
hal·i·but *n* (**halibut**) **:** large flattened fish with both eyes on the upper side
hall *n* **1 :** large public or college or university building **2 :** lobby **3 :** auditorium
hal·le·lu·jah *interj* — used to express praise, joy, or thanks
hall·mark *n* **:** distinguishing characteristic
hal·low *vb* **:** consecrate — **hal·lowed** *adj*
Hal·low·een *n* **:** evening of October 31 observed esp. by children in merrymaking and masquerading
hal·lu·ci·na·tion *n* **:** perception of objects that are not real — **hal·lu·ci·nate** *vb* — **hal·lu·ci·na·to·ry** *adj*
ha·lo *n* **:** circle of light appearing to surround a shining body
halt *vb* **:** stop or cause to stop — **halt** *n*
hal·ter *n* **1 :** rope or strap for leading or tying an animal **2 :** brief blouse held up by straps ~ *vb* **:** catch (an animal) with a halter
halve *vb* **1 :** divide into halves **2 :** reduce to half
halves *pl of* HALF
ham *n* **1 :** thigh — usu. pl. **2 :** cut esp. of pork from the thigh **3 :** showy actor **4 :** amateur radio operator ~ *vb* **:** overplay a part — **ham** *adj*
ham·burg·er, ham·burg *n* **:** ground beef or a sandwich made with this
ham·mer *n* **1 :** hand tool for pounding **2 :** gun part whose striking explodes the charge ~ *vb* **:** beat, drive, or shape with a hammer — **hammer out** *vb* **:** produce with effort
ham·mock *n* **:** swinging bed hung by cords at each end
¹ham·per *vb* **:** impede
²hamper *n* **:** large covered basket
ham·ster *n* **:** thickly built shorttailed rodent
ham·string *vb* **1 :** cripple by cutting the leg tendons **2 :** make ineffective or powerless
hand *n* **1 :** end of a front limb adapted for grasping **2 :** side **3 :** promise of marriage **4 :** handwriting **5 :** assistance or participation **6 :** applause **7 :** cards held by a player **8 :** worker ~ *vb* **:** lead, assist, give, or pass with the hand — **hand·clasp** *n* — **hand·craft** *vb* — **hand·ful** *n* — **hand·gun** *n* — **hand·less** *adj* — **hand·made** *adj* — **hand·rail** *n* — **hand·saw** *n* — **hand·shake** *n* — **hand·wo·ven** *adj* — **hand·writ·ing** *n* — **hand·writ·ten** *adj*
hand·bag *n* **:** woman's purse
hand·book *n* **:** concise reference book
hand·cuffs *n pl* **:** locking bracelets that bind the wrists together — **handcuff** *vb*
hand·i·cap *n* **1 :** advantage given or disadvantage imposed to equalize a competition **2 :** disadvantage — **handicap** *vb* — **hand·i·capped** *adj* — **hand·i·cap·per** *n*

hand•i•craft *n* **1 :** manual skill **2 :** article made by hand — **hand•i•craft•er** *n*

hand•ker•chief *n* **:** small piece of cloth carried for personal use

han•dle *n* **:** part to be grasped ~ *vb* **1 :** touch, hold, or manage with the hands **2 :** deal with **3 :** deal or trade in — **han•dle•bar** *n* — **han•dled** *adj* — **han•dler** *n*

hand•some *adj* **1 :** sizable **2 :** generous **3 :** having a pleasing appearance — **hand•some•ly** *adv* — **hand•some•ness** *n*

hand•spring *n* **:** somersault on the hands

handy *adj* **1 :** conveniently near **2 :** easily used **3 :** dexterous — **hand•i•ly** *adv* — **hand•i•ness** *n*

handy•man *n* **:** one who does odd jobs

hang *vb* **1 :** fasten or remain fastened to an elevated point without support from below **2 :** suspend by the neck until dead — past tense often *hanged* **3 :** droop ~ *n* **1 :** way a thing hangs **2 :** an understanding of something — **hang•er** *n* — **hang•ing** *n*

han•gar *n* **:** airplane shelter

hang•nail *n* **:** loose skin near a fingernail

hang•out *n* **:** place where one likes to spend time

han•ker *vb* **:** desire strongly — **han•ker•ing** *n*

han•ky–pan•ky *n* **:** questionable or underhanded activity

Ha•nuk•kah *n* **:** 8-day Jewish holiday commemorating the rededication of the Temple of Jerusalem after its defilement by Antiochus of Syria

hap•haz•ard *adj* **:** having no plan or order — **hap•haz•ard•ly** *adv*

hap•pen *vb* **1 :** take place **2 :** be fortunate to encounter something unexpectedly — often used with infinitive

hap•pen•ing *n* **:** occurrence

hap•py *adj* **1 :** fortunate **2 :** content, pleased, or joyous — **hap•pi•ly** *adv* — **hap•pi•ness** *n*

ha•rass *vb* **1 :** disturb and impede by repeated raids **2 :** annoy continually — **ha•rass•ment** *n*

har•bor *n* **:** protected body of water suitable for anchorage ~ *vb* **1 :** give refuge to **2 :** hold as a thought or feeling

hard *adj* **1 :** not easily penetrated **2 :** firm or definite **3 :** close or searching **4 :** severe or without apparent feelings **5 :** strenuous or difficult **6 :** physically strong or intense — **hard** *adv* — **hard•ness** *n*

hard•en *vb* **:** make or become hard or harder — **hard•en•er** *n*

hard•head•ed *adj* **1 :** stubborn **2 :** realistic — **hard•head•ed•ly** *adv* — **hard•head•ed•ness** *n*

hard–heart•ed *adj* **:** lacking sympathy — **hard–heart•ed•ly** *adv* — **hard–heart•ed•ness** *n*

hard•ly *adv* **1 :** only just **2 :** certainly not

hard•ship *n* **:** suffering or privation

hard•ware *n* **1 :** cutlery or tools made of metal **2 :** physical components of a vehicle or apparatus

har•dy *adj* **:** able to withstand adverse conditions — **har•di•ly** *adv* — **har•di•ness** *n*

hark *vb* **:** listen

harm *n* **1 :** physical or mental damage **2 :** mischief ~ *vb* **:** cause harm — **harm•ful** *adj* — **harm•ful•ly** *adv* — **harm•ful•ness** *n* — **harm•less** *adj* — **harm•less•ly** *adv* — **harm•less•ness** *n*

har•mon•i•ca *n* **:** small wind instrument with metallic reeds

har•mo•ny *n* **1 :** musical combination of sounds **2 :** pleasing arrangement of parts **3 :** lack of conflict **4 :** internal calm — **har•mon•ic** *adj* — **har•mon•i•cal•ly** *adv* — **har•mo•ni•ous** *adj* — **har•mo•ni•ous•ly** *adv* — **har•mo•ni•ous•ness** *n* — **har•mo•ni•za•tion** *n* — **har•mo•nize** *vb*

har•ness *n* **:** gear of a draft animal ~ *vb* **1 :** put a harness on **2 :** put to use

harp *n* **:** musical instrument with many strings plucked by the fingers ~ *vb* **1 :** play on a harp **2 :** dwell on a subject tiresomely — **harp•er** *n* — **harp•ist** *n*

har•row *n* **:** implement used to break up soil ~ *vb* **1 :** cultivate with a harrow **2 :** distress

harsh *adj* **1 :** disagreeably rough **2 :** severe — **harsh•ly** *adv* — **harsh•ness** *n*

har•vest *n* **1 :** act or time of gathering in a crop **2 :** mature crop — **harvest** *vb* — **har•vest•er** *n*

has *pres 3d sing of* HAVE

hash *vb* **:** chop into small pieces ~ *n* **:** chopped meat mixed with potatoes and browned

has•sle *n* **1 :** quarrel **2 :** struggle **3 :** cause of annoyance — **hassle** *vb*

haste *n* **1 :** rapidity of motion **2 :** rash action **3 :** excessive eagerness — **hast•i•ly** *adv* — **hast•i•ness** *n* — **hasty** *adj*

has•ten *vb* **:** hurry

hat *n* : covering for the head

[1]hatch *n* : small door or opening — **hatch·way** *n*

[2]hatch *vb* : emerge from an egg — **hatch·ery** *n*

hatch·et *n* : short-handled ax

hate *n* : intense hostility and aversion ~ *vb* **1** : express or feel hate **2** : dislike — **hate·ful** *adj* — **hate·ful·ly** *adv* — **hate·ful·ness** *n* — **hat·er** *n*

ha·tred *n* : hate

haugh·ty *adj* : disdainfully proud — **haugh·ti·ly** *adv* — **haugh·ti·ness** *n*

haul *vb* **1** : draw or pull **2** : transport or carry ~ *n* **1** : amount collected **2** : load or the distance it is transported — **haul·er** *n*

haunt *vb* **1** : visit often **2** : visit or inhabit as a ghost ~ *n* : place frequented — **haunt·er** *n* — **haunt·ing·ly** *adv*

have *vb* (**had; had**) **1** : hold in possession, service, or affection **2** : be compelled or forced — used with *to* **3** — used as an auxiliary with the past participle to form the present perfect, past perfect, or future perfect **4** : obtain or receive **5** : undergo **6** : cause to **7** : bear — **have to do with** : have in the way of connection or relation with or effect on

hav·oc *n* **1** : wide destruction **2** : great confusion

[1]hawk *n* : bird of prey with a strong hooked bill and sharp talons

[2]hawk *vb* : offer for sale by calling out in the street — **hawk·er** *n*

hay *n* : herbs (as grass) cut and dried for use as fodder — **hay** *vb* — **hay·loft** *n* — **hay·mow** *n* — **hay·stack** *n*

hay·wire *adj* : being out of order

haz·ard *n* **1** : source of danger **2** : chance ~ *vb* : venture or risk — **haz·ard·ous** *adj*

[1]haze *n* : fine dust, smoke, or light vapor in the air that reduces visibility

[2]haze *vb* : harass by abusive and humiliating tricks

ha·zel *n* **1** : shrub or small tree bearing edible nuts (**ha·zel·nuts**) **2** : light brown color

hazy *adj* **1** : obscured by haze **2** : vague or indefinite — **haz·i·ly** *adv* — **haz·i·ness** *n*

he *pron* **1** : that male one **2** : a or the person

head *n* **1** : front or upper part of the body **2** : mind **3** : upper or higher end **4** : director or leader **5** : place of leadership or honor ~ *adj* : principal or chief ~ *vb* **1** : provide with or form a head **2** : put, stand, or be at the head **3** : point or proceed in a certain direction — **head·ache** *n* — **head·band** *n* — **head·dress** *n* — **head·ed** *adj* — **head·first** *adv or adj* — **head·gear** *n* — **head·less** *adj* — **head·rest** *n* — **head·ship** *n* — **head·wait·er** *n*

head·ing *n* **1** : direction in which a plane or ship heads **2** : something (as a title) standing at the top or beginning

head·light *n* : light on the front of a vehicle

head·line *n* : introductory line of a newspaper story printed in large type

head–on *adj* : having the front facing in the direction of initial contact — **head–on** *adv*

head·phone *n* : an earphone held on by a band over the head — usu. pl.

head·quar·ters *n sing or pl* : command or administrative center

head·strong *adj* : stubborn or willful

heady *adj* **1** : tending to make one giddy or elated **2** : shrewd

heal *vb* : make or become sound or whole — **heal·er** *n*

health *n* : sound physical or mental condition

health·ful *adj* : beneficial to health — **health·ful·ly** *adv* — **health·ful·ness** *n*

healthy *adj* : enjoying or typical of good health — **health·i·ly** *adv* — **health·i·ness** *n*

heap *n* : pile ~ *vb* : throw or lay in a heap

hear *vb* **1** : perceive by the ear **2** : heed **3** : learn

hear·ing *n* **1** : process or power of perceiving sound **2** : earshot **3** : session in which witnesses are heard

hear·say *n* : rumor

hearse *n* : vehicle for carrying the dead to the grave

heart *n* **1** : hollow muscular organ that keeps up the circulation of the blood **2** : playing card of a suit marked with a red heart **3** : whole personality or the emotional or moral part of it **4** : courage **5** : essential part — **heart·beat** *n* — **heart·ed** *adj*

heart·ache *n* : anguish of mind

heart·break *n* : crushing grief — **heart·break·er** *n* — **heart·break·ing** *adj* — **heart·bro·ken** *adj*

heart·burn *n* : burning distress in the heart area after eating

heart·en *vb* : encourage

hearth *n* **1** : area in front of a fireplace **2** : home — **hearth·stone** *n*

heart·less *adj* : cruel

heart•warm•ing *adj* : inspiring sympathetic feeling

hearty *adj* **1 :** vigorously healthy **2 :** nourishing — **heart•i•ly** *adv* — **heart•i•ness** *n*

heat *vb* : make or become warm or hot ∼ *n* **1 :** condition of being hot **2 :** form of energy that causes a body to rise in temperature **3 :** intensity of feeling — **heat•ed•ly** *adv* — **heat•er** *n*

hea•then *n* : person who is godless or not civilized — **heathen** *adj*

heave *vb* **1 :** rise or lift upward **2 :** throw **3 :** rise and fall ∼ *n* **1 :** an effort to lift or raise **2 :** throw

heav•en *n* **1** *pl* **:** sky **2 :** abode of the Deity and of the blessed dead **3 :** place of supreme happiness — **heav•en•ly** *adj* — **heav•en•ward** *adv or adj*

heavy *adj* **1 :** having great weight **2 :** hard to bear **3 :** greater than the average — **heav•i•ly** *adv* — **heavi•ness** *n* — **heavy•weight** *n*

heck•le *vb* : harass with gibes — **heck•ler** *n*

hec•tic *adj* : filled with excitement, activity, or confusion — **hec•ti•cal•ly** *adv*

hedge *n* **1 :** fence or boundary of shrubs or small trees **2 :** means of protection ∼ *vb* **1 :** protect oneself against loss **2 :** evade the risk of commitment — **hedg•er** *n*

heed *vb* : pay attention ∼ *n* : attention — **heed•ful** *adj* — **heed•ful•ly** *adv* — **heed•ful•ness** *n* — **heed•less** *adj* — **heed•less•ly** *adv* — **heed•less•ness** *n*

heel *n* **1 :** back of the foot **2 :** crusty end of a loaf of bread **3 :** solid piece forming the back of the sole of a shoe — **heel•less** *adj*

hefty *adj* : big and bulky

height *n* **1 :** highest part or point **2 :** distance from bottom to top **3 :** altitude

height•en *vb* : increase in amount or degree

heir *n* : one who inherits or is entitled to inherit property

heir•ess *n* : female heir esp. to great wealth

held *past of* HOLD

he•li•cop•ter *n* : aircraft supported in the air by rotors

he•li•um *n* : very light nonflammable gaseous chemical element

hell *n* **1 :** nether world in which the dead continue to exist **2 :** realm of the devil **3 :** place or state of torment or destruction — **hell•ish** *adj*

hel•lo *n* : expression of greeting

helm *n* : lever or wheel for steering a ship — **helms•man** *n*

hel•met *n* : protective covering for the head

help *vb* **1 :** supply what is needed **2 :** be of use **3 :** refrain from or prevent ∼ *n* **1 :** something that helps or is a source of help **2 :** one who helps another — **help•er** *n* — **help•ful** *adj* — **help•ful•ly** *adv* — **help•ful•ness** *n* — **help•less** *adj* — **help•less•ly** *adv* — **help•less•ness** *n*

help•ing *n* : portion of food

hem *n* : border of an article of cloth doubled back and stitched down ∼ *vb* **1 :** sew a hem **2 :** surround restrictively — **hem•line** *n*

hemi•sphere *n* : one of the halves of the earth divided by the equator into northern and southern parts (**northern hemisphere, southern hemisphere**) or by a meridian into eastern and western parts (**eastern hemisphere, western hemisphere**) — **hemi•spher•ic, hemi•spher•i•cal** *adj*

hem•or•rhage *n* : large discharge of blood — **hemorrhage** *vb* — **hem•or•rhag•ic** *adj*

hen *n* : female domestic fowl

hence *adv* **1 :** away **2 :** therefore **3 :** from this source or origin

hence•forth *adv* : from this point on

her *adj* : of or relating to her or herself ∼ *pron objective case of* SHE

herb *n* **1 :** seed plant that lacks woody tissue **2 :** plant or plant part valued for medicinal or savory qualities — **her•ba•ceous** *adj* — **herb•age** *n* — **herb•al** *n or adj* — **herb•al•ist** *n*

her•bi•cide *n* : agent that destroys plants — **her•bi•cid•al** *adj*

herd *n* : group of animals of one kind ∼ *vb* : assemble or move in a herd — **herd•er** *n* — **herds•man** *n*

here *adv* **1 :** in, at, or to this place **2 :** now **3 :** at or in this point or particular **4 :** in the present life or state ∼ *n* : this place — **here•abouts, here•about** *adv*

here•af•ter *adv* : in some future time or state ∼ *n* : existence beyond earthly life

he•red•i•tary *adj* **1 :** genetically passed or passable from parent to offspring **2 :** passing by inheritance — **he•red•i•ty** *n*

her•e•sy *n* : opinion or doctrine contrary to church dogma — **her•e•tic** *n* — **he•re•ti•cal** *adj*

here•to•fore *adv* : up to this time

her•i•tage *n* **1 :** inheritance **2 :** birthright

her•mit *n* : one who lives in solitude

he•ro *n* **:** one that is much admired or shows great courage — **he•ro•ic** *adj* — **he•ro•i•cal•ly** *adv* — **he•ro•ics** *n pl* — **her•o•ism** *n*
her•o•in *n* **:** strongly addictive narcotic
her•o•ine *n* **:** woman of heroic achievements or qualities
her•on *n* **:** long-legged long-billed wading bird
hers *pron* **:** one or the ones belonging to her
her•self *pron* **:** she, her — used reflexively or for emphasis
hertz *n* **hertz :** unit of frequency equal to one cycle per second
hes•i•tant *adj* **:** tending to hesitate — **hes•i•tance** *n* — **hes•i•tan•cy** *n* — **hes•i•tant•ly** *adv*
hes•i•tate *vb* **1 :** hold back esp. in doubt **2 :** pause — **hes•i•ta•tion** *n*
hew *vb* **1 :** cut or shape with or as if with an ax **2 :** conform strictly — **hew•er** *n*
hex *vb* **:** put an evil spell on — **hex** *n*
hexa•gon *n* **:** 6-sided polygon — **hex•ag•o•nal** *adj*
hi•ber•nate *vb* **:** pass the winter in a torpid or resting state — **hi•ber•na•tion** *n* — **hi•ber•na•tor** *n*
hic•cup *vb* **:** to inhale spasmodically and make a peculiar sound ∼ *n pl* **:** attack of hiccuping
[1]**hide** *vb* **hid; hid•den/hid :** put or remain out of sight — **hid•er** *n*
[2]**hide** *n* **:** animal skin
hid•eous *adj* **:** very ugly — **hid•eous•ly** *adv* — **hid•eous•ness** *n*
hi•er•ar•chy *n* **:** persons or things arranged in a graded series — **hi•er•ar•chi•cal** *adj*
high *adj* **1 :** having large extension upward **2 :** elevated in pitch **3 :** exalted in character **4 :** of greater degree or amount than average **5 :** expensive **6 :** excited or stupefied by alcohol or a drug ∼ *adv* **:** at or to a high place or degree ∼ *n* **1 :** elevated point or level **2 :** automobile gear giving the highest speed — **high•ly** *adv* — **high•ness** *n*
high–definition *adj* **:** being or relating to a television system with twice as many scan lines per frame as a conventional system
high•light *n* **:** event or detail of major importance ∼ *vb* **1 :** emphasize **2 :** be a highlight of
high school *n* **:** school usu. including grades 9 to 12 or 10 to 12
high–strung *adj* **:** very nervous or sensitive
high•way *n* **:** public road
hi•jack *vb* **:** steal esp. by commandeering a vehicle — **hijack** *n* — **hi•jack•er** *n*
hike *vb* **1 :** raise quickly **2 :** take a long walk ∼ *n* **1 :** long walk **2 :** increase — **hik•er** *n*
hi•lar•i•ous *adj* **:** extremely funny — **hi•lar•i•ous•ly** *adv* — **hi•lar•i•ty** *n*
hill *n* **:** place where the land rises — **hill•side** *n* — **hill•top** *n* — **hilly** *adj*
him *pron, objective case of* HE
him•self *pron* **:** he, him — used reflexively or for emphasis
hind *adj* **:** back — **hind•most** *adj*
hin•der *vb* **:** obstruct or hold back
hin•drance *n* **:** something that hinders
hind•sight *n* **:** understanding of an event after it has happened
Hin•du•ism *n* **:** body of religious beliefs and practices native to India — **Hin•du** *n or adj*
hinge *n* **:** jointed piece on which a swinging part (as a door) turns ∼ *vb* **1 :** attach by or furnish with hinges **2 :** depend
hint *n* **1 :** indirect suggestion **2 :** clue **3 :** very small amount — **hint** *vb*
hip *n* **:** part of the body on either side just below the waist — **hip•bone** *n*
hip•po•pot•a•mus *n* **:** large thick-skinned African river animal
hire *n* **1 :** payment for labor **2 :** employment **3 :** one who is hired ∼ *vb* **:** employ for pay
his *adj* **:** of or belonging to him ∼ *pron* **:** ones belonging to him
hiss *vb* **1 :** make a sibilant sound **2 :** show dislike by hissing — **hiss** *n*
his•to•ry *n* **1 :** chronological record of significant events **2 :** study of past events **3 :** an established record — **his•to•ri•an** *n* — **his•tor•ic, his•tor•i•cal** *adj* — **his•tor•i•cal•ly** *adv*
hit *vb* **hit; hit 1 :** reach with a blow **2 :** come or cause to come in contact **3 :** affect detrimentally ∼ *n* **1 :** blow **2 :** great success — **hit•ter** *n*
hitch *vb* **1 :** move by jerks **2 :** catch by a hook **3 :** hitchhike ∼ *n* **1 :** jerk **2 :** sudden halt
hitch•hike *vb* **:** travel by securing free rides from passing vehicles — **hitch•hik•er** *n*
hive *n* **1 :** container housing honeybees **2 :** colony of bees — **hive** *vb*
HMO *n* **:** comprehensive health-care organization financed by clients
hoard *n* **:** hidden accumulation — **hoard** *vb* — **hoard•er** *n*
hoarse *adj* **1 :** harsh in sound **2 :** speaking in

a harsh strained voice — **hoarse·ly** *adv* — **hoarse·ness** *n*

hoax *n* **:** act intended to trick or dupe — **hoax** *vb* — **hoax·er** *n*

hob·ble *vb* **:** limp along ~ *n* **:** hobbling movement

hob·by *n* **:** interest engaged in for relaxation — **hob·by·ist** *n*

hob·nail *n* **:** short nail for studding shoe soles — **hob·nailed** *adj*

hock·ey *n* **:** game played on ice or a field by 2 teams

hodge·podge *n* **:** heterogeneous mixture

hoe *n* **:** long-handled tool for cultivating or weeding — **hoe** *vb*

hog *n* **1 :** domestic adult swine **2 :** glutton ~ *vb* **:** take selfishly — **hog·gish** *adj*

hoist *vb* **:** lift ~ *n* **1 :** lift **2 :** apparatus for hoisting

hold *vb* (**held; held**) **1 :** possess **2 :** restrain **3 :** have a grasp on **4 :** remain or keep in a particular situation or position **5 :** contain **6 :** regard **7 :** cause to occur **8 :** occupy esp. by appointment or election ~ *n* **1 :** act or manner of holding **2 :** restraining or controlling influence — **hold·er** *n* — **hold forth :** speak at length — **hold to :** adhere to — **hold with :** agree with

hold·up *n* **1 :** robbery at the point of a gun **2 :** delay

hole *n* **1 :** opening into or through something **2 :** hollow place (as a pit) **3 :** den — **hole** *vb*

hol·i·day *n* **1 :** day of freedom from work **2 :** vacation — **holiday** *vb*

ho·lis·tic *adj* **:** relating to a whole (as the body)

hol·ler *vb* **:** cry out — **hol·ler** *n*

hol·low *adj* **1 :** somewhat depressed **2 :** having a cavity within **3 :** sounding like a noise made in an empty place **4 :** empty of value or meaning ~ *vb* **:** make or become hollow ~ *n* **1 :** surface depression **2 :** cavity — **hol·low·ness** *n*

hol·ly *n* **:** evergreen tree or shrub with glossy leaves

ho·lo·caust *n* **:** thorough destruction esp. by fire

ho·ly *adj* **1 :** sacred **2 :** spiritually pure — **ho·li·ness** *n*

hom·age *n* **:** reverent regard

home *n* **1 :** residence **2 :** congenial environment **3 :** place of origin or refuge ~ *vb* **:** go or return home — **home·bred** *adj* — **home·com·ing** *n* — **hom·ey** *adj* — **home·grown** *adj* — **home·land** *n* — **home·less** *adj* — **home·made** *adj*

home·ly *adj* **:** plain or unattractive — **home·li·ness** *n*

home·sick *adj* **:** longing for home — **home·sick·ness** *n*

home·stead *n* **:** home and land occupied and worked by a family — **home·stead·er** *n*

home·work *n* **:** school lessons to be done outside the classroom

ho·mo·ge·neous *adj* **:** of the same or a similar kind — **ho·mo·ge·ne·i·ty** *n* — **ho·mo·ge·neous·ly** *adv*

ho·mog·e·nize *vb* **:** make the particles in (as milk) of uniform size and even distribution — **ho·mog·e·ni·za·tion** *n* — **ho·mog·e·niz·er** *n*

Ho·mo sa·pi·ens *n* **:** humankind

hon·est *adj* **1 :** free from deception **2 :** trustworthy **3 :** frank — **hon·est·ly** *adv* — **hon·esty** *n*

hon·ey *n* **:** sweet sticky substance made by bees (**hon·ey·bees**) from the nectar of flowers — **hon·ey·comb** *n*

hon·ey·moon *n* **:** holiday taken by a newly married couple — **honeymoon** *vb*

honk *n* **:** cry of a goose or a similar sound — **honk** *vb* — **honk·er** *n*

hon·or *n* **1 :** good name **2 :** outward respect or symbol of this **3 :** privilege **4 :** person of superior rank or position — used esp. as a title **5 :** something or someone worthy of respect **6 :** integrity ~ *vb* **1 :** regard with honor **2 :** confer honor on **3 :** fulfill the terms of — **hon·or·able** *adj* — **hon·or·ably** *adv* — **hon·or·ari·ly** *adv* — **hon·or·ary** *adj* — **hon·or·ee** *n*

hood *n* **1 :** part of a garment that covers the head **2 :** covering over an automobile engine compartment — **hood·ed** *adj*

hood·wink *vb* **:** deceive

hoof *n* **:** horny covering of the toes of some mammals (as horses or cattle) — **hoofed** *adj*

hook *n* **:** curved or bent device for catching, holding, or pulling ~ *vb* **:** seize or make fast with a hook — **hook·er** *n*

hoop *n* **:** circular strip, figure, or object

hoot *vb* **1 :** shout in contempt **2 :** make the cry of an owl — **hoot** *n* — **hoot·er** *n*

hop *vb* **:** move by quick springy leaps — **hop** *n*

hope *vb* **:** desire with expectation of fulfillment ~ *n* **1 :** act of hoping **2 :** something hoped for — **hope·ful** *adj* — **hope·ful·ly** *adv* —

hope•ful•ness *n* — **hope•less** *adj* — **hope•less•ly** *adv* — **hope•less•ness** *n*

ho•ri•zon *n* : apparent junction of earth and sky — **hor•i•zon•tal** *adj* — **hor•i•zon•tal•ly** *adv*

hor•mone *n* : cell product in body fluids that has a specific effect on other cells — **hor•mon•al** *adj*

horn *n* **1** : hard bony projection on the head of a hoofed animal **2** : brass wind instrument — **horned** *adj* — **horn•less** *adj* — **horny** *adj*

hor•net *n* : large social wasp

hor•ren•dous *adj* : horrible

hor•ri•ble *adj* **1** : having or causing horror **2** : highly disagreeable — **hor•ri•ble•ness** *n* — **hor•ri•bly** *adv*

hor•ri•fy *vb* : cause to feel horror

hor•ror *n* **1** : intense fear, dread, or dismay **2** : intense repugnance **3** : something horrible

horse *n* : large solid-hoofed domesticated mammal — **horse•back** *n or adv* — **horse•hair** *n* — **horse•hide** *n* — **horse•less** *adj* — **horse•man** *n* — **horse•man•ship** *n* — **horse•wom•an** *n* — **hors•ey, horsy** *adj*

horse•play *n* : rough boisterous play

horse•pow•er *n* : unit of mechanical power

horse•shoe *n* : U-shaped protective metal plate fitted to the rim of a horse's hoof

hor•ti•cul•ture *n* : science of growing fruits, vegetables, and flowers — **hor•ti•cul•tur•al** *adj* — **hor•ti•cul•tur•ist** *n*

hose *n* **1** *pl* **hose** : stocking or sock **2** *pl* **hos•es** : flexible tube for conveying fluids ~ *vb* : spray, water, or wash with a hose

hos•pi•ta•ble *adj* : given to generous and cordial reception of guests — **hos•pi•ta•bly** *adv*

hos•pi•tal *n* : institution where the sick or injured receive medical care — **hos•pi•tal•i•za•tion** *n* — **hos•pi•tal•ize** *vb*

hos•pi•tal•i•ty *n* : hospitable treatment, reception, or disposition

[1]host *n* **1** : army **2** : multitude

[2]host *n* : one who receives or entertains guests — **host** *vb*

[3]host *n* : eucharistic bread

hos•tage *n* : person held to guarantee that promises be kept or demands met

host•ess *n* : woman who is host

hos•tile *adj* : openly or actively unfriendly or opposed to someone or something — **hostile** *n* — **hos•tile•ly** *adv* — **hos•til•i•ty** *n*

hot *adj* **1** : having a high temperature **2** : giving a sensation of heat or burning **3** : ardent **4** : pungent — **hot** *adv* — **hot•ly** *adv* — **hot•ness** *n*

hot dog *n* : frankfurter

ho•tel *n* : building where lodging and personal services are provided

hound *n* : long-eared hunting dog ~ *vb* : pursue relentlessly

hour *n* **1** : 24th part of a day **2** : time of day — **hour•ly** *adv or adj*

hour•glass *n* : glass vessel for measuring time

house *n* **1** : building to live in **2** : household **3** : legislative body **4** : business firm ~ *vb* : provide with or take shelter — **house•boat** *n* — **house•clean** *vb* — **house•clean•ing** *n* — **house•ful** *n* — **house•keep•er** *n* — **house•keep•ing** *n* — **house•maid** *n* — **house•wares** *n pl* — **house•work** *n*

house•bro•ken *adj* : trained in excretory habits acceptable in indoor living

house•fly *n* : two-winged fly common about human habitations

house•hold *n* : those who dwell as a family under the same roof ~ *adj* **1** : domestic **2** : common or familiar — **house•hold•er** *n*

house•wife *n* (**house•wives**) : married woman in charge of a household — **house•wife•ly** *adj* — **house•wif•ery** *n*

hov•er *vb* **1** : remain suspended in the air **2** : move about in the vicinity

how *adv* **1** : in what way or condition **2** : for what reason **3** : to what extent ~ *conj* : the way or manner in which

how•ev•er *conj* : in whatever manner ~ *adv* **1** : to whatever degree or in whatever manner **2** : in spite of that

howl *vb* : emit a loud long doleful sound like a dog — **howl** *n* — **howl•er** *n*

hub *n* : central part of a circular object (as of a wheel) — **hub•cap** *n*

hud•dle *vb* **1** : crowd together **2** : confer — **hud•dle** *n*

hue *n* : color or gradation of color — **hued** *adj*

hug *vb* **1** : press tightly in the arms **2** : stay close to — **hug** *n*

huge *adj* : very large or extensive — **huge•ly** *adv* — **huge•ness** *n*

hulk *n* **1** : bulky or unwieldy person or thing **2** : old ship unfit for service — **hulk•ing** *adj*

hull *n* **1** : outer covering of a fruit or seed **2** : frame or body of a ship or boat ~ *vb* : remove the hulls of — **hull•er** *n*

hum *vb* **1** : make a prolonged sound like that of the speech sound /m/ **2** : be busily active **3**

: run smoothly **4 :** sing with closed lips — **hum** *n* — **hum•mer** *n*

hu•man *adj* **1 :** of or relating to the species people belong to **2 :** by, for, or like people — **human** *n* — **hu•man•kind** *n* — **hu•man•ly** *adv* — **hu•man•ness** *n*

hu•mane *adj* **:** showing compassion or consideration for others — **hu•mane•ly** *adv* — **hu•mane•ness** *n*

hu•man•ism *n* **:** doctrine or way of life centered on human interests or values — **hu•man-ist** *n or adj* — **hu•man•is•tic** *adj*

hu•man•i•tar•i•an *n* **:** person promoting human welfare — **hu•man•i•tar•i•an** *adj* — **hu•man•i•tari•an•ism** *n*

hu•man•i•ty *n* **1 :** human or humane quality or state **2 :** the human race

hum•ble *adj* **1 :** not proud or haughty **2 :** not pretentious ~ *vb* **:** make humble — **hum•ble•ness** *n* — **hum•bler** *n* — **hum•bly** *adv*

hu•mid *adj* **:** containing or characterized by moisture — **hu•mid•i•fi•ca•tion** *n* — **hu•mid•i•fi•er** *n* — **hu•mid•i•fy** *vb* — **hu•mid•ly** *adv*

hu•mid•i•ty *n* **:** atmospheric moisture

hu•mil•i•ate *vb* **:** injure the self-respect of — **hu•mil•i•at•ing•ly** *adv* — **hu•mil•i•ation** *n*

hu•mil•i•ty *n* **:** humble quality or state

hu•mor *n* **1 :** mood **2 :** quality of being laughably ludicrous or incongruous **3 :** appreciation of what is ludicrous or incongruous **4 :** something intended to be funny ~ *vb* **:** comply with the wishes or mood of — **hu•mor•ist** *n* — **hu•mor•less** *adj* — **hu•mor•less•ly** *adv* — **hu•mor•less•ness** *n* — **hu•mor•ous** *adj* — **hu•mor•ous•ly** *adv* — **hu•mor•ous•ness** *n*

hump *n* **:** rounded protuberance — **humped** *adj*

hunch *vb* **:** assume or cause to assume a bent or crooked posture ~ *n* **:** strong intuitive feeling

hun•dred *n* **:** 10 times 10 — **hundred** *adj* — **hun•dredth** *adj or n*

hun•ger *n* **1 :** craving or urgent need for food **2 :** strong desire — **hunger** *vb* — **hun•gri•ly** *adv* — **hun•gry** *adj*

hunk *n* **:** large piece

hunt *vb* **1 :** pursue for food or sport **2 :** try to find ~ *n* **:** act or instance of hunting — **hunt•er** *n*

hur•dle *n* **1 :** barrier to leap over in a race **2 :** obstacle — **hur•dle** *vb* — **hur•dler** *n*

hurl *vb* **:** throw with violence — **hurl** *n* — **hurl•er** *n*

hur•rah *interj* — used to express joy or approval

hur•ri•cane *n* **:** tropical storm with winds of 74 miles per hour or greater

hur•ry *vb* **:** go or cause to go with haste ~ *n* **:** extreme haste — **hur•ried•ly** *adv* — **hur•ried•ness** *n*

hurt *vb* **hurt; hurt 1 :** feel or cause pain **2 :** do harm to ~ *n* **1 :** bodily injury **2 :** harm — **hurt•ful** *adj* — **hurt•ful•ness** *n*

hur•tle *vb* **:** move rapidly or forcefully

hus•band *n* **:** married man ~ *vb* **:** manage prudently

hus•band•ry *n* **1 :** careful use **2 :** agriculture

hush *vb* **:** make or become quiet ~ *n* **:** silence

husk *n* **:** outer covering of a seed or fruit ~ *vb* **:** strip the husk from — **husk•er** *n*

[1]**hus•ky** *adj* **:** hoarse — **hus•ki•ly** *adv* — **hus•ki•ness** *n*

[2]**husky** *adj* **:** burly — **husk•i•ness** *n*

hus•tle *vb* **1 :** hurry **2 :** work energetically — **hustle** *n* — **hus•tler** *n*

hut *n* **:** small often temporary dwelling

hy•brid *n* **:** offspring of genetically differing parents — **hybrid** *adj* — **hy•brid•iza•tion** *n* — **hy•brid•ize** *vb* — **hy•brid•iz•er** *n*

hy•drant *n* **:** pipe from which water may be drawn to fight fires

hy•dro•elec•tric *adj* **:** producing electricity by waterpower — **hy•dro•elec•tric•i•ty** *n*

hy•dro•gen *n* **:** very light gaseous colorless odorless flammable chemical element

hy•giene *n* **:** conditions or practices conducive to health — **hy•gien•ic** *adj* — **hy•gien•i•cal•ly** *adv* — **hy•gien•ist** *n*

hying *pres part of* HIE

hymn *n* **:** song of praise esp. to God — **hymn** *vb*

hym•nal *n* **:** book of hymns

hype *vb* **:** publicize extravagantly — **hype** *n*

hy•phen *n* **:** punctuation mark - used to divide or compound words — **hyphen** *vb*

hy•phen•ate *vb* **:** connect or divide with a hyphen — **hy•phen•ation** *n*

hyp•no•sis *n* **:** induced state like sleep in which the subject is responsive to suggestions of the inducer (**hyp•no•tist**) — **hyp•no•tism** *n* — **hyp•no•tiz•able** *adj* — **hyp•no•tize** *vb*

hy•poc•ri•sy *n* **:** a feigning to be what one is not — **hyp•o•crite** *n* — **hyp•o•crit•i•cal** *adj* — **hyp•o•crit•i•cal•ly** *adv*

hy•pot•e•nuse *n* **:** side of a right-angled triangle opposite the right angle

hy•poth•e•sis *n* **:** assumption made in order to

test its consequences — **hy•poth•e•size** *vb* — **hy•po•thet•i•cal** *adj* — **hy•po•thet•i•cal•ly** *adv*

hys•te•ria *n* : uncontrollable fear or outburst of emotion — **hys•ter•i•cal** *adj* — **hys•ter•i•cal•ly** *adv*

hys•ter•ics *n pl* : uncontrollable laughter or crying

I

i *n* : 9th letter of the alphabet

I *pron* : the speaker

ice *n* **1** : frozen water **2** : flavored frozen dessert ~ *vb* **1** : freeze **2** : chill **3** : cover with icing

ice•berg *n* : large floating mass of ice

ice cream *n* : sweet frozen food

ice–skate *vb* : skate on ice — **ice skater** *n*

ici•cle *n* : hanging mass of ice

ic•ing *n* : sweet usu. creamy coating for baked goods

icon *n* **1** : religious image **2** : small picture on a computer screen identified with an available function

icy *adj* **1** : covered with or consisting of ice **2** : very cold — **ic•i•ly** *adv* — **ic•i•ness** *n*

idea *n* **1** : something imagined in the mind **2** : purpose or plan

ide•al *adj* **1** : imaginary **2** : perfect ~ *n* **1** : standard of excellence **2** : model **3** : aim — **ide•al•ly** *adv*

ide•al•ize *vb* : think of or represent as ideal — **ide•al•ism** *n* — **ide•al•ist** *n* — **ide•al•is•tic** *adj* — **ide•al•is•ti•cal•ly** *adv* — **ide•al•i•za•tion** *n*

iden•ti•cal *adj* **1** : being the same **2** : exactly or essentially alike

iden•ti•fy *vb* **1** : associate **2** : establish the identity of — **iden•ti•fi•able** *adj* — **iden•ti•fi•ca•tion** *n* — **iden•ti•fi•er** *n*

iden•ti•ty *n* **1** : sameness of essential character **2** : individuality **3** : fact of being what is supposed

id•i•om *n* **1** : language peculiar to a person or group **2** : expression with a special meaning — **id•i•om•at•ic** *adj* — **id•i•om•at•i•cal•ly** *adv*

id•i•ot *n* : mentally retarded or foolish person — **id•i•o•cy** *n* — **id•i•ot•ic** *adj* — **id•i•ot•i•cal•ly** *adv*

idle *adj* **1** : worthless **2** : inactive **3** : lazy ~ *vb* : spend time doing nothing — **idle•ness** *n* — **idler** *n* — **idly** *adv*

idol *n* **1** : image of a god **2** : object of devotion — **idol•iza•tion** *n* — **idol•ize** *vb*

idyll *n* : period of peace and contentment — **idyl•lic** *adj*

if *conj* **1** : in the event that **2** : whether **3** : even though

ig•loo *n* : hut made of snow blocks

ig•nite *vb* : set afire or catch fire — **ig•nit•able** *adj* — **ig•ni•tion** *n*

ig•no•rant *adj* **1** : lacking knowledge **2** : showing a lack of knowledge or intelligence **3** : unaware — **ig•no•rance** *n* — **ig•no•rant•ly** *adv*

ig•nore *vb* : refuse to notice

ill *adj* **worse; worst** **1** : sick **2** : bad **3** : rude or unacceptable **4** : hostile ~ *adv* **1** : with displeasure **2** : harshly **3** : scarcely **4** : badly ~ *n* **1** : evil **2** : misfortune **3** : sickness — **ill•ness** *n*

il•le•gal *adj* : not lawful — **il•le•gal•i•ty** *n* — **il•le•gal•ly** *adv*

il•leg•i•ble *adj* : not legible — **il•leg•i•bil•i•ty** *n* — **il•leg•i•bly** *adv*

il•le•git•i•mate *adj* **1** : born of unmarried parents **2** : illegal — **il•le•git•i•ma•cy** *n* — **il•le•git•i•mate•ly** *adv*

il•lic•it *adj* : not lawful — **il•lic•it•ly** *adv*

il•lit•er•ate *adj* : unable to read or write — **il•lit•er•a•cy** *n* — **il•lit•er•ate** *n*

il•log•i•cal *adj* : contrary to sound reasoning — **il•log•i•cal•ly** *adv*

il•lu•mi•nate *vb* **1** : light up **2** : make clear — **il•lu•mi•nat•ing•ly** *adv* — **il•lu•mi•na•tion** *n*

il•lu•sion *n* **1** : mistaken idea **2** : misleading visual image — **il•lu•so•ry** *adj*

il•lus•trate *vb* **1** : explain by example **2** : provide with pictures or figures — **il•lus•tra•tion** *n* — **il•lus•tra•tive** *adj* — **il•lus•tra•tive•ly** *adv* — **il•lus•tra•tor** *n*

il•lus•tri•ous *adj* : notably or brilliantly outstanding — **il•lus•tri•ous•ness** *n*

im•age *n* **1** : likeness **2** : visual counterpart of an object formed by a lens or mirror **3** : mental picture ~ *vb* : create a representation of — **im•ag•ery** *n*

imag·i·nary *adj* **:** existing only in the imagination

imag·i·na·tion *n* **1 :** act or power of forming a mental image **2 :** creative ability

imag·ine *vb* **:** form a mental picture of something not present — **imag·in·able** *adj* — **imag·in·ably** *adv* — **imag·i·na·tive** *adj* — **imag·i·na·tive·ly** *adv*

im·be·cile *n* **:** idiot — **imbecile, im·be·cil·ic** *adj* — **im·be·cil·i·ty** *n*

im·i·tate *vb* **1 :** follow as a model **2 :** mimic — **im·i·ta·tion** *n or adj* — **im·i·ta·tive** *adj* — **im·i·ta·tor** *n*

im·mac·u·late *adj* **:** without stain or blemish — **im·mac·u·late·ly** *adv*

im·ma·te·ri·al *adj* **1 :** spiritual **2 :** not relevant — **im·ma·te·ri·al·i·ty** *n*

im·ma·ture *adj* **:** not yet mature — **im·ma·tu·ri·ty** *n*

im·me·di·a·cy *n* **:** quality or state of being urgent

im·me·di·ate *adj* **1 :** direct **2 :** being next in line **3 :** made or done at once **4 :** not distant — **im·me·di·ate·ly** *adv*

im·mense *adj* **:** vast — **im·mense·ly** *adv* — **im·men·si·ty** *n*

im·merse *vb* **1 :** plunge or dip esp. into liquid **2 :** engross — **im·mer·sion** *n*

im·mi·grate *vb* **:** come into a place and take up residence — **im·mi·grant** *n* — **im·mi·gra·tion** *n*

im·mo·late *vb* **:** offer in sacrifice — **im·mo·la·tion** *n*

im·mor·al *adj* **:** not moral — **im·mo·ral·i·ty** *n* — **im·mor·al·ly** *adv*

im·mor·tal *adj* **1 :** not mortal **2 :** having lasting fame ~ *n* **:** one exempt from death or oblivion — **im·mor·tal·i·ty** *n* — **im·mor·tal·ize** *vb*

im·mune *adj* **:** not liable esp. to disease — **im·mu·ni·ty** *n* — **im·mu·ni·za·tion** *n* — **im·mu·nize** *vb*

im·mu·nol·o·gy *n* **:** science of immunity to disease — **im·mu·no·log·ic, im·mu·no·log·i·cal** *adj* — **im·mu·nol·o·gist** *n*

im·pact *vb* **1 :** press close **2 :** have an effect on ~ *n* **1 :** forceful contact **2 :** influence

im·pair *vb* **:** diminish in quantity, value, or ability — **im·pair·ment** *n*

im·pale *vb* **:** pierce with something pointed

im·par·tial *adj* **:** not partial — **im·par·tial·i·ty** *n* — **im·par·tial·ly** *adv*

im·passe *n* **:** inescapable predicament

im·pas·sive *adj* **:** showing no feeling or interest — **im·pas·sive·ly** *adv* — **im·pas·siv·i·ty** *n*

im·pa·tient *adj* **:** not patient — **im·pa·tience** *n* — **im·pa·tient·ly** *adv*

im·peach *vb* **1 :** charge (an official) with misconduct **2 :** cast doubt on **3 :** remove from office for misconduct — **im·peach·ment** *n*

im·pec·ca·ble *adj* **:** faultless — **im·pec·ca·bly** *adv*

im·pede *vb* **:** interfere with

im·ped·i·ment *n* **1 :** hindrance **2 :** speech defect

im·per·a·tive *adj* **1 :** expressing a command **2 :** urgent ~ *n* **1 :** imperative mood or verb form **2 :** unavoidable fact, need, or obligation — **im·per·a·tive·ly** *adv*

im·per·cep·ti·ble *adj* **:** not perceptible — **im·per·cep·ti·bly** *adv*

im·per·fect *adj* **:** not perfect — **im·per·fec·tion** *n* — **im·per·fect·ly** *adv*

im·pe·ri·al *adj* **1 :** relating to an empire or an emperor **2 :** royal

im·pe·ri·al·ism *n* **:** policy of controlling other nations — **im·pe·ri·al·ist** *n or adj* — **im·pe·ri·al·is·tic** *adj* — **im·pe·ri·al·is·ti·cal·ly** *adv*

im·per·ma·nent *adj* **:** not permanent — **im·per·ma·nent·ly** *adv*

im·per·son·al *adj* **:** not involving human personality or emotion — **im·per·son·al·i·ty** *n* — **im·per·son·al·ly** *adv*

im·per·son·ate *vb* **:** assume the character of — **im·per·son·a·tion** *n* — **im·per·son·a·tor** *n*

im·per·ti·nent *adj* **1 :** irrelevant **2 :** insolent — **im·per·ti·nence** *n* — **im·per·ti·nent·ly** *adv*

im·per·vi·ous *adj* **:** incapable of being penetrated or affected

im·pe·tus *n* **:** driving force

im·plant *vb* **1 :** set firmly or deeply **2 :** fix in the mind or spirit ~ *n* **:** something implanted in tissue — **im·plan·ta·tion** *n*

im·plau·si·ble *adj* **:** not plausible — **im·plau·si·bil·i·ty** *n*

im·ple·ment *n* **:** tool, utensil ~ *vb* **:** put into practice — **im·ple·men·ta·tion** *n*

im·pli·cate *vb* **:** involve

im·pli·ca·tion *n* **1 :** an implying **2 :** something implied

im·plic·it *adj* **1 :** understood though only implied **2 :** complete and unquestioning — **im·plic·it·ly** *adv*

im·plode *vb* : burst inward — **im·plo·sion** *n* — **im·plo·sive** *adj*
im·ply *vb* : express indirectly
im·po·lite *adj* : not polite
im·pon·der·able *adj* : incapable of being precisely evaluated — **im·pon·der·able** *n*
im·port *vb* **1** : mean **2** : bring in from an external source ~ *n* **1** : meaning **2** : importance **3** : something imported — **im·por·ta·tion** *n* — **im·port·er** *n*
im·por·tant *adj* : having great worth, significance, or influence — **im·por·tance** *n* — **im·por·tant·ly** *adv*
im·pose *vb* **1** : establish as compulsory **2** : take unwarranted advantage of — **im·po·si·tion** *n*
im·pos·ing *adj* : impressive — **im·pos·ing·ly** *adv*
im·pos·si·ble *adj* **1** : incapable of occurring **2** : enormously difficult — **im·pos·si·bil·i·ty** *n* — **im·pos·si·bly** *adv*
im·pos·tor, im·pos·ter *n* : one who assumes an identity or title to deceive — **im·pos·ture** *n*
im·prac·ti·cal *adj* : not practical
im·pre·cise *adj* : not precise — **im·pre·cise·ly** *adv* — **im·pre·cise·ness** *n* — **im·pre·ci·sion** *n*
im·preg·nate *vb* **1** : make pregnant **2** : cause to be filled, permeated, or saturated — **im·preg·na·tion** *n*
im·press *vb* **1** : apply with or produce by pressure **2** : press, stamp, or print in or upon **3** : produce a vivid impression of **4** : affect (as the mind) forcibly — **im·pres·sive** *adj* — **im·pres·sive·ly** *adv* — **im·pres·sive·ness** *n* — **im·pres·sion** *n* — **im·pres·sion·able** *adj*
im·pris·on *vb* : put in prison — **im·pris·on·ment** *n*
im·prob·able *adj* : unlikely to be true or to occur — **im·prob·a·bil·i·ty** *n* — **im·prob·a·bly** *adv*
im·prop·er *adj* : not proper — **im·prop·er·ly** *adv*
im·prove *vb* : grow or make better — **im·prov·able** *adj* — **im·prove·ment** *n*
im·pro·vise *vb* : make, invent, or arrange without prior planning — **im·pro·vi·sa·tion** *n* — **im·pro·vis·er, im·pro·vi·sor** *n*
im·pu·dent *adj* : insolent — **im·pu·dence** *n* — **im·pu·dent·ly** *adv*
im·pugn *vb* : attack as false
im·pulse *n* **1** : moving force **2** : sudden inclination — **im·pul·sive** *adj* — **im·pul·sive·ly** *adv* — **im·pul·sive·ness** *n*
im·pure *adj* : not pure — **im·pu·ri·ty** *n*
in *prep* **1** — used to indicate location, inclusion, situation, or manner **2** : into **3** : during ~ *adv* : to or toward the inside ~ *adj* : located inside
in·act·ive *adj* : not active or in use
in·an·i·mate *adj* : not animate or animated — **in·an·i·mate·ly** *adv* — **in·an·i·mate·ness** *n*
in·au·gu·rate *vb* **1** : install in office **2** : start — **in·au·gu·ral** *adj* — **in·au·gu·ra·tion** *n*
in·cal·cu·la·ble *adj* : too large to be calculated — **in·cal·cu·la·bly** *adv*
in·can·ta·tion *n* : use of spoken or sung charms or spells as a magic ritual
in·ca·pac·i·tate *vb* : disable
in·car·cer·ate *vb* : imprison — **in·car·cer·a·tion** *n*
in·cen·tive *n* : inducement to do something
in·cep·tion *n* : beginning
in·ces·sant *adj* : continuing without interruption — **in·ces·sant·ly** *adv*
inch *n* : unit of length equal to $\frac{1}{12}$ foot ~ *vb* : move by small degrees
in·ci·dent *n* : occurrence — **in·ci·dence** *n* — **in·ci·dent** *adj*
in·ci·den·tal *adj* **1** : subordinate, nonessential, or attendant **2** : met by chance ~ *n* **1** : something incidental **2** *pl* : minor expenses that are not itemized — **in·ci·den·tal·ly** *adv*
in·cite *vb* : arouse to action — **in·cite·ment** *n*
in·cline *vb* **1** : bow **2** : tend toward an opinion **3** : slope ~ *n* : slope — **in·cli·na·tion** *n* — **in·clin·er** *n*
in·clude *vb* : take in or comprise — **in·clu·sion** *n* — **in·clu·sive** *adj*
in·come *n* : money gained (as from work or investment)
in·com·pa·ra·ble *adj* : eminent beyond comparison
in·com·pe·tent *adj* : lacking sufficient knowledge or skill — **in·com·pe·tence** *n* — **in·com·pe·ten·cy** *n* — **in·com·pe·tent** *n*
in·con·ceiv·able *adj* **1** : impossible to comprehend **2** : unbelievable — **in·con·ceiv·ably** *adv*
in·con·se·quen·tial *adj* : not important — **in·con·se·quence** *n* — **in·con·se·quen·tial·ly** *adv*
in·con·ve·nience *n* **1** : discomfort **2** : something that causes trouble or annoyance ~ *vb*

: cause inconvenience to — **in·con·ve·nient** *adj* — **in·con·ve·nient·ly** *adv*

in·cor·po·rate *vb* **1 :** blend **2 :** form into a legal body — **in·cor·po·rat·ed** *adj* — **in·cor·po·ra·tion** *n*

in·cor·rect *adj* **:** not correct or proper — **in·cor·rect·ly** *adv*

in·crease *vb* **:** make or become greater ∼ *n* **1 :** enlargement in size **2 :** something added — **in·creas·ing·ly** *adv*

in·cred·i·ble *adj* **:** too extraordinary to be believed — **in·cred·ibil·i·ty** *n* — **in·cred·i·bly** *adv*

in·crim·i·nate *vb* **:** show to be guilty of a crime — **in·crim·i·na·tion** *n* — **in·crim·i·na·to·ry** *adj*

in·cur *vb* **:** become liable or subject to

in·deed *adv* **:** without question

in·def·i·nite *adj* **1 :** not defining or identifying **2 :** not precise **3 :** having no fixed limit — **in·def·i·nite·ly** *adv*

in·den·ta·tion *n* **1 :** notch, recess, or dent **2 :** action of indenting **3 :** space at the beginning of a paragraph — **in·dent** *vb*

Independence Day *n* **:** July 4 observed as a legal holiday in commemoration of the adoption of the Declaration of Independence in 1776

in·de·pen·dent *adj* **1 :** not governed by another **2 :** not requiring or relying on something or somebody else **3 :** not easily influenced — **in·de·pen·dence** *n* — **in·de·pen·dent** *n* — **in·de·pen·dent·ly** *adv*

in·dex *n* **1 :** alphabetical list of items (as topics in a book) **2 :** a number that serves as a measure or indicator of something ∼ *vb* **1 :** provide with an index **2 :** serve as an index of

in·di·cate *vb* **1 :** point out or to **2 :** show indirectly **3 :** state briefly — **in·di·ca·tion** *n* — **in·dic·a·tive** *adj* — **in·di·ca·tor** *n*

in·dict *vb* **:** charge with a crime — **in·dict·able** *adj* — **in·dict·ment** *n*

in·dif·fer·ent *adj* **1 :** having no preference **2 :** showing neither interest nor dislike **3 :** mediocre — **in·dif·fer·ence** *n* — **in·dif·fer·ent·ly** *adv*

in·dig·e·nous *adj* **:** native to a particular region

in·di·ges·tion *n* **:** discomfort from inability to digest food

in·dig·na·tion *n* **:** anger aroused by something unjust or unworthy — **in·dig·nant** *adj* — **in·dig·nant·ly** *adv* — **in·dig·ni·ty** *n*

in·di·rect *adj* **:** not straight or straightforward — **in·di·rec·tion** *n* — **in·di·rect·ly** *adv* — **in·di·rect·ness** *n*

in·dis·crim·i·nate *adj* **1 :** not careful or discriminating **2 :** haphazard — **in·dis·crim·i·nate·ly** *adv*

in·dis·tinct *adj* **:** not clearly recognizable or understandable — **in·dis·tinct·ly** *adv*

in·di·vid·u·al *n* **1 :** single member of a category **2 :** person — **in·di·vid·u·al** *adj* — **in·di·vid·u·al·i·ty** *n* — **in·di·vid·u·al·ly** *adv*

in·di·vid·u·al·ize *vb* **1 :** make individual **2 :** treat individually

in·doc·tri·nate *vb* **:** instruct in fundamentals (as of a doctrine) — **in·doc·tri·na·tion** *n*

in·doors *adv* **:** in or into a building

in·duce *vb* **1 :** persuade **2 :** bring about — **in·duce·ment** *n* — **in·duc·er** *n*

in·duct *vb* **1 :** put in office **2 :** admit as a member **3 :** enroll (as for military service) — **in·duct·ee** *n* — **in·duc·tion** *n*

in·dulge *vb* **:** yield to the desire of or for — **in·dul·gence** *n* — **in·dul·gent** *adj* — **in·dul·gent·ly** *adv*

in·dus·tri·ous *adj* **:** diligent or busy — **in·dus·tri·ous·ly** *adv* — **in·dus·tri·ous·ness** *n*

in·dus·try *n* **1 :** diligence **2 :** manufacturing enterprises or activity — **in·dus·tri·al** *adj* — **in·dus·tri·al·ist** *n* — **in·dus·tri·al·iza·tion** *n* — **in·dus·tri·al·ize** *vb* — **in·dus·tri·al·ly** *adv*

in·ept *adj* **1 :** inappropriate or foolish **2 :** generally incompetent — **in·ep·ti·tude** *n* — **in·ept·ly** *adv* — **in·ept·ness** *n*

in·equal·i·ty *n* **:** quality of being unequal or uneven

in·ert *adj* **1 :** powerless to move or act **2 :** sluggish — **in·ert·ly** *adv* — **in·ert·ness** *n*

in·ev·i·ta·ble *adj* **:** incapable of being avoided or escaped — **in·ev·i·ta·bil·i·ty** *n* — **in·ev·i·ta·bly** *adv*

in·ex·cus·able *adj* **:** being without excuse or justification — **in·ex·cus·ably** *adv*

in·fa·mous *adj* **:** having the worst kind of reputation — **in·fa·mous·ly** *adv* — **in·fa·my** *n*

in·fant *n* **:** baby — **in·fan·cy** *n* — **in·fan·tile** *adj*

in·fat·u·ate *vb* **:** inspire with foolish love or admiration — **in·fat·u·a·tion** *n*

in·fect *vb* **:** contaminate with disease-producing matter — **in·fec·tion** *n* — **in·fec·tious** *adj* — **in·fec·tive** *adj*

in·fer *vb* **:** deduce — **in·fer·ence** *n* — **in·fer·en·tial** *adj*

in·fe·ri·or *adj* **1 :** being lower in position, degree, rank, or merit **2 :** of lesser quality — **inferior** *n* — **in•fe•ri•or•i•ty** *n*

in•fest *vb* **:** swarm or grow in or over — **in•fes•ta•tion** *n*

in•fi•del•i•ty *n* **:** lack of faithfulness

in•fil•trate *vb* **:** enter or become established in without being noticed — **in•fil•tra•tion** *n*

in•fi•nite *adj* **1 :** having no limit or extending indefinitely **2 :** vast — **in•fi•nite** *n* — **in•fi•nite•ly** *adv* — **in•fin•i•tude** *n*

in•fin•i•tive *n* **:** verb form in English usu. used with *to*

in•fin•i•ty *n* **1 :** quality or state of being infinite **2 :** indefinitely great number or amount

in•flame *vb* **1 :** excite to intense action or feeling **2 :** affect or become affected with red and painful response to injury — **in•flam•ma•tion** *n* — **in•flam•ma•to•ry** *adj*

in•flam•ma•ble *adj* **:** flammable

in•flate *vb* **1 :** swell or puff up (as with gas) **2 :** expand or increase abnormally — **in•flat•able** *adj*

in•fla•tion *n* **1 :** act of inflating **2 :** continual rise in prices — **in•fla•tion•ary** *adj*

in•flec•tion *n* **1 :** change in pitch or loudness of the voice **2 :** change in form of a word — **in•flect** *vb* — **in•flec•tion•al** *adj*

in•flu•ence *n* **1 :** power or capacity of causing an effect in indirect or intangible ways **2 :** one that exerts influence ∼ *vb* **:** affect or alter by influence — **in•flu•en•tial** *adj*

in•flux *n* **:** a flowing in

in•form *vb* **:** give information or knowledge to — **in•for•mant** *n* — **in•for•ma•tion** *n* — **in•for•ma•tion•al** *adj* — **in•for•ma•tive** *adj* — **in•form•er** *n*

in•for•mal *adj* **1 :** without formality or ceremony **2 :** for ordinary or familiar use — **in•for•mal•i•ty** *n* — **in•for•mal•ly** *adv*

in•fringe *vb* **:** violate another's right or privilege — **in•fringe•ment** *n*

in•fu•ri•ate *vb* **:** make furious — **in•fu•ri•at•ing•ly** *adv*

in•ge•nious *adj* **:** very clever — **in•ge•nious•ly** *adv* — **in•ge•nious•ness** *n*

in•ge•nu•ity *n* **:** skill or cleverness in planning or inventing

in•gen•u•ous *adj* **:** innocent and candid — **in•gen•u•ous•ly** *adv* — **in•gen•u•ous•ness** *n*

in•gre•di•ent *n* **:** one of the substances that make up a mixture

in•hab•it *vb* **:** live or dwell in — **in•hab•it•able** *adj* — **in•hab•it•ant** *n*

in•hale *vb* **:** breathe in — **in•hal•ant** *n* — **in•ha•la•tion** *n* — **in•hal•er** *n*

in•her•ent *adj* **:** being an essential part of something — **in•her•ent•ly** *adv*

in•her•it *vb* **:** receive from one's ancestors — **in•her•it•able** *adj* — **in•her•i•tance** *n* — **in•her•i•tor** *n*

in•hib•it *vb* **:** hold in check — **in•hi•bi•tion** *n*

in•hu•man *adj* **:** cruel or impersonal — **in•hu•man•i•ty** *n* — **in•hu•man•ly** *adv* — **in•hu•man•ness** *n*

ini•tial *adj* **1 :** of or relating to the beginning **2 :** first ∼ *n* **:** 1st letter of a word or name ∼ *vb* **:** put initials on — **ini•tial•ly** *adv*

ini•ti•ate *vb* **1 :** start **2 :** induct into membership **3 :** instruct in the rudiments of something — **ini•ti•ate** *n* — **ini•ti•a•tion** *n* — **ini•tia•to•ry** *adj*

ini•tia•tive *n* **1 :** first step **2 :** readiness to undertake something on one's own

in•ject *vb* **:** force or introduce into something — **in•jec•tion** *n*

in•junc•tion *n* **:** court writ requiring one to do or to refrain from doing a specified act

in•jure *vb* **:** do damage, hurt, or a wrong to

in•ju•ry *n* **1 :** act that injures **2 :** hurt, damage, or loss sustained — **in•ju•ri•ous** *adj*

in•jus•tice *n* **:** unjust act

ink *n* **:** usu. liquid and colored material for writing and printing ∼ *vb* **:** put ink on — **ink•well** *n* — **inky** *adj*

in–law *n* **:** relative by marriage

in•lay *vb* **:** set into a surface for decoration ∼ *n* **1 :** inlaid work **2 :** shaped filling cemented into a tooth

inn *n* **:** hotel — **inn•keep•er** *n*

in•ner *adj* **:** being on the inside

in•no•cent *adj* **1 :** free from guilt **2 :** harmless **3 :** not sophisticated — **in•no•cence** *n* — **in•no•cent** *n* — **in•no•cent•ly** *adv*

in•no•va•tion *n* **:** new idea or method — **in•no•vate** *vb* — **in•no•va•tive** *adj* — **in•no•va•tor** *n*

in•or•di•nate *adj* **:** unusual or excessive — **in•or•di•nate•ly** *adv*

in•or•gan•ic *adj* **:** made of mineral matter

in•put *n* **:** something put in — **in•put** *vb*

in•quire *vb* **1 :** ask **2 :** investigate — **in•quir•er** *n* — **in•quir•ing•ly** *adv* — **in•qui•ry** *n*

in•quis•i•tive *adj* **:** curious — **in•quis•i•tive•ly** *adv* — **in•quis•i•tive•ness** *n*

in•sane *adj* **1 :** not sane **2 :** absurd — **in•sane•ly** *adv* — **in•san•i•ty** *n*

in·scribe *vb* **1 :** write **2 :** engrave **3 :** dedicate (a book) to someone — **in·scrip·tion** *n*
in·sect *n* **:** small usu. winged animal with 6 legs
in·sec·ti·cide *n* **:** insect poison — **in·sec·ti·cid·al** *adj*
in·se·cure *adj* **1 :** not certain **2 :** not safe **3 :** fearful — **in·se·cure·ly** *adv* — **in·se·cu·ri·ty** *n*
in·sen·si·ble *adj* **1 :** unconscious **2 :** unable to feel **3 :** unaware — **in·sen·si·bil·i·ty** *n* — **in·sen·si·bly** *adv*
in·sert *vb* **:** put in — **in·sert** *n* — **in·ser·tion** *n*
in·side *n* **1 :** inner side **2** *pl* **:** internal organs ~ *prep* **1 :** in or into the inside of **2 :** within ~ *adv* **1 :** on the inner side **2 :** into the interior — **in·side** *adj* — **in·sid·er** *n*
in·sight *n* **:** understanding — **in·sight·ful** *adj*
in·sin·u·ate *vb* **1 :** imply **2 :** bring in artfully — **in·sin·u·a·tion** *n*
in·sist *vb* **:** be firmly demanding — **in·sis·tence** *n* — **in·sis·tent** *adj* — **in·sis·tent·ly** *adv*
in·so·lent *adj* **:** bold and contemptuous — **in·so·lence** *n*
in·sol·vent *adj* **:** unable or insufficient to pay debts — **in·sol·ven·cy** *n*
in·som·nia *n* **:** inability to sleep — **in·som·ni·ac** *n*
in·spect *vb* **:** view closely and critically — **in·spec·tion** *n* — **in·spec·tor** *n*
in·spire *vb* **1 :** inhale **2 :** influence by example **3 :** bring about **4 :** stir to action — **in·spi·ra·tion** *n* — **in·spi·ra·tion·al** *adj* — **in·spir·er** *n*
in·stall, in·stal *vb* **1 :** induct into office **2 :** set up for use — **in·stal·la·tion** *n*
in·stall·ment *n* **:** partial payment
in·stance *n* **1 :** request or instigation **2 :** example
in·stant *n* **:** moment ~ *adj* **1 :** immediate **2 :** ready to mix — **in·stan·ta·neous** *adj* — **in·stan·ta·neous·ly** *adv* — **in·stant·ly** *adv*
in·stead *adv* **:** as a substitute or alternative
instead of *prep* **:** as a substitute for or alternative to
in·stinct *n* **1 :** natural talent **2 :** natural inherited or subconsciously motivated behavior — **in·stinc·tive** *adj* — **in·stinc·tive·ly** *adv* — **in·stinc·tu·al** *adj*
in·sti·tute *vb* **:** establish, start, or organize ~ *n* **1 :** organization promoting a cause **2 :** school
in·sti·tu·tion *n* **1 :** act of instituting **2 :** custom **3 :** corporation or society of a public character — **in·sti·tu·tion·al** *adj* — **in·sti·tu·tion·al·ize** *vb* — **in·sti·tu·tion·al·ly** *adv*
in·struct *vb* **1 :** teach **2 :** give an order to — **in·struc·tion** *n* — **in·struc·tion·al** *adj* — **in·struc·tive** *adj* — **in·struc·tor** *n* — **in·struc·tor·ship** *n*
in·stru·ment *n* **1 :** something that produces music **2 :** means **3 :** device for doing work and esp. precision work **4 :** legal document — **in·stru·men·tal** *adj* — **in·stru·men·tal·ist** *n* — **in·stru·men·tal·i·ty** *n* — **in·stru·men·ta·tion** *n*
in·su·late *vb* **:** protect from heat loss or electricity — **in·su·la·tion** *n* — **in·su·la·tor** *n*
in·sult *vb* **:** treat with contempt ~ *n* **:** insulting act or remark — **in·sult·ing·ly** *adv*
in·sure *vb* **1 :** guarantee against loss **2 :** make certain — **in·sur·able** *adj* — **in·sur·ance** *n* — **in·sured** *n* — **in·sur·er** *n*
in·tact *adj* **:** not damaged
in·take *n* **1 :** opening through which something enters **2 :** act of taking in **3 :** amount taken in
in·te·ger *n* **:** number that is not a fraction and does not include a fraction
in·te·grate *vb* **1 :** unite **2 :** end segregation of or at — **in·te·gra·tion** *n*
in·teg·ri·ty *n* **1 :** soundness **2 :** adherence to a code of values **3 :** completeness
in·tel·lect *n* **:** power of knowing or thinking — **in·tel·lec·tu·al** *adj or n* — **in·tel·lec·tu·al·ism** *n* — **in·tel·lec·tu·al·ly** *adv*
in·tel·li·gence *n* **1 :** ability to learn and understand **2 :** mental acuteness **3 :** information — **in·tel·li·gent** *adj* — **in·tel·li·gent·ly** *adv*
in·tend *vb* **:** have as a purpose — **in·tend·ed** *n or adj*
in·tense *adj* **1 :** extreme **2 :** deeply felt — **in·tense·ly** *adv* — **in·ten·si·fi·ca·tion** *n* — **in·ten·si·fy** *vb* — **in·ten·si·ty** *n* — **in·ten·sive** *adj* — **in·ten·sive·ly** *adv*
[1]in·tent *n* **:** purpose — **in·ten·tion** *n* — **in·ten·tion·al** *adj* — **in·ten·tion·al·ly** *adv*
[2]in·tent *adj* **:** concentrated — **in·tent·ly** *adv* — **in·tent·ness** *n*
in·ter·ac·tion *n* **:** mutual influence — **in·ter·act** *vb* — **in·ter·ac·tive** *adj*
in·ter·breed *vb* **:** breed together
in·ter·cede *vb* **:** act to reconcile — **in·ter·ces·sion** *n* — **in·ter·ces·sor** *n*
in·ter·cept *vb* **:** interrupt the progress of — **in·ter·cept** *n* — **in·ter·cep·tion** *n* — **in·ter·cep·tor** *n*

in•ter•change *vb* **1 :** exchange **2 :** change places **~** *n* **1 :** exchange **2 :** junction of highways — **in•ter•change•able** *adj*

in•ter•est *n* **1 :** right **2 :** benefit **3 :** charge for borrowed money **4 :** readiness to pay special attention **5 :** quality that causes interest **~** *vb* **1 :** concern **2 :** get the attention of — **in•ter•est•ing** *adj* — **in•ter•est•ing•ly** *adv*

in•ter•fere *vb* **1 :** collide or be in opposition **2 :** try to run the affairs of others — **in•ter•fer•ence** *n*

in•te•ri•or *adj* **:** being on the inside **~** *n* **1 :** inside **2 :** inland area

in•ter•jec•tion *n* **:** an exclamatory word — **in•ter•jec•tion•al•ly** *adv*

in•ter•lock *vb* **1 :** unite by or as by lacing together **2 :** connect for mutual effect — **in•ter•lock** *n*

in•ter•me•di•ary *n* **:** agent between individuals or groups — **intermediary** *adj*

in•ter•me•di•ate *adj* **:** between extremes — **in•ter•me•di•ate** *n*

in•ter•mis•sion *n* **:** break in a performance

in•ter•mix *vb* **:** mix together — **in•ter•mix•ture** *n*

in•tern *n* **:** advanced student (as in medicine) gaining supervised experience **~** *vb* **:** act as an intern — **in•tern•ship** *n*

in•ter•nal *adj* **1 :** inward **2 :** inside of the body **3 :** relating to or existing in the mind — **in•ter•nal•ly** *adv*

in•ter•na•tion•al *adj* **:** affecting 2 or more nations **~** *n* **:** something having international scope — **in•ter•na•tion•al•ism** *n* — **in•ter•na•tion•al•ize** *vb* — **in•ter•na•tion•al•ly** *adv*

In•ter•net *n* **:** network that connects computer networks worldwide

in•ter•pret *vb* **:** explain the meaning of — **in•ter•pre•ta•tion** *n* — **in•ter•pre•ta•tive** *adj* — **in•ter•pret•er** *n* — **in•ter•pre•tive** *adj*

in•ter•ro•gate *vb* **:** question — **in•ter•ro•ga•tion** *n* — **in•ter•rog•a•tive** *adj or n* — **in•ter•ro•ga•tor** *n* — **in•ter•rog•a•to•ry** *adj*

in•ter•rupt *vb* **:** intrude so as to hinder or end continuity — **in•ter•rupt•er** *n* — **in•ter•rup•tion** *n* — **in•ter•rup•tive** *adv*

in•ter•sect *vb* **1 :** cut across or divide **2 :** cross — **in•ter•sec•tion** *n*

in•ter•twine *vb* **:** twist together — **in•ter•twine•ment** *n*

in•ter•val *n* **1 :** time between **2 :** space between

in•ter•vene *vb* **1 :** happen between events **2 :** intercede — **in•ter•ven•tion** *n*

in•ter•view *n* **:** a meeting to get information — **in•ter•view** *vb* — **in•ter•view•er** *n*

in•tes•tine *n* **:** tubular part of the digestive system after the stomach including a long narrow upper part (**small intestine**) followed by a broader shorter lower part (**large intestine**) — **in•tes•ti•nal** *adj*

in•ti•mate *vb* **:** hint **~** *adj* **1 :** very friendly **2 :** suggesting privacy **3 :** very personal **~** *n* **:** close friend — **in•ti•ma•cy** *n* — **in•ti•mate•ly** *adv* — **in•ti•ma•tion** *n*

in•tim•i•date *vb* **:** make fearful — **in•tim•i•da•tion** *n*

in•to *prep* **1 :** to the inside of **2 :** to the condition of **3 :** against

in•to•na•tion *n* **:** way of singing or speaking

in•tox•i•cate *vb* **:** make drunk — **in•tox•i•cant** *n or adj* — **in•tox•i•ca•tion** *n*

in•tri•cate *adj* **:** very complex and delicate — **in•tri•ca•cy** *n* — **in•tri•cate•ly** *adv*

in•trigue *vb* **1 :** scheme **2 :** arouse curiosity of **~** *n* **:** secret scheme — **in•trigu•ing•ly** *adv*

in•tro•duce *vb* **1 :** bring in esp. for the 1st time **2 :** cause to be acquainted **3 :** bring to notice **4 :** put in — **in•tro•duc•tion** *n* — **in•tro•duc•to•ry** *adj*

in•tro•vert *n* **:** shy or reserved person — **in•tro•ver•sion** *n* — **in•tro•vert** *adj* — **in•tro•vert•ed** *adj*

in•trude *vb* **1 :** thrust in **2 :** go beyond usual or proper limits — **in•trud•er** *n* — **in•tru•sion** *n* — **in•tru•sive** *adj* — **in•tru•sive•ness** *n*

in•tu•i•tion *n* **:** quick and ready insight — **in•tu•it** *vb* — **in•tu•i•tive** *adj* — **in•tu•i•tive•ly** *adv*

in•vade *vb* **:** enter for conquest — **in•vad•er** *n* — **in•va•sion** *n*

[1]in•val•id *adj* **:** not true or legal — **in•va•lid•i•ty** *n* — **in•val•id•ly** *adv*

[2]in•va•lid *adj* **:** sickly **~** *n* **:** one chronically ill

in•val•i•date *vb* **:** make invalid — **in•val•i•da•tion** *n*

in•valu•able *adj* **:** extremely valuable

in•vent *vb* **1 :** think up **2 :** create for the 1st time — **in•ven•tion** *n* — **in•ven•tive** *adj* — **in•ven•tive•ness** *n* — **in•ven•tor** *n*

in•ven•to•ry *n* **1 :** list of goods **2 :** stock — **in•ven•to•ry** *vb*

in•vert *vb* **1 :** turn upside down or inside out **2 :** reverse — **in•ver•sion** *n*

in•ver•te•brate *adj* **:** lacking a backbone **~** *n* **:** invertebrate animal

in•vest *vb* **1 :** give power or authority to **2 :** endow with a quality **3 :** commit money to someone else's use in hope of profit — **in•vest•ment** *n* — **in•ves•tor** *n*

in•ves•ti•gate *vb* **:** study closely and systematically — **in•ves•ti•ga•tion** *n* — **in•ves•ti•ga•tive** *adj* — **in•ves•ti•ga•tor** *n*

in•vig•o•rate *vb* **:** give life and energy to — **in•vig•o•ra•tion** *n*

in•vis•ible *adj* **:** not visible

in•vite *vb* **1 :** entice **2 :** increase the likelihood of **3 :** request the presence or participation of **4 :** encourage — **in•vi•ta•tion** *n* — **in•vit•ing** *adj*

in•vo•ca•tion *n* **1 :** prayer **2 :** incantation

in•voice *n* **:** itemized bill for goods shipped ~ *vb* **:** bill

in•vol•un•tary *adj* **:** done without control or choice — **in•vol•un•tari•ly** *adv*

in•volve *vb* **1 :** draw in as a participant **2 :** relate closely **3 :** require as a necessary part **4 :** occupy fully — **in•volve•ment** *n*

in•volved *adj* **:** intricate

inward, in•wards *adv* **:** toward the inside, center, or inner being — **in•ward•ly** *adv*

io•dine *n* **1 :** nonmetallic chemical element **2 :** solution of iodine used as an antiseptic

ion *n* **:** electrically charged particle — **ion•ic** *adj* — **ion•iz•able** *adj* — **ion•i•za•tion** *n* — **ion•ize** *vb* — **ion•iz•er** *n*

IOU *n* **:** acknowledgment of a debt

irate *adj* **:** aroused to intense anger — **irate•ly** *adv*

ire *n* **:** anger

iris *n* **1 :** colored part around the pupil of the eye **2 :** plant with long leaves and large showy flowers

irk *vb* **:** annoy — **irk•some** *adj* — **irk•some•ly** *adv*

iron *n* **1 :** heavy metallic chemical element **2 :** something made of iron **3 :** heated device for pressing clothes **4 :** hardness, determination ~ *vb* **:** press or smooth out with an iron — **iron•ware** *n* — **iron•work** *n* — **iron•work•er** *n* — **iron•works** *n pl*

iro•ny *n* **1 :** use of words to express the opposite of the literal meaning **2 :** incongruity between the actual and expected result of events — **iron•ic, iron•i•cal** *adj* — **iron•i•cal•ly** *adv*

ir•ra•tio•nal *adj* **1 :** incapable of reasoning **2 :** not based on reason — **ir•ra•tio•nal•i•ty** *n* — **ir•ra•tio•nal•ly** *adv*

ir•reg•u•lar *adj* **:** not regular or normal — **ir•reg•u•lar** *n* — **ir•reg•u•lar•i•ty** *n* — **ir•reg•u•lar•ly** *adv*

ir•rel•e•vant *adj* **:** not relevant — **ir•rel•e•vance** *n*

ir•re•place•able *adj* **:** not replaceable

ir•re•sist•ible *adj* **:** impossible to successfully resist — **ir•re•sist•ibly** *adv*

ir•re•spon•si•ble *adj* **:** not responsible — **ir•re•spon•si•bil•i•ty** *n* — **ir•re•spon•si•bly** *adv*

ir•rev•er•ence *n* **1 :** lack of reverence **2 :** irreverent act or utterance — **ir•rev•er•ent** *adj*

ir•re•vers•ible *adj* **:** incapable of being reversed

ir•ri•gate *vb* **:** supply with water by artificial means — **ir•ri•ga•tion** *n*

ir•ri•tate *vb* **1 :** excite to anger **2 :** make sore or inflamed — **ir•ri•ta•bil•i•ty** *n* — **ir•ri•ta•ble** *adj* — **ir•ri•ta•bly** *adv* — **ir•ri•tant** *adj or n* — **ir•ri•tat•ing•ly** *adv* — **ir•ri•ta•tion** *n*

is *pres 3d sing of* BE

Is•lam *n* **:** religious faith of Muslims — **Is•lam•ic** *adj*

is•land *n* **:** body of land surrounded by water — **is•land•er** *n*

isle *n* **:** small island

iso•late *vb* **:** place or keep by itself — **iso•la•tion** *n*

isos•ce•les *adj* **:** having 2 equal sides

is•sue *vb* **1 :** go, come, or flow out **2 :** descend from a specified ancestor **3 :** emanate or result **4 :** put forth or distribute officially ~ *n* **1 :** action of issuing **2 :** offspring **3 :** result **4 :** point of controversy **5 :** act of giving out or printing **6 :** quantity given out or printed — **is•su•ance** *n* — **is•su•er** *n*

it *pron* **1 :** that one — used of a lifeless thing or an abstract entity **2** — used as an anticipatory subject or object ~ *n* **:** player who tries to catch others (as in a game of tag)

itch *n* **1 :** uneasy irritating skin sensation **2 :** skin disorder **3 :** persistent desire — **itch** *vb* — **itchy** *adj*

item *n* **1 :** particular in a list, account, or series **2 :** piece of news — **item•iza•tion** *n* — **item•ize** *vb*

itin•er•ary *n* **:** route or outline of a journey

its *adj* **:** relating to it

it•self *pron* **:** it — used reflexively or for emphasis

ivo•ry *n* **1 :** hard creamy-white material of elephants' tusks **2 :** pale yellow color

ivy *n* **:** trailing woody vine with evergreen leaves

J

j *n* **:** 10th letter of the alphabet

jab *vb* **:** thrust quickly or abruptly ~ *n* **:** short straight punch

jab·ber *vb* **:** talk rapidly or unintelligibly — **jabber** *n*

jack *n* **1 :** mechanical device to raise a heavy body **2 :** small flag **3 :** small 6-pointed metal object used in a game (**jacks**) **4 :** electrical socket ~ *vb* **1 :** raise with a jack **2 :** increase

jack·ass *n* **1 :** male ass **2 :** stupid person

jack·et *n* **:** garment for the upper body

jack·ham·mer *n* **:** pneumatic tool for drilling

jack·knife *n* **jack·knives :** pocketknife ~ *vb* **:** fold like a jackknife

jack–o'–lan·tern *n* **:** lantern made of a carved pumpkin

jack·pot *n* **:** sum of money won

jade *n* **:** usu. green gemstone

jad·ed *adj* **:** dulled or bored by having too much

jag·ged *adj* **:** sharply notched

jail *n* **:** prison — **jail** *vb* — **jail·break** *n* — **jail·er, jail·or** *n*

ja·la·pe·ño *n* **:** Mexican hot pepper

jam *vb* **1 :** press into a tight position **2 :** cause to become wedged and unworkable ~ *n* **1 :** crowded mass that blocks or impedes **2 :** difficult situation **3 :** thick sweet food made of cooked fruit

jan·gle *vb* **:** make a harsh ringing sound — **jangle** *n*

jan·i·tor *n* **:** person who has the care of a building — **jan·i·to·ri·al** *adj*

Jan·u·ary *n* **:** 1st month of the year having 31 days

[1]**jar** *vb* **1 :** have a harsh or disagreeable effect **2 :** vibrate or shake ~ *n* **1 :** jolt **2 :** painful effect

[2]**jar** *n* **:** wide-mouthed container

jar·gon *n* **:** special vocabulary of a group

jaw *n* **1 :** either of the bony or cartilaginous structures that support the mouth **2 :** one of 2 movable parts for holding or crushing ~ *vb* **:** talk indignantly or at length — **jaw·bone** *n* — **jawed** *adj*

jay *n* **:** noisy brightly colored bird

jay·walk *vb* **:** cross a street carelessly — **jay·walk·er** *n*

jazz *vb* **:** enliven ~ *n* **1 :** kind of American music involving improvisation **2 :** empty talk — **jazzy** *adj*

jeal·ous *adj* **:** suspicious of a rival or of one believed to enjoy an advantage — **jeal·ous·ly** *adv* — **jeal·ou·sy** *n*

jeans *n pl* **:** pants made of durable twilled cotton cloth

jeep *n* **:** 4-wheel army vehicle

jeer *vb* **1 :** speak or cry out in derision **2 :** ridicule ~ *n* **:** taunt

Je·ho·vah *n* **:** God

jell *vb* **1 :** come to the consistency of jelly **2 :** take shape

jel·ly *n* **:** a substance (as food) with a soft somewhat elastic consistency — **jelly** *vb*

jel·ly·fish *n* **:** sea animal with a saucer-shaped jellylike body

jeop·ar·dize *vb* **:** exposure to death, loss, or injury — **jeop·ar·dy** *n*

jerk *vb* **1 :** give a sharp quick push, pull, or twist **2 :** move in short abrupt motions ~ *n* **1 :** short quick pull or twist **2 :** stupid or foolish person — **jerk·i·ly** *adv* — **jerky** *adj*

jest *n* **:** witty remark — **jest** *vb*

jest·er *n* **:** one employed to entertain a court

jet *vb* **1 :** spout or emit in a stream **2 :** travel by jet ~ *n* **1 :** forceful rush of fluid through a narrow opening **2 :** jet-propelled airplane

jet–propelled *adj* **:** driven by an engine (**jet engine**) that produces propulsion (**jet propulsion**) by the rearward discharge of a jet of fluid

Jew *n* **:** one whose religion is Judaism — **Jewish** *adj*

jew·el *n* **1 :** ornament of precious metal **2 :** gem ~ *vb* **:** adorn with jewels — **jew·el·er, jew·el·ler** *n* — **jew·el·ry** *n*

jibe *vb* **:** be in agreement

jif·fy *n* **:** short time

jig·gle *vb* **:** move with quick little jerks — **jiggle** *n*

jilt *vb* **:** drop (a lover) without apparent feelings

jim·my *n* **:** small crowbar ~ *vb* **:** pry open

jin·gle *vb* **:** make a light tinkling sound ~ *n* **1 :** light tinkling sound **2 :** short verse or song

jinx *n* **:** one that brings bad luck — **jinx** *vb*

jit·ters *n pl* **:** extreme nervousness — **jit·tery** *adj*

job *n* **1 :** something that has to be done **2 :** regular employment — **job•hold•er** *n* — **job-less** *adj*

jock•ey *n* : one who rides a horse in a race ~ *vb* : manipulate or maneuver adroitly

jog *vb* **1** : give a slight shake or push to **2** : run or ride at a slow pace ~ *n* **1** : slight shake **2** : slow pace — **jog•ger** *n*

join *vb* **1** : come or bring together **2** : become a member of — **join•er** *n*

joint *n* **1** : point of contact between bones **2** : place where 2 parts connect **3** : often disreputable place ~ *adj* : common to 2 or more — **joint•ed** *adj* — **joint•ly** *adv*

joke *n* : something said or done to provoke laughter ~ *vb* : make jokes — **jok•er** *n* — **jok•ing•ly** *adv*

jol•ly *adj* : full of high spirits — **jol•li•ty** *n*

jolt *vb* **1** : move with a sudden jerky motion **2** : give a jolt to ~ *n* **1** : abrupt jerky blow or movement **2** : sudden shock — **jolt•er** *n*

jos•tle *vb* : push or shove

jot *n* : least bit ~ *vb* : write briefly and hurriedly

jour•nal *n* **1** : brief account of daily events **2** : periodical (as a newspaper) — **jour•nal•ism** *n* — **jour•nal•ist** *n* — **jour•nal•is•tic** *adj*

jour•ney *n* : a going from one place to another ~ *vb* : make a journey

joy *n* **1** : feeling of happiness **2** : source of happiness — **joy** *vb* — **joy•ful** *adj* — **joy•ful•ly** *adv* — **joy•less** *adj* — **joy•ous** *adj* — **joy•ous•ly** *adv* — **joy•ous•ness** *n*

joy•ride *n* : reckless ride for pleasure — **joy•rid•er** *n* — **joy•rid•ing** *n*

ju•bi•lant *adj* : expressing great joy — **ju•bi•lant•ly** *adv* — **ju•bi•la•tion** *n*

Ju•da•ism *n* : religion developed among the ancient Hebrews — **Ju•da•ic** *adj*

judge *vb* **1** : form an opinion **2** : decide as a judge ~ *n* **1** : public official authorized to decide questions brought before a court **2** : one who gives an authoritative opinion — **judg•ment, judge•ment** *n* — **judg•men•tal** *adj* — **judg•men•tal•ly** *adv* — **judge•ship** *n*

ju•di•cial *adj* : relating to the judiciary — **ju•di•cial•ly** *adv*

ju•di•cia•ry *n* : system of courts of law or the judges of them — **ju•di•cial** *adj* — **ju•di•cial•ly** *adv* — **ju•di•cia•ry** *adj*

ju•di•cious *adj* : having or characterized by sound judgment — **ju•di•cious•ly** *adv*

ju•do *n* : form of wrestling — **ju•do•ist** *n*

jug *n* : large deep container with a narrow mouth and a handle

jug•gle *vb* **1** : keep several objects in motion in the air at the same time **2** : manipulate for an often tricky purpose — **jug•gler** *n*

juice *n* **1** : extractable fluid contents of cells or tissues **2** : electricity — **juic•er** *n* — **juic•i•ly** *adv* — **juic•i•ness** *n* — **juicy** *adj*

ju•jube *n* : gummy candy

juke•box *n* : coin-operated machine for playing music recordings

Ju•ly *n* : 7th month of the year having 31 days

jum•ble *vb* : mix in a confused mass — **jumble** *n*

jum•bo *n* : very large version — **jum•bo** *adj*

jump *vb* **1** : rise into or through the air esp. by muscular effort **2** : pass over **3** : give a start **4** : rise or increase sharply ~ *n* **1** : a jumping **2** : sharp sudden increase **3** : initial advantage

[1]jump•er *n* : one that jumps

[2]jumper *n* : sleeveless one-piece dress

jumpy *adj* : nervous or jittery

junc•tion *n* **1** : a joining **2** : place or point of meeting

June *n* : 6th month of the year having 30 days

jun•gle *n* : thick tangled mass of tropical vegetation

ju•nior *n* **1** : person who is younger or of lower rank than another **2** : student in the next-to-last year ~ *adj* : younger or lower in rank

junk *n* **1** : discarded articles **2** : shoddy product ~ *vb* : discard or scrap — **junky** *adj*

ju•ris•dic•tion *n* **1** : right or authority to interpret and apply the law **2** : limits within which authority may be exercised — **ju•ris•dic•tion•al** *adj*

ju•ry *n* : body of persons sworn to give a verdict on a matter — **ju•ror** *n*

just *adj* **1** : reasonable **2** : correct or proper **3** : morally or legally right **4** : deserved ~ *adv* **1** : exactly **2** : very recently **3** : barely **4** : only **5** : quite **6** : possibly — **just•ly** *adv* — **just•ness** *n*

jus•tice *n* **1** : administration of what is just **2** : judge **3** : administration of law **4** : fairness

jus•ti•fy *vb* : prove to be just, right, or reasonable — **jus•ti•fi•able** *adj* — **jus•ti•fi•ca•tion** *n*

ju•ve•nile *adj* : relating to children or young people ~ *n* : young person

K

k *n* : 11th letter of the alphabet

ka·lei·do·scope *n* : device containing loose bits of colored material reflecting in many patterns — **ka·lei·do·scop·ic** *adj* — **ka·lei·do·scop·i·cal·ly** *adv*

kan·ga·roo *n* : large leaping Australian mammal

kar·a·o·ke *n* : device that plays accompaniments for singers

kar·at *n* : unit of gold content

ka·ra·te *n* : art of self-defense by crippling kicks and punches

keen *adj* **1** : sharp **2** : severe **3** : enthusiastic **4** : mentally alert — **keen·ly** *adv* — **keen·ness** *n*

keep *vb* (**kept; kept**) **1** : perform **2** : guard **3** : maintain **4** : retain in one's possession **5** : detain **6** : continue in good condition **7** : refrain ~ *n* **1** : fortress **2** : means by which one is kept — **keep·er** *n*

keep·sake *n* : souvenir

keg *n* : small cask or barrel

ken·nel *n* : dog shelter — **ken·nel** *vb*

ker·nel *n* **1** : inner softer part of a seed or nut **2** : whole seed of a cereal **3** : central part

ketch·up *n* : spicy tomato sauce

ket·tle *n* : vessel for boiling liquids

key *n* **1** : usu. metal piece to open a lock **2** : explanation **3** : lever pressed by a finger in playing an instrument or operating a machine **4** : leading individual or principle **5** : system of musical tones or pitch ~ *vb* : cause to be in tune ~ *adj* : basic — **key·hole** *n* — **key up** *vb* : make nervous

key·board *n* : arrangement of keys

kha·ki *n* : light yellowish brown color

kick *vb* **1** : strike out or hit with the foot **2** : object strongly ~ *n* : thrust with the foot **2** : stimulating effect — **kick·er** *n*

kid *n* **1** : young goat **2** : child ~ *vb* **1** : deceive as a joke **2** : tease — **kid·der** *n* — **kid·ding·ly** *adv*

kid·nap *vb* : carry a person away by illegal force — **kid·nap·per, kid·nap·er** *n*

kid·ney *n* : either of a pair of organs that excrete urine

kill *vb* **1** : deprive of life **2** : finish **3** : use up (time) ~ *n* : act of killing — **kill·er** *n*

ki·lo *n* : kilogram

ki·lo·gram *n* : metric unit of weight equal to 2.2 pounds

ki·lo·hertz *n* : 1000 hertz

ki·lo·me·ter *n* : 1000 meters

kilo·watt *n* : 1000 watts

kin *n* **1** : one's relatives **2** : kinsman

kind *n* **1** : essential quality **2** : group with common traits **3** : variety ~ *adj* **1** : of a sympathetic nature **2** : arising from sympathy — **kind·heart·ed** *adj* — **kind·ness** *n*

kin·der·gar·ten *n* : class for young children — **kin·der·gart·ner** *n*

kin·dle *vb* **1** : set on fire or start burning **2** : stir up — **kin·dling** *n*

kind·ly *adj* : of a sympathetic nature ~ *adv* **1** : sympathetically **2** : courteously — **kind·li·ness** *n*

kin·folk, kinfolks *n pl* : kin — **kins·man** *n* — **kins·wom·an** *n*

king *n* : male sovereign — **king·dom** *n* — **king·less** *adj* — **king·ly** *adj* — **king·ship** *n*

kink *n* **1** : short tight twist or curl **2** : cramp — **kinky** *adj*

kin·ship *n* : relationship

kiss *vb* : touch with the lips as a mark of affection — **kiss** *n*

kit *n* : set of articles (as tools or parts)

kitch·en *n* : room with cooking facilities

kite *n* **1** : small hawk **2** : covered framework flown at the end of a string

kit·ten *n* : young cat — **kit·ten·ish** *adj*

[1]**kit·ty** *n* : kitten

[2]**kitty** *n* : fund or pool (as in a card game)

kit·ty–cor·ner, kit·ty–cor·nered *var of* CATERCORNER

klep·to·ma·nia *n* : neurotic impulse to steal — **klep·to·ma·ni·ac** *n*

knack *n* **1** : clever way of doing something **2** : natural aptitude

knead *vb* **1** : work and press with the hands **2** : massage — **knead·er** *n*

knee *n* : joint in the middle part of the leg — **knee·cap** *n* — **kneed** *adj*

kneel *vb* (**knelt; knelt**) : rest on one's knees

knew *past of* KNOW

knick·knack *n* : small decorative object

knife *n* **knives** : sharp blade with a handle ~ *vb* : stab or cut with a knife

knight *n* **1** : mounted warrior of feudal times

2 : man honored by a sovereign ~ *vb* **:** make a knight of — **knight·hood** *n* — **knight·ly** *adv*

knit *vb* **1 :** link firmly or closely **2 :** form a fabric by interlacing yarn or thread ~ *n* **:** knitted garment — **knit·ter** *n*

knob *n* **:** rounded protuberance or handle — **knobbed** *adj* — **knob·by** *adj*

knock *vb* **1 :** strike with a sharp blow **2 :** collide **3 :** find fault with ~ *n* **:** sharp blow — **knock·er** *n* — **knock out** *vb* **:** make unconscious

knot *n* **1 :** interlacing (as of string) that forms a lump **2 :** base of a woody branch in the stem **3 :** group **4 :** one nautical mile per hour ~ *vb* **:** tie in or with a knot — **knot·ty** *adj*

know *vb* **knew; known 1 :** perceive directly or understand **2 :** be familiar with — **know·able** *adj* — **know·er** *n*

know·ing *adj* **:** shrewdly and keenly alert — **know·ing·ly** *adv*

knowl·edge *n* **1 :** understanding gained by experience **2 :** range of information — **knowl·edge·able** *adj*

knuck·le *n* **:** rounded knob at a finger joint

Ko·ran *n* **:** book of Islam containing revelations made to Muhammad by Allah

ko·sher *adj* **:** ritually fit for use according to Jewish law

Kwan·zaa, Kwan·za *n* **:** African-American festival held from December 26 to January 1

L

l *n* **:** 12th letter of the alphabet

lab *n* **:** laboratory

la·bel *n* **1 :** identification slip **2 :** identifying word or phrase ~ *vb* **:** put a label on

la·bor *n* **1 :** physical or mental effort **2 :** physical efforts of childbirth **3 :** task **4 :** people who work manually ~ *vb* **:** work esp. with great effort — **la·bor·er** *n* — **la·bo·ri·ous** *adj* — **la·bo·ri·ous·ly** *adv*

lab·o·ra·to·ry *n* **:** place for experimental testing

Labor Day *n* **:** 1st Monday in September observed as a legal holiday in recognition of working people

lab·y·rinth *n* **:** maze — **lab·y·rin·thine** *adj*

lace *n* **1 :** cord or string for tying **2 :** fine net usu. figured fabric ~ *vb* **1 :** tie **2 :** adorn with lace — **lacy** *adj*

lac·er·ate *vb* **:** tear roughly — **lac·er·a·tion** *n*

lack *vb* **:** be missing or deficient in ~ *n* **:** deficiency

lack·lus·ter *adj* **:** dull

lac·tate *vb* **:** secrete milk — **lac·ta·tion** *n*

lad *n* **:** boy

lad·der *n* **:** device with steps or rungs for climbing

la·dle *n* **:** spoon with a deep bowl — **ladle** *vb*

la·dy *n* **1 :** woman of rank or authority **2 :** woman

lag *vb* **:** fail to keep up ~ *n* **1 :** a falling behind **2 :** interval — **lag·gard** *n* — **lag·gard·ly** *adv or adj*

la·goon *n* **:** shallow sound, channel, or pond near or connecting with a larger body of water

laid *past of* LAY

lain *past part of* LIE

lair *n* **:** den

la·ity *n* **:** people of a religious faith who are not clergy members

lake *n* **:** inland body of water

la·ma *n* **:** Buddhist monk

lamb *n* **:** young sheep or its flesh used as food

lam·baste, lam·bast *vb* **1 :** beat **2 :** censure

lame *adj* **1 :** having a limb disabled **2 :** weak ~ *vb* **:** make lame — **lame·ly** *adv* — **lame·ness** *n*

la·ment *vb* **1 :** mourn **2 :** express sorrow for ~ *n* **1 :** mourning **2 :** complaint — **lam·en·ta·ble** *adj* — **lam·en·ta·bly** *adv* — **lam·en·ta·tion** *n*

lam·i·nat·ed *adj* **:** made of thin layers of material — **lam·i·nate** *vb* — **lam·i·nate** *n or adj* — **lam·i·na·tion** *n*

lamp *n* **:** device for producing light or heat

lam·poon *n* **:** satire — **lam·poon** *vb*

lance *n* **:** spear ~ *vb* **:** pierce or open with a lancet

land *n* **1 :** solid part of the surface of the earth **2 :** country ~ *vb* **1 :** go ashore **2 :** catch or gain **3 :** touch the ground or a surface — **land·less** *adj* — **land·own·er** *n*

land·fill *n* **:** dump

land·ing *n* **1 :** action of one that lands **2 :** place for loading passengers and cargo **3 :** level part of a staircase

land·lord *n* **:** owner of property

land·mark *n* **1 :** object that marks a boundary

or serves as a guide **2 :** event that marks a turning point
land•scape *n* **:** view of natural scenery ~ *vb* **:** beautify a piece of land (as by decorative planting)
land•slide *n* **1 :** slipping down of a mass of earth **2 :** overwhelming victory
lane *n* **:** narrow way
lan•guage *n* **:** words and the methods of combining them for communication
lanky *adj* **:** tall and thin
lan•tern *n* **:** enclosed portable light
[1]**lap** *n* **1 :** front part of the lower trunk and thighs of a seated person **2 :** overlapping part **3 :** one complete circuit completing a course (as around a track or pool) ~ *vb* **:** fold over
[2]**lap** *vb* **1 :** scoop up with the tongue **2 :** splash gently
la•pel *n* **:** fold of the front of a coat
lapse *n* **1 :** slight error **2 :** termination of a right or privilege **3 :** interval ~ *vb* **1 :** slip **2 :** become less **3 :** cease
lap•top *adj* **:** of a size that may be used on one's lap
lar•ce•ny *n* **:** theft — **lar•ce•nous** *adj*
large *adj* **:** greater than average — **large•ly** *adv* — **large•ness** *n*
lar•i•at *n* **:** lasso
lar•va *n* **:** wormlike form of an insect — **lar•val** *adj*
lar•yn•gi•tis *n* **:** inflammation of the upper part of the throat
la•sa•gna *n* **:** flat noodles baked usu. with tomato sauce, meat, and cheese
la•ser *n* **:** device that produces an intense light beam
lash *vb* **:** whip ~ *n* **1 :** stroke esp. of a whip **2 :** eyelash
lass *n* **:** girl
lass•ie *n* **:** girl
las•so *n* **:** rope with a noose for catching livestock — **las•so** *vb*
[1]**last** *vb* **:** continue in existence or operation
[2]**last** *adj* **1 :** final **2 :** previous **3 :** least likely ~ *adv* **1 :** at the end **2 :** most recently **3 :** in conclusion ~ *n* **:** something that is last — **last•ly** *adv* — **at last :** finally
latch *vb* **:** catch or get hold ~ *n* **:** catch that holds a door closed
late *adj* **1 :** coming or staying after the proper time **2 :** advanced toward the end **3 :** recently deceased **4 :** recent — **late** *adv* — **late•comer** *n* — **late•ly** *adv* — **late•ness** *n*
la•tent *adj* **:** present but not visible or expressed — **la•ten•cy** *n*
lat•er *adv* **:** at some time after the present time
lat•er•al *adj* **:** on or toward the side — **lat•er•al•ly** *adv*
la•tex *n* **:** emulsion of synthetic rubber or plastic
lath•er *n* **:** foam ~ *vb* **:** form or spread lather
lat•i•tude *n* **1 :** distance north or south from the earth's equator **2 :** freedom of action
lat•ter *adj* **1 :** more recent **2 :** being the second of 2 — **lat•ter•ly** *adv*
lat•tice *n* **:** framework of crossed strips
laud *vb or n* **:** praise — **laud•able** *adj* — **laud•ably** *adv*
laugh *vb* **:** show mirth, joy, or scorn with a smile and explosive sound — **laugh** *n* — **laugh•able** *adj* — **laugh•ing•ly** *adv* — **laugh•ter** *n*
laugh•ing•stock *n* **:** object of ridicule
launch *vb* **1 :** hurl or send off **2 :** set afloat **3 :** start — **launch** *n* — **launch•er** *n*
laun•der *vb* **:** wash or iron fabrics — **laun•der•er** *n* — **laun•dress** *n* — **laun•dry** *n*
lau•rel *n* **1 :** small evergreen tree **2 :** honor
la•va *n* **:** volcanic molten rock
lav•a•to•ry *n* **:** bathroom
lav•ish *adj* **:** expended profusely ~ *vb* **:** expend or give freely — **lav•ish•ly** *adv* — **lav•ish•ness** *n*
law *n* **1 :** established rule of conduct **2 :** body of such rules **3 :** principle of construction or procedure **4 :** rule stating uniform behavior under uniform conditions **5 :** lawyer's profession — **law•break•er** *n* — **law•ful** *adj* — **law•ful•ly** *adv* — **law•giv•er** *n* — **law•less** *adj* — **law•less•ly** *adv* — **law•less•ness** *n* — **law•mak•er** *n* — **law•man** *n* — **law•suit** *n*
lawn *n* **:** grass-covered yard
law•yer *n* **:** legal practitioner
lax *adj* **:** not strict or tense — **lax•i•ty** *n* — **lax•ly** *adv*
[1]**lay** *vb* **laid; laid 1 :** put or set down **2 :** produce eggs **3 :** bet **4 :** impose as a duty or burden **5 :** put forward ~ *n* **:** way something lies or is laid
[2]**lay** *past of* LIE
[3]**lay** *adj* **:** of the laity — **lay•man** *n* — **lay•wom•an** *n*
lay•er *n* **1 :** one that lays **2 :** one thickness over or under another
lay•off *n* **:** temporary dismissal of a worker
lay•out *n* **:** arrangement

la•zy *adj* : disliking activity or exertion — **la•zi•ly** *adv* — **la•zi•ness** *n*

lead led; led *vb* **1 :** guide on a way **2 :** direct the activity of **3 :** go at the head of **4 :** tend to a definite result ~ *n* : position in front — **lead•er** *n* — **lead•er•less** *adj* — **lead•er•ship** *n*

leaf *n* (**leaves**) **1 :** green outgrowth of a plant stem **2 :** leaflike thing ~ *vb* **1 :** produce leaves **2 :** turn book pages — **leaf•age** *n* — **leafed** *adj* — **leaf•less** *adj* — **leafy** *adj* — **leaved** *adj*

leaf•let *n* : pamphlet

league *n* : association for a common purpose — **league** *vb* — **leagu•er** *n*

leak *vb* **1 :** enter or escape through a leak **2 :** become or make known ~ *n* : opening that accidentally admits or lets out a substance — **leak•age** *n* — **leaky** *adj*

[1]lean *vb* **1 :** bend from a vertical position **2 :** rely on for support **3 :** incline in opinion — **lean** *n*

[2]lean *adj* **1 :** lacking in flesh **2 :** lacking richness — **lean•ness** *n*

leap *vb* : jump — **leap** *n*

leap year *n* : 366-day year

learn *vb* **1 :** gain understanding or skill by study or experience **2 :** memorize **3 :** find out — **learn•er** *n*

learn•ed *adj* : having great learning — **learn•ed•ness** *n*

learn•ing *n* : knowledge

lease *n* : contract transferring real estate for a term and usu. for rent ~ *vb* : grant by or hold under a lease

leash *n* : line to hold an animal — **leash** *vb*

least *adj* **1 :** lowest in importance or position **2 :** smallest **3 :** scantiest ~ *n* : one that is least ~ *adv* : in the smallest or lowest degree

leath•er *n* : dressed animal skin — **leath•ern** *adj* — **leath•ery** *adj*

[1]leave *vb* **left; left 1 :** bequeath **2 :** allow or cause to remain **3 :** have as a remainder **4 :** go away ~ *n* **1 :** permission **2 :** authorized absence **3 :** departure

[2]leave *vb* : produce leaves

leaves *pl of* LEAF

lech•ery *n* : inordinate indulgence in sex — **lech•er** *n* — **lech•er•ous** *adj* — **lech•er•ous•ly** *adv* — **lech•er•ous•ness** *n*

lec•ture *n* **1 :** instructive talk **2 :** reprimand — **lec•ture** *vb* — **lec•tur•er** *n* — **lec•ture•ship** *n*

led *past of* LEAD

ledge *n* : shelflike projection

leery *adj* : suspicious or wary

lee•ward *adj* : situated away from the wind ~ *n* : the lee side

lee•way *n* : allowable margin

[1]left *adj* : on the same side of the body as the heart ~ *n* : left hand — **left** *adv*

[2]left *past of* LEAVE

leg *n* **1 :** limb of an animal that supports the body **2 :** something like a leg **3 :** clothing to cover the leg ~ *vb* : walk or run — **leg•ged** *adj* — **leg•less** *adj*

leg•a•cy *n* : inheritance

le•gal *adj* **1 :** relating to law or lawyers **2 :** lawful — **le•gal•is•tic** *adj* — **le•gal•i•ty** *n* — **le•gal•ize** *vb* — **le•gal•ly** *adv*

leg•end *n* **1 :** story handed down from the past **2 :** inscription **3 :** explanation of map symbols — **leg•end•ary** *adj*

leg•i•ble *adj* : capable of being read — **leg•i•bil•i•ty** *n* — **leg•i•bly** *adv*

le•gion *n* **1 :** large army unit **2 :** multitude **3 :** association of former servicemen — **le•gion•ary** *n* — **le•gion•naire** *n*

leg•is•late *vb* : enact or bring about with laws — **leg•is•la•tion** *n* — **leg•is•la•tive** *adj* — **leg•is•la•tor** *n* — **leg•is•la•ture** *n*

le•git•i•mate *adj* **1 :** lawfully begotten **2 :** genuine **3 :** conforming with law or accepted standards — **le•git•i•ma•cy** *n* — **le•git•i•mate•ly** *adv* — **le•git•i•mize** *vb*

lei•sure *n* **1 :** free time **2 :** ease **3 :** convenience — **lei•sure•ly** *adj or adv*

lem•on *n* : yellow citrus fruit — **lem•on•ade** *n* — **lem•ony** *adj*

lend *vb* (**lent; lent**) **1 :** give for temporary use **2 :** furnish — **lend•er** *n*

length *n* **1 :** longest dimension **2 :** duration in time **3 :** piece to be joined to others — **length•en** *vb* — **length•wise** *adv or adj* — **lengthy** *adj*

le•nient *adj* : of mild and tolerant disposition or effect — **le•ni•en•cy** *n* — **le•ni•ent•ly** *adv*

lens *n* **1 :** curved piece for forming an image in an optical instrument **2 :** transparent body in the eye that focuses light rays

lent *past of* LEND

Lent *n* : 40-day period of penitence and fasting from Ash Wednesday to Easter — **Lent•en** *adj*

leop•ard *n* : large tawny black-spotted cat

less *adj* **1 :** fewer **2 :** of lower rank, degree, or importance **3 :** smaller ~ *adv* : to a lesser de-

gree ~ *n, pl* **less** : smaller portion ~ *prep* : minus — **less•en** *vb*
less•er *adj* : of less size, quality, or significance
les•son *n* **1** : reading or exercise to be studied by a pupil **2** : something learned
let *vb* **let; let** **1** : cause to **2** : rent **3** : permit
le•thal *adj* : deadly — **le•thal•ly** *adv*
let•ter *n* **1** : unit of an alphabet **2** : written or printed communication **3** *pl* : literature or learning **4** : literal meaning ~ *vb* : mark with letters — **let•ter•er** *n*
let•tuce *n* : garden plant with crisp leaves
lev•ee *n* : embankment to prevent flooding
lev•el *n* **1** : device for establishing a flat surface **2** : horizontal surface **3** : position in a scale ~ *vb* **1** : make flat or level **2** : aim **3** : tear down ~ *adj* **1** : having an even surface **2** : of the same height or rank — **lev•el•er** *n* — **lev•el•ly** *adv* — **lev•el•ness** *n*
le•ver *n* : bar for prying or dislodging something — **le•ver•age** *n*
li•a•ble *adj* **1** : legally obligated **2** : probable **3** : likely to be affected — **li•a•bil•i•ty** *n*
li•ar *n* : one who lies
li•bel *n* : action, crime, or an instance of injuring a person's reputation esp. by something written ~ *vb* : make or publish a libel — **li•bel•er** *n* — **li•bel•ist** *n* — **li•bel•ous, li•bel•lous** *adj*
lib•er•al *adj* : not stingy, narrow, or conservative — **liberal** *n* — **lib•er•al•ism** *n* — **lib•er•al•i•ty** *n* — **lib•er•al•ize** *vb* — **lib•er•al•ly** *adv*
lib•er•ate *vb* : set free — **lib•er•a•tion** *n* — **lib•er•a•tor** *n*
lib•er•ty *n* **1** : quality or state of being free **2** : action going beyond normal limits
li•brary *n* **1** : place where books are kept for use **2** : collection of books — **li•brar•i•an** *n*
lice *pl of* LOUSE
li•cense, li•cence *n* **1** : legal permission to engage in some activity **2** : document or tag providing proof of a license **3** : irresponsible use of freedom — **license** *vb* — **li•cens•ee** *n*
lick *vb* **1** : draw the tongue over **2** : beat ~ *n* **1** : stroke of the tongue **2** : small amount
lic•o•rice *n* : dried root of a European legume or candy flavored by it
lid *n* **1** : movable cover **2** : eyelid
¹lie *vb* **lay; lain** **1** : be in, rest in, or assume a horizontal position **2** : occupy a certain relative position ~ *n* : position in which something lies
²lie *vb* : tell a lie ~ *n* : untrue statement
life *n* (**lives**) **1** : quality that distinguishes a vital and functional being from a dead body or inanimate matter **2** : physical and mental experiences of an individual **3** : biography **4** : period of existence **5** : way of living **6** : liveliness — **life•guard** *n or vb* — **life•less** *adj* — **life•like** *adj* — **life•time** *n*
life•blood *n* : basic source of strength and vitality
life•sav•ing *n* : art or practice of saving lives — **life•sav•er** *n*
lift *vb* **1** : move upward or cause to move upward **2** : put an end to — **lift** *n* — **lift•er** *n*
lift•off *n* : vertical takeoff by a rocket
¹light *n* **1** : radiation that makes vision possible **2** : daylight **3** : source of light **4** : public knowledge **5** : aspect **6** : celebrity **7** : flame for lighting ~ *adj* **1** : bright **2** : weak in color ~ *vb* **1** : make or become light **2** : cause to burn — **light•en** *vb* — **light•er** *n* — **light•ness** *n* — **light•proof** *adj*
²light *adj* : not heavy, serious, or abundant — **light** *adv* — **light•en** *vb* — **light•ly** *adv* — **light•ness** *n* — **light•weight** *adj*
light•heart•ed *adj* : free from worry — **light•heart•ed•ly** *adv* — **light•heart•ed•ness** *n*
light•ning *n* : flashing discharge of atmospheric electricity
¹like *vb* **1** : enjoy **2** : desire ~ *n* : preference — **lik•able, like•able** *adj*
²like *adj* : similar ~ *prep* **1** : similar or similarly to **2** : typical of **3** : such as ~ *n* : counterpart ~ *conj* : as or as if — **like•ness** *n* — **like•wise** *adv*
like•ly *adj* **1** : probable **2** : believable ~ *adv* : in all probability — **like•li•hood** *n*
lik•en *vb* : compare
lily *n* : tall bulbous herb with funnel-shaped flowers
limb *n* **1** : projecting appendage used in moving or grasping **2** : tree branch — **limb•less** *adj*
lim•ber *adj* : supple or agile ~ *vb* : make or become limber
lime *n* : small green lemonlike citrus fruit — **lime•ade** *n*
lim•er•ick *n* : light poem of 5 lines
lim•it *n* **1** : boundary **2** : something that restrains or confines ~ *vb* : set limits on — **lim•i•ta•tion** *n* — **lim•it•less** *adj*
lim•ou•sine *n* : large luxurious sedan
limp *vb* : walk lamely ~ *n* : limping movement

or gait ~ *adj* **:** lacking firmness and body — **limp·ly** *adv* — **limp·ness** *n*

[1]**line** *vb* **:** cover the inner surface of — **lin·ing** *n*

[2]**line** *n* **1 :** cord, rope, or wire **2 :** row or something like a row **3 :** note **4 :** course of action or thought **5 :** state of agreement **6 :** occupation **7 :** limit **8 :** transportation system **9 :** long narrow mark ~ *vb* **1 :** mark with a line **2 :** place in a line **3 :** form a line — **lin·er** *n*

lin·e·ar *adj* **1 :** straight **2 :** long and narrow

lin·en *n* **1 :** cloth or thread made of flax **2 :** household articles made of linen cloth

lin·ger *vb* **:** be slow to leave or act — **lin·ger·er** *n*

lin·guist *n* **1 :** person skilled in speech or languages **2 :** student of language — **lin·guis·tic** *adj* — **lin·guis·tics** *n pl*

link *n* **1 :** connecting structure (as a ring of a chain) **2 :** bond — **link** *vb* — **link·age** *n* — **link·er** *n*

lint *n* **:** fine fluff or loose short fibers from fabric

li·on *n* **:** large cat of Africa and Asia — **li·on·ess** *n*

lip *n* **1 :** either of the 2 fleshy folds surrounding the mouth **2 :** edge of something hollow — **lipped** *adj* — **lip·read·ing** *n*

lip·stick *n* **:** stick of cosmetic to color lips

liq·ue·fy *vb* **:** make or become liquid — **liq·ue·fi·er** *n*

liq·uid *adj* **1 :** flowing freely like water **2 :** neither solid nor gaseous **3 :** of or convertible to cash — **liquid** *n* — **li·quid·i·ty** *n*

liq·ui·date *vb* **1 :** pay off **2 :** dispose of — **liq·ui·da·tion** *n*

li·quor *n* **:** usu. distilled liquid containing alcohol

lisp *vb* **:** pronounce *s* and *z* imperfectly — **lisp** *n*

list *n* **1 :** series of names or items ~ *vb* **1 :** make a list of **2 :** put on a list

lis·ten *vb* **1 :** pay attention in order to hear **2 :** heed — **lis·ten·er** *n*

list·less *adj* **:** having no desire to act — **list·less·ly** *adv* — **list·less·ness** *n*

lit *past of* LIGHT

li·ter *n* **:** unit of liquid measure equal to about 1.06 quarts

lit·er·al *adj* **:** being exactly as stated — **lit·er·al·ly** *adv*

lit·er·ary *adj* **:** relating to literature

lit·er·ate *adj* **:** able to read and write — **lit·er·a·cy** *n*

lit·er·a·ture *n* **:** writings of enduring interest

lit·i·gate *vb* **:** carry on a lawsuit — **lit·i·gant** *n* — **lit·i·ga·tion** *n* — **li·ti·gious** *adj* — **li·ti·gious·ness** *n*

lit·ter *n* **1 :** animal offspring of one birth **2 :** stretcher **3 :** rubbish **4 :** material to absorb animal waste ~ *vb* **1 :** give birth to young **2 :** strew with litter

lit·tle *adj* **lit·tler/less/less·er; lit·tlest/least 1 :** not big **2 :** not much **3 :** not important ~ *adv* **1 :** slightly **2 :** not often ~ *n* **:** small amount — **lit·tle·ness** *n*

[1]**live** *vb* **1 :** be alive **2 :** conduct one's life **3 :** nourish oneself **4 :** reside — **liv·able** *adj* — **liv·a·bil·i·ty** *n*

[2]**live** *adj* **1 :** having life **2 :** burning **3 :** connected to electric power **4 :** not exploded **5 :** of continuing interest **6 :** involving the actual presence of real people

live·li·hood *n* **:** means of supporting one's life

live·ly *adj* **:** full of life and vigor — **live·li·ness** *n*

liv·er *n* **:** organ that secretes bile

lives *pl of* LIFE

liv·ing *adj* **:** having life ~ *n* **:** livelihood

load *n* **1 :** cargo **2 :** supported weight **3 :** burden **4 :** a large quantity — usu. pl. ~ *vb* **1 :** put a load on **2 :** burden **3 :** put ammunition in

[1]**loaf** *n* **:** mass of bread

[2]**loaf** *vb* **:** waste time — **loaf·er** *n*

loan *n* **1 :** money borrowed at interest **2 :** something lent temporarily **3 :** grant of use ~ *vb* **:** lend

loath·ing *n* **:** extreme disgust

lob *vb* **:** throw or hit in a high arc — **lob** *n*

lob·by *n* **1 :** public waiting room at the entrance of a building **2 :** persons lobbying ~ *vb* **:** try to influence legislators — **lob·by·ist** *n*

lob·ster *n* **:** marine crustacean with 2 large pincerlike claws

lo·cal *adj* **:** confined to or serving a limited arca — **lo·cal** *n* — **lo·cal·i·za·tion** *n* — **lo·cal·ize** *vb* — **lo·cal·ly** *adv*

lo·cale *n* **:** setting for an event — **lo·cal·i·ty** *n*

lo·cate *vb* **1 :** settle **2 :** find a site for **3 :** discover the place of — **lo·ca·tion** *n*

lock *n* **1 :** fastener using a bolt **2 :** enclosure in a canal to raise or lower boats ~ *vb* **1 :** make fast with a lock **2 :** confine **3 :** interlock

lock·er *n* **:** storage compartment

lo·co·mo·tion *n* **:** power of moving — **lo·co·mo·tive** *adj*

lodge *vb* **1 :** provide quarters for **2 :** come to rest **3 :** file ~ *n* **1 :** special house (as for hunters) **2 :** animal's den **3 :** branch of a fraternal organization — **lodg•er** *n* — **lodg•ing** *n* — **lodg•ment, lodge•ment** *n*

loft *n* **1 :** attic **2 :** upper floor (as of a warehouse)

lofty *adj* **1 :** noble **2 :** proud **3 :** tall or high — **loft•i•ly** *adv* — **loft•i•ness** *n*

log *n* **1 :** unshaped timber **2 :** daily record of a ship's or plane's progress ~ *vb* **1 :** cut (trees) for lumber **2 :** enter in a log — **log•ger** *n*

log•ic *n* **1 :** science of reasoning **2 :** sound reasoning — **log•i•cal** *adj* — **log•i•cal•ly** *adv* — **lo•gi•cian** *n*

lo•gis•tics *n sing or pl* **:** procurement and movement of people and supplies — **lo•gis•tic** *adj*

loin *n* **1 :** part of the body on each side of the spine between the hip and lower ribs **2** *pl* **:** pubic regions

loi•ter *vb* **:** remain around a place idly — **loi•ter•er** *n*

lol•li•pop, lol•ly•pop *n* **:** hard candy on a stick

lone *adj* **1 :** alone or isolated **2 :** only — **lone•li•ness** *n* — **lone•ly** *adj* — **lon•er** *n*

lone•some *adj* **:** sad from lack of company — **lone•some•ly** *adv* — **lone•some•ness** *n*

long *adj* **1 :** extending far or for a considerable time **2 :** having a specified length **3 :** tedious **4 :** well supplied — used with *on* ~ *adv* **:** for a long time ~ *n* **:** long period ~ *vb* **:** feel a strong desire — **long•ing** *n* — **long•ing•ly** *adv*

lon•gev•i•ty *n* **:** long life

lon•gi•tude *n* **:** angular distance east or west from a meridian

look *vb* **1 :** see **2 :** seem **3 :** direct one's attention **4 :** face ~ *n* **1 :** action of looking **2 :** appearance of the face **3 :** aspect — **look after :** take care of — **look for 1 :** expect **2 :** search for

look•out *n* **1 :** one who watches **2 :** careful watch

[1]**loom** *n* **:** frame or machine for weaving

[2]**loom** *vb* **:** appear large and indistinct or impressive

loop *n* **1 :** doubling of a line that leaves an opening **2 :** something like a loop — **loop** *vb*

loop•hole *n* **:** means of evading

loose *adj* **1 :** not fixed tight **2 :** not restrained **3 :** not dense **4 :** slack **5 :** not exact ~ *vb* **1 :** release **2 :** untie or relax — **loose** *adv* — **loose•ly** *adv* — **loos•en** *vb* — **loose•ness** *n*

loot *n or vb* **:** plunder — **loot•er** *n*

lop•sid•ed *adj* **1 :** leaning to one side **2 :** not symmetrical — **lop•sid•ed•ly** *adv* — **lop•sid•ed•ness** *n*

lord *n* **1 :** one with authority over others **2 :** British nobleman — **lord•ship** *n*

lord•ly *adj* **:** haughty

lore *n* **:** traditional knowledge

lose *vb* **lost; lost 1 :** have pass from one's possession **2 :** be deprived of **3 :** waste **4 :** be defeated in **5 :** fail to keep to or hold **6 :** get rid of — **los•er** *n*

loss *n* **1 :** something lost **2** *pl* **:** killed, wounded, or captured soldiers **3 :** failure to win

lost *adj* **1 :** not used, won, or claimed **2 :** unable to find the way

lot *n* **1 :** object used in deciding something by chance **2 :** share **3 :** fate **4 :** plot of land **5 :** much

lo•tion *n* **:** liquid to rub on the skin

lot•tery *n* **:** drawing of lots with prizes going to winners

loud *adj* **1 :** high in volume of sound **2 :** noisy **3 :** obtrusive in color or pattern — **loud** *adv* — **loud•ly** *adv* — **loud•ness** *n* — **loud-speak•er** *n*

lounge *vb* **:** act or move lazily ~ *n* **:** room with comfortable furniture

louse *n* **lice :** parasitic wingless usu. flat insect

lousy *adj* **1 :** infested with lice **2 :** not good — **lous•i•ly** *adv* — **lous•i•ness** *n*

love *n* **1 :** strong affection **2 :** warm attachment **3 :** beloved person ~ *vb* **1 :** feel affection for **2 :** enjoy greatly — **lov•able** *adj* — **love•less** *adj* — **lov•er** *n* — **lov•ing•ly** *adv*

love•ly *adj* **:** beautiful — **love•li•ness** *n* — **lovely** *adv*

low *adj* **1 :** not high or tall **2 :** below normal level **3 :** not loud **4 :** humble **5 :** sad **6 :** less than usual **7 :** falling short of a standard **8 :** unfavorable ~ *n* **1 :** something low **2 :** automobile gear giving the slowest speed — **low** *adv* — **low•ness** *n*

low•er *vb* **1 :** drop **2 :** let descend **3 :** reduce in amount

low•ly *adj* **1 :** humble **2 :** low in rank — **low•li•ness** *n*

loy•al *adj* **:** faithful to a country, cause, or friend — **loy•al•ist** *n* — **loy•al•ly** *adv* — **loy•al•ty** *n*

lu•bri•cate *vb* : apply a lubricant to — **lu•bri•cant** *n* — **lu•bri•ca•tion** *n* — **lu•bri•ca•tor** *n*
lu•cid *adj* **1** : mentally sound **2** : easily understood — **lu•cid•i•ty** *n* — **lu•cid•ly** *adv* — **lu•cid•ness** *n*
luck *n* **1** : chance **2** : good fortune — **luck•i•ly** *adv* — **luck•i•ness** *n* — **luck•less** *adj* — **lucky** *adj*
lu•cra•tive *adj* : profitable — **lu•cra•tive•ly** *adv* — **lu•cra•tive•ness** *n*
lu•di•crous *adj* : comically ridiculous — **lu•di•crous•ly** *adv* — **lu•di•crous•ness** *n*
lug *vb* : drag or carry laboriously
lug•gage *n* : baggage
lull *vb* : make or become quiet or relaxed ~ *n* : temporary calm
lul•la•by *n* : song to lull children to sleep
lum•ber *n* : timber dressed for use ~ *vb* : cut logs — **lum•ber•man** *n* — **lum•ber•yard** *n*
lu•mi•nous *adj* : emitting light — **lu•mi•nance** *n* — **lu•mi•nos•i•ty** *n* — **lu•mi•nous•ly** *adv*
lump *n* **1** : mass of irregular shape **2** : abnormal swelling ~ *vb* : heap together — **lump•ish** *adj* — **lumpy** *adj*
lu•na•cy *n* : state of insanity
lu•nar *adj* : of the moon
lu•na•tic *adj* : insane — **lu•na•tic** *n*
lunch *n* : noon meal ~ *vb* : eat lunch
lung *n* : breathing organ in the chest — **lunged** *adj*
lunge *n* **1** : sudden thrust **2** : sudden move forward — **lunge** *vb*
lurch *n* : sudden swaying — **lurch** *vb*
lure *n* **1** : something that attracts **2** : artificial fish bait ~ *vb* : attract
lu•rid *adj* **1** : gruesome **2** : sensational — **lu•rid•ly** *adv*
lurk *vb* : lie in wait
lus•cious *adj* **1** : pleasingly sweet in taste or smell **2** : sensually appealing — **lus•cious•ly** *adv* — **lus•cious•ness** *n*
lush *adj* : covered with abundant growth
lust *n* **1** : intense sexual desire **2** : intense longing — **lust** *vb* — **lust•ful** *adj*
lus•ter, lus•tre *n* **1** : brightness from reflected light **2** : magnificence — **lus•ter•less** *adj* — **lus•trous** *adj*
lusty *adj* : full of vitality — **lust•i•ly** *adv* — **lust•i•ness** *n*
lux•u•ri•ant *adj* **1** : growing plentifully **2** : rich and varied — **lux•u•ri•ance** *n* — **lux•u•ri•ant•ly** *adv* — **lux•u•ri•ate** *vb*
lux•u•ry *n* **1** : great comfort **2** : something adding to pleasure or comfort — **lux•u•ri•ous** *adj* — **lux•u•ri•ous•ly** *adv*
lye *n* : caustic alkaline substance
lying *pres part of* LIE
lynch *vb* : put to death by mob action — **lynch•er** *n*
lyr•ic *adj* **1** : suitable for singing **2** : expressing direct personal emotion ~ *n* **1** : lyric poem **2** *pl* : words of a song — **lyr•i•cal** *adj*

M

m *n* : 13th letter of the alphabet
ma'am *n* : madam
ma•ca•bre *adj* : gruesome
mac•a•ro•ni *n* : tube-shaped pasta
mac•a•roon *n* : cookie of ground almonds or coconut
mace *n* : spice from the fibrous coating of the nutmeg
ma•chete *n* : large heavy knife
ma•chine *n* : combination of mechanical or electrical parts ~ *vb* : modify by machine-operated tools — **ma•chin•able** *adj* — **ma•chin•ery** *n* — **ma•chin•ist** *n*
mac•ra•mé *n* : coarse lace or fringe made by knotting
mad *adj* **1** : insane or rabid **2** : rash and foolish **3** : angry **4** : carried away by enthusiasm — **mad•den** *vb* — **mad•den•ing•ly** *adv* — **mad•ly** *adv* — **mad•ness** *n*
mad•am *n* — used in polite address to a woman
made *past of* MAKE
ma•de•moi•selle *n* : an unmarried girl or woman — used as a title for a woman esp. of French nationality
mad•house *n* **1** : insane asylum **2** : place of great uproar or confusion
Ma•fia *n* : secret criminal organization
mag•a•zine *n* **1** : storehouse **2** : publication issued at regular intervals **3** : cartridge container in a gun
mag•ic *n* **1** : art of using supernatural powers

2 : extraordinary power or influence **3 :** sleight of hand — **magic, mag•i•cal** *adj* — **mag•i•cal•ly** *adv* — **ma•gi•cian** *n*

mag•is•trate *n* **:** judge — **mag•is•te•ri•al** *adj* — **mag•is•tra•cy** *n*

mag•net *n* **1 :** body that attracts iron **2 :** something that attracts — **mag•net•ic** *adj* — **mag•net•i•cal•ly** *adv* — **mag•ne•tism** *n*

mag•ne•tize *vb* **1 :** attract like a magnet **2 :** give magnetic properties to — **mag•ne•tiz•able** *adj* — **mag•ne•ti•za•tion** *n* — **mag•ne•tiz•er** *n*

mag•nif•i•cent *adj* **:** splendid — **mag•nif•i•cence** *n* — **mag•nif•i•cent•ly** *adv*

mag•ni•fy *vb* **1 :** intensify **2 :** enlarge — **mag•ni•fi•ca•tion** *n* — **mag•ni•fi•er** *n*

mag•ni•tude *n* **1 :** greatness of size or extent **2 :** quantity

ma•hog•a•ny *n* **:** tropical evergreen tree or its reddish brown wood

maid *n* **1 :** unmarried young woman **2 :** female servant

mail *n* **1 :** something sent or carried in the postal system **2 :** postal system ~ *vb* **:** send by mail — **mail•box** *n* — **mail•man** *n*

main *n* **1 :** force **2 :** ocean **3 :** principal pipe, duct, or circuit of a utility system ~ *adj* **:** chief — **main•ly** *adv*

main•land *n* **:** part of a country on a continent

main•stream *n* **:** prevailing current or direction of activity or influence — **main•stream** *adj*

main•tain *vb* **1 :** keep in an existing state (as of repair) **2 :** sustain **3 :** declare — **main•tain•abil•i•ty** *n* — **main•tain•able** *adj* — **main•te•nance** *n*

maj•es•ty *n* **1 :** sovereign power or dignity — used as a title **2 :** grandeur or splendor — **ma•jes•tic** *adj* — **ma•jes•ti•cal•ly** *adv*

ma•jor *adj* **1 :** larger or greater **2 :** noteworthy or conspicuous ~ *n* **1 :** commissioned officer (as in the army) ranking next below a lieutenant colonel **2 :** main field of study ~ *vb* **:** pursue an academic major

ma•jor•i•ty *n* **1 :** age of full civil rights **2 :** quantity more than half

make *vb* **(made; made) 1 :** cause to exist, occur, or appear **2 :** fashion or manufacture **3 :** formulate in the mind **4 :** constitute **5 :** prepare **6 :** cause to be or become **7 :** carry out or perform **8 :** compel **9 :** gain **10 :** have an effect — used with *for* ~ *n* **:** brand — **mak•er** *n* — **make do** *vb* **:** get along with what is available — **make good** *vb* **1 :** repay **2 :** succeed — **make out** *vb* **1 :** draw up or write **2 :** discern or understand **3 :** fare — **make up** *vb* **1 :** invent **2 :** become reconciled **3 :** compensate for

make–be•lieve *n* **:** a pretending to believe ~ *adj* **:** imagined or pretended

make•shift *n* **:** temporary substitute — **makeshift** *adj*

make•up *n* **1 :** way in which something is constituted **2 :** cosmetics

mal•a•dy *n* **:** disease or disorder

male *adj* **1 :** relating to the sex that performs a fertilizing function **2 :** masculine ~ *n* **:** male individual — **male•ness** *n*

ma•lev•o•lent *adj* **:** malicious or spiteful — **ma•lev•o•lence** *n*

mal•for•ma•tion *n* **:** distortion or faulty formation — **mal•formed** *adj*

mal•func•tion *vb* **:** fail to operate properly — **mal•func•tion** *n*

mal•ice *n* **:** desire to cause pain or injury to another — **ma•li•cious** *adj* — **ma•li•cious•ly** *adv*

ma•lig•nant *adj* **1 :** harmful **2 :** likely to cause death — **ma•lig•nan•cy** *n* — **ma•lig•nant•ly** *adv* — **ma•lig•ni•ty** *n*

mall *n* **1 :** shaded promenade **2 :** concourse providing access to rows of shops

mal•let *n* **:** hammerlike tool

mal•nu•tri•tion *n* **:** inadequate nutrition — **mal•nour•ished** *adj*

mal•prac•tice *n* **:** failure of professional duty

ma•ma, mam•ma *n* **:** mother

mam•mal *n* **:** warm-blooded vertebrate animal that nourishes its young with milk — **mam•ma•li•an** *adj or n*

mam•mo•gram *n* **:** X-ray photograph of the breasts

man *n* **(men) 1 :** human being **2 :** adult male **3 :** mankind ~ *vb* **:** supply with people for working — **man•hood** *n* — **man•hunt** *n* — **man•like** *adj* — **man•li•ness** *n* — **man•ly** *adj or adv* — **man–made** *adj* — **man•nish** *adj* — **man•nish•ly** *adv* — **man•nish•ness** *n* — **man–size, man–sized** *adj*

man•age *vb* **1 :** control **2 :** direct or carry on business or affairs **3 :** cope — **man•age•abil•i•ty** *n* — **man•age•able** *adj* — **man•age•able•ness** *n* — **man•age•ably** *adv* —

man•age•ment *n* — **man•ag•er** *n* — **man•a•ge•ri•al** *adj*
man•date *n* : authoritative command
man•da•to•ry *adj* : obligatory
mane *n* : animal's neck hair — **maned** *adj*
ma•neu•ver *n* **1** : planned movement of troops or ships **2** : military training exercise **3** : clever or skillful move or action — **maneuver** *vb* — **ma•neu•ver•abil•i•ty** *n*
man•gle *vb* **1** : mutilate **2** : bungle — **mangler** *n*
man•hole *n* : entry to a sewer
ma•nia *n* **1** : insanity marked by uncontrollable emotion or excitement **2** : excessive enthusiasm — **ma•ni•ac** *n* — **ma•ni•a•cal** *adj* — **man•ic** *adj or n*
man•i•cure *n* : treatment for the fingernails ~ *vb* **1** : do manicure work on **2** : trim precisely — **man•i•cur•ist** *n*
man•i•fest *adj* : clear to the senses or to the mind ~ *vb* : make evident — **man•i•fes•ta•tion** *n* — **man•i•fest•ly** *adv*
ma•nip•u•late *vb* **1** : treat or operate manually or mechanically **2** : influence esp. by cunning — **ma•nip•u•la•tion** *n* — **ma•nip•u•la•tive** *adj* — **ma•nip•u•la•tor** *n*
man•kind *n* : human race
man•ne•quin *n* : dummy used to display clothes
man•ner *n* **1** : kind **2** : usual way of acting **3** : artistic method **4** *pl* : social conduct
man•ner•ism *n* : individual peculiarity of action
man•ner•ly *adj* : polite — **man•ner•li•ness** *n* — **mannerly** *adv*
man•or *n* : country estate — **ma•no•ri•al** *adj*
man•pow•er *n* : supply of people available for service
man•sion *n* : very big house
man•slaugh•ter *n* : unintentional killing of a person
man•tle *n* **1** : sleeveless cloak **2** : something that covers, enfolds, or envelops — **man•tle** *vb*
man•u•al *adj* : involving the hands or physical force ~ *n* : handbook — **man•u•al•ly** *adv*
man•u•fac•ture *n* : process of making atricles by hand or by machinery ~ *vb* : make from raw materials — **man•u•fac•tur•er** *n*
ma•nure *n* : animal excrement used as fertilizer
manu•script *n* **1** : something written or typed **2** : document submitted for publication
many *adj* **more; most** : consisting of a large number — **many** *n or pron*
map *n* : representation of a geographical area ~ *vb* **1** : make a map of **2** : plan in detail — **map•pa•ble** *adj* — **map•per** *n*
ma•ple *n* : tree with hard light-colored wood
mar *vb* : damage
mar•a•thon *n* **1** : long-distance race **2** : test of endurance — **mar•a•thon•er** *n*
mar•ble *n* **1** : crystallized limestone **2** : small glass ball used in a children's game (**marbles**)
march *vb* : move with regular steps or in a purposeful manner ~ *n* **1** : distance covered in a march **2** : measured stride **3** : forward movement **4** : music for marching — **march•er** *n*
March *n* : 3d month of the year having 31 days
mar•ga•rine *n* : butter substitute made usu. from vegetable oils
mar•gin *n* **1** : edge **2** : spare amount, measure, or degree — **mar•gin•al** *adj* — **mar•gin•al•ly** *adv*
ma•ri•na *n* : place for mooring pleasure boats
ma•rine *adj* **1** : relating to the sea **2** : relating to marines ~ *n* : infantry soldier associated with a navy
mar•i•tal *adj* : relating to marriage
mar•i•time *adj* : relating to the sea or commerce on the sea
mark *n* **1** : something aimed at **2** : something (as a line) designed to record position **3** : visible sign **4** : written symbol **5** : grade **6** : lasting impression **7** : blemish ~ *vb* **1** : designate or set apart by a mark or make a mark on **2** : characterize **3** : remark — **mark•er** *n*
mar•ket *n* **1** : buying and selling of goods or the place this happens **2** : demand for commodities **3** : store ~ *vb* : sell — **mar•ket•able** *adj* — **mar•ket•place** *n*
ma•roon *vb* : isolate without hope of escape
mar•riage *n* **1** : state of being married **2** : wedding ceremony — **mar•riage•able** *adj*
mar•ry *vb* **1** : join as husband and wife **2** : take or give in marriage — **mar•ried** *adj or n*
marsh *n* : soft wet land — **marshy** *adj*
mar•shal *n* **1** : leader of ceremony **2** : usu. high military or administrative officer ~ *vb* **1** : arrange in order, rank, or position **2** : lead with ceremony
marsh•mal•low *n* : spongy candy
mart *n* : market
mar•tial *adj* **1** : relating to war or an army **2** : warlike
mar•tyr *n* : one who dies or makes a great sac-

rifice for a cause ~ *vb* : make a martyr of — **mar•tyr•dom** *n*

mar•vel *vb* : feel surprise or wonder ~ *n* : something amazing — **mar•vel•ous, mar•vel•lous** *adj* — **mar•vel•ous•ly** *adv* — **mar•vel•ous•ness** *n*

mas•cara *n* : eye cosmetic

mas•cot *n* : one believed to bring good luck

mas•cu•line *adj* : relating to the male sex — **mas•cu•lin•i•ty** *n*

mash *n* **1 :** crushed steeped grain for fermenting **2 :** soft pulpy mass ~ *vb* **1 :** reduce to a pulpy mass **2 :** smash — **mash•er** *n*

mask *n* : disguise for the face ~ *vb* **1 :** disguise **2 :** cover to protect — **mask•er** *n*

mas•quer•ade *n* **1 :** costume party **2 :** disguise ~ *vb* **1 :** disguise oneself **2 :** take part in a costume party — **mas•quer•ad•er** *n*

mass *n* **1 :** large amount of matter or number of things **2 :** expanse or magnitude **3 :** great body of people — usu. pl. ~ *vb* : form into a mass — **mass•less** *adj* — **massy** *adj*

Mass *n* : worship service of the Roman Catholic Church

mas•sa•cre *n* : wholesale slaughter — **mas•sa•cre** *vb*

mas•sage *n* : a rubbing of the body — **mas•sage** *vb*

mas•sive *adj* **1 :** being a large mass **2 :** large in scope — **mas•sive•ly** *adv* — **mas•sive•ness** *n*

mast *n* : tall pole esp. for supporting sails — **mast•ed** *adj*

mas•ter *n* **1 :** male teacher **2 :** holder of an academic degree between a bachelor's and a doctor's **3 :** one highly skilled **4 :** one in authority ~ *vb* **1 :** subdue **2 :** become proficient in — **mas•ter•ful** *adj* — **mas•ter•ful•ly** *adv* — **mas•ter•ly** *adj* — **mas•tery** *n*

mas•ter•piece *n* : great piece of work

mat *n* **1 :** coarse woven or plaited fabric **2 :** mass of tangled strands **3 :** thick pad ~ *vb* : form into a mat

[1]**match** *n* **1 :** one equal to another **2 :** one able to cope with another **3 :** suitable pairing **4 :** game **5 :** marriage ~ *vb* **1 :** set in competition **2 :** marry **3 :** be or provide the equal of **4 :** fit or go together — **match•less** *adj* — **match•mak•er** *n*

[2]**match** *n* : piece of wood or paper material with a combustible tip

mate *n* **1 :** companion **2 :** subordinate officer on a ship **3 :** one of a pair ~ *vb* **1 :** fit together **2 :** come together as a pair esp. for reproduction

ma•te•ri•al *adj* **1 :** natural **2 :** relating to matter **3 :** important **4 :** of a physical or worldly nature ~ *n* : stuff something is made of — **ma•te•ri•al•ism** *n* — **ma•te•ri•al•ist** *n or adj* — **ma•te•ri•al•is•tic** *adj* — **ma•te•ri•al•ize** *vb* — **ma•te•ri•al•i•za•tion** *n* — **ma•te•ri•al•ly** *adv*

ma•ter•nal *adj* : motherly — **ma•ter•nal•ly** *adv*

ma•ter•ni•ty *n* **1 :** state of being a mother **2 :** hospital's childbirth facility ~ *adj* **1 :** worn during pregnancy **2 :** relating to the period close to childbirth

math *n* : mathematics

math•e•mat•ics *n pl* : science of numbers and of shapes in space — **math•e•mat•i•cal** *adj* — **math•e•mat•i•cal•ly** *adv* — **math•e•ma•ti•cian** *n*

mat•i•nee, mat•i•née *n* : afternoon performance

mat•ri•mo•ny *n* : marriage — **mat•ri•mo•ni•al** *adj* — **mat•ri•mo•ni•al•ly** *adv*

ma•trix *n* : something (as a mold) that gives form, foundation, or origin to something else enclosed in it

mat•ter *n* **1 :** subject of interest **2** *pl* **:** circumstances **3 :** trouble **4 :** physical substance ~ *vb* : be important

mat•tress *n* : pad to sleep on

ma•ture *adj* **1 :** carefully considered **2 :** fully grown or developed **3 :** due for payment ~ *vb* : become mature — **mat•u•ra•tion** *n* — **ma•ture•ly** *adv* — **ma•tu•ri•ty** *n*

maul *n* : heavy hammer ~ *vb* **1 :** beat **2 :** handle roughly

mau•so•le•um *n* : large above-ground tomb

max•i•mum *n* **1 :** greatest quantity **2 :** upper limit **3 :** largest number — **maximum** *adj* — **max•i•mize** *vb*

may *verbal auxiliary, past* **might 1 :** have permission **2 :** be likely to **3** — used to express desire, purpose, or contingency

May *n* : 5th month of the year having 31 days

may•be *adv* : perhaps

may•on•naise *n* : creamy white sandwich spread

may•or *n* : chief city official — **may•or•al** *adj* — **may•or•al•ty** *n*

maze *n* : confusing network of passages — **mazy** *adj*

me *pron, objective case of* I

mead•ow *n* : low-lying usu. level grassland — **mead•ow•land** *n*

mea•ger, mea•gre *adj* **1 :** thin **2 :** lacking richness or strength — **mea•ger•ly** *adv* — **mea•ger•ness** *n*

[1]**meal** *n* **1 :** food to be eaten at one time **2 :** act of eating — **meal•time** *n*

[2]**meal** *n* : ground grain — **mealy** *adj*

[1]**mean** *adj* **1 :** humble **2 :** worthy of or showing little regard **3 :** stingy **4 :** malicious — **mean•ly** *adv* — **mean•ness** *n*

[2]**mean** *vb* **meant; meant 1 :** intend **2 :** serve to convey, show, or indicate **3 :** be important — **mean•ing** *n* — **mean•ing•ful** *adj* — **mean•ing•ful•ly** *adv* — **mean•ing•less** *adj*

[3]**mean** *n* **1 :** middle point **2** *pl* **:** something that helps gain an end **3** *pl* **:** material resources **4 :** sum of several quantities divided by the number of quantities ~ *adj* **:** being a mean

mean•time *n* : intervening time — **meantime** *adv*

mean•while *n* : meantime ~ *adv* **1 :** meantime **2 :** at the same time

mea•sles *n pl* **:** disease that is marked by red spots on the skin

mea•sure *n* **1 :** moderate amount **2 :** dimensions or amount **3 :** something to show amount **4 :** unit or system of measurement **5 :** act of measuring **6 :** means to an end ~ *vb* **1 :** find out or mark off size or amount of **2 :** have a specified measurement — **mea•sur•able** *adj* — **mea•sur•ably** *adv* — **mea•sure•less** *adj* — **mea•sure•ment** *n* — **mea•sur•er** *n*

meat *n* **1 :** food **2 :** animal flesh used as food — **meat•ball** *n* — **meaty** *adj*

me•chan•ic *n* : worker who repairs machinery

me•chan•i•cal *adj* **1 :** relating to machines or mechanics **2 :** involuntary — **me•chan•i•cal•ly** *adv*

me•chan•ics *n sing or pl* **1 :** branch of physics dealing with energy and forces in relation to bodies **2 :** mechanical details

mech•a•nism *n* **1 :** piece of machinery **2 :** technique for gaining a result **3 :** basic processes producing a phenomenon — **mech•a•nis•tic** *adj* — **mech•a•ni•za•tion** *n* — **mech•a•nize** *vb* — **mech•a•niz•er** *n*

med•al *n* **1 :** religious pin or pendant **2 :** coinlike commemorative metal piece

med•dle *vb* : interfere — **med•dler** *n* — **med•dle•some** *adj*

me•dia *n pl* **:** communications organizations

me•di•an *n* : middle value in a range — **me•di•an** *adj*

me•di•ate *vb* : help settle a dispute — **me•di•a•tion** *n* — **me•di•a•tor** *n*

med•i•cal *adj* : relating to medicine — **med•i•cal•ly** *adv*

med•i•ca•tion *n* **1 :** act of medicating **2 :** medicine — **med•i•cate** *vb*

med•i•cine *n* **1 :** preparation used to treat disease **2 :** science dealing with the cure of disease — **me•dic•i•nal** *adj* — **me•dic•i•nal•ly** *adv*

me•di•e•val, me•di•ae•val *adj* **:** of or relating to the Middle Ages — **me•di•e•val•ist** *n*

me•di•o•cre *adj* : not very good — **me•di•oc•ri•ty** *n*

med•i•tate *vb* : contemplate — **med•i•ta•tion** *n* — **med•i•ta•tive** *adj* — **med•i•ta•tive•ly** *adv*

me•di•um *n* **1 :** middle position or degree **2 :** means of effecting or conveying something **3 :** surrounding substance **4 :** means of communication **5 :** mode of artistic expression — **me•di•um** *adj*

meek *adj* **1 :** having a mild manner or personality **2 :** lacking spirit — **meek•ly** *adv* — **meek•ness** *n*

meet *vb* **met; met 1 :** run into **2 :** join **3 :** oppose **4 :** assemble **5 :** satisfy **6 :** be introduced to ~ *n* **:** sports team competition

meet•ing *n* **:** a getting together — **meet•ing•house** *n*

mega•byte *n* : unit of computer storage capacity

mega•hertz *n* : one million hertz

mel•an•choly *n* **:** depression — **mel•an•chol•ic** *adj* — **melancholy** *adj*

mel•low *adj* **1 :** grown gentle or mild **2 :** rich and full — **mel•low** *vb* — **mel•low•ness** *n*

mel•o•dy *n* **1 :** agreeable sound **2 :** succession of musical notes — **me•lod•ic** *adj* — **me•lod•i•cal•ly** *adv* — **me•lo•di•ous** *adj* — **me•lo•di•ous•ly** *adv* — **me•lo•di•ous•ness** *n*

mel•on *n* : gourdlike fruit

melt *vb* **1 :** change from solid to liquid usu. by heat **2 :** dissolve or disappear gradually **3 :** move or be moved emotionally

mem•ber *n* **1 :** part of a person, animal, or plant **2 :** one of a group **3 :** part of a whole — **mem•ber•ship** *n*

memo *n* : memorandum

mem•o•ra•bil•ia *n pl* **1 :** memorable things **2 :** souvenirs

mem•o•ra•ble *adj* **:** worth remembering —

mem•o•ra•bil•i•ty *n* — **mem•o•ra•ble•ness** *n* — **mem•o•ra•bly** *adv*
mem•o•ran•dum *n* **:** informal note
me•mo•ri•al *n* **:** something (as a monument) meant to keep remembrance alive — **memorial** *adj* — **me•mo•ri•al•ize** *vb*
Memorial Day *n* **:** last Monday in May or formerly May 30 observed as a legal holiday in commemoration of dead servicemen
mem•o•ry *n* **1 :** power of remembering **2 :** something remembered **3 :** commemoration **4 :** time within which past events are remembered — **mem•o•ri•za•tion** *n* — **mem•o•rize** *vb* — **mem•o•riz•er** *n*
men *pl of* MAN
men•ace *n* **:** threat of danger ~ *vb* **1 :** threaten **2 :** endanger — **men•ac•ing•ly** *adv*
mend *vb* **1 :** improve **2 :** repair **3 :** heal — **mend** *n* — **mend•er** *n*
me•nial *adj* **1 :** relating to servants **2 :** humble ~ *n* **:** domestic servant — **me•ni•al•ly** *adv*
meno•pause *n* **:** time when menstruation ends — **meno•paus•al** *adj*
me•no•rah *n* **:** candelabrum used in Jewish worship
men•stru•a•tion *n* **:** monthly discharge of blood from the uterus — **men•stru•al** *adj* — **men•stru•ate** *vb*
men•tal *adj* **:** relating to the mind or its disorders — **men•tal•i•ty** *n* — **men•tal•ly** *adv*
men•tion *vb* **:** refer to — **men•tion** *n*
men•tor *n* **:** instructor
menu *n* **1 :** restaurant's list of food **2 :** list of offerings
me•ow *n* **:** characteristic cry of a cat — **meow** *vb*
mer•chan•dise *n* **:** goods bought and sold ~ *vb* **:** buy and sell — **mer•chan•dis•er** *n*
mer•chant *n* **:** one who buys and sells
mer•cu•ry *n* **:** heavy liquid metallic chemical element
mer•cy *n* **1 :** show of pity or leniency **2 :** divine blessing — **mer•ci•ful** *adj* — **mer•ci•ful•ly** *adv* — **mer•ci•less** *adj* — **mer•ci•less•ly** *adv* — **mercy** *adj*
mere *adj, superlative* **mer•est :** nothing more than — **mere•ly** *adv*
merge *vb* **1 :** unite **2 :** blend — **merg•er** *n*
me•rid•i•an *n* **:** imaginary circle on the earth's surface passing through the poles — **me•rid•i•an** *adj*
mer•it *n* **1 :** praiseworthy quality **2** *pl* **:** rights and wrongs of a legal case ~ *vb* **:** deserve — **mer•i•to•ri•ous** *adj* — **mer•i•to•ri•ous•ly** *adv* — **mer•i•to•ri•ous•ness** *n*
mer•ry *adj* **:** full of high spirits — **mer•ri•ly** *adv* — **mer•ri•ment** *n* — **mer•ry•mak•er** *n* — **mer•ry•mak•ing** *n*
merry–go–round *n* **:** revolving amusement ride
mesdames *pl of* MADAM *or of* MADAME *or of* MRS.
mesdemoiselles *pl of* MADEMOISELLE
mesh *n* **1 :** one of the openings in a net **2 :** net fabric **3 :** working contact ~ *vb* **:** fit together properly — **meshed** *adj*
mes•mer•ize *vb* **:** hypnotize
mess *n* **1 :** meal eaten by a group **2 :** confused, dirty, or offensive state ~ *vb* **1 :** make dirty or untidy **2 :** work at something in a casual manner **3 :** interfere — **messy** *adj*
mes•sage *n* **:** news, information, or a command sent by one person to another
mes•sen•ger *n* **:** one who carries a message or does an errand
messieurs *pl of* MONSIEUR
Messrs. *pl of* MR.
met *past of* MEET
me•tab•o•lism *n* **:** biochemical processes necessary to life — **met•a•bol•ic** *adj* — **me•tab•o•lize** *vb*
met•al *n* **:** shiny substance that can be melted and shaped and conducts heat and electricity — **me•tal•lic** *adj* — **met•al•ware** *n* — **met•al•work** *n* — **met•al•work•er** *n* — **met•al•work•ing** *n*
met•a•phor *n* **:** use of a word denoting one kind of object or idea in place of another to suggest a likeness between them — **met•a•phor•i•cal** *adj*
me•te•or *n* **:** small body that produces a streak of light as it burns up in the atmosphere
me•te•or•ic *adj* **1 :** relating to a meteor **2 :** sudden and spectacular — **me•te•or•i•cal•ly** *adv*
me•te•o•rol•o•gy *n* **:** science of weather — **me•te•o•ro•log•ic, me•te•o•ro•log•i•cal** *adj* — **me•te•o•rol•o•gist** *n*
[1]**me•ter** *n* **:** unit of length equal to 39.37 inches
[2]**me•ter** *n* **:** measuring instrument
meth•od *n* **1 :** procedure for achieving an end **2 :** orderly arrangement or plan — **me•thod•i•cal** *adj* — **me•thod•i•cal•ly** *adv* — **me•thod•i•cal•ness** *n*
met•ric, met•ri•cal *adj* **:** relating to meter or the metric system — **met•ri•cal•ly** *adv*

metric system *n* **:** system of weights and measures using the meter and kilogram

me•trop•o•lis *n* **:** major city — **met•ro•pol•i•tan** *adj*

mice *pl of* MOUSE

mi•cro•or•gan•ism *n* **:** very tiny living thing

mi•cro•phone *n* **:** instrument for changing sound waves into variations of an electric current

mi•cro•scope *n* **:** optical device for magnifying tiny objects — **mi•cro•scop•ic** *adj* — **mi•cro•scop•i•cal•ly** *adv* — **mi•cros•copy** *n*

mi•cro•wave *n* **1 :** short radio wave **2 :** oven that cooks food using microwaves ~ *vb* **:** heat or cook in a microwave oven — **mi•cro•wav•able, mi•cro•wave•able** *adj*

mid *adj* **:** middle — **mid•point** *n* — **mid•stream** *n* — **mid•sum•mer** *n* — **mid•town** *n or adj* — **mid•week** *n* — **mid•win•ter** *n* — **mid•year** *n*

mid•air *n* **:** a point in the air well above the ground

mid•day *n* **:** noon

mid•dle *adj* **1 :** equally distant from the extremes **2 :** being at neither extreme ~ *n* **:** middle part or point

Middle Ages *n pl* **:** period from about A.D. 500 to about 1500

midg•et *n* **:** very small person or thing

mid•night *n* **:** 12 o'clock at night

midst *n* **:** position close to or surrounded by others — **midst** *prep*

[1]**might** *past of* MAY — used to express permission or possibility or as a polite alternative to *may*

[2]**might** *n* **:** power or resources

mighty *adj* **1 :** very strong **2 :** great — **might•i•ly** *adv* — **might•i•ness** *n* — **mighty** *adv*

mi•graine *n* **:** severe headache often with nausea

mi•grate *vb* **1 :** move from one place to another **2 :** pass periodically from one region or climate to another — **mi•grant** *n* — **mi•gra•tion** *n* — **mi•gra•to•ry** *adj*

mild *adj* **1 :** gentle in nature or behavior **2 :** moderate in action or effect — **mild•ly** *adv* — **mild•ness** *n*

mil•dew *n* **:** whitish fungal growth — **mil•dew** *vb*

mile *n* **:** unit of length equal to 5280 feet

mile•age *n* **1 :** allowance per mile for traveling expenses **2 :** amount or rate of use expressed in miles

mile•stone *n* **:** significant point in development

mil•i•tant *adj* **:** aggressively active or hostile — **mil•i•tan•cy** *n* — **militant** *n* — **mil•i•tant•ly** *adv*

mil•i•tary *adj* **1 :** relating to soldiers, arms, or war **2 :** relating to or performed by armed forces ~ *n* **:** armed forces or the people in them — **mil•i•tar•i•ly** *adv* — **mil•i•tar•ism** *n* — **mil•i•ta•rist** *n* — **mil•i•tar•is•tic** *adj*

mi•li•tia *n* **:** civilian soldiers — **mi•li•tia•man** *n*

milk *n* **:** white nutritive fluid secreted by female mammals for feeding their young ~ *vb* **1 :** draw off the milk of **2 :** draw something from as if by milking — **milk•er** *n* — **milk•i•ness** *n* — **milky** *adj*

mill *n* **1 :** building in which grain is ground into flour **2 :** manufacturing plant **3 :** machine used esp. for forming or processing ~ *vb* **1 :** subject to a process in a mill **2 :** move in a circle — **mill•er** *n*

mil•len•ni•um *n* **:** a period of 1000 years

mil•li•gram *n* **:** $\frac{1}{1000}$ gram

mil•li•li•ter *n* **:** $\frac{1}{1000}$ liter

mil•li•me•ter : $\frac{1}{1000}$ meter

mil•lion *n* **:** 1000 thousands — **mil•lion** *adj* — **mil•lionth** *adj or n*

mil•lion•aire *n* **:** person worth a million or more (as of dollars)

mime *n* **1 :** mimic **2 :** pantomime — **mime** *vb*

mim•ic *n* **:** one that mimics ~ *vb* **1 :** imitate closely **2 :** ridicule by imitation — **mim•ic•ry** *n*

mince *vb* **1 :** cut into small pieces **2 :** choose (one's words) carefully **3 :** walk in a prim affected manner

mind *n* **1 :** memory **2 :** the part of an individual that feels, perceives, and esp. reasons **3 :** intention **4 :** normal mental condition **5 :** opinion **6 :** intellectual ability ~ *vb* **1 :** attend to **2 :** obey **3 :** be concerned about **4 :** be careful — **mind•ed** *adj* — **mind•less** *adj* — **mind•less•ly** *adv* — **mind•less•ness** *n*

mind•ful *adj* **:** aware or attentive — **mind•ful•ly** *adv* — **mind•ful•ness** *n*

[1]**mine** *pron* **:** that which belongs to me

[2]**mine** *n* **1 :** excavation from which minerals are taken **2 :** explosive device placed in the ground or water for destroying enemy vehicles or vessels that later pass ~ *vb* **1 :** get ore from **2 :** place military mines in — **mine•field** *n* — **min•er** *n*

min•er•al *n* **1 :** crystalline substance not of organic origin **2 :** useful natural substance (as

coal) obtained from the ground — **min•er•al** *adj* — **min•er•al•o•gy** *n* — **min•er•al•o•gist** *n*
min•gle *vb* : bring together or mix
min•ia•ture *n* : tiny copy or very small version — **miniature** *adj* — **min•ia•tur•ist** *n* — **min•ia•tur•ize** *vb*
min•i•mal *adj* : relating to or being a minimum — **min•i•mal•ly** *adv*
min•i•mize *vb* **1** : reduce to a minimum **2** : underestimate intentionally
min•i•mum *n* : lowest quantity or amount — **min•i•mum** *adj*
mini•skirt *n* : very short skirt
min•is•ter *n* **1** : Protestant member of the clergy **2** : high officer of state **3** : diplomatic representative ~ *vb* : give aid or service — **min•is•te•ri•al** *adj* — **min•is•tra•tion** *n*
min•is•try *n* **1** : office or duties of a minister **2** : body of ministers **3** : government department headed by a minister
mini•van *n* : small van
mi•nor *adj* **1** : less in size, importance, or value **2** : not serious ~ *n* **1** : person not yet of legal age **2** : secondary field of academic specialization
mi•nor•i•ty *n* **1** : time or state of being a minor **2** : smaller number (as of votes) **3** : part of a population differing from others (as in race or religion)
[1]**mint** *n* **1** : fragrant herb that yields a flavoring oil **2** : mint-flavored piece of candy — **minty** *adj*
[2]**mint** *n* **1** : place where coins are made **2** : vast sum ~ *adj* : unused — **mint** *vb* — **mint•er** *n*
mi•nus *prep* **1** : diminished by **2** : lacking ~ *n* : negative quantity or quality
mi•nus•cule, min•is•cule *adj* : very small
[1]**min•ute** *n* **1** : 60th part of an hour or of a degree **2** : short time **3** *pl* : official record of a meeting
[2]**mi•nute** *adj* **1** : very small **2** : marked by close attention to details — **mi•nute•ly** *adv* — **mi•nute•ness** *n*
mir•a•cle *n* **1** : extraordinary event taken as a sign of divine intervention in human affairs **2** : marvel — **mi•rac•u•lous** *adj* — **mi•rac•u•lous•ly** *adv*
mir•ror *n* : smooth surface (as of glass) that reflects images ~ *vb* : reflect in or as if in a mirror
mirth *n* : gladness and laughter — **mirth•ful** *adj* — **mirth•ful•ly** *adv* — **mirth•ful•ness** *n* — **mirth•less** *adj*
mis•be•have *vb* : behave improperly — **mis•be•hav•er** *n* — **mis•be•hav•ior** *n*
mis•cel•la•neous *adj* : consisting of many things of different kinds — **mis•cel•la•ny** *n* — **mis•cel•la•neous•ly** *adv* — **mis•cel•la•neous•ness** *n*
mis•chief *n* : conduct esp. of a child that annoys or causes minor damage
mis•chie•vous *adj* **1** : causing annoyance or minor injury **2** : irresponsibly playful — **mis•chie•vous•ly** *adv* — **mis•chie•vous•ness** *n*
mis•de•mean•or *n* : crime less serious than a felony
mi•ser *n* : person who hoards and is stingy with money — **mi•ser•li•ness** *n* — **mi•ser•ly** *adj*
mis•er•a•ble *adj* **1** : wretchedly deficient **2** : causing extreme discomfort **3** : shameful — **mis•er•a•ble•ness** *n* — **mis•er•a•bly** *adv*
mis•ery *n* : suffering and want caused by distress or poverty
mis•fit *n* : person poorly adjusted to his environment
mis•for•tune *n* **1** : bad luck **2** : unfortunate condition or event
mis•giv•ing *n* : doubt or concern
mis•in•ter•pret *vb* : understand or explain wrongly — **mis•in•ter•pre•ta•tion** *n*
mis•lay *vb* : misplace
mis•lead *vb* : lead in a wrong direction or into error — **mis•lead•ing** *adj* — **mis•lead•ing•ly** *adv*
mis•place *vb* : put in a wrong or unremembered place
mis•pro•nounce *vb* : pronounce incorrectly — **mis•pro•nun•ci•a•tion** *n*
mis•quote *vb* : quote incorrectly — **mis•quo•ta•tion** *n*
mis•rep•re•sent *vb* : represent falsely or unfairly — **mis•rep•re•sen•ta•tion** *n*
[1]**miss** *vb* **1** : fail to hit, reach, or contact **2** : notice the absence of **3** : fail to obtain **4** : avoid **5** : omit — **miss** *n*
[2]**miss** *n* : young unmarried woman or girl — often used as a title
mis•sile *n* : object (as a stone or rocket) thrown or shot
miss•ing *adj* : absent or lost
mis•sion *n* **1** : ministry sent by a church to spread its teaching **2** : group of diplomats sent to a foreign country **3** : task
mis•sion•ary *adj* : relating to religious missions ~ *n* : person sent to spread religious faith

mis•spell *vb* : spell incorrectly — **mis•spell•ing** *n*
mis•step *n* **1 :** wrong step **2 :** mistake
mist *n* : particles of water falling as fine rain
mis•take *n* **1 :** misunderstanding or wrong belief **2 :** wrong action or statement — **mis•take** *vb* — **mis•tak•en** *adj* — **mis•tak•en•ly** *adv*
mis•ter *n* : sir — used without a name in addressing a man
mis•treat *vb* : treat badly — **mis•treat•ment** *n*
mis•tress *n* **1 :** woman in control **2 :** a woman not his wife with whom a married man has recurrent sexual relations
misty *adj* **1 :** obscured by mist **2 :** tearful — **mist•i•ly** *adv* — **mist•i•ness** *n*
mis•un•der•stand *vb* **1 :** fail to understand **2 :** interpret incorrectly — **mis•un•der•stand•ing** *n*
mis•use *vb* **1 :** use incorrectly **2 :** mistreat — **mis•use** *n*
mitt *n* : mittenlike baseball glove
mit•ten *n* : hand covering without finger sections
mix *vb* : combine or join into one mass or group ~ *n* : commercially prepared food mixture — **mix•able** *adj* — **mix•er** *n* — **mix up** *vb* : confuse
mix•ture *n* : act or product of mixing
mix–up *n* : instance of confusion
moan *n* : low prolonged sound of pain or grief — **moan** *vb*
mob *n* **1 :** large disorderly crowd **2 :** criminal gang ~ *vb* : crowd around and attack or annoy
mo•bile *adj* : capable of moving or being moved ~ *n* : suspended art construction with freely moving parts — **mo•bil•i•ty** *n*
mo•bi•lize *vb* : assemble and make ready for war duty — **mo•bi•li•za•tion** *n*
moc•ca•sin *n* **1 :** heelless shoe **2 :** venomous U.S. snake
mock *vb* **1 :** ridicule **2 :** mimic in derision ~ *adj* **1 :** simulated **2 :** phony — **mock•er** *n* — **mock•ery** *n* — **mock•ing•ly** *adv*
mode *n* **1 :** particular form or variety **2 :** style — **mod•al** *adj* — **mod•ish** *adj*
mod•el *n* **1 :** structural design **2 :** miniature representation **3 :** something worthy of copying **4 :** one who poses for an artist or displays clothes **5 :** type or design ~ *vb* **1 :** shape **2 :** work as a model ~ *adj* **1 :** serving as a pattern **2 :** being a miniature representation of
mo•dem *n* : device by which a computer communicates with another computer over telephone lines
mod•er•ate *adj* : avoiding extremes ~ *vb* **1 :** lessen the intensity of **2 :** act as one who presides — **mod•er•ate** *n* — **mod•er•ate•ly** *adv* — **mod•er•ate•ness** *n* — **mod•er•a•tor** *n* — **mod•er•a•tion** *n*
mod•ern *adj* : relating to or characteristic of the present — **modern** *n* — **mo•der•ni•ty** *n* — **mod•ern•i•za•tion** *n* — **mod•ern•ize** *vb* — **mod•ern•iz•er** *n* — **mod•ern•ly** *adv* — **mod•ern•ness** *n*
mod•est *adj* **1 :** having a moderate estimate of oneself **2 :** reserved or decent in thoughts or actions **3 :** limited in size, amount, or aim — **mod•est•ly** *adv* — **mod•es•ty** *n*
mod•i•fy *vb* **1 :** limit the meaning of **2 :** change — **mod•i•fi•ca•tion** *n* — **mod•i•fi•er** *n*
mod•u•late *vb* **1 :** keep in proper measure or proportion **2 :** vary a radio wave — **mod•u•la•tion** *n* — **mod•u•la•tor** *n* — **mod•u•la•to•ry** *adj*
moist *adj* : slightly or moderately wet — **moist•en** *vb* — **moist•en•er** *n* — **moist•ly** *adv* — **moist•ness** *n*
mois•ture *n* : small amount of liquid that causes dampness — **mois•tur•ize** *vb* — **mois•tur•iz•er** *n*
mo•lar *n* : grinding tooth — **mo•lar** *adj*
mo•las•ses *n* : thick brown syrup from raw sugar
¹mold *n* : frame or cavity for forming ~ *vb* : shape in or as if in a mold — **mold•er** *n*
²mold *n* : surface growth of fungus ~ *vb* : become moldy — **mold•i•ness** *n* — **moldy** *adj*
¹mole *n* : spot on the skin
²mole *n* : small burrowing mammal — **mole•hill** *n*
mo•lest *vb* **1 :** annoy or disturb **2 :** force physical and usu. sexual contact on — **mo•les•ta•tion** *n* — **mo•lest•er** *n*
mol•li•fy *vb* : soothe in temper — **mol•li•fi•ca•tion** *n*
mom *n* : mother
mo•ment *n* **1 :** tiny portion of time **2 :** time of excellence **3 :** importance
mo•men•tary *adj* : continuing only a moment — **mo•men•tar•i•ly** *adv* — **mo•men•tar•i•ness** *n*
mo•men•tous *adj* : very important — **mo•men•tous•ly** *adv* — **mo•men•tous•ness** *n*
mo•men•tum *n* : force of a moving body

mon·arch *n* : ruler of a kingdom or empire — **mo·nar·chi·cal** *adj* — **mon·ar·chy** *n*

mon·as·tery *n* : house for monks — **mo·nas·tic** *adj or n* — **mo·nas·ti·cal·ly** *adv* — **mo·nas·ti·cism** *n*

Mon·day *n* : 2d day of the week

mon·ey *n* **1 :** something (as coins or paper currency) used in buying **2 :** wealth — **mon·e·tary** *adj* — **mon·eyed** *adj* — **mon·ey·lend·er** *n*

mon·i·tor *n* **1 :** student assistant **2 :** television screen ~ *vb* : watch or observe esp. for quality

monk *n* : member of a religious order living in a monastery — **monk·ish** *adj*

mon·key *n* : small long-tailed arboreal primate

mono·logue *n* : long speech — **mono·logu·ist, mo·no·lo·gist** *n*

mo·nop·o·ly *n* **1 :** exclusive ownership or control of a commodity **2 :** one controlling a monopoly — **mo·nop·o·list** *n* — **mo·nop·o·lis·tic** *adj* — **mo·nop·o·li·za·tion** *n* — **mo·nop·o·lize** *vb*

mo·not·o·nous *adj* **1 :** sounded in one unvarying tone **2 :** tediously uniform — **mo·not·o·nous·ly** *adv* — **mo·not·o·nous·ness** *n* — **mo·not·o·ny** *n*

mon·ster *n* **1 :** abnormal or terrifying animal **2 :** ugly, wicked, or cruel person — **mon·stros·i·ty** *n* — **mon·strous** *adj* — **mon·strous·ly** *adv*

month *n* : 12th part of a year — **month·ly** *adv or adj or n*

mon·u·ment *n* : structure erected in remembrance

mon·u·men·tal *adj* **1 :** serving as a monument **2 :** outstanding **3 :** very great — **mon·u·men·tal·ly** *adv*

moo *vb* : make the noise of a cow — **moo** *n*

mood *n* : state of mind or emotion

moody *adj* **1 :** sad **2 :** subject to changing moods and esp. to bad moods — **mood·i·ly** *adv* — **mood·i·ness** *n*

moon *n* : natural satellite (as of earth) — **moon·beam** *n* — **moon·light** *n* — **moon·lit** *adj*

moor *vb* : fasten with line or anchor

moor·ing *n* : place where boat can be moored

moose *n* (**moose**) : large heavy-antlered deer

moot *adj* : open to question

mop *n* : floor-cleaning implement ~ *vb* : use a mop on

mope *vb* : be sad or listless

mor·al *adj* **1 :** relating to principles of right and wrong **2 :** conforming to a standard of right behavior **3 :** relating to or acting on the mind, character, or will ~ *n* **1 :** point of a story **2** *pl* **:** moral practices or teachings — **mor·al·ist** *n* — **mor·al·is·tic** *adj* — **mor·al·i·ty** *n* — **mor·al·ize** *vb* — **mor·al·ly** *adv*

mo·rale *n* : emotional attitude

mor·a·to·ri·um *n* : suspension of activity

mor·bid *adj* **1 :** relating to disease **2 :** gruesome — **mor·bid·i·ty** *n* — **mor·bid·ly** *adv* — **mor·bid·ness** *n*

more *adj* **1 :** greater **2 :** additional ~ *adv* **1 :** in addition **2 :** to a greater degree ~ *n* **1 :** greater quantity **2 :** additional amount ~ *pron* : additional ones

morgue *n* : temporary holding place for dead bodies

morn *n* : morning

morn·ing *n* : time from sunrise to noon

mo·ron *n* **1 :** mentally retarded person **2 :** very stupid person — **mo·ron·ic** *adj* — **mo·ron·i·cal·ly** *adv*

mor·sel *n* : small piece or quantity

mor·tal *adj* **1 :** causing or subject to death **2 :** extreme — **mortal** *n* — **mor·tal·i·ty** *n* — **mor·tal·ly** *adv*

mort·gage *n* : transfer of property rights as security for a loan — **mortgage** *vb* — **mort·gag·ee** *n* — **mort·ga·gor** *n*

mo·sa·ic *n* : inlaid stone decoration — **mosaic** *adj*

Mos·lem *var of* MUSLIM

mosque *n* : building where Muslims worship

mos·qui·to *n* : biting bloodsucking insect

moss *n* : green seedless plant — **mossy** *adj*

most *adj* **1 :** majority of **2 :** greatest ~ *adv* : to the greatest or a very great degree ~ *n* : greatest amount ~ *pron* : greatest number or part

most·ly *adv* : mainly

mo·tel *n* : hotel with rooms accessible from the parking lot

moth *n* : small pale insect related to the butterflies

moth·er *n* **1 :** female parent **2 :** source ~ *vb* **1 :** give birth to **2 :** cherish or protect — **moth·er·hood** *n* — **moth·er·land** *n* — **moth·er·less** *adj* — **moth·er·ly** *adj*

moth·er–in–law *n* **mothers–in–law :** spouse's mother

mo·tif *n* : dominant theme

mo·tion *n* **1 :** act or instance of moving **2**

: proposal for action ~ *vb* : direct by a movement — **mo•tion•less** *adj* — **mo•tion•less•ly** *adv* — **mo•tion•less•ness** *n*
motion picture *n* : movie
mo•ti•vate *vb* : provide with a motive — **mo•ti•va•tion** *n* — **mo•ti•va•tor** *n*
mo•tive *n* : cause of a person's action ~ *adj* **1** : moving to action **2** : relating to motion — **mo•tive•less** *adj*
mo•tor *n* : unit that supplies power or motion ~ *vb* : travel by automobile — **mo•tor•bike** *n* — **mo•tor•boat** *n* — **mo•tor•cy•cle** *n* — **mo•tor•ist** *n* — **mo•tor•ize** *vb*
mot•to *n* : brief guiding rule
mould *var of* MOLD
mound *n* : pile (as of earth)
mount *vb* **1** : increase in amount **2** : get up on **3** : put in position ~ *n* **1** : frame or support **2** : horse to ride — **mount•able** *adj* — **mount•er** *n*
moun•tain *n* : elevated land higher than a hill — **moun•tain•ous** *adj* — **moun•tain•top** *n*
mourn *vb* : feel or express grief — **mourn•er** *n* — **mourn•ful** *adj* — **mourn•ful•ly** *adv* — **mourn•ful•ness** *n* — **mourn•ing** *n*
mouse *n* (**mice**) **1** : small rodent **2** : device for controlling cursor movement on a computer display — **mouse•trap** *n or vb* — **mousy, mous•ey** *adj*
mousse *n* **1** : light chilled dessert **2** : foamy hair-styling preparation
mous•tache *var of* MUSTACHE
mouth *n* : opening through which an animal takes in food ~ *vb* **1** : speak **2** : repeat without comprehension or sincerity **3** : form soundlessly with the lips — **mouthed** *adj* — **mouth•ful** *n*
mouth•piece *n* **1** : part (as of a musical instrument) held in or to the mouth **2** : person who speaks for another
move *vb* **1** : go or cause to go to another point **2** : change residence **3** : change or cause to change position **4** : take or cause to take action **5** : make a formal request **6** : stir the emotions ~ *n* **1** : act or instance of moving **2** : step taken to achieve a goal — **mov•able, move•able** *adj* — **move•ment** *n* — **mov•er** *n*
mov•ie *n* : projected picture in which persons and objects seem to move
mow *vb* : cut with a machine — **mow•er** *n*
Mr. *n* (**Messrs.**) — conventional title for a man
Mrs. *n* (**Mes•dames**) — conventional title for a married woman
Ms. *n* — conventional title for a woman
much *adj* **more; most** : great in quantity, extent, or degree ~ *adv* **more; most** : to a great degree or extent ~ *n* : great quantity, extent, or degree
muck *n* : manure, dirt, or mud — **mucky** *adj*
mu•cus *n* : slippery protective secretion of membranes (**mucous membranes**) lining body cavities — **mu•cous** *adj*
mud *n* : soft wet earth — **mud•di•ly** *adv* — **mud•di•ness** *n* — **mud•dy** *adj or vb*
mud•dle *vb* **1** : make, be, or act confused **2** : make a mess of — **muddle** *n* — **mud•dle•head•ed** *adj*
muf•fin *n* : soft cake baked in a cup-shaped container
muf•fle *vb* **1** : wrap up **2** : dull the sound of — **muf•fler** *n*
[1]**mug** *n* : drinking cup ~ *vb* : make faces
[2]**mug** *vb* : assault with intent to rob — **mug•ger** *n*
mug•gy *adj* : hot and humid — **mug•gi•ness** *n*
[1]**mule** *n* **1** : offspring of a male ass and a female horse **2** : stubborn person — **mul•ish** *adj* — **mul•ish•ly** *adv* — **mu•lish•ness** *n*
[2]**mule** *n* : backless shoe
mull *vb* : ponder
mul•ti•ple *adj* **1** : several or many **2** : various ~ *n* : product of one number by another
mul•ti•pli•ca•tion *n* **1** : increase **2** : short method of repeated addition
mul•ti•ply *vb* **1** : increase in number **2** : perform multiplication — **mul•ti•pli•er** *n*
mul•ti•tude *n* : great number — **mul•ti•tu•di•nous** *adj*
mum•ble *vb* : speak indistinctly — **mum•ble** *n* — **mum•bler** *n*
mum•my *n* : embalmed body — **mum•mi•fi•ca•tion** *n* — **mum•mi•fy** *vb*
mumps *n sing or pl* : virus disease with swelling esp. of the salivary glands
munch *vb* : chew
mun•dane *adj* **1** : relating to the world **2** : lacking concern for the ideal or spiritual — **mun•dane•ly** *adv*
mu•nic•i•pal *adj* : of or relating to a town or city — **mu•nic•i•pal•i•ty** *n*
mur•der *n* : unlawful killing of a person ~ *vb* : commit a murder — **mur•der•er** *n* — **mur•der•ess** *n* — **mur•der•ous** *adj* — **mur•der•ous•ly** *adv*

mur·mur *n* **1 :** muttered complaint **2 :** low indistinct sound — **murmur** *vb* — **mur·mur·er** *n* — **mur·mur·ous** *adj*

mus·cle *n* **1 :** body tissue capable of contracting to produce motion **2 :** strength ~ *vb* **:** force one's way — **mus·cled** *adj* — **mus·cu·lar** *adj* — **mus·cu·lar·i·ty** *n*

¹muse *vb* **:** ponder — **mus·ing·ly** *adv*

²muse *n* **:** source of inspiration

mu·se·um *n* **:** institution displaying objects of interest

mush *n* **1 :** corn meal boiled in water or something of similar consistency **2 :** sentimental nonsense — **mushy** *adj*

mush·room *n* **:** caplike organ of a fungus ~ *vb* **:** grow rapidly

mu·sic *n* **:** vocal or instrumental sounds — **mu·si·cal** *adj or n* — **mu·si·cal·ly** *adv*

mu·si·cian *n* **:** composer or performer of music — **mu·si·cian·ly** *adj* — **mu·si·cian·ship** *n*

musk *n* **:** strong-smelling substance from an Asiatic deer used in perfume — **musk·i·ness** *n* — **musky** *adj*

Mus·lim *n* **:** adherent of Islam — **Mus·lim** *adj*

mus·lin *n* **:** cotton fabric

muss *n* **:** untidy state ~ *vb* **:** mess up the arrangement of — **muss·i·ly** *adv* — **muss·i·ness** *n* — **mussy** *adj*

must *vb* — used as an auxiliary esp. to express a command, obligation, or necessity ~ *n* **:** something necessary

mus·tache *n* **:** hair of the human upper lip

mus·tard *n* **:** pungent yellow seasoning

mus·ter *vb* **1 :** assemble **2 :** arouse ~ *n* **:** assembled group

musty *adj* **:** stale — **must·i·ly** *adv* — **must·i·ness** *n*

mu·tate *vb* **:** undergo change in a hereditary character — **mu·tant** *adj or n* — **mu·ta·tion** *n* — **mu·ta·tive** *adj*

mute *adj* **1 :** unable to speak **2 :** silent ~ *n* **1 :** one who is mute **2 :** muffling device ~ *vb* **:** muffle — **mute·ly** *adv* — **mute·ness** *n*

mu·ti·late *vb* **:** damage seriously (as by cutting off or altering an essential part) — **mu·ti·la·tion** *n* — **mu·ti·la·tor** *n*

mu·ti·ny *n* **:** rebellion — **mu·ti·neer** *n* — **mu·ti·nous** *adj* — **mu·ti·nous·ly** *adv* — **mutiny** *vb*

mutt *n* **:** dog that is of mixed breed

mut·ter *vb* **1 :** speak indistinctly or softly **2 :** grumble — **mutter** *n*

mu·tu·al *adj* **1 :** given or felt by one another in equal amount **2 :** common — **mu·tu·al·ly** *adv*

muz·zle *n* **1 :** nose and jaws of an animal **2 :** muzzle covering to immobilize an animal's jaws **3 :** discharge end of a gun ~ *vb* **:** restrain with or as if with a muzzle

my *adj* **1 :** relating to me or myself **2** — used interjectionally esp. to express surprise

myr·i·ad *n* **:** indefinitely large number — **myriad** *adj*

my·self *pron* **:** I, me — used reflexively or for emphasis

mys·tery *n* **1 :** religious truth **2 :** something not understood **3 :** puzzling or secret quality or state — **mys·te·ri·ous** *adj* — **mys·te·ri·ous·ly** *adv* — **mys·te·ri·ous·ness** *n*

mys·tic *adj* **:** spiritual or mysterious ~ *n* **:** one who has spiritual experiences — **mys·ti·cal** *adj* — **mys·ti·cal·ly** *adj* — **mys·ti·cism** *n*

mys·ti·fy *vb* **:** perplex — **mys·ti·fi·ca·tion** *n*

myth *n* **1 :** legendary narrative explaining a belief or phenomenon **2 :** imaginary person or thing — **myth·i·cal** *adj*

my·thol·o·gy *n* **:** body of myths — **myth·o·log·i·cal** *adj* — **my·thol·o·gist** *n*

N

n *n* **:** 14th letter of the alphabet

nab *vb* **:** seize or arrest

na·cho *n* **:** tortilla chip topped with a savory mixture and cheese and broiled

nag *vb* **1 :** complain **2 :** scold or urge continually **3 :** be persistently annoying ~ *n* **:** one who nags habitually

nail *n* **1 :** horny sheath at the end of each finger and toe **2 :** pointed metal fastener ~ *vb* **:** fasten with a nail — **nail·er** *n*

na·ive, na·ïve *adj* **1 :** innocent and unsophisticated **2 :** easily deceived — **na·ive·ly** *adv* — **na·ive·ness** *n* — **na·ïve·té** *n*

na·ked *adj* **1 :** having no clothes on **2 :** not covered **3 :** plain or obvious **4 :** without aid — **na·ked·ly** *adv* — **na·ked·ness** *n*

name *n* **1 :** word by which a person or thing is known **2 :** disparaging word for someone **3 :** distinguished reputation ~ *vb* **1 :** give a name to **2 :** mention or identify by name **3**

: nominate or appoint ~ *adj* **1** : relating to a name **2** : prominent — **name•able** *adj* — **name•less** *adj* — **name•less•ly** *adv*

name•ly *adv* : that is to say

nap *vb* **1** : sleep briefly **2** : be off guard ~ *n* : short sleep

nape *n* : back of the neck

nap•kin *n* : small cloth for use at the table

nar•cot•ic *n* : painkilling addictive drug — **nar•cot•ic** *adj*

nar•rate *vb* : tell (a story) — **nar•ra•tion** *n* — **nar•ra•tive** *n or adj* — **nar•ra•tor** *n*

nar•row *adj* **1** : of less than standard width **2** : limited **3** : not liberal **4** : barely successful ~ *vb* : make narrow — **nar•row•ly** *adv* — **nar•row•ness** *n*

nar•row–mind•ed *adj* : shallow, provincial, or bigoted

nasal *adj* : relating to or uttered through the nose — **na•sal•ly** *adv*

nas•ty *adj* **1** : filthy **2** : extremely improper or offensive **3** : malicious or spiteful **4** : difficult or disagreeable **5** : unfair — **nas•ti•ly** *adv* — **nas•ti•ness** *n*

na•tion *n* **1** : people of similar characteristics **2** : community with its own territory and government — **na•tion•al** *adj or n* — **na•tion•al•ly** *adv* — **na•tion•hood** *n* — **na•tion•wide** *adj*

na•tion•al•ism *n* : devotion to national interests, unity, and independence — **na•tion•al•ist** *n or adj* — **na•tion•al•is•tic** *adj*

na•tion•al•i•ty *n* **1** : national character **2** : membership in a nation **3** : political independence **4** : ethnic group

na•tion•al•ize *vb* **1** : make national **2** : place under government control — **na•tion•al•i•za•tion** *n*

na•tive *adj* **1** : belonging to a person at or by way of birth **2** : born or produced in a particular place ~ *n* : one who belongs to a country by birth

Na•tiv•i•ty *n* **1** : birth of Christ **2** *not cap* : birth

nat•u•ral *adj* **1** : relating to or determined by nature **2** : not artificial **3** : simple and sincere **4** : lifelike ~ *n* : one having an innate talent — **nat•u•ral•ness** *n*

nat•u•ral•ism *n* : realism in art and literature — **nat•u•ral•ist** *n* — **nat•u•ral•is•tic** *adj*

nat•u•ral•ize *vb* **1** : become or cause to become established **2** : confer citizenship on — **nat•u•ral•i•za•tion** *n*

nat•u•ral•ly *adv* **1** : in a natural way **2** : as might be expected

na•ture *n* **1** : basic quality of something **2** : kind **3** : disposition **4** : physical universe **5** : natural environment

naugh•ty *adj* **1** : disobedient or misbehaving **2** : improper — **naught•i•ly** *adv* — **naught•i•ness** *n*

nau•sea *n* **1** : sickness of the stomach with a desire to vomit **2** : extreme disgust — **nau•se•ate** *vb* — **nau•seous** *adj*

nau•ti•cal *adj* : relating to ships and sailing — **nau•ti•cal•ly** *adv*

na•val *adj* : relating to a navy

na•vel *n* : depression in the abdomen

nav•i•gate *vb* **1** : sail on or through **2** : direct the course of — **nav•i•ga•ble** *adj* — **nav•i•ga•bil•i•ty** *n* — **nav•i•ga•tion** *n* — **nav•i•ga•tor** *n*

na•vy *n* **1** : fleet **2** : nation's organization for sea warfare

near *adv* : at or close to ~ *prep* : close to ~ *adj* **1** : not far away **2** : very much like ~ *vb* : approach — **near•ly** *adv* — **near•ness** *n*

near•by *adv or adj* : near

near•sight•ed *adj* : seeing well at short distances only — **near•sight•ed•ly** *adv* — **near•sight•ed•ness** *n*

neat *adj* **1** : not diluted **2** : tastefully simple **3** : orderly and clean — **neat** *adv* — **neat•ly** *adv* — **neat•ness** *n*

nec•es•sary *n* : indispensable item ~ *adj* **1** : inevitable **2** : compulsory **3** : positively needed — **nec•es•sar•i•ly** *adv* — **ne•ces•si•tate** *vb* — **ne•ces•si•ty** *n*

neck *n* **1** : body part connecting the head and trunk **2** : part of a garment at the neck **3** : narrow part ~ *vb* : kiss and caress — **necked** *adj*

neck•lace *n* : ornament worn around the neck

neck•tie *n* : ornamental cloth tied under a collar

nec•tar•ine *n* : smooth-skinned peach

need *n* **1** : obligation **2** : lack of something or what is lacking **3** : poverty ~ *vb* **1** : be in want **2** : have cause for **3** : be under obligation — **need•ful** *adj* — **need•less** *adj* — **need•less•ly** *adv* — **needy** *adj*

nee•dle *n* **1** : pointed sewing implement or something like it **2** : movable bar in a compass **3** : hollow instrument for injecting or withdrawing material ~ *vb* : incite to action by repeated gibes — **nee•dle•work** *n*

ne•gate *vb* **1** : deny **2** : nullify — **ne•ga•tion** *n*

neg·a·tive *adj* **1 :** marked by denial or refusal **2 :** showing a lack of something suspected or desirable **3 :** less than zero **4 :** having more electrons than protons **5 :** having light and shadow images reversed ~ *n* **1 :** negative word or vote **2 :** a negative number **3 :** negative photographic image — **neg·a·tive·ly** *adv* — **neg·a·tive·ness** *n* — **neg·a·tiv·i·ty** *n*

ne·glect *vb* **1 :** disregard **2 :** leave unattended to ~ *n* **1 :** act of neglecting **2 :** condition of being neglected — **ne·glect·ful** *adj*

neg·li·gent *adj* **:** marked by neglect — **neg·li·gence** *n* — **neg·li·gent·ly** *adv*

ne·go·ti·ate *vb* **1 :** confer with another to settle a matter **2 :** obtain cash for **3 :** get through successfully — **ne·go·tia·ble** *adj* — **ne·go·ti·a·tion** *n* — **ne·go·ti·a·tor** *n*

neigh·bor *n* **1 :** one living nearby **2 :** fellowman ~ *vb* **:** be near or next to — **neigh·bor·hood** *n* — **neigh·bor·li·ness** *n* — **neigh·bor·ly** *adv*

nei·ther *pron or adj* **:** not the one or the other ~ *conj* **1 :** not either **2 :** nor

neph·ew *n* **:** a son of one's brother, sister, brother-in-law, or sister-in-law

nerd *n* **:** one who is not stylish or socially at ease — **nerdy** *adj*

nerve *n* **1 :** strand of body tissue that connects the brain with other parts of the body **2 :** self-control **3 :** daring **4** *pl* **:** nervousness — **nerved** *adj* — **nerve·less** *adj* — **nervy** *adj*

ner·vous *adj* **1 :** relating to or made up of nerves **2 :** easily excited **3 :** timid or fearful — **ner·vous·ly** *adv* — **ner·vous·ness** *n*

nest *n* **1 :** shelter prepared by a bird for its eggs **2 :** place where eggs (as of insects or fish) are laid and hatched **3 :** snug retreat **4 :** set of objects fitting one inside or under another ~ *vb* **:** build or occupy a nest

nes·tle *vb* **:** settle snugly (as in a nest)

net *n* **:** fabric with spaces between strands or something made of this ~ *vb* **:** cover with or catch in a net

net·work *n* **:** system of crossing or connected elements

neu·rot·ic *adj* **:** relating to neurosis ~ *n* **:** unstable person — **neu·rot·i·cal·ly** *adv*

neu·tral *adj* **1 :** not favoring either side **2 :** being neither one thing nor the other **3 :** not decided in color **4 :** not electrically charged ~ *n* **1 :** one that is neutral **2 :** position of gears that are not engaged — **neu·tral·i·za·tion** *n* — **neu·tral·ize** *vb*

nev·er *adv* **1 :** not ever **2 :** not in any degree, way, or condition

nev·er·the·less *adv* **:** in spite of that

new *adj* **1 :** not old or familiar **2 :** different from the former **3 :** recently discovered or learned **4 :** not accustomed **5 :** refreshed or regenerated **6 :** being such for the first time ~ *adv* **:** newly — **new·ish** *adj* — **new·ly** *adv* — **new·ness** *n*

news *n* **:** report of recent events — **news·cast** *n* — **news·cast·er** *n* — **news·let·ter** *n* — **news·mag·a·zine** *n* — **news·man** *n* — **news·pa·per** *n* — **news·pa·per·man** *n* — **news·stand** *n* — **news·wom·an** *n* — **news·wor·thy** *adj*

New Year's Day *n* **:** January 1 observed as a legal holiday

next *adj* **:** immediately preceding or following ~ *adv* **1 :** in the time or place nearest **2 :** at the first time yet to come ~ *prep* **:** nearest to

nib·ble *vb* **:** bite gently or bit by bit ~ *n* **:** small bite

nice *adj* **1 :** exhibiting or requiring excessive care **2 :** very precise or delicate **3 :** pleasing **4 :** respectable — **nice·ly** *adv* — **nice·ness** *n* — **nice·ty** *n*

niche *n* **1 :** recess in a wall **2 :** fitting place, work, or use

nick *n* **1 :** small broken area or chip **2 :** critical moment ~ *vb* **:** make a nick in

nick·el *n* **1 :** hard silver-white metallic chemical element used in alloys **2 :** U.S. 5-cent piece

nick·name *n* **:** informal substitute name — **nick·name** *vb*

niece *n* **:** a daughter of one's brother, sister, brother-in-law, or sister-in-law

night *n* **1 :** period between dusk and dawn **2 :** the coming of night — **night** *adj* — **night·ly** *adj or adv* — **night·time** *n*

night·club *n* **:** place for drinking and entertainment open at night

night·mare *n* **:** frightening dream — **night·mare** *adj* — **night·mar·ish** *adj*

nil *n* **:** nothing

nim·ble *adj* **1 :** agile **2 :** clever — **nim·ble·ness** *n* — **nim·bly** *adv*

nine *n* **1 :** one more than 8 **2 :** 9th in a set or series — **nine** *adj or pron* — **ninth** *adj or adv or n*

nine·teen *n* **:** one more than 18 — **nine·teen** *adj or pron* — **nine·teenth** *adj or n*

nine•ty *n* : 9 times 10 — **nine•ti•eth** *adj or n* — **nine•ty** *adj or pron*

nip *vb* **1 :** catch hold of and squeeze tightly **2 :** pinch or bite off **3 :** destroy the growth or fulfillment of ~ *n* **1 :** biting cold **2 :** pungent flavor **3 :** pinch or bite

nip•per *n* **1 :** one that nips **2** *pl* **:** pincers **3 :** small boy

nip•py *adj* **1 :** pungent **2 :** chilly

ni•tro•gen *n* : tasteless odorless gaseous chemical element

nit•wit *n* : stupid person

no *adv* **1** — used to express the negative **2 :** in no respect or degree **3 :** not so **4** — used as an interjection of surprise or doubt ~ *adj* **1 :** not any **2 :** not a ~ *n* **1 :** refusal **2 :** negative vote

no•ble *adj* **1 :** illustrious **2 :** aristocratic **3 :** marked by much dignity **4 :** of outstanding character ~ *n* : nobleman — **no•ble•ness** *n* — **no•bly** *adv*

no•ble•man *n* : a person of aristocratic rank

no•body *pron* : no person ~ *n* : person of no influence or importance

no–brain•er : something that requires a minimum of thought

nod *vb* **1 :** bend the head downward or forward (as in bowing or going to sleep or as a sign of assent) **2 :** move up and down **3 :** show by a nod of the head — **nod** *n*

no•el *n* **1 :** Christmas carol **2** *cap* : Christmas season

noes *pl of* NO

noise *n* : loud or unpleasant sound ~ *vb* : spread by rumor — **noise•less** *adj* — **noise•less•ly** *adv* — **noise•mak•er** *n* — **nois•i•ly** *adv* — **nois•i•ness** *n* — **noisy** *adj*

no•mad *n* : one who has no permanent home — **no•mad** *adj* — **no•mad•ic** *adj*

nom•i•nate *vb* : propose or choose as a candidate — **nom•i•na•tion** *n* — **nom•i•nee** *n*

non•cha•lant *adj* : showing indifference — **non•cha•lance** *n* — **non•cha•lant•ly** *adv*

non•con•form•ist *n* : one who does not conform to an established belief or mode of behavior — **non•con•for•mi•ty** *n*

none *pron* : not any ~ *adv* : not at all

non•per•son *n* : person without social or legal status

non•sense *n* : foolish or meaningless words or actions — **non•sen•si•cal** *adj* — **non•sen•si•cal•ly** *adv*

noo•dle *n* : ribbon-shaped food paste

nook *n* **1 :** inside corner **2 :** private place

noon *n* : middle of the day — **noon** *adj* — **noon•time** *n*

noose *n* : rope loop that slips down tight

nor *conj* : and not — used esp. after *neither* to introduce and negate the 2d member of a series

norm *n* **1 :** standard usu. derived from an average **2 :** typical widespread practice or custom

nor•mal *adj* : average, regular, or standard — **nor•mal•cy** *n* — **nor•mal•i•ty** *n* — **nor•mal•i•za•tion** *n* — **nor•mal•ize** *vb* — **nor•mal•ly** *adv*

north *adv* : to or toward the north ~ *adj* : situated toward, at, or coming from the north ~ *n* **1 :** direction to the left of one facing east **2** *cap* : regions to the north — **north•er•ly** *adv or adj* — **north•ern** *adj* — **North•ern•er** *n* — **north•ern•most** *adj* — **north•ward** *adv or adj* — **north•wards** *adv*

north•east *n* **1 :** direction between north and east **2** *cap* : regions to the northeast — **north•east** *adj or adv* — **north•east•er•ly** *adv or adj* — **north•east•ern** *adj*

north pole *n* : northernmost point of the earth

north•west *n* **1 :** direction between north and west **2** *cap* : regions to the northwest — **northwest** *adj or adv* — **north•west•er•ly** *adv or adj* — **north•west•ern** *adj*

nose *n* **1 :** part of the face containing the nostrils **2 :** sense of smell **3 :** front part ~ *vb* **1 :** detect by smell **2 :** push aside with the nose **3 :** pry **4 :** inch ahead — **nose•bleed** *n* — **nosed** *adj* — **nose out** *vb* : narrowly defeat

nos•tal•gia *n* : wistful yearning for something past — **nos•tal•gic** *adj*

nos•tril *n* : opening of the nose

nosy, nos•ey *adj* : tending to pry

not *adv* — used to make a statement negative

no•ta•ble *adj* **1 :** noteworthy **2 :** distinguished ~ *n* : notable person — **no•ta•bil•i•ty** *n* — **no•ta•bly** *adv*

no•ta•ry public *n* : public official who attests writings to make them legally authentic

notch *n* : V-shaped hollow — **notch** *vb*

note *vb* **1 :** notice **2 :** write down ~ *n* **1 :** musical tone **2 :** written comment or record **3 :** short informal letter **4 :** notice or heed — **note•book** *n*

note•wor•thy *adj* : worthy of special mention

noth•ing *pron* **1 :** no thing **2 :** no part **3 :** one of no value or importance ~ *adv* : not at all ~ *n* **1 :** something that does not exist **2 :** zero

3 : one of little or no importance — **noth•ing•ness** *n*

no•tice *n* 1 : warning or announcement 2 : attention ~ *vb* : take notice of — **no•tice•able** *adj* — **no•tice•ably** *adv*

no•ti•fy *vb* : give notice of or to — **no•ti•fi•ca•tion** *n*

no•tion *n* 1 : idea or opinion 2 : whim

no•to•ri•ous *adj* : widely and unfavorably known — **no•to•ri•e•ty** *n* — **no•to•ri•ous•ly** *adv*

not•with•stand•ing *prep* : in spite of ~ *adv* : nevertheless ~ *conj* : although

noun *n* : word that is the name of a person, place, or thing

nour•ish *vb* : promote the growth of — **nour•ish•ing** *adj* — **nour•ish•ment** *n*

nov•el *adj* : new or strange ~ *n* : long invented prose story — **nov•el•ist** *n*

nov•el•ty *n* 1 : something new or unusual 2 : newness 3 : small manufactured article — usu. pl.

No•vem•ber *n* : 11th month of the year having 30 days

nov•ice *n* 1 : one preparing to take vows in a religious order 2 : one who does not have experience or training

now *adv* 1 : at the present time or moment 2 : immediately 3 : under these circumstances ~ *conj* : in view of the fact ~ *n* : present time

no•where *adv* : not anywhere — **no•where** *n*

nu•cle•ar *adj* 1 : relating to the atomic nucleus or atomic energy 2 : relating to a weapon whose power is from a nuclear reaction

nu•cle•us *n* : central mass or part (as of a cell or an atom)

nude *adj* : naked ~ *n* : nude human figure — **nu•di•ty** *n*

nudge *vb* : touch or push gently — **nudge** *n*

nui•sance *n* : something annoying

null *adj* : having no legal or binding force — **nul•li•ty** *n*

nul•li•fy *vb* : make valueless or of no legal force — **nul•li•fi•ca•tion** *n*

numb *adj* : lacking feeling — **numb** *vb* — **numb•ly** *adv* — **numbness** *n*

num•ber *n* 1 : total of individuals taken together 2 : indefinite total 3 : unit of a mathematical system 4 : numeral 5 : one in a sequence ~ *vb* 1 : count 2 : assign a number to 3 : comprise in number — **num•ber•less** *adj* — **nu•mer•i•cal** *adj* — **nu•mer•i•cal•ly** *adv*

nu•mer•al *n* : conventional symbol representing a number

nu•mer•a•tor *n* : part of a fraction above the line

nu•mer•ous *adj* : consisting of a great number

nun *n* : woman belonging to a religious order — **nun•nery** *n*

nurse *n* 1 : one hired to care for children 2 : person trained to care for sick people ~ *vb* 1 : provide with milk from the breast 2 : care for

nurs•ery *n* 1 : place where children are cared for 2 : place where young plants are grown

nur•ture *n* 1 : training or upbringing 2 : food or nourishment ~ *vb* 1 : care for or feed 2 : educate

nut *n* 1 : dry hard-shelled fruit or seed with a firm inner kernel 2 : metal block with a screw hole through it 3 : foolish, eccentric, or crazy person 4 : enthusiast — **nut•crack•er** *n* — **nut•shell** *n* — **nut•ty** *adj*

nu•tri•tion *n* : act or process of nourishing esp. with food — **nu•tri•tion•al** *adj* — **nu•tri•tious** *adj* — **nu•tri•tive** *adj*

nuts *adj* 1 : enthusiastic 2 : crazy

nuz•zle *vb* 1 : touch with or as if with the nose 2 : snuggle

ny•lon *n* 1 : tough synthetic material used esp. in textiles 2 *pl* : stockings made of nylon

O

o *n* 1 : 15th letter of the alphabet 2 : zero

oaf *n* : stupid or awkward person — **oaf•ish** *adj*

oak *n* : tree bearing a thin-shelled nut or its wood — **oak•en** *adj*

oar *n* : pole with a blade at the end used to propel a boat

oa•sis *n* : fertile area in a desert

oat *n* : cereal grass or its edible seed — **oat•cake** *n* — **oat•en** *adj* — **oat•meal** *n*

oath *n* 1 : solemn appeal to God as a pledge of sincerity 2 : profane utterance

obe•di•ent *adj* : willing to obey — **obe•di•ence** *n* — **obe•di•ent•ly** *adv*

obese *adj* : extremely fat — **obe•si•ty** *n*

obey *vb* **1 :** follow the commands or guidance of **2 :** behave in accordance with

obit•u•ary *n* **:** death notice

[1]ob•ject *n* **1 :** something that may be seen or felt **2 :** purpose **3 :** noun or equivalent toward which the action of a verb is directed or which follows a preposition

[2]object *vb* **:** offer opposition or disapproval — **ob•jec•tion** *n* — **ob•jec•tion•able** *adj* — **ob•jec•tion•ably** *adv* — **ob•jec•tor** *n*

ob•jec•tive *adj* **1 :** relating to an object or end **2 :** existing outside an individual's thoughts or feelings **3 :** treating facts without distortion **4 :** relating to or being a grammatical case marking objects ~ *n* **:** aim or end of action — **ob•jec•tive•ly** *adv* — **ob•jec•tive•ness** *n* — **ob•jec•tiv•i•ty** *n*

ob•li•gate *vb* **:** bind legally or morally — **ob•li•ga•tion** *n* — **oblig•a•to•ry** *adj*

oblige *vb* **1 :** compel **2 :** do a favor for — **oblig•ing** *adj* — **oblig•ing•ly** *adv*

oblit•er•ate *vb* **:** completely remove or destroy — **oblit•er•a•tion** *n*

obliv•i•on *n* **1 :** state of having lost conscious awareness **2 :** state of being forgotten

obliv•i•ous *adj* **:** not aware or mindful — used with *to* or *of* — **obliv•i•ous•ly** *adv* — **obliv•i•ous•ness** *n*

ob•long *adj* **:** longer in one direction than in the other with opposite sides parallel — **oblong** *n*

ob•nox•ious *adj* **:** repugnant — **ob•nox•ious•ly** *adv* — **ob•nox•ious•ness** *n*

ob•scene *adj* **:** repugnantly improper or offensive — **ob•scene•ly** *adv* — **ob•scen•i•ty** *n*

ob•scure *adj* **1 :** dim or hazy **2 :** not well known **3 :** vague ~ *vb* **:** make indistinct or unclear — **ob•scure•ly** *adv* — **ob•scu•ri•ty** *n*

ob•ser•va•to•ry *n* **:** place for observing astronomical phenomena

ob•serve *vb* **1 :** conform to **2 :** celebrate **3 :** see, watch, or notice **4 :** remark — **ob•serv•able** *adj* — **ob•ser•vance** *n* — **ob•ser•vant** *adj* — **ob•ser•va•tion** *n*

ob•sess *vb* **:** preoccupy intensely or abnormally — **ob•ses•sion** *n* — **ob•ses•sive** *adj* — **ob•ses•sive•ly** *adv*

ob•so•lete *adj* **:** no longer in use

ob•sta•cle *n* **:** something that stands in the way or opposes

ob•sti•nate *adj* **:** stubborn — **ob•sti•na•cy** *n* — **ob•sti•nate•ly** *adv*

ob•struct *vb* **:** block or impede — **ob•struc•tion** *n* — **ob•struc•tive** *adj* — **ob•struc•tor** *n*

ob•tain *vb* **1 :** gain by effort **2 :** be generally recognized — **ob•tain•able** *adj*

ob•vi•ous *adj* **:** plain or unmistakable — **ob•vi•ous•ly** *adv* — **ob•vi•ous•ness** *n*

oc•ca•sion *n* **1 :** favorable opportunity **2 :** cause **3 :** time of an event **4 :** special event ~ *vb* **:** cause — **oc•ca•sion•al** *adj* — **oc•ca•sion•al•ly** *adv*

oc•cu•pa•tion *n* **1 :** vocation **2 :** action or state of occupying — **oc•cu•pa•tion•al** *adj* — **oc•cu•pa•tion•al•ly** *adv*

oc•cu•py *vb* **1 :** engage the attention of **2 :** fill up **3 :** take or hold possession of **4 :** reside in — **oc•cu•pan•cy** *n* — **oc•cu•pant** *n* — **oc•cu•pi•er** *n*

oc•cur *vb* **1 :** be found or met with **2 :** take place **3 :** come to mind

oc•cur•rence *n* **:** something that takes place

ocean *n* **1 :** whole body of salt water **2 :** very large body of water — **ocean•front** *n* — **ocean•go•ing** *adj* — **oce•an•ic** *adj*

o'•clock *adv* **:** according to the clock

oc•ta•gon *n* **:** 8-sided polygon — **oc•tag•o•nal** *adj*

Oc•to•ber *n* **:** 10th month of the year having 31 days

oc•to•pus *n* **:** sea mollusk with 8 arms

odd *adj* **1 :** being only one of a pair or set **2 :** not divisible by two without a remainder **3 :** additional to what is usual or to the number mentioned **4 :** queer — **odd•i•ty** *n* — **odd•ly** *adv* — **odd•ness** *n*

odds *n pl* **1 :** difference by which one thing is favored **2 :** disagreement **3 :** ratio between winnings and the amount of the bet

odor *n* **:** quality that affects the sense of smell — **odor•less** *adj* — **odor•ous** *adj*

of *prep* **1 :** from **2 :** distinguished by **3 :** because of **4 :** made or written by **5 :** made with, being, or containing **6 :** belonging to or connected with **7 :** about **8 :** that is **9 :** concerning **10 :** before

off *adv* **1 :** from a place **2 :** unattached or removed **3 :** to a state of being no longer in use **4 :** away from work **5 :** at a distance in time or space ~ *prep* **1 :** away from **2 :** at the expense of **3 :** not engaged in or abstaining from **4 :** below the usual level of ~ *adj* **1 :** not operating, up to standard, or correct **2 :** remote **3 :** provided for

of•fend *vb* **1 :** sin or act in violation **2 :** hurt, annoy, or insult — **of•fend•er** *n*

of•fense, of•fence *n* **:** attack, misdeed, or insult — **of•fen•sive** *adj* — **of•fen•sive•ly** *adv* — **of•fen•sive•ness** *n*

of•fer *vb* **1 :** present for acceptance **2 :** propose **3 :** put up (an effort) ~ *n* **1 :** proposal **2 :** bid — **of•fer•ing** *n*

of•fice *n* **1 :** position of authority (as in government) **2 :** rite **3 :** place where a business is transacted — **of•fice•hold•er** *n*

of•fi•cer *n* **1 :** one charged with law enforcement **2 :** one who holds an office of trust or authority **3 :** one who holds a commission in the armed forces

of•fi•cial *n* **:** one in office ~ *adj* **:** authorized or authoritative — **of•fi•cial•dom** *n* — **of•fi•cial•ly** *adv*

of•fi•ci•ate *vb* **:** perform a ceremony or function

off•spring *n* **offspring :** one coming into being through animal or plant reproduction

of•ten *adv* **:** many times — **of•ten•times, oft•times** *adv*

oh *interj* **1** — used to express an emotion **2** — used in direct address

oil *n* **1 :** greasy liquid substance **2 :** petroleum ~ *vb* **:** put oil in or on — **oil•er** *n* — **oil•i•ness** *n* — **oily** *adj*

oint•ment *n* **:** oily medicinal preparation

OK *or* **okay** *adv or adj* **:** all right ~ *vb* **:** approve ~ *n* **:** approval

old *adj* **1 :** of long standing **2 :** of a specified age **3 :** relating to a past era **4 :** having existed a long time — **old•ish** *adj*

old–fash•ioned *adj* **1 :** out-of-date **2 :** conservative

ol•fac•to•ry *adj* **:** relating to the sense of smell

ol•ive *n* **1 :** evergreen tree bearing small edible fruit or the fruit **2 :** dull yellowish green color

om•e•let, om•e•lette *n* **:** beaten eggs lightly fried and folded

omen *n* **:** sign or warning of the future

om•i•nous *adj* **:** presaging evil — **om•i•nous•ly** *adv* — **om•i•nous•ness** *n*

omit *vb* **1 :** leave out **2 :** fail to perform — **omis•si•ble** *adj* — **omis•sion** *n*

om•nip•o•tent *adj* **:** almighty — **om•nip•o•tence** *n* — **om•nip•o•tent•ly** *adv*

on *prep* **1 :** in or to a position over and in contact with **2 :** at or to **3 :** about **4 :** from **5 :** with regard to **6 :** in a state or process **7 :** during the time of ~ *adv* **1 :** in or into contact with **2 :** forward **3 :** into operation

once *adv* **1 :** one time only **2 :** at any one time **3 :** formerly ~ *n* **:** one time ~ *conj* **:** as soon as ~ *adj* **:** former — **at once 1 :** simultaneously **2 :** immediately

one *adj* **1 :** being a single thing **2 :** being one in particular **3 :** being the same in kind ~ *pron* **1 :** certain indefinitely indicated person or thing **2 :** a person in general ~ *n* **1 :** 1st in a series **2 :** single person or thing — **one•ness** *n*

oner•ous *adj* **:** imposing a burden

one•self *pron* **:** one's own self — usu. used reflexively or for emphasis

one•time *adj* **:** former

one–way *adj* **:** made or for use in only one direction

on•ion *n* **:** plant grown for its pungent edible bulb or this bulb

on•ly *adj* **:** alone in its class ~ *adv* **1 :** merely or exactly **2 :** solely **3 :** at the very least **4 :** as a result ~ *conj* **:** but

on•set *n* **:** start

on•to *prep* **:** to a position or point on

on•ward *adv or adj* **:** forward

ooze *n* **:** soft mud ~ *vb* **:** flow or leak out slowly — **oozy** *adj*

opaque *adj* **1 :** blocking light **2 :** not easily understood — **opaque•ly** *adv*

open *adj* **1 :** not shut or shut up **2 :** not secret or hidden **3 :** frank or generous **4 :** extended **5 :** free from controls **6 :** not decided ~ *vb* **1 :** make or become open **2 :** make or become functional **3 :** start ~ *n* **:** outdoors — **open•er** *n* — **open•ly** *adv* — **open•ness** *n*

open•hand•ed *adj* **:** generous — **open•hand•ed•ly** *adv*

open•ing *n* **1 :** act or instance of making open **2 :** something that is open **3 :** opportunity

op•era *n* **:** drama set to music — **op•er•at•ic** *adj*

op•er•ate *vb* **1 :** perform work **2 :** perform an operation **3 :** manage — **op•er•a•ble** *adj* — **op•er•a•tive** *adj* — **op•er•a•tor** *n*

op•er•a•tion *n* **1 :** act or process of operating **2 :** surgical work on a living body **3 :** military action or mission — **op•er•a•tion•al** *adj*

opin•ion *n* **1 :** belief **2 :** judgment **3 :** formal statement by an expert

opin•ion•at•ed *adj* **:** stubborn in one's opinions

op•po•nent *n* **:** one that opposes

op•por•tune *adj* **:** suitable or timely — **op•por•tune•ly** *adv*

op•por•tun•ism *n* **:** a taking advantage of opportunities — **op•por•tun•ist** *n* — **op•por•tu•nis•tic** *adj*

op•por•tu•ni•ty *n* : favorable time
op•pose *vb* **1 :** place opposite or against something **2 :** resist — **op•po•si•tion** *n*
op•po•site *n* : one that is opposed ~ *adj* **1 :** set facing something that is at the other side or end **2 :** opposed or contrary ~ *adv* : on opposite sides ~ *prep* : across from — **op•po•site•ly** *adv*
op•press *vb* **1 :** persecute **2 :** weigh down — **op•pres•sion** *n* — **op•pres•sive** *adj* — **op•pres•sive•ly** *adv* — **op•pres•sor** *n*
op•ti•cal *adj* : relating to optics, vision, or the eye
op•ti•mism *n* : tendency to hope for the best — **op•ti•mist** *n* — **op•ti•mis•tic** *adj* — **op•ti•mis•ti•cal•ly** *adv*
op•tion *n* **1 :** ability to choose **2 :** right to buy or sell a stock **3 :** alternative — **op•tion•al** *adj*
or *conj* — used to indicate an alternative
oral *adj* **1 :** spoken **2 :** relating to the mouth — **oral•ly** *adv*
or•ange *n* **1 :** reddish yellow citrus fruit **2 :** color between red and yellow — **or•ange•ade** *n*
ora•tion *n* : elaborate formal speech — **or•a•tor** *n*
or•bit *n* : path made by one body revolving around another ~ *vb* : revolve around — **or•bit•al** *adj* — **or•bit•er** *n*
or•chard *n* : place where fruit or nut trees are grown — **or•chard•ist** *n*
or•ches•tra *n* **1 :** group of musicians **2 :** front seats of a theater's main floor — **or•ches•tral** *adj* — **or•ches•tral•ly** *adv*
or•deal *n* : severely trying experience
or•der *n* **1 :** rank, class, or special group **2 :** arrangement **3 :** rule of law **4 :** authoritative regulation or instruction **5 :** working condition **6 :** special request for a purchase or what is purchased ~ *vb* **1 :** arrange **2 :** give an order to **3 :** place an order for
or•der•ly *adj* **1 :** being in order or tidy **2 :** well behaved ~ *n* **1 :** officer's attendant **2 :** hospital attendant — **or•der•li•ness** *n*
or•di•nal *n* : number indicating order in a series
or•di•nance *n* : municipal law
or•di•nary *adj* : of common occurrence, quality, or ability — **or•di•nar•i•ly** *adv*
ore *n* : mineral containing a valuable constituent
or•gan *n* **1 :** air-powered or electronic keyboard instrument **2 :** animal or plant structure with special function **3 :** periodical
or•gan•ic *adj* **1 :** relating to a bodily organ **2 :** relating to living things **3 :** relating to or containing carbon or its compounds **4 :** relating to foods produced without the use of laboratory-made products — **or•gan•i•cal•ly** *adv*
or•gan•ism *n* : a living thing
or•ga•nize *vb* : form parts into a functioning whole — **or•ga•ni•za•tion** *n* — **or•ga•ni•za•tion•al** *adj* — **or•ga•niz•er** *n*
ori•ent *vb* **1 :** set in a definite position **2 :** acquaint with a situation — **ori•en•ta•tion** *n*
or•i•fice *n* : opening
or•i•gin *n* **1 :** ancestry **2 :** rise, beginning, or derivation from a source — **orig•i•nate** *vb* — **orig•i•na•tor** *n*
orig•i•nal *n* : something from which a copy is made ~ *adj* **1 :** first **2 :** not copied from something else **3 :** inventive — **orig•i•nal•i•ty** *n* — **orig•i•nal•ly** *adv*
or•na•ment *n* : something that adorns ~ *vb* : provide with ornament — **or•na•men•tal** *adj* — **or•na•men•ta•tion** *n*
or•nate *adj* : elaborately decorated — **or•nate•ly** *adv* — **or•nate•ness** *n*
or•phan *n* : child whose parents are dead — **orphan** *vb* — **or•phan•age** *n*
or•tho•dox *adj* **1 :** conforming to established doctrine **2** *cap* : of or relating to a Christian church originating in the Eastern Roman Empire — **or•tho•doxy** *n*
os•mo•sis *n* : diffusion esp. of water through a membrane — **os•mot•ic** *adj*
os•ten•ta•tion *n* : pretentious display — **os•ten•ta•tious** *adj* — **os•ten•ta•tious•ly** *adv*
os•tra•cize *vb* : exclude by common consent — **os•tra•cism** *n*
oth•er *adj* **1 :** being the one left **2 :** alternate **3 :** additional ~ *pron* **1 :** remaining one **2 :** different one
oth•er•wise *adv* **1 :** in a different way **2 :** in different circumstances **3 :** in other respects — **oth•er•wise** *adj*
ought *verbal auxiliary* — used to express obligation, advisability, or expectation
ounce *n* **1 :** unit of weight equal to about 28.3 grams **2 :** unit of capacity equal to about 29.6 milliliters
our *adj* : of or relating to us
ours *pron* : that which belongs to us
our•selves *pron* : we, us — used reflexively or for emphasis
out *adv* **1 :** away from the inside or center **2 :** beyond control **3 :** to extinction, exhaustion,

or completion **4 :** in or into the open ~ *vb* **:** become known ~ *adj* **1 :** situated outside **2 :** absent ~ *prep* **1 :** out through **2 :** outward on or along — **out•bound** *adj* — **out•build•ing** *n*

out•break *n* **:** sudden occurrence

out•burst *n* **:** violent expression of feeling

out•cast *n* **:** person cast out by society

out•come *n* **:** result

out•dat•ed *adj* **:** out-of-date

out•do *vb* **:** do better than

out•doors *adv* **:** in or into the open air ~ *n* **:** open air — **out•door** *adj*

out•er *adj* **1 :** external **2 :** farther out — **out•er•most** *adj*

out•fit *n* **1 :** equipment for a special purpose **2 :** group ~ *vb* **:** equip — **out•fit•ter** *n*

out•ing *n* **:** excursion

outlast *vb* **:** last longer than

out•law *n* **:** lawless person ~ *vb* **:** make illegal

out•lay *n* **:** expenditure

out•let *n* **1 :** exit **2 :** means of release **3 :** market for goods **4 :** electrical device that gives access to wiring

out•line *n* **1 :** line marking the outer limits **2 :** summary ~ *vb* **1 :** draw the outline of **2 :** indicate the chief parts of

out•look *n* **1 :** viewpoint **2 :** prospect for the future

out of *prep* **1 :** out from within **2 :** beyond the limits of **3 :** among **4** — used to indicate absence or loss **5 :** because of **6 :** from or with

out–of–date *adj* **:** no longer current or useful

out•put *n* **:** amount produced ~ *vb* **:** produce

out•rage *n* **1 :** violent or shameful act **2 :** injury or insult **3 :** extreme anger ~ *vb* **1 :** subject to violent injury **2 :** make very angry

out•ra•geous *adj* **:** extremely offensive or shameful — **out•ra•geous•ly** *adv* — **out•ra•geous•ness** *n*

out•right *adv* **1 :** completely **2 :** instantly ~ *adj* **1 :** complete **2 :** given without reservation

out•side *n* **1 :** place beyond a boundary **2 :** exterior **3 :** utmost limit ~ *adj* **1 :** outer **2 :** coming from without **3 :** remote ~ *adv* **:** on or to the outside ~ *prep* **1 :** on or to the outside of **2 :** beyond the limits of

out•sid•er *n* **:** one who does not belong to a group

out•smart *vb* **:** outwit

out•spo•ken *adj* **:** direct and open in speech — **out•spo•ken•ness** *n*

out•stand•ing *adj* **1 :** not yet paid **2 :** very good — **out•stand•ing•ly** *adv*

out•strip *vb* **1 :** go faster than **2 :** surpass

out•ward *adj* **1 :** being toward the outside **2 :** showing outwardly — **out•ward** *adv* — **out•ward•ly** *adv*

out•wit *vb* **:** get the better of by superior cleverness

oval *adj* **:** having the shape of an egg — **oval** *n*

ova•tion *n* **:** enthusiastic applause

ov•en *n* **:** chamber (as in a stove) for baking

over *adv* **1 :** across **2 :** upside down **3 :** in excess or addition **4 :** above **5 :** at an end **6 :** again ~ *prep* **1 :** above in position or authority **2 :** more than **3 :** along, through, or across **4 :** because of ~ *adj* **1 :** upper **2 :** remaining **3 :** ended

over•age *n* **:** surplus

over•all *adj* **:** including everything

over•alls *n pl* **:** pants with an extra piece covering the chest

over•bear•ing *adj* **:** arrogant

over•blown *adj* **:** pretentious

over•cast *adj* **:** clouded over ~ *n* **:** cloud covering

over•coat *n* **:** outer coat

over•come *vb* **1 :** defeat **2 :** make helpless or exhausted

over•do *vb* **:** do too much

over•flow *vb* **1 :** flood **2 :** flow over — **over•flow** *n*

over•hang *vb* **:** jut out over ~ *n* **:** something that overhangs

over•haul *vb* **1 :** repair **2 :** overtake

over•head *adv* **:** aloft ~ *adj* **:** situated above ~ *n* **:** general business expenses

over•hear *vb* **:** hear without the speaker's knowledge

over•joyed *adj* **:** filled with joy

over•lap *vb* **:** lap over — **overlap** *n*

over•look *vb* **1 :** look down on **2 :** fail to see **3 :** ignore **4 :** pardon **5 :** supervise ~ *n* **:** observation point

over•ly *adv* **:** excessively

over•night *adv* **1 :** through the night **2 :** suddenly — **overnight** *adj*

over•pass *n* **:** bridge over a road

over•pow•er *vb* **:** conquer

over•rule *vb* **:** rule against or set aside

over•run *vb* **1 :** swarm or flow over **2 :** go beyond ~ *n* **:** an exceeding of estimated costs

over•see *vb* **:** supervise — **over•seer** *n*

over•sight *n* **:** inadvertent omission or error

over·take *vb* : catch up with

over·throw *vb* **1 :** upset **2 :** defeat — **over·throw** *n*

over·time *n* : extra working time — **overtime** *adv*

over·turn *vb* **1 :** turn over **2 :** nullify

over·view *n* : brief survey

over·whelm *vb* : overcome completely — **over·whelm·ing·ly** *adv*

owe *vb* **1 :** have an obligation to pay **2 :** be indebted to or for

owl *n* : nocturnal bird of prey — **owl·ish** *adj* — **owl·ish·ly** *adv*

own *adj* : belonging to oneself ~ *vb* **1 :** have as property **2 :** acknowledge ~ *pron* : one or ones belonging to oneself — **own·er** *n* — **own·er·ship** *n*

ox *n* (**ox·en**) : bovine mammal and esp. a castrated bull

ox·y·gen *n* : gaseous chemical element essential for life

ozone *n* : very reactive bluish form of oxygen

P

p *n* : 16th letter of the alphabet

pace *n* **1 :** walking step **2 :** rate of progress ~ *vb* **1 :** go at a pace **2 :** cover with slow steps **3 :** set the pace of

pace·mak·er *n* : electrical device to regulate heartbeat

pa·cif·ic *adj* : calm or peaceful

pac·i·fy *vb* : make calm — **pac·i·fi·ca·tion** *n* — **pac·i·fi·er** *n* — **pac·i·fism** *n* — **pac·i·fist** *n or adj* — **pac·i·fis·tic** *adj*

pack *n* **1 :** compact bundle **2 :** group of animals ~ *vb* **1 :** put into a container **2 :** fill tightly or completely **3 :** send without ceremony — **pack·er** *n*

pack·age *n* : items bundled together ~ *vb* : enclose in a package

pack·et *n* : small package

pact *n* : agreement

pad *n* **1 :** cushioning part or thing **2 :** floating leaf of a water plant **3 :** tablet of paper ~ *vb* **1 :** furnish with a pad **2 :** expand with needless matter — **pad·ding** *n*

pad·dle *n* : implement with a flat blade ~ *vb* : move, beat, or stir with a paddle

pad·lock *n* : lock with a U-shaped catch — **padlock** *vb*

pa·gan *n or adj* : heathen — **pa·gan·ism** *n*

[1]**page** *n* : messenger ~ *vb* : summon by repeated calls — **pag·er** *n*

[2]**page** *n* **1 :** single leaf (as of a book) or one side of the leaf **2 :** information at a single World Wide Web address

pag·eant *n* : elaborate spectacle or procession — **pag·eant·ry** *n*

pa·go·da *n* : tower with roofs curving upward

paid *past of* PAY

pail *n* : cylindrical container with a handle — **pail·ful** *n*

pain *n* **1 :** punishment or penalty **2 :** suffering of body or mind **3** *pl* **:** great care ~ *vb* : cause or experience pain — **pain·ful** *adj* — **pain·ful·ly** *adv* — **pain·kill·er** *n* — **pain·kill·ing** *adj* — **pain·less** *adj* — **pain·less·ly** *adv*

pains·tak·ing *adj* : taking great care — **pains·tak·ing** *n* — **pains·tak·ing·ly** *adv*

paint *vb* **1 :** apply color or paint to **2 :** portray esp. in color ~ *n* : mixture of pigment and liquid — **paint·brush** *n* — **paint·er** *n* — **paint·ing** *n*

pair *n* : a set of two ~ *vb* : put or go together as a pair

pa·ja·mas *n pl* : loose suit for sleeping

pal *n* : close friend

pal·ace *n* **1 :** residence of a chief of state **2 :** mansion — **pa·la·tial** *adj*

pal·ate *n* **1 :** roof of the mouth **2 :** taste — **pal·at·able** *adj* — **pal·a·tal** *adj*

pale *adj* **1 :** lacking in color or brightness **2 :** light in color or shade ~ *vb* : make or become pale — **pale·ness** *n*

pal·ette *n* : board on which paints are laid and mixed

pall *n* **1 :** cloth draped over a coffin **2 :** something that produces gloom

pall·bear·er *n* : one who attends the coffin at a funeral

pal·let *n* **1 :** makeshift bed **2 :** portable storage platform

pal·lor *n* : paleness

[1]**palm** *n* **1 :** tall tropical tree crowned with large leaves **2 :** symbol of victory

[2]**palm** *n* : underside of the hand ~ *vb* **1 :** conceal in the hand **2 :** impose by fraud

pal·pa·ble *adj* **1 :** capable of being touched **2 :** obvious — **pal·pa·bly** *adv*

pal·pi·tate *vb* : beat rapidly — **pal·pi·ta·tion** *n*

pam•per *vb* **:** spoil or indulge

pam•phlet *n* **:** unbound publication — **pam•phle•teer** *n*

pan *n* **:** broad, shallow, and open container ~ *vb* **1 :** wash gravel in a pan to search for gold **2 :** criticize severely

pan•cake *n* **:** fried flat cake

pan•cre•as *n* **:** gland that produces insulin — **pan•cre•at•ic** *adj*

pan•da *n* **:** black-and-white bearlike animal

pan•de•mo•ni•um *n* **:** wild uproar

pan•der *n* **:** one who caters to others' desires or weaknesses ~ *vb* **:** act as a pander

pane *n* **:** sheet of glass

pan•el *n* **1 :** list of persons (as jurors) **2 :** discussion group **3 :** flat piece of construction material **4 :** board with instruments or controls ~ *vb* **:** decorate with panels — **pan•el•ing** *n* — **pan•el•ist** *n*

pan•han•dle *vb* **:** ask for money on the street — **pan•han•dler** *n*

pan•ic *n* **:** sudden overpowering fright ~ *vb* **:** affect or be affected with panic — **pan•icky** *adj*

pan•o•ra•ma *n* **:** view in every direction — **pan•o•ram•ic** *adj*

pant *vb* **1 :** breathe with great effort **2 :** yearn ~ *n* **:** panting sound

pant•ies *n pl* **:** woman's or child's short underpants

pan•to•mime *n* **1 :** play without words **2 :** expression by bodily or facial movements ~ *vb* **:** represent by pantomime

pan•try *n* **:** storage room for food and dishes

pants *n pl* **1 :** 2-legged outer garment **2 :** panties

pa•pal *adj* **:** relating to the pope

pa•per *n* **1 :** pliable substance used to write or print on, to wrap things in, or to cover walls **2 :** printed or written document **3 :** newspaper — **paper** *adj or vb* — **pa•per•hang•er** *n* — **pa•per•weight** *n* — **pa•pery** *adj*

pa•pier–mâ•ché *n* **:** molding material of waste paper

par *n* **1 :** stated value **2 :** common level **3 :** accepted standard or normal condition — **par** *adj*

para•chute *n* **:** large umbrella-shaped device for making a descent through air — **para•chute** *vb* — **para•chut•ist** *n*

pa•rade *n* **1 :** pompous display **2 :** ceremonial formation and march ~ *vb* **1 :** march in a parade **2 :** show off

par•a•dise *n* **:** place of bliss

par•a•dox *n* **:** statement that seems contrary to common sense yet is perhaps true — **par•a•dox•i•cal** *adj* — **par•a•dox•i•cal•ly** *adv*

para•graph *n* **:** unified division of a piece of writing ~ *vb* **:** divide into paragraphs

par•al•lel *adj* **1 :** lying or moving in the same direction but always the same distance apart **2 :** similar ~ *n* **1 :** parallel line, curve, or surface **2 :** line of latitude **3 :** similarity ~ *vb* **1 :** compare **2 :** correspond to — **par•al•lel•ism** *n*

par•al•lel•o•gram *n* **:** 4-sided polygon with opposite sides equal and parallel

pa•ral•y•sis *n* **:** loss of function and esp. of voluntary motion — **par•a•lyt•ic** *adj or n*

par•a•lyze *vb* **:** affect with paralysis — **par•a•lyz•ing•ly** *adv*

para•med•ic *n* **:** person trained to provide initial emergency medical treatment

para•noia *n* **:** mental disorder marked by irrational suspicion — **para•noid** *adj or n*

par•a•pher•na•lia *n sing or pl* **:** equipment

para•phrase *n* **:** restatement of a text giving the meaning in different words — **para•phrase** *vb*

par•a•site *n* **:** organism living on another — **par•a•sit•ic** *adj* — **par•a•sit•ism** *n*

par•cel *n* **1 :** lot **2 :** package ~ *vb* **:** divide into portions

parch *vb* **:** toast or shrivel with dry heat

par•don *n* **:** excusing of an offense ~ *vb* **:** free from penalty — **par•don•able** *adj* — **par•don•er** *n*

pare *vb* **1 :** trim off an outside part **2 :** reduce as if by paring — **par•er** *n*

par•ent *n* **:** one that begets or brings up offspring — **par•ent•age** *n* — **pa•ren•tal** *adj* — **par•ent•hood** *n*

pa•ren•the•sis *n* **1 :** word or phrase inserted in a passage **2 :** one of a pair of punctuation marks ( ) — **par•en•thet•ic, par•en•thet•i•cal** *adj* — **par•en•thet•i•cal•ly** *adv*

par•ish *n* **:** local church community

pa•rish•io•ner *n* **:** member of a parish

park *n* **:** land set aside for recreation or for its beauty ~ *vb* **:** leave a vehicle standing

par•ka *n* **:** usu. hooded heavy jacket

park•way *n* **:** broad landscaped thoroughfare

par•lay *n* **:** the risking of a stake plus its winnings — **par•lay** *vb*

par•ley *n* **:** conference about a dispute — **par•ley** *vb*

par·lia·ment *n* : legislative assembly — **par·lia·men·tar·i·an** *n* — **par·lia·men·ta·ry** *adj*
par·lor *n* **1** : reception room **2** : place of business
par·o·dy *n* : humorous or satirical imitation — **par·o·dy** *vb*
pa·role *n* : conditional release of a prisoner — **pa·role** *vb* — **pa·rol·ee** *n*
par·ra·keet *var of* PARAKEET
par·rot *n* : bright-colored tropical bird
pars·ley *n* : garden plant used as a seasoning or garnish
par·son *n* : minister
par·son·age *n* : parson's house
part *n* **1** : one of the units into which a larger whole is divided **2** : function or role ~ *vb* **1** : take leave **2** : separate **3** : go away **4** : give up
par·take *vb* : have or take a share — **par·tak·er** *n*
par·tial *adj* **1** : favoring one over another **2** : affecting a part only — **par·tial·i·ty** *n* — **par·tial·ly** *adv*
par·tic·i·pate *vb* : take part in something — **par·tic·i·pant** *adj or n* — **par·tic·i·pa·tion** *n* — **par·tic·i·pa·to·ry** *adj*
par·ti·cle *n* : small bit
par·tic·u·lar *adj* **1** : relating to a specific person or thing **2** : individual **3** : hard to please ~ *n* : detail — **par·tic·u·lar·ly** *adv*
par·ti·san *n* **1** : adherent **2** : guerrilla — **par·ti·san** *adj* — **par·ti·san·ship** *n*
par·ti·tion *n* **1** : distribution **2** : something that divides — **partition** *vb*
part·ly *adv* : in some degree
part·ner *n* **1** : associate **2** : companion **3** : business associate — **part·ner·ship** *n*
part of speech : class of words distinguished esp. according to function
par·ty *n* **1** : political organization **2** : participant **3** : company of persons esp. with a purpose **4** : social gathering
pass *vb* **1** : move past, over, or through **2** : go away or die **3** : allow to elapse **4** : go unchallenged **5** : transfer or undergo transfer **6** : render a judgment **7** : occur **8** : enact **9** : undergo testing successfully **10** : be regarded **11** : decline ~ *n* **1** : low place in a mountain range **2** : act of passing **3** : accomplishment **4** : permission to leave, enter, or move about — **pass·able** *adj* — **pass·ably** *adv* — **pass·er** *n* — **pass·er·by** *n*
pas·sage *n* **1** : process of passing **2** : means of passing **3** : voyage **4** : right to pass **5** : literary selection — **pas·sage·way** *n*
pas·sé *adj* : out-of-date
pas·sen·ger *n* : traveler in a conveyance
pas·sion *n* **1** : strong feeling esp. of anger, love, or desire **2** : object of affection or enthusiasm — **pas·sion·ate** *adj* — **pas·sion·ate·ly** *adv* — **pas·sion·less** *adj*
pas·sive *adj* **1** : not active but acted upon **2** : submissive — **pas·sive** *n* — **pas·sive·ly** *adv* — **pas·siv·i·ty** *n*
Pass·over *n* : Jewish holiday celebrated in March or April in commemoration of the Hebrews' liberation from slavery in Egypt
pass·port *n* : government document needed for travel abroad
pass·word *n* **1** : word or phrase spoken to pass a guard **2** : sequence of characters needed to get into a computer system
past *adj* **1** : ago **2** : just gone by **3** : having existed before the present **4** : expressing past time ~ *prep or adv* : beyond ~ *n* **1** : time gone by **2** : verb tense expressing time gone by **3** : past life
pas·ta *n* : fresh or dried shaped dough
paste *n* **1** : smooth ground food **2** : moist adhesive ~ *vb* : attach with paste — **pasty** *adj*
pas·tel *n* : light color — **pas·tel** *adj*
pas·teur·ize *vb* : heat (as milk) so as to kill germs — **pas·teur·i·za·tion** *n*
pas·time *n* : amusement
pas·tor *n* : priest or minister serving a church or parish — **pas·tor·ate** *n*
past·ry *n* : sweet baked goods
pas·ture *n* : land used for grazing ~ *vb* : graze
pat *n* **1** : light tap **2** : small mass ~ *vb* : tap gently ~ *adj or adv* **1** : apt or glib **2** : not yielding
patch *n* **1** : piece used for mending **2** : small area distinct from surrounding area ~ *vb* **1** : mend with a patch **2** : make of fragments **3** : repair hastily — **patchy** *adj*
pa·tent *adj* **1** : obvious **2** : protected by a patent ~ *n* : document conferring or securing a right ~ *vb* : secure by patent — **pat·ent·ly** *adv*
pa·ter·nal *adj* **1** : fatherly **2** : related through or inherited from a father — **pa·ter·nal·ly** *adv*
pa·ter·ni·ty *n* : fatherhood
path *n* **1** : trodden way **2** : route or course — **path·find·er** *n* — **path·way** *n* — **path·less** *adj*
pa·thet·ic *adj* : pitiful — **pa·thet·i·cal·ly** *adv*

pa•tience *n* **:** habit or fact of being patient
pa•tient *adj* **:** bearing pain or trials without complaint ~ *n* **:** one under medical care — **pa•tient•ly** *adv*
pa•tio *n* **1 :** courtyard **2 :** paved recreation area near a house
pa•tri•arch *n* **1 :** man revered as father or founder **2 :** venerable old man — **pa•tri•ar•chal** *adj* — **pa•tri•ar•chy** *n*
pa•tri•ot *n* **:** one who loves his or her country — **pa•tri•ot•ic** *adj* — **pa•tri•ot•i•cal•ly** *adv* — **pa•tri•o•tism** *n*
pa•trol *n* **1 :** a going around for observation or security **2 :** group on patrol ~ *vb* **:** carry out a patrol
pa•tron *n* **1 :** special protector **2 :** wealthy supporter **3 :** customer — **pa•tron•age** *n*
pa•tron•ize *vb* **1 :** be a customer of **2 :** treat with condescension
pat•tern *n* **1 :** model for imitation or for making things **2 :** artistic design **3 :** noticeable formation or set of characteristics ~ *vb* **:** form according to a pattern
pat•ty *n* **:** small flat cake
paunch *n* **:** large belly — **paunchy** *adj*
pau•per *n* **:** poor person — **pau•per•ism** *n* — **pau•per•ize** *vb*
pause *n* **:** temporary stop ~ *vb* **:** stop briefly
pave *vb* **:** cover to smooth or firm the surface — **pave•ment** *n* — **pav•ing** *n*
pa•vil•ion *n* **1 :** large tent **2 :** light structure used for entertainment or shelter
paw *n* **:** foot of a 4-legged clawed animal ~ *vb* **1 :** handle clumsily or rudely **2 :** touch or strike with a paw
pawn *n* **1 :** goods deposited as security for a loan **2 :** state of being pledged ~ *vb* **:** deposit as a pledge — **pawn•bro•ker** *n* — **pawn•shop** *n*
pay *vb* **(paid; paid) 1 :** make due return for goods or services **2 :** discharge indebtedness for **3 :** retaliate for **4 :** give freely or as fitting **5 :** be profitable ~ *n* **1 :** status of being paid **2 :** something paid — **pay•able** *adj* — **pay•check** *n* — **pay•ee** *n* — **pay•er** *n* — **pay•ment** *n*
PC *n* **:** small personal computer
pea *n* **:** round edible seed of a leguminous vine
peace *n* **1 :** state of calm and quiet **2 :** absence of war or strife — **peace•able** *adj* — **peace•ably** *adv* — **peace•ful** *adj* — **peace•ful•ly** *adv* — **peace•keep•er** *n* — **peace•keep•ing** *n* — **peace•mak•er** *n* — **peace•time** *n*
peach *n* **:** sweet juicy fruit of a flowering tree or this tree
peak *n* **1 :** pointed or projecting part **2 :** top of a hill **3 :** highest level ~ *vb* **:** reach a maximum — **peak** *adj*
pea•nut *n* **:** annual herb that bears underground pods or the pod or the edible seed inside
pear *n* **:** fleshy fruit of a tree related to the apple
pearl *n* **:** gem formed within an oyster — **pearly** *adj*
peas•ant *n* **:** tiller of the soil — **peas•ant•ry** *n*
peat *n* **:** decayed organic deposit often dried for fuel — **peaty** *adj*
peb•ble *n* **:** small stone — **peb•bly** *adj*
pe•can *n* **:** hickory tree bearing a smooth-shelled nut or the nut
[1]**peck** *n* **:** unit of dry measure equal to 8 quarts
[2]**peck** *vb* **:** strike or pick up with the bill ~ *n* **:** quick sharp stroke
pe•cu•liar *adj* **1 :** characteristic of only one **2 :** strange — **pe•cu•liar•i•ty** *n* — **pe•cu•liar•ly** *adv*
ped•al *n* **:** lever worked by the foot ~ *adj* **:** relating to the foot ~ *vb* **:** use a pedal
ped•dle *vb* **:** offer for sale — **ped•dler** *n*
ped•es•tal *n* **:** support or foot of something upright
pe•des•tri•an *adj* **1 :** ordinary **2 :** walking ~ *n* **:** person who walks
peek *vb* **1 :** look furtively **2 :** glance — **peek** *n*
peel *vb* **1 :** strip the skin or rind from **2 :** lose the outer layer ~ *n* **:** skin or rind — **peel•ing** *n*
[1]**peep** *vb* **:** utter faint shrill sounds — **cheep** *n*
[2]**peep** *vb* **1 :** look slyly **2 :** begin to emerge ~ *n* **:** brief look — **peep•er** *n* — **peep•hole** *n*
[1]**peer** *n* **1 :** one's equal **2 :** nobleman — **peer•age** *n*
[2]**peer** *vb* **:** look intently or curiously
peer•less *adj* **:** having no equal
peeve *vb* **:** make resentful ~ *n* **:** complaint — **peev•ish** *adj* — **peev•ish•ly** *adv* — **peev•ish•ness** *n*
peg *n* **:** small pinlike piece ~ *vb* **1 :** put a peg into **2 :** fix or mark with or as if with pegs
pel•let *n* **:** little ball — **pel•let•al** *adj* — **pel•let•ize** *vb*
[1]**pelt** *n* **:** skin of a fur-bearing animal
[2]**pelt** *vb* **:** strike with blows or missiles
pel•vis *n* **:** cavity formed by the hip bones — **pel•vic** *adj*

[1]**pen** *n* **:** enclosure for animals ~ *vb* **:** shut in a pen

[2]**pen** *n* **:** tool for writing with ink ~ *vb* **:** write

pe·nal *adj* **:** relating to punishment — **pe·nal·ize** *vb* — **pen·al·ty** *n*

pen·cil *n* **:** writing or drawing tool with a solid marking substance (as graphite) as its core ~ *vb* **:** draw or write with a pencil

pen·dant *n* **:** hanging ornament

pen·dent, pen·dant *adj* **:** hanging

pend·ing *prep* **:** while awaiting ~ *adj* **:** not yet decided

pen·du·lum *n* **:** a hanging weight that is free to swing

pen·e·trate *vb* **1 :** enter into **2 :** permeate **3 :** see into — **pen·e·tra·ble** *adj* — **pen·e·tra·tion** *n* — **pen·e·tra·tive** *adj*

pen·guin *n* **:** short-legged flightless seabird

pen·in·su·la *n* **:** land extending out into the water — **pen·in·su·lar** *adj*

pen·i·ten·tia·ry *n* **:** state or federal prison

pen·nant *n* **:** nautical or championship flag

pen·ny *n* **1 :** monetary unit equal to $\frac{1}{100}$ pound **2 :** cent — **pen·ni·less** *adj*

pen·sion *n* **:** retirement income ~ *vb* **:** pay a pension to — **pen·sion·er** *n*

pen·sive *adj* **:** thoughtful — **pen·sive·ly** *adv*

pent·a·gon *n* **:** 5-sided polygon — **pen·tag·o·nal** *adj*

peo·ple *n* **1 people** *pl* **:** human beings in general **2 people** *pl* **:** human beings in a certain group (as a family) or community **3** *pl* **peoples :** tribe, nation, or race ~ *vb* **:** constitute the population of

pep *n* **:** brisk energy ~ *vb* **:** put pep into — **pep·py** *adj*

pep·per *n* **1 :** pungent seasoning from the berry (**peppercorn**) of a shrub **2 :** vegetable grown for its hot or sweet fruit ~ *vb* **:** season with pepper — **pep·pery** *adj*

pep·per·mint *n* **:** pungent aromatic mint

per *prep* **1 :** by means of **2 :** for each **3 :** according to

per·ceive *vb* **1 :** realize **2 :** become aware of through the senses — **per·ceiv·able** *adj* — **per·cep·ti·ble** *adj* — **per·cep·ti·bly** *adv* — **per·cep·tion** *n* — **per·cep·tive** *n* — **per·cep·tive·ly** *adv*

per·cent *adv* **:** in each hundred ~ *n* **per·cent 1 :** one part in a hundred **2 :** percentage

per·cent·age *n* **:** part expressed in hundredths

per·cen·tile *n* **:** a standing on a scale of 0–100

perch *n* **:** resting place for birds ~ *vb* **:** settle on a resting place

per·co·late *vb* **:** trickle or filter down through a substance — **per·co·la·tor** *n*

per·cus·sion *n* **1 :** sharp blow **2 :** musical instrument sounded by striking

pe·ren·ni·al *adj* **1 :** present at all seasons **2 :** continuing from year to year **3 :** recurring regularly ~ *n* **:** perennial plant — **pe·ren·ni·al·ly** *adv*

per·fect *adj* **1 :** being without fault or defect **2 :** exact **3 :** complete ~ *vb* **:** make perfect — **per·fect·ibil·i·ty** *n* — **per·fect·ible** *adj* — **per·fect·ly** *adv* — **per·fect·ness** *n*

per·fec·tion *n* **1 :** quality or state of being perfect **2 :** highest degree of excellence — **per·fec·tion·ist** *n*

per·fo·rate *vb* **:** make a hole in — **per·fo·ra·tion** *n*

per·form *vb* **1 :** carry out **2 :** do in a set manner **3 :** give a public presentation — **per·for·mance** *n* — **per·form·er** *n*

per·fume *n* **1 :** pleasant odor **2 :** something that gives a scent ~ *vb* **:** add scent to

per·haps *adv* **:** possibly but not certainly

per·il *n* **:** danger — **per·il·ous** *adj* — **per·il·ous·ly** *adv*

pe·rim·e·ter *n* **:** outer boundary of a body or figure

pe·ri·od *n* **1 :** punctuation mark . used esp. to mark the end of a declarative sentence or an abbreviation **2 :** division of time **3 :** stage in a process or development

pe·ri·od·ic *adj* **:** occurring at regular intervals — **pe·ri·od·i·cal** *n* — **pe·ri·od·i·cal·ly** *adv*

pe·riph·ery *n* **:** outer boundary — **pe·riph·er·al** *adj*

per·ish *vb* **:** die or spoil — **per·ish·able** *adj or n*

per·ju·ry *n* **:** lying under oath — **per·jure** *vb* — **per·jur·er** *n*

perk *vb* **1 :** thrust (as the head) up jauntily **2 :** freshen **3 :** gain vigor or spirit — **perky** *adj*

per·ma·nent *adj* **:** lasting ~ *n* **:** hair wave — **per·ma·nence** *n* — **per·ma·nent·ly** *adv*

per·me·ate *vb* **1 :** seep through **2 :** become spread throughout — **per·me·able** *adj* — **per·me·a·bil·i·ty** *n* — **per·me·ation** *n*

per·mit *vb* **1 :** approve **2 :** make possible ~ *n* **:** license — **per·mis·si·ble** *adj* — **per·mis·sion** *n* — **per·mis·sive** *adj* — **per·miss·ive·ly** *adv* — **per·mis·sive·ness** *n*

per·pen·dic·u·lar *adj* **1 :** vertical **2 :** meeting at a right angle — **perpendicular** *n* — **per·pen·dic·u·lar·i·ty** *n* — **per·pen·dic·u·lar·ly** *adv*

per·pe·trate *vb* **:** be guilty of doing — **per·pe·tra·tion** *n* — **per·pe·tra·tor** *n*

per·pet·u·al *adj* **1 :** continuing forever **2 :** occurring continually — **per·pet·u·al·ly** *adv* — **per·pet·u·ate** *vb* — **per·pe·tu·ity** *n*

per·plex *vb* **:** confuse — **per·plex·i·ty** *n*

per·se·cute *vb* **:** harass, afflict — **per·se·cu·tion** *n* — **per·se·cu·tor** *n*

per·se·vere *vb* **:** persist — **per·se·ver·ance** *n*

per·sist *vb* **1 :** go on resolutely in spite of difficulties **2 :** continue to exist — **per·sis·tence** *n* — **per·sis·ten·cy** *n* — **per·sis·tent** *adj* — **per·sis·tent·ly** *adv*

per·son *n* **1 :** human being **2 :** human being's body or individuality **3 :** reference to the speaker, one spoken to, or one spoken of

per·son·able *adj* **:** having a pleasing personality

per·son·al *adj* **1 :** relating to a particular person **2 :** done in person **3 :** affecting one's body **4 :** offensive to a certain individual — **per·son·al·ize** *vb* — **per·son·al·ly** *adv*

per·son·al·i·ty *n* **1 :** manner and disposition of an individual **2 :** distinctive or well-known person

per·son·i·fy *vb* **1 :** represent as a human being **2 :** be the embodiment of — **per·son·i·fi·ca·tion** *n*

per·son·nel *n* **:** body of persons employed

per·spec·tive *n* **1 :** apparent depth and distance in painting **2 :** view of things in their true relationship or importance

per·spire *vb* **:** sweat — **per·spi·ra·tion** *n*

per·suade *vb* **:** win over to a belief or course of action by argument or entreaty — **per·sua·sion** *n* — **per·sua·sive** *adj* — **per·sua·sive·ly** *adv* — **per·sua·sive·ness** *n*

per·tain *vb* **1 :** belong **2 :** relate

per·ti·nent *adj* **:** relevant — **per·ti·nence** *n*

per·verse *adj* **1 :** corrupt **2 :** unreasonably contrary — **per·verse·ly** *adv* — **per·verse·ness** *n* — **per·ver·sion** *n* — **per·ver·si·ty** *n*

per·vert *vb* **:** corrupt or distort ∼ *n* **:** one that is perverted

pes·si·mism *n* **:** inclination to expect the worst — **pes·si·mist** *n* — **pes·si·mis·tic** *adj*

pest *n* **1 :** nuisance **2 :** plant or animal detrimental to humans or their crops — **pes·ti·cide** *n*

pes·ter *vb* **:** harass with petty matters

pet *n* **1 :** domesticated animal kept for pleasure **2 :** favorite ∼ *vb* **:** stroke gently or lovingly

pet·al *n* **:** modified leaf of a flower head

pe·ti·tion *n* **:** formal written request ∼ *vb* **:** make a request — **pe·ti·tion·er** *n*

pet·ri·fy *vb* **1 :** change into stony material **2 :** make rigid or inactive (as from fear) — **pet·ri·fac·tion** *n*

pe·tro·leum *n* **:** raw oil obtained from the ground

pet·ty *adj* **1 :** minor **2 :** of no importance **3 :** narrow-minded or mean — **pet·ti·ly** *adv* — **pet·ti·ness** *n*

pew *n* **:** bench with a back used in a church

pH *n* **:** number expressing relative acidity and alkalinity

phantasy *var of* FANTASY

phan·tom *n* **:** something that only appears to be real — **phan·tom** *adj*

phar·ma·ceu·ti·cal *adj* **:** relating to pharmacy or the making and selling of medicinal drugs — **phar·ma·ceu·ti·cal** *n*

phar·ma·cy *n* **1 :** art or practice of preparing and dispensing medical drugs **2 :** drugstore — **phar·ma·cist** *n*

phar·ynx *n* **:** space behind the mouth into which the nostrils, esophagus, and windpipe open — **pha·ryn·ge·al** *adj*

phase *n* **1 :** particular appearance or stage in a recurring series of changes **2 :** stage in a process — **phase in** *vb* **:** introduce in stages — **phase out** *vb* **:** discontinue gradually

phe·nom·e·non *n* **1** *pl* **phe·nom·e·na :** observable fact or event **2** *pl* **phe·nom·e·nons :** prodigy — **phe·nom·e·nal** *adj*

phi·los·o·phy *n* **1 :** critical study of fundamental beliefs **2 :** sciences and liberal arts exclusive of medicine, law, and theology **3 :** system of ideas **4 :** sum of personal convictions — **phil·o·soph·ic, phil·o·soph·i·cal** *adj* — **phil·o·soph·i·cal·ly** *adv* — **phi·los·o·phize** *vb* — **phi·los·o·pher** *n*

pho·bia *n* **:** irrational persistent fear

phone *n* **:** telephone ∼ *vb* **:** call on a telephone

pho·no·graph *n* **:** instrument that reproduces sounds from a grooved disc

pho·ny, pho·ney *adj* **:** not sincere or genuine — **phony** *n*

pho·to *n* **:** photograph — **pho·to** *vb or adj*

pho·to·copy *n* **:** photographic copy (as of a printed page) — **pho·to·copy** *vb*

pho·to·graph *n* **:** picture taken by photography — **pho·to·graph** *vb* — **pho·tog·ra·pher** *n*

— **pho·to·graph·ic** *adj* — **pho·to·graph·i·cal·ly** *adv* — **pho·tog·ra·phy** *n*
phrase *n* **1 :** brief expression **2 :** group of related words that express a thought ∼ *vb* **:** express in a particular manner
phys·i·cal *adj* **1 :** relating to nature **2 :** material as opposed to mental or spiritual **3 :** relating to the body ∼ *n* **:** medical examination — **phys·i·cal·ly** *adv*
phy·si·cian *n* **:** doctor of medicine
phys·i·cist *n* **:** specialist in physics
phys·ics *n* **:** science that deals with matter and motion
phy·sique *n* **:** build of a person's body
pi·ano *n* **:** musical instrument with strings sounded by hammers operated from a keyboard — **pi·a·nist** *n*
[1]**pick** *vb* **1 :** break up with a pointed instrument **2 :** remove bit by bit **3 :** gather by plucking **4 :** select **5 :** rob **6 :** provoke **7 :** unlock with a wire **8 :** eat sparingly ∼ *n* **1 :** act of choosing **2 :** choicest one — **pick·er** *n* — **pick up** *vb* **1 :** improve **2 :** put in order
[2]**pick** *n* **:** pointed digging tool
pick·le *n* **1 :** brine or vinegar solution for preserving foods or a food preserved in a pickle **2 :** bad state — **pickle** *vb*
pick·up *n* **1 :** revival or acceleration **2 :** light truck with an open body
pic·nic *n* **:** outing with food usu. eaten in the open ∼ *vb* **:** go on a picnic
pic·ture *n* **1 :** representation by painting, drawing, or photography **2 :** vivid description **3 :** copy **4 :** movie ∼ *vb* **:** form a mental image of — **pic·to·ri·al** *adj* — **pic·tur·esque** *adj*
pie *n* **:** pastry crust and a filling
piece *n* **1 :** part of a whole **2 :** one of a group or set **3 :** single item **4 :** product of creative work ∼ *vb* **:** join into a whole
pier *n* **1 :** support for a bridge span **2 :** deck or wharf built out over water **3 :** pillar
pierce *vb* **1 :** enter or thrust into or through **2 :** penetrate **3 :** see through
pig *n* **1 :** young swine **2 :** dirty or greedy individual **3 :** iron casting — **pig·gish** *adj* — **pig·let** *n* — **pig·pen** *n* — **pig·sty** *n*
pi·geon *n* **:** stout-bodied short-legged bird
pig·gy·back *adv or adj* **:** up on the back and shoulders
pig·ment *n* **:** coloring matter — **pig·men·ta·tion** *n*
pig·tail *n* **:** tight braid of hair
pike *n* **:** turnpike
pile *n* **:** quantity of things thrown on one another ∼ *vb* **:** heap up, accumulate
pil·grim *n* **1 :** one who travels to a shrine or holy place in devotion **2** *cap* **:** one of the English settlers in America in 1620
pil·grim·age *n* **:** pilgrim's journey
pill *n* **:** small rounded mass of medicine — **pill·box** *n*
pil·lar *n* **:** upright usu. supporting column — **pil·lared** *adj*
pil·low *n* **:** soft cushion for the head — **pil·low·case** *n*
pi·lot *n* **1 :** helmsman **2 :** person licensed to take ships into and out of a port **3 :** guide **4 :** one that flies an aircraft or spacecraft ∼ *vb* **:** act as pilot of — **pi·lot·less** *adj*
pim·ple *n* **:** small inflamed swelling on the skin — **pim·ply** *adj*
pin *n* **1 :** fastener made of a small pointed piece of wire **2 :** ornament or emblem fastened to clothing with a pin **3 :** wooden object used as a target in bowling ∼ *vb* **1 :** fasten with a pin **2 :** hold fast or immobile — **pin·hole** *n*
pin·a·fore *n* **:** sleeveless dress or apron fastened at the back
pin·cer *n* **1** *pl* **:** gripping tool with 2 jaws **2 :** pincerlike claw
pinch *vb* **1 :** squeeze between the finger and thumb or between the jaws of a tool **2 :** compress painfully **3 :** restrict **4 :** steal ∼ *n* **1 :** emergency **2 :** painful effect **3 :** act of pinching **4 :** very small quantity
pin·cush·ion *n* **:** cushion for storing pins
[1]**pine** *n* **:** evergreen cone-bearing tree or its wood
[2]**pine** *vb* **1 :** lose health through distress **2 :** yearn for intensely
pine·ap·ple *n* **:** tropical plant bearing an edible juicy fruit
pink *n* **:** light red color — **pink** *adj* — **pink·ish** *adj*
pin·point *vb* **:** locate, hit, or aim with great precision
pint *n* **:** one-half quart
pi·o·neer *n* **1 :** one that originates or helps open up a new line of thought or activity **2 :** early settler ∼ *vb* **:** act as a pioneer
pi·ous *adj* **1 :** conscientious in religious practices **2 :** affectedly religious — **pi·ous·ly** *adv*
pipe *n* **1 :** tube that produces music when air is forced through **2 :** bagpipe **3 :** long tube for conducting a fluid **4 :** smoking tool ∼ *vb* **1**

: play on a pipe **2 :** speak in a high voice **3 :** convey by pipes — **pip•er** *n*

pipe•line *n* **1 :** line of pipe **2 :** channel for information

pi•ra•cy *n* **1 :** robbery on the seas **2 :** unauthorized use of another's production or invention

pi•rate *n* **:** one who commits piracy — **pi•rate** *vb* — **pi•rat•i•cal** *adj*

pis *pl of* PI

pis•tol *n* **:** firearm held with one hand

pis•ton *n* **:** sliding piece that receives and transmits motion usu. inside a cylinder

[1]pit *n* **1 :** hole or shaft in the ground **2 :** depressed or enclosed place for a special purpose **3 :** hell **4 :** hollow or indentation ~ *vb* **1 :** form pits in **2 :** become marred with pits

[2]pit *n* **:** stony seed of some fruits ~ *vb* **:** remove the pit from

pitch *vb* **1 :** erect and fix firmly in place **2 :** throw **3 :** set at a particular tone level **4 :** fall headlong ~ *n* **1 :** action or manner of pitching **2 :** degree of slope **3 :** relative highness of a tone **4 :** sales talk — **pitched** *adj*

[1]pitch•er *n* **:** container for liquids

[2]pitcher *n* **:** one that pitches (as in baseball)

pitch•fork *n* **:** long-handled fork for pitching hay

pit•tance *n* **:** small portion or amount

pity *n* **1 :** sympathetic sorrow **2 :** something to be regretted ~ *vb* **:** feel pity for — **piti•able** *adj* — **piti•ful** *adj* — **piti•ful•ly** *adv* — **piti•less** *adj* — **piti•less•ly** *adv*

piv•ot *n* **:** fixed pin on which something turns ~ *vb* **:** turn on or as if on a pivot — **piv•ot•al** *adj*

piz•za *n* **:** thin pie of bread dough spread with a spiced mixture (as of tomatoes, cheese, and meat)

piz•zazz, pi•zazz *n* **:** glamour

piz•ze•ria *n* **:** pizza restaurant

pla•cate *vb* **:** appease — **pla•ca•ble** *adj*

place *n* **1 :** space or room **2 :** indefinite area **3 :** a particular building, locality, area, or part **4 :** relative position in a scale or sequence **5 :** seat **6 :** job ~ *vb* **1 :** put in a place **2 :** identify — **place•ment** *n*

plac•id *adj* **:** undisturbed or peaceful — **pla•cid•i•ty** *n* — **plac•id•ly** *adv*

pla•gia•rize *vb* **:** use (words or ideas) of another as if your own — **pla•gia•rism** *n* — **pla•gia•rist** *n*

plague *n* **1 :** disastrous evil **2 :** destructive contagious bacterial disease ~ *vb* **1 :** afflict with disease or disaster **2 :** harass

plaid *n* **:** woolen fabric with a pattern of crossing stripes or the pattern itself — **plaid** *adj*

plain *n* **:** expanse of relatively level treeless country ~ *adj* **1 :** lacking ornament **2 :** not concealed or disguised **3 :** easily understood **4 :** frank **5 :** not fancy or pretty — **plain•ly** *adv* — **plain•ness** *n*

plain•tiff *n* **:** complaining party in a lawsuit

plait *n* **1 :** pleat **2 :** braid of hair or straw — **plait** *vb*

plan *n* **1 :** drawing or diagram **2 :** method for accomplishing something ~ *vb* **1 :** form a plan of **2 :** intend — **plan•less** *adj* — **plan•ner** *n*

plane *n* **1 :** level surface **2 :** level of existence, consciousness, or development **3 :** airplane ~ *adj* **1 :** flat **2 :** dealing with flat surfaces or figures

plan•et *n* **:** celestial body that revolves around the sun — **plan•e•tary** *adj*

plank *n* **1 :** heavy thick board **2 :** article in the platform of a political party — **plank•ing** *n*

plant *vb* **1 :** set in the ground to grow **2 :** place firmly or forcibly ~ *n* **1 :** living thing without sense organs that cannot move about **2 :** land, buildings, and machinery used esp. in manufacture

plan•tain *n* **:** banana plant with starchy greenish fruit

plan•ta•tion *n* **:** agricultural estate usu. worked by resident laborers

plant•er *n* **1 :** plantation owner **2 :** plant container

plasma TV *n* **:** television screen in which cells of ionized gas emit light upon receiving an electric current

plas•ter *n* **1 :** medicated dressing **2 :** hardening paste for coating walls and ceilings ~ *vb* **:** cover with plaster — **plas•ter•er** *n*

plas•tic *adj* **:** capable of being molded ~ *n* **:** material that can be formed into rigid objects, films, or filaments — **plas•tic•i•ty** *n*

plate *n* **1 :** flat thin piece **2 :** plated metalware **3 :** shallow usu. circular dish **4 :** denture or the part of it that fits to the mouth **5 :** something printed from an engraving ~ *vb* **:** overlay with metal — **plat•ing** *n*

pla•teau *n* **:** large level area of high land

plat•form *n* **1 :** raised flooring or stage **2 :** declaration of principles for a political party

plat•i•num *n* : heavy grayish-white metallic chemical element
plat•ter *n* : large serving plate
plau•si•ble *adj* : reasonable or believeable — **plau•si•bil•i•ty** *n* — **plau•si•bly** *adv*
play *n* **1** : action in a game **2** : recreational activity **3** : light or fitful movement **4** : free movement **5** : stage representation of a drama ~ *vb* **1** : engage in recreation **2** : move or toy with aimlessly **3** : perform music **4** : act in a drama — **play•act•ing** *n* — **play•er** *n* — **play•ful** *adj* — **play•ful•ly** *adv* — **play•ful•ness** *n* — **play•ground** *n* — **play•mate** *n* — **play•pen** *n* — **play•suit** *n* — **play•thing** *n*
play•house *n* **1** : theater **2** : small house for children to play in
play•wright *n* : writer of plays
pla•za *n* **1** : public square **2** : shopping mall
plea *n* **1** : defendant's answer to charges **2** : urgent request
plead *vb* **1** : argue for or against in court **2** : answer to a charge or indictment **3** : appeal earnestly — **plead•er** *n*
pleas•ant *adj* **1** : giving pleasure **2** : marked by pleasing behavior or appearance — **pleas•ant•ly** *adv* — **pleas•ant•ness** *n* — **pleas•ant•ry** *n*
please *vb* **1** : give pleasure or satisfaction to **2** : desire or intend
pleas•ing *adj* : giving pleasure — **pleas•ing•ly** *adv*
plea•sure *n* **1** : desire or inclination **2** : enjoyment **3** : source of delight — **plea•sur•able** *adj* — **plea•sur•ably** *adv*
pleat *vb* : arrange in pleats ~ *n* : fold in cloth
pledge *n* **1** : something given as security **2** : promise or vow ~ *vb* **1** : offer as or bind by a pledge **2** : promise
plen•ty *n* : more than adequate number or amount — **plen•ti•ful** *adj* — **plen•ti•ful•ly** *adv*
pli•able *adj* : flexible
pli•ant *adj* : flexible — **pli•an•cy** *n*
pli•ers *n pl* : pinching or gripping tool
plight *n* : bad state
plod *vb* **1** : walk heavily or slowly **2** : work laboriously and monotonously — **plod•der** *n* — **plod•ding•ly** *adv*
plot *n* **1** : small area of ground **2** : ground plan **3** : main story development (as of a book or movie) **4** : secret plan for doing something ~ *vb* **1** : make a plot or plan of **2** : plan or contrive — **plot•ter** *n*
plow, plough *n* **1** : tool used to turn soil **2** : device for pushing material aside ~ *vb* **1** : break up with a plow **2** : cleave or move through like a plow — **plow•man** *n*
ploy *n* : clever maneuver
pluck *vb* **1** : pull off or out **2** : tug or twitch ~ *n* **1** : act or instance of plucking **2** : spirit or courage
plucky *adj* : courageous or spirited
plug *n* **1** : something for sealing an opening **2** : electrical connector at the end of a cord **3** : piece of favorable publicity ~ *vb* **1** : stop or make tight or secure by inserting a plug **2** : publicize
plum *n* **1** : smooth-skinned juicy fruit **2** : fine reward
plumb *n* : weight on the end of a line (**plumb line**) to show vertical direction ~ *adv* **1** : vertically **2** : completely ~ *vb* : sound or test with a plumb ~ *adj* : vertical
plumb•er *n* : one who repairs usu. water pipes and fixtures
plumb•ing *n* : system of water pipes in a building
plume *n* : large, conspicuous, or showy feather ~ *vb* **1** : provide or deck with feathers **2** : indulge in pride — **plumed** *adj*
plum•met *vb* : drop straight down
plump *adj* : having a full rounded form — **plump•ness** *n*
plun•der *vb* : rob or take goods by force (as in war) ~ *n* : something taken in plundering — **plun•der•er** *n*
plunge *vb* **1** : thrust or drive with force **2** : leap or dive into water **3** : begin an action suddenly **4** : dip or move suddenly forward or down ~ *n* : act or instance of plunging — **plung•er** *n*
plu•ral *adj* : relating to a word form denoting more than one — **plu•ral** *n* — **plu•ral•i•za•tion** *n* — **plu•ral•ize** *vb*
plu•ral•i•ty *n* : greatest number of votes cast when not a majority
plus *prep* : with the addition of ~ *n* **1** : sign + (**plus sign**) in mathematics to indicate addition **2** : added or positive quantity **3** : advantage ~ *adj* : being more or in addition ~ *conj* : and
plush *n* : fabric with a long pile ~ *adj* : luxurious — **plush•ly** *adv* — **plushy** *adj* — **plush•ness** *n*
[1]**ply** *n* : fold, thickness, or strand of which something is made — **ply•wood** *n*

[2]ply *vb* **1 :** use or work at **2 :** keep supplying something to **3 :** travel regularly usu. by sea

pneu•mat•ic *adj* **1 :** moved by air pressure **2 :** filled with compressed air — **pneu•mat•i•cal•ly** *adv*

pneu•mo•nia *n* **:** inflammatory lung disease

pock•et *n* **1 :** small open bag sewn into a garment **2 :** container or receptacle **3 :** isolated area or group ~ *vb* **:** put in a pocket — **pock•et•ful** *n* — **pock•et•knife** *n*

pock•et•book *n* **1 :** purse **2 :** financial resources

pod *n* **1 :** dry fruit that splits open when ripe **2 :** compartment on a ship or craft

po•et•ry *n* **1 :** metrical writing **2 :** poems — **po•em** *n* — **po•et** *n* — **po•et•ic, po•et•i•cal** *adj*

point *n* **1 :** individual often essential detail **2 :** purpose **3 :** particular place, time, or stage **4 :** sharp end **5 :** projecting piece of land **6 :** dot or period **7 :** division of the compass **8 :** unit of counting ~ *vb* **1 :** sharpen **2 :** indicate direction by extending a finger **3 :** direct attention to **4 :** aim — **point•ed•ly** *adv* — **point•less** *adj*

point•er *n* **1 :** one that points out **2 :** large short-haired hunting dog **3 :** hint or tip

poise *vb* **:** balance ~ *n* **:** self-possessed calmness

poi•son *n* **:** chemical that can injure or kill ~ *vb* **1 :** injure or kill with poison **2 :** apply poison to **3 :** affect destructively — **poi•son•er** *n* — **poi•son•ous** *adj*

poke *vb* **1 :** prod **2 :** dawdle ~ *n* **:** quick thrust

[1]pok•er *n* **:** rod for stirring a fire

[2]poker *n* **:** card game for gambling

po•lar *adj* **:** relating to a geographical or magnetic pole

po•lar•ize *vb* **1 :** cause to have magnetic poles **2 :** break up into opposing groups — **po•lar•i•za•tion** *n*

[1]pole *n* **:** long slender piece of wood or metal

[2]pole *n* **1 :** either end of the earth's axis **2 :** battery terminal **3 :** either end of a magnet

po•lice *n* **(police) 1 :** department of government that keeps public order and enforces the laws **2 :** members of the police ~ *vb* **:** regulate and keep in order — **po•lice•man** *n* — **po•lice•wom•an** *n*

[1]pol•i•cy *n* **:** course of action selected to guide decisions

[2]policy *n* **:** insurance contract — **pol•i•cy•hold•er** *n*

pol•ish *vb* **1 :** make smooth and glossy **2 :** develop or refine ~ *n* **1 :** shiny surface **2 :** refinement

po•lite *adj* **:** marked by courteous social conduct — **po•lite•ly** *adv* — **po•lite•ness** *n*

pol•i•tics *n sing or pl* **:** practice of government and managing of public affairs — **po•lit•i•cal** *adj* — **po•lit•i•cal•ly** *adv* — **pol•i•ti•cian** *n*

pol•ka dot *n* **:** one of a series of regular dots in a pattern

poll *n* **1 :** head **2 :** place where votes are cast — usu. pl. **3 :** a sampling of opinion ~ *vb* **1 :** cut off **2 :** receive or record votes **3 :** question in a poll — **poll•ster** *n*

pol•len *n* **:** spores of a seed plant

pol•li•na•tion *n* **:** the carrying of pollen to fertilize the seed — **pol•li•nate** *vb* — **pol•li•na•tor** *n*

pol•lute *vb* **:** contaminating with waste products — **pol•lut•ant** *n* — **pol•lut•er** *n* — **pol•lu•tion** *n*

poly•es•ter *n* **:** synthetic fiber

poly•gon *n* **:** closed plane figure with straight sides

pom•mel *n* **1 :** knob on the hilt of a sword **2 :** knob at the front of a saddle ~ *vb* **:** pummel

pomp•ous *adj* **:** pretentiously dignified — **pom•pos•i•ty** *n* — **pomp•ous•ly** *adv*

pon•cho *n* **:** blanketlike cloak

pond *n* **:** small body of water

pon•der *vb* **:** consider

pon•der•ous *adj* **1 :** very heavy **2 :** clumsy **3 :** oppressively dull

pon•tiff *n* **:** pope — **pon•tif•i•cal** *adj*

pon•tif•i•cate *vb* **:** talk pompously

po•ny *n* **:** small horse

po•ny•tail *n* **:** hair arrangement like the tail of a pony

poo•dle *n* **:** dog with a curly coat

pool *n* **1 :** small body of water **2 :** puddle

poor *adj* **1 :** lacking material possessions **2 :** less than adequate **3 :** arousing pity **4 :** unfavorable — **poor•ly** *adv*

[1]pop *vb* **1 :** move suddenly **2 :** burst with or make a sharp sound **3 :** protrude ~ *n* **1 :** sharp explosive sound **2 :** flavored soft drink

[2]pop *adj* **:** popular

pop•corn *n* **:** corn whose kernels burst open into a light mass when heated

pope *n, often cap* **:** head of the Roman Catholic Church

pop•u•lar *adj* **1 :** relating to the general public **2 :** widely accepted **3 :** commonly liked — **pop•u•lar•i•ty** *n* — **pop•u•lar•ize** *vb* — **pop•u•lar•ly** *adv*

pop•u•la•tion *n* **:** people or number of people in an area

porch *n* **:** covered entrance

pore *n* **:** tiny hole (as in the skin) — **pored** *adj*

pork *n* **:** pig meat

po•rous *adj* **:** permeable to fluids — **po•ros•i•ty** *n*

port *n* **1 :** harbor **2 :** city with a harbor

por•ta•ble *adj* **:** capable of being carried — **por•ta•ble** *n*

por•tent *n* **:** something that foreshadows a coming event — **por•ten•tous** *adj*

por•ter *n* **:** baggage carrier

port•fo•lio *n* **1 :** portable case for papers **2 :** office or function of a diplomat **3 :** investor's securities

por•tion *n* **:** part or share of a whole ~ *vb* **:** divide into or allot portions

por•trait *n* **:** picture of a person — **por•trait•ist** *n* — **por•trai•ture** *n*

por•tray *vb* **1 :** make a picture of **2 :** describe in words **3 :** play the role of — **por•tray•al** *n*

pose *vb* **1 :** assume a posture or attitude **2 :** propose **3 :** pretend to be what one is not ~ *n* **1 :** sustained posture **2 :** pretense — **pos•er** *n*

po•si•tion *n* **1 :** stand taken on a question **2 :** place or location **3 :** status **4 :** job — **position** *vb*

pos•i•tive *adj* **1 :** definite **2 :** confident **3 :** relating to or being an adjective or adverb form that denotes no increase **4 :** greater than zero **5 :** having a deficiency of electrons **6 :** affirmative — **pos•i•tive•ly** *adv* — **pos•i•tive•ness** *n*

pos•sess *vb* **1 :** have as property or as a quality **2 :** control — **pos•ses•sion** *n* — **pos•ses•sor** *n*

pos•ses•sive *adj* **1 :** relating to a grammatical case denoting ownership **2 :** jealous — **pos•ses•sive** *n* — **pos•ses•sive•ness** *n*

pos•si•ble *adj* **1 :** that can be done **2 :** potential — **pos•si•bil•i•ty** *n* — **pos•si•bly** *adv*

[1]**post** *n* **:** upright stake serving to support or mark ~ *vb* **:** put up or announce by a notice

[2]**post** *vb* **1 :** mail **2 :** inform

[3]**post** *n* **1 :** sentry's station **2 :** assigned task **3 :** army camp ~ *vb* **:** station

post•age *n* **:** fee for mail

post•al *adj* **:** relating to the mail

post•er *n* **:** large usu. printed notice

post•hu•mous *adj* **:** occurring after one's death — **post•hu•mous•ly** *adv*

post•mark *n* **:** official mark on mail — **postmark** *vb*

post office *n* **:** agency or building for mail service

post•pone *vb* **:** put off to a later time — **post•pone•ment** *n*

pos•tu•late *vb* **:** assume as true ~ *n* **:** assumption

pos•ture *n* **:** bearing of the body ~ *vb* **:** strike a pose

pot *n* **:** rounded container ~ *vb* **:** place in a pot — **pot•ful** *n*

po•ta•to *n* **:** edible plant tuber

po•tent *adj* **:** powerful or effective — **po•ten•cy** *n*

po•ten•tial *adj* **:** capable of becoming actual ~ *n* **1 :** something that can become actual **2 :** degree of electrification with reference to a standard — **po•ten•ti•al•i•ty** *n* — **po•ten•tial•ly** *adv*

pot•hole *n* **:** large hole in a road surface

pot•luck *n* **:** whatever food is available

pot•pour•ri *n* **1 :** mix of flowers, herbs, and spices used for scent **2 :** miscellaneous collection

pot•shot *n* **1 :** casual or easy shot **2 :** random critical remark

pot•tery *n* **:** objects (as dishes) made from clay — **pot•ter** *n*

pouch *n* **1 :** small bag **2 :** bodily sac

poul•try *n* **:** domesticated fowl

pounce *vb* **:** spring or swoop upon and seize

[1]**pound** *n* **1 :** unit of weight equal to 16 ounces **2 :** monetary unit (as of the United Kingdom) — **pound•age** *n*

[2]**pound** *vb* **1 :** crush by beating **2 :** strike heavily **3 :** drill **4 :** move along heavily

pour *vb* **1 :** flow or supply esp. copiously **2 :** rain hard

pout *vb* **:** look sullen — **pout** *n*

pov•er•ty *n* **1 :** lack of money or possessions **2 :** poor quality

pow•der *n* **:** dry material of fine particles ~ *vb* **:** sprinkle or cover with powder — **pow•dery** *adj*

pow•er *n* **1 :** position of authority **2 :** ability to act **3 :** one that has power **4 :** physical might **5 :** force or energy used to do work ~ *vb*

: supply with power — **pow•er•ful** *adj* — **pow•er•ful•ly** *adv* — **pow•er•less** *adj*
prac•ti•cal *adj* **1 :** relating to practice **2 :** virtual **3 :** capable of being put to use **4 :** inclined to action as opposed to speculation — **prac•ti•cal•i•ty** *n* — **prac•ti•cal•ly** *adv*
prac•tice, prac•tise *vb* **1 :** perform repeatedly to become proficient **2 :** do or perform customarily **3 :** be professionally engaged in ~ *n* **1 :** actual performance **2 :** habit **3 :** exercise for proficiency **4 :** exercise of a profession
prag•ma•tism *n* **:** practical approach to problems — **prag•mat•ic** *adj* — **prag•mat•i•cal•ly** *adv* — **prag•ma•tist** *n*
prai•rie *n* **:** broad grassy rolling tract of land
praise *vb* **1 :** express approval of **2 :** glorify — **praise** *n* — **praise•wor•thy** *adj*
prance *vb* **1 :** spring from the hind legs **2 :** swagger — **prance** *n* — **pranc•er** *n*
prank *n* **:** playful or mischievous act — **prank•ster** *n*
pray *vb* **1 :** entreat **2 :** ask earnestly for something **3 :** address God or a god
prayer *n* **1 :** earnest request **2 :** an addressing of God or a god **3 :** words used in praying — **prayer•ful** *adj* — **prayer•ful•ly** *adv*
preach *vb* **1 :** deliver a sermon **2 :** advocate earnestly — **preach•er** *n* — **preach•ment** *n*
pre•car•i•ous *adj* **:** dangerously insecure — **pre•car•i•ous•ly** *adv* — **pre•car•i•ous•ness** *n*
pre•cau•tion *n* **:** care taken beforehand — **pre•cau•tion•ary** *adj*
pre•cede *vb* **:** be, go, or come ahead of — **pre•ce•dence** *n* — **prec•e•dent** *n*
pre•cinct *n* **1 :** district of a city **2** *pl* **:** vicinity
pre•cious *adj* **1 :** of great value **2 :** greatly cherished **3 :** affected
pre•cip•i•tate *vb* **1 :** cause to happen quickly or abruptly **2 :** cause to separate out of a liquid **3 :** fall as rain, snow, or hail ~ *n* **:** solid matter precipitated from a liquid ~ *adj* **:** unduly hasty — **pre•cip•i•tate•ly** *adv* — **pre•cip•i•tate•ness** *n* — **pre•cip•i•tous** *adj* — **pre•cip•i•tous•ly** *adv*
pre•cip•i•ta•tion *n* **1 :** rash haste **2 :** rain, snow, or hail
pre•cise *adj* **1 :** definite **2 :** highly accurate — **pre•cise•ly** *adv* — **pre•cise•ness** *n*
pre•ci•sion *n* **:** quality or state of being precise
pre•clude *vb* **:** make impossible
pre•co•cious *adj* **:** exceptionally advanced — **pre•co•cious•ly** *adv* — **pre•coc•i•ty** *n*
pred•a•to•ry *adj* **:** preying upon others — **pred•a•tor** *n*
pre•de•ces•sor *n* **:** a previous holder of a position
pre•des•tine *vb* **:** settle beforehand — **pre•des•ti•na•tion** *n*
pre•dic•a•ment *n* **:** difficult situation
pred•i•cate *n* **:** part of a sentence that states something about the subject ~ *vb* **1 :** affirm **2 :** establish — **pred•i•ca•tion** *n*
pre•dict *vb* **:** declare in advance — **pre•dict•abil•i•ty** *n* — **pre•dict•able** *adj* — **pre•dict•ably** *adv* — **pre•dic•tion** *n*
pre•dis•pose *vb* **:** cause to be favorable or likely to respond to something beforehand — **pre•dis•po•si•tion** *n*
pre•dom•i•nate *vb* **:** be superior — **pre•dom•i•nance** *n* — **pre•dom•i•nant** *adj* — **pre•dom•i•nant•ly** *adv*
pre•em•i•nent *adj* **:** having highest rank — **pre•em•i•nence** *n* — **pre•em•i•nent•ly** *adv*
pre•empt *vb* **1 :** seize for oneself **2 :** take the place of — **pre•emp•tion** *n* — **pre•emp•tive** *adj*
pre•fab•ri•cat•ed *adj* **:** manufactured for rapid assembly elsewhere — **pre•fab•ri•ca•tion** *n*
pref•ace *n* **:** introductory comments ~ *vb* **:** introduce with a preface — **pref•a•to•ry** *adj*
pre•fer *vb* **1 :** like better **2 :** bring (as a charge) against a person — **pref•er•a•ble** *adj* — **pref•er•a•bly** *adv* — **pref•er•ence** *n* — **pref•er•en•tial** *adj*
[1]**pre•fix** *vb* **:** place before
[2]**pre•fix** *n* **:** affix at the beginning of a word
preg•nant *adj* **1 :** containing unborn young **2 :** meaningful — **preg•nan•cy** *n*
pre•his•tor•ic, pre•his•tor•i•cal *adj* **:** relating to the period before written history
prej•u•dice *n* **1 :** damage esp. to one's rights **2 :** unreasonable attitude for or against something ~ *vb* **1 :** damage **2 :** cause to have prejudice — **prej•u•di•cial** *adj*
pre•lim•i•nary *n* **:** something that precedes or introduces — **pre•lim•i•nary** *adj*
pre•lude *n* **:** introductory performance, event, or musical piece
pre•ma•ture *adj* **:** coming before the usual or proper time — **pre•ma•ture•ly** *adv*
pre•mier *adj* **:** first in rank or importance ~ *n* **:** prime minister — **pre•mier•ship** *n*
pre•miere *n* **:** 1st performance ~ *vb* **:** give a 1st performance of
prem•ise *n* **1 :** statement made or implied as a

basis of argument **2** *pl* **:** piece of land with the structures on it

pre·mi·um *n* **1 :** bonus **2 :** sum over the stated value **3 :** sum paid for insurance **4 :** high value

pre·mo·ni·tion *n* **:** feeling that something is about to happen — **pre·mon·i·to·ry** *adj*

pre·oc·cu·py *vb* **:** occupy the attention of — **pre·oc·cu·pa·tion** *n* — **pre·oc·cu·pied** *adj*

pre·pare *vb* **1 :** make or get ready often beforehand **2 :** put together or compound — **prep·a·ra·tion** *n* — **pre·pa·ra·to·ry** *adj* — **pre·pared·ness** *n*

prep·o·si·tion *n* **:** word that combines with a noun or pronoun to form a phrase — **prep·o·si·tion·al** *adj*

pre·req·ui·site *n* **:** something required beforehand — **prerequisite** *adj*

pre·rog·a·tive *n* **:** special right or power

pre·scribe *vb* **1 :** lay down as a guide **2 :** direct the use of as a remedy

pre·scrip·tion *n* **:** written direction for the preparation and use of a medicine or the medicine prescribed

pres·ence *n* **1 :** fact or condition of being present **2 :** appearance or bearing

[1]**pres·ent** *n* **:** gift

[2]**pre·sent** *vb* **1 :** introduce **2 :** bring before the public **3 :** make a gift to or of **4 :** bring before a court for inquiry — **pre·sent·able** *adj* — **pre·sen·ta·tion** *n* — **pre·sent·ment** *n*

[3]**pres·ent** *adj* **:** now existing, in progress, or attending ~ *n* **:** the time or moment now existing — **pres·ent·ly** *adv*

present participle *n* **:** participle that typically expresses present action

pre·serve *vb* **1 :** keep safe from danger or spoilage **2 :** maintain ~ *n* **1 :** preserved fruit — often in pl. **2 :** area for protection of natural resources — **pres·er·va·tion** *n* — **pre·ser·va·tive** *adj or n* — **pre·serv·er** *n*

pre·side *vb* **1 :** act as chairman **2 :** exercise control

pres·i·dent *n* **1 :** one chosen to preside **2 :** chief official (as of a company or nation) — **pres·i·den·cy** *n* — **pres·i·den·tial** *adj*

press *n* **1 :** crowded condition **2 :** machine or device for exerting pressure and esp. for printing **3 :** pressure **4 :** printing or publishing establishment **5 :** news media and esp. newspapers ~ *vb* **1 :** lie against and exert pressure on **2 :** smooth with an iron or squeeze with something heavy **3 :** urge **4 :** crowd **5 :** force one's way — **press·er** *n*

press·ing *adj* **:** urgent

pres·sure *n* **1 :** burden of distress or urgent business **2 :** direct application of force — **pres·sure** *vb* — **pres·sur·i·za·tion** *n* — **pres·sur·ize** *vb*

pres·tige *n* **:** estimation in the eyes of people — **pres·ti·gious** *adj*

pres·to *adv or adj* **:** quickly

pre·sume *vb* **1 :** assume authority without right to do so **2 :** take for granted — **pre·sum·able** *adj* — **pre·sum·ably** *adv* — **pre·sump·tion** *n* — **pre·sump·tive** *adj*

pre·sump·tu·ous *adj* **:** too bold or forward — **pre·sump·tu·ous·ly** *adv*

pre·sup·pose *vb* **:** take for granted — **pre·sup·po·si·tion** *n*

pre·tend *vb* **1 :** act as if something is real or true when it is not **2 :** act in a way that is false **3 :** lay claim — **pre·tend·er** *n*

pre·tense, pre·tence *n* **1 :** insincere effort **2 :** deception — **pre·ten·sion** *n*

pre·ten·tious *adj* **:** overly showy or self-important — **pre·ten·tious·ly** *adv* — **pre·ten·tious·ness** *n*

pre·text *n* **:** falsely stated purpose

pret·ty *adj* **:** pleasing by delicacy or attractiveness ~ *adv* **:** in some degree ~ *vb* **:** make pretty — **pret·ti·ly** *adv* — **pret·ti·ness** *n*

pre·vail *vb* **1 :** triumph **2 :** urge successfully **3 :** be frequent, widespread, or dominant

prev·a·lent *adj* **:** widespread — **prev·a·lence** *n*

pre·vent *vb* **:** keep from happening or acting — **pre·vent·able** *adj* — **pre·ven·tion** *n* — **pre·ven·tive** *adj or n* — **pre·ven·ta·tive** *adj or n*

pre·view *vb* **:** view or show beforehand — **pre·view** *n*

pre·vi·ous *adj* **:** having gone, happened, or existed before — **pre·vi·ous·ly** *adv*

prey *n* **1 :** animal taken for food by another **2 :** victim ~ *vb* **1 :** seize and devour animals as prey **2 :** have a harmful effect on

price *n* **:** cost ~ *vb* **:** set a price on — **pric·ey** *adj* — **price·less** *adj*

prick *n* **1 :** tear or small wound made by a point **2 :** something sharp or pointed ~ *vb* **:** pierce slightly with a sharp point — **prick·er** *n*

pride *n* **:** quality or state of being proud ~ *vb* **:** indulge in pride — **pride·ful** *adj*

priest *n* **:** person having authority to perform

the sacred rites of a religion — **priest•ess** *n* — **priest•hood** *n* — **priest•li•ness** *n* — **priest•ly** *adj*

pri•ma•ry *adj* **:** first in order of time, rank, or importance ~ *n* **:** preliminary election — **pri•mar•i•ly** *adv*

pri•mate *n* **1 :** highest-ranking bishop **2 :** mammal of the group that includes humans and monkeys

prime *n* **:** earliest or best part or period ~ *adj* **:** standing first (as in significance or quality) ~ *vb* **1 :** fill or load **2 :** lay a preparatory coating on

prime minister *n* **:** chief executive of a parliamentary government

[1]prim•er *n* **:** small introductory book

[2]prim•er *n* **1 :** device for igniting an explosive **2 :** material for priming a surface

prim•i•tive *adj* **1 :** relating to or characteristic of an early stage of development **2 :** of or relating to a tribal people or culture ~ *n* **:** one that is primitive — **prim•i•tive•ly** *adv* — **prim•i•tive•ness** *n*

prince *n* **1 :** ruler **2 :** son of a king or queen — **prince•ly** *adj*

prin•cess *n* **1 :** daughter of a king or queen **2 :** wife of a prince

prin•ci•pal *adj* **:** most important ~ *n* **1 :** leading person **2 :** head of a school **3 :** sum lent at interest — **prin•ci•pal•ly** *adv*

prin•ci•pal•i•ty *n* **:** territory of a prince

prin•ci•ple *n* **1 :** general or fundamental law **2 :** rule or code of conduct or devotion to such a code

print *n* **1 :** mark or impression made by pressure **2 :** printed state or form **3 :** printed matter **4 :** copy made by printing **5 :** cloth with a figure stamped on it ~ *vb* **1 :** produce impressions of (as from type) **2 :** write in letters like those of printer's type — **print•able** *adj* — **print•er** *n* — **print•out** *n* — **print out** *vb*

prior *adj* **:** coming before in time, order, or importance — **pri•or•i•ty** *n*

prism *n* **:** transparent 3-sided object that separates light into colors — **pris•mat•ic** *adj*

pris•on *n* **:** place where criminals are confined — **pris•on•er** *n*

pris•sy *adj* **:** overly prim — **pris•si•ness** *n*

pris•tine *adj* **:** pure

pri•va•cy *n* **:** quality or state of being apart from others

pri•vate *adj* **1 :** belonging to a particular individual or group **2 :** carried on independently **3 :** withdrawn from company or observation ~ *n* **:** enlisted person of the lowest rank in the marine corps or of one of the two lowest ranks in the army — **pri•vate•ly** *adv*

priv•i•lege *n* **:** right granted as an advantage or favor — **priv•i•leged** *adj*

[1]prize *n* **1 :** something offered or striven for in competition or in contests of chance **2 :** something very desirable — **prize** *adj* — **prize•win•ner** *n* — **prize•win•ning** *adj*

[2]prize *vb* **:** value highly

[1]pro *n* **:** favorable argument or person ~ *adv* **:** in favor

[2]pro *n or adj* **:** professional

prob•a•ble *adj* **:** seeming true or real or to have a good chance of happening — **prob•a•bil•i•ty** *n* — **prob•a•bly** *adv*

pro•bate *n* **:** judicial determination of the validity of a will ~ *vb* **:** establish by probate

pro•ba•tion *n* **1 :** period of testing and trial **2 :** freedom for a convict during good behavior under supervision — **pro•ba•tion•ary** *adj* — **pro•ba•tion•er** *n*

probe *n* **1 :** slender instrument for examining a cavity **2 :** investigation ~ *vb* **1 :** examine with a probe **2 :** investigate

prob•lem *n* **1 :** question to be solved **2 :** source of perplexity or vexation — **prob•lem** *adj* — **prob•lem•at•ic** *adj* — **prob•lem•at•i•cal** *adj*

pro•ce•dure *n* **1 :** way of doing something **2 :** series of steps in regular order — **pro•ce•dur•al** *adj*

pro•ceed *vb* **1 :** come forth **2 :** go on in an orderly way **3 :** begin and carry on an action **4 :** advance

pro•ceeds *n pl* **:** total money taken in

pro•cess *n* **1 :** something going on **2 :** natural phenomenon marked by gradual changes **3 :** series of actions or operations directed toward a result **4 :** summons **5 :** projecting part ~ *vb* **:** subject to a process — **pro•ces•sor** *n*

pro•ces•sion *n* **:** group moving along in an orderly way

pro•claim *vb* **:** announce publicly or with conviction — **proc•la•ma•tion** *n*

pro•cras•ti•nate *vb* **:** put something off until later — **pro•cras•ti•na•tion** *n* — **pro•cras•ti•na•tor** *n*

pro•cure *vb* **:** get possession of — **pro•cur•able** *adj* — **pro•cure•ment** *n* — **pro•cur•er** *n*

prod *vb* **:** push with or as if with a pointed instrument — **prod** *n*

prod•i•gal *adj* **:** recklessly extravagant or wasteful — **prodigal** *n* — **prod•i•gal•i•ty** *n*

prod•i•gy *n* **:** extraordinary person or thing

pro•duce *vb* **1 :** present to view **2 :** give birth to **3 :** bring into existence ~ *n* **1 :** product **2 :** agricultural products — **pro•duc•er** *n*

prod•uct *n* **1 :** number resulting from multiplication **2 :** something produced

pro•duc•tion *n* **:** act, process, or result of producing — **pro•duc•tive** *adj* — **pro•duc•tive•ness** *n* — **pro•duc•tiv•i•ty** *n*

pro•fane *vb* **:** treat with irreverence ~ *adj* **1 :** not concerned with religion **2 :** serving to debase what is holy — **pro•fane•ly** *adv* — **pro•fane•ness** *n* — **pro•fan•i•ty** *n*

pro•fes•sion *n* **1 :** open declaration of belief **2 :** occupation requiring specialized knowledge and academic training

pro•fes•sion•al *adj* **1 :** of, relating to, or engaged in a profession **2 :** playing sport for pay — **pro•fes•sion•al** *n* — **pro•fes•sion•al•ism** *n* — **pro•fes•sion•al•ize** *vb* — **pro•fes•sion•al•ly** *adv*

pro•fes•sor *n* **:** university or college teacher — **pro•fes•so•ri•al** *adj* — **pro•fes•sor•ship** *n*

pro•fi•cient *adj* **:** very good at something — **pro•fi•cien•cy** *n* — **proficient** *n* — **pro•fi•cient•ly** *adv*

pro•file *n* **:** picture in outline — **profile** *vb*

prof•it *n* **1 :** valuable return **2 :** excess of the selling price of goods over cost ~ *vb* **:** gain a profit — **prof•it•able** *adj* — **prof•it•ably** *adv* — **prof•it•less** *adj*

pro•found *adj* **1 :** marked by intellectual depth or insight **2 :** deeply felt — **pro•found•ly** *adv* — **pro•fun•di•ty** *n*

prog•no•sis *n* **:** prospect of recovery from disease

pro•gram *n* **1 :** outline of the order to be pursued or the subjects included (as in a performance) **2 :** plan of procedure **3 :** coded instructions for a computer ~ *vb* **1 :** enter in a program **2 :** provide a computer with a program — **pro•gram•ma•bil•i•ty** *n* — **pro•gram•ma•ble** *adj* — **pro•gram•mer** *n*

prog•ress *n* **:** movement forward or to a better condition ~ *vb* **1 :** move forward **2 :** improve — **pro•gres•sion** *n* — **pro•gres•sive** *adj* — **pro•gres•sive•ly** *adv*

pro•hib•it *vb* **:** prevent by authority — **pro•hi•bi•tion** *n* — **pro•hi•bi•tion•ist** *n* — **pro•hib•i•tive** *adj* — **pro•hib•i•tive•ly** *adv* — **pro•hib•i•to•ry** *adj*

proj•ect *n* **:** planned undertaking ~ *vb* **1 :** design or plan **2 :** protrude **3 :** throw forward — **pro•jec•tion** *n*

pro•jec•tor *n* **:** device for projecting pictures on a screen

pro•le•tar•i•at *n* **:** laboring class

pro•lif•er•ate *vb* **:** grow or increase in number rapidly — **pro•lif•er•a•tion** *n*

pro•lif•ic *adj* **:** producing abundantly — **pro•lif•i•cal•ly** *adv*

pro•logue *n* **:** preface

pro•long *vb* **:** lengthen in time or extent — **pro•lon•ga•tion** *n*

prom *n* **:** formal school dance

prom•e•nade *n* **1 :** leisurely walk **2 :** place for strolling — **promenade** *vb*

prom•i•nence *n* **1 :** quality, state, or fact of being readily noticeable or distinguished **2 :** something that stands out — **prom•i•nent** *adj* — **prom•i•nent•ly** *adv*

prom•ise *n* **1 :** statement that one will do or not do something **2 :** basis for expectation — **prom•ise** *vb* — **prom•is•so•ry** *adj*

prom•is•ing *adj* **:** likely to succeed — **prom•is•ing•ly** *adv*

pro•mote *vb* **1 :** advance in rank **2 :** contribute to the growth, development, or prosperity of — **pro•mot•er** *n* — **pro•mo•tion** *n* — **pro•mo•tion•al** *adj*

[1]**prompt** *vb* **1 :** incite **2 :** give a cue to (an actor or singer) — **prompt•er** *n*

[2]**prompt** *adj* **:** ready and quick — **prompt•ly** *adv* — **prompt•ness** *n*

prone *adj* **1 :** having a tendency **2 :** lying face downward — **prone•ness** *n*

pro•noun *n* **:** word used as a substitute for a noun

pro•nounce *vb* **1 :** utter officially or as an opinion **2 :** say or speak esp. correctly — **pro•nounce•able** *adj* — **pro•nounce•ment** *n* — **pro•nun•ci•a•tion** *n*

proof *n* **1 :** evidence of a truth or fact **2 :** trial impression or print

prop *vb* **1 :** support **2 :** sustain — **prop** *n*

pro•pa•gan•da *n* **:** the spreading of ideas or information to further or damage a cause — **pro•pa•gan•dist** *n* — **pro•pa•gan•dize** *vb*

prop•a•gate *vb* **1 :** reproduce biologically **2 :** cause to spread — **prop•a•ga•tion** *n*

pro•pel *vb* **:** drive forward — **pro•pel•lant, pro•pel•lent** *n or adj*

pro•pel•ler *n* **:** hub with revolving blades that propels a craft

prop•er *adj* **1 :** suitable or right **2 :** limited to a specified thing **3 :** correct **4 :** strictly adhering to standards of social manners, dignity, or good taste — **prop•er•ly** *adv*

prop•er•ty *n* **1 :** quality peculiar to an individual **2 :** something owned **3 :** piece of real estate **4 :** ownership

proph•et *n* **:** one who utters revelations or predicts events — **proph•e•cy** *n* — **proph•et•ess** *n* — **pro•phet•ic** *adj* — **pro•phet•i•cal•ly** *adv*

pro•por•tion *n* **1 :** relation of one part to another or to the whole with respect to magnitude, quantity, or degree **2 :** symmetry **3 :** share ~ *vb* **:** adjust in size in relation to others — **pro•por•tion•al** *adj* — **pro•por•tion•al•ly** *adv* — **pro•por•tion•ate** *adj* — **pro•por•tion•ate•ly** *adv*

pro•pose *vb* **1 :** plan or intend **2 :** make an offer of marriage **3 :** present for consideration — **pro•pos•al** *n* — **prop•o•si•tion** *n*

pro•pri•etor *n* **:** owner — **pro•pri•etary** *adj* — **pro•pri•etor•ship** *n* — **pro•pri•etress** *n* — **pro•pri•ety** *n*

pro•pul•sion *n* **1 :** action of propelling **2 :** driving power — **pro•pul•sive** *adj*

pro•scribe *vb* **:** prohibit — **pro•scrip•tion** *n*

prose *n* **:** ordinary language

pros•e•cute *vb* **1 :** follow to the end **2 :** seek legal punishment of — **pros•e•cu•tion** *n* — **pros•e•cu•tor** *n*

pros•pect *n* **1 :** extensive view **2 :** something awaited **3 :** potential buyer ~ *vb* **:** look for mineral deposits — **pro•spec•tive** *adj* — **pro•spec•tive•ly** *adv* — **pros•pec•tor** *n*

pros•per *vb* **:** thrive or succeed — **pros•per•ous** *adj*

pros•per•i•ty *n* **:** economic well-being

pros•trate *adj* **:** stretched out with face on the ground ~ *vb* **1 :** fall or throw (oneself) into a prostrate position **2 :** reduce to helplessness — **pros•tra•tion** *n*

pro•tect *vb* **:** shield from injury — **pro•tec•tion** *n* — **pro•tec•tive** *adj* — **pro•tec•tor** *n*

pro•tein *n* **:** complex combination of amino acids present in living matter

pro•test *n* **1 :** organized public demonstration of disapproval **2 :** strong objection ~ *vb* **1 :** assert positively **2 :** object strongly — **pro•tes•ta•tion** *n* — **pro•test•er, pro•tes•tor** *n*

Prot•es•tant *n* **:** Christian not of a Catholic or Orthodox church — **Prot•es•tant•ism** *n*

pro•to•type *n* **:** original model

pro•trac•tor *n* **:** instrument for drawing and measuring angles

pro•trude *vb* **:** stick out or cause to stick out — **pro•tru•sion** *n*

pro•tu•ber•ance *n* **:** something that protrudes — **pro•tu•ber•ant** *adj*

proud *adj* **1 :** having or showing excessive self-esteem **2 :** highly pleased **3 :** having proper self-respect **4 :** glorious — **proud•ly** *adv*

prove *vb* (**proved; proved/prov•en**) **1 :** test by experiment or by a standard **2 :** establish the truth of by argument or evidence **3 :** turn out esp. after trial or test — **prov•able** *adj*

prov•erb *n* **:** short meaningful popular saying — **pro•ver•bi•al** *adj*

pro•vide *vb* **1 :** take measures beforehand **2 :** make a stipulation **3 :** supply what is needed — **pro•vid•er** *n*

prov•i•dence *n* **1** *often cap* **:** divine guidance **2** *cap* **:** God **3 :** quality of being provident

prov•i•dent *adj* **1 :** making provision for the future **2 :** thrifty — **prov•i•dent•ly** *adv*

prov•ince *n* **1 :** administrative district **2** *pl* **:** all of a country outside the metropolis **3 :** sphere

pro•vin•cial *adj* **1 :** relating to a province **2 :** limited in outlook — **pro•vin•cial•ism** *n*

pro•vi•sion *n* **1 :** act of providing **2 :** stock of food — usu. in pl. **3 :** stipulation ~ *vb* **:** supply with provisions

pro•vi•sion•al *adj* **:** provided for a temporary need — **pro•vi•sion•al•ly** *adv*

pro•voke *vb* **1 :** incite to anger **2 :** stir up on purpose — **prov•o•ca•tion** *n* — **pro•voc•a•tive** *adj*

prowl *vb* **:** roam about stealthily — **prowl** *n* — **prowl•er** *n*

prox•im•i•ty *n* **:** nearness

proxy *n* **:** authority to act for another — **proxy** *adj*

prude *n* **:** one who shows extreme modesty — **prud•ery** *n* — **prud•ish** *adj*

pru•dent *adj* **1 :** shrewd **2 :** cautious **3 :** thrifty — **pru•dence** *n* — **pru•den•tial** *adj* — **pru•dent•ly** *adv*

¹prune *n* **:** dried plum

²prune *vb* **:** cut off unwanted parts

¹pry *vb* **:** look closely or inquisitively

²pry *vb* **:** raise, move, or pull apart with a lever

psalm *n* **:** sacred song or poem — **psalm•ist** *n*

psy•che *n* **:** soul or mind

psy•chi•a•try *n* **:** branch of medicine dealing

with mental, emotional, and behavioral disorders — **psy·chi·at·ric** *adj* — **psy·chi·a·trist** *n*

psy·chic *adj* **1 :** relating to the psyche **2 :** sensitive to supernatural forces ~ *n* **:** person sensitive to supernatural forces — **psy·chi·cal·ly** *adv*

psy·chol·o·gy *n* **1 :** science of mind and behavior **2 :** mental and behavioral aspect (as of an individual) — **psy·cho·log·i·cal** *adj* — **psy·cho·log·i·cal·ly** *adv* — **psy·chol·o·gist** *n*

pub·lic *adj* **1 :** relating to the people as a whole **2 :** civic **3 :** not private **4 :** open to all **5 :** well-known ~ *n* **:** people as a whole — **pub·lic·ly** *adv*

pub·lic·i·ty *n* **1 :** news information given out to gain public attention **2 :** public attention

pub·li·cize *vb* **:** bring to public attention — **pub·li·cist** *n*

pub·lish *vb* **1 :** announce publicly **2 :** reproduce for sale esp. by printing — **pub·li·ca·tion** *n* — **pub·lish·er** *n*

pud·ding *n* **:** creamy dessert

pud·dle *n* **:** very small pool of water

puff *vb* **1 :** blow in short gusts **2 :** pant **3 :** enlarge ~ *n* **1 :** short discharge (as of air) **2 :** slight swelling **3 :** something light and fluffy — **puffy** *adj*

puke *vb* **:** vomit — **puke** *n*

pull *vb* **1 :** exert force so as to draw (something) toward or out **2 :** move **3 :** stretch or tear ~ *n* **1 :** act of pulling **2 :** influence **3 :** device for pulling something — **pull·er** *n*

pul·ley *n* **:** wheel with a grooved rim

pulp *n* **1 :** soft part of a fruit or vegetable **2 :** soft moist mass (as of mashed wood) — **pulpy** *adj*

pul·pit *n* **:** raised desk used in preaching

pul·sate *vb* **:** expand and contract rhythmically — **pul·sa·tion** *n*

pulse *n* **:** arterial throbbing caused by heart contractions — **pulse** *vb*

pul·ver·ize *vb* **:** beat or grind into a powder

pum·mel *vb* **:** beat

[1]**pump** *n* **:** device for moving or compressing fluids ~ *vb* **1 :** raise (as water) with a pump **2 :** fill by means of a pump — with *up* **3 :** move like a pump — **pump·er** *n*

[2]**pump** *n* **:** woman's low shoe

pump·kin *n* **:** large usu. orange fruit of a vine related to the gourd

pun *n* **:** humorous use of a word in a way that suggests two or more interpretations — **pun** *vb*

[1]**punch** *vb* **1 :** strike with the fist **2 :** perforate with a punch ~ *n* **:** quick blow with the fist — **punch·er** *n*

[2]**punch** *n* **:** mixed beverage often including fruit juice

punc·tu·al *adj* **:** prompt — **punc·tu·al·i·ty** *n* — **punc·tu·al·ly** *adv*

punc·tu·ate *vb* **:** mark with symbols to clarify meaning — **punc·tu·a·tion** *n*

punc·ture *n* **:** act or result of puncturing ~ *vb* **:** make a hole in

pun·gent *adj* **:** having a sharp or stinging odor or taste — **pun·gen·cy** *n* — **pun·gent·ly** *adv*

pun·ish *vb* **:** impose a penalty on or for — **pun·ish·able** *adj* — **pun·ish·ment** *n*

punt *vb* **:** kick a ball dropped from the hands ~ *n* **:** act of punting a ball

pu·ny *adj* **:** slight in power or size

pup *n* **:** young dog

[1]**pu·pil** *n* **:** young person in school

[2]**pu·pil** *n* **:** dark central opening of the iris of the eye

pup·pet *n* **:** small doll moved by hand or by strings — **pup·pe·teer** *n*

pup·py *n* **:** young dog

pur·chase *vb* **:** obtain in exchange for money ~ *n* **1 :** act of purchasing **2 :** something purchased **3 :** secure grasp — **pur·chas·er** *n*

pure *adj* **:** free of foreign matter, contamination, or corruption — **pure·ly** *adv*

purge *vb* **1 :** purify esp. from sin **2 :** have or cause emptying of the bowels **3 :** get rid of ~ *n* **1 :** act or result of purging **2 :** something that purges — **pur·ga·tive** *adj or n*

pu·ri·fy *vb* **:** make or become pure — **pu·ri·fi·ca·tion** *n* — **pu·ri·fi·er** *n*

Pu·rim *n* **:** Jewish holiday celebrated in February or March in commemoration of the deliverance of the Jews from the massacre plotted by Haman

pu·ri·ty *n* **:** quality or state of being pure

pur·ple *n* **:** bluish red color — **pur·plish** *adj*

pur·pose *n* **1 :** something (as a result) aimed at **2 :** resolution ~ *vb* **:** intend — **pur·pose·ful** *adj* — **pur·pose·ful·ly** *adv* — **pur·pose·less** *adj* — **pur·pose·ly** *adv*

purse *n* **1 :** bag or pouch for money and small objects **2 :** financial resource **3 :** prize money

pur·su·ant to *prep* **:** according to

pur·sue *vb* **1 :** follow in order to overtake **2**

: seek to accomplish **3 :** proceed along **4 :** engage in — **pur·su·er** *n*

pur·suit *n* **1 :** act of pursuing **2 :** occupation

pur·vey *vb* **:** supply (as provisions) usu. as a business — **pur·vey·or** *n*

push *vb* **1 :** press against to move forward **2 :** urge on or provoke ~ *n* **1 :** vigorous effort **2 :** act of pushing — **push·cart** *n* — **push·er** *n*

pushy *adj* **:** objectionably aggressive

put *vb* (**put; put**) **1 :** bring to a specified position or condition **2 :** subject to pain, suffering, or death **3 :** impose or cause to exist **4 :** express **5 :** cause to be used or employed — **put off** *vb* **:** postpone or delay — **put out** *vb* **:** bother or inconvenience — **put up** *vb* **1 :** prepare for storage **2 :** lodge **3 :** contribute or pay — **put up with :** endure

pu·tre·fy *vb* **:** make or become rotten — **pu·tre·fac·tion** *n* — **pu·trid** *adj* — **pu·trid·i·ty** *n*

puz·zle *vb* **1 :** confuse **2 :** attempt to solve — used with *out* or *over* ~ *n* **:** something that confuses or tests ingenuity — **puz·zle·ment** *n* — **puz·zler** *n*

pyg·my *n* **:** dwarf — **pyg·my** *adj*

py·lon *n* **:** tower or tall post

pyr·a·mid *n* **:** structure with a square base and 4 triangular sides meeting at a point

py·ro·ma·nia *n* **:** irresistible impulse to start fires — **py·ro·ma·ni·ac** *n*

py·ro·tech·nics *n pl* **:** spectacular display (as of fireworks) — **py·ro·tech·nic** *adj*

Q

q *n* **:** 17th letter of the alphabet

[1]**quack** *vb* **:** make a cry like that of a duck — **quack** *n*

[2]**quack** *n* **:** one who pretends to have medical or healing skill — **quack** *adj* — **quack·ery** *n*

quad·ran·gle *n* **:** rectangular courtyard

quad·ri·lat·er·al *n* **:** 4-sided polygon

quad·ru·ped *n* **:** animal having 4 feet

qua·dru·ple *vb* **:** multiply by 4 ~ *adj* **:** being 4 times as great or as many

qua·dru·plet *n* **:** one of 4 offspring born at one birth

quail *n* (**quail**) **:** short-winged plump game bird

quaint *adj* **:** pleasingly old-fashioned or odd — **quaint·ly** *adv* — **quaint·ness** *n*

quake *vb* **:** shake or tremble ~ *n* **:** earthquake

qual·i·fy *vb* **1 :** modify or limit **2 :** fit by skill or training for some purpose **3 :** become eligible — **qual·i·fi·ca·tion** *n* — **qual·i·fied** *adj* — **qual·i·fi·er** *n*

qual·i·ty *n* **1 :** peculiar and essential character, nature, or feature **2 :** excellence or distinction

quan·ti·ty *n* **1 :** something that can be measured or numbered **2 :** considerable amount

quar·an·tine *n* **1 :** restraint on the movements of persons or goods to prevent the spread of pests or disease **2 :** place or period of quarantine — **quarantine** *vb*

quar·rel *n* **:** basis of conflict — **quarrel** *vb* — **quar·rel·some** *adj*

[1]**quar·ry** *n* **:** prey

[2]**quar·ry** *n* **:** excavation for obtaining stone — **quar·ry** *vb*

quart *n* **:** unit of liquid measure equal to .95 liter or of dry measure equal to 1.10 liters

quar·ter *n* **1 :** $\frac{1}{4}$ part **2 :** $\frac{1}{4}$ of a dollar **3 :** city district **4** *pl* **:** place to live esp. for a time **5 :** mercy ~ *vb* **:** divide into 4 equal parts

quar·ter·ly *adv or adj* **:** at 3-month intervals ~ *n* **:** periodical published 4 times a year

quar·tet *n* **1 :** music for 4 performers **2 :** group of 4

quay *n* **:** wharf

quea·sy *adj* **:** nauseated — **quea·si·ly** *adv* — **quea·si·ness** *n*

queen *n* **1 :** wife or widow of a king **2 :** female monarch **3 :** woman of rank, power, or attractiveness **4 :** fertile female of a social insect — **queen·ly** *adj*

queer *adj* **:** differing from the usual or normal — **queer·ly** *adv* — **queer·ness** *n*

quench *vb* **1 :** put out **2 :** satisfy (a thirst) — **quench·able** *adj* — **quench·er** *n*

que·ry *n* **:** question — **que·ry** *vb*

quest *n or vb* **:** search

ques·tion *n* **1 :** something asked **2 :** subject for debate **3 :** dispute ~ *vb* **1 :** ask questions **2 :** doubt or dispute **3 :** subject to analysis — **ques·tion·er** *n*

ques·tion·able *adj* **1 :** not certain **2 :** of doubtful truth or morality — **ques·tion·ably** *adv*

ques·tion·naire *n* **:** set of questions

queue *n* **1 :** braid of hair **2 :** a waiting line ~ *vb* **:** line up

quib•ble *n* : minor objection — **quib•ble** *vb* — **quib•bler** *n*

quick *adj* **1 :** rapid **2 :** alert or perceptive ~ *n* : sensitive area of living flesh — **quick** *adv* — **quick•ly** *adv* — **quick•ness** *n*

quick•en *vb* **1 :** come to life **2 :** increase in speed

qui•et *adj* **1 :** marked by little motion or activity **2 :** gentle **3 :** free from noise **4 :** not showy **5 :** isolated ~ *vb* : pacify — **quiet** *adv or n* — **qui•et•ly** *adv* — **qui•et•ness** *n*

quilt *n* : padded bedspread ~ *vb* : stitch or sew in layers with padding in between

quin•tet *n* **1 :** music for 5 performers **2 :** group of 5

quin•tu•ple *adj* **1 :** having 5 units or members **2 :** being 5 times as great or as many — **quintuple** *n or vb*

quip *vb* : make a clever remark — **quip** *n*

quirk *n* : peculiarity of action or behavior — **quirky** *adj*

quit *vb* **quit; quit 1 :** stop **2 :** leave — **quitter** *n*

quite *adv* **1 :** completely **2 :** to a considerable extent

quiv•er *vb* : shake or tremble — **quiv•er** *n*

quiz *n* : short test ~ *vb* : question closely

quiz•zi•cal *adj* **1 :** teasing **2 :** curious

quo•rum *n* : required number of members present

quo•ta *n* : proportional part or share

quote *vb* **1 :** repeat (another's words) exactly **2 :** state (a price) — **quot•able** *adj* — **quo•ta•tion** *n* — **quote** *n*

quo•tient *n* : number obtained from division

R

r *n* : 18th letter of the alphabet

rab•bet *n* : groove in a board

rab•bi *n* : Jewish religious leader — **rab•bin•ate** *n* — **rab•bin•ic, rab•bin•i•cal** *adj*

rab•bit *n* : long-eared burrowing mammal

ra•bid *adj* **1 :** violent **2 :** fanatical **3 :** affected with rabies — **ra•bid•ly** *adv*

ra•bies *n* : acute deadly virus disease

rac•coon *n* : tree-dwelling mammal with a black mask and a bushy ringed tail

[1]race *n* **1 :** strong current of water **2 :** contest of speed **3 :** election campaign ~ *vb* **1 :** run in a race **2 :** rush — **race•course** *n* — **race•horse** *n* — **rac•er** *n* — **race•track** *n*

[2]race *n* **1 :** family, tribe, people, or nation of the same stock **2 :** division of mankind based on hereditary traits — **ra•cial** *adj* — **ra•cial•ly** *adv*

rac•ism *n* : discrimination based on the belief that some races are by nature superior — **rac•ist** *n*

rack *n* **1 :** framework for display or storage **2 :** instrument that stretches the body for torture ~ *vb* : torture with or as if with a rack

[1]rack•et *n* : bat with a tight netting across an open frame

[2]racket *n* **1 :** confused noise **2 :** fraudulent scheme — **rack•e•teer** *n* — **rack•e•teer•ing** *n*

racy *adj* : being or bordering on being highly improper or offensive — **rac•i•ly** *adv* — **rac•i•ness** *n*

ra•dar *n* : radio device for determining distance and direction of distant objects

ra•di•ant *adj* **1 :** glowing **2 :** beaming with happiness **3 :** transmitted by radiation — **ra•di•ance** *n* — **ra•di•ant•ly** *adv*

ra•di•ate *vb* **1 :** issue rays or in rays **2 :** spread from a center — **ra•di•a•tion** *n*

ra•di•a•tor *n* : cooling or heating device

rad•i•cal *adj* **1 :** fundamental **2 :** extreme ~ *n* : person favoring extreme changes — **rad•i•cal•ism** *n* — **rad•i•cal•ly** *adv*

radii *pl of* RADIUS

ra•dio *n* **1 :** wireless transmission or reception of sound by means of electric waves **2 :** radio receiving set ~ *vb* : send a message to by radio — **radio** *adj*

ra•dio•ac•tiv•i•ty *n* : property of an element that emits energy through nuclear disintegration — **ra•dio•ac•tive** *adj*

rad•ish *n* : pungent fleshy root usu. eaten raw

ra•di•us (**ra•dii**) *n* **1 :** line from the center of a circle or sphere to the circumference or surface **2 :** area defined by a radius

[1]raft *n* : flat floating platform ~ *vb* : travel or transport by raft

[2]raft *n* : large amount or number

raf•ter *n* : beam supporting a roof

rag *n* : waste piece of cloth

rage *n* **1 :** violent anger **2 :** state of being currently widely popular ~ *vb* **1 :** be extremely angry or violent **2 :** be out of control

rag•ged *adj* : torn — **rag•ged•ly** *adv* — **rag•ged•ness** *n*

raid *n* : sudden usu. surprise attack — **raid** *vb* — **raid•er** *n*

rail *n* **1** : bar serving as a guard or barrier **2** : bar forming a track for wheeled vehicles **3** : railroad

rail•ing *n* : rail or a barrier of rails

rail•road *n* : road for a train laid with iron rails and wooden ties ~ *vb* : force something hastily — **rail•road•er** *n* — **rail•road•ing** *n*

rain **1** : water falling in drops from the clouds **2** : shower of objects ~ *vb* : fall as or like rain — **rain•bow** *n* — **rain•coat** *n* — **rain•drop** *n* — **rain•fall** *n* — **rain•mak•er** *n* — **rain•mak•ing** *n* — **rain•storm** *n* — **rain•water** *n* — **rainy** *adj*

raise *vb* **1** : lift **2** : arouse **3** : erect **4** : collect **5** : breed, grow, or bring up **6** : increase **7** : make light ~ *n* : increase esp. in pay — **rais•er** *n*

rai•sin *n* : dried grape

rake *n* : garden tool for smoothing or sweeping ~ *vb* **1** : gather, loosen, or smooth with or as if with a rake **2** : sweep with gunfire

ral•ly *vb* **1** : bring or come together **2** : revive or recover **3** : make a comeback ~ *n* **1** : act of rallying **2** : mass meeting

ram *n* **1** : male sheep **2** : beam used in battering down walls or doors ~ *vb* **1** : force or drive in or through **2** : strike against violently

RAM *n* : main internal storage area in a computer

ram•ble *vb* : wander — **ram•ble** *n* — **ram•bler** *n*

ramp *n* : sloping passage or connecting roadway

ram•page *vb* : rush about wildly ~ *n* : violent or riotous action or behavior

ran *past of* RUN

ranch *n* **1** : establishment for the raising of cattle, sheep, or horses **2** : specialized farm ~ *vb* : operate a ranch — **ranch•er** *n*

ran•cid *adj* : smelling or tasting as if spoiled — **ran•cid•i•ty** *n*

ran•dom *adj* : occurring by chance — **ran•dom•ize** *vb* — **ran•dom•ly** *adv* — **ran•dom•ness** *n* — **at random** : without definite aim or method

rang *past of* RING

range *n* **1** : series of things in a row **2** : open land for grazing **3** : cooking stove **4** : variation within limits **5** : place for target practice **6** : extent ~ *vb* **1** : arrange **2** : roam at large, freely, or over **3** : vary within limits

rang•er *n* : officer who manages and protects public lands

rank *n* **1** : line of soldiers **2** : orderly arrangement **3** : grade of official standing **4** : position within a group ~ *vb* **1** : arrange in formation or according to class **2** : take or have a relative position

ran•sack *vb* : search through and rob

ran•som *n* : something demanded for the freedom of a captive ~ *vb* : gain the freedom of by paying a price — **ran•som•er** *n*

rant *vb* : talk or scold violently — **rant•er** *n* — **rant•ing•ly** *adv*

¹rap *n* : sharp blow or rebuke ~ *vb* : strike or criticize sharply

²rap *vb* : talk freely

rape *vb* : force to have sexual intercourse — **rape** *n* — **rap•er** *n* — **rap•ist** *n*

rap•id *adj* : very fast — **ra•pid•i•ty** *n* — **rap•id•ly** *adv*

rap•ture *n* : spiritual or emotional ecstasy — **rap•tur•ous** *adj* — **rap•tur•ous•ly** *adv*

¹rare *adj* : having a portion relatively uncooked

²rare *adj* **1** : not dense **2** : unusually fine **3** : seldom met with — **rare•ly** *adv* — **rare•ness** *n* — **rar•i•ty** *n*

ras•cal *n* : mean, dishonest, or mischievous person — **ras•cal•i•ty** *n* — **ras•cal•ly** *adj*

¹rash *adj* : too hasty in decision or action — **rash•ly** *adv* — **rash•ness** *n*

²rash *n* : a breaking out of the skin with red spots

rasp *vb* **1** : rub with or as if with a rough file **2** : speak in a grating tone ~ *n* : coarse file

rasp•ber•ry *n* : edible red or black berry

rat *n* : destructive rodent larger than the mouse ~ *vb* : betray or inform on

rate *n* **1** : quantity, amount, or degree measured in relation to some other quantity **2** : rank ~ *vb* **1** : estimate or determine the rank or quality of **2** : deserve — **rat•ing** *n*

rath•er *adv* **1** : preferably **2** : on the other hand **3** : more properly **4** : somewhat

rat•i•fy *vb* : approve and accept formally — **rat•i•fi•ca•tion** *n*

ra•tio *n* : relation in number, quantity, or degree between things

ra•tion *n* : share or allotment (as of food) ~ *vb* : use or allot sparingly

ra•tio•nal *adj* **1** : having reason or sanity **2** : relating to reason — **ra•tio•nal•ly** *adv*

ra•tio•nale *n* **1 :** explanation of principles of belief or practice **2 :** underlying reason

ra•tio•nal•ize *vb* **:** justify (as one's behavior or weaknesses) esp. to oneself — **ra•tio•nal•i•za•tion** *n*

rat•tle *vb* **1 :** make a series of clattering sounds **2 :** say briskly **3 :** confuse or upset ~ *n* **1 :** series of clattering sounds **2 :** something (as a toy) that rattles

rat•ty *adj* **:** shabby

rave *vb* **1 :** talk wildly in or as if in delirium **2 :** talk with extreme enthusiasm ~ *n* **1 :** act of raving **2 :** enthusiastic praise

rav•el *vb* **1 :** have threads become separated **2 :** tangle ~ *n* **1 :** something tangled **2 :** loose thread

raw *adj* **1 :** not cooked **2 :** not processed **3 :** not trained **4 :** having the surface rubbed off **5 :** cold and damp **6 :** vulgar — **raw•ness** *n*

ray *n* **1 :** thin beam of radiant energy (as light) **2 :** tiny bit

ray•on *n* **:** fabric made from cellulose fiber

ra•zor *n* **:** sharp cutting instrument used to shave off hair

reach *vb* **1 :** stretch out **2 :** touch or try to touch or grasp **3 :** extend to or arrive at **4 :** communicate with ~ *n* **1 :** act of reaching **2 :** distance one can reach **3 :** ability to reach — **reach•able** *adj* — **reach•er** *n*

re•act *vb* **1 :** act in response to some influence or stimulus **2 :** undergo chemical change — **re•ac•tion** *n* — **re•ac•tion•ary** *adj or n* — **re•ac•tive** *adj* — **re•ac•tor** *n*

read *vb* **1 :** understand written language **2 :** utter aloud printed words **3 :** interpret **4 :** study **5 :** indicate ~ *adj* **:** informed by reading — **read•a•bil•i•ty** *n* — **read•able** *adj* — **read•ably** *adv* — **read•er** *n* — **read•er•ship** *n* — **read•ing** *n*

ready *adj* **1 :** prepared or available for use or action **2 :** willing to do something ~ *vb* **:** make ready ~ *n* **:** state of being ready — **read•i•ly** *adv* — **read•i•ness** *n*

re•al *adj* **1 :** relating to fixed or immovable things (as land) **2 :** genuine **3 :** not imaginary ~ *adv* **:** very — **re•al•ness** *n* — **for real 1 :** in earnest **2 :** genuine — **re•al•i•ty** *n* — **re•al•ly** *adv*

real estate *n* **:** property in houses and land

re•al•ism *n* **1 :** disposition to deal with facts practically **2 :** faithful portrayal of reality — **re•al•ist** *adj or n* — **re•al•is•tic** *adj* — **re•al•is•ti•cal•ly** *adv*

re•al•ize *vb* **1 :** make actual **2 :** obtain **3 :** be aware of — **re•al•iz•able** *adj* — **re•al•i•za•tion** *n*

reap *vb* **:** cut or clear (as a crop) with a scythe or machine — **reap•er** *n*

[1]rear *vb* **1 :** raise upright **2 :** breed or bring up **3 :** rise on the hind legs

[2]rear *n* **1 :** back **2 :** position at the back of something ~ *adj* **:** being at the back — **rear•ward** *adj or adv*

rea•son *n* **1 :** explanation or justification **2 :** motive for action or belief **3 :** power or process of thinking ~ *vb* **1 :** use the faculty of reason **2 :** try to persuade another — **rea•son•er** *n* — **rea•son•ing** *n*

rea•son•able *adj* **1 :** being within the bounds of reason **2 :** not expensive — **rea•son•able•ness** *n* — **rea•son•ably** *adv*

re•bate *n* **:** return of part of a payment — **re•bate** *vb*

reb•el *n* **:** one that resists authority ~ *vb* **1 :** resist authority **2 :** feel or exhibit anger — **reb•el** *adj* — **re•bel•lion** *n* — **re•bel•lious** *adj* — **re•bel•lious•ly** *adv* — **re•bel•lious•ness** *n*

re•bound *vb* **1 :** spring back on striking something **2 :** recover from a reverse ~ *n* **1 :** action of rebounding **2 :** reaction to a reverse

re•buke *vb* **:** criticize sharply

re•call *vb* **1 :** call back **2 :** remember **3 :** revoke ~ *n* **1 :** a summons to return **2 :** remembrance **3 :** act of revoking

re•cede *vb* **1 :** move back or away **2 :** slant backward

re•ceipt *n* **1 :** act of receiving **2 :** something (as payment) received — usu. in pl. **3 :** writing acknowledging something received

re•ceive *vb* **1 :** take in or accept **2 :** greet or entertain (visitors) **3 :** pick up radio waves and convert into sounds or pictures — **re•ceiv•able** *adj* — **re•ceiv•er** *n*

re•cent *adj* **1 :** having lately come into existence **2 :** of the present time or time just past — **re•cent•ly** *adv* — **re•cent•ness** *n*

re•cep•ta•cle *n* **:** container

re•cep•tion *n* **1 :** act of receiving **2 :** social gathering at which guests are formally welcomed

re•cep•tion•ist *n* **:** person employed to greet callers

re•cep•tive *adj* **:** open and responsive to ideas, impressions, or suggestions — **re•cep•tive•ly** *adv* — **re•cep•tive•ness** *n* — **re•cep•tiv•i•ty** *n*

re•cess *n* **1 :** indentation in a line or surface **2 :** suspension of a session for rest ~ *vb* **1 :** make a recess in or put into a recess **2 :** interrupt a session for a recess

re•ces•sion *n* **1 :** departing procession **2 :** period of reduced economic activity

rec•i•pe *n* **:** instructions for making something

re•cip•i•ent *n* **:** one that receives

re•cip•ro•cal *adj* **1 :** affecting each in the same way **2 :** so related that one is equivalent to the other — **re•cip•ro•cal•ly** *adv* — **re•ci•proc•i•ty** *n*

re•cip•ro•cate *vb* **:** make a return for something done or given — **re•cip•ro•ca•tion** *n*

re•cit•al *n* **1 :** public reading or recitation **2 :** music or dance concert or exhibition by pupils — **re•cit•al•ist** *n*

re•cite *vb* **1 :** repeat verbatim **2 :** recount — **rec•i•ta•tion** *n* — **re•cit•er** *n*

reck•less *adj* **:** lacking caution — **reck•less•ly** *adv* — **reck•less•ness** *n*

reck•on *vb* **1 :** count or calculate **2 :** consider — **reck•on•ing** *n*

re•claim *vb* **1 :** change to a desirable condition **2 :** obtain from a waste product or by-product **3 :** demand or obtain the return of — **re•claim•able** *adj* — **rec•la•ma•tion** *n*

re•cline *vb* **:** lean backward or lie down

rec•og•nize *vb* **1 :** identify as previously known **2 :** take notice of **3 :** acknowledge esp. with appreciation — **rec•og•ni•tion** *n* — **rec•og•niz•able** *adj* — **rec•og•niz•ably** *adv*

rec•ol•lect *vb* **:** remember

rec•ol•lec•tion *n* **1 :** act or power of recollecting **2 :** something recollected

rec•om•mend *vb* **1 :** present as deserving of acceptance or trial **2 :** advise — **rec•om•mend•able** *adj* — **rec•om•men•da•tion** *n*

rec•on•cile *vb* **1 :** cause to be friendly again **2 :** adjust or settle **3 :** bring to acceptance — **rec•on•cil•able** *adj* — **rec•on•cile•ment** *n* — **rec•on•cil•er** *n* — **rec•on•cil•i•a•tion** *n*

re•con•di•tion *vb* **:** restore to good condition

re•cord *vb* **1 :** set down in writing **2 :** register permanently **3 :** indicate **4 :** preserve (as sound or images) for later reproduction ~ *n* **1 :** something recorded **2 :** best performance — **re•cord•er** *n*

[1]re•count *vb* **:** relate in detail

[2]re•count *vb* **:** count again — **re•count** *n*

re•cov•er *vb* **1 :** regain position, poise, or health **2 :** gain compensation for a loss — **re•cov•er•able** *adj* — **re•cov•ery** *n*

rec•re•a•tion *n* **:** a refreshing of strength or spirits as a change from work or study — **rec•re•a•tion•al** *adj*

re•cruit *n* **:** newly enlisted member ~ *vb* **:** enlist the membership or services of — **re•cruit•er** *n* — **re•cruit•ment** *n*

rect•an•gle *n* **:** 4-sided figure with 4 right angles — **rect•an•gu•lar** *adj*

rec•ti•fy *vb* **:** make or set right — **rec•ti•fi•ca•tion** *n*

rec•tor *n* **:** pastor

rec•to•ry *n* **:** rector's residence

re•cu•per•ate *vb* **:** recover (as from illness) — **re•cu•per•a•tion** *n* — **re•cu•per•a•tive** *adj*

re•cur *vb* **1 :** return in thought or talk **2 :** occur again — **re•cur•rence** *n* — **re•cur•rent** *adj*

re•cy•cle *vb* **:** process (as glass or cans) in order to regain a material for human use — **re•cy•cla•ble** *adj*

red *n* **1 :** color of blood or of the ruby **2** *cap* **:** communist — **red** *adj* — **red•dish** *adj* — **red•ness** *n*

red•den *vb* **:** make or become red or reddish

re•deem *vb* **1 :** regain, free, or rescue by paying a price **2 :** atone for **3 :** free from sin **4 :** convert into something of value — **re•deem•able** *adj* — **re•deem•er** *n*

re•demp•tion *n* **:** act of redeeming — **re•demp•tive** *adj* — **re•demp•to•ry** *adj*

re•duce *vb* **1 :** lessen **2 :** put in a lower rank **3 :** lose weight — **re•duc•er** *n* — **re•duc•ible** *adj*

re•duc•tion *n* **1 :** act of reducing **2 :** amount lost in reducing **3 :** something made by reducing

re•dun•dant *adj* **:** using more words than necessary — **re•dun•dan•cy** *n* — **re•dun•dant•ly** *adv*

reed *n* **1 :** tall slender grass of wet areas **2 :** thin springy strip that vibrates to produce tones in certain wind instruments — **reedy** *adj*

reef *n* **:** ridge of rocks or sand at or near the surface of the water

reek *n* **:** strong or disagreeable fume or odor ~ *vb* **:** give off a reek

reel *n* **:** revolvable device on which something flexible is wound or a quantity of something wound on it ~ *vb* **1 :** wind on a reel **2 :** pull in by reeling — **reel•able** *adj* — **reel•er** *n*

re•fer *vb* **1 :** direct or send to some person or place **2 :** submit for consideration or action **3**

: have connection **4 :** mention or allude to something — **re·fer·able** *adj* — **re·fer·ral** *n*

ref·er·ee *n* **1 :** one to whom an issue is referred for settlement **2 :** sports official ~ *vb* : act as referee

ref·er·ence *n* **1 :** act of referring **2 :** a bearing on a matter **3 :** consultation for information **4 :** person who can speak for one's character or ability or a recommendation given by such a person

ref·er·en·dum *n* **:** a submitting of legislative measures for voters' approval or rejection

re·fill *vb* **:** fill again — **re·fill** *n* — **re·fill·able** *adj*

re·fine *vb* **1 :** free from impurities or waste matter **2 :** improve or perfect **3 :** free or become free of what is coarse or uncouth — **re·fine·ment** *n* — **re·fin·er** *n*

re·flect *vb* **1 :** bend or cast back (as light or heat) **2 :** bring as a result **3 :** cast reproach or blame **4 :** ponder — **re·flec·tion** *n* — **re·flec·tive** *adj* — **re·flec·tor** *n*

re·flex *n* **:** automatic response to a stimulus ~ *adj* **1 :** bent back **2 :** relating to a reflex — **re·flex·ly** *adv*

re·flex·ive *adj* **:** of or relating to an action directed back upon the doer or the grammatical subject — **reflexive** *n* — **re·flex·ive·ly** *adv* — **re·flex·ive·ness** *n*

re·form *vb* **:** make or become better esp. by correcting bad habits — **reform** *n* — **re·form·able** *adj* — **re·for·ma·tive** *adj* — **re·form·er** *n*

re·frac·tion *n* **:** the bending of a ray (as of light) when it passes from one medium into another — **re·frac·tive** *adj*

re·frain *vb* **:** hold oneself back ~ *n* **:** verse recurring regularly in a song — **re·frain·ment** *n*

re·fresh *vb* **1 :** make or become fresh or fresher **2 :** supply or take refreshment — **re·fresh·er** *n* — **re·fresh·ing·ly** *adv*

re·fresh·ment *n* **1 :** act of refreshing **2** *pl* **:** light meal

re·frig·er·ate *vb* **:** chill or freeze (food) for preservation — **re·frig·er·ant** *adj or n* — **re·frig·er·a·tion** *n* — **re·frig·er·a·tor** *n*

ref·uge *n* **1 :** protection from danger **2 :** place that provides protection

ref·u·gee *n* **:** person who flees for safety

re·fund *vb* **:** give or put back (money) ~ *n* **1 :** act of refunding **2 :** sum refunded — **re·fund·able** *adj*

[1]re·fuse *vb* **:** decline to accept, do, or give — **re·fus·al** *n*

[2]ref·use *n* **:** worthless matter

re·gal *adj* **1 :** befitting a king **2 :** marked by much dignity — **re·gal·ly** *adv*

re·gard *n* **1 :** consideration **2 :** feeling of approval and liking **3** *pl* **:** friendly greetings **4 :** relation ~ *vb* **1 :** pay attention to **2 :** show respect for **3 :** have an opinion of **4 :** look at **5 :** relate to — **re·gard·ful** *adj* — **re·gard·less** *adj*

re·gard·ing *prep* **:** concerning

re·gen·er·ate *adj* **1 :** formed or created again **2 :** spiritually reborn ~ *vb* **1 :** reform completely **2 :** replace (a lost body part) by new tissue growth **3 :** give new life to — **re·gen·er·a·tion** *n* — **re·gen·er·a·tive** *adj* — **re·gen·er·a·tor** *n*

re·gent *n* **1 :** person who rules during the childhood, absence, or incapacity of the sovereign **2 :** member of a governing board — **re·gen·cy** *n*

re·gime *n* **:** government in power

reg·i·men *n* **:** systematic course of treatment or training

re·gion *n* **:** indefinitely defined area — **re·gion·al** *adj* — **re·gion·al·ly** *adv*

reg·is·ter *n* **1 :** record of items or details or a book for keeping such a record **2 :** device to regulate ventilation **3 :** counting or recording device **4 :** range of a voice or instrument ~ *vb* **1 :** enter in a register **2 :** record automatically **3 :** get special care for mail by paying more postage

reg·is·tra·tion *n* **1 :** act of registering **2 :** entry in a register

reg·is·try *n* **1 :** enrollment **2 :** place of registration **3 :** official record book

re·gret *vb* **1 :** mourn the loss or death of **2 :** be very sorry for ~ *n* **1 :** sorrow or the expression of sorrow **2** *pl* **:** message declining an invitation — **re·gret·ful** *adj* — **re·gret·ful·ly** *adv* — **re·gret·ta·ble** *adj* — **re·gret·ta·bly** *adv* — **re·gret·ter** *n*

reg·u·lar *adj* **1 :** conforming to what is usual, normal, or average **2 :** steady, uniform, or unvarying — **regular** *n* — **reg·u·lar·i·ty** *n* — **reg·u·lar·ize** *vb* — **reg·u·lar·ly** *adv*

reg·u·late *vb* **1 :** govern according to rule **2 :** adjust to a standard — **reg·u·la·tion** *n* — **reg·u·la·tive** *adj* — **reg·u·la·tor** *n* — **reg·u·la·to·ry** *adj*

re·ha·bil·i·tate *vb* **1 :** restore to a previous

state or position **2 :** make good or usable again — **re•ha•bil•i•ta•tion** *n*

re•hearse *vb* **1 :** repeat or recount **2 :** engage in a practice performance of — **re•hears•al** *n* — **re•hears•er** *n*

reign *n* **:** sovereign's authority or rule ~ *vb* **:** rule as a sovereign

re•im•burse *vb* **:** repay — **re•im•burs•able** *adj* — **re•im•burse•ment** *n*

rein *n* **1 :** strap fastened to a bit to control an animal **2 :** restraining influence ~ *vb* **:** direct by reins

rein•deer *n* **:** large deer

re•in•force *vb* **:** strengthen or support — **re•in•force•ment** *n* — **re•in•forc•er** *n*

re•ject *vb* **1 :** refuse to grant or consider **2 :** refuse to admit, believe, or receive **3 :** throw out as useless or unsatisfactory ~ *n* **:** rejected person or thing — **re•jec•tion** *n*

re•joice *vb* **:** feel joy — **re•joic•er** *n*

re•join *vb* **1 :** join again **2 :** say in answer

re•ju•ve•nate *vb* **:** make young again — **re•ju•ve•na•tion** *n*

re•lapse *n* **:** recurrence of illness after a period of improvement ~ *vb* **:** suffer a relapse

re•late *vb* **1 :** give a report of **2 :** show a connection between **3 :** have a relationship — **re•lat•able** *adj* — **re•lat•er, re•la•tor** *n* — **re•la•tion** *n*

re•la•tion•ship *n* **:** state of being related or interrelated

rel•a•tive *n* **:** person connected with another by blood or marriage ~ *adj* **:** considered in comparison with something else — **rel•a•tive•ly** *adv* — **rel•a•tive•ness** *n*

re•lax *vb* **1 :** make or become less tense or rigid **2 :** make less severe **3 :** seek rest or recreation — **re•lax•er** *n*

re•lax•a•tion *n* **1 :** lessening of tension **2 :** recreation

re•lay *n* **:** fresh supply (as of horses or people) arranged to relieve others ~ *vb* **:** pass along in stages

re•lease *vb* **1 :** free from confinement or oppression **2 :** give up claim to or control over **3 :** permit publication, performance, exhibition, or sale ~ *n* **1 :** relief from trouble **2 :** discharge from an obligation **3 :** act of releasing or what is released

re•lent *vb* **:** become less severe

re•lent•less *adj* **:** mercilessly severe or persistent — **re•lent•less•ly** *adv* — **re•lent•less•ness** *n*

rel•e•vance *n* **:** relation to the matter at hand — **rel•e•vant** *adj* — **rel•e•vant•ly** *adv*

re•li•able *adj* **:** fit to be trusted — **re•li•abil•i•ty** *n* — **re•li•able•ness** *n* — **re•li•ably** *adv*

re•li•ant *adj* **:** dependent — **re•li•ance** *n*

re•lieve *vb* **1 :** free from a burden or distress **2 :** release from a post or duty **3 :** break the monotony of — **re•lief** *n* — **re•liev•er** *n*

re•li•gion *n* **1 :** service and worship of God **2 :** set or system of religious beliefs — **re•li•gion•ist** *n*

re•li•gious *adj* **1 :** relating or devoted to an ultimate reality or deity **2 :** relating to religious beliefs or observances **3 :** marked by intense feelings — **re•li•gious•ly** *adv*

rel•ish *n* **1 :** keen enjoyment **2 :** highly seasoned sauce (as of pickles) ~ *vb* **:** enjoy — **rel•ish•able** *adj*

re•luc•tant *adj* **:** feeling or showing doubt or unwillingness — **re•luc•tance** *n* — **re•luc•tant•ly** *adv*

re•ly *vb* **:** place faith or confidence — often with *on*

re•main *vb* **1 :** be left after others have been removed **2 :** be something yet to be done **3 :** stay behind **4 :** continue unchanged — **re•mains** *n* — **re•main•der** *n*

re•mark *vb* **:** express as an observation ~ *n* **:** passing comment

re•mark•able *adj* **:** extraordinary — **re•mark•able•ness** *n* — **re•mark•ably** *adv*

rem•e•dy *n* **1 :** medicine that cures **2 :** something that corrects an evil or compensates for a loss ~ *vb* **:** provide or serve as a remedy for

re•mem•ber *vb* **1 :** think of again **2 :** keep from forgetting **3 :** convey greetings from

re•mem•brance *n* **1 :** act of remembering **2 :** something that serves to bring to mind

re•mind *vb* **:** cause to remember — **re•mind•er** *n*

rem•nant *n* **:** small part or trace remaining

re•mod•el *vb* **:** alter the structure of

re•mon•strate *vb* **:** speak in protest, reproof, or opposition — **re•mon•strance** *n* — **re•mon•stra•tion** *n*

re•morse *n* **:** distress arising from a sense of guilt — **re•morse•ful** *adj* — **re•morse•less** *adj*

re•mote *adj* **1 :** far off in place or time **2 :** hard to reach or find **3 :** acting, acted on, or controlled indirectly or from afar **4 :** slight **5 :** distant in manner — **re•mote•ly** *adv* — **re•mote•ness** *n*

re•move *vb* **1 :** move by lifting or taking off or away **2 :** get rid of — **re•mov•able** *adj* — **re•mov•al** *n* — **re•mov•er** *n*
re•mu•ner•ate *vb* **:** pay — **re•mu•ner•a•tion** *n* — **re•mu•ner•a•tor** *n*
rend *vb* (**rent; rent**) **:** tear apart forcibly
ren•der *vb* **1 :** extract by heating **2 :** hand over or give up **3 :** do (a service) for another **4 :** cause to be or become
ren•dez•vous *n* **1 :** place appointed for a meeting **2 :** meeting at an appointed place ~ *vb* **:** meet at a rendezvous
ren•e•gade *n* **:** deserter of one faith or cause for another
re•new *vb* **1 :** make or become new, fresh, or strong again **2 :** begin again **3 :** grant or obtain an extension of — **re•new•able** *adj* — **re•new•al** *n* — **re•new•er** *n*
re•nounce *vb* **:** give up, refuse, or resign — **re•nounce•ment** *n*
ren•o•vate *vb* **:** make like new again — **ren•o•va•tion** *n* — **ren•o•va•tor** *n*
re•nown *n* **:** state of being widely known and honored — **renowned** *adj*
rent *n* **:** money paid or due periodically for the use of another's property ~ *vb* **:** hold or give possession and use of for rent — **rent•al** *n or adj* — **rent•er** *n*
repair *vb* **:** restore to good condition ~ *n* **1 :** act or instance of repairing **2 :** condition — **re•pair•er** *n* — **re•pair•man** *n*
re•pay *vb* **:** pay back — **re•pay•able** *adj* — **re•pay•ment** *n*
re•peal *vb* **:** annul by legislative action — **re•peal** *n* — **re•peal•er** *n*
re•peat *vb* **:** say or do again ~ *n* **1 :** act of repeating **2 :** something repeated — **re•peat•able** *adj* — **re•peat•ed•ly** *adv* — **re•peat•er** *n*
re•pel *vb* **1 :** drive away **2 :** disgust — **re•pel•lent** *adj or n*
re•pent *vb* **1 :** turn from sin **2 :** regret — **re•pen•tance** *n* — **re•pen•tant** *adj*
rep•e•ti•tion *n* **:** act or instance of repeating
rep•e•ti•tious *adj* **:** tediously repeating — **rep•e•ti•tious•ly** *adv* — **rep•e•ti•tious•ness** *n*
re•pet•i•tive *adj* **:** repetitious — **re•pet•i•tive•ly** *adv* — **re•pet•i•tive•ness** *n*
re•place *vb* **1 :** restore to a former position **2 :** take the place of **3 :** put something new in the place of — **re•place•able** *adj* — **re•place•ment** *n* — **re•plac•er** *n*
re•plen•ish *vb* **:** stock or supply anew — **re•plen•ish•ment** *n*
rep•li•ca *n* **:** exact copy
rep•li•cate *vb* **:** duplicate or repeat — **rep•li•cate** *n* — **rep•li•ca•tion** *n*
re•ply *vb* **:** say or do in answer ~ *n* **:** answer
re•port *n* **1 :** rumor **2 :** statement of information (as events or causes) **3 :** explosive noise ~ *vb* **1 :** give an account of **2 :** present an account of (an event) as news **3 :** present oneself **4 :** make known to authorities — **re•port•age** *n* — **re•port•ed•ly** *adv* — **re•port•er** *n* — **re•por•to•ri•al** *adj*
re•pose *vb* **:** lay or lie at rest ~ *n* **1 :** state of resting **2 :** calm or peace — **re•pose•ful** *adj*
re•pos•sess *vb* **:** regain possession and legal ownership of — **re•pos•ses•sion** *n*
rep•re•sent *vb* **1 :** serve as a sign or symbol of **2 :** act or speak for **3 :** describe as having a specified quality or character — **rep•re•sen•ta•tion** *n*
rep•re•sen•ta•tive *adj* **1 :** standing or acting for another **2 :** carried on by elected representatives ~ *n* **1 :** typical example **2 :** one that represents another **3 :** member of usu. the lower house of a legislature — **rep•re•sen•ta•tive•ly** *adv* — **rep•re•sen•ta•tive•ness** *n*
re•press *vb* **:** restrain or suppress — **re•pres•sion** *n* — **re•pres•sive** *adj*
rep•ri•mand *n* **:** formal or severe criticism — **rep•ri•mand** *vb*
re•proach *n* **1 :** disgrace **2 :** rebuke ~ *vb* **:** express disapproval to — **re•proach•ful** *adj* — **re•proach•ful•ly** *adv* — **re•proach•ful•ness** *n*
re•pro•duce *vb* **1 :** produce again or anew **2 :** produce offspring — **re•pro•duc•ible** *adj* — **re•pro•duc•tion** *n* — **re•pro•duc•tive** *adj*
rep•tile *n* **:** air-breathing scaly vertebrate — **rep•til•ian** *adj or n*
re•pub•lic *n* **:** country with representative government
re•pub•li•can *adj* **1 :** relating to or resembling a republic **2 :** supporting a republic — **repub•lican** *n* — **re•pub•li•can•ism** *n*
re•pug•nant *adj* **:** contrary to one's tastes or principles — **re•pug•nance** *n* — **re•pug•nant•ly** *adv*
re•pulse *vb* **1 :** drive or beat back **2 :** treat with contempt **3 :** be repugnant to — **repulse** *n* — **re•pul•sion** *n*
re•pul•sive *adj* **:** arousing aversion or disgust — **re•pul•sive•ly** *adv* — **re•pul•sive•ness** *n*
rep•u•ta•ble *adj* **:** having a good reputation — **rep•u•ta•bly** *adv*

rep·u·ta·tion *n* : one's character or public esteem

re·quest *n* : act or instance of asking for something or a thing asked for ~ *vb* **1 :** make a request of **2 :** ask for — **re·quest·er** *n*

re·quire *vb* **1 :** insist on **2 :** call for as essential — **re·quire·ment** *n*

res·cue *vb* : set free from danger or confinement — **rescue** *n* — **res·cu·er** *n*

re·search *n* : careful or diligent search esp. for new knowledge — **research** *vb* — **re·search·er** *n*

re·sem·ble *vb* : be like or similar to — **re·sem·blance** *n*

re·sent *vb* : feel or show annoyance at — **re·sent·ful** *adj* — **re·sent·ful·ly** *adv* — **re·sent·ment** *n*

res·er·va·tion *n* **1 :** act of reserving or something reserved **2 :** limiting condition

re·serve *vb* **1 :** store for future use **2 :** set aside for special use ~ *n* **1 :** something reserved **2 :** restraint in words or bearing **3 :** military forces withheld from action or not part of the regular services — **re·served** *adj*

res·er·voir *n* : place where something (as water) is kept in store

re·side *vb* **1 :** make one's home **2 :** be present

res·i·dence *n* **1 :** act or fact of residing in a place **2 :** place where one lives — **res·i·dent** *adj or n* — **res·i·den·tial** *adj*

res·i·due *n* : part remaining — **re·sid·u·al** *adj*

re·sign *vb* **1 :** give up deliberately **2 :** give (oneself) over without resistance — **res·ig·na·tion** *n* — **re·sign·ed·ly** *adv*

res·in *n* : substance from the gum or sap of trees — **res·in·ous** *adj*

re·sist *vb* **1 :** withstand the force or effect of **2 :** fight against — **re·sist·ible** *adj* — **re·sist·less** *adj*

re·sis·tance *n* **1 :** act of resisting **2 :** ability of an organism to resist disease **3 :** opposition to electric current

re·sis·tant *adj* : giving resistance

res·o·lute *adj* : having a fixed purpose — **res·o·lute·ly** *adv* — **res·o·lute·ness** *n*

res·o·lu·tion *n* **1 :** process of resolving **2 :** firmness of purpose **3 :** statement of the opinion, will, or intent of a body

re·solve *vb* **1 :** find an answer to **2 :** make a formal resolution ~ *n* **1 :** something resolved **2 :** steadfast purpose — **re·solv·able** *adj*

res·o·nant *adj* **1 :** continuing to sound **2 :** relating to intensification or prolongation of sound (as by a vibrating body) — **res·o·nance** *n* — **res·o·nant·ly** *adv*

re·sort *n* **1 :** source of help **2 :** place to go for vacation ~ *vb* **1 :** go often or habitually **2 :** have recourse

re·source *n* **1 :** new or reserve source **2** *pl* **:** available funds **3 :** ability to handle situations — **re·source·ful** *adj* — **re·source·ful·ness** *n*

re·spect *n* **1 :** relation to something **2 :** high or special regard **3 :** detail ~ *vb* : consider deserving of high regard — **re·spect·able** *adj* — **re·spect·abil·i·ty** *n* — **re·spect·ably** *adv* — **re·spect·er** *n* — **re·spect·ful** *adj* — **re·spect·ful·ly** *adv* — **re·spect·ful·ness** *n*

re·spec·tive *adj* : individual and specific — **re·spec·tive·ly** *adv*

res·pi·ra·tion *n* : act or process of breathing — **re·spi·ra·to·ry** *adj* — **re·spire** *vb*

res·pi·ra·tor *n* : device for artificial respiration

re·spond *vb* **1 :** answer **2 :** react — **re·spon·dent** *n or adj* — **re·spond·er** *n*

re·sponse *n* **1 :** act of responding **2 :** answer

re·spon·si·ble *adj* **1 :** answerable for acts or decisions **2 :** able to fulfill obligations **3 :** having important duties — **re·spon·si·bil·i·ty** *n* — **re·spon·si·ble·ness** *n* — **re·spon·si·bly** *adv*

re·spon·sive *adj* : quick to respond — **re·spon·sive·ly** *adv* — **re·spon·sive·ness** *n*

¹rest *n* **1 :** sleep **2 :** freedom from work or activity **3 :** state of inactivity **4 :** something used as a support ~ *vb* **1 :** get rest **2 :** cease action or motion **3 :** give rest to **4 :** sit or lie fixed or supported **5 :** depend — **rest·ful** *adj* — **rest·ful·ly** *adv*

²rest *n* : remainder

res·tau·rant *n* : public eating place

rest·less *adj* **1 :** lacking or giving no rest **2 :** always moving **3 :** uneasy — **rest·less·ly** *adv* — **rest·less·ness** *n*

re·store *vb* **1 :** give back **2 :** put back into use or into a former state — **re·stor·able** *adj* — **res·to·ra·tion** *n* — **re·stor·ative** *n or adj* — **re·stor·er** *n*

re·strain *vb* : limit or keep under control — **re·strain·able** *adj* — **re·strained** *adj* — **re·strain·ed·ly** *adv* — **re·strain·er** *n* — **re·straint** *n*

re·strict *vb* **1 :** confine within bounds **2 :** limit use of — **re·stric·tion** *n* — **re·stric·tive** *adj* — **re·stric·tive·ly** *adv*

re·sult *vb* : come about because of something

else ~ *n* **1 :** thing that results **2 :** something obtained by calculation or investigation — **re•sul•tant** *adj or n*

re•sume *vb* **:** return to or take up again after interruption — **re•sump•tion** *n*

ré•su•mé, re•su•me, re•su•mé *n* **:** summary of one's career and qualifications

res•ur•rect *vb* **1 :** raise from the dead **2 :** bring to attention or use again — **res•ur•rec•tion** *n*

re•sus•ci•tate *vb* **:** bring back from apparent death — **re•sus•ci•ta•tion** *n* — **re•sus•ci•ta•tor** *n*

re•tail *vb* **:** sell in small quantities directly to the consumer ~ *n* **:** business of selling to consumers — **retail** *adj or adv* — **re•tail•er** *n*

re•tain *vb* **1 :** keep or hold onto **2 :** engage the services of

re•tain•er *n* **1 :** household servant **2 :** retaining fee

re•tal•i•ate *vb* **:** return (as an injury) in kind — **re•tal•i•a•tion** *n* — **re•tal•ia•to•ry** *adj*

re•tard *vb* **:** hold back — **re•tar•da•tion** *n*

re•tard•ed *adj* **:** slow or limited in intellectual development

retch *vb* **:** try to vomit

re•ten•tion *n* **1 :** state of being retained **2 :** ability to retain — **re•ten•tive** *adj*

ret•i•na *n* **:** sensory membrane lining the eye — **ret•i•nal** *adj*

re•tire *vb* **1 :** withdraw for privacy **2 :** end a career **3 :** go to bed — **re•tir•ee** *n* — **re•tire•ment** *n*

re•tort *vb* **:** say in reply ~ *n* **:** quick, witty, or cutting answer

re•trace *vb* **:** go over again or in reverse

re•tract *vb* **1 :** draw back or in **2 :** withdraw a charge or promise — **re•tract•able** *adj* — **re•trac•tion** *n*

re•treat *n* **1 :** act of withdrawing **2 :** place of privacy or safety or meditation and study ~ *vb* **:** make a retreat

ret•ri•bu•tion *n* **:** retaliation — **re•trib•u•tive** *adj* — **re•trib•u•to•ry** *adj*

re•trieve *vb* **1 :** search for and bring in game **2 :** recover — **re•triev•able** *adj* — **re•triev•al** *n*

ret•ro•ac•tive *adj* **:** made effective as of a prior date — **ret•ro•ac•tive•ly** *adv*

ret•ro•spect *n* **:** review of past events — **ret•ro•spec•tion** *n* — **ret•ro•spec•tive** *adj* — **ret•ro•spec•tive•ly** *adv*

re•turn *vb* **1 :** go or come back **2 :** pass, give, or send back to an earlier possessor **3 :** answer **4 :** bring in as a profit **5 :** give or do in return ~ *n* **1 :** act of returning or something returned **2** *pl* **:** report of balloting results **3 :** statement of taxable income **4 :** profit — **re•turn** *adj* — **re•turn•able** *adj or n* — **re•turn•er** *n*

re•union *n* **1 :** act of reuniting **2 :** a meeting of persons after a separation

re•veal *vb* **1 :** make known **2 :** show plainly

rev•el *vb* **1 :** take part in a revel **2 :** take great pleasure ~ *n* **:** wild party or celebration — **rev•el•er, rev•el•ler** *n* — **rev•el•ry** *n*

rev•e•la•tion *n* **1 :** act of revealing **2 :** something enlightening or astonishing

re•venge *vb* **:** avenge ~ *n* **1 :** desire for retaliation **2 :** act of retaliation — **re•venge•ful** *adj* — **re•veng•er** *n*

rev•e•nue *n* **:** money collected by a government

re•ver•ber•ate *vb* **:** sound in a series of echoes — **re•ver•ber•a•tion** *n*

re•vere *vb* **:** show honor and devotion to — **rev•er•ence** *n* — **rev•er•ent** *adj* — **rev•er•ent•ly** *adv*

rev•er•end *adj* **:** worthy of reverence ~ *n* **:** clergy member

rev•er•ie *n* **:** daydream

re•verse *adj* **1 :** opposite to a previous or normal condition **2 :** acting in an opposite way ~ *vb* **1 :** turn upside down or completely around **2 :** change to the contrary or in the opposite direction ~ *n* **1 :** something contrary **2 :** change for the worse **3 :** back of something — **re•ver•sal** *n* — **re•verse•ly** *adv* — **re•vers•ible** *adj*

re•view *n* **1 :** formal inspection **2 :** general survey **3 :** critical evaluation **4 :** second or repeated study or examination ~ *vb* **1 :** examine or study again **2 :** reexamine judicially **3 :** look back over **4 :** examine critically **5 :** inspect — **re•view•er** *n*

re•vise *vb* **1 :** look over something written to correct or improve **2 :** make a new version of — **re•vis•able** *adj* — **revise** *n* — **re•vis•er, re•vi•sor** *n* — **re•vi•sion** *n*

re•vive *vb* **:** bring back to life or consciousness or into use — **re•viv•al** *n* — **re•viv•er** *n*

re•voke *vb* **:** annul by recalling — **re•vok•er** *n*

re•volt *vb* **1 :** throw off allegiance **2 :** cause or experience disgust or shock ~ *n* **:** rebellion or revolution — **re•volt•er** *n*

re•volt•ing *adj* **:** extremely offensive — **re•volt•ing•ly** *adv*

rev•o•lu•tion *n* **1 :** rotation **2 :** progress in an orbit **3 :** sudden, radical, or complete change (as overthrow of a government) — **rev•o•lu•tion•ary** *adj or n* — **rev•o•lu•tion•ize** *vb*

re•volve *vb* **1 :** ponder **2 :** move in an orbit **3 :** rotate — **re•volv•able** *adj*

re•volv•er *n* **:** pistol with a revolving cylinder

re•vul•sion *n* **:** complete dislike or repugnance

re•ward *vb* **:** give a reward to or for ~ *n* **:** something offered for service or achievement

re•write *vb* **:** revise — **rewrite** *n*

rhap•so•dy *n* **1 :** expression of extravagant praise **2 :** flowing free-form musical composition — **rhap•sod•ic** *adj* — **rhap•sod•i•cal•ly** *adv* — **rhap•so•dize** *vb*

rho•do•den•dron *n* **:** flowering evergreen shrub

rhyme *n* **1 :** correspondence in terminal sounds **2 :** verse that rhymes ~ *vb* **:** make or have rhymes

rhythm *n* **:** regular succession of sounds or motions — **rhyth•mic, rhyth•mi•cal** *adj* — **rhyth•mi•cal•ly** *adv*

rib *n* **1 :** curved bone joined to the spine **2 :** riblike thing ~ *vb* **1 :** furnish or mark with ribs **2 :** tease — **rib•ber** *n*

rib•bon *n* **1 :** narrow strip of fabric used esp. for decoration **2 :** strip of inked cloth (as in a typewriter)

rice *n* **:** starchy edible seeds of an annual cereal grass

rich *adj* **1 :** having a lot of money or possessions **2 :** valuable **3 :** containing much sugar, fat, or seasoning **4 :** abundant **5 :** deep and pleasing in color or tone **6 :** fertile — **rich•ly** *adv* — **rich•ness** *n*

rich•es *n pl* **:** wealth

rid *vb* **:** make free of something unwanted — **rid•dance** *n*

rid•dle *n* **:** puzzling question ~ *vb* **:** speak in riddles

ride *vb* (**rode; rid•den**) **1 :** be carried along **2 :** sit on and cause to move **3 :** travel over a surface **4 :** tease or nag ~ *n* **1 :** trip on an animal or in a vehicle **2 :** mechanical device ridden for amusement — **rid•er** *n* — **rid•er•less** *adj*

ridge *n* **1 :** range of hills **2 :** raised line or strip **3 :** line of intersection of 2 sloping surfaces — **ridgy** *adj*

rid•i•cule *vb* **:** laugh at or make fun of — **ridicule** *n*

ri•dic•u•lous *adj* **:** arousing ridicule — **ri•dic•u•lous•ly** *adv* — **ri•dic•u•lous•ness** *n*

rifle *n* **:** long shoulder weapon with spiral grooves in the bore — **ri•fle•man** *n* — **ri•fling** *n*

[1]rig *vb* **1 :** fit out with rigging **2 :** set up esp. as a makeshift ~ *n* **1 :** distinctive shape, number, and arrangement of sails and masts of a sailing ship **2 :** equipment **3 :** carriage with its horse

[2]rig *vb* **:** manipulate esp. by deceptive or dishonest means

right *adj* **1 :** meeting a standard of conduct **2 :** correct **3 :** genuine **4 :** normal **5 :** opposite of left ~ *n* **1 :** something that is correct, just, proper, or honorable **2 :** something to which one has a just claim **3 :** something that is on the right side ~ *adv* **1 :** according to what is right **2 :** immediately **3 :** completely **4 :** on or to the right ~ *vb* **1 :** restore to a proper state **2 :** bring or become upright again — **right•er** *n* — **right•ness** *n* — **right•ward** *adj*

righ•teous *adj* **:** acting or being in accordance with what is just or moral — **righ•teous•ly** *adv* — **righ•teous•ness** *n*

rig•id *adj* **:** lacking flexibility — **ri•gid•i•ty** *n* — **rig•id•ly** *adv*

rig•or *n* **:** severity — **rig•or•ous** *adj* — **rig•or•ous•ly** *adv*

rim *n* **:** edge esp. of something curved ~ *vb* **:** border

rind *n* **:** usu. hard or tough outer layer

[1]ring *n* **1 :** circular band used as an ornament or for holding or fastening **2 :** something circular **3 :** place for contest or display **4 :** group with a selfish or dishonest aim ~ *vb* **:** surround — **ringed** *adj* — **ring•like** *adj*

[2]ring *vb* **1 :** sound resonantly when struck **2 :** cause to make a metallic sound by striking **3 :** produce a strong echoing sound **4 :** call esp. by a bell ~ *n* **1 :** resonant sound or tone **2 :** act or instance of ringing — **ring•er** *n*

ring•tone *n* **:** sound of a cell phone to indicate an incoming call

rink *n* **:** enclosed place for skating

rinse *vb* **1 :** cleanse usu. with water only **2 :** treat (hair) with a rinse ~ *n* **:** liquid used for rinsing — **rins•er** *n*

ri•ot *n* **1 :** violent public disorder **2 :** random or disorderly lavish display — **riot** *vb* — **ri•ot•er** *n* — **ri•ot•ous** *adj*

rip *vb* **:** cut or tear open ~ *n* **:** rent made by ripping — **rip•per** *n*

ripe *adj* **:** fully grown, developed, or prepared — **ripe•ly** *adv* — **rip•en** *vb* — **ripe•ness** *n*

rip·ple *vb* **1 :** become lightly ruffled on the surface **2 :** sound like rippling water — **ripple** *n*

rise *vb* (**rose; ris·en**) **1 :** get up from sitting, kneeling, or lying **2 :** take arms **3 :** appear above the horizon **4 :** move upward **5 :** gain a higher position or rank **6 :** increase ∼ *n* **1 :** act of rising **2 :** origin **3 :** elevation **4 :** increase **5 :** upward slope **6 :** area of high ground — **ris·er** *n*

risk *n* **:** exposure to loss or injury — **risk** *vb* — **risk·i·ness** *n* — **risky** *adj*

rite *n* **1 :** set form for conducting a ceremony **2 :** customary ceremonies of a church **3 :** ceremonial action

rit·u·al *n* **:** rite — **ritual** *adj* — **rit·u·al·ism** *n* — **rit·u·al·is·tic** *adj* — **rit·u·al·is·ti·cal·ly** *adv* — **rit·u·al·ly** *adv*

ri·val *n* **1 :** competitor **2 :** peer ∼ *vb* **1 :** be in competition with **2 :** equal — **rival** *adj* — **ri·val·ry** *n*

riv·er *n* **:** large natural stream of water — **riv·er·bank** *n* — **riv·er·bed** *n* — **riv·er·boat** *n* — **riv·er·side** *n*

road *n* **:** open way for vehicles, persons, and animals — **road·bed** *n* — **road·block** *n* — **road·side** *n or adj* — **road·way** *n*

roam *vb* **:** wander

roar *vb* **:** utter a full loud prolonged sound — **roar** *n* — **roar·er** *n*

roast *vb* **1 :** cook by dry heat **2 :** criticize severely ∼ *n* **:** piece of meat suitable for roasting — **roast** *adj* — **roast·er** *n*

rob *vb* **1 :** steal from **2 :** commit robbery — **rob·ber** *n*

rob·bery *n* **:** theft of something from a person by use of violence or threat

robe *n* **1 :** long flowing outer garment **2 :** covering for the lower body ∼ *vb* **:** clothe with or as if with a robe

rob·in *n* **:** No. American thrush with a reddish breast

ro·bot *n* **1 :** machine that looks and acts like a human being **2 :** efficient but insensitive person — **ro·bot·ic** *adj*

[1]**rock** *vb* **:** sway or cause to sway back and forth ∼ *n* **1 :** rocking movement **2 :** popular music marked by repetition and a strong beat

[2]**rock** *n* **:** mass of hard mineral material — **rock** *adj* — **rocky** *adj*

rock·er *n* **1 :** curved piece on which a chair rocks **2 :** chair that rocks

rock·et *n* **1 :** self-propelled firework or missile **2 :** jet engine that carries its own oxygen ∼ *vb* **:** rise abruptly and rapidly — **rock·et·ry** *n*

rod *n* **1 :** straight slender stick **2 :** unit of length equal to 5 yards

rode *past of* RIDE

ro·deo *n* **:** contest of cowboy skills

rogue *n* **:** dishonest or mischievous person — **rogu·ery** *n* — **rogu·ish** *adj* — **rogu·ish·ly** *adv* — **rogu·ish·ness** *n*

role *n* **1 :** part to play **2 :** function

roll *n* **1 :** official record or list of names **2 :** something rolled up or rounded **3 :** bread baked in a small rounded mass **4 :** sound of rapid drum strokes **5 :** heavy reverberating sound **6 :** rolling movement ∼ *vb* **1 :** move by turning over **2 :** move on wheels **3 :** flow in a continuous stream **4 :** swing from side to side **5 :** shape or be shaped in rounded form **6 :** press with a revolving cylinder — **roll·er** *n*

Ro·man Cath·o·lic *n* **:** member of a Christian church led by a pope — **Ro·man Cath·o·lic** *adj* — **Ro·man Ca·thol·i·cism** *n*

ro·mance *n* **1 :** medieval tale of knightly adventure **2 :** love story **3 :** love affair ∼ *vb* **1 :** have romantic fancies **2 :** have a love affair with — **ro·manc·er** *n*

ro·man·tic *adj* **1 :** visionary or imaginative **2 :** appealing to one's emotions — **ro·man·ti·cal·ly** *adv*

romp *vb* **:** play actively and noisily — **romp** *n*

roof *n* **:** upper covering part of a building ∼ *vb* **:** cover with a roof — **roofed** *adj* — **roof·ing** *n* — **roof·less** *adj* — **roof·top** *n*

rook *n* **:** crowlike bird

rook·ie *n* **:** novice

room *n* **1 :** sufficient space **2 :** partitioned part of a building ∼ *vb* **:** occupy lodgings — **room·er** *n* — **room·ful** *n* — **roomy** *adj*

roost·er *n* **:** adult male domestic chicken

root *n* **1 :** leafless underground part of a seed plant **2 :** rootlike thing or part **3 :** source **4 :** essential core ∼ *vb* **:** form, fix, or become fixed by roots — **root·less** *adj* — **root·let** *n* — **root·like** *adj*

[3]**root** *vb* **:** applaud or encourage noisily — **root·er** *n*

rope *n* **:** large strong cord of strands of fiber ∼ *vb* **1 :** tie with a rope **2 :** lasso

ro·sa·ry *n* **1 :** string of beads used in praying **2 :** Roman Catholic devotion

[1]**rose** *past of* RISE

[2]**rose** *n* **1 :** prickly shrub with bright flowers **2**

: purplish red — **rose** *adj* — **rose•bud** *n* — **rose•bush** *n*

Rosh Ha•sha•nah *n* : Jewish New Year observed as a religious holiday in September or October

rosy *adj* **1 :** of the color rose **2 :** hopeful — **ros•i•ly** *adv* — **ros•i•ness** *n*

rot *vb* : undergo decomposition ~ *n* **1 :** decay **2 :** disease in which tissue breaks down

ro•ta•ry *adj* **1 :** turning on an axis **2 :** having a rotating part

ro•tate *vb* **1 :** turn about an axis or a center **2 :** alternate in a series — **ro•ta•tion** *n* — **ro•ta•tor** *n*

ro•tor *n* **1 :** part that rotates **2 :** system of rotating horizontal blades for supporting a helicopter

rot•ten *adj* **1 :** having rotted **2 :** corrupt **3 :** extremely unpleasant or inferior — **rot•ten•ness** *n*

rough *adj* **1 :** not smooth **2 :** not calm **3 :** harsh, violent, or rugged **4 :** crudely or hastily done ~ *n* : rough state or something in that state ~ *vb* **1 :** roughen **2 :** handle roughly **3 :** make roughly — **rough•en** *vb* — **rough•ly** *adv* — **rough•ness** *n*

round *adj* **1 :** having every part the same distance from the center **2 :** cylindrical **3 :** complete **4 :** approximate **5 :** blunt **6 :** moving in or forming a circle ~ *n* **1 :** round or curved thing **2 :** series of recurring actions or events **3 :** period of time or a unit of action **4 :** fired shot **5 :** cut of beef ~ *vb* **1 :** make or become round **2 :** go around **3 :** finish **4 :** express as an approximation — **round•ish** *adj* — **round•ly** *adv* — **round•ness** *n*

rout *n* **1 :** state of wild confusion **2 :** disastrous defeat ~ *vb* : defeat decisively

route *n* : line of travel ~ *vb* : send by a selected route

rou•tine *n* **1 :** regular course of procedure **2 :** an often repeated speech, formula, or part — **routine** *adj* — **rou•tine•ly** *adv*

rove *vb* : wander or roam — **rov•er** *n*

[1]**row** *vb* **1 :** propel a boat with oars **2 :** carry in a rowboat ~ *n* : act of rowing — **row•boat** *n* — **row•er** *n*

[2]**row** *n* : number of objects in a line

[3]**row** *n* : noisy quarrel — **row** *vb*

row•dy *adj* : coarse or boisterous in behavior — **row•di•ness** *n* — **rowdy** *n*

roy•al *adj* : relating to or befitting a king ~ *n* : person of royal blood — **roy•al•ly** *adv* — **roy•al•ty** *n*

rub *vb* **1 :** use pressure and friction on a body **2 :** scour, polish, erase, or smear by pressure and friction **3 :** chafe with friction ~ *n* : difficulty

rub•ber *n* **1 :** one that rubs **2 :** waterproof elastic substance or something made of it — **rub•ber** *adj* — **rub•ber•ize** *vb* — **rub•bery** *adj*

rub•bish *n* : waste or trash

ru•by *n* : precious red stone or its color — **ruby** *adj*

rude *adj* **1 :** roughly made **2 :** impolite — **rude•ly** *adv* — **rude•ness** *n*

rue *vb* : feel regret for ~ *n* : regret — **rue•ful** *adj* — **rue•ful•ly** *adv* — **rue•ful•ness** *n*

ruf•fle *vb* **1 :** draw into or provide with pleats **2 :** roughen the surface of **3 :** irritate ~ *n* : strip of fabric pleated on one edge — **ruf•fly** *adj*

rug *n* : piece of heavy fabric used as a floor covering

rug•ged *adj* **1 :** having a rough uneven surface **2 :** severe **3 :** strong — **rug•ged•ly** *adv* — **rug•ged•ness** *n*

ru•in *n* **1 :** complete collapse or destruction **2 :** remains of something destroyed — usu. in pl. **3 :** cause of destruction ~ *vb* **1 :** destroy **2 :** damage beyond repair **3 :** bankrupt

ru•in•ous *adj* : causing ruin — **ruin•ous•ly** *adv*

rule *n* **1 :** guide or principle for governing action **2 :** usual way of doing something **3 :** government **4 :** straight strip (as of wood or metal) marked off in units for measuring ~ *vb* **1 :** govern **2 :** give as a decision — **rul•er** *n*

rum *n* : liquor made from molasses or sugarcane

rum•ble *vb* : make a low heavy rolling sound — **rumble** *n*

ru•mor *n* **1 :** common talk **2 :** widespread statement not authenticated — **rumor** *vb*

rump *n* : rear part of an animal

rum•ple *vb* : tousle or wrinkle — **rumple** *n*

run *vb* **ran; run 1 :** go rapidly or hurriedly **2 :** enter a race or election **3 :** operate **4 :** continue in force **5 :** flow rapidly **6 :** take a certain direction **7 :** manage **8 :** incur ~ *n* **1 :** act of running **2 :** brook **3 :** continuous series **4 :** usual kind **5 :** freedom of movement **6 :** lengthwise ravel

run•away *n* : fugitive ~ *adj* **1 :** fugitive **2 :** out of control

¹rung *past part of* RING
²rung *n* : horizontal piece of a chair or ladder
run·ner *n* **1 :** one that runs **2 :** thin piece or part on which something slides **3 :** slender creeping branch of a plant
run·ning *adj* **1 :** flowing **2 :** continuous
runt *n* : small person or animal — **runty** *adj*
rup·ture *n* **1 :** breaking or tearing apart ~ *vb* : cause or undergo rupture
ru·ral *adj* : relating to the country or agriculture
rush *vb* **1 :** move forward or act with too great haste **2 :** perform in a short time ~ *n* : violent forward motion ~ *adj* : requiring speed — **rush·er** *n*
rust *n* **1 :** reddish coating on exposed iron **2 :** reddish brown color — **rust** *vb* — **rusty** *adj*
rus·tic *adj* : relating to or suitable for the country or country dwellers ~ *n* : rustic person — **rus·ti·cal·ly** *adv*
rus·tle *vb* **1 :** make or cause a rustle **2 :** forage food **3 :** steal cattle from the range ~ *n* : series of small sounds — **rus·tler** *n*
rut *n* **1 :** track worn by wheels or feet **2 :** set routine — **rut·ted** *adj*
ruth·less *adj* : having no pity — **ruth·less·ly** *adv* — **ruth·less·ness** *n*
RV *n* recreational vehicle
rye *n* **1 :** cereal grass grown for grain **2 :** whiskey from rye

S

s *n* : 19th letter of the alphabet
Sab·bath *n* **1 :** Saturday observed as a day of worship by Jews and some Christians **2 :** Sunday observed as a day of worship by Christians
sab·o·tage *n* : deliberate destruction or hampering ~ *vb* : wreck through sabotage
sack *n* : bag ~ *vb* : fire
sac·ra·ment *n* : formal religious act or rite — **sac·ra·men·tal** *adj*
sa·cred *adj* **1 :** set apart for or worthy of worship **2 :** worthy of reverence **3 :** relating to religion — **sa·cred·ly** *adv* — **sa·cred·ness** *n*
sac·ri·fice *n* **1 :** the offering of something precious to a deity or the thing offered **2 :** loss or deprivation ~ *vb* : offer or give up as a sacrifice — **sac·ri·fi·cial** *adj*
sac·ri·lege *n* : violation of something sacred — **sac·ri·le·gious** *adj*
sad *adj* **1 :** affected with grief or sorrow **2 :** causing sorrow — **sad·den** *vb* — **sad·ly** *adv* — **sad·ness** *n*
sad·dle *n* : seat for riding on horseback ~ *vb* : put a saddle on
sa·dism *n* : delight in cruelty — **sa·dist** *n* — **sa·dis·tic** *adj* — **sa·dis·ti·cal·ly** *adv*
sa·fa·ri *n* : hunting expedition in Africa
safe *adj* **1 :** free from harm **2 :** providing safety ~ *n* : container to keep valuables safe — **safe·keep·ing** *n* — **safe·ly** *adv*
safe·guard *n* : measure or device for preventing accidents — **safe·guard** *vb*
safe·ty *n* **1 :** freedom from danger **2 :** protective device
sag *vb* : droop, sink, or settle — **sag** *n*
sage *adj* : wise or prudent ~ *n* : wise man — **sage·ly** *adv*
said *past of* SAY
sail *n* **1 :** fabric used to catch the wind and move a boat or ship **2 :** trip on a sailboat ~ *vb* **1 :** travel on a ship or sailboat **2 :** move with ease or grace — **sail·boat** *n* — **sail·or** *n*
saint *n* : holy or godly person — **saint·ed** *adj* — **saint·hood** *n* — **saint·li·ness** *n* — **saint·ly** *adj*
sake *n* **1 :** purpose or reason **2 :** one's good or benefit
sal·ad *n* : dish usu. of raw lettuce, vegetables, or fruit
sa·la·mi *n* : highly seasoned dried sausage
sal·a·ry *n* : regular payment for services
sale *n* **1 :** transfer of ownership of property for money **2 :** selling at bargain prices **3** *pl* : activities involved in selling — **sal·able, sale·able** *adj* — **sales·man** *n* — **sales·per·son** *n* — **sales·wom·an** *n*
sa·li·va *n* : liquid secreted into the mouth — **sal·i·vary** *adj* — **sal·i·vate** *vb* — **sal·i·va·tion** *n*
salm·on *n* (**salmon**) **1 :** food fish with pink or red flesh **2 :** deep yellowish pink color
sa·lon *n* : elegant room or shop
sa·loon *n* **1 :** public cabin on a passenger ship **2 :** barroom
sal·sa *n* : spicy sauce of tomatoes, onions, and hot peppers
salt *n* **1 :** white crystalline substance that consists of sodium and chlorine **2 :** compound

formed usu. from acid and metal — **salt** *vb or adj* — **salt•i•ness** *n* — **salty** *adj*
sa•lute *vb* : honor by ceremony or formal movement — **salute** *n*
sal•vage *n* : something saved from destruction ~ *vb* : rescue or save
sal•va•tion *n* : saving of a person from sin or danger
same *adj* : being the one referred to ~ *pron* : the same one or ones ~ *adv* : in the same manner — **same•ness** *n*
sam•ple *n* : piece or part that shows the quality of a whole ~ *vb* : judge by a sample
sanc•ti•mo•nious *adj* : hypocritically pious — **sanc•ti•mo•nious•ly** *adv*
sanc•tion *n* **1** : authoritative approval **2** : coercive measure — usu. pl ~ *vb* : approve
sanc•tu•ary *n* **1** : consecrated place **2** : place of refuge
sand *n* : loose granular particles of rock ~ *vb* : smooth with an abrasive — **sand•bank** *n* — **sand•er** *n* — **sand•storm** *n* — **sandy** *adj*
san•dal *n* : shoe consisting of a sole strapped to the foot
sand•wich *n* : bread surrounding a filling ~ *vb* : squeeze or crowd in
sane *adj* **1** : mentally healthy **2** : sensible — **sane•ly** *adv*
sang *past of* SING
san•i•tary *adj* **1** : relating to health **2** : free from filth or infective matter
san•i•ta•tion *n* : protection of health by maintenance of sanitary conditions
san•i•ty *n* : soundness of mind
sank *past of* SINK
[1]**sap** *n* **1** : fluid that circulates through a plant **2** : gullible person
[2]**sap** *vb* **1** : undermine **2** : weaken or exhaust gradually
sap•py *adj* **1** : full of sap **2** : overly sentimental
sar•casm *n* **1** : cutting remark **2** : ironical criticism or reproach — **sar•cas•tic** *adj* — **sar•cas•ti•cal•ly** *adv*
[1]**sash** *n* : broad band worn around the waist or over the shoulder
[2]**sash** *n* **1** : frame for a pane of glass in a door or window **2** : movable part of a window
sassy *adj* : insolent
sat *past of* SIT
Sa•tan *n* : devil — **sa•tan•ic** *adj* — **sa•tan•i•cal•ly** *adv*
satch•el *n* : small bag
sate *vb* : satisfy fully
sat•el•lite *n* : body or object that revolves around a larger celestial body
sat•in *n* : glossy fabric — **sat•iny** *adj*
sat•ire *n* : literary ridicule done with humor — **sa•tir•ic, sa•tir•i•cal** *adj* — **sa•tir•i•cal•ly** *adv* — **sat•i•rist** *n* — **sat•i•rize** *vb*
sat•is•fac•tion *n* : state of being satisfied — **sat•is•fac•to•ri•ly** *adv* — **sat•is•fac•to•ry** *adj* — **sat•is•fy** *vb* — **sat•is•fy•ing•ly** *adv*
sat•u•rate *vb* : soak or charge thoroughly — **sat•u•ra•tion** *n*
Sat•ur•day *n* : 7th day of the week
sauce *n* : fluid dressing or topping for food — **sauce•pan** *n*
sau•cer *n* : small shallow dish under a cup
sau•na *n* : steam or dry heat bath or a room or cabinet used for such a bath
sau•sage *n* : minced and highly seasoned meat
sau•té *vb* : fry in a little fat — **sauté** *n*
sav•age *adj* **1** : wild **2** : cruel ~ *n* : person belonging to a primitive society — **sav•age•ly** *adv* — **sav•age•ness** *n* — **sav•age•ry** *n*
save *vb* **1** : rescue from danger **2** : guard from destruction **3** : redeem from sin **4** : put aside as a reserve — **sav•er** *n*
sav•ior, sav•iour *n* **1** : one who saves **2** *cap* : Jesus Christ
[1]**saw** *past of* SEE
[2]**saw** *n* : cutting tool with teeth ~ *vb* : cut with a saw — **saw•dust** *n* — **saw•mill** *n* — **saw•yer** *n*
say *vb* **said; said 1** : express in words **2** : state positively ~ *n* **1** : expression of opinion **2** : power of decision
say•ing *n* : commonly repeated statement
scab *n* **1** : protective crust over a sore or wound **2** : worker taking a striker's job ~ *vb* **1** : become covered with a scab **2** : work as a scab — **scab•by** *adj*
scald *vb* **1** : burn with hot liquid or steam **2** : heat to the boiling point
[1]**scale** *n* : weighing device ~ *vb* : weigh
[2]**scale** *n* **1** : thin plate esp. on the body of a fish or reptile **2** : thin coating or layer ~ *vb* : strip of scales — **scaled** *adj* — **scale•less** *adj* — **scaly** *adj*
[3]**scale** *n* **1** : graduated series **2** : size of a sample (as a model) in proportion to the size of the actual thing **3** : standard of estimation or judgment **4** : series of musical tones ~ *vb* **1** : climb by a ladder **2** : arrange in a graded series
scalp *n* : skin and flesh of the head ~ *vb* **1**

: remove the scalp from **2 :** resell at a greatly increased price — **scalp•er** *n*

scam•per *vb* : run nimbly — **scam•per** *n*

scan *vb* **1 :** read (verses) so as to show meter **2 :** examine closely or hastily **3 :** examine with a sensing device — **scan** *n* — **scan•ner** *n*

scan•dal *n* **1 :** disgraceful situation **2 :** malicious gossip — **scan•dal•ize** *vb* — **scan•dal•ous** *adj*

scant *adj* : barely sufficient ~ *vb* : hold back from being generous — **scant•i•ly** *adv* — **scanty** *adj*

scar *n* : mark where a wound has healed — **scar** *vb*

scarce *adj* : lacking in quantity or number — **scar•ci•ty** *n*

scarce•ly *adv* **1 :** barely **2 :** almost not

scare *vb* : frighten ~ *n* : fright — **scary** *adj*

scarf *n* : cloth worn about the shoulders or the neck

scat•ter *vb* **1 :** spread about irregularly **2 :** disperse

scav•en•ger *n* **1 :** person that collects refuse or waste **2 :** animal that feeds on decayed matter — **scav•enge** *vb*

scene *n* **1 :** single situation in a play or movie **2 :** stage setting **3 :** view **4 :** display of emotion — **sce•nic** *adj*

scen•ery *n* **1 :** painted setting for a stage **2 :** picturesque view

scent *vb* **1 :** smell **2 :** fill with odor ~ *n* **1 :** odor **2 :** sense of smell **3 :** perfume — **scent•ed** *adj*

sched•ule *n* : list showing sequence of events ~ *vb* : make a schedule of

scheme *n* **1 :** crafty plot **2 :** systematic design ~ *vb* : form a plot — **sche•mat•ic** *adj* — **schem•er** *n*

schol•ar *n* : student or learned person — **schol•ar•ly** *adj*

schol•ar•ship *n* **1 :** qualities or learning of a serious student **2 :** money given to a student to pay for education

scho•las•tic *adj* : relating to schools, scholars, or scholarship

¹school *n* **1 :** institution for learning **2 :** pupils in a school **3 :** group with shared beliefs ~ *vb* : teach — **school•boy** *n* — **school•girl** *n* — **school•house** *n* — **school•mate** *n* — **school•room** *n* — **school•teach•er** *n*

²school *n* : large number of fish swimming together

sci•ence *n* : branch of systematic study esp. of the physical world — **sci•en•tif•ic** *adj* — **sci•en•tif•i•cal•ly** *adv* — **sci•en•tist** *n*

scis•sors *n pl* : small shears

scold *n* : person who scolds ~ *vb* : criticize severely

scoop *n* : shovellike utensil ~ *vb* **1 :** take out with a scoop **2 :** dig out

scoot•er *n* : child's foot-propelled vehicle

scope *n* **1 :** extent **2 :** room for development

scorch *vb* : burn the surface of

score *n* **1** *pl* **score** : twenty **2 :** cut **3 :** record of points made (as in a game) **4 :** debt **5 :** music of a composition ~ *vb* **1 :** record **2 :** mark with lines **3 :** gain in a game **4 :** assign a grade to **5 :** compose a score for — **score•less** *adj* — **scor•er** *n*

scorn *n* : emotion involving both anger and disgust ~ *vb* : hold in contempt — **scorn•er** *n* — **scorn•ful** *adj* — **scorn•ful•ly** *adv*

scout *vb* : inspect or observe to get information ~ *n* : person sent out to get information

scowl *vb* : make a frowning expression of displeasure — **scowl** *n*

scram *vb* : go away at once

scram•ble *vb* **1 :** clamber clumsily around **2 :** struggle for possession of something **3 :** mix together **4 :** cook (eggs) by stirring during frying — **scram•ble** *n*

scrap *n* **1 :** fragment **2 :** discarded material ~ *vb* : get rid of as useless

scrape *vb* **1 :** remove by drawing a knife over **2 :** clean or smooth by rubbing **3 :** draw across a surface with a grating sound **4 :** damage by contact with a rough surface **5 :** gather or proceed with difficulty ~ *n* **1 :** act of scraping **2 :** predicament — **scrap•er** *n*

scratch *vb* **1 :** scrape or dig with or as if with claws or nails **2 :** cause to move gratingly **3 :** delete by or as if by drawing a line through ~ *n* : mark or sound made in scratching — **scratchy** *adj*

scrawl *vb* : write hastily and carelessly — **scrawl** *n*

scream *vb* : cry out loudly and shrilly ~ *n* : loud shrill cry

screen *n* **1 :** device or partition used to protect or decorate **2 :** surface on which pictures appear (as in movies) ~ *vb* : shield or separate with or as if with a screen

screw *n* **1 :** grooved fastening device **2 :** propeller ~ *vb* **1 :** fasten by means of a screw **2 :** move spirally

screw•driv•er *n* **:** tool for turning screws
scrib•ble *vb* **:** write hastily or carelessly — **scrib•ble** *n* — **scrib•bler** *n*
script *n* **:** text (as of a play)
scrip•ture *n* **:** sacred writings of a religion — **scrip•tur•al** *adj*
scroll *n* **1 :** roll of paper for writing a document **2 :** spiral or coiled design
scrub *vb* **:** clean or wash by rubbing — **scrub** *n*
scru•ple *n* **:** reluctance due to ethical considerations — **scru•ple** *vb* — **scru•pu•lous** *adj* — **scru•pu•lous•ly** *adv*
scru•ti•ny *n* **:** careful inspection — **scru•ti•nize** *vb*
scuff *vb* **:** scratch, scrape, or wear away — **scuff** *n*
scuf•fle *vb* **1 :** struggle at close quarters **2 :** shuffle one's feet — **scuf•fle** *n*
sculp•ture *n* **:** work of art carved or molded ∼ *vb* **:** form as sculpture — **sculp•tor** *n* — **sculp•tur•al** *adj*
scum *n* **:** slimy film on a liquid
sea *n* **1 :** large body of salt water **2 :** ocean **3 :** rough water — **sea** *adj* — **sea•bird** *n* — **sea•coast** *n* — **sea•food** *n* — **sea•port** *n* — **sea•shore** *n* — **sea•wa•ter** *n* — **sea•weed** *n*
[1]**seal** *n* **:** large sea mammal of cold regions — **seal•skin** *n*
[2]**seal** *n* **1 :** device for stamping a design **2 :** something that closes ∼ *vb* **1 :** affix a seal to **2 :** close up securely **3 :** determine finally — **seal•ant** *n* — **seal•er** *n*
seam *n* **1 :** line of junction of 2 edges **2 :** layer of a mineral ∼ *vb* **:** join by sewing — **seam•less** *adj*
search *vb* **1 :** look through **2 :** seek — **search** *n* — **search•er** *n* — **search•light** *n*
search engine *n* **:** computer software used to search for specified information on the World Wide Web
[1]**sea•son** *n* **1 :** division of the year **2 :** customary time for something — **sea•son•al** *adj* — **sea•son•al•ly** *adv*
[2]**season** *vb* **1 :** add spice to (food) **2 :** make strong or fit for use — **sea•son•ing** *n*
seat *n* **1 :** place to sit **2 :** chair, bench, or stool for sitting on **3 :** place that serves as a capital or center ∼ *vb* **1 :** place in or on a seat **2 :** provide seats for
[1]**sec•ond** *adj* **:** next after the 1st ∼ *n* **1 :** one that is second **2 :** one who assists (as in a duel) — **sec•ond, se•cond•ly** *adv* — **sec•ond•ary** *adj*
[2]**sec•ond** *n* **1 :** 60th part of a minute **2 :** moment
sec•ond•hand *adj* **1 :** not original **2 :** used before
se•cret *adj* **1 :** hidden **2 :** kept from general knowledge — **se•cre•cy** *n* — **secret** *n* — **se•cre•tive** *adj* — **se•cret•ly** *adv*
sec•re•tary *n* **1 :** one hired to handle correspondence and other tasks for a superior **2 :** official in charge of correspondence or records **3 :** head of a government department — **sec•re•tari•al** *adj*
[1]**se•crete** *vb* **:** produce from or as if from a gland — **se•cre•tion** *n*
[2]**se•crete** *vb* **:** hide
sect *n* **:** religious group — **sec•tar•i•an** *adj*
sec•tion *n* **:** distinct part — **sec•tion•al** *adj*
sec•u•lar *adj* **1 :** not sacred **2 :** not monastic
se•cure *adj* **:** free from danger or loss ∼ *vb* **1 :** fasten safely **2 :** get — **se•cure•ly** *adv* — **se•cu•ri•ty** *n*
se•dan *n* **1 :** chair carried by 2 men **2 :** enclosed automobile
[1]**se•date** *adj* **:** quiet and dignified — **se•date•ly** *adv*
[2]**sedate** *vb* **:** dose with sedatives — **se•da•tion** *n* — **sed•a•tive** *n*
sed•i•ment *n* **:** material that settles to the bottom of a liquid or is deposited by water or a glacier — **sed•i•men•ta•ry** *adj* — **sed•i•men•ta•tion** *n*
se•duce *vb* **1 :** lead astray **2 :** entice to sexual intercourse — **se•duc•er** *n* — **se•duc•tion** *n* — **se•duc•tive** *adj*
see *vb* **saw; seen 1 :** perceive by the eye **2 :** have experience of **3 :** understand **4 :** make sure **5 :** meet with or escort
seed *n* **1 :** part by which a plant is propagated **2 :** source ∼ *vb* **1 :** sow **2 :** remove seeds from — **seed•less** *adj*
seed•ling *n* **:** young plant grown from seed
seedy *adj* **1 :** full of seeds **2 :** shabby
seek *vb* (**sought; sought**) **1 :** search for **2 :** try to reach or obtain — **seek•er** *n*
seem *vb* **:** give the impression of being — **seem•ing•ly** *adv*
seem•ly *adj* **:** proper or fit
seep *vb* **:** leak through fine pores or cracks — **seep•age** *n*
see•saw *n* **:** board balanced in the middle — **seesaw** *vb*

seg·ment *n* : division of a thing — **seg·ment·ed** *adj*
seg·re·gate *vb* **1 :** cut off from others **2 :** separate by races — **seg·re·ga·tion** *n*
seize *vb* : take by force — **sei·zure** *n*
sel·dom *adv* : not often
se·lect *adj* **1 :** favored **2 :** discriminating ~ *vb* : take by preference — **se·lec·tive** *adj* — **se·lec·tion** *n*
self *n* **selves :** essential person distinct from others
self–con·fi·dent *adj* : confident in oneself and in one's powers and abilities — **self–con·fi·dence** *n*
self–con·scious *adj* : uncomfortably aware of oneself as an object of observation — **self-con·scious·ly** *adv* — **self–con·scious·ness** *n*
self–con·trol *n* : restraint over one's own impulses, emotions, or desires
self–es·teem *n* : respect for and confidence in oneself
self·ish *adj* : excessively or exclusively concerned with one's own well-being — **self·ish·ly** *adv* — **self·ish·ness** *n*
self·less *adj* : unselfish — **self·less·ness** *n*
sell *vb* (**sold; sold**) **1 :** transfer (property) esp. for money **2 :** deal in as a business **3 :** be sold — **sell·er** *n*
selves *pl of* SELF
se·man·tic *adj* : relating to meaning in language — **se·man·tics** *n sing or pl*
se·mes·ter *n* : half a school year
semi·co·lon *n* : punctuation mark ;
semi·fi·nal *adj* : being next to the final — **semifinal** *n*
sen·ate *n* : upper branch of a legislature — **sen·a·tor** *n* — **sen·a·to·rial** *adj*
send *vb* (**sent; sent**) **1 :** cause to go **2 :** propel — **send·er** *n*
se·nior *adj* : older or higher ranking — **se·nior** *n* — **se·nior·i·ty** *n*
sen·sa·tion *n* **1 :** bodily feeling **2 :** condition of excitement or the cause of it — **sen·sa·tion·al** *adj*
sense *n* **1 :** meaning **2 :** faculty of perceiving something physical **3 :** sound mental capacity ~ *vb* **1 :** perceive by the senses **2 :** detect automatically — **sense·less** *adj* — **sense·less·ly** *adv*
sen·si·bil·i·ty *n* : delicacy of feeling
sen·si·ble *adj* **1 :** capable of sensing or being sensed **2 :** aware or conscious **3 :** reasonable — **sen·si·bly** *adv*
sen·si·tive *adj* **1 :** subject to excitation by or responsive to stimuli **2 :** having power of feeling **3 :** easily affected — **sen·si·tive·ness** *n* — **sen·si·tiv·i·ty** *n*
sen·si·tize *vb* : make or become sensitive
sen·so·ry *adj* : relating to sensation or the senses
sen·su·al *adj* **1 :** pleasing the senses **2 :** devoted to the pleasures of the senses — **sen·su·al·ist** *n* — **sen·su·al·i·ty** *n* — **sen·su·al·ly** *adv*
sen·su·ous *adj* : having strong appeal to the senses
sent *past of* SEND
sen·tence *n* **1 :** judgment of a court **2 :** grammatically self-contained speech unit ~ *vb* : impose a sentence on
sen·ti·ment *n* **1 :** belief **2 :** feeling
sen·ti·men·tal *adj* : influenced by tender feelings — **sen·ti·men·tal·ism** *n* — **sen·ti·men·tal·ist** *n* — **sen·ti·men·tal·i·ty** *n* — **sen·ti·men·tal·ize** *vb* — **sen·ti·men·tal·ly** *adv*
sep·a·rate *vb* **1 :** set or keep apart **2 :** become divided or detached ~ *adj* **1 :** not connected or shared **2 :** distinct from each other — **sep·a·ra·ble** *adj* — **sep·a·rate·ly** *adv* — **sep·a·ra·tion** *n* — **sep·a·ra·tor** *n*
Sep·tem·ber *n* : 9th month of the year having 30 days
se·quel *n* **1 :** consequence or result **2 :** continuation of a story
se·quence *n* : continuous or connected series — **se·quen·tial** *adj* — **se·quen·tial·ly** *adv*
ser·e·nade *n* : music sung or played esp. to a woman being courted — **serenade** *vb*
se·rene *adj* : tranquil — **se·rene·ly** *adv* — **se·ren·i·ty** *n*
ser·geant *n* : noncommissioned officer (as in the army)
se·ri·al *adj* : being or relating to a series or sequence ~ *n* : story appearing in parts — **se·ri·al·ly** *adv*
se·ries *n* : number of things in order
se·ri·ous *adj* **1 :** subdued in appearance or manner **2 :** sincere **3 :** of great importance — **se·ri·ous·ly** *adv* — **se·ri·ous·ness** *n*
ser·mon *n* : lecture on religion or behavior
ser·pent *n* : snake — **ser·pen·tine** *adj*
ser·vant *n* : person employed for domestic work
serve *vb* **1 :** work through or perform a term of service **2 :** be of use **3 :** prove adequate **4**

: hand out (food or drink) **5** : be of service to — **serv•er** *n*

ser•vice *n* **1** : act or means of serving **2** : meeting for worship **3** : branch of public employment or the persons in it **4** : set of dishes or table utensils **5** : benefit ∼ *vb* : repair — **ser•vice•able** *adj* — **ser•vice•man** *n* — **ser•vice•wom•an** *n*

ses•sion *n* : meeting

set *vb* **set; set** **1** : cause to sit **2** : place **3** : settle, arrange, or adjust **4** : cause to be or do **5** : become fixed or solid **6** : sink below the horizon ∼ *adj* : settled ∼ *n* **1** : group classed together **2** : setting for the scene of a play or film **3** : electronic apparatus **4** : collection of mathematical elements — **set forth** : begin a trip — **set off** *vb* : set forth — **set out** *vb* : begin a trip or undertaking — **set up** *vb* **1** : assemble or erect **2** : cause

set•back *n* : reverse

set•ting *n* : the time, place, and circumstances in which something occurs

set•tle *vb* **1** : come to rest **2** : sink gradually **3** : establish in residence **4** : adjust or arrange **5** : calm **6** : dispose of (as by paying) **7** : decide or agree on — **set•tle•ment** *n* — **set•tler** *n*

sev•en *n* : one more than 6 — **sev•en** *adj or pron* — **sev•enth** *adj or adv or n*

sev•en•teen *n* : one more than 16 — **seventeen** *adj or pron* — **sev•en•teenth** *adj or n*

sev•en•ty *n* : 7 times 10 — **sev•en•ti•eth** *adj or n* — **sev•en•ty** *adj or pron*

sev•er *vb* : cut off or apart — **sev•er•ance** *n*

sev•er•al *adj* **1** : distinct **2** : consisting of an indefinite but not large number — **sev•er•al•ly** *adv*

se•vere *adj* **1** : strict **2** : restrained or unadorned **3** : painful or distressing **4** : hard to endure — **se•vere•ly** *adv* — **se•ver•i•ty** *n*

sew *vb* : join or fasten by stitches — **sew•ing** *n*

sew•age *n* : liquid household waste

[1]sew•er *n* : one that sews

[2]sew•er *n* : pipe or channel to carry off waste matter

sex *n* : either of 2 divisions into which organisms are grouped according to their reproductive roles — **sexed** *adj* — **sex•less** *adj* — **sex•u•al** *adj* — **sex•u•al•i•ty** *n* — **sex•u•al•ly** *adv* — **sexy** *adj*

sex•ism *n* : discrimination based on sex and esp. against women — **sex•ist** *adj or n*

shab•by *adj* **1** : worn and faded **2** : dressed in worn clothes **3** : not generous or fair — **shabbi•ly** *adv* — **shab•bi•ness** *n*

shack *n* : hut

shade *n* **1** : space sheltered from the light esp. of the sun **2** : gradation of color **3** : small difference **4** : something that shades ∼ *vb* **1** : shelter from light and heat **2** : add shades of color to **3** : show slight differences esp. in color or meaning

shad•ow *n* **1** : shade cast upon a surface by something blocking light **2** : trace **3** : gloomy influence ∼ *vb* **1** : cast a shadow **2** : follow closely — **shad•owy** *adj*

shady *adj* **1** : giving shade **2** : of dubious honesty

shaft *n* **1** : long slender cylindrical part **2** : deep vertical opening (as of a mine)

shag•gy *adj* **1** : covered with long hair or wool **2** : not neat and combed

shake *vb* **shook; shak•en** **1** : move or cause to move quickly back and forth **2** : distress **3** : clasp (hands) as friendly gesture — **shake** *n* — **shak•er** *n*

shaky *adj* : not sound, stable, or reliable — **shak•i•ly** *adv* — **shak•i•ness** *n*

shall *vb, past* **should** — used as an auxiliary to express a command, futurity, or determination

shal•low *adj* **1** : not deep **2** : not intellectually profound

sham•bles *n* : state of disorder

shame *n* **1** : distress over guilt or disgrace **2** : cause of shame or regret ∼ *vb* **1** : make ashamed **2** : disgrace — **shame•ful** *adj* — **shame•ful•ly** *adv* — **shame•less** *adj* — **shame•less•ly** *adv*

sham•poo *vb* : wash one's hair ∼ *n* : act of or preparation used in shampooing

shape *vb* : form esp. in a particular structure or appearance ∼ *n* **1** : distinctive appearance or arrangement of parts **2** : condition — **shapeless** *adj* — **shape•li•ness** *n* — **shape•ly** *adj*

share *n* **1** : portion belonging to one **2** : interest in a company's stock ∼ *vb* : divide or use with others — **share•hold•er** *n* — **shar•er** *n*

shark *n* : voracious sea fish

sharp *adj* **1** : having a good point or cutting edge **2** : alert, clever, or sarcastic **3** : vigorous or fierce **4** : having prominent angles or a sudden change in direction **5** : distinct **6** : higher than the true pitch ∼ *adv* : exactly ∼ *n* : sharp note — **shar•pen** *vb* — **sharp•en•er** *n* — **sharp•ly** *adv* — **sharp•ness** *n*

shat·ter *vb* : smash or burst into fragments — **shat·ter·proof** *adj*
shave *vb* **1 :** cut off with a razor **2 :** make bare by cutting the hair from **3 :** slice very thin ~ *n* : act or instance of shaving — **shav·er** *n*
shawl *n* : loose covering for the head or shoulders
she *pron* : that female one
shear *vb* **1 :** trim wool from **2 :** cut off with scissorlike action
shears *n pl* : cutting tool with 2 blades fastened so that the edges slide by each other
shed *vb* **1 :** give off (as tears or hair) **2 :** cause to flow or diffuse ~ *n* : small storage building
sheen *n* : subdued luster
sheep *n* (**sheep**) : domesticated mammal covered with wool — **sheep·skin** *n*
sheep·ish *adj* : embarrassed by awareness of a fault
sheer *adj* **1 :** pure **2 :** very steep **3 :** very thin or transparent
sheet *n* : broad flat piece (as of cloth or paper)
shelf *n* (**shelves**) **1 :** flat narrow structure used for storage or display **2 :** sandbank or rock ledge
shell *n* **1 :** hard or tough outer covering **2 :** case holding explosive powder and projectile for a weapon **3 :** light racing boat with oars ~ *vb* **1 :** remove the shell of **2 :** bombard — **shelled** *adj* — **shell·er** *n*
shel·ter *n* : something that gives protection ~ *vb* : give refuge to
shep·herd *n* : one that tends sheep ~ *vb* : act as a shepherd or guardian
sher·bet, sher·bert *n* : fruit-flavored frozen dessert
sher·iff *n* : county law officer
shield *n* **1 :** broad piece of armor carried on the arm **2 :** something that protects — **shield** *vb*
shier *comparative of* SHY
shiest *superlative of* SHY
shift *vb* **1 :** change place, position, or direction **2 :** get by ~ *n* **1 :** loose-fitting dress **2 :** an act or instance of shifting **3 :** scheduled work period
shift·less *adj* : lazy
shifty *adj* : tricky or untrustworthy
shin *n* : front part of the leg below the knee ~ *vb* : climb by sliding the body close along
shine *vb* **1 :** give off or cause to give off light **2 :** be outstanding **3 :** polish ~ *n* : brilliance
shiny *adj* : bright or polished
ship *n* **1 :** large oceangoing vessel **2 :** aircraft or spacecraft ~ *vb* **1 :** put on a ship **2 :** transport by carrier — **ship·board** *n* — **ship·build·er** *n* — **ship·per** *n* — **ship·wreck** *n or vb* — **ship·yard** *n*
ship·ment *n* : an act of shipping or the goods shipped
shirk *vb* : evade — **shirk·er** *n*
shirt *n* : garment for covering the torso — **shirt·less** *adj*
shiv·er *vb* : tremble — **shiv·er** *n* — **shiv·ery** *adj*
shock *n* **1 :** forceful impact **2 :** violent mental or emotional disturbance **3 :** effect of a charge of electricity **4 :** depression of the vital bodily processes ~ *vb* **1 :** strike with surprise, horror, or disgust **2 :** subject to an electrical shock — **shock·proof** *adj*
shod·dy *adj* : poorly made or done — **shod·di·ly** *adv* — **shod·di·ness** *n*
shoe *n* **1 :** covering for the human foot **2 :** horseshoe ~ *vb* **shod; shod:** put horseshoes on — **shoe·lace** *n* — **shoe·ma·ker** *n*
shone *past of* SHINE
shook *past of* SHAKE
shoot *vb* **shot; shot 1 :** propel (as an arrow or bullet) **2 :** wound or kill with a missile **3 :** discharge (a weapon) **4 :** drive (as a ball) at a goal **5 :** photograph **6 :** move swiftly ~ *n* : new plant growth — **shoot·er** *n*
shop *n* : place where things are made or sold ~ *vb* : visit stores — **shop·keep·er** *n* — **shop·per** *n*
shop·lift *vb* : steal goods from a store — **shop·lift·er** *n*
[1]**shore** *n* : land along the edge of water — **shore·bird** *n* — **shore·line** *n*
[2]**shore** *vb* : prop up ~ *n* : something that props
short *adj* **1 :** not long or tall or extending far **2 :** brief in time **3 :** curt **4 :** not having or being enough ~ *adv* : curtly ~ *n* **1** *pl* : short drawers or trousers **2 :** short circuit — **short·en** *vb* — **short·ly** *adv* — **short·ness** *n*
short·age *n* : deficiency
short·cut *n* **1 :** more direct route than that usu. taken **2 :** quicker way of doing something
short·hand *n* : method of speed writing
shot *n* **1 :** act of shooting **2 :** attempt (as at making a goal) **3 :** small pellets forming a charge **4 :** range or reach **5 :** photograph **6 :** injection of medicine **7 :** small serving of liquor — **shot·gun** *n*

should *past of* SHALL — used as an auxiliary to express condition, obligation, or probability

shoul·der *n* **1 :** part of the body where the arm joins the trunk **2 :** part that projects or lies to the side ~ *vb* **:** push with or bear on the shoulder

shout *vb* **:** give voice loudly — **shout** *n*

shove *vb* **:** push along or away — **shove** *n*

shov·el *n* **:** broad tool for digging or lifting ~ *vb* **:** take up or dig with a shovel

show *vb* **1 :** present to view **2 :** reveal or demonstrate **3 :** teach **4 :** prove **5 :** conduct or escort **6 :** appear or be noticeable ~ *n* **1 :** demonstrative display **2 :** spectacle **3 :** theatrical, radio, or television program — **show·case** *n* — **show off** *vb* **1 :** display proudly **2 :** act so as to attract attention — **show up** *vb* **:** arrive

show·er *n* **1 :** brief fall of rain **2 :** bath in which water sprinkles down on the person or a facility for such a bath **3 :** party at which someone gets gifts ~ *vb* **1 :** rain or fall in a shower **2 :** bathe in a shower — **show·ery** *adj*

showy *adj* **:** very noticeable or overly elaborate — **show·i·ly** *adv* — **show·i·ness** *n*

shrank *past of* SHRINK

shred *n* **:** narrow strip cut or torn off ~ *vb* **:** cut or tear into shreds

shrewd *adj* **:** clever — **shrewd·ly** *adv* — **shrewd·ness** *n*

shriek *n* **:** shrill cry — **shriek** *vb*

shrill *adj* **:** piercing and high-pitched — **shril·ly** *adv*

shrimp *n* **:** small sea crustacean

shrine *n* **1 :** tomb of a saint **2 :** hallowed place

shrink *vb* **shrank/shrunk; shrunk/shrunk·en 1 :** draw back or away **2 :** become smaller — **shrink·able** *adj*

shriv·el *vb* **:** shrink or wither into wrinkles

shrub *n* **:** low woody plant — **shrub·by** *adj*

shrub·bery *n* **:** growth of shrubs

shrug *vb* **:** hunch the shoulders up in doubt, indifference, or uncertainty — **shrug** *n*

shrunk *past part* of SHRINK

shrunk·en *past part* of SHRINK

shud·der *vb* **:** tremble — **shud·der** *n*

shuf·fle *vb* **1 :** mix together **2 :** walk with a sliding movement — **shuf·fle** *n*

shun *vb* **:** keep away from

shut *vb* (**shut; shut**) **1 :** bar passage into or through (as by moving a lid or door) **2 :** suspend activity — **shut out** *vb* **:** exclude — **shut up** *vb* **:** stop or cause to stop talking

shut·ter *n* **1 :** movable cover for a window **2 :** camera part that exposes film

shut·tle *n* **1 :** part of a weaving machine that carries thread back and forth **2 :** vehicle traveling back and forth over a short route ~ *vb* **:** move back and forth frequently

shy *adj* **1 :** sensitive and hesitant in dealing with others **2 :** wary **3 :** lacking ~ *vb* **:** draw back (as in fright) — **shy·ly** *adv* — **shy·ness** *n*

sick *adj* **1 :** not in good health **2 :** nauseated **3 :** relating to or meant for the sick — **sick·bed** *n* — **sick·en** *vb* — **sick·ly** *adj* — **sick·ness** *n*

side *n* **1 :** part to left or right of an object or the torso **2 :** edge or surface away from the center or at an angle to top and bottom or ends **3 :** contrasting or opposing position or group — **sid·ed** *adj*

side·swipe *vb* **:** strike with a glancing blow — **side·swipe** *n*

side·track *vb* **:** lead aside or astray

side·walk *n* **:** paved walk at the side of a road

side·ways *adv or adj* **1 :** to or from the side **2 :** with one side to the front

sift *vb* **1 :** pass through a sieve **2 :** examine carefully — **sift·er** *n*

sigh *n* **:** audible release of the breath (as to express weariness) — **sigh** *vb*

sight *n* **1 :** something seen or worth seeing **2 :** process, power, or range of seeing **3 :** device used in aiming **4 :** view or glimpse ~ *vb* **:** get sight of — **sight·ed** *adj* — **sight·less** *adj* — **sight–see·ing** *adj* — **sight·seer** *n*

sign *n* **1 :** symbol **2 :** gesture expressing a command or thought **3 :** public notice to advertise or warn **4 :** trace ~ *vb* **1 :** mark with or make a sign **2 :** write one's name on — **sign·er** *n*

sig·nal *n* **1 :** sign of command or warning **2 :** electronic transmission ~ *vb* **:** communicate or notify by signals ~ *adj* **:** distinguished

sig·na·ture *n* **:** one's name written by oneself

sig·ni·fy *vb* **1 :** show by a sign **2 :** mean — **sig·nif·i·cance** *n* — **sig·nif·i·cant** *adj* — **sig·nif·i·cant·ly** *adv* — **sig·ni·fi·ca·tion** *n*

si·lence *n* **:** state of being without sound ~ *vb* **:** keep from making noise or sound — **si·lenc·er** *n* — **si·lent** *adj* — **si·lent·ly** *adv*

silk *n* **1 :** fine strong lustrous protein fiber from moth larvae (**silkworms**) **2 :** thread or cloth made from silk — **silk·en** *adj* — **silky** *adj*

sil·ly *adj* **:** foolish or stupid — **sil·li·ness** *n*

sil·ver *n* **1 :** white ductile metallic chemical element **2 :** table utensils ~ *adj* **:** having the color of silver — **sil•very** *adj*

sim•i•lar *adj* **:** resembling each other in some ways — **sim•i•lar•i•ty** *n* — **sim•i•lar•ly** *adv*

sim•ple *adj* **1 :** free from dishonesty, vanity, or pretense **2 :** of humble origin or modest position **3 :** not complex **4 :** lacking education, experience, or intelligence — **sim•ple•ness** *n* — **sim•ply** *adv*

sim•plic•i•ty *n* **:** state or fact of being simple

sim•pli•fy *vb* **:** make easier — **sim•pli•fi•ca•tion** *n*

sim•u•late *vb* **:** create the effect or appearance of — **sim•u•la•tion** *n* — **sim•u•la•tor** *n*

si•mul•ta•ne•ous *adj* **:** occurring or operating at the same time — **si•mul•ta•ne•ous•ly** *adv* — **simul•ta•ne•ous•ness** *n*

sin *n* **:** offense against God ~ *vb* **:** commit a sin — **sin•ful** *adj* — **sin•less** *adj* — **sin•ner** *n*

since *adv* **1 :** from a past time until now **2 :** backward in time ~ *prep* **1 :** in the period after **2 :** continuously from ~ *conj* **1 :** from the time when **2 :** because

sin•cere *adj* **:** genuine or honest — **sin•cere•ly** *adv* — **sin•cer•i•ty** *n*

sing *vb* **sang; sung :** produce musical tones with the voice — **sing•er** *n*

sin•gle *adj* **1 :** one only **2 :** unmarried ~ *n* **:** separate one — **sin•gle•ness** *n* — **sin•gly** *adv* — **single out** *vb* **:** select or set aside

sin•gu•lar *adj* **1 :** relating to a word form denoting one **2 :** outstanding or superior **3 :** queer — **sin•gu•lar** *n* — **sin•gu•lar•i•ty** *n* — **sin•gu•lar•ly** *adv*

sink *vb* **(sank; sunk) 1 :** go or put underwater **2 :** grow worse **3 :** make by digging or boring **4 :** invest ~ *n* **:** basin with a drain

sip *vb* **:** drink in small quantities — **sip** *n*

sir *n* **1** — used before the first name of a knight or baronet **2** — used as a respectful form of address

si•ren *n* **1 :** seductive woman **2 :** wailing warning whistle

sis•sy *n* **:** timid or effeminate boy

sis•ter *n* **:** female sharing one or both parents with another person — **sis•ter•hood** *n* — **sis•ter•ly** *adj*

sis•ter–in–law *n* **sis•ters–in–law :** sister of one's spouse or wife of one's brother

sit *vb* **sat; sat 1 :** rest on the buttocks **2 :** settle on a resting place **3 :** hold a session **4 :** pose for a portrait **5 :** have a location **6 :** rest or fix in place — **sit•ter** *n*

site *n* **1 :** place **2 :** Web site

sit•u•a•tion *n* **1 :** location **2 :** condition **3 :** job

six *n* **:** one more than 5 — **six** *adj or pron* — **sixth** *adj or adv or n*

six•teen *n* **:** one more than 15 — **sixteen** *adj or pron* — **six•teenth** *adj or n*

six•ty *n* **:** 6 times 10 — **six•ti•eth** *adj or n* — **sixty** *adj or pron*

size *n* **:** measurement of the amount of space something takes up ~ *vb* **:** grade according to size — **siz•able** *adj* — **siz•ably** *adv*

skate *n* **1 :** metal runner on a shoe for gliding over ice **2 :** roller skate — **skate** *vb* — **skat•er** *n*

skel•e•ton *n* **:** bony framework — **skel•e•tal** *adj*

skep•tic *n* **:** one who is critical or doubting — **skep•ti•cal** *adj* — **skep•ti•cism** *n*

sketch *n* **1 :** rough drawing **2 :** short story or essay — **sketch** *vb* — **sketchy** *adj*

ski *n* **:** long strip for gliding over snow or water — **ski** *vb* — **ski•er** *n*

skid *n* **1 :** plank for supporting something or on which it slides **2 :** act of skidding ~ *vb* **:** slide sideways

skill *n* **:** developed or learned ability — **skilled** *adj* — **skill•ful** *adj* — **skill•ful•ly** *adv*

skim *vb* **1 :** take off from the top of a liquid **2 :** read or move over swiftly ~ *adj* **:** having the cream removed — **skim•mer** *n*

skin *n* **1 :** outer layer of an animal body **2 :** rind ~ *vb* **:** take the skin from — **skin•less** *adj* — **skinned** *adj* — **skin•tight** *adj*

skin•ny *adj* **:** very thin

skip *vb* **1 :** move with leaps **2 :** read past or ignore — **skip** *n*

skirt *n* **:** garment or part of a garment that hangs below the waist ~ *vb* **:** pass around the edge of

skull *n* **:** bony case that protects the brain

sky *n* **1 :** upper air **2 :** heaven — **sky•line** *n* — **sky•ward** *adv or adj*

sky•scrap•er *n* **:** very tall building

slab *n* **:** thick slice

slack *adj* **1 :** careless **2 :** not taut **3 :** not busy ~ *n* **1 :** part hanging loose **2** *pl* **:** casual trousers — **slack•en** *vb* — **slack•ly** *adv* — **slack•ness** *n*

slain *past part of* SLAY

slam *n* **:** heavy jarring impact ~ *vb* **:** shut, strike, or throw violently and loudly

slang *n* **:** informal nonstandard vocabulary — **slangy** *adj*

slant *vb* **1 :** slope **2 :** present with a special

viewpoint ~ *n* : sloping direction, line, or plane

slap *vb* : strike sharply with the open hand — **slap** *n*

slash *vb* **1 :** cut with sweeping strokes **2 :** reduce sharply ~ *n* : gash

slaugh•ter *n* **1 :** butchering of livestock for market **2 :** great and cruel destruction of lives ~ *vb* : commit slaughter upon — **slaugh•ter•house** *n*

slave *n* : one owned and forced into service by another ~ *vb* : work as or like a slave — **slave** *adj* — **slav•ery** *n* — **slav•ish** *adj* — **slav•ish•ly** *adv*

slay *vb* (**slew/slayed; slain**) **1** *past slew* : kill **2** *past slayed* : overwhelm with amusement — **slay•er** *n*

sled *n* : vehicle on runners — **sled** *vb*

sleek *adj* : smooth or glossy — **sleek** *vb*

sleep *n* : natural suspension of consciousness ~ *vb* (**slept; slept**) : rest in a state of sleep — **sleep•er** *n* — **sleep•i•ly** *adv* — **sleep•i•ness** *n* — **sleep•less** *adj* — **sleep•walk•er** *n* — **sleepy** *adj*

sleeve *n* : part of a garment for the arm — **sleeve•less** *adj*

sleigh *n* : horse-drawn sled with seats ~ *vb* : drive or ride in a sleigh

slen•der *adj* **1 :** thin esp. in physique **2 :** scanty

slew *past of* SLAY

slice *n* : thin flat piece ~ *vb* : cut a slice from

slick *adj* **1 :** very smooth **2 :** clever — **slick** *vb*

slide *vb* : move smoothly along a surface ~ *n* **1 :** act of sliding **2 :** surface on which something slides **3 :** transparent picture for projection

slier *comparative of* SLY

sliest *superlative of* SLY

slight *adj* **1 :** slender **2 :** frail **3 :** small in degree ~ *vb* **1 :** ignore or treat as not important — **slight** *n* — **slight•ly** *adv*

slim *adj* **1 :** slender **2 :** scanty ~ *vb* : make or become slender

slime *n* : dirty slippery film (as on water) — **slimy** *adj*

sling *vb* (**slung; slung**) : hurl with or as if with a sling ~ *n* **1 :** strap for swinging and hurling stones **2 :** looped strap or bandage to lift or support

slink *vb* (**slunk; slunk**) : move stealthily or sinuously — **slinky** *adj*

¹slip *vb* **1 :** escape quietly or secretly **2 :** slide along smoothly **3 :** make a mistake **4 :** to pass without being noticed or done **5 :** fall off from a standard ~ *n* **1 :** ship's berth **2 :** sudden mishap **3 :** mistake **4 :** woman's undergarment

²slip *n* **1 :** plant shoot **2 :** small strip (as of paper)

slip•per *n* : shoe that slips on easily

slip•pery *adj* **1 :** slick enough to slide on **2 :** tricky — **slip•peri•ness** *n*

slit *vb* (**slit; slit**) : make a slit in ~ *n* : long narrow cut

slob *n* : untidy person

slob•ber *vb* : dribble saliva — **slob•ber** *n*

slo•gan *n* : word or phrase expressing the aim of a cause

slop *n* : food waste for animal feed ~ *vb* : spill

slope *vb* : deviate from the vertical or horizontal ~ *n* : upward or downward slant

slop•py *adj* **1 :** muddy **2 :** untidy

slot *n* : narrow opening

slow *adj* **1 :** sluggish or stupid **2 :** moving, working, or happening at less than the usual speed ~ *vb* **1 :** make slow **2 :** go slower — **slow** *adv* — **slow•ly** *adv* — **slow•ness** *n*

slug•gish *adj* : slow in movement or flow — **slug•gish•ly** *adv* — **slug•gish•ness** *n*

slum *n* : thickly populated area marked by poverty

slum•ber *vb or n* : sleep

slump *vb* **1 :** sink suddenly **2 :** assume an extremely relaxed or stooped posture — **slump** *n*

slung *past of* SLING

slunk *past of* SLINK

slur *vb* : run (words or notes) together — **slur** *n*

sly *adj* : given to or showing secrecy and deception — **sly•ly** *adv* — **sly•ness** *n*

smack *vb* **1 :** move (the lips) so as to make a sharp noise **2 :** kiss or slap with a loud noise ~ *n* **1 :** sharp noise made by the lips **2 :** noisy slap

small *adj* **1 :** little in size or amount **2 :** few in number **3 :** trivial — **small•ish** *adj* — **small•ness** *n*

smart *vb* **1 :** cause or feel stinging pain **2 :** endure distress ~ *adj* **1 :** intelligent or resourceful **2 :** stylish — **smart** *n* — **smart•ly** *adv* — **smart•ness** *n*

smash *vb* : break or be broken into pieces ~ *n* **1 :** smashing blow **2 :** act or sound of smashing

smear *n* : greasy stain ~ *vb* **1 :** spread (something sticky) **2 :** smudge **3 :** spread malicious gossip about someone

smell *vb* **1 :** perceive the odor of **2 :** have or give off an odor ~ *n* **1 :** sense by which one perceives odor **2 :** odor — **smelly** *adj*

smelt *vb* : melt or fuse (ore) in order to separate the metal — **smelt•er** *n*

smile *n* : facial expression with the mouth turned up usu. to show pleasure — **smile** *vb*

smog *n* : fog and smoke — **smog•gy** *adj*

smoke *n* : sooty gas from burning ~ *vb* **1 :** give off smoke **2 :** inhale the fumes of burning tobacco **3 :** cure (as meat) with smoke — **smoke•less** *adj* — **smok•er** *n* — **smoky** *adj*

smooth *adj* **1 :** having a surface without irregularities **2 :** not jarring or jolting ~ *vb* : make smooth — **smooth•ly** *adv* — **smooth•ness** *n*

smoth•er *vb* **1 :** kill by depriving of air **2 :** cover thickly

smudge *vb* : soil or blur by rubbing ~ *n* **1 :** thick smoke **2 :** dirty spot

smug•gle *vb* : import or export secretly or illegally — **smug•gler** *n*

snack *n* : light meal

snag *n* : unexpected difficulty ~ *vb* : become caught on something that sticks out

snake *n* : long-bodied limbless reptile — **snake•bite** *n*

snap *vb* **1 :** bite at something **2 :** utter angry words **3 :** break suddenly with a sharp sound ~ *n* **1 :** act or sound of snapping **2 :** fastening that closes with a click **3 :** something easy to do — **snap•per** *n* — **snap•pish** *adj* — **snap•py** *adj*

snap•shot *n* : casual photograph

snare *n* : trap for catching game ~ *vb* : capture or hold with or as if with a snare

[1]**snarl** *n* : tangle ~ *vb* : cause to become knotted

[2]**snarl** *vb or n* : growl

snatch *vb* **1 :** try to grab something suddenly **2 :** seize or take away suddenly ~ *n* **1 :** act of snatching **2 :** something brief or fragmentary

sneak *vb* : move or take in a furtive manner ~ *n* : one who acts in a furtive manner — **sneak•i•ly** *adv* — **sneak•ing•ly** *adv* — **sneaky** *adj*

sneak•er *n* : sports shoe

sneer *vb* : smile scornfully — **sneer** *n*

sneeze *vb* : force the breath out with sudden and involuntary violence — **sneeze** *n*

snick•er *n* : partly suppressed laugh — **snicker** *vb*

sniff *vb* **1 :** draw air audibly up the nose **2 :** detect by smelling — **sniff** *n*

snob *n* : one who acts superior to others — **snob•bery** *n* — **snob•bish** *adj* — **snob•bish•ly** *adv* — **snob•bish•ness** *n*

snoop *vb* : pry in a furtive way ~ *n* : prying person

snooze *vb* : take a nap — **snooze** *n*

snore *vb* : breathe with a hoarse noise while sleeping — **snore** *n*

snort *vb* : force air noisily through the nose — **snort** *n*

snow *n* : crystals formed from water vapor ~ *vb* : fall as snow — **snow•ball** *n* — **snow•bank** *n* — **snow•drift** *n* — **snow•fall** *n* — **snow•plow** *n* — **snow•storm** *n* — **snowy** *adj*

snuff *vb* : put out (a candle) — **snuff•er** *n*

snug *adj* **1 :** warm, secure, and comfortable **2 :** fitting closely — **snug•ly** *adv* — **snug•ness** *n*

snug•gle *vb* : curl up comfortably

so *adv* **1 :** in the manner or to the extent indicated **2 :** in the same way **3 :** therefore **4 :** finally **5 :** thus ~ *conj* : for that reason

soak *vb* **1 :** lie in a liquid **2 :** absorb ~ *n* : act of soaking

soap *n* : cleaning substance — **soap** *vb* — **soapy** *adj*

soar *vb* : fly upward on or as if on wings

sob *vb* : weep with convulsive heavings of the chest — **sob** *n*

so•ber *adj* **1 :** not drunk **2 :** serious or solemn — **so•ber•ly** *adv*

soc•cer *n* : game played by kicking a ball

so•cia•ble *adj* : friendly — **so•cia•bil•i•ty** *n* — **so•cia•bly** *adv*

so•cial *adj* **1 :** relating to pleasant companionship **2 :** naturally living or growing in groups **3 :** relating to human society ~ *n* : social gathering — **so•cial•ly** *adv*

so•cial•ism *n* : social system based on government control of the production and distribution of goods — **so•cial•ist** *n or adj* — **so•cial•is•tic** *adj*

so•cial•ize *vb* **1 :** regulate by socialism **2 :** adapt to social needs **3 :** participate in a social gathering — **so•cial•i•za•tion** *n*

so•ci•ety *n* **1 :** companionship **2 :** community life **3 :** rich or fashionable class **4 :** voluntary group

so•ci•ol•o•gy *n* : study of social relationships — **so•ci•o•log•i•cal** *adj* — **so•ci•ol•o•gist** *n*
[1]**sock** *n* : short stocking
[2]**sock** *vb or n* : punch
sock•et *n* : hollow part that holds something
so•da *n* **1 :** carbonated water or a soft drink **2 :** ice cream drink made with soda
so•fa *n* : wide padded chair
soft *adj* **1 :** not hard, rough, or harsh **2 :** containing no alcohol — **soft•en** *vb* — **soft•en•er** *n* — **soft•ly** *adv* — **soft•ness** *n*
soft•ball *n* : game like baseball
soft•ware *n* : computer programs
sog•gy *adj* : heavy with moisture — **sog•gi•ness** *n*
[1]**soil** *vb* : make or become dirty ~ *n* : embedded dirt
[2]**soil** *n* : loose surface material of the earth
so•lar *adj* : relating to the sun or the energy in sunlight
sold *past of* SELL
sol•dier *n* : person in military service ~ *vb* : serve as a soldier — **sol•dier•ly** *adj or adv*
[1]**sole** *n* : bottom of the foot or a shoe — **soled** *adj*
[2]**sole** *adj* : single or only — **sole•ly** *adv*
sol•emn *adj* **1 :** dignified and ceremonial **2 :** highly serious — **so•lem•ni•ty** *n* — **sol•emn•ly** *adv*
so•lic•it *vb* : ask for — **so•lic•i•ta•tion** *n*
so•lic•i•tor *n* **1 :** one that solicits **2 :** lawyer
sol•id *adj* **1 :** not hollow **2 :** having 3 dimensions **3 :** hard **4 :** of good quality **5 :** of one character ~ *n* **1 :** 3-dimensional figure **2 :** substance in solid form — **solid** *adv* — **so•lid•i•ty** *n* — **sol•id•ly** *adv* — **sol•id•ness** *n*
sol•i•dar•i•ty *n* : unity of purpose
sol•i•tary *adj* **1 :** alone **2 :** isolated **3 :** single
so•lo *n* : performance by only one person ~ *adv* : alone — **solo** *adj or vb* — **so•lo•ist** *n*
so•lu•tion *n* **1 :** answer to a problem **2 :** homogeneous liquid mixture
solve *vb* : find a solution for — **solv•able** *adj*
sol•vent *adj* **1 :** able to pay all debts **2 :** dissolving or able to dissolve ~ *n* : substance that dissolves or disperses another substance — **sol•ven•cy** *n*
some *adj* **1 :** one unspecified **2 :** unspecified or indefinite number of **3 :** at least a few or a little ~ *pron* : a certain number or amount
som•er•sault *n* : body flip — **som•er•sault** *vb*
some•what *adv* : in some degree
son *n* : male offspring
song *n* : music and words to be sung
son–in–law *n* **sons–in–law** : husband of one's daughter
soon *adv* **1 :** before long **2 :** promptly **3 :** early
soot *n* : fine black substance formed by combustion — **sooty** *adj*
soothe *vb* : calm or comfort — **sooth•er** *n*
so•phis•ti•cat•ed *adj* **1 :** complex **2 :** wise, cultured, or shrewd in human affairs — **so•phis•ti•ca•tion** *n*
soph•o•more *n* : 2d-year student
so•pra•no *n* : highest singing voice
sore *adj* **1 :** causing pain or distress **2 :** severe or intense **3 :** angry ~ *n* : sore usu. infected spot on the body — **sore•ly** *adv* — **sore•ness** *n*
sor•row *n* : deep distress, sadness, or regret or a cause of this — **sor•row•ful** *adj* — **sor•row•ful•ly** *adv*
sor•ry *adj* **1 :** feeling sorrow, regret, or penitence **2 :** dismal
sort *n* **1 :** kind **2 :** nature ~ *vb* : classify — **out of sorts** : grouchy
SOS *n* : call for help
so–so *adj or adv* : barely acceptable
sought *past of* SEEK
soul *n* **1 :** immaterial essence of an individual life **2 :** essential part **3 :** person
soul•ful *adj* : full of or expressing deep feeling — **soul•ful•ly** *adv*
[1]**sound** *adj* **1 :** free from fault, error, or illness **2 :** firm or hard **3 :** showing good judgment — **sound•ly** *adv* — **sound•ness** *n*
[2]**sound** *n* **1 :** sensation of hearing **2 :** energy of vibration sensed in hearing **3 :** something heard ~ *vb* **1 :** make or cause to make a sound **2 :** seem — **sound•less** *adj* — **sound•less•ly** *adv* — **sound•proof** *adj or vb*
soup *n* : broth usu. containing pieces of solid food — **soupy** *adj*
sour *adj* **1 :** having an acid or tart taste **2 :** disagreeable ~ *vb* : become or make sour — **sour•ish** *adj* — **sour•ly** *adv* — **sour•ness** *n*
source *n* **1 :** point of origin **2 :** one that provides something needed
souse *vb* **1 :** pickle **2 :** immerse **3 :** intoxicate ~ *n* **1 :** something pickled **2 :** drunkard
south *adv* : to or toward the south ~ *adj* : situated toward, at, or coming from the south ~ *n* **1 :** direction to the right of sunrise **2** *cap* : regions to the south — **south•er•ly** *adv or adj* — **south•ern** *adj* — **South•ern•er** *n* —

south•ern•most *adj* — **southward** *adv or adj* — **south•wards** *adv*

south•east *n* **1 :** direction between south and east **2** *cap* : regions to the southeast — **south-east** *adj or adv* — **south•east•er•ly** *adv or adj* — **south•east•ern** *adj*

south pole *n* : the southernmost point of the earth

south•west *n* **1 :** direction between south and west **2** *cap* : regions to the southwest — **south•west** *adj or adv* — **south•west•er•ly** *adv or adj* — **south•west•ern** *adj*

sou•ve•nir *n* : something that is a reminder of a place or event

sow *vb* **1 :** plant or strew with seed **2 :** scatter abroad — **sow•er** *n*

sox *pl of* SOCK

space *n* **1 :** period of time **2 :** area in, around, or between **3 :** region beyond earth's atmosphere **4 :** accommodations ~ *vb* : place at intervals — **space•craft** *n* — **space•flight** *n* — **space•man** *n* — **space•ship** *n*

spa•cious *adj* : large or roomy — **spa•cious•ly** *adv* — **spa•cious•ness** *n*

[1]spade *n or vb* : shovel — **spade•ful** *n*

[2]spade *n* : playing card marked with a black figure like an inverted heart

spa•ghet•ti *n* : pasta strings

spam *n* : unsolicited commercial e-mail

span *n* **1 :** amount of time **2 :** distance between supports ~ *vb* : extend across

spank *vb* : hit on the buttocks with an open hand

spare *adj* **1 :** held in reserve **2 :** thin or scanty ~ *vb* **1 :** reserve or avoid using **2 :** avoid punishing or killing — **spare** *n*

spark *n* **1 :** tiny hot and glowing particle **2 :** smallest beginning or germ **3 :** visible electrical discharge ~ *vb* **1 :** emit or produce sparks **2 :** stir to activity

spar•kle *vb* **1 :** flash **2 :** effervesce ~ *n* : gleam — **spark•ler** *n*

sparse *adj* : thinly scattered — **sparse•ly** *adv*

spasm *n* **1 :** involuntary muscular contraction **2 :** sudden, violent, and temporary effort or feeling — **spas•mod•ic** *adj* — **spas•mod•i•cal•ly** *adv*

spa•tial *adj* : relating to space — **spa•tial•ly** *adv*

spat•ter *vb* : splash with drops of liquid — **spat•ter** *n*

spawn *vb* **1 :** produce eggs or offspring **2 :** bring forth ~ *n* : egg cluster — **spawn•er** *n*

speak *vb* (**spoke; spo•ken**) **1 :** utter words **2 :** express orally **3 :** address an audience **4 :** use (a language) in talking — **speak•er** *n*

spear *n* : long pointed weapon ~ *vb* : strike or pierce with a spear

spe•cial *adj* **1 :** unusual or unique **2 :** particularly favored **3 :** set aside for a particular use — **special** *n* — **spe•cial•ly** *adv*

spe•cial•ist *n* **1 :** person who specializes in a particular branch of learning or activity **2 :** any of four enlisted ranks in the army corresponding to the grades of corporal through sergeant first class

spe•cial•ize *vb* : concentrate one's efforts — **spe•cial•i•za•tion** *n*

spe•cial•ty *n* : area or field in which one specializes

spe•cies *n* : biological grouping of closely related organisms

spe•cif•ic *adj* : definite or exact — **spe•cif•i•cal•ly** *adv*

spec•i•fy *vb* : mention precisely or by name — **spec•i•fi•ca•tion** *n*

spec•i•men *n* : typical example

speck *n* : tiny particle or blemish — **speck** *vb*

spec•ta•cle *n* **1 :** impressive public display **2** *pl* : eyeglasses

spec•tac•u•lar *adj* : sensational or showy

spec•ta•tor *n* : person who looks on

spec•u•late *vb* **1 :** think about things yet unknown **2 :** risk money in a business deal in hope of high profit — **spec•u•la•tion** *n* — **spec•u•la•tive** *adj* — **spec•u•la•tor** *n*

speech *n* **1 :** power, act, or manner of speaking **2 :** talk given to an audience — **speech-less** *adj*

speed *n* **1 :** quality of being fast **2 :** rate of motion or performance ~ *vb* **sped; sped:** go at a great or excessive rate of speed — **speed-boat** *n* — **speed•er** *n* — **speed•i•ly** *adv* — **speed•up** *n* — **speedy** *adj*

[1]spell *n* : influence of or like magic

[2]spell *vb* **1 :** name, write, or print the letters of **2 :** mean — **spell•er** *n*

spend *vb* (**spent; spent**) **1 :** pay out **2 :** cause or allow to pass — **spend•er** *n*

sperm *n* : semen or a germ cell in it

sphere *n* **1 :** figure with every point on its surface at an equal distance from the center **2 :** round body **3 :** range of action or influence — **spher•i•cal** *adj*

spice *n* **1 :** aromatic plant product for seasoning food **2 :** interesting quality — **spice** *vb* — **spicy** *adj*

spi•der *n* : small insectlike animal with 8 legs — **spi•dery** *adj*
spike *n* : very large nail ~ *vb* : fasten or pierce with a spike — **spiked** *adj*
spill *vb* **1 :** fall, flow, or run out unintentionally **2 :** divulge ~ *n* **1 :** act of spilling **2 :** something spilled — **spill•able** *adj*
spin *vb* (**spun; spun**) **1 :** draw out fiber and twist into thread **2 :** form thread from a sticky body fluid **3 :** revolve or cause to revolve extremely fast ~ *n* : rapid rotating motion — **spin•ner** *n*
spin•ach *n* : garden herb with edible leaves
spine *n* **1 :** backbone **2 :** stiff sharp projection on a plant or animal — **spine•less** *adj* — **spiny** *adj*
spi•ral *adj* : circling or winding around a single point or line — **spiral** *n or vb* — **spi•ral•ly** *adv*
spire *n* : usu. tapering church tower — **spiry** *adj*
spir•it *n* **1 :** life-giving force **2** *cap* **:** presence of God **3 :** ghost **4 :** mood **5 :** vivacity or enthusiasm **6** *pl* **:** alcoholic liquor ~ *vb* : carry off secretly — **spir•it•ed** *adj* — **spir•it•less** *adj*
spir•i•tu•al *adj* **1 :** relating to the spirit or sacred matters **2 :** deeply religious ~ *n* : religious folk song — **spir•i•tu•al•i•ty** *n* — **spir•i•tu•al•ly** *adv*
spit *vb* (**spit/spat; spit/spat**) : eject saliva from the mouth ~ *n* **1 :** saliva **2 :** perfect likeness
spite *n* : petty ill will ~ *vb* : annoy or offend — **spite•ful** *adj* — **spite•ful•ly** *adv* — **in spite of :** in defiance or contempt of
splash *vb* : scatter a liquid on — **splash** *n*
splat•ter *vb* : spatter — **splat•ter** *n*
splen•did *adj* **1 :** impressive in beauty or brilliance **2 :** outstanding — **splen•did•ly** *adv*
splen•dor *n* **1 :** brilliance **2 :** magnificence
splice *vb* : join (2 things) end to end — **splice** *n*
splint *n* **1 :** thin strip of wood **2 :** something that keeps an injured body part in place
splin•ter *n* : thin needlelike piece ~ *vb* : break into splinters
split *vb* **split; split** : divide lengthwise or along a grain — **split** *n*
spoil *n* : plunder ~ *vb* **1 :** ruin **2 :** rot **3 :** pamper excessively — **spoil•age** *n* — **spoil•er** *n*
spoke *past of* SPEAK
spo•ken *past part of* SPEAK
sponge *n* **1 :** porous water-absorbing mass that forms the skeleton of some marine animals **2 :** spongelike material used for wiping ~ *vb* **1 :** wipe with a sponge **2 :** live at another's expense — **spongy** *adj*
spon•sor *n* : one who assumes responsibility for another or who provides financial support — **spon•sor** *vb* — **spon•sor•ship** *n*
spon•ta•ne•ous *adj* : done, produced, or occurring naturally or without planning — **spon•ta•ne•i•ty** *n* — **spon•ta•ne•ous•ly** *adv*
spook *n* : ghost ~ *vb* : frighten — **spooky** *adj*
spool *n* : cylinder on which something is wound
spoon *n* : utensil consisting of a small shallow bowl with a handle — **spoon** *vb* — **spoon•ful** *n*
sport *vb* **1 :** frolic **2 :** show off ~ *n* **1 :** physical activity engaged in for pleasure **2 :** jest **3 :** person who shows good sportsmanship — **sport•ive** *adj* — **sporty** *adj*
sports•man•ship *n* : ability to be gracious in winning or losing
spot *n* **1 :** blemish **2 :** distinctive small part **3 :** location ~ *vb* **1 :** mark with spots **2 :** see or recognize ~ *adj* : made at random or in limited numbers — **spot•less** *adj* — **spot•less•ly** *adv*
spouse *n* : one's husband or wife
spout *vb* **1 :** shoot forth in a stream **2 :** say pompously ~ *n* **1 :** opening through which liquid spouts **2 :** jet of liquid
sprain *n* : twisting injury to a joint ~ *vb* : injure with a sprain
sprawl *vb* : lie or sit with limbs spread out — **sprawl** *n*
spray *n* **1 :** mist **2 :** device that discharges liquid as a mist — **spray** *vb* — **spray•er** *n*
spread *vb* **1 :** open up or unfold **2 :** scatter or smear over a surface **3 :** cause to be known or to exist over a wide area ~ *n* **1 :** extent to which something is spread **2 :** cloth cover **3 :** something intended to be spread — **spread•er** *n*
spring *vb* **1 :** move or grow quickly or by elastic force **2 :** come from by descent **3 :** make known suddenly ~ *n* **1 :** source **2 :** flow of water from underground **3 :** season between winter and summer **4 :** elastic body or device (as a coil of wire) **5 :** leap **6 :** elastic power — **springy** *adj*
sprin•kle *vb* : scatter in small drops or particles ~ *n* : light rainfall — **sprin•kler** *n*
sprite *n* : elf or elfish person

sprout *vb* **:** send out new growth ∼ *n* **:** plant shoot
spruce *adj* **:** neat and stylish in appearance ∼ *vb* **:** make or become neat
spun *past of* SPIN
spur *n* **1 :** pointed device used to urge on a horse **2 :** something that urges to action **3 :** projecting part ∼ *vb* **:** urge on — **spurred** *adj*
[1]**spurt** *n* **:** burst of effort, speed, or activity ∼ *vb* **:** make a spurt
[2]**spurt** *vb* **:** gush out ∼ *n* **:** sudden gush
sput·ter *vb* **1 :** talk hastily and indistinctly in excitement **2 :** make popping sounds — **sputter** *n*
spy *vb* **:** watch or try to gather information secretly — **spy** *n*
squab·ble *n or vb* **:** dispute
squad *n* **:** small group
square *n* **1 :** instrument for measuring right angles **2 :** flat figure that has 4 equal sides and 4 right angles **3 :** open area in a city **4 :** product of number multiplied by itself ∼ *adj* **1 :** being a square in form **2 :** having sides meet at right angles **3 :** multiplied by itself **4 :** being a square unit of area **5 :** honest ∼ *vb* **1 :** form into a square **2 :** multiply (a number) by itself **3 :** conform **4 :** settle — **square·ly** *adv*
[1]**squash** *vb* **1 :** press flat **2 :** suppress
[2]**squash** *n* **:** garden vegetable
squat *vb* **1 :** stoop or sit on one's heels **2 :** settle on land one does not own ∼ *n* **:** act or posture of squatting ∼ *adj* **:** short and thick — **squat·ter** *n*
squeak *vb* **:** make a thin high-pitched sound — **squeak** *n* — **squeaky** *adj*
squeal *vb* **1 :** make a shrill sound or cry **2 :** protest — **squeal** *n*
squeeze *vb* **1 :** apply pressure to **2 :** extract by pressure — **squeeze** *n* — **squeez·er** *n*
squint *vb* **:** look with the eyes partly closed — **squint** *n or adj*
squirm *vb* **:** wriggle
squir·rel *n* **:** rodent with a long bushy tail
squirt *vb* **:** eject liquid in a spurt — **squirt** *n*
stab *n* **1 :** wound made by a pointed weapon **2 :** quick thrust **3 :** attempt ∼ *vb* **:** pierce or wound with or as if with a pointed weapon
[1]**sta·ble** *n* **:** building for domestic animals ∼ *vb* **:** keep in a stable
[2]**stable** *adj* **1 :** firmly established **2 :** mentally and emotionally healthy **3 :** steady — **sta·bil·i·ty** *n* — **sta·bil·iza·tion** *n* — **sta·bi·lize** *vb* — **sta·bi·liz·er** *n*
stack *n* **:** large pile ∼ *vb* **:** pile up
sta·di·um *n* **:** outdoor sports arena
staff *n* **1 :** rod or supporting cane **2 :** people assisting a leader **3 :** 5 horizontal lines on which music is written ∼ *vb* **:** supply with workers — **staff·er** *n*
stag *n* **:** male deer ∼ *adj* **:** only for men ∼ *adv* **:** without a date
stage *n* **1 :** raised platform for a speaker or performers **2 :** theater **3 :** step in a process ∼ *vb* **:** produce (a play)
stag·ger *vb* **1 :** reel or cause to reel from side to side **2 :** overlap or alternate — **stagger** *n* — **stag·ger·ing·ly** *adv*
stag·nant *adj* **:** not moving or active — **stagnate** *vb* — **stag·na·tion** *n*
staid *past of* STAY
stain *vb* **1 :** discolor **2 :** dye (as wood) **3 :** disgrace ∼ *n* **1 :** discolored area **2 :** mark of guilt **3 :** coloring preparation — **stain·less** *adj*
stair *n* **1 :** step in a series for going from one level to another **2** *pl* **:** flight of steps — **stairway** *n* — **stair·case** *n*
stake *n* **1 :** usu. small post driven into the ground **2 :** bet **3 :** prize in a contest ∼ *vb* **1 :** mark or secure with a stake **2 :** bet
stale *adj* **1 :** having lost good taste and quality from age **2 :** no longer new, strong, or effective — **stale·ness** *n*
stale·mate *n* **:** deadlock — **stale·mate** *vb*
[1]**stalk** *vb* **1 :** walk stiffly or proudly **2 :** pursue stealthily
[2]**stalk** *n* **:** plant stem — **stalked** *adj*
[1]**stall** *n* **1 :** compartment in a stable **2 :** booth where articles are sold
[2]**stall** *vb* **:** bring or come to a standstill unintentionally
[3]**stall** *vb* **:** delay, evade, or keep a situation going to gain advantage or time
stam·i·na *n* **:** endurance
stam·mer *vb* **:** hesitate in speaking — **stammer** *n*
stamp *vb* **1 :** pound with the sole of the foot or a heavy implement **2 :** impress or imprint **3 :** cut out with a die **4 :** attach a postage stamp to ∼ *n* **1 :** device for stamping **2 :** act of stamping **3 :** government seal showing a tax or fee has been paid
stance *n* **:** way of standing
stand *vb* **(stood; stood) 1 :** be at rest in or assume an upright position **2 :** remain un-

changed **3 :** be steadfast **4 :** maintain a relative position or rank **5 :** set upright **6 :** undergo or endure ~ *n* **1 :** act or place of standing, staying, or resisting **2 :** sales booth **3 :** structure for holding something upright **4 :** group of plants growing together **5** *pl* **:** tiered seats **6 :** opinion or viewpoint

stan•dard *n* **1 :** symbolic figure or flag **2 :** model, rule, or guide **3 :** upright support — **stan•dard** *adj* — **stan•dard•i•za•tion** *n* — **stan•dard•ize** *vb*

stank *past of* STINK

[1]sta•ple *n* **:** U-shaped wire fastener — **staple** *vb* — **sta•pler** *n*

[2]sta•ple *n* **:** chief commodity or item — **staple** *adj*

star *n* **1 :** celestial body visible as a point of light **2 :** 5- or 6-pointed figure representing a star **3 :** leading performer ~ *vb* **1 :** mark with a star **2 :** play the leading role — **stardom** *n* — **star•less** *adj* — **star•light** *n* — **star•ry** *adj*

starch *n* **:** nourishing carbohydrate from plants also used in adhesives and laundering ~ *vb* **:** stiffen with starch — **starchy** *adj*

stare *vb* **:** look intently with wide-open eyes — **stare** *n* — **star•er** *n*

start *vb* **1 :** twitch or jerk (as from surprise) **2 :** perform or show performance of the first part of an action or process ~ *n* **1 :** sudden involuntary motion **2 :** beginning — **start•er** *n*

star•tle *vb* **:** frighten or surprise suddenly

starve *vb* **1 :** suffer or die from hunger **2 :** kill with hunger — **star•va•tion** *n*

stash *vb* **:** store in a secret place for future use — **stash** *n*

state *n* **1 :** condition of being **2 :** condition of mind **3 :** nation or a political unit within it ~ *vb* **1 :** express in words **2 :** establish — **statehood** *n* — **state•ment** *n*

stat•ic *adj* **1 :** relating to bodies at rest or forces in equilibrium **2 :** not moving **3 :** relating to stationary charges of electricity ~ *n* **:** noise on radio or television from electrical disturbances

sta•tion *n* **1 :** place of duty **2 :** regular stop on a bus or train route **3 :** social standing **4 :** place where radio or television programs originate ~ *vb* **:** assign to a station

sta•tion•ary *adj* **1 :** not moving or not movable **2 :** not changing

sta•tio•nery *n* **:** letter paper with envelopes

sta•tis•tics *n pl* **:** numerical facts collected for study — **sta•tis•ti•cal** *adj* — **sta•tis•ti•cal•ly** *adv* — **stat•is•ti•cian** *n*

stat•ue *n* **:** solid 3-dimensional likeness — **stat•u•ette** *n*

stat•ure *n* **1 :** height **2 :** status gained by achievement

sta•tus *n* **:** relative situation or condition

sta•tus quo *n* **:** existing state of affairs

stat•ute *n* **:** law — **stat•u•to•ry** *adj*

[1]stay *n* **:** support ~ *vb* **:** prop up

[2]stay *vb* **1 :** pause **2 :** remain **3 :** reside **4 :** stop or postpone **5 :** satisfy for a time ~ *n* **:** a staying

stead•fast *adj* **:** faithful or determined — **stead•fast•ly** *adv*

steady *adj* **1 :** firm in position or sure in movement **2 :** calm or reliable **3 :** constant **4 :** regular ~ *vb* **:** make or become steady — **steadily** *adv* — **steadi•ness** *n* — **steady** *adv*

steak *n* **:** thick slice of meat

steal *vb* (**stole; sto•len**) **1 :** take and carry away wrongfully and with intent to keep **2 :** move secretly or slowly

steam *n* **:** vapor of boiling water ~ *vb* **:** give off steam — **steam•boat** *n* — **steam•ship** *n* — **steamy** *adj*

steel *n* **:** tough carbon-containing iron ~ *vb* **:** fill with courage — **steel** *adj* — **steely** *adj*

steep *adj* **:** having a very sharp slope or great elevation — **steep•ly** *adv* — **steep•ness** *n*

steer *vb* **1 :** direct the course of (as a ship or car) **2 :** guide

stem *n* **:** main upright part of a plant ~ *vb* **1 :** derive **2 :** make progress against — **stemless** *adj* — **stemmed** *adj*

stem cell *n* **:** undifferentiated cell that may give rise to many different types of cells

step *n* **1 :** single action of a leg in walking or running **2 :** rest for the foot in going up or down **3 :** degree, rank, or stage **4 :** way of walking ~ *vb* **1 :** move by steps **2 :** press with the foot

ste•reo•phon•ic *adj* **:** relating to a 3-dimensional effect of reproduced sound — **ste•reo** *adj or n*

ste•reo•type *n* **:** gross often mistaken generalization — **stereotype** *vb* — **ste•reo•typ•i•cal** *adj* — **ste•reo•typi•cal•ly** *adv*

ster•ile *adj* **1 :** unable to bear fruit, crops, or offspring **2 :** free from disease germs — **steril•i•ty** *n* — **ster•il•i•za•tion** *n* — **ster•il•ize** *vb* — **ster•il•iz•er** *n*

stern *adj* **:** severe — **stern·ly** *adv* — **stern·ness** *n*
stew *n* **1 :** dish of boiled meat and vegetables **2 :** state of worry or agitation — **stew** *vb*
stew·ard *n* **1 :** manager of an estate or an organization **2 :** person on a ship or airliner who looks after passenger comfort — **stew·ard·ship** *n*
stew·ard·ess *n* **:** woman who is a steward (as on an airplane)
[1]**stick** *n* **1 :** cut or broken branch **2 :** long thin piece of wood or something resembling it
[2]**stick** *vb* **stuck; stuck 1 :** stab **2 :** thrust or project **3 :** hold fast to something **4 :** attach **5 :** become jammed or fixed
stick·er *n* **:** adhesive label
sticky *adj* **1 :** adhesive or gluey **2 :** muggy **3 :** difficult
stiff *adj* **1 :** not bending easily **2 :** tense **3 :** formal **4 :** strong **5 :** severe — **stiff·en** *vb* — **stiff·en·er** *n* — **stiff·ly** *adv* — **stiff·ness** *n*
still *adj* **1 :** motionless **2 :** silent ~ *vb* **:** make or become still ~ *adv* **1 :** without motion **2 :** up to and during this time **3 :** in spite of that ~ *n* **:** silence — **still·ness** *n*
stim·u·late *vb* **:** make active — **stim·u·lant** *n or adj* — **stim·u·la·tion** *n*
stim·u·lus *n* **:** something that stimulates
sting *vb* (**stung; stung**) **1 :** prick painfully **2 :** cause to suffer acutely ~ *n* **:** act of stinging or a resulting wound — **sting·er** *n*
stin·gy *adj* **:** not generous — **stin·gi·ness** *n*
stink *vb* (**stank/stunk; stunk**) **:** have a strong offensive odor — **stink** *n* — **stink·er** *n*
stip·u·late *vb* **:** demand as a condition — **stip·u·la·tion** *n*
stir *vb* **1 :** move slightly **2 :** prod or push into activity **3 :** mix by continued circular movement ~ *n* **:** act or result of stirring
stitch *n* **1 :** loop formed by a needle in sewing **2 :** sudden sharp pain ~ *vb* **1 :** fasten or decorate with stitches **2 :** sew
stock *n* **1 :** block or part of wood **2 :** original from which others derive **3 :** farm animals **4 :** supply of goods **5 :** money invested in a large business **6** *pl* **:** instrument of punishment like a pillory with holes for the feet or feet and hands ~ *vb* **:** provide with stock
stock·ing *n* **:** close-fitting covering for the foot and leg
stock·pile *n* **:** reserve supply — **stockpile** *vb*
stole *past of* STEAL
stolen *past part of* STEAL
stom·ach *n* **1 :** saclike digestive organ **2 :** abdomen **3 :** appetite or desire ~ *vb* **:** put up with — **stom·ach·ache** *n*
stomp *vb* **:** stamp
stone *n* **1 :** hardened earth or mineral matter **2 :** small piece of rock **3 :** seed that is hard or has a hard covering ~ *vb* **:** pelt or kill with stones — **stony** *adj*
stood *past of* STAND
stool *n* **1 :** seat usu. without back or arms **2 :** footstool **3 :** discharge of feces
stoop *vb* **1 :** bend over **2 :** lower oneself ~ *n* **1 :** act of bending over **2 :** bent position of shoulders
stop *vb* **1 :** block an opening **2 :** end or cause to end **3 :** pause for rest or a visit in a journey ~ *n* **1 :** plug **2 :** act or place of stopping **3 :** delay in a journey — **stop·light** *n* — **stop·page** *n* — **stop·per** *n*
stor·age *n* **:** safekeeping of goods (as in a warehouse)
store *vb* **:** put aside for future use ~ *n* **1 :** something stored **2 :** retail business establishment — **store·house** *n* — **store·keep·er** *n* — **store·room** *n*
storm *n* **1 :** heavy fall of rain or snow **2 :** violent outbreak ~ *vb* **1 :** rain or snow heavily **2 :** rage **3 :** make an attack against — **stormy** *adj*
[1]**sto·ry** *n* **1 :** narrative **2 :** report — **sto·ry·tell·er** *n*
[2]**story** *n* **:** floor of a building
stove *n* **:** apparatus for providing heat (as for cooking or heating)
strad·dle *vb* **:** stand over or sit on with legs on opposite sides — **strad·dle** *n*
strag·gle *vb* **:** wander or become separated from others — **strag·gler** *n*
straight *adj* **1 :** having no bends, turns, or twists **2 :** just, proper, or honest **3 :** neat and orderly ~ *adv* **:** in a straight manner — **straight·en** *vb*
straight·for·ward *adj* **:** frank or honest
[1]**strain** *n* **1 :** line of descent from common ancestors **2 :** trace
[2]**strain** *vb* **1 :** exert to the utmost **2 :** filter or remove by filtering **3 :** injure by improper use ~ *n* **1 :** excessive tension or exertion **2 :** bodily injury from excessive effort — **strain·er** *n*
strait *n* **1 :** narrow channel connecting 2 bodies of water **2** *pl* **:** distress
[1]**strand** *vb* **1 :** drive or cast upon the shore **2 :** leave helpless

[2]**strand** *n* **1 :** twisted fiber of a rope **2 :** length of something ropelike

strange *adj* **1 :** unusual or queer **2 :** new — **strang•er** *n* — **strange•ly** *adv* — **strange•ness** *n*

stran•gle *vb* **:** choke to death — **stran•gler** *n* — **stran•gu•la•tion** *n*

strap *n* **:** narrow strip of flexible material used esp. for fastening ~ *vb* **1 :** secure with a strap **2 :** beat with a strap — **strap•less** *n*

strat•e•gy *n* **:** carefully worked out plan of action — **stra•te•gic** *adj* — **strat•e•gist** *n*

straw *n* **1 :** grass stems after grain is removed **2 :** tube for drinking ~ *adj* **:** made of straw

straw•ber•ry *n* **:** juicy red pulpy fruit

stray *vb* **:** wander or deviate ~ *n* **:** person or animal that strays ~ *adj* **:** separated from or not related to anything close by

streak *n* **1 :** mark of a different color **2 :** narrow band of light **3 :** trace **4 :** run (as of luck) or series ~ *vb* **1 :** form streaks in or on **2 :** move fast

stream *n* **1 :** flow of water on land **2 :** steady flow (as of water or air) ~ *vb* **1 :** flow in a stream **2 :** pour out streams

stream•lined *adj* **1 :** made with contours to reduce air or water resistance **2 :** simplified **3 :** modernized — **streamline** *vb*

street *n* **:** thoroughfare esp. in a city or town

strength *n* **1 :** quality of being strong **2 :** toughness **3 :** intensity

strength•en *vb* **:** make, grow, or become stronger — **strength•en•er** *n*

stress *n* **1 :** pressure or strain that tends to distort a body **2 :** relative prominence given to one thing among others **3 :** state of physical or mental tension or something inducing it ~ *vb* **:** put stress on — **stress•ful** *adj*

stretch *vb* **1 :** spread or reach out **2 :** draw out in length or breadth **3 :** make taut **4 :** exaggerate **5 :** become extended without breaking ~ *n* **:** act of extending beyond normal limits

stretch•er *n* **:** device for carrying a sick or injured person

strew *vb* **1 :** scatter **2 :** cover by scattering something over

strict *adj* **1 :** allowing no escape or evasion **2 :** precise — **strict•ly** *adv* — **strict•ness** *n*

stride *vb* (**strode; strid•den**) **:** walk or run with long steps ~ *n* **1 :** long step **2 :** manner of striding

strike *vb* (**struck; struck**) **1 :** hit sharply **2 :** delete **3 :** produce by impressing **4 :** cause to sound **5 :** afflict **6 :** occur to or impress **7 :** cause (a match) to ignite by rubbing **8 :** refrain from working **9 :** find **10 :** take on (as a pose) ~ *n* **1 :** act or instance of striking **2 :** work stoppage **3 :** military attack — **strik•er** *n* — **strike out** *vb* **:** start out vigorously — **strike up** *vb* **:** start

string *n* **1 :** line usu. of twisted threads **2 :** series **3** *pl* **:** stringed instruments ~ *vb* **strung; strung 1 :** thread on or with a string **2 :** hang or fasten by a string

strin•gent *adj* **:** severe

stringy *adj* **:** tough or fibrous

[1]**strip** *vb* **1 :** take the covering or clothing from **2 :** undress — **strip•per** *n*

[2]**strip** *n* **:** long narrow flat piece

stripe *n* **:** distinctive line or long narrow section ~ *vb* **:** make stripes on — **striped** *adj*

strive *vb* (**strove; stri•ven/strived**) **1 :** struggle **2 :** try hard

strode *past of* STRIDE

stroke *vb* **:** rub gently ~ *n* **1 :** act of swinging or striking **2 :** sudden action

stroll *vb* **:** walk leisurely — **stroll** *n* — **stroll•er** *n*

strong *adj* **1 :** capable of exerting great force or of withstanding stress or violence **2 :** healthy **3 :** having intense feelings for a cause — **strong•ly** *adv*

struck *past of* STRIKE

struc•ture *n* **1 :** building **2 :** arrangement of elements ~ *vb* **:** make into a structure — **struc•tur•al** *adj*

strug•gle *vb* **1 :** make strenuous efforts to overcome an adversary **2 :** proceed with great effort ~ *n* **1 :** strenuous effort **2 :** intense competition for superiority

strung *past of* STRING

strut *vb* **:** walk in a proud or showy manner ~ *n* **1 :** proud walk **2 :** supporting bar or rod

stub•born *adj* **1 :** determined not to yield **2 :** hard to control — **stub•born•ly** *adv* — **stub•born•ness** *n*

stuck *past of* STICK

stuck–up *adj* **:** conceited

[1]**stud** *n* **:** male horse kept for breeding

[2]**stud** *n* **1 :** upright beam for holding wall material **2 :** projecting nail, pin, or rod ~ *vb* **:** supply or dot with studs

stu•dent *n* **:** one who studies

stu•dio *n* **1 :** artist's workroom **2 :** place where movies are made or television or radio shows are broadcast

stu·di·ous *adj* : devoted to study — **stu·di·ous·ly** *adv*
study *n* **1 :** act or process of learning about something **2 :** branch of learning **3 :** careful examination **4 :** room for reading or studying ~ *vb* : apply the attention and mind to a subject
stuff *n* **1 :** personal property **2 :** raw or fundamental material **3 :** unspecified material or things ~ *vb* : fill by packing things in — **stuff·ing** *n*
stuffy *adj* **1 :** lacking fresh air **2 :** unimaginative or pompous
stum·ble *vb* **1 :** lose one's balance or fall in walking or running **2 :** speak or act clumsily **3 :** happen by chance — **stum·ble** *n*
stump *n* : part left when something is cut off ~ *vb* : confuse — **stumpy** *adj*
stun *vb* **1 :** make senseless or dizzy by or as if by a blow **2 :** bewilder
stung *past of* STING
stunk *past of* STINK
stun·ning *adj* **1 :** astonishing or incredible **2 :** strikingly beautiful — **stun·ning·ly** *adv*
[1]stunt *vb* : hinder the normal growth or progress of
[2]stunt *n* : spectacular feat
stu·pid *adj* : not sensible or intelligent — **stu·pid·i·ty** *n* — **stu·pid·ly** *adv*
stur·dy *adj* : strong — **stur·di·ly** *adv* — **stur·di·ness** *n*
stut·ter *vb or n* : stammer
sty *n* : pig pen
style *n* **1 :** distinctive way of speaking, writing, or acting **2 :** elegant or fashionable way of living ~ *vb* **1 :** name **2 :** give a particular design or style to — **styl·ish** *adj* — **styl·ish·ly** *adv* — **styl·ish·ness** *n* — **styl·ist** *n* — **styl·ize** *vb*
[1]sub *n or vb* : substitute
[2]sub *n* : submarine
sub·con·scious *adj* : existing without conscious awareness ~ *n* : part of the mind concerned with subconscious activities — **sub·con·scious·ly** *adv*
sub·due *vb* **1 :** bring under control **2 :** reduce the intensity of
sub·ject *n* **1 :** person under the authority of another **2 :** something being discussed or studied **3 :** word or word group about which something is said in a sentence ~ *adj* **1 :** being under one's authority **2 :** prone **3 :** dependent on some condition or act ~ *vb* **1 :** bring under control **2 :** cause to undergo — **sub·jec·tion** *n*
sub·jec·tive *adj* : deriving from an individual viewpoint or bias — **sub·jec·tive·ly** *adv* — **sub·jec·tiv·i·ty** *n*
sub·ma·rine *adj* : existing, acting, or growing under the sea ~ *n* : underwater boat
sub·mit *vb* **1 :** yield **2 :** give or offer — **sub·mis·sion** *n* — **sub·mis·sive** *adj*
sub·or·di·nate *adj* : lower in rank ~ *n* : one that is subordinate ~ *vb* : place in a lower rank or class — **sub·or·di·na·tion** *n*
sub·scribe *vb* **1 :** give consent or approval **2 :** agree to support or to receive and pay for — **sub·scrib·er** *n*
sub·scrip·tion *n* : order for regular receipt of a publication
sub·se·quent *adj* : following after — **sub·se·quent·ly** *adv*
sub·sid·iary *adj* **1 :** furnishing support **2 :** of secondary importance ~ *n* : company controlled by another company
sub·si·dy *n* : gift of supporting funds — **sub·si·dize** *vb*
sub·stance *n* **1 :** essence or essential part **2 :** physical material **3 :** wealth
sub·stan·tial *adj* **1 :** plentiful **2 :** considerable — **sub·stan·tial·ly** *adv*
sub·stan·ti·ate *vb* : verify — **sub·stan·ti·a·tion** *n*
sub·sti·tute *n* : replacement ~ *vb* : put or serve in place of another — **substitute** *adj* — **sub·sti·tu·tion** *n*
sub·tle *adj* **1 :** hardly noticeable **2 :** clever — **sub·tle·ty** *n* — **sub·tly** *adv*
sub·tract *vb* : take away (as one number from another) — **sub·trac·tion** *n*
sub·urb *n* : residential area adjacent to a city — **sub·ur·ban** *adj or n* — **sub·ur·ban·ite** *n*
sub·way *n* : underground electric railway
suc·ceed *vb* **1 :** follow (someone) in a job, role, or title **2 :** attain a desired object or end
suc·cess *n* **1 :** favorable outcome **2 :** gaining of wealth and fame **3 :** one that succeeds — **suc·cess·ful** *adj* — **suc·cess·ful·ly** *adv*
suc·ces·sion *n* **1 :** order, act, or right of succeeding **2 :** series
such *adj* **1 :** of this or that kind **2 :** having a specified quality — **such** *pron or adv*
suck *vb* **1 :** draw in liquid with the mouth **2 :** draw liquid from by or as if by mouth — **suck** *n* — **suc·tion** *n*
sud·den *adj* **1 :** happening unexpectedly **2**

: steep **3 :** hasty — **sud•den•ly** *adv* — **sud•den•ness** *n*
suds *n pl* **:** soapy water esp. when frothy — **sudsy** *adj*
sue *vb* **1 :** petition **2 :** bring legal action against
suf•fer *vb* **1 :** experience pain, loss, or hardship **2 :** permit — **suf•fer•er** *n*
suf•fer•ing *n* **:** pain or hardship
suf•fi•cient *adj* **:** adequate — **suf•fi•cien•cy** *n* — **suf•ficient•ly** *adv*
suf•fix *n* **:** letters added at the end of a word — **suffix** *vb* — **suf•fix•a•tion** *n*
suf•fo•cate *vb* **:** suffer or die or cause to die from lack of air — **suf•fo•cat•ing•ly** *adv* — **suf•fo•ca•tion** *n*
sug•ar *n* **:** sweet substance ~ *vb* **:** mix, cover, or sprinkle with sugar — **sug•ar•cane** *n* — **sug•ary** *adj*
sug•gest *vb* **1 :** put into someone's mind **2 :** remind one by association of ideas — **sug•gest•ible** *adj* — **sug•ges•tion** *n* — **sug•ges•tive** *adj* — **sug•ges•tive•ly** *adv* — **sug•ges•tive•ness** *n*
sui•cide *n* **1 :** act of killing oneself purposely **2 :** one who commits suicide — **sui•cid•al** *adj*
suit *n* **1 :** action in court to recover a right or claim **2 :** number of things used or worn together **3 :** one of the 4 sets of playing cards ~ *vb* **1 :** be appropriate or becoming to **2 :** meet the needs of — **suit•abil•i•ty** *n* — **suit•able** *adj* — **suit•ably** *adv*
suite *n* **1 :** group of rooms **2 :** set of matched furniture
sul•len *adj* **1 :** gloomily silent **2 :** dismal — **sul•len•ly** *adv* — **sul•len•ness** *n*
sum *n* **1 :** amount **2 :** gist **3 :** result of addition ~ *vb* **:** find the sum of
sum•ma•ry *adj* **1 :** concise **2 :** done without delay or formality ~ *n* **:** concise statement — **sum•mar•i•ly** *adv* — **sum•ma•rize** *vb* — **sum•ma•tion** *n*
sum•mer *n* **:** season in which the sun shines most directly — **sum•mery** *adj*
sum•mon *vb* **1 :** send for or call together **2 :** order to appear in court — **sum•mon•er** *n*
sun *n* **1 :** shining celestial body around which the planets revolve **2 :** light of the sun ~ *vb* **:** expose to the sun — **sun•beam** *n* — **sun•block** *n* — **sun•burn** *n or vb* — **sun•glass•es** *n pl* — **sun•light** *n* — **sun•ny** *adj* — **sun•rise** *n* — **sun•set** *n* — **sun•shine** *n* — **sun•tan** *n*
Sun•day *n* **:** 1st day of the week
sung *past of* SING
sunk *past of* SINK
super *adj* **:** very fine
su•perb *adj* **:** outstanding — **su•perb•ly** *adv*
su•per•fi•cial *adj* **:** relating to what is only apparent — **su•per•fi•ci•al•i•ty** *n* — **su•per•fi•cial•ly** *adv*
su•per•in•tend *vb* **:** have charge and oversight of — **su•per•in•ten•dence** *n* — **su•per•in•ten•den•cy** *n* — **su•per•in•ten•dent** *n*
su•pe•ri•or *adj* **1 :** higher, better, or more important **2 :** haughty — **superior** *n* — **su•pe•ri•or•i•ty** *n*
su•per•la•tive *adj* **1 :** relating to or being an adjective or adverb form that denotes an extreme level **2 :** surpassing others — **superlative** *n* — **su•per•la•tive•ly** *adv*
su•per•nat•u•ral *adj* **:** beyond the observable physical world — **su•per•nat•u•ral•ly** *adv*
su•per•pow•er *n* **:** politically and militarily dominant nation
su•per•sede *vb* **:** take the place of
su•per•sti•tion *n* **:** beliefs based on ignorance, fear of the unknown, or trust in magic — **su•per•sti•tious** *adj*
su•per•vise *vb* **:** have charge of — **su•per•vi•sion** *n* — **su•per•vi•sor** *n* — **su•per•vi•so•ry** *adj*
sup•per *n* **:** evening meal
sup•ple•ment *n* **:** something that adds to or makes up for a lack — **supplement** *vb* — **sup•ple•men•tal** *adj* — **sup•ple•men•ta•ry** *adj*
sup•ply *vb* **:** furnish ~ *n* **1 :** amount needed or available **2** *pl* **:** provisions — **sup•pli•er** *n*
sup•port *vb* **1 :** take sides with **2 :** provide with food, clothing, and shelter **3 :** hold up or serve as a foundation for — **support** *n* — **sup•port•able** *adj* — **sup•port•er** *n*
sup•pose *vb* **1 :** assume to be true **2 :** expect **3 :** think probable — **sup•po•si•tion** *n*
sup•press *vb* **1 :** put an end to by authority **2 :** keep from being known **3 :** hold back — **sup•pres•sant** *n* — **sup•pres•sion** *n*
su•preme *adj* **1 :** highest in rank or authority **2 :** greatest possible — **su•preme•ly** *adv*
Supreme Being *n* **:** God
sur•charge *n* **1 :** excessive load or burden **2 :** extra fee or cost
sure *adj* **1 :** confident **2 :** reliable **3 :** not to be disputed **4 :** bound to happen ~ *adv* **:** surely — **sure•ness** *n*

sure·ly *adv* **1 :** in a sure manner **2 :** without doubt **3 :** indeed

surf *n* **:** waves that break on the shore ~ *vb* **:** ride the surf — **surf·board** *n* — **surf·er** *n* — **surf·ing** *n*

sur·face *n* **1 :** the outside of an object **2 :** outward aspect ~ *vb* **:** rise to the surface

sur·geon *n* **:** physician who specializes in surgery

sur·gery *n* **:** medical treatment involving cutting open the body

sur·gi·cal *adj* **:** relating to surgeons or surgery — **sur·gi·cal·ly** *adv*

sur·name *n* **:** family name

sur·pass *vb* **:** go beyond or exceed — **sur·pass·ing·ly** *adv*

sur·plus *n* **:** quantity left over

sur·prise *vb* **1 :** come upon or affect unexpectedly **2 :** amaze — **surprise** *n* — **sur·pris·ing** *adj* — **sur·pris·ing·ly** *adv*

sur·ren·der *vb* **:** give up oneself or a possession to another ~ *n* **:** act of surrendering

sur·round *vb* **:** enclose on all sides

sur·round·ings *n pl* **:** objects, conditions, or area around something

sur·veil·lance *n* **:** careful watch

sur·vey *vb* **1 :** look over and examine closely **2 :** make a survey of (as a tract of land) ~ *n* **1 :** inspection **2 :** process of measuring (as land) — **sur·vey·or** *n*

sur·vive *vb* **1 :** remain alive or in existence **2 :** outlive or outlast — **sur·viv·al** *n* — **sur·vi·vor** *n*

sus·pect *adj* **1 :** regarded with suspicion **2 :** questionable ~ *n* **:** one who is suspected (as of a crime) ~ *vb* **1 :** have doubts of **2 :** believe guilty without proof **3 :** guess

sus·pend *vb* **1 :** temporarily stop or keep from a function or job **2 :** withhold (judgment) temporarily **3 :** hang

sus·pense *n* **:** excitement and uncertainty as to outcome — **sus·pense·ful** *adj*

sus·pen·sion *n* **:** act of suspending or the state or period of being suspended

sus·pi·cion *n* **1 :** act of suspecting something **2 :** trace

sus·pi·cious *adj* **1 :** arousing suspicion **2 :** inclined to suspect — **sus·pi·cious·ly** *adv*

sus·tain *vb* **1 :** provide with nourishment **2 :** keep going **3 :** hold up **4 :** suffer **5 :** support or prove

swag·ger *vb* **1 :** walk with a conceited swing **2 :** boast — **swag·ger** *n*

¹swal·low *n* **:** small migratory bird

²swal·low *vb* **1 :** take into the stomach through the throat **2 :** envelop or take in **3 :** accept too easily — **swal·low** *n*

swam *past of* SWIM

swamp *n* **:** wet spongy land ~ *vb* **:** deluge (as with water) — **swampy** *adj*

swan *n* **:** white long-necked swimming bird

swap *vb* **:** trade — **swap** *n*

swat *vb* **:** hit sharply — **swat** *n* — **swat·ter** *n*

sway *vb* **1 :** swing gently from side to side **2 :** influence ~ *n* **1 :** gentle swinging from side to side **2 :** controlling power or influence

swear *vb* **(swore; sworn) 1 :** make or cause to make a solemn statement under oath **2 :** use profane language — **swear·er** *n* — **swear·ing** *n*

sweat *vb* **1 :** excrete salty moisture from skin glands **2 :** form drops of moisture on the surface **3 :** work or cause to work hard — **sweat** *n* — **sweaty** *adj*

sweat·er *n* **:** knitted jacket or pullover

sweat·shirt *n* **:** loose collarless heavy cotton jersey pullover

sweep *vb* **(swept; swept) 1 :** remove or clean by a brush or a single forceful wipe (as of the hand) **2 :** move over with speed and force (as of the hand) **3 :** move or extend in a wide curve ~ *n* **1 :** a clearing off or away **2 :** single forceful wipe or swinging movement **3 :** scope — **sweep·er** *n* — **sweep·ing** *adj*

sweet *adj* **1 :** being or causing the pleasing taste typical of sugar **2 :** not stale or spoiled **3 :** not salted **4 :** pleasant **5 :** much loved ~ *n* **:** something sweet — **sweet·en** *vb* — **sweet·ly** *adv* — **sweet·ness** *n* — **sweet·en·er** *n*

sweet·heart *n* **:** person one loves

swell *vb* **(swelled; swelled/swol·len) 1 :** enlarge **2 :** bulge **3 :** fill or be filled with emotion ~ *n* **1 :** long rolling ocean wave **2 :** condition of bulging — **swell·ing** *n*

swept *past of* SWEEP

swerve *vb* **:** move abruptly aside from a course — **swerve** *n*

swift *adj* **1 :** moving with great speed **2 :** occurring suddenly — **swift·ly** *adv* — **swift·ness** *n*

swim *vb* **(swam; swum) 1 :** propel oneself in water **2 :** float in or be surrounded with a liquid **3 :** be dizzy ~ *n* **:** act or period of swimming — **swim·mer** *n*

swin·dle *vb* **:** cheat (someone) of money or property — **swindle** *n* — **swin·dler** *n*

swine *n* (**swine**) **:** short-legged hoofed mammal with a snout — **swin•ish** *adj*

swing *vb* (**swung; swung**) **1 :** move or cause to move rapidly in an arc **2 :** sway or cause to sway back and forth **3 :** hang so as to sway or sag **4 :** turn on a hinge or pivot **5 :** manage or handle successfully ~ *n* **1 :** act or instance of swinging **2 :** swinging movement (as in trying to hit something) **3 :** suspended seat for swinging — **swing** *adj* — **swing•er** *n*

swipe *n* **:** strong sweeping blow ~ *vb* **1 :** strike or wipe with a sweeping motion **2 :** steal esp. with a quick movement

swirl *vb* **:** move or cause to move in a circle — **swirl** *n*

switch *n* **1 :** slender flexible whip or twig **2 :** blow with a switch **3 :** shift, change, or reversal **4 :** device that opens or closes an electrical circuit ~ *vb* **1 :** punish or urge on with a switch **2 :** change or reverse roles, positions, or subjects **3 :** operate a switch of

switch•board *n* **:** panel of switches to make and break telephone connections

swiv•el *vb* **:** swing or turn on a pivot — **swivel** *n*

swollen *past part of* SWELL

swoop *vb* **:** make a swift diving attack — **swoop** *n*

sword *n* **:** thrusting or cutting weapon with a long blade

swore *past of* SWEAR

sworn *past part of* SWEAR

swum *past part of* SWIM

swung *past of* SWING

syl•la•ble *n* **:** unit of a spoken word — **syl•lab•ic** *adj*

sym•bol *n* **:** something that represents or suggests another thing — **sym•bol•ic** *adj* — **sym•bol•i•cal•ly** *adv* — **sym•bol•ism** *n* — **sym•bol•ize** *vb*

sym•me•try *n* **:** regularity and balance in the arrangement of parts — **sym•met•ri•cal** *adj* — **sym•met•ri•cal•ly** *adv*

sym•pa•thy *n* **1 :** ability to understand or share the feelings of another **2 :** expression of sorrow for another's misfortune — **sym•pa•thet•ic** *adj* — **sym•pa•thet•i•cal•ly** *adv* — **sym•pa•thize** *vb*

sym•pho•ny *n* **:** composition for an orchestra or the orchestra itself — **sym•phon•ic** *adj*

symp•tom *n* **:** unusual feeling or reaction that is a sign of disease — **symp•tom•at•ic** *adj*

syn•a•gogue, syn•a•gog *n* **:** Jewish house of worship

syn•chro•nize *vb* **1 :** occur or cause to occur at the same instant **2 :** cause to agree in time — **syn•chro•ni•za•tion** *n*

syn•drome *n* **:** particular group of symptoms

syn•onym *n* **:** word with the same meaning as another — **syn•on•y•mous** *adj* — **syn•on•y•my** *n*

syn•the•sis *n* **:** combination of parts or elements into a whole — **syn•the•size** *vb*

syn•thet•ic *adj* **:** artificially made — **synthetic** *n* — **syn•thet•i•cal•ly** *adv*

syr•up *n* **:** thick sticky sweet liquid — **syr•upy** *adj*

sys•tem *n* **1 :** arrangement of units that function together **2 :** regular order — **sys•tem•at•ic** *adj* — **sys•tem•at•i•cal•ly** *adv* — **sys•tem•a•tize** *vb* — **sys•tem•ic** *adj*

T

t *n* **:** 20th letter of the alphabet

tab•by *n* **:** domestic cat

ta•ble *n* **1 :** piece of furniture having a smooth slab fixed on legs **2 :** supply of food **3 :** arrangement of data in columns **4 :** short list — **ta•ble•cloth** *n* — **ta•ble•top** *n* — **ta•ble•ware** *n* — **tab•u•lar** *adj*

ta•ble•spoon *n* **1 :** large serving spoon **2 :** measuring spoon holding ½ fluid ounce — **ta•ble•spoon•ful** *n*

tab•let *n* **1 :** flat slab suited for an inscription **2 :** collection of sheets of paper glued together at one edge **3 :** disk-shaped pill

tab•loid *n* **:** newspaper of small page size

tack *n* **1 :** small sharp nail **2 :** course of action ~ *vb* **1 :** fasten with tacks **2 :** add on

tack•le *n* **1 :** equipment **2 :** arrangement of ropes and pulleys **3 :** act of tackling ~ *vb* **1 :** seize or throw down **2 :** start dealing with

tacky *adj* **:** cheap or gaudy

tact *n* **:** sense of the proper thing to say or do — **tact•ful** *adj* — **tact•ful•ly** *adv* — **tact•less** *adj* — **tact•less•ly** *adv*

tac•tic *n* **:** action as part of a plan

taf•fy *n* **:** candy stretched until porous

[1]tag *n* **:** piece of hanging or attached material

~ *vb* **1 :** provide or mark with a tag **2 :** follow closely

²tag *n* **:** children's game of trying to catch one another ~ *vb* **:** touch a person in tag

tail *n* **1 :** rear end or a growth extending from the rear end of an animal **2 :** back or last part **3 :** the reverse of a coin ~ *vb* **:** follow — **tailed** *adj* — **tail•less** *adj* — **tail•light** *n*

tai•lor *n* **:** one who makes or alters garments ~ *vb* **1 :** fashion or alter (clothes) **2 :** make or adapt for a special purpose

take *vb* (**took; tak•en**) **1 :** get into one's possession **2 :** become affected by **3 :** receive into one's body (as by eating) **4 :** pick out or remove **5 :** use for transportation **6 :** need or make use of **7 :** lead, carry, or cause to go to another place **8 :** undertake and do, make, or perform ~ *n* **:** amount taken — **take•over** *n* — **tak•er** *n* — **take advantage of :** profit by — **take exception :** object — **take off** *vb* **1 :** remove **2 :** go away **3 :** mimic **4 :** begin flight — **take over** *vb* **:** assume control or possession of or responsibility for — **take place :** happen

tale *n* **1 :** story or anecdote **2 :** falsehood

tal•ent *n* **:** natural mental or creative ability — **tal•ent•ed** *adj*

talk *vb* **1 :** express one's thoughts in speech **2 :** discuss **3 :** influence to a position or course of action by talking ~ *n* **1 :** act of talking **2 :** formal discussion **3 :** rumor **4 :** informal lecture — **talk•a•tive** *adj* — **talk•er** *n*

tall *adj* **:** extending to a great or specified height — **tall•ness** *n*

tame *adj* **1 :** changed from being wild to being controllable by man **2 :** docile **3 :** dull ~ *vb* **:** make or become tame — **tam•able, tame•able** *adj* — **tame•ly** *adv* — **tam•er** *n*

tan *vb* **1 :** change (hide) into leather esp. by soaking in a liquid containing tannin **2 :** make or become brown (as by exposure to the sun) ~ *n* **1 :** brown skin color induced by the sun **2 :** light yellowish brown — **tan•ner** *n* — **tan•nery** *n*

tan•gi•ble *adj* **1 :** able to be touched **2 :** substantially real — **tan•gi•bly** *adv*

tan•gle *vb* **:** unite in intricate confusion ~ *n* **:** tangled twisted mass

tank *n* **1 :** large artificial receptacle for liquids **2 :** armored military vehicle — **tank•ful** *n*

tank•er *n* **:** vehicle or vessel with tanks for transporting a liquid

¹tap *n* **1 :** faucet **2 :** act of tapping ~ *vb* **1 :** pierce so as to draw off fluid **2 :** connect into — **tap•per** *n*

²tap *vb* **:** rap lightly ~ *n* **:** light stroke or its sound

tape *n* **1 :** narrow flexible strip (as of cloth, plastic, or metal) **2 :** tape measure ~ *vb* **1 :** fasten with tape **2 :** record on tape

ta•per *n* **1 :** slender wax candle **2 :** gradual lessening of width in a long object ~ *vb* **1 :** make or become smaller toward one end **2 :** diminish gradually

tar *n* **:** thick dark sticky liquid distilled (as from coal) ~ *vb* **:** treat or smear with tar

tar•dy *adj* **:** late — **tar•di•ly** *adv* — **tar•di•ness** *n*

tar•get *n* **1 :** mark to shoot at **2 :** goal to be achieved ~ *vb* **1 :** make a target of **2 :** establish as a goal

tar•iff *n* **1 :** duty or rate of duty imposed on imported goods **2 :** schedule of tariffs, rates, or charges

¹tart *adj* **1 :** pleasantly sharp to the taste **2 :** caustic — **tart•ly** *adv* — **tart•ness** *n*

²tart *n* **:** small pie

task *n* **:** assigned work

taste *vb* **1 :** test or determine the flavor of **2 :** eat or drink in small quantities **3 :** have a specific flavor ~ *n* **1 :** small amount tasted **2 :** bit **3 :** special sense that identifies sweet, sour, bitter, or salty qualities **4 :** individual preference **5 :** critical appreciation of quality — **taste•ful** *adj* — **taste•ful•ly** *adv* — **taste•less** *adj* — **taste•less•ly** *adv* — **tast•er** *n*

tasty *adj* **:** pleasing to the sense of taste — **tast•i•ness** *n*

tat•tle•tale *n* **:** one that tattles

taught *past of* TEACH

taunt *n* **:** hurtful challenge or insult — **taunt** *vb* — **taunt•er** *n*

taut *adj* **:** tightly drawn — **taut•ly** *adv* — **taut•ness** *n*

tax *vb* **1 :** impose a tax on **2 :** charge **3 :** put under stress ~ *n* **1 :** charge by authority for public purposes **2 :** strain — **tax•able** *adj* — **tax•a•tion** *n* — **tax•pay•er** *n* — **tax•pay•ing** *adj*

taxi *n* **:** automobile transporting passengers for a fare ~ *vb* **1 :** transport or go by taxi **2 :** move along the ground before takeoff or after landing

tea *n* **:** cured leaves of an Asian shrub or a drink made from these — **tea•cup** *n* — **tea•ket•tle** *n* — **tea•pot** *n*

teach *vb* (**taught; taught**) **1 :** tell or show the fundamentals or skills of something **2 :** cause to know the consequences **3 :** impart knowledge of — **teach•able** *adj* — **teach•er** *n* — **teach•ing** *n*

team *n* **1 :** draft animals harnessed together **2 :** number of people organized for a game or work ~ *vb* : form or work together as a team — **team** *adj* — **team•mate** *n* — **team•work** *n*

¹tear *n* : drop of salty liquid that moistens the eye — **tear•ful** *adj* — **tear•ful•ly** *adv*

²tear *vb* (**tore; torn**) **1 :** separate or pull apart by force **2 :** move or act with violence or haste ~ *n* : act or result of tearing

tease *vb* : annoy by goading, coaxing, or tantalizing ~ *n* **1 :** act of teasing or state of being teased **2 :** one that teases

tea•spoon *n* **1 :** small spoon for stirring or sipping **2 :** measuring spoon holding 1/6 fluid ounce — **tea•spoon•ful** *n*

tech•ni•cal *adj* **1 :** having or relating to special mechanical or scientific knowledge **2 :** by strict interpretation of rules — **tech•ni•cal•ly** *adv*

tech•ni•cal•i•ty *n* : detail meaningful only to a specialist

tech•nique *n* : manner of accomplishing something

tech•nol•o•gy *n* : applied science — **tech•no•log•i•cal** *adj*

te•dious *adj* : wearisome from length or dullness — **te•dious•ly** *adv* — **te•dious•ness** *n*

tee *n* : mound or peg on which a golf ball is placed before beginning play — **tee** *vb*

teen•age, teen•aged *adj* : relating to people in their teens — **teen•ag•er** *n*

teens *n pl* : years 13 to 19 in a person's life

tee•pee *var of* TEPEE

teeth *pl of* TOOTH

teethe *vb* : grow teeth

tele•cast *vb* : broadcast by television — **tele•cast** *n* — **tele•cast•er** *n*

tele•com•mu•ni•ca•tion *n* : communication at a distance (as by radio or telephone)

tele•phone *n* : instrument or system for electrical transmission of spoken words ~ *vb* : communicate with by telephone — **tele•phon•er** *n*

tele•scope *n* : tube-shaped optical instrument for viewing distant objects ~ *vb* : slide or cause to slide inside another similar section — **tele•scop•ic** *adj*

tele•vise *vb* : broadcast by television

tele•vi•sion *n* : transmission and reproduction of images by radio waves

tell *vb* (**told; told**) **1 :** count **2 :** relate in detail **3 :** reveal **4 :** give information or an order to **5 :** find out by observing

tem•per *vb* **1 :** dilute or soften **2 :** toughen ~ *n* **1 :** characteristic attitude or feeling **2 :** toughness **3 :** disposition or control over one's emotions

tem•per•a•ment *n* : characteristic frame of mind — **tem•per•a•men•tal** *adj*

tem•per•a•ture *n* **1 :** degree of hotness or coldness **2 :** fever

¹tem•ple *n* : place of worship

²temple *n* : flattened space on each side of the forehead

tem•po•rary *adj* : lasting for a short time only — **tem•po•rar•i•ly** *adv*

tempt *vb* **1 :** coax or persuade to do wrong **2 :** attract or provoke — **tempt•er** *n* — **tempt•ing•ly** *adv* — **tempt•ress** *n*

temp•ta•tion *n* **1 :** act of tempting **2 :** something that tempts

ten *n* **1 :** one more than 9 **2 :** 10th in a set or series **3 :** thing having 10 units — **ten** *adj or pron* — **tenth** *adj or adv or n*

ten•ant *n* : one who occupies a rented dwelling — **ten•an•cy** *n*

¹tend *vb* : take care of or supervise something

²tend *vb* **1 :** move in a particular direction **2 :** show a tendency

ten•den•cy *n* : likelihood to move, think, or act in a particular way

¹ten•der *adj* **1 :** soft or delicate **2 :** expressing or responsive to love or sympathy **3 :** sensitive (as to touch) — **ten•der•ly** *adv* — **ten•der•ness** *n*

²ten•der *n* **1 :** offer of a bid for a contract **2 :** something that may be offered in payment — **tender** *vb*

ten•der•ize *vb* : make (meat) tender — **ten•der•iz•er** *n*

ten•nis *n* : racket-and-ball game played across a net

ten•or *n* **1 :** general drift or meaning **2 :** highest natural adult male voice

¹tense *n* : distinct verb form that indicates time

²tense *adj* **1 :** stretched tight **2 :** marked by nervous tension — **tense** *vb* — **tense•ly** *adv* — **tense•ness** *n* — **ten•si•ty** *n*

ten•sion *n* **1 :** tense condition **2 :** state of mental unrest or of potential hostility or opposition

tent *n* **:** collapsible shelter

ten•ta•tive *adj* **:** subject to change or discussion — **ten•ta•tive•ly** *adv*

te•pee *n* **:** conical tent

term *n* **1 :** period of time **2 :** mathematical expression **3 :** special word or phrase **4** *pl* **:** conditions **5** *pl* **:** relations ~ *vb* **:** name

ter•min•al *n* **1 :** end **2 :** device for making an electrical connection **3 :** station at end of a transportation line — **ter•min•al** *adj*

ter•mi•nate *vb* **:** bring or come to an end — **ter•mi•na•ble** *adj* — **ter•mi•na•tion** *n*

ter•mi•nol•o•gy *n* **:** terms used in a particular subject

ter•race *n* **1 :** balcony or patio **2 :** bank with a flat top ~ *vb* **:** landscape in a series of banks

ter•ri•ble *adj* **1 :** exciting terror **2 :** distressing **3 :** intense **4 :** of very poor quality — **ter•ri•bly** *adv*

ter•rif•ic *adj* **1 :** exciting terror **2 :** extraordinary

ter•ri•fy *vb* **:** fill with terror — **ter•ri•fy•ing•ly** *adv*

ter•ri•to•ry *n* **:** particular geographical region — **ter•ri•to•ri•al** *adj*

ter•ror *n* **:** intense fear and panic or a cause of it

ter•ror•ize *vb* **1 :** fill with terror **2 :** coerce by threat or violence — **ter•ror•ism** *n* — **ter•ror•ist** *adj or n*

test *n* **:** examination or evaluation ~ *vb* **:** examine by a test — **test•er** *n*

tes•ti•fy *vb* **1 :** give testimony **2 :** serve as evidence

tes•ti•mo•ni•al *n* **1 :** favorable recommendation **2 :** tribute — **tes•ti•mo•ni•al** *adj*

tes•ti•mo•ny *n* **:** statement given as evidence in court

text *n* **1 :** author's words **2 :** main body of printed or written matter on a page **3 :** textbook **4 :** scriptural passage used as the theme of a sermon **5 :** topic — **tex•tu•al** *adj*

text•book *n* **:** book on a school subject

tex•tile *n* **:** fabric

tex•ture *n* **1 :** feel and appearance of something **2 :** structure

than *conj or prep* — used in comparisons

thank *vb* **:** express gratitude to — **thank•ful** *adj* — **thank•ful•ly** *adv* — **thank•ful•ness** *n* — **thank•less** *adj* — **thanks** *n pl*

Thanks•giv•ing *n* **:** fourth Thursday in November observed as a legal holiday for giving thanks for divine goodness

that *pron, pl* **those 1 :** something indicated or understood **2 :** the one farther away ~ *adj pl* **those :** being the one mentioned or understood or farther away ~ *conj or pron* — used to introduce a clause ~ *adv* **:** to such an extent

the *definite article* **:** that particular one ~ *adv* — used before a comparative or superlative

the•ater, the•atre *n* **1 :** building or room for viewing a play or movie **2 :** dramatic arts — **the•at•ri•cal** *adj*

theft *n* **:** act of stealing

their *adj* **:** relating to them

theirs *pron* **:** their one or ones

them *pron, objective case of* THEY

theme *n* **1 :** subject matter **2 :** essay **3 :** melody developed in a piece of music — **the•mat•ic** *adj*

them•selves *pron pl* **:** they, them — used reflexively or for emphasis

then *adv* **1 :** at that time **2 :** soon after that **3 :** in addition **4 :** in that case **5 :** consequently ~ *n* **:** that time ~ *adj* **:** existing at that time

the•o•ry *n* **1 :** general principles of a subject **2 :** plausible or scientifically acceptable explanation **3 :** judgment, guess, or opinion — **the•o•ret•i•cal** *adj* — **the•o•rize** *vb* — **the•o•rist** *n*

ther•a•py *n* **:** treatment for mental or physical disorder — **ther•a•peu•tic** *adj* — **ther•a•peu•ti•cal•ly** *adv* — **ther•a•pist** *n*

there *adv* **1 :** in, at, or to that place **2 :** in that respect ~ *pron* — used to introduce a sentence or clause ~ *n* **:** that place or point

there•fore *adv* **:** for that reason

there•of *adv* **1 :** of that or it **2 :** from that

ther•mal *adj* **:** relating to, caused by, or conserving heat — **ther•mal•ly** *adv*

ther•mom•e•ter *n* **:** instrument for measuring temperature — **ther•mo•met•ric** *adj*

ther•mo•stat *n* **:** automatic temperature control — **ther•mo•stat•ic** *adj* — **ther•mo•stat•i•cal•ly** *adv*

these *pl of* THIS

the•sis *n* **1 :** proposition to be argued for **2 :** essay embodying results of original research

they *pron* **1 :** those ones **2 :** people in general

thick *adj* **1 :** having relatively great mass from front to back or top to bottom **2 :** having a tendency to flow very slowly ~ *n* **:** most crowded or thickest part — **thick•en** *vb* — **thick•en•er** *n* — **thick•ly** *adv* — **thick•ness** *n*

thief *n* **:** one that steals

thigh *n* **:** upper part of the leg

thin *adj* **1 :** having relatively little mass from

front to back or top to bottom **2 :** not closely set or placed **3 :** relatively free flowing **4 :** lacking substance, fullness, or strength ~ *vb* **:** make or become thin — **thin·ly** *adv* — **thin·ness** *n*

thing *n* **1 :** matter of concern **2 :** event or act **3 :** object **4** *pl* **:** possessions

think *vb* (**thought; thought**) **1 :** form or have in the mind **2 :** have as an opinion **3 :** ponder **4 :** devise by thinking **5 :** imagine — **think·er** *n*

third *adj* **:** being number 3 in a countable series ~ *n* **1 :** one that is third **2 :** one of 3 equal parts — **third, third·ly** *adv*

thirst *n* **1 :** dryness in mouth and throat **2 :** intense desire ~ *vb* **:** feel thirst — **thirsty** *adj*

thir·teen *n* **:** one more than 12 — **thir·teen** *adj or pron* — **thir·teenth** *adj or n*

thir·ty *n* **:** 3 times 10 — **thir·ti·eth** *adj or n* — **thirty** *adj or pron*

this *pron, pl* **:** something close or under immediate discussion ~ *adj pl* **these :** being the one near, present, just mentioned, or more immediately under observation ~ *adv* **:** to such an extent or degree

thorn *n* **:** sharp spike on a plant or a plant bearing these — **thorny** *adj*

thor·ough *adj* **:** omitting or overlooking nothing — **thor·ough·ly** *adv* — **thor·ough·ness** *n*

thor·ough·fare *n* **:** a main road or route for passage

those *pl of* THAT

though *adv* **:** however ~ *conj* **1 :** despite the fact that **2 :** granting that

thought *past of* THINK *n* **1 :** process of thinking **2 :** serious consideration **3 :** idea

thought·ful *adj* **1 :** absorbed in or showing thought **2 :** considerate of others — **thought·ful·ly** *adv* — **thought·ful·ness** *n*

thought·less *adj* **1 :** careless or reckless **2 :** lacking concern for others — **thought·less·ly** *adv*

thou·sand *n* **:** 10 times 100 — **thou·sand** *adj* — **thou·sandth** *adj or n*

thread *n* **1 :** fine line of fibers **2 :** train of thought **3 :** ridge around a screw ~ *vb* **1 :** pass thread through **2 :** put together on a thread **3 :** make one's way through or between

threat *n* **1 :** expression of intention to harm **2 :** thing that threatens

threat·en *vb* **1 :** utter threats **2 :** show signs of being near or impending — **threat·en·ing·ly** *adv*

three *n* **1 :** one more than 2 **2 :** 3d in a set or series — **three** *adj or pron*

threw *past of* THROW

thrift *n* **:** careful management or saving of money — **thrift·i·ly** *adv* — **thrifty** *adj*

thrill *vb* **1 :** have or cause to have a sudden sharp feeling of excitement **2 :** tremble — **thrill** *n* — **thrill·er** *n* — **thrill·ing·ly** *adv*

thrive *vb* **1 :** grow vigorously **2 :** prosper

throat *n* **1 :** front part of the neck **2 :** passage to the stomach — **throat·ed** *adj* — **throaty** *adj*

throb *vb* **:** pulsate — **throb** *n*

throne *n* **:** chair representing power or sovereignty

throt·tle *vb* **:** choke ~ *n* **:** valve regulating volume of fuel and air delivered to engine cylinders

through *prep* **1 :** into at one side and out at the other side of **2 :** by way of **3 :** among, between, or all around **4 :** because of **5 :** throughout the time of ~ *adv* **1 :** from one end or side to the other **2 :** from beginning to end **3 :** to the core **4 :** into the open ~ *adj* **1 :** going directly from origin to destination **2 :** finished

through·out *adv* **1 :** everywhere **2 :** from beginning to end ~ *prep* **1 :** in or to every part of **2 :** during the whole of

throw *vb* (**threw; thrown**) **1 :** propel through the air **2 :** cause to fall or fall off **3 :** put suddenly in a certain position or condition **4 :** move quickly as if throwing **5 :** put on or off hastily — **throw** *n* — **throw·er** *n* — **throw up** *vb* **:** vomit

thrust *vb* (**thrust; thrust**) **1 :** shove forward **2 :** stab or pierce — **thrust** *n*

thumb *n* **1 :** short thick division of the hand opposing the fingers **2 :** glove part for the thumb ~ *vb* **:** leaf through with the thumb — **thumb·nail** *n*

thun·der *n* **:** sound following lightning — **thunder** *vb* — **thun·der·clap** *n* — **thun·der·ous** *adj* — **thun·der·ous·ly** *adv*

Thurs·day *n* **:** 5th day of the week

thus *adv* **1 :** in this or that way **2 :** to this degree or extent **3 :** because of this or that

[1]tick *n* **:** small 8-legged blood-sucking animal

[2]tick *n* **1 :** light rhythmic tap or beat **2 :** check mark ~ *vb* **1 :** make ticks **2 :** mark with a tick **3 :** operate

tick•et *n* **1 :** tag showing price, payment of a fee or fare, or a traffic offense **2 :** list of candidates ~ *vb* **:** put a ticket on

tick•le *vb* **1 :** please or amuse **2 :** touch lightly causing uneasiness, laughter, or spasmodic movements — **tick•le** *n*

tick•lish *adj* **1 :** sensitive to tickling **2 :** requiring delicate handling — **tick•lish•ness** *n*

tide *n* **:** alternate rising and falling of the sea ~ *vb* **:** be enough to allow (one) to get by for a time — **tid•al** *adj* — **tide•wa•ter** *n*

ti•dy *adj* **1 :** well ordered and cared for **2 :** large or substantial — **ti•di•ness** *n* — **ti•dy** *vb*

tie *n* **1 :** line or ribbon for fastening, uniting, or closing **2 :** cross support to which railroad rails are fastened **3 :** uniting force **4 :** equality in score or tally or a deadlocked contest **5 :** necktie ~ *vb* **1 :** fasten or close by wrapping and knotting a tie **2 :** form a knot in **3 :** gain the same score or tally as an opponent

tier *n* **:** one of a steplike series of rows

ti•ger *n* **:** very large black-striped cat — **ti•ger•ish** *adj* — **ti•gress** *n*

tight *adj* **1 :** fitting close together esp. so as not to allow air or water in **2 :** held very firmly **3 :** taut **4 :** fitting too snugly **5 :** difficult **6 :** stingy **7 :** evenly contested **8 :** low in supply — **tight** *adv* — **tight•en** *vb* — **tight•ly** *adv* — **tight•ness** *n*

tights *n pl* **:** skintight garments

tile *n* **:** thin piece of stone or fired clay used on roofs, floors, or walls ~ *vb* **:** cover with tiles

[1]**till** *prep or conj* **:** until

[2]**till** *vb* **:** cultivate (soil) — **till•able** *adj*

tilt *vb* **:** cause to incline ~ *n* **:** slant

tim•ber *n* **1 :** cut wood for building **2 :** large squared piece of wood **3 :** wooded land or trees for timber ~ *vb* **:** cover, frame, or support with timbers — **tim•bered** *adj* — **tim•ber•land** *n*

time *n* **1 :** period during which something exists or continues or can be accomplished **2 :** point at which something happens **3 :** customary hour **4 :** age **5 :** rate of speed **6 :** moment, hour, day, or year as indicated by a clock or calendar **7 :** one's experience during a particular period ~ *vb* **1 :** arrange or set the time of **2 :** determine or record the time, duration, or rate of — **time•keep•er** *n* — **time•less** *adj* — **time•less•ness** *n* — **time•li•ness** *n* — **time•ly** *adv* — **tim•er** *n*

times *prep* **:** multiplied by

time•ta•ble *n* **:** table of departure and arrival times

tim•id *adj* **:** lacking in courage or self-confidence — **ti•mid•i•ty** *n* — **tim•id•ly** *adv*

tin *n* **1 :** soft white metallic chemical element **2 :** metal food can

tine *n* **:** one of the points of a fork

tin•gle *vb* **:** feel a ringing, stinging, or thrilling sensation — **tingle** *n*

tin•kle *vb* **:** make or cause to make a high ringing sound — **tinkle** *n*

tint *n* **1 :** slight or pale coloration **2 :** color shade ~ *vb* **:** give a tint to

ti•ny *adj* **:** very small

[1]**tip** *vb* **1 :** overturn **2 :** lean ~ *n* **:** act or state of tipping

[2]**tip** *n* **:** pointed end of something ~ *vb* **1 :** furnish with a tip **2 :** cover the tip of

[3]**tip** *n* **:** small sum given for a service performed ~ *vb* **:** give a tip to

[4]**tip** *n* **:** piece of confidential information ~ *vb* **:** give confidential information to

tip•toe *n* **:** the toes of the feet ~ *adv or adj* **:** supported on tiptoe ~ *vb* **:** walk quietly or on tiptoe

tip–top *n* **:** highest point ~ *adj* **:** excellent

[1]**tire** *vb* **1 :** make or become weary **2 :** wear out the patience of — **tire•less** *adj* — **tire•less•ly** *adv* — **tire•some** *adj* — **tire•some•ly** *adv*

[2]**tire** *n* **:** rubber cushion encircling a car wheel

tired *adj* **:** weary

tis•sue *n* **1 :** soft absorbent paper **2 :** layer of cells forming a basic structural element of an animal or plant body

ti•tle *n* **1 :** legal ownership **2 :** distinguishing name **3 :** designation of honor, rank, or office **4 :** championship — **ti•tled** *adj*

TNT *n* **:** high explosive

to *prep* **1 :** in the direction of **2 :** at, on, or near **3 :** resulting in **4 :** before or until **5** — used to show a relationship or object of a verb **6** — used with an infinitive ~ *adv* **1 :** forward **2 :** to a state of consciousness

toast *vb* **1 :** make (as a slice of bread) crisp and brown **2 :** drink in honor of someone or something **3 :** warm ~ *n* **1 :** toasted sliced bread **2 :** act of drinking in honor of someone — **toast•er** *n*

to•bac•co *n* **:** broad-leaved herb or its leaves prepared for smoking or chewing

to•day *adv* **1 :** on or for this day **2 :** at the present time ~ *n* **:** present day or time

to–do *n* **:** disturbance or fuss

toe *n* : one of the 5 end divisions of the foot — **toe•nail** *n*
tof•fee, tof•fy *n* : candy made of boiled sugar and butter
to•geth•er *adv* **1 :** in or into one place or group **2 :** in or into contact or association **3 :** at one time **4 :** as a group — **to•geth•er•ness** *n*
toil *vb* : work hard and long — **toil** *n* — **toil•er** *n* — **toil•some** *adj*
toi•let *n* **1 :** dressing and grooming oneself **2 :** bathroom **3 :** water basin to urinate and defecate in
to•ken *n* **1 :** outward sign or expression of something **2 :** small part representing the whole **3 :** piece resembling a coin
told *past of* TELL
tol•er•ance *n* **1 :** lack of opposition for beliefs or practices differing from one's own **2 :** capacity for enduring **3 :** allowable deviation — **tol•er•ant** *adj* — **tol•er•ant•ly** *adv*
tol•er•ate *vb* **1 :** allow to be or to be done without opposition **2 :** endure or resist the action of — **tol•er•a•ble** *adj* — **tol•er•a•bly** *adv* — **tol•er•a•tion** *n*
toll *n* **1 :** fee paid for a privilege or service **2 :** cost of achievement in loss or suffering — **toll•booth** *n* — **toll•gate** *n*
to•ma•to *n* : tropical American herb or its fruit
tomb *n* : house, vault, or grave for burial — **tomb•stone** *n*
tom•boy *n* : girl who behaves in a manner usu. considered boyish
to•mor•row *adv* : on or for the day after today — **tomorrow** *n*
ton *n* : unit of weight equal to 2000 pounds
tone *n* **1 :** vocal or musical sound **2 :** sound of definite pitch **3 :** manner of speaking that expresses an emotion or attitude **4 :** color quality **5 :** healthy condition **6 :** general character or quality ~ *vb* : soften or muffle — often used with *down* — **ton•al** *adj* — **to•nal•i•ty** *n*
tongue *n* **1 :** fleshy movable organ of the mouth **2 :** language **3 :** something long and flat and fastened at one end — **tongued** *adj* — **tongue•less** *adj*
to•night *adv* : on this night ~ *n* : present or coming night
too *adv* **1 :** in addition **2 :** excessively
took *past of* TAKE
tool *n* : device worked by hand ~ *vb* : shape or finish with a tool
tool•bar *n* : strip of icons on a computer display providing quick access to pictured functions
toot *vb* : sound or cause to sound esp. in short blasts — **toot** *n*
tooth *n pl* **teeth 1 :** one of the hard structures in the jaws for chewing **2 :** one of the projections on the edge of a gear wheel — **tooth•ache** *n* — **tooth•brush** *n* — **toothed** *adj* — **tooth•less** *adj* — **tooth•paste** *n* — **tooth•pick** *n*
[1]top *n* **1 :** highest part or level of something **2 :** lid or covering ~ *vb* **1 :** cover with a top **2 :** surpass **3 :** go over the top of ~ *adj* : being at the top — **topped** *adj* — **top•most** *adj*
[2]top *n* : spinning toy
top•ic *n* : subject for discussion or study
top•i•cal *adj* **1 :** relating to or arranged by topics **2 :** relating to current or local events — **top•i•cal•ly** *adv*
top•ple *vb* : fall or cause to fall
torch *n* : flaming light — **torch•bear•er** *n* — **torch•light** *n*
tore *past of* TEAR
tor•ment *n* : extreme pain or anguish or a source of this ~ *vb* **1 :** cause severe anguish to **2 :** harass — **tor•men•tor** *n*
torn *past part of* TEAR
tor•na•do *n* : violent destructive whirling wind
tor•ti•lla *n* : round flat cornmeal or wheat flour bread
tor•ture *n* **1 :** use of pain to punish or force **2 :** agony ~ *vb* : inflict torture on — **tor•tur•er** *n*
toss *vb* **1 :** move to and fro or up and down violently **2 :** throw with a quick light motion **3 :** move restlessly — **toss** *n*
toss–up *n* **1 :** a deciding by flipping a coin **2 :** even chance
to•tal *n* : entire amount ~ *vb* **1 :** add up **2 :** amount to — **to•tal** *adj* — **to•tal•ly** *adv*
to•tal•i•ty *n* : whole amount or entirety
tote *vb* : carry
touch *vb* **1 :** make contact with so as to feel **2 :** be or cause to be in contact **3 :** take into the hands or mouth **4 :** treat or mention a subject **5 :** relate or concern **6 :** move to sympathetic feeling ~ *n* **1 :** light stroke **2 :** act or fact of touching or being touched **3 :** sense of feeling **4 :** trace **5 :** state of being in contact — **touch up** *vb* : improve with minor changes
touch•down *n* : scoring of 6 points in football
touchy *adj* **1 :** easily offended **2 :** requiring tact
tough *adj* **1 :** strong but elastic **2 :** not easily chewed **3 :** severe or disciplined **4 :** stubborn

~ *n* : rowdy — **tough•en** *vb* — **tough•ly** *adv* — **tough•ness** *n*

tour *n* **1 :** period of time spent at work or on an assignment **2 :** journey with a return to the starting point ~ *vb* **:** travel over to see the sights — **tour•ist** *n*

tour•na•ment *n* **1 :** medieval jousting competition **2 :** championship series of games

tow *vb* **:** pull along behind — **tow** *n*

to•ward, to•wards *prep* **1 :** in the direction of **2 :** with respect to **3 :** in part payment on

tow•el *n* **:** absorbent cloth or paper for wiping or drying

tow•er *n* **:** tall structure ~ *vb* **:** rise to a great height — **tow•ered** *adj* — **tow•er•ing** *adj*

town *n* **1 :** small residential area **2 :** city — **towns•peo•ple** *n pl*

tox•ic *adj* **:** poisonous — **tox•ic•i•ty** *n*

tox•in *n* **:** poison produced by an organism

toy *n* **:** something for a child to play with ~ *vb* **:** amuse oneself or play with something ~ *adj* **1 :** designed as a toy **2 :** very small

trace *vb* **1 :** mark over the lines of (a drawing) **2 :** follow the trail or the development of ~ *n* **1 :** track **2 :** tiny amount or residue — **trace•able** *adj* — **trac•er** *n*

track *n* **1 :** trail left by wheels or footprints **2 :** racing course **3 :** train rails **4 :** awareness of a progression **5 :** looped belts propelling a vehicle ~ *vb* **1 :** follow the trail of **2 :** make tracks on — **track•er** *n*

track–and–field *adj* **:** relating to athletic contests of running, jumping, and throwing events

trac•tion *n* **:** gripping power to permit movement — **trac•tion•al** *adj* — **trac•tive** *adj*

trac•tor *n* **1 :** farm vehicle used esp. for pulling **2 :** truck for hauling a trailer

trade *n* **1 :** one's regular business **2 :** occupation requiring skill **3 :** the buying and selling of goods **4 :** act of trading ~ *vb* **1 :** give in exchange for something **2 :** buy and sell goods **3 :** be a regular customer — **trades•peo•ple** *n pl*

trade•mark *n* **:** word or mark identifying a manufacturer — **trade•mark** *vb*

tra•di•tion *n* **:** belief or custom passed from generation to generation — **tra•di•tion•al** *adj* — **tra•di•tion•al•ly** *adv*

traf•fic *n* **1 :** business dealings **2 :** movement along a route ~ *vb* **:** do business — **traf•fick•er** *n* — **traffic light** *n*

trag•e•dy *n* **1 :** serious drama describing a conflict and having a sad end **2 :** disastrous event

trag•ic *adj* **:** being a tragedy — **trag•i•cal•ly** *adv*

trail *vb* **1 :** hang down and drag along the ground **2 :** draw along behind **3 :** follow the track of **4 :** dwindle ~ *n* **1 :** something that trails **2 :** path or evidence left by something

trail•er *n* **1 :** vehicle intended to be hauled **2 :** dwelling designed to be towed to a site

train *n* **1 :** trailing part of a gown **2 :** connected series **3 :** group of linked railroad cars ~ *vb* **1 :** cause to grow as desired **2 :** make or become prepared or skilled **3 :** point — **train•ee** *n* — **train•er** *n* — **train•load** *n*

trai•tor *n* **:** one who betrays a trust or commits treason — **trai•tor•ous** *adj*

tramp *vb* **1 :** walk or hike **2 :** tread on ~ *n* **:** beggar or vagrant

tram•ple *vb* **:** walk or step on so as to bruise or crush — **tram•ple** *n* — **tram•pler** *n*

trance *n* **1 :** sleeplike condition **2 :** state of mystical absorption

tran•quil *adj* **:** quiet and undisturbed — **tran•quil•ize** *vb* — **tran•quil•iz•er** *n* — **tran•quil•li•ty, tran•quil•i•ty** *n* — **tran•quil•ly** *adv*

trans•ac•tion *n* **1 :** business deal **2** *pl* **:** records of proceedings — **trans•act** *vb*

trans•fer *vb* **1 :** move from one person, place, or situation to another **2 :** convey ownership of **3 :** print or copy by contact **4 :** change to another vehicle or transportation line ~ *n* **1 :** act or process of transferring **2 :** one that transfers or is transferred **3 :** ticket permitting one to transfer — **trans•fer•able** *adj* — **trans•fer•al** *n* — **trans•fer•ence** *n*

trans•form *vb* **1 :** change in structure, appearance, or character **2 :** change (an electric current) in potential or type — **trans•for•ma•tion** *n* — **trans•form•er** *n*

tran•sit *n* **1 :** movement over, across, or through **2 :** local and esp. public transportation **3 :** surveyor's instrument

tran•si•tion *n* **:** passage from one state, stage, or subject to another — **tran•si•tion•al** *adj*

tran•si•to•ry *adj* **:** of brief duration

trans•late *vb* **:** change into another language — **trans•lat•able** *adj* — **trans•la•tion** *n* — **trans•la•tor** *n*

trans•lu•cent *adj* **:** not transparent but clear enough to allow light to pass through — **trans•lu•cence** *n* — **trans•lu•cen•cy** *n* — **trans•lu•cent•ly** *adv*

trans•mit *vb* **1 :** transfer from one person or place to another **2 :** pass on by inheritance **3**

: broadcast — **trans•mis•si•ble** *adj* — **trans•mis•sion** *n* — **trans•mit•ta•ble** *adj* — **trans•mit•tal** *n* — **trans•mit•ter** *n*

trans•par•ent *adj* **1 :** clear enough to see through **2 :** obvious — **trans•par•en•cy** *n* — **trans•par•ent•ly** *adv*

trans•plant *vb* **1 :** dig up and move to another place **2 :** transfer from one body part or person to another — **transplant** *n* — **trans•plan•ta•tion** *n*

trans•port *vb* **1 :** carry or deliver to another place **2 :** carry away by emotion ∼ *n* **1 :** act of transporting **2 :** rapture **3 :** ship or plane for carrying troops or supplies — **trans•por•ta•tion** *n* — **trans•port•er** *n*

trans•pose *vb* **:** change the position, sequence, or key — **trans•po•si•tion** *n*

trap *n* **1 :** device for catching animals **2 :** something by which one is caught unawares **3 :** device to allow one thing to pass through while keeping other things out ∼ *vb* **:** catch in a trap — **trap•per** *n*

trap•e•zoid *n* **:** plane 4-sided figure with 2 parallel sides — **trap•e•zoi•dal** *adj*

trash *n* **:** something that is no good — **trashy** *adj*

trav•el *vb* **1 :** take a trip or tour **2 :** move or be carried from point to point ∼ *n* **:** journey — often pl. — **trav•el•er, trav•el•ler** *n*

trawl *vb* **:** fish or catch with a trawl ∼ *n* **:** large cone-shaped net — **trawl•er** *n*

tray *n* **:** shallow flat-bottomed receptacle for holding or carrying something

treach•er•ous *adj* **:** disloyal or dangerous — **treach•er•ous•ly** *adv*

treach•ery *n* **:** betrayal of a trust

tread *vb* (**trod; trod•den/trod**) **1 :** step on or over **2 :** walk **3 :** press or crush with the feet ∼ *n* **1 :** way of walking **2 :** sound made in walking **3 :** part on which a thing runs

trea•son *n* **:** attempt to overthrow the government — **trea•son•able** *adj* — **trea•son•ous** *adj*

trea•sure *n* **1 :** wealth stored up **2 :** something of great value ∼ *vb* **:** keep as precious

trea•sury *n* **:** place or office for keeping and distributing funds — **trea•sur•er** *n*

treat *vb* **1 :** have as a topic **2 :** pay for the food or entertainment of **3 :** act toward or regard in a certain way **4 :** give medical care to ∼ *n* **1 :** food or entertainment paid for by another **2 :** something special and enjoyable — **treat•ment** *n*

trea•ty *n* **:** agreement between governments

tree *n* **:** tall woody plant ∼ *vb* **:** force up a tree — **tree•less** *adj*

trem•ble *vb* **1 :** shake from fear or cold **2 :** move or sound as if shaken

tre•men•dous *adj* **:** amazingly large, powerful, or excellent — **tre•men•dous•ly** *adv*

trench *n* **:** long narrow cut in land

trend *n* **:** prevailing tendency, direction, or style ∼ *vb* **:** move in a particular direction — **trendy** *adj*

tres•pass *n* **1 :** sin **2 :** unauthorized entry onto someone's property ∼ *vb* **1 :** sin **2 :** enter illegally — **tres•pass•er** *n*

tri•al *n* **1 :** hearing and judgment of a matter in court **2 :** source of great annoyance **3 :** test use or experimental effort — **trial** *adj*

tri•an•gle *n* **:** plane figure with 3 sides and 3 angles — **tri•an•gu•lar** *adj*

tribe *n* **:** social group of numerous families — **trib•al** *adj* — **tribes•man** *n* — **tribes•peo•ple** *n pl*

trib•ute *n* **1 :** payment to acknowledge submission **2 :** tax **3 :** gift or act showing respect

trick *n* **1 :** scheme to deceive **2 :** prank **3 :** deceptive or ingenious feat **4 :** mannerism **5 :** knack **6 :** tour of duty ∼ *vb* **:** deceive by cunning — **trick•ery** *n* — **trick•ster** *n*

trick•le *vb* **:** run in drops or a thin stream — **trickle** *n*

tricky *adj* **1 :** inclined to trickery **2 :** requiring skill or caution

tri•cy•cle *n* **:** 3-wheeled bicycle

tri•fle *n* **:** something of little value or importance ∼ *vb* **1 :** speak or act in a playful or flirting way **2 :** toy — **tri•fler** *n* — **tri•fling** *adj*

trig•ger *n* **:** finger-piece of a firearm lock that fires the gun ∼ *vb* **:** set into motion — **trigger** *adj* — **trig•gered** *adj*

tril•lion *n* **:** 1000 billions — **tril•lion** *adj* — **trillionth** *adj or n*

trim *vb* **1 :** decorate **2 :** make neat or reduce by cutting ∼ *adj* **:** neat and compact ∼ *n* **1 :** state or condition **2 :** ornaments — **trim•ly** *adv* — **trim•mer** *n* — **trim•ming** *n*

Trin•i•ty *n* **:** divine unity of Father, Son, and Holy Spirit

trio *n* **1 :** music for 3 performers **2 :** group of 3

trip *vb* **1 :** step lightly **2 :** stumble or cause to stumble **3 :** make or cause to make a mistake **4 :** release (as a spring or switch) ∼ *n* **1**

: journey **2 :** stumble **3 :** drug-induced experience

tri•ple *vb* : make 3 times as great ~ *n* : group of 3 ~ *adj* **1 :** having 3 units **2 :** being 3 times as great or as many

trip•let *n* **1 :** group of 3 **2 :** one of 3 offspring born together

tri•umph *n* : victory or great success ~ *vb* : obtain or celebrate victory — **tri•um•phal** *adj* — **tri•um•phant** *adj* — **tri•um•phant•ly** *adv*

triv•i•al *adj* : of little importance — **triv•i•al•i•ty** *n*

trod *past of* TREAD

trodden *past part of* TREAD

trol•ley *n* : streetcar run by overhead electric wires

troop *n* **1 :** cavalry unit **2** *pl* **:** soldiers **3 :** collection of people or things ~ *vb* : move or gather in crowds

troop•er *n* **1 :** cavalry soldier **2 :** police officer on horseback or state police officer

tro•phy *n* : prize gained by a victory

trop•ic *n* **1 :** either of the 2 parallels of latitude one 23½ degrees north of the equator (**tropic of Cancer**) and one 23½ degrees south of the equator (**tropic of Cap•ri•corn**) **2** *pl* **:** region lying between the tropics — **tropic, trop•i•cal** *adj*

trou•ble *vb* **1 :** disturb **2 :** afflict **3 :** make an effort ~ *n* **1 :** cause of mental or physical distress **2 :** effort — **trou•ble•mak•er** *n* — **trou•ble•some** *adj* — **trou•ble•some•ly** *adv*

trou•sers *n pl* : long pants — **trouser** *adj*

truce *n* : agreement to halt fighting

truck *n* **1 :** wheeled frame for moving heavy objects **2 :** automotive vehicle for transporting heavy loads ~ *vb* : transport on a truck — **truck•er** *n* — **truck•load** *n*

trudge *vb* : walk or march steadily and with difficulty

true *adj* **1 :** loyal **2 :** in agreement with fact or reality **3 :** genuine ~ *adv* **1 :** truthfully **2 :** accurately ~ *vb* : make balanced or even — **tru•ly** *adv*

trum•pet *n* : tubular brass wind instrument with a flaring end ~ *vb* **1 :** blow a trumpet **2 :** proclaim loudly — **trum•pet•er** *n*

trunk *n* **1 :** main part (as of a body or tree) **2 :** long muscular nose of an elephant **3 :** storage chest **4 :** storage space in a car **5** *pl* **:** shorts

trust *n* **1 :** reliance on another **2 :** assured hope **3 :** credit **4 :** property held or managed in behalf of another **5 :** combination of firms that reduces competition **6 :** something entrusted to another's care **7 :** custody ~ *vb* **1 :** depend **2 :** hope **3 :** entrust **4 :** have faith in — **trust•ful** *adj* — **trust•ful•ly** *adv* — **trust•ful•ness** *n* — **trust•worth•i•ness** *n* — **trust•wor•thy** *adj*

truth *n* **1 :** real state of things **2 :** true or accepted statement **3 :** agreement with fact or reality — **truth•ful** *adj* — **truth•ful•ly** *adv* — **truth•ful•ness** *n*

try *vb* **1 :** conduct the trial of **2 :** put to a test **3 :** strain **4 :** make an effort at ~ *n* : act of trying

try•out *n* : competitive test of performance esp. for athletes or actors — **try out** *vb*

tsar *var of* CZAR

T–shirt *n* : collarless pullover shirt with short sleeves

tub *n* **1 :** wide bucketlike vessel **2 :** bathtub

tube *n* **1 :** hollow cylinder **2 :** round container from which a substance can be squeezed **3 :** airtight circular tube of rubber inside a tire — **tubed** *adj* — **tube•less** *adj* — **tu•bu•lar** *adj*

tuck *vb* **1 :** pull up into a fold **2 :** put into a snug often concealing place **3 :** make snug in bed — used with *in* ~ *n* : fold in a cloth

Tues•day *n* : 3d day of the week

tuft *n* : clump (as of hair or feathers) — **tuft•ed** *adj*

tug *vb* **1 :** pull hard **2 :** move by pulling ~ *n* : act of tugging

tug–of–war *n* (**tugs–of–war**) : pulling contest between 2 teams

tu•ition *n* : cost of instruction

tu•lip *n* : herb with cup-shaped flowers

tum•ble *vb* **1 :** perform gymnastic feats of rolling and turning **2 :** fall or cause to fall suddenly **3 :** toss ~ *n* : act of tumbling

tum•my *n* : belly

tu•mor *n* : abnormal and useless growth of tissue — **tu•mor•ous** *adj*

tu•mult *n* **1 :** uproar **2 :** violent agitation of mind or feelings — **tu•mul•tu•ous** *adj*

tu•na *n* : large seafood fish

tune *n* **1 :** melody **2 :** correct musical pitch **3 :** harmonious relationship ~ *vb* **1 :** bring or come into harmony **2 :** adjust in musical pitch **3 :** adjust a receiver so as to receive a broadcast **4 :** put in first-class working order — **tun•able** *adj* — **tune•ful** *adj* — **tun•er** *n*

tun•nel *n* **:** underground passageway ~ *vb* **:** make a tunnel through or under something
tur•bine *n* **:** engine turned by the force of gas or water on fan blades
tur•bu•lent *adj* **1 :** causing violence or disturbance **2 :** marked by agitation or tumult — **tur•bu•lence** *n* — **tur•bu•lent•ly** *adv*
turf *n* **:** upper layer of soil bound by grass and roots
tur•key *n* **:** large American bird raised for food
turn *vb* **1 :** move or cause to move around an axis **2 :** twist (a mechanical part) to operate **3 :** wrench **4 :** cause to face or move in a different direction **5 :** reverse the sides or surfaces of **6 :** upset **7 :** go around **8 :** become or cause to become **9 :** seek aid from a source ~ *n* **1 :** act or instance of turning **2 :** change **3 :** place at which something turns **4 :** place, time, or opportunity to do something in order — **turn•er** *n* — **turn down** *vb* **:** decline to accept — **turn in** *vb* **1 :** deliver or report to authorities **2 :** go to bed — **turn off** *vb* **:** stop the functioning of — **turn out** *vb* **1 :** expel **2 :** produce **3 :** come together **4 :** prove to be in the end — **turn over** *vb* **:** transfer — **turn up** *vb* **1 :** discover or appear **2 :** happen unexpectedly
turn•out *n* **1 :** gathering of people for a special purpose **2 :** size of a gathering
turn•over *n* **1 :** upset or reversal **2 :** filled pastry **3 :** volume of business **4 :** movement (as of goods or people) into, through, and out of a place
turn•pike *n* **:** expressway on which tolls are charged
tur•tle *n* **:** reptile with the trunk enclosed in a bony shell
tur•tle•neck *n* **:** high close-fitting collar that can be turned over or a sweater or shirt with this collar
tu•tor *n* **:** private teacher ~ *vb* **:** teach usu. individually
TV *n* **:** television
tweak *vb* **:** pinch and pull playfully — **tweak** *n*
tweed *n* **1 :** rough woolen fabric **2** *pl* **:** tweed clothing — **tweedy** *adj*
tweet *n* **:** chirping note — **tweet** *vb*
twee•zers *n pl* **:** small pincerlike tool
twelve *n* **1 :** one more than 11 **2 :** 12th in a set or series **3 :** something having 12 units — **twelfth** *adj or n* — **twelve** *adj or pron*
twen•ty *n* **:** 2 times 10 — **twen•ti•eth** *adj or n* — **twenty** *adj or pron*
twen•ty–twen•ty, 20–20 *adj* **:** being vision of normal sharpness
twice *adv* **1 :** on 2 occasions **2 :** 2 times
twig *n* **:** small branch — **twig•gy** *adj*
twi•light *n* **:** light from the sky at dusk or dawn — **twi•light** *adj*
twin *n* **:** either of 2 offspring born together ~ *adj* **1 :** born with one another or as a pair at one birth **2 :** made up of 2 similar parts
twine *n* **:** strong twisted thread ~ *vb* **1 :** twist together **2 :** coil about a support — **twin•er** *n* — **twiny** *adj*
twinge *vb* **:** affect with or feel a sudden sharp pain ~ *n* **:** sudden sharp stab (as of pain)
twin•kle *vb* **:** shine with a flickering light ~ *n* **1 :** wink **2 :** intermittent shining — **twin•kler** *n*
twirl *vb* **:** whirl round ~ *n* **1 :** act of twirling **2 :** coil — **twirl•er** *n*
twist *vb* **1 :** unite by winding (threads) together **2 :** wrench **3 :** move in or have a spiral shape **4 :** follow a winding course ~ *n* **1 :** act or result of twisting **2 :** unexpected development
twist•er *n* **:** tornado
twit *n* **:** fool
twitch *vb* **:** move or pull with a sudden motion ~ *n* **:** act of twitching
twit•ter *vb* **:** make chirping noises ~ *n* **:** small intermittent noise
two *n* **1 :** one more than one **2 :** the 2d in a set or series **3 :** something having 2 units — **two** *adj or pron*
two•fold *adj* **:** double — **two•fold** *adv*
two•some *n* **:** couple
tying *pres part of* TIE
type *n* **1 :** class, kind, or group set apart by common characteristics **2 :** special design of printed letters ~ *vb* **1 :** write with a typewriter **2 :** identify or classify as a particular type
typ•i•cal *adj* **:** having the essential characteristics of a group — **typ•i•cal•i•ty** *n* — **typ•i•cal•ly** *adv* — **typ•i•cal•ness** *n*
typ•i•fy *vb* **:** be typical of
tyr•an•ny *n* **:** unjust use of absolute governmental power — **ty•ran•ni•cal** *adj* — **ty•ran•ni•cal•ly** *adv* — **tyr•an•nize** *vb*
ty•rant *n* **:** harsh ruler having absolute power
tzar *var of* CZAR

U

u *n* **:** 21st letter of the alphabet

ug•ly *adj* **1 :** offensive to look at **2 :** mean or quarrelsome — **ug•li•ness** *n*

uku•le•le *n* **:** small 4-string guitar

ul•cer *n* **:** eroded sore — **ul•cer•ate** *vb* — **ul•cer•a•tion** *n* — **ul•cer•ous** *adj*

ul•ti•mate *adj* **:** final, maximum, or extreme — **ultimate** *n* — **ul•ti•mate•ly** *adv*

ul•ti•ma•tum *n* **:** final proposition or demand carrying or implying a threat

um•brel•la *n* **:** collapsible fabric device to protect from sun or rain

um•pire *n* **1 :** arbitrator **2 :** sport official — **um•pire** *vb*

un•ac•cept•able *adj* **:** not acceptable or pleasing — **un•ac•cept•ably** *adv*

un•af•fect•ed *adj* **1 :** not influenced or changed by something **2 :** natural and sincere — **un•af•fect•ed•ly** *adv*

unan•i•mous *adj* **1 :** showing no disagreement **2 :** formed with the agreement of all — **una•nim•i•ty** *n* — **unan•i•mous•ly** *adv*

un•armed *adj* **:** not armed or armored

un•at•tached *adj* **1 :** not attached **2 :** not married or engaged

un•aware *adv* **:** unawares ~ *adj* **:** not aware

un•awares *adv* **1 :** without warning **2 :** unintentionally

un•bal•anced *adj* **1 :** not balanced **2 :** mentally unstable

un•beat•en *adj* **:** not beaten

un•be•liev•able *adj* **1 :** improbable **2 :** superlative — **un•be•liev•ably** *adv*

un•bro•ken *adj* **1 :** not damaged **2 :** not interrupted

un•buck•le *vb* **:** unfasten the buckle of

un•but•ton *vb* **:** unfasten the buttons of

un•called–for *adj* **:** too harsh or rude for the occasion

un•cer•tain *adj* **1 :** not determined, sure, or definitely known **2 :** subject to chance or change — **un•cer•tain•ly** *adv* — **un•cer•tain•ty** *n*

un•cle *n* **1 :** brother of one's father or mother **2 :** husband of one's aunt

un•clean *adj* **:** not clean or pure — **un•clean•ness** *n*

un•com•mon *adj* **1 :** rare **2 :** superior — **un•com•mon•ly** *adv*

un•con•cerned *adj* **1 :** disinterested **2 :** not anxious or upset — **un•con•cerned•ly** *adv*

un•con•di•tion•al *adj* **:** not limited in any way — **un•con•di•tion•al•ly** *adv*

un•con•scious *adj* **1 :** not awake or aware of one's surroundings **2 :** not consciously done ~ *n* **:** part of one's mental life that one is not aware of — **un•con•scious•ly** *adv* — **un•con•scious•ness** *n*

un•con•trol•la•ble *adj* **:** incapable of being controlled — **un•con•trol•la•bly** *adv*

un•cov•er *vb* **1 :** reveal **2 :** expose by removing a covering

un•cut *adj* **1 :** not cut down, into, off, or apart **2 :** not shaped by cutting **3 :** not abridged

un•de•ni•able *adj* **:** plainly true — **un•de•ni•ably** *adv*

un•der *adv* **:** below or beneath something ~ *prep* **1 :** lower than and sheltered by **2 :** below the surface of **3 :** covered or concealed by **4 :** subject to the authority of **5 :** less than ~ *adj* **1 :** lying below or beneath **2 :** subordinate **3 :** less than usual, proper, or desired

un•der•age *adj* **:** of less than legal age

un•der•clothes *n pl* **:** underwear

un•der•cloth•ing *n* **:** underwear

un•der•cov•er *adj* **:** employed or engaged in secret investigation

un•der•de•vel•oped *adj* **:** not normally or adequately developed esp. economically

un•der•dog *n* **:** contestant given least chance of winning

un•der•es•ti•mate *vb* **:** estimate too low

un•der•feed *vb* **:** feed inadequately

un•der•foot *adv* **1 :** under the feet **2 :** in the way of another

un•der•go *vb* **1 :** endure **2 :** go through (as an experience)

un•der•grad•u•ate *n* **:** university or college student

un•der•ground *adv* **1 :** beneath the surface of the earth **2 :** in secret ~ *adj* **1 :** being or growing under the surface of the ground **2 :** secret ~ *n* **:** secret political movement or group

un•der•hand *adv or adj* **1 :** with secrecy and deception **2 :** with the hand kept below the waist

un·der·line *vb* **1 :** draw a line under **2 :** stress — **underline** *n*
un·der·mine *vb* **1 :** excavate beneath **2 :** weaken or wear away secretly or gradually
un·der·neath *prep* **:** directly under ∼ *adv* **1 :** below a surface or object **2 :** on the lower side
un·der·pants *n pl* **:** short undergarment for the lower trunk
un·der·priv·i·leged *adj* **:** poor
un·der·rate *vb* **:** rate or value too low
un·der·sea *adj* **:** being, carried on, or used beneath the surface of the sea ∼ *adv* **un·der·seas :** beneath the surface of the sea
un·der·shirt *n* **:** shirt worn as underwear
un·der·shorts *n pl* **:** short underpants
un·der·side *n* **:** side or surface lying underneath
un·der·stand *vb* **1 :** be aware of the meaning of **2 :** deduce **3 :** have a sympathetic attitude — **un·der·stand·able** *adj* — **un·der·stand·ably** *adv*
un·der·stand·ing *n* **1 :** intelligence **2 :** ability to comprehend and judge **3 :** mutual agreement ∼ *adj* **:** sympathetic
un·der·stood *adj* **1 :** agreed upon **2 :** implicit
un·der·take *vb* **1 :** attempt (a task) or assume (a responsibility) **2 :** guarantee — **un·der·tak·ing** *n*
un·der·tak·er *n* **:** one in the funeral business
un·der·wa·ter *adj* **:** being or used below the surface of the water — **underwater** *adv*
under way *adv* **:** in motion or in progress
un·der·wear *n* **:** clothing worn next to the skin and under ordinary clothes
un·der·write *vb* **1 :** provide insurance for **2 :** guarantee financial support of — **un·der·writ·er** *n*
un·dies *n pl* **:** underwear
un·do *vb* **1 :** unfasten **2 :** reverse **3 :** ruin — **un·do·ing** *n*
un·dress *vb* **:** remove one's clothes ∼ *n* **:** state of being naked
un·due *adj* **:** excessive — **un·du·ly** *adv*
un·dy·ing *adj* **:** immortal or perpetual
un·earth *vb* **:** dig up or discover
un·easy *adj* **1 :** awkward or embarrassed **2 :** disturbed or worried — **un·eas·i·ly** *adv* — **un·eas·i·ness** *n*
un·em·ployed *adj* **:** not having a job — **un·em·ploy·ment** *n*
un·equal *adj* **:** not equal or uniform — **un·equal·ly** *adv*
un·equiv·o·cal *adj* **:** leaving no doubt — **un·equiv·o·cal·ly** *adv*
un·even *adj* **1 :** not smooth **2 :** not regular or consistent — **un·even·ly** *adv* — **un·even·ness** *n*
un·event·ful *adj* **:** lacking interesting or noteworthy incidents — **un·event·ful·ly** *adv*
un·ex·pect·ed *adj* **:** not expected — **un·ex·pect·ed·ly** *adv*
un·fair *adj* **:** marked by injustice, partiality, or deception — **un·fair·ly** *adv*
un·faith·ful *adj* **:** not loyal — **un·faith·ful·ly** *adv* — **un·faith·ful·ness** *n*
un·fa·mil·iar *adj* **1 :** not well known **2 :** not acquainted — **un·fa·mil·iar·i·ty** *n*
un·fas·ten *vb* **:** release a catch or lock
un·fav·or·able *adj* **:** not pleasing, advantageous, or agreeable — **un·fav·or·ably** *adv*
un·fit *adj* **:** not suitable — **un·fit·ness** *n*
un·fold *vb* **1 :** open the folds of **2 :** reveal **3 :** develop
un·for·get·ta·ble *adj* **:** memorable — **un·for·get·ta·bly** *adv*
un·for·tu·nate *adj* **1 :** not lucky or successful **2 :** deplorable — **un·for·tu·nate** *n* — **un·for·tu·nate·ly** *adv*
un·found·ed *adj* **:** lacking a sound basis
un·friend·ly *adj* **:** not friendly or kind — **un·friend·li·ness** *n*
un·grate·ful *adj* **:** not thankful for favors — **un·grate·ful·ly** *adv* — **un·grate·ful·ness** *n*
un·hap·py *adj* **1 :** unfortunate **2 :** sad — **un·hap·pi·ly** *adv* — **un·hap·pi·ness** *n*
un·healthy *adj* **1 :** not wholesome **2 :** not well
un·heard–of *adj* **:** not known or experienced before
un·hinge *vb* **1 :** take from the hinges **2 :** make unstable esp. mentally
un·ho·ly *adj* **:** sinister or shocking — **un·ho·li·ness** *n*
uni·form *adj* **:** not changing or showing any variation ∼ *n* **:** distinctive dress worn by members of a particular group — **uni·for·mi·ty** *n* — **uni·form·ly** *adv*
uni·fy *vb* **:** make into a coherent whole — **uni·fi·ca·tion** *n*
un·in·hib·it·ed *adj* **:** free of restraint — **un·in·hib·it·ed·ly** *adv*
un·in·ten·tion·al *adj* **:** not done willingly — **un·in·ten·tion·al·ly** *adv*
un·in·ter·est·ing *adj* **:** not interesting — **un·in·ter·est·ing·ly** *adv*

union *n* **1 :** act or instance of joining two or more things into one or the state of being so joined **2 :** confederation of nations or states **3 :** organization of workers (**labor union, trade union**) — **union•ize** *vb* — **union•i•za•tion** *n*

unique *adj* **1 :** being the only one of its kind **2 :** very unusual — **unique•ly** *adv* — **unique•ness** *n*

unit *n* **1 :** smallest whole number **2 :** definite amount or quantity used as a standard of measurement **3 :** single part of a whole — **unit** *adj*

unite *vb* **:** put or join together

uni•ty *n* **1 :** quality or state of being united or a unit **2 :** harmony

uni•ver•sal *adj* **1 :** relating to or affecting everyone or everything **2 :** present or occurring everywhere — **uni•ver•sal•ly** *adv*

uni•verse *n* **:** the complete system of all things that exist

uni•ver•si•ty *n* **:** institution of higher learning

un•kind *adj* **:** not kind or sympathetic — **un•kind•li•ness** *n* — **un•kind•ly** *adv* — **un•kind•ness** *n*

un•law•ful *adj* **:** illegal — **un•law•ful•ly** *adv*

un•less *conj* **:** except on condition that

un•like *adj* **1 :** not similar **2 :** not equal ~ *prep* **:** different from — **un•like•ly** *adv* — **un•like•ness** *n* — **un•like•li•hood** *n*

un•load *vb* **1 :** take (cargo) from a vehicle, vessel, or plane **2 :** take a load from **3 :** discard

un•lock *vb* **1 :** unfasten through release of a lock **2 :** release or reveal

un•lucky *adj* **1 :** experiencing bad luck **2 :** likely to bring misfortune — **un•luck•i•ly** *adv*

un•married *adj* **:** not married

un•mis•tak•able *adj* **:** not capable of being mistaken or misunderstood — **un•mis•tak•ably** *adv*

un•nat•u•ral *adj* **1 :** not natural or spontaneous **2 :** abnormal — **un•nat•u•ral•ly** *adv* — **un•nat•u•ral•ness** *n*

un•oc•cu•pied *adj* **1 :** not busy **2 :** not occupied

un•pack *vb* **1 :** remove (things packed) from a container **2 :** remove the contents of (a package)

un•pleas•ant *adj* **:** not pleasing or agreeable

un•plug *vb* **1 :** remove a clog or plug in **2 :** disconnect from an electric circuit by removing a plug

un•re•al *adj* **:** not real or genuine — **un•re•al•i•ty** *n*

un•roll *vb* **1 :** unwind a roll of **2 :** become unrolled

un•ruly *adj* **:** not readily controlled or disciplined — **un•rul•i•ness** *n*

un•sci•en•tif•ic *adj* **:** not in accord with the principles and methods of science

un•screw *vb* **:** loosen or remove by withdrawing screws or by turning

un•self•ish *adj* **:** generous — **un•sef•ish•ly** *adv*

un•set•tle *vb* **:** disturb — **un•set•tled** *adj*

un•sta•ble *adj* **1 :** not mentally or physically balanced **2 :** tending to change

un•stop•pa•ble *adj* **:** not capable of being stopped

un•tan•gle *vb* **1 :** free from a state of being tangled **2 :** find a solution to

un•think•able *adj* **:** not to be thought of or considered possible

un•tidy *adj* **:** not neat or orderly

un•tie *vb* **:** open by releasing ties

un•til *prep* **:** up to the time of ~ *conj* **:** to the time that

un•to *prep* **:** to

un•used *adj* **1 :** not accustomed **2 :** not used

un•usu•al *adj* **:** not usual or common — **un•usu•al•ly** *adv*

un•well *adj* **:** sick

un•wind *vb* **1 :** undo something that is wound **2 :** become unwound **3 :** relax

un•wrap *vb* **:** remove the wrappings from

un•writ•ten *adj* **:** made or passed on only in speech or through tradition

un•zip *vb* **:** zip open

up *adv* **1 :** in or to a higher position or level **2 :** from beneath a surface or level **3 :** in or into an upright position **4 :** out of bed **5 :** to or with greater intensity **6 :** into existence, evidence, or knowledge **7 :** away **8** — used to indicate a degree of success, completion, or finality ~ *adj* **1 :** in the state of having risen **2 :** raised to or at a higher level **3 :** moving, inclining, or directed upward **4 :** in a state of greater intensity **5 :** at an end ~ *vb* **1 up; upped :** act abruptly **2 upped; upped :** move or cause to move upward ~ *prep* **1 :** to, toward, or at a higher point of **2 :** along or toward the beginning of

up•date *vb* **:** bring up to date — **up•date** *n*

up•grade *n* **1 :** upward slope **2 :** increase ~ *vb* **:** raise to a higher position

up•hill *adv* **:** upward on a hill or incline ~ *adj* **1 :** going up **2 :** difficult

up•hold *vb* : support or defend — **up•hold•er** *n*

up•keep *n* : act or cost of keeping up or maintaining

up•on *prep* : on

up•per *adj* : higher in position, rank, or order ~ *n* : top part of a shoe

up•right *adj* **1** : vertical **2** : erect in posture **3** : morally correct ~ *n* : something that stands upright — **up•right** *adv* — **up•right•ly** *adv* — **up•right•ness** *n*

up•ris•ing *n* : revolt

up•roar *n* : state of commotion or violent disturbance

up•roar•i•ous *adj* **1** : marked by uproar **2** : extremely funny — **up•roar•i•ous•ly** *adv*

up•root *vb* : remove by or as if by pulling up by the roots

up•set *vb* **1** : force or be forced out of the usual position **2** : disturb emotionally or physically ~ *n* **1** : act of throwing into disorder **2** : minor physical disorder ~ *adj* : emotionally disturbed or agitated

up•side down *adv* **1** : turned so that the upper and lower parts are reversed **2** : in or into confusion or disorder — **up•side–down** *adj*

up•stairs *adv* : up the stairs or to the next floor ~ *adj* : situated on the floor above ~ *n sing or pl* : part of a building above the ground floor

up•tight *adj* **1** : tense **2** : angry **3** : rigidly conventional

up–to–date *adj* : current — **up–to–date•ness** *n*

up•town *n* : upper part of a town or city — **up•town** *adj or adv*

up•ward, up•wards *adv* **1** : in a direction from lower to higher **2** : toward a higher or greater state or number ~ *adj* : directed toward or situated in a higher place — **up•ward•ly** *adv*

ur•ban *adj* : characteristic of a city

ur•bane *adj* : polished in manner — **ur•ban•i•ty** *n*

ur•ban•ite *n* : city dweller

ur•chin *n* : mischievous youngster

urge *vb* **1** : earnestly plead for or insist on (an action) **2** : try to persuade **3** : impel to a course of activity ~ *n* : force or impulse that moves one to action

ur•gent *adj* **1** : calling for immediate attention **2** : urging insistently — **ur•gen•cy** *n* — **ur•gent•ly** *adv*

urine *n* : liquid waste material from the kidneys — **uri•nary** *adj*

URL *n* : address on the Internet

urn *n* **1** : vaselike or cuplike vessel on a pedestal **2** : large coffee pot

us *pron, objective case of* WE

us•age *n* **1** : customary practice **2** : way of doing or of using something

use *n* **1** : act or practice of putting something into action **2** : state of being used **3** : way of using **4** : privilege, ability, or power to use something **5** : utility or function **6** : occasion or need to use ~ *vb* **1** : put into action or service **2** : consume **3** : behave toward **4** : to make use of **5** — used in the past tense with *to* to indicate a former practice — **us•abil•i•ty** *n* — **us•able** *adj* — **use•ful** *adj* — **use•ful•ly** *adv* — **use•ful•ness** *n* — **use•less** *adj* — **use•less•ly** *adv* — **use•less•ness** *n* — **us•er** *n*

used *adj* **1** : not new **2** : accustomed — used with *to*

usu•al *adj* : being what is expected according to custom or habit — **usu•al•ly** *adv*

uten•sil *n* **1** : eating or cooking tool **2** : useful tool

util•i•ty *n* **1** : usefulness **2** : regulated business providing a public service (as electricity)

uti•lize *vb* : make use of — **uti•li•za•tion** *n*

ut•most *adj* **1** : most distant **2** : of the greatest or highest degree or amount — **utmost** *n*

ut•ter *adj* : absolute ~ *vb* : express with the voice — **ut•ter•ance** *n* — **ut•ter•er** *n* — **ut•ter•ly** *adv*

V

v *n* : 22d letter of the alphabet

va•cant *adj* **1** : not occupied, filled, or in use **2** : devoid of thought or expression — **va•can•cy** *n* — **va•cant•ly** *adv*

va•cate *vb* **1** : annul **2** : leave unfilled or unoccupied

va•ca•tion *n* : period of rest from routine — **va•ca•tion** *vb* — **va•ca•tion•er** *n*

vac•ci•nate *vb* : administer a vaccine usu. by injection — **vac•ci•na•tion** *n*

vac•cine *n* : substance to induce immunity to a disease

vac•u•um *n* **:** empty space with no air ~ *vb* **:** clean with a machine (**vacuum cleaner**) that cleans by suction
va•gi•na *n* **:** canal that leads out from the uterus — **vag•i•nal** *adj*
vague *adj* **:** not clear, definite, or distinct — **vague•ly** *adv* — **vague•ness** *n*
vain *adj* **1 :** of no value **2 :** not successful **3 :** conceited — **vain•ly** *adv*
vale•dic•to•ri•an *n* **:** student giving the farewell address at commencement — **vale•dic•to•ry** *adj or n*
val•en•tine *n* **:** sweetheart or a card sent to a sweetheart or friend on St. Valentine's Day
val•id *adj* **1 :** proper and legally binding **2 :** founded on truth or fact — **va•lid•i•ty** *n* — **val•id•ly** *adv*
val•i•date *vb* **:** establish as valid — **val•i•da•tion** *n*
val•ley *n* **:** long depression between ranges of hills
val•or *n* **:** bravery or heroism — **val•or•ous** *adj*
valu•able *adj* **1 :** worth a lot of money **2 :** being of great importance or use — **valuable** *n*
val•ue *n* **1 :** fair return or equivalent for something exchanged **2 :** how much something is worth **3 :** distinctive quality (as of a color or sound) **4 :** guiding principle or ideal — usu. pl. ~ *vb* **1 :** estimate the worth of **2 :** appreciate the importance of — **val•ue•less** *adj* — **val•u•er** *n*
valve *n* **:** structure or device to control flow of a liquid or gas — **valved** *adj* — **valve•less** *adj*
vam•pire *n* **1 :** legendary night-wandering dead body that sucks human blood **2 :** bat that feeds on the blood of animals
van *n* **:** enclosed truck
van•dal *n* **:** person who willfully defaces or destroys property — **van•dal•ism** *n* — **van•dal•ize** *vb*
vane *n* **:** bladelike device designed to be moved by force of the air or water
van•guard *n* **1 :** troops moving at the front of an army **2 :** forefront of an action or movement
va•nil•la *n* **:** a flavoring made from the pods of a tropical orchid or this orchid
van•ish *vb* **:** disappear suddenly
van•i•ty *n* **1 :** futility or something that is futile **2 :** undue pride in oneself **3 :** makeup case or table
va•por *n* **1 :** fine separated particles floating in and clouding the air **2 :** gaseous form of an ordinarily liquid substance — **va•por•ize** *vb* — **va•por•i•za•tion** *n* — **va•por•iz•er** *n* — **va•por•ous** *adj*
var•i•able *adj* **:** apt to vary — **var•i•abil•i•ty** *n* — **var•i•able** *n* — **var•i•ably** *adv*
vari•a•tion *n* **:** instance or extent of varying
var•ied *adj* **:** showing variety — **var•ied•ly** *adv*
va•ri•ety *n* **1 :** state of being different **2 :** collection of different things **3 :** something that differs from others of its kind
var•i•ous *adj* **:** being many and unlike — **var•i•ous•ly** *adv*
var•nish *n* **:** liquid that dries to a hard glossy protective coating ~ *vb* **:** cover with varnish
var•si•ty *n* **:** principal team representing a school
vary *vb* **1 :** alter **2 :** make or be of different kinds
vase *n* **:** tall usu. ornamental container to hold flowers
vast *adj* **:** very great in size, extent, or amount — **vast•ly** *adv* — **vast•ness** *n*
[1]**vault** *n* **1 :** masonry arch **2 :** usu. underground storage or burial room ~ *vb* **:** form or cover with a vault — **vault•ed** *adj* — **vaulty** *adj*
[2]**vault** *vb* **:** spring over esp. with the help of the hands or a pole ~ *n* **:** act of vaulting — **vault•er** *n*
VCR *n* **:** a device that records and plays videotapes
veg•e•ta•ble *adj* **1 :** relating to or obtained from plants **2 :** like that of a plant ~ *n* **1 :** plant **2 :** plant grown for food
veg•e•tar•i•an *n* **:** person who eats no meat — **veg•e•tar•i•an** *adj* — **veg•e•tar•i•an•ism** *n*
veg•e•ta•tion *n* **:** plant life — **veg•e•ta•tion•al** *adj* — **veg•e•ta•tive** *adj*
ve•hi•cle *n* **1 :** medium through which something is expressed, applied, or administered **2 :** structure for transporting something esp. on wheels — **ve•hic•u•lar** *adj*
veil *n* **1 :** sheer material to hide something or to cover the face and head **2 :** something that hides ~ *vb* **:** cover with a veil
vein *n* **1 :** rock fissure filled with deposited mineral matter **2 :** vessel that carries blood toward the heart **3 :** sap-carrying tube in a leaf **4 :** distinctive element or style of expression — **veined** *adj*
vel•vet *n* **:** fabric with a short soft pile — **vel•vet** *adj* — **vel•vety** *adj*
vend *vb* **:** sell — **vend•ible** *adj* — **ven•dor** *n*

ven·geance *n* : punishment in retaliation for an injury or offense

venge·ful *adj* : filled with a desire for revenge — **venge·ful·ly** *adv*

ven·om *n* **1** : poison secreted by certain animals **2** : ill will — **ven·om·ous** *adj*

vent *vb* **1** : provide with or let out at a vent **2** : give expression to ~ *n* : opening for passage or for relieving pressure

ven·ti·late *vb* : allow fresh air to circulate through — **ven·ti·la·tion** *n* — **ven·ti·la·tor** *n*

ven·ture *vb* **1** : risk or take a chance on **2** : put forward (an opinion) ~ *n* : speculative business enterprise

ven·ture·some *adj* : brave or daring — **ven·ture·some·ly** *adv* — **ven·ture·some·ness** *n*

verb *n* : word that expresses action or existence

ver·bal *adj* **1** : having to do with or expressed in words **2** : oral **3** : relating to or formed from a verb — **ver·bal·i·za·tion** *n* — **ver·bal·ize** *vb* — **ver·bal·ly** *adv*

verbal auxiliary *n* : auxiliary verb

ver·dict *n* : decision of a jury

ver·i·fy *vb* : establish the truth, accuracy, or reality of — **ver·i·fi·able** *adj* — **ver·i·fi·ca·tion** *n*

ver·min *n* (**vermin**) : small animal pest

ver·sa·tile *adj* : having many abilities or uses — **ver·sa·til·i·ty** *n*

verse *n* **1** : line or stanza of poetry **2** : poetry **3** : short division of a chapter in the Bible

ver·sion *n* **1** : translation of the Bible **2** : account or description from a particular point of view

ver·sus *prep* : opposed to or against

ver·te·brate *n* : animal with a backbone — **verte·brate** *adj*

ver·ti·cal *adj* : rising straight up from a level surface — **vertical** *n* — **ver·ti·cal·i·ty** *n* — **ver·ti·cal·ly** *adv*

very *adj* **1** : exact **2** : exactly suitable **3** : mere or bare **4** : precisely the same ~ *adv* **1** : to a high degree **2** : in actual fact

ves·pers *n pl* : late afternoon or evening worship service

ves·sel *n* **1** : a container (as a barrel, bottle, bowl, or cup) for a liquid **2** : craft for navigation esp. on water **3** : tube in which a body fluid is circulated

[1]**vest** *vb* **1** : give a particular authority, right, or property to **2** : clothe with or as if with a garment

[2]**vest** *n* : sleeveless garment usu. worn under a suit coat

vet·er·an *n* **1** : former member of the armed forces **2** : person with long experience — **veteran** *adj*

Veterans Day *n* : 4th Monday in October or formerly November 11 observed as a legal holiday in commemoration of the end of war in 1918 and 1945

vet·er·i·nar·i·an *n* : doctor of animals — **vet·er·i·nary** *adj*

ve·to *n* **1** : power to forbid and esp. the power of a chief executive to prevent a bill from becoming law **2** : exercise of the veto ~ *vb* **1** : forbid **2** : reject a legislative bill

vex *vb* : trouble, distress, or annoy — **vex·a·tion** *n* — **vex·a·tious** *adj*

via *prep* : by way of

vi·brant *adj* **1** : vibrating **2** : pulsing with vigor or activity **3** : sounding from vibration — **vi·bran·cy** *n*

vi·brate *vb* **1** : move or cause to move quickly back and forth or side to side **2** : respond sympathetically — **vi·bra·tion** *n* — **vi·bra·tor** *n* — **vi·bra·tory** *adj*

vice *n* **1** : immoral habit **2** : depravity

vice ver·sa *adv* : with the order reversed

vi·cin·i·ty *n* : surrounding area

vi·cious *adj* **1** : wicked **2** : savage **3** : malicious — **vi·cious·ly** *adv* — **vi·cious·ness** *n*

vic·tim *n* : person killed, hurt, or abused — **vic·tim·i·za·tion** *n* — **vic·tim·ize** *vb* — **vic·tim·iz·er** *n*

vic·tor *n* : winner

vic·to·ry *n* : success in defeating an enemy or opponent or in overcoming difficulties — **vic·to·ri·ous** *adj* — **vic·to·ri·ous·ly** *adv*

vid·eo *adj* : relating to the television image

vid·eo·tape *vb* : make a recording of (a television production) on special tape — **videotape** *n*

vie *vb* : contend — **vi·er** *n*

view *n* **1** : process of seeing or examining **2** : opinion **3** : area of landscape that can be seen **4** : range of vision **5** : purpose or object ~ *vb* **1** : look at **2** : think about or consider — **view·er** *n*

view·point *n* : position from which something is considered

vig·il *n* **1** : day of devotion before a religious feast **2** : act or time of keeping awake **3** : long period of keeping watch (as over a sick or dying person)

vig·i·lant *adj* : alert esp. to avoid danger — **vig·i·lance** *n* — **vig·i·lant·ly** *adv*
vig·or *n* **1** : energy or strength **2** : intensity or force — **vig·or·ous** *adj* — **vig·or·ous·ly** *adv* — **vig·or·ous·ness** *n*
vile *adj* : thoroughly bad or contemptible — **vile·ly** *adv* — **vile·ness** *n*
vil·la *n* : country estate
vil·lage *n* : small country town — **vil·lag·er** *n*
vil·lain *n* : bad person — **vil·lain·ess** *n* — **vil·lain·ous** *adj* — **vil·lain·ous·ly** *adv* — **vil·lain·ous·ness** *n* — **vil·lainy** *n*
vin·di·cate *vb* **1** : avenge **2** : exonerate **3** : justify — **vin·di·ca·tion** *n* — **vin·di·ca·tor** *n*
vin·dic·tive *adj* : seeking or meant for revenge — **vin·dic·tive·ly** *adv* — **vin·dic·tive·ness** *n*
vine *n* : climbing or trailing plant
vin·e·gar *n* : acidic liquid obtained by fermentation — **vin·e·gary** *adj*
vin·tage *n* **1** : season's yield of grapes or wine **2** : period of origin ~ *adj* : of enduring interest
vi·nyl *n* : strong plastic
vi·o·late *vb* **1** : act with disrespect or disregard of **2** : rape **3** : desecrate — **vi·o·la·tion** *n* — **vi·o·la·tor** *n*
vi·o·lence *n* : intense physical force that causes or is intended to cause injury or destruction — **vi·o·lent** *adj* — **vi·o·lent·ly** *adv*
vi·o·let *n* **1** : small flowering plant **2** : reddish blue
vi·o·lin *n* : bowed stringed instrument — **vi·o·lin·ist** *n*
VIP *n* : very important person
vir·gin *n* **1** : unmarried woman **2** : a person who has never had sexual intercourse ~ *adj* **1** : chaste **2** : natural and unspoiled — **vir·gin·al** *adj* — **vir·gin·al·ly** *adv* — **vir·gin·i·ty** *n*
vir·tu·al *adj* : being in effect but not in fact or name — **vir·tu·al·ly** *adv*
vir·tue *n* **1** : moral excellence **2** : effective or commendable quality **3** : chastity — **vir·tu·ous** *adj* — **vir·tu·ous·ly** *adv*
vi·rus *n* **1** : tiny disease-causing agent **2** : a computer program that performs a malicious action (as destroying data)
vi·sa *n* : authorization to enter a foreign country
vise *n* : device for clamping something being worked on
vis·i·ble *adj* **1** : capable of being seen **2** : manifest or apparent — **vis·i·bil·i·ty** *n* — **vis·i·bly** *adv*
vi·sion *n* **1** : vivid picture seen in a dream or trance or in the imagination **2** : foresight **3** : power of seeing ~ *vb* : imagine
vis·it *vb* **1** : go or come to see **2** : stay with for a time as a guest **3** : cause or be a reward, affliction, or punishment ~ *n* : short stay as a guest — **vis·it·able** *adj* — **vis·i·tor** *n*
vi·sor *n* **1** : front piece of a helmet **2** : part (as on a cap or car windshield) that shades the eyes
vis·ta *n* : distant view
vi·su·al *adj* **1** : relating to sight **2** : visible — **vi·su·al·ly** *adv*
vi·su·al·ize *vb* : form a mental image of — **vi·su·al·i·za·tion** *n* — **vi·su·al·iz·er** *n*
vi·tal *adj* **1** : relating to, necessary for, or characteristic of life **2** : full of life and vigor **3** : fatal **4** : very important — **vi·tal·ly** *adv*
vi·tal·i·ty *n* **1** : life force **2** : energy
vi·ta·min *n* : natural organic substance essential to health
viv·id *adj* **1** : lively **2** : brilliant **3** : intense or sharp — **viv·id·ly** *adv* — **viv·id·ness** *n*
vo·cab·u·lary *n* **1** : list or collection of words **2** : stock of words used by a person or about a subject
vo·cal *adj* **1** : relating to or produced by or for the voice **2** : speaking out freely and usu. emphatically — **vo·cal·ize** *vb*
vo·ca·tion *n* : regular employment — **vo·ca·tion·al** *adj*
voice *n* **1** : sound produced through the mouth by humans and many animals **2** : power of speaking **3** : right of choice or opinion ~ *vb* : express in words — **voiced** *adj*
voice mail *n* : an electronic system for recording and playing back telephone messages
void *adj* **1** : containing nothing **2** : lacking — with *of* **3** : not legally binding ~ *n* **1** : empty space **2** : feeling of hollowness ~ *vb* **1** : discharge (as body waste) **2** : make (as a contract) void — **void·able** *adj* — **void·er** *n*
vol·a·tile *adj* **1** : readily vaporizing at a relatively low temperature **2** : likely to change suddenly — **vol·a·til·i·ty** *n* — **vol·a·til·ize** *vb*
vol·ca·no *n* : opening in the earth's crust from which molten rock and steam come out — **vol·ca·nic** *adj*
vol·ley *n* **1** : flight of missiles (as arrows) **2** : simultaneous shooting of many weapons
vol·ley·ball *n* : game of batting a large ball over a net
volt *n* : unit for measuring the force that moves an electric current — **volt·age** *n*

vol•ume *n* **1 :** book **2 :** space occupied as measured by cubic units **3 :** amount **4 :** loudness of a sound

vol•un•tary *adj* **1 :** done, made, or given freely and without expecting compensation **2 :** relating to or controlled by the will — **vol•un•tar•i•ly** *adv*

vol•un•teer *n* **:** person who offers to help or work without expecting payment or reward ~ *vb* **1 :** offer or give voluntarily **2 :** offer oneself as a volunteer

vom•it *vb* **:** throw up the contents of the stomach — **vom•it** *n*

vote *n* **1 :** individual expression of preference in choosing or reaching a decision **2 :** right to indicate one's preference or the preference expressed ~ *vb* **1 :** cast a vote **2 :** choose or defeat by vote — **vote•less** *adj* — **vot•er** *n*

vouch•er *n* **:** written record or receipt that serves as proof of a transaction

vow *n* **:** solemn promise to do something or to live or act a certain way — **vow** *vb*

vow•el *n* **1 :** speech sound produced without obstruction or friction in the mouth **2 :** letter representing such a sound

voy•age *n* **:** long journey esp. by water or through space ~ *vb* **:** make a voyage — **voy•ag•er** *n*

vul•gar *adj* **1 :** relating to the common people **2 :** lacking refinement **3 :** offensive in manner or language — **vul•gar•ism** *n* — **vul•gar•i•ty** *n* — **vul•gar•ize** *vb* — **vul•gar•ly** *adv*

vul•ner•a•ble *adj* **:** exposed to attack or damage — **vul•ner•a•bil•i•ty** *n* — **vul•ner•a•bly** *adv*

vul•ture *n* **:** large flesh-eating bird

vying *pres part of* VIE

W

w *n* **:** 23d letter of the alphabet

wad *n* **1 :** little mass **2 :** soft mass of fibrous material **3 :** pliable plug to retain a powder charge **4 :** considerable amount ~ *vb* **1 :** form into a wad **2 :** stuff with a wad

wade *vb* **1 :** step in or through (as water) **2 :** move with difficulty — **wade** *n* — **wad•er** *n*

wa•fer *n* **1 :** thin crisp cake or cracker **2 :** waferlike thing

waf•fle *n* **:** crisped cake of batter cooked in a hinged utensil (**waffle iron**) ~ *vb* **:** hesitate in deciding

wag *vb* **:** sway or swing from side to side or to and fro — **wag** *n*

wage *vb* **:** engage in ~ *n* **1 :** payment for labor or services **2 :** compensation

wa•ger *n or vb* **:** bet

wag•gle *vb* **:** wag — **waggle** *n*

wag•on *n* **1 :** 4-wheeled vehicle drawn by animals **2 :** child's 4-wheeled cart

waist *n* **1 :** narrowed part of the body between chest and hips **2 :** waistlike part — **waist•line** *n*

wait *vb* **1 :** remain in readiness or expectation **2 :** delay **3 :** attend as a waiter ~ *n* **1 :** concealment **2 :** act or period of waiting

wait•er *n* **:** person who serves others at tables

wait•ress *n* **:** woman who serves others at tables

[1]**wake** *vb* (**woke; wo•ken**) **1 :** keep watch **2 :** bring or come back to consciousness after sleep ~ *n* **1 :** state of being awake **2 :** watch held over a dead body

[2]**wake** *n* **:** track left by a ship

wak•en *vb* **:** wake

walk *vb* **1 :** move or cause to move on foot **2 :** pass over, through, or along by walking ~ *n* **1 :** a going on foot **2 :** place or path for walking **3 :** distance to be walked **4 :** way of living **5 :** way of walking **6 :** slow 4-beat gait of a horse — **walk•er** *n*

wall *n* **1 :** structure for defense or for enclosing something **2 :** upright enclosing part of a building or room **3 :** something like a wall ~ *vb* **:** provide, separate, surround, or close with a wall — **walled** *adj*

wal•let *n* **:** pocketbook with compartments

wal•low *vb* **1 :** roll about in deep mud **2 :** indulge oneself excessively ~ *n* **:** place for wallowing

wal•nut *n* **1 :** nut with a furrowed shell and adherent husk **2 :** tree on which this nut grows or its brown wood

wand *n* **:** slender staff

wan•der *vb* **1 :** move about aimlessly **2 :** stray **3 :** become delirious — **wan•der•er** *n*

wane *vb* **1 :** grow smaller or less **2 :** lose power, prosperity, or influence — **wane** *n*

want *vb* **1 :** lack **2 :** need **3 :** desire earnestly ~ *n* **1 :** deficiency **2 :** dire need **3 :** something wanted

war *n* **1 :** armed fighting between nations **2**

: state of hostility or conflict **3 :** struggle between opposing forces or for a particular end ~ *vb* : engage in warfare — **war·less** *adj* — **war·time** *n*

war·ble *n* **1 :** melodious succession of low pleasing sounds **2 :** musical trill ~ *vb* : sing or utter in a trilling way

ward *n* **1 :** a guarding or being under guard or guardianship **2 :** division of a prison or hospital **3 :** electoral or administrative division of a city **4 :** person under protection of a guardian or a law court ~ *vb* : turn aside — **ward·ship** *n*

war·den *n* **1 :** guardian **2 :** official charged with supervisory duties or enforcement of laws **3 :** official in charge of a prison

ward·robe *n* **1 :** clothes closet **2 :** collection of wearing apparel

ware·house *n* : place for storage of merchandise — **ware·house** *vb* — **ware·house·man** *n* — **ware·hous·er** *n*

war·fare *n* **1 :** military operations between enemies **2 :** struggle

war·like *adj* : fond of, relating to, or used in war

warm *adj* **1 :** having or giving out moderate or adequate heat **2 :** serving to retain heat **3 :** showing strong feeling **4 :** giving a pleasant impression of warmth, cheerfulness, or friendliness ~ *vb* **1 :** make or become warm **2 :** give warmth or energy to **3 :** experience feelings of affection **4 :** become increasingly ardent, interested, or competent — **warm·er** *n* — **warm·ly** *adv* — **warm up** *vb* : make ready by preliminary activity

warmth *n* **1 :** quality or state of being warm **2 :** enthusiasm

warn *vb* **1 :** put on guard **2 :** notify in advance — **warn·ing** *n or adj*

warp *n* **1 :** lengthwise threads in a woven fabric **2 :** twist ~ *vb* **1 :** twist out of shape **2 :** lead astray **3 :** distort

war·rant *n* **1 :** authorization **2 :** legal writ authorizing action ~ *vb* **1 :** declare or maintain positively **2 :** guarantee **3 :** approve **4 :** justify

war·ran·ty *n* : guarantee of the integrity of a product

war·rior *n* : one engaged or experienced in warfare

wart *n* **1 :** small projection on the skin caused by a virus **2 :** wartlike protuberance — **warty** *adj*

wary *adj* : careful in guarding against danger or deception

was *past 1st & 3d sing of* BE

wash *vb* **1 :** cleanse with or as if with a liquid (as water) **2 :** wet thoroughly with liquid **3 :** flow along the border of **4 :** flow in a stream **5 :** move or remove by or as if by the action of water **6 :** cover or daub lightly with a liquid **7 :** undergo laundering ~ *n* **1 :** act of washing or being washed **2 :** articles to be washed **3 :** surging action of water or disturbed air — **wash·able** *adj* — **wash·cloth** *n*

wash·er *n* **1 :** machine for washing **2 :** ring used around a bolt or screw to ensure tightness or relieve friction

wash·ing *n* : articles to be washed

Washington's Birthday *n* : the 3d Monday in February or formerly February 22 observed as a legal holiday

waste *n* **1 :** sparsely settled or barren region **2 :** act or an instance of wasting **3 :** refuse (as garbage or rubbish) **4 :** material (as feces) produced but not used by a living body ~ *vb* **1 :** ruin **2 :** spend or use carelessly **3 :** lose substance or energy ~ *adj* **1 :** wild and uninhabited **2 :** being of no further use — **waste·bas·ket** *n* — **wast·er** *n* — **waste·ful** *adj* — **waste·ful·ly** *adv* — **waste·ful·ness** *n* — **waste·land** *n*

watch *vb* **1 :** be or stay awake intentionally **2 :** be on the lookout for danger **3 :** observe **4 :** keep oneself informed about ~ *n* **1 :** act of keeping awake to guard **2 :** close observation **3 :** one that watches **4 :** period of duty on a ship or those on duty during this period **5 :** timepiece carried on the person — **watch·dog** *n* — **watch·er** *n* — **watch·ful** *adj* — **watch·ful·ly** *adv* — **watch·ful·ness** *n* — **watch·man** *n*

wa·ter *n* **1 :** liquid that descends as rain and forms rivers, lakes, and seas **2 :** liquid containing or resembling water ~ *vb* **1 :** supply with or get water **2 :** dilute with or as if with water **3 :** form or secrete watery matter

wa·ter·fall *n* : steep descent of the water of a stream

wa·ter·mel·on *n* : large fruit with sweet juicy usu. red pulp

wa·ter·proof *adj* : not letting water through ~ *vb* : make waterproof — **wa·ter·proof·ing** *n*

wa·ter·tight *adj* **1 :** so tight as not to let water in **2 :** allowing no possibility for doubt or uncertainty

wa•tery *adj* **1 :** containing, full of, or giving out water **2 :** being like water **3 :** soft and soggy
watt *n* **:** unit of electric power — **watt•age** *n*
wave *vb* **1 :** flutter **2 :** signal with the hands **3 :** wave to and fro with the hand **4 :** curve up and down like a wave ~ *n* **1 :** moving swell on the surface of water **2 :** wavelike shape **3 :** waving motion **4 :** sudden temporary increase **5 :** disturbance that transfers energy from point to point — **wave•length** *n* — **wave•let** *n* — **wave•like** *adj* — **wavy** *adj*
wa•ver *vb* **1 :** fluctuate in opinion, allegiance, or direction **2 :** flicker **3 :** falter — **waver** *n* — **wa•ver•er** *n* — **wa•ver•ing•ly** *adv*
[1]**wax** *n* **1 :** yellowish plastic substance secreted by bees **2 :** substance like beeswax ~ *vb* **:** treat or rub with wax esp. for polishing — **waxy** *adj*
[2]**wax** *vb* **1 :** grow larger **2 :** become
way *n* **1 :** thoroughfare for travel or passage **2 :** route **3 :** course of action **4 :** method **5 :** detail **6 :** usual or characteristic state of affairs **7 :** condition **8 :** distance **9 :** progress along a course — **by the way :** in a digression — **by way of 1 :** for the purpose of **2 :** by the route through — **out of the way :** remote
way•ward *adj* **1 :** following one's own capricious inclinations **2 :** not predictable
we *pron* — used of a group that includes the speaker or writer
weak *adj* **1 :** lacking strength or vigor **2 :** deficient in vigor of mind or character **3 :** of less than usual strength **4 :** not having or exerting authority — **weak•en** *vb* — **weak•ly** *adv* — **weak•ness** *n*
weak•ling *n* **:** person who is physically, mentally, or morally weak
wealth *n* **1 :** abundant possessions or resources **2 :** great quantity
wealthy *adj* **:** having wealth
weap•on *n* **1 :** something (as a gun) that may be used to fight with **2 :** means by which one contends against another — **weap•on•less** *adj*
wear *vb* (**wore; worn**) **1 :** use as an article of clothing or adornment **2 :** carry on the person **3 :** show an appearance of **4 :** decay by use or by scraping **5 :** lessen the strength of **6 :** endure use ~ *n* **1 :** act of wearing **2 :** clothing **3 :** lasting quality **4 :** result of use — **wear•able** *adj* — **wear•er** *n* — **wear out** *vb* **1 :** make or become useless by wear **2 :** tire
wea•ry *adj* **1 :** worn out in strength, freshness, or patience **2 :** expressing or characteristic of weariness ~ *vb* **:** make or become weary — **wea•ri•ly** *adv* — **wea•ri•ness** *n* — **wea•ri•some** *adj* — **wea•ri•some•ly** *adv*
weath•er *n* **:** state of the atmosphere ~ *vb* **1 :** expose to or endure the action of weather **2 :** endure — **weath•er•man** *n* — **weath•er•proof** *adj or vb*
weave *vb* (**wove; wo•ven**) **1 :** form by interlacing strands of material **2 :** to make as if by weaving together parts **3 :** follow a winding course ~ *n* **:** pattern or method of weaving — **weav•er** *n*
web *n* **1 :** cobweb **2 :** animal or plant membrane **3 :** network **4** *cap* **:** World Wide Web ~ *vb* **:** cover or provide with a web — **webbed** *adj*
web•bing *n* **:** strong closely woven tape
Web site *n* **:** group of World Wide Web pages available online
wed *vb* **1 :** marry **2 :** unite
wed•ding *n* **:** marriage ceremony and celebration
wedge *n* **:** V-shaped object used for splitting, raising, forcing open, or tightening ~ *vb* **1 :** tighten or split with a wedge **2 :** force into a narrow space
Wednes•day *n* **:** 4th day of the week
wee *adj* **:** very small
weed *n* **:** unwanted plant ~ *vb* **1 :** remove weeds **2 :** get rid of — **weed•er** *n* — **weedy** *adj*
weeds *n pl* **:** mourning clothes
week *n* **1 :** 7 successive days **2 :** calendar period of 7 days beginning with Sunday and ending with Saturday **3 :** the working or school days of the calendar week
week•day *n* **:** any day except Sunday and often Saturday
week•end *n* **:** Saturday and Sunday ~ *vb* **:** spend the weekend
week•ly *adj* **:** occurring, appearing, or done every week ~ *n* **:** weekly publication — **week•ly** *adv*
weep *vb* (**wept; wept**) **:** shed tears — **weep•er** *n* — **weepy** *adj*
weigh *vb* **1 :** determine the heaviness of **2 :** have a specified weight **3 :** consider carefully **4 :** raise (an anchor) off the sea floor **5 :** press down or burden
weight *n* **1 :** amount that something weighs **2 :** relative heaviness **3 :** heavy object **4 :** bur-

den or pressure **5 :** importance ~ *vb* **1 :** load with a weight **2 :** oppress — **weight·less** *adj* — **weight·less·ness** *n* — **weighty** *adj*

weird *adj* **1 :** unearthly or mysterious **2 :** strange — **weird·ly** *adv* — **weird·ness** *n*

wel·come *vb* **:** accept or greet cordially ~ *adj* **:** received or permitted gladly ~ *n* **:** cordial greeting or reception

wel·fare *n* **1 :** prosperity **2 :** government aid for those in need

[1]**well** *n* **1 :** spring **2 :** hole sunk in the earth to obtain a natural deposit (as of oil) **3 :** source of supply **4 :** open space extending vertically through floors ~ *vb* **:** flow forth

[2]**well** *adv* (**bet·ter; best**) **1 :** in a good or proper manner **2 :** satisfactorily **3 :** fully **4 :** intimately **5 :** considerably ~ *adj* **1 :** satisfactory **2 :** prosperous **3 :** desirable **4 :** healthy

well–adjusted *adj* **:** not psychologically troubled

well–be·ing *n* **:** state of being happy, healthy, or prosperous

well–known *adj* **:** widely known or acknowledged

well–mean·ing *adj* **:** having good intentions

well–off *adj* **:** being in good condition esp. financially

well–to–do *adj* **:** prosperous

went *past of* GO

wept *past of* WEEP

were *past 2d sing, past pl, or past subjunctive of* BE

west *adv* **:** to or toward the west ~ *adj* **:** situated toward or at or coming from the west ~ *n* **1 :** direction of sunset **2** *cap* **:** regions to the west — **west·er·ly** *adv or adj* — **west·ward** *adv or adj* — **west·wards** *adv*

west·ern *adj* **1** *cap* **:** of a region designated West **2 :** lying toward or coming from the west — **West·ern·er** *n*

wet *adj* **1 :** consisting of or covered or soaked with liquid **2 :** not dry ~ *n* **:** moisture ~ *vb* **:** make or become moist — **wet·ly** *adv* — **wet·ness** *n*

whack *vb* **:** strike sharply ~ *n* **1 :** sharp blow **2 :** proper working order **3 :** chance **4 :** try

whale *n* **:** large marine mammal ~ *vb* **:** hunt for whales — **whale·boat** *n* — **whal·er** *n*

wharf *n* **:** structure alongside which boats lie to load or unload

what *pron* **1** — used to inquire the identity or nature of something **2 :** that which **3 :** whatever ~ *adv* **:** in what respect ~ *adj* **1** — used to inquire about the identity or nature of something **2 :** how remarkable or surprising **3 :** whatever

what·ev·er *pron* **1 :** anything or everything that **2 :** no matter what ~ *adj* **:** of any kind at all

wheat *n* **:** cereal grain that yields flour — **wheat·en** *adj*

wheel *n* **1 :** disk or circular frame capable of turning on a central axis **2 :** device of which the main part is a wheel ~ *vb* **1 :** convey or move on wheels or a wheeled vehicle **2 :** rotate **3 :** turn so as to change direction — **wheeled** *adj* — **wheel·er** *n* — **wheel·less** *adj*

wheeze *vb* **:** breathe with difficulty and with a whistling sound — **wheeze** *n* — **wheezy** *adj*

when *adv* — used to inquire about or designate a particular time ~ *conj* **1 :** at or during the time that **2 :** every time that **3 :** if **4 :** although ~ *pron* **:** what time

when·ev·er *conj or adv* **:** at whatever time

where *adv* **1 :** at, in, or to what place **2 :** at, in, or to what situation, position, direction, circumstances, or respect ~ *conj* **1 :** at, in, or to what place, position, or circumstance **2 :** at, in, or to which place ~ *n* **:** place

where·abouts *adv* **:** about where ~ *n sing or pl* **:** place where a person or thing is

where·as *conj* **1 :** while on the contrary **2 :** since

wher·ev·er *adv* **:** where ~ *conj* **:** at, in, or to whatever place or circumstance

whether *conj* **1 :** if it is or was true that **2 :** if it is or was better **3 :** whichever is the case

which *adj* **1 :** being what one or ones out of a group **2 :** whichever ~ *pron* **1 :** which one or ones **2 :** whichever

which·ev·er *pron or adj* **:** no matter what one

whiff *n* **1 :** slight gust **2 :** inhalation of odor, gas, or smoke **3 :** slight trace ~ *vb* **:** inhale an odor

while *n* **1 :** period of time **2 :** time and effort used ~ *conj* **1 :** during the time that **2 :** as long as **3 :** although ~ *vb* **:** cause to pass esp. pleasantly

whim *n* **:** sudden wish, desire, or change of mind

whim·sy, whim·sey *n* **1 :** whim **2 :** fanciful creation — **whim·si·cal** *adj* — **whim·si·cal·ly** *adv*

whine *vb* **1 :** utter a usu. high-pitched plaintive

cry **2** : complain — **whine** *n* — **whin•er** *n* — **whiny** *adj*

whip *vb* **1** : move quickly **2** : strike with something slender and flexible **3** : defeat **4** : incite **5** : beat into a froth ~ *n* **1** : flexible device used for whipping **2** : party leader responsible for discipline **3** : beating motion — **whip•per** *n*

whip•lash *n* : injury from a sudden sharp movement of the neck and head

whir *vb* : move, fly, or revolve with a whir ~ *n* : continuous fluttering or vibratory sound

whirl *vb* **1** : move or drive in a circle **2** : spin **3** : move or turn quickly **4** : reel ~ *n* **1** : rapid circular movement **2** : state of commotion or confusion **3** : try

whirl•pool *n* : a current of water flowing in a circle

whisk *n* **1** : quick light sweeping or brushing motion **2** : usu. wire kitchen implement for beating ~ *vb* **1** : move or convey briskly **2** : beat **3** : brush lightly

whis•ker *n* **1** *pl* : beard **2** : long bristle or hair near an animal's mouth — **whis•kered** *adj*

whis•key, whis•ky *n* : liquor distilled from a fermented mash of grain

whis•per *vb* **1** : speak softly **2** : tell by whispering ~ *n* **1** : soft low sound **2** : rumor

whis•tle *n* **1** : device by which a shrill sound is produced **2** : shrill clear sound made by a whistle or through the lips ~ *vb* **1** : make or utter a whistle **2** : signal or call by a whistle **3** : produce by whistling — **whis•tler** *n*

white *adj* **1** : free from color **2** : of the color of new snow or milk **3** : having light skin ~ *n* **1** : color of maximum lightness **2** : white part or thing **3** : person who is light-skinned — **white•ness** *n* — **whit•ish** *adj*

white–col•lar *adj* : relating to salaried employees with duties not requiring protective or work clothing

whit•en *vb* : make or become white — **whit•en•er** *n*

whit•tle *vb* **1** : pare **2** : shape by paring **3** : reduce gradually

whiz, whizz *vb* : make a sound like a speeding object — **whiz, whizz** *n*

who *pron* **1** : what or which person or persons **2** : person or persons that **3** — used to introduce a relative clause

who•ev•er *pron* : no matter who

whole *adj* **1** : being in healthy or sound condition **2** : having all its parts or elements **3** : constituting the total sum of ~ *n* **1** : complete amount or sum **2** : something whole or entire — **on the whole 1** : considering all circumstances **2** : in general — **whole•ness** *n*

whole•heart•ed *adj* : sincere

whole•sale *n* : sale of goods in quantity usu. for resale by a retail merchant ~ *adj* **1** : of or relating to wholesaling **2** : performed on a large scale ~ *vb* : sell at wholesale — **wholesale** *adv* — **whole•sal•er** *n*

whole•some *adj* **1** : promoting mental, spiritual, or bodily health **2** : healthy — **wholesome•ness** *n*

whol•ly *adv* **1** : totally **2** : solely

whom *pron, objective case of* WHO

whom•ev•er *pron, objective case of* WHOEVER

whoop *vb* : shout loudly ~ *n* : shout

whop•per *n* **1** : something unusually large or extreme of its kind **2** : monstrous lie

whose *adj* : of or relating to whom or which ~ *pron* : whose one or ones

why *adv* : for what reason, cause, or purpose ~ *conj* **1** : reason for which **2** : for which ~ *n* : reason ~ *interj* — used esp. to express surprise

wick *n* : cord that draws up oil, tallow, or wax to be burned

wick•ed *adj* **1** : morally bad **2** : harmful or troublesome **3** : very unpleasant **4** : very impressive — **wick•ed•ly** *adv* — **wick•ed•ness** *n*

wide *adj* **1** : covering a vast area **2** : measured at right angles to the length **3** : having a great measure across **4** : opened fully **5** : far from the thing in question ~ *adv* **1** : over a great distance **2** : so as to leave considerable space between **3** : fully — **wide•ly** *adv* — **wid•en** *vb*

wide–awake *adj* : alert

wides•pread *adj* : generally known or spread out

wid•ow *n* : woman who has lost her husband by death and has not married again ~ *vb* : cause to become a widow — **wid•ow•hood** *n*

wid•ow•er *n* : man who has lost his wife by death and has not married again

width *n* **1** : distance from side to side **2** : largeness of extent **3** : measured and cut piece of material

wield *vb* **1** : use or handle esp. effectively **2** : exert — **wield•er** *n*

wife *n* (**wives**) : married woman — **wife•hood** *n* — **wife•less** *adj* — **wife•ly** *adj*

wig *n* **:** manufactured covering of hair for the head
wig•gle *vb* **1 :** move with quick jerky or shaking movements **2 :** wriggle — **wig•gle** *n* — **wig•gler** *n*
wild *adj* **1 :** living or being in a state of nature and not domesticated or cultivated **2 :** showing lack of restraint **3 :** turbulent **4 :** crazy **5 :** not civilized **6 :** erratic ~ *n* **1 :** wilderness **2 :** undomesticated state ~ *adv* **:** without control — **wild•ly** *adv* — **wild•ness** *n*
wil•der•ness *n* **:** uncultivated and uninhabited region
wild•fire *n* **:** sweeping and destructive fire
wild•life *n* **:** undomesticated animals
will *vb past* **would 1 :** wish to **2** — used as an auxiliary verb to express (1) desire or willingness, (2) customary action, (3) simple future time, (4) capability, (5) determination, (6) probability, (7) inevitability, or (8) a command **3 :** dispose of by a will ~ *n* **1 :** often determined wish **2 :** act, process, or experience of willing **3 :** power of controlling one's actions or emotions **4 :** legal document disposing of property after death
will•ful, wil•ful *adj* **1 :** governed by will without regard to reason **2 :** intentional — **will•ful•ly** *adv*
will•ing *adj* **1 :** inclined or favorably disposed in mind **2 :** prompt to act **3 :** done, borne, or accepted voluntarily or without reluctance — **will•ing•ly** *adv* — **will•ing•ness** *n*
will•pow•er *n* **:** energetic determination
wilt *vb* **1 :** lose or cause to lose freshness and become limp esp. from lack of water **2 :** grow weak
win *vb* (**won; won**) **1 :** get possession of esp. by effort **2 :** gain victory in battle or a contest **3 :** make friendly or favorable ~ *n* **:** victory
[1]**wind** *n* **1 :** movement of the air **2 :** breath **3 :** gas in the stomach or intestines **4 :** air carrying a scent **5 :** intimation ~ *vb* **1 :** get a scent of **2 :** cause to be out of breath
[2]**wind** *vb* **1 :** have or follow a curving course **2 :** move or lie to encircle **3 :** encircle or cover with something pliable **4 :** tighten the spring of ~ *n* **wound; wound :** turn or coil — **wind•er** *n*
wind•fall *n* **1 :** thing blown down by wind **2 :** unexpected benefit
wind•mill *n* **:** machine worked by the wind turning vanes
win•dow *n* **1 :** opening in the wall of a building to let in light and air **2 :** pane in a window **3 :** span of time for something **4 :** area of a computer display — **win•dow•less** *adj*
wind•shield *n* **:** transparent screen in front of the occupants of a vehicle
wind•up *n* **:** end — **wind up** *vb*
wind•ward *adj* **:** being in or facing the direction from which the wind is blowing ~ *n* **:** direction from which the wind is blowing
windy *adj* **1 :** having wind **2 :** indulging in useless talk
wing *n* **1 :** movable paired appendage for flying **2 :** winglike thing **3** *pl* **:** area at the side of the stage out of sight **4 :** faction ~ *vb* **1 :** fly **2 :** propel through the air — **winged** *adj* — **wing•less** *adj* — **on the wing :** in flight — **under one's wing :** in one's charge or care
wink *vb* **1 :** close and open the eyes quickly **2 :** avoid seeing or noticing something **3 :** twinkle **4 :** close and open one eye quickly as a signal or hint ~ *n* **1 :** brief sleep **2 :** act of winking **3 :** instant — **wink•er** *n*
win•ner *n* **:** one that wins
win•ning *n* **1 :** victory **2 :** money won at gambling ~ *adj* **1 :** victorious **2 :** charming
win•ter *n* **:** season between autumn and spring ~ *adj* **:** sown in autumn for harvest the next spring or summer — **win•ter•time** *n*
wipe *vb* **1 :** clean or dry by rubbing **2 :** remove by rubbing **3 :** erase completely **4 :** destroy **5 :** pass over a surface ~ *n* **:** act or instance of wiping — **wip•er** *n*
wire *n* **1 :** thread of metal **2 :** work made of wire **3 :** telegram or one sent through a cable under the sea ~ *vb* **1 :** provide with wire **2 :** bind or mount with wire — **wire•less** *adj*
wiry *adj* **1 :** resembling wire **2 :** slender yet strong and sinewy — **wir•i•ness** *n*
wis•dom *n* **1 :** accumulated learning **2 :** good sense
wise *adj* **1 :** having or showing wisdom, good sense, or good judgment **2 :** aware of what is going on — **wise•ly** *adv*
wise•crack *n* **:** clever, smart, or flippant remark ~ *vb* **:** make a wisecrack
wish *vb* **1 :** have a desire **2 :** express a wish concerning **3 :** request ~ *n* **1 :** a wishing or desire **2 :** expressed will or desire
wish•ful *adj* **1 :** expressive of a wish **2 :** according with wishes rather than fact
wit *n* **1 :** reasoning power **2 :** mental soundness — *usu. pl.* **3 :** quickness and cleverness in handling words and ideas **4 :** talent for

clever remarks or one noted for witty remarks — **wit·less** *adj* — **wit·less·ly** *adv* — **wit·less·ness** *n* — **wit·ted** *adj*

witch *n* **1 :** person believed to have magic power **2 :** ugly old woman ~ *vb* **:** bewitch

witch·craft *n* **:** power or practices of a witch

with *prep* **1 :** against, to, or toward **2 :** in support of **3 :** because of **4 :** in the company of **5 :** having **6 :** despite **7 :** containing **8 :** by means of

with·draw *vb* **1 :** take back or away **2 :** call back or retract **3 :** go away **4 :** terminate one's participation in or use of — **with·draw·al** *n*

with·er *vb* **1 :** shrivel **2 :** lose or cause to lose energy, force, or freshness

with·hold *vb* **1 :** hold back **2 :** refrain from giving

with·in *adv* **1 :** in or into the interior **2 :** inside oneself ~ *prep* **1 :** in or to the inner part of **2 :** in the limits or compass of

with·out *prep* **1 :** outside **2 :** lacking **3 :** unaccompanied or unmarked by — **with·out** *adv*

wit·ness *n* **1 :** testimony **2 :** one who testifies **3 :** one present at a transaction to testify that it has taken place **4 :** one who has personal knowledge or experience **5 :** something serving as proof ~ *vb* **1 :** bear witness **2 :** act as legal witness of **3 :** furnish proof of **4 :** be a witness of **5 :** be the scene of

wit·ty *adj* **:** marked by or full of wit — **wit·ti·ly** *adv* — **wit·ti·ness** *n*

wives *pl of* WIFE

wiz·ard *n* **1 :** magician **2 :** very clever person — **wiz·ard·ry** *n*

wob·ble *vb* **1 :** move or cause to move with an irregular rocking motion **2 :** tremble **3 :** waver — **wob·ble** *n* — **wob·bly** *adj*

woe *n* **1 :** deep suffering **2 :** misfortune

woke *past of* WAKE

woken *past part of* WAKE

wolf *n* (**wolves**) **:** large doglike predatory mammal ~ *vb* **:** eat greedily — **wolf·ish** *adj*

wom·an *n* (**wom·en**) **1 :** adult female person **2 :** women in general **3 :** feminine nature — **wom·an·hood** *n* — **wom·an·ish** *adj* — **wom·an·li·ness** *n* — **wom·an·ly** *adv*

won *past of* WIN

won·der *n* **1 :** cause of astonishment or surprise **2 :** feeling (as of astonishment) aroused by something extraordinary ~ *vb* **1 :** feel surprise **2 :** feel curiosity or doubt

won·der·ful *adj* **1 :** exciting wonder **2 :** unusually good — **won·der·ful·ly** *adv* — **won·der·ful·ness** *n*

won·drous *adj* **:** wonderful — **won·drous·ly** *adv* — **won·drous·ness** *n*

wood *n* **1 :** dense growth of trees usu. smaller than a forest — often pl. **2 :** hard fibrous substance of trees and shrubs beneath the bark **3 :** wood prepared for some use (as burning) ~ *adj* **1 :** wooden **2 :** suitable for working with wood **3 :** living or growing in woods — **wood·chop·per** *n* — **wood·pile** *n* — **wood·shed** *n*

wood·en *adj* **1 :** made of wood **2 :** lacking resilience **3 :** lacking ease, liveliness or interest — **wood·en·ly** *adv* — **wood·en·ness** *n*

wood·work *n* **:** work (as interior house fittings) made of wood

woody *adj* **1 :** abounding with woods **2 :** of, containing, or like wood fibers — **wood·i·ness** *n*

wool *n* **1 :** soft hair of some mammals and esp. the sheep **2 :** something (as a textile) made of wool — **wooled** *adj*

wool·en, wool·len *adj* **1 :** made of wool **2 :** relating to the manufacture of woolen products ~ *n* **1 :** woolen fabric **2 :** woolen garments — *usu. pl.*

wool·ly *adj* **1 :** of, relating to, or bearing wool **2 :** consisting of or resembling wool **3 :** confused or turbulent

woo·zy *adj* **1 :** confused **2 :** somewhat dizzy, nauseated, or weak — **woo·zi·ness** *n*

word *n* **1 :** brief remark **2 :** speech sound or series of speech sounds that communicates a meaning **3 :** written representation of a word **4 :** order **5 :** news **6 :** promise **7** *pl* **:** dispute ~ *vb* **:** express in words — **word·less** *adj*

word processing *n* **:** production of structured and printed documents through a computer program (**word processor**) — **word process** *vb*

wordy *adj* **:** using many words — **word·i·ness** *n*

wore *past of* WEAR

work *n* **1 :** labor **2 :** employment **3 :** task **4 :** something (as an artistic production) produced by mental effort or physical labor **5** *pl* **:** place where industrial labor is done **6** *pl* **:** moving parts of a mechanism **7 :** workmanship ~ *adj* **1 :** suitable for wear while working **2 :** used for work ~ *vb* **1 :** bring to pass **2 :** create by expending labor upon **3 :** bring or get into a form or condition **4 :** set or keep in operation **5 :** solve **6 :** cause to labor **7 :** arrange **8 :** excite **9 :** labor **10 :** perform work regularly for wages **11 :** function according to plan or design **12 :** produce a desired effect — **work·able** *adj* — **work·bench** *n* — **work·er** *n* — **work·man** *n* — **work·room** *n* — **in the works :** in preparation

work·day *n* **1 :** day on which work is done **2 :** period of time during which one is working

work·ing *adj* **1 :** adequate to allow work to be done **2 :** adopted or assumed to help further work or activity ~ *n* **:** operation — usu. used in pl.

work·man·ship *n* **1 :** art or skill of a workman **2 :** quality of a piece of work

work·out *n* **:** exercise to improve one's fitness

work out *vb* **1 :** bring about by effort **2 :** solve **3 :** develop **4 :** to be successful **5 :** perform exercises

work·shop *n* **1 :** small establishment for manufacturing or handicrafts **2 :** seminar emphasizing exchange of ideas and practical methods

world *n* **1 :** universe **2 :** earth with its inhabitants and all things upon it **3 :** people in general **4 :** great number or quantity **5 :** class of persons or their sphere of interest

world·ly *adj* **1 :** devoted to this world and its pursuits rather than to religion **2 :** sophisticated — **world·li·ness** *n*

world·wide *adj* **:** extended throughout the entire world — **worldwide** *adv*

World Wide Web *n* **:** part of the Internet accessible through a browser

worm *n* **1 :** earthworm or a similar animal **2** *pl* **:** disorder caused by parasitic worms ~ *vb* **1 :** move or cause to move in a slow and indirect way **2 :** to free from worms — **wormy** *adj*

worn *past part of* WEAR

worn–out *adj* **:** exhausted or used up by or as if by wear

wor·ry *vb* **1 :** shake and mangle with the teeth **2 :** disturb **3 :** feel or express anxiety ~ *n* **1 :** anxiety **2 :** cause of anxiety — **wor·ri·er** *n* — **wor·ri·some** *adj*

worse *adj, comparative of* BAD *or of* ILL **1 :** bad or evil in a greater degree **2 :** more unwell ~ *n* **1 :** one that is worse **2 :** greater degree of badness ~ *adv comparative of* BAD *or of* ILL **:** in a worse manner

wors·en *vb* **:** make or become worse

wor·ship *n* **1 :** reverence toward a divine being or supernatural power **2 :** expression of reverence **3 :** extravagant respect or devotion ~ *vb* **1 :** honor or reverence **2 :** perform or take part in worship — **wor·ship·er, wor·ship·per** *n*

worst *adj, superlative of* BAD *or of* ILL **1 :** most bad, evil, ill, or corrupt **2 :** most unfavorable, unpleasant, or painful ~ *n* **:** one that is worst ~ *adv superlative of* ILL *or* BAD *or* BADLY **:** to the extreme degree of badness ~ *vb* **:** defeat

worth *prep* **1 :** equal in value to **2 :** deserving of ~ *n* **1 :** monetary value **2 :** value of something measured by its qualities **3 :** moral or personal merit — **worth·less** *adj*

worth·while *adj* **:** being worth the time or effort spent

wor·thy *adj* **1 :** having worth or value **2 :** having sufficient worth ~ *n* **:** worthy person — **wor·thi·ly** *adv* — **wor·thi·ness** *n*

would *past of* WILL — used to express (1) preference, (2) intent, (3) habitual action, (4) contingency, (5) probability, or (6) a request

[1]**wound** *n* **1 :** injury in which the skin is broken **2 :** mental hurt ~ *vb* **:** inflict a wound to or in

[2]**wound** *past of* WIND

wove *past of* WEAVE

woven *past part of* WEAVE

wrap *vb* **1 :** cover esp. by winding or folding **2 :** envelop and secure for transportation or storage **3 :** enclose, surround, or conceal wholly **4 :** coil, fold, draw, or twine about something ~ *n* **1 :** wrapper or wrapping **2 :** outer garment (as a shawl)

wrap·per *n* **1 :** that in which something is wrapped **2 :** one that wraps

wreath *n* **:** something (as boughs) intertwined into a circular shape

wreathe *vb* **1 :** shape into or take on the shape of a wreath **2 :** decorate or cover with a wreath

wreck *n* **1 :** broken remains (as of a ship or vehicle) after heavy damage **2 :** something disabled or in a state of ruin **3 :** an individual who has become weak or infirm **4 :** action of breaking up or destroying something ~ *vb* **:** ruin or damage by breaking up

wreck·age *n* **1 :** act of wrecking **2 :** remains of a wreck

wreck·er *n* **1 :** automotive vehicle for removing disabled cars **2 :** one that wrecks or tears down and removes buildings

wrench *vb* **1 :** pull with violent twisting or force **2 :** injure or disable by a violent twisting or straining ~ *n* **1 :** forcible twisting **2 :** tool for exerting a twisting force

wres·tle *vb* **1 :** scuffle with and attempt to

throw and pin an opponent **2 :** compete against in wrestling **3 :** struggle (as with a problem) ~ *n* **:** action or an instance of wrestling — **wres·tler** *n*

wres·tling *n* **:** sport in which 2 opponents try to throw and pin each other

wretch·ed *adj* **1 :** deeply afflicted, dejected, or distressed **2 :** grievous **3 :** inferior — **wretch·ed·ly** *adv* — **wretch·ed·ness** *n*

wrig·gle *vb* **1 :** twist and turn restlessly **2 :** move along by twisting and turning — **wrig·gle** *n* — **wrig·gler** *n*

wring *vb* **wrung; wrung 1 :** squeeze or twist out moisture **2 :** get by or as if by twisting or pressing **3 :** twist together in anguish **4 :** pain — **wring·er** *n*

wrin·kle *n* **:** crease or small fold on a surface (as in the skin or in cloth) ~ *vb* **:** develop or cause to develop wrinkles — **wrin·kly** *adj*

wrist *n* **:** joint or region between the hand and the arm

writ *n* **1 :** something written **2 :** legal order in writing

write *vb* (**wrote; writ·ten**) **1 :** form letters or words on a surface **2 :** form the letters or the words of (as on paper) **3 :** make up and set down for others to read **4 :** write a letter to — **write off** *vb* **:** cancel

writ·er *n* **:** one that writes esp. as a business or occupation

writ·ing *n* **1 :** act of one that writes **2 :** handwriting **3 :** something written or printed

wrong *n* **1 :** unfair or unjust act **2 :** something that is contrary to justice **3 :** state of being or doing wrong ~ *adj* **1 :** sinful **2 :** not right according to a standard **3 :** not suitable **4 :** incorrect ~ *adv* **1 :** in a wrong direction or manner **2 :** incorrectly ~ *vb* **1 :** do wrong to **2 :** treat unjustly — **wrong·do·er** *n* — **wrong·do·ing** *n* — **wrong·ful** *adj* — **wrong·ful·ly** *adv* — **wrong·ful·ness** *n* — **wrong·ly** *adv*

wrote *past of* WRITE

wrung *past of* WRING

x *n* **1 :** 24th letter of the alphabet **2 :** unknown quantity ~ *vb* **:** cancel with a series of *x*'s — usu. with *out*

Xmas *n* **:** Christmas

x–ray *vb* **:** examine, treat, or photograph with X rays

X ray *n* **1 :** radiation of short wavelength that is able to penetrate solids **2 :** photograph taken with X rays — **X–ray** *adj*

xy·lo·phone *n* **:** musical instrument with wooden bars that are struck — **xy·lo·phon·ist** *n*

y *n* **:** 25th letter of the alphabet

yacht *n* **:** luxurious pleasure boat ~ *vb* **:** race or cruise in a yacht

yam *n* **1 :** edible root of a tropical vine **2 :** deep orange sweet potato

yank *n* **:** strong sudden pull — **yank** *vb*

Yan·kee *n* **:** native or inhabitant of New England, the northern U.S., or the U.S.

[1]**yard** *n* **1 :** 3 feet **2 :** long spar for supporting and spreading a sail — **yard·age** *n* — **yard·stick** *n*

[2]**yard** *n* **1 :** enclosed roofless area **2 :** grounds of a building **3 :** work area

yar·mul·ke *n* **:** a small brimless cap worn by Jewish males in a synagogue

yarn *n* **1 :** spun fiber for weaving or knitting **2 :** tale

yawn *vb* **:** open the mouth wide ~ *n* **:** deep breath through a wide-open mouth — **yawn·er** *n*

year *n* **1 :** period of about 365 days **2** *pl* **:** age

year·book *n* **:** annual report of the year's events

year·ly *adj* **:** annual — **year·ly** *adv*

yearn *vb* **1 :** feel desire esp. for what one cannot have **2 :** feel tenderness or compassion

yearn·ing *n* **:** tender or urgent desire

yeast *n* **:** froth or sediment in sugary liquids containing a tiny fungus and used in making alcoholic liquors and as a leaven in baking — **yeasty** *adj*

yell *vb* **:** utter a loud cry — **yell** *n*
yel·low *adj* **1 :** of the color yellow **2 :** sensational **3 :** cowardly ~ *vb* **:** make or turn yellow ~ *n* **1 :** color of lemons **2 :** yolk of an egg — **yel·low·ish** *adj*
yen *n* **:** strong desire
yes *adv* — used to express consent or agreement ~ *n* **:** affirmative answer
ye·shi·va, ye·shi·vah *n* **:** Jewish school
yes·ter·day *adv* **1 :** on the day preceding today **2 :** only a short time ago ~ *n* **1 :** day last past **2 :** time not long past
yet *adv* **1 :** in addition **2 :** up to now **3 :** so soon as now **4 :** nevertheless ~ *conj* **:** but
yield *vb* **1 :** surrender **2 :** grant **3 :** bear as a crop **4 :** produce **5 :** cease opposition or resistance ~ *n* **:** quantity produced or returned
yo·ga *n* **:** system of exercises for attaining bodily or mental control and well-being
yo·gurt *n* **:** fermented slightly acid soft food made from milk
yoke *n* **1 :** neck frame for coupling draft animals or for carrying loads **2 :** clamp **3 :** slavery **4 :** tie or link **5 :** piece of a garment esp. at the shoulder ~ *vb* **1 :** couple with a yoke **2 :** join
yolk *n* **:** yellow part of an egg — **yolked** *adj*
Yom Kip·pur *n* **:** Jewish holiday observed in September or October with fasting and prayer as a day of atonement
you *pron* **1 :** person or persons addressed **2 :** person in general
young *adj* **1 :** being in the first or an early stage of life, growth, or development **2 :** recently come into being **3 :** youthful ~ *n* **young :** persons or animals that are young — **young·ish** *adj*
young·ster *n* **1 :** young person **2 :** child
your *adj* **:** relating to you or yourself
yours *pron* **:** the ones belonging to you
your·self *pron* (**your·selves**) **:** you — used reflexively or for emphasis
youth *n* **1 :** period between childhood and maturity **2 :** young man **3 :** young persons **4 :** state or quality of being young, fresh, or vigorous
youth·ful *adj* **1 :** relating to or appropriate to youth **2 :** young **3 :** vigorous and fresh — **youth·ful·ly** *adv* — **youth·ful·ness** *n*
yo–yo *n* **:** toy that falls from or rises to the hand as it unwinds and rewinds on a string
yule *n* **:** Christmas — **yule·tide** *n*
yum·my *adj* **:** highly attractive or pleasing

Z

z *n* **:** 26th letter of the alphabet
za·ny *n* **1 :** clown **2 :** silly person ~ *adj* **:** crazy or foolish — **za·ni·ly** *adv* — **za·ni·ness** *n*
zeal *n* **:** enthusiasm
ze·bra *n* **:** horselike African mammal marked with light and dark stripes
ze·nith *n* **:** highest point
ze·ro *n* **1 :** number represented by the symbol 0 or the symbol itself **2 :** starting point **3 :** lowest point ~ *adj* **:** having no size or quantity
zest *n* **1 :** quality of enhancing enjoyment **2 :** keen enjoyment — **zest·ful** *adj* — **zest·ful·ly** *adv* — **zest·ful·ness** *n*
zig·zag *n* **:** one of a series of short sharp turns or angles ~ *adj* **:** having zigzags ~ *adv* **:** in or by a zigzag path ~ *vb* **:** proceed along a zigzag path
zil·lion *n* **:** large indeterminate number
[1]**zip** *vb* **:** move or act with speed ~ *n* **:** energy
[2]**zip** *vb* **:** close or open with a zipper
zip code *n* **:** number that identifies a U.S. postal delivery area
zip·per *n* **:** fastener consisting of 2 rows of interlocking teeth
zip·py *adj* **:** brisk
zo·di·ac *n* **:** imaginary belt in the heavens encompassing the paths of the planets and divided into 12 signs used in astrology — **zo·di·a·cal** *adj*
zone *n* **1 :** division of the earth's surface based on latitude and climate **2 :** distinctive area ~ *vb* **1 :** mark off into zones **2 :** reserve for special purposes — **zon·al** *adj* — **zon·al·ly** *adv* — **zo·na·tion** *n*
zoo *n* **:** collection of living animals usu. for public display — **zoo·keep·er** *n*
zo·ol·o·gy *n* **:** science of animals — **zo·o·log·i·cal** *adj* — **zo·ol·o·gist** *n*
zoom *vb* **1 :** move with a loud hum or buzz **2 :** move or increase with great speed — **zoom** *n*

THE DECEPTION IN A KISS

Noel moved closer, probing her eyes with his own, trying to divine her secrets—for secrets he was certain she had. At the same time, he felt another, stronger compulsion to tell her everything.

"Miss Riverstone . . . Rowena," he murmured.

She swayed toward him, almost imperceptibly, clearly eager to hear whatever he might say. Trapped between warring temptations, he gave in to the less dangerous of the two.

Noel thought to just brush her lips—a quick kiss to confuse her senses and keep her off balance, the better to question her later. Instead, her sweet softness captivated him.

With a tiny sigh, she lifted her arms to his shoulders, clinging to him as though for support. Her answering kiss was innocent, inexperienced, but that made it all the sweeter.

He found himself exulting that he was the first man to awaken this side of the serious Miss Riverstone . . .

Other AVON ROMANCES

HER SCANDALOUS INTENTIONS *by Sari Robins*
HIGHLAND ROGUES: THE WARRIOR BRIDE
by Lois Greiman
HIS BRIDE *by Gayle Callen*
INTO TEMPTATION *by Kathryn Smith*
THE MACKENZIES: COLE *by Ana Leigh*
ONCE A DREAMER *by Candice Hern*
THE WARRIOR'S GAME *by Denise Hampton*

Coming Soon

A NECESSARY BRIDE *by Debra Mullins*
TO WED A STRANGER *by Edith Layton*

And Don't Miss These
ROMANTIC TREASURES
from Avon Books

BORN IN SIN *by Kinley MacGregor*
CAPTURED INNOCENCE *by Susan Sizemore*
THE IRRESISTIBLE MACRAE: BOOK THREE OF
THE HIGHLAND LORDS *by Karen Ranney*

BRENDA HIATT

Innocent Passions

AVON BOOKS
An Imprint of HarperCollins*Publishers*

This is a work of fiction. Names, characters, places, and incidents are products of the author's imagination or are used fictitiously and are not to be construed as real. Any resemblance to actual events, locales, organizations, or persons, living or dead, is entirely coincidental.

AVON BOOKS
An Imprint of HarperCollins*Publishers*
10 East 53rd Street
New York, New York 10022-5299

ISBN: 0-06-050758-6
www.avonromance.com

First Avon Books paperback printing: February 2003

Printed in the U.S.A.

10 9 8 7 6 5 4 3 2 1

For INDYWITTS,
my wonderful critique group.
Thank you for all of your help!

Chapter 1

August 1816

"We'll be murdered in our beds, miss, just see if we won't."

Rowena Riverstone smiled indulgently at her maid, though in truth she was rather overwhelmed herself by the teeming streets of London on this, her first visit to the metropolis.

"Nonsense, Matthilda. My brother's house is in the nicer part of Town and quite secure. As long as we refrain from wandering the streets alone and at night, we should be perfectly safe."

But Matthilda shook her head and continued to mutter dire predictions for their visit. "The sooner we can return to River Chase, the happier I'll be."

"Especially since that will mean returning to your Jeb," Rowena said, chuckling at the maid's blush. "Very well, I won't tease any more."

In fact it was partly for the sake of Jeb's future that

Rowena had felt it necessary to come to Town, his future and that of other tenants like him. As for her own future . . .

Rowena stifled a sigh. After twenty-one years immured in the country, her future was all too easy to predict: year after year of spinsterhood, perhaps to be enlivened one day by the role of maiden aunt, should her brother Nelson ever marry and have children.

She refused to give in to regrets, however. She led a full life, what with her studies, the management of Nelson's country household and the writing of her political essays—essays that would become more timely once she was established in London.

She smiled a secret smile, for not even Matthilda had any clue that Rowena was the mysterious MRR, regular—and controversial—contributor to William Cobbett's *Political Register.* If she stayed in London long enough, she might meet Mr. Cobbett himself, as well as some of the other men whose views she admired, such as essayist Leigh Hunt and her idol, the fiery Spencean reformer Lester Richards.

She had actually corresponded with the latter early in the year—not that he was likely to remember, of course. Still, she cherished his two letters, and had all but committed them to memory. To meet him face to face would be—

"This be Hay Street, miss," the coachman called down to them. "What number did you say?"

"Number twelve," Rowena replied, adjusting her spectacles and leaning forward to peer out of the window.

Her father had maintained this Town residence for fifteen years and her brother for two, but this would be her first glimpse of it, as neither of them had ever allowed her to visit London. Now that she was mistress of her own funds, however, her brother could no longer prevent her doing as she wished.

"I hope Nelson is in," she remarked to Matthilda. "And that he has room for us."

The maid stared at her in horror. "Is he not expecting you, miss? But you said—"

"I said I was needed in London—but not by my brother."

Matthilda sputtered her dismay as the coach pulled to a halt, but Rowena ignored her to stare with interest at the tall, narrow house, virtually identical to all of the other tall, narrow houses on Hay Street.

"I can't say it looks like much," she commented as the coachman lowered the steps and assisted her from the coach.

"Shall I knock, miss?" he asked.

"Please." Head high, trailed by her maid, Rowena mounted the steps to the door, trying to look as though she'd done so every day of her life.

A portly butler answered the knock. Regarding the young lady on the doorstep without recognition, he raised a supercilious eyebrow but Rowena refused to be cowed by a mere retainer when she had fiercer dragons to face.

"Pray inform Sir Nelson that his sister, Miss Riverstone, has come to visit." She rather enjoyed the blank astonishment that replaced the butler's original haughtiness.

"Of . . . of course, miss." He stood aside so that she and her maid could enter. "If you'll wait in the parlor while I inform Sir Nelson, I can have tea brought."

"That would be lovely," Rowena said graciously. She directed the coachman to have her trunk brought in, sent Matthilda off to the servants' hall, then followed the butler across the wooden parquet floor of the front hall to the indicated room.

The small, pleasant parlor was furnished in ruby and cream—favorite colors, she recalled, of her mother, who had died seven years earlier. No doubt she'd had a hand in decorating the house when her father had first taken it for his extended stays in London, where he had held a position of some importance in the Home Office.

"Rubbish!" came a familiar voice from the hall. "My sister never comes to Town. It must be some supplicant pretending—" Entering the parlor, he broke off, sandy eyebrows ascending into carefully disordered sandy hair as he spotted her. "Ro? What the devil are you doing here?"

"Good afternoon, Nelson," she responded calmly to the stocky young man some three years her senior. "I am delighted to see you, too."

His brows now drew down to a frown. "You didn't answer my question. Nor did you send word you were coming."

"If I had, you would have forbidden it." She glanced at the listening butler, who, catching her eye, suddenly seemed to realize he was needed elsewhere and hurried off.

"With good reason." Sir Nelson's frown deepened to a scowl. "You and your radical ideas." Belatedly, he glanced behind him.

Seeing no listening servants, he closed the parlor door. "I won't have you spouting your seditious theories here in London, Ro. It could do irreparable damage to my position. The politics at Whitehall are dicey right now. Besides—"

"You've been saying that for two years, and Father for years before that," she reminded him. "And my theories are *not* seditious. They are mere common sense, if you'd only—"

He held up a hand. "Not another word. If you can't promise to hold your Whiggish tongue on such matters, I'll pack you straight back to River Chase in the morning."

That had always been the sticking point. Their father had demanded just such a promise as a condition of Rowena visiting London and she had never been willing to give it. After all, what would have been the point in coming to the seat of England's power if she had to compromise her principles to get there?

Now, however, she smiled. "Perhaps you have forgotten that I celebrated a birthday five days since. If you are unwilling to house me, I am quite capable of setting up an establishment of my own—nor can you prevent me doing so."

Nelson stared. "Devil take it, I *had* forgotten." He ran a hand through his hair in agitation.

"Don't worry, Nelson. I haven't come here with the express purpose of embarrassing you. I simply wish to see London."

Her brother frowned again, clearly disbelieving. "I know you better than that, Ro. That time Lord Sidmouth came to the Chase to see Father while he was ill—you hadn't been in the room with him ten minutes before you started talking about the plight of the soldiers released from service after the Treaty of Paris."

"I remember. But it was important that—" At her brother's alarmed expression, she stopped. "I'm older and wiser now, Nelson, and I can't stay buried in the country forever."

Though he still looked skeptical, her brother shrugged. "I suppose it's only fair you should have your chance before you're permanently on the shelf," he said grudgingly.

Rowena ignored the hurt and resentment his words produced, focusing instead on her real goal. "I'm glad you understand." She was pleased with the evenness of her voice.

A tap on the door heralded the arrival of tea.

"If you're going to stay here, you'll need a companion," said Sir Nelson, his expression softening slightly. "I'll order a room made up while you have a bite to eat."

"Thank you," she said, "but I may not need it. I mean to send a note round to Lady Pearl directly, telling her I'm here. She has frequently invited me to stay with her—and I'm sure she can give me pointers on how to behave properly, as well."

Her brother brightened noticeably. "That would be capital!" Then he pulled out his pocket watch and consulted it. "I'm expected at Whitehall," he said. "You can tell me this evening what your plans are."

When he had gone, Rowena carried her cup and a plate of biscuits to the writing desk near the window and proceeded to write her note to Lady Pearl—now Lady Hardwyck—her best friend in the world.

She and Pearl had practically grown up together, as River Chase bordered the main estate of the imposing Duke of Oakshire, Pearl's father. She and Pearl had shared many interests as well as a strong bond of friendship, and the disparity in their social stations had never mattered to anyone except Pearl's stepmother.

Now, however, Rowena's pen hesitated. That was in the country. Here in London, where Pearl was not only daughter to a duke but also a countess, wife of one of the wealthiest men in England . . . Would it be terribly forward of her to write?

"Nonsense," she told herself sternly. "This is Pearl. Besides, when have you ever cared about other people's opinions?" She wrote quickly, then rang for a footman to deliver the note before she could reconsider.

Noel Paxton signed his report, set his pen down on the battered oak writing desk, and sighed. This had become the most frustrating investigation of his career, and not because he'd failed to apprehend the notorious Saint of Seven Dials. In fact, the legendary thief would be in prison now, had Noel chosen it, but that would have brought him no closer to his true goal—a goal his "superiors" at Bow Street knew nothing about.

"Will you be wanting anything else, sir?" Kemp, Noel's aide, manservant, and confidante, refilled the empty teacup on the corner of the desk.

"A clue, Kemp. A clue. I can't help feeling we're missing something obvious."

Abandoning his proper servant pose, the wiry young man leaned against the mantelpiece, balancing the chipped teapot between his hands, handle in one, spout in the other. "Can't see how, sir. You've picked up on things Runners, with years of experience, missed. Had the Saint in the palm of your hand."

Noel wished he could share his henchman's unswerving faith in his abilities. "At least I've verified that the Saint—Saints, I should say—and the Bishop are not the same man. Which means those anonymous essays are again my only lead."

It was damnably frustrating. He'd been so certain the author of those essays was the Saint, as well as the soulless Black Bishop, that vile traitor who had cost so many English lives during the recent war.

Who had killed at least two men Noel had called friend.

Posing as a British agent in France, the Black Bishop had in fact sold information to Napoleon. His treason had endangered more than one true agent, including Noel himself. Twice, fellow agents had come close to identifying the man and both of those agents had died violently before revealing what they'd learned.

Based on certain evidence found on the battlefield, the Foreign Office had believed the Bishop perished at Waterloo. Noel reluctantly retired to his Derbyshire estate, his services as Puss in Boots, the Foreign Office's top spy, no longer required. He had finally accepted that the Bishop was beyond justice—until portions of a certain essay in the *Political Register* had struck him as eerily familiar.

Noel told the Foreign Office of his suspicion that the Bishop was in fact alive and in England, only to learn that his superiors had already come to the same conclusion. Another agent, investigating the disappearance of certain documents from the Home Office pertaining to the Bishop, had recently died in an all-too-convenient accident. Noel was recalled to service to hunt down the traitor, a task he was more than willing to resume.

A visit to the offices of the *Political Register* revealed that the essay which had aroused Noel's suspicions had been posted from Oakshire—and that the handwriting of the original bore striking similarities to the Bishop's letters to the Foreign Office during the war.

"Mr. R," the anonymous essayist, was so passionate in his defense of the Saint of Seven Dials that Noel had postulated a link. With the approval of the Foreign Office, he offered his services to Bow Street to help apprehend the thief—an offer the magistrate eagerly accepted.

At first, it had appeared he was on the right track. Bow Street's primary suspect seemed to fit everything Noel knew of the Black Bishop. Going by the names of Luke St. Clair, Lucio di Santo, and now the Earl of Hardwyck, the man possessed a genius for disguise, a Continental background, and even an Oakshire connection, through his wife.

But further investigation revealed that Hardwyck had never been in France, had never left England, in fact. His supposed Continental ties were fictitious, invented to allow him to fit in at Oxford and, later, in Society, to further his larcenous ends. Nor had he written those essays.

Frustrated as he was, Noel couldn't find it in him to condemn Lord Hardwyck, nor his successor as Saint,

Lord Marcus Northrup. Both had given the lion's share of their booty to London's poor, and had stolen only from the most undeserving of the *ton*. No, he'd prefer not to be known as the man who brought Robin Hood to justice.

"I don't fancy myself a modern-day Sheriff of Nottingham, Kemp," he said aloud. "The Saint is free to continue his work—not that it sounds as though he plans to do so."

Lord Hardwyck had given up the role upon his marriage two months since, and it appeared that Lord Marcus, also recently wed, had now done the same. Which presented Noel with a definite problem.

"London won't be the same without the Saint of Seven Dials," said Kemp, echoing his thoughts. "Lots of folks count on him, from what I hear. And didn't the bloke gather evidence against real criminals, as well? Useful, that."

Noel nodded. "Useful indeed." Lord Marcus had given him enough evidence to break up a ring of crimps—men profiting from the kidnapping and selling of young boys into service aboard ships—and to put three of them in prison. A valuable resource gone, along with Noel's ostensible reason for nosing about London.

Without the cover of hunting down the Saint, how was he to track down the Black Bishop without giving himself away to his crafty nemesis? Discovery would likely mean the same fate as the last agent—not that fear of death would stop him. His pursuit of the Bishop had long passed from the patriotic to the personal.

"You're right, Kemp," he said slowly, thinking

hard. "London needs the Saint of Seven Dials—and so do I."

If Lord Marcus was unwilling to take up that mantle again, perhaps the answer was to do so himself. As the Saint, surely he could ferret out the real identity of the essayist Mr. R, now his only link to the Black Bishop. With the Saint still active, he could continue his public investigation, which would allow him to pursue his covert one as well.

His decision made, Noel stood. "I'll be back in a few hours," he told his manservant.

The next Saint of Seven Dials would need more information from his predecessors before he could step fully into their shoes.

Rowena finished her tea. No doubt Matthilda was getting something to eat in the kitchens, but perhaps she should—

No, this was London, where the division between mistress and servant would be more rigidly enforced. She must remember that, as well as countless other items of protocol, if she was to remain long enough to further her goals.

Should she have sent that note to Pearl? She recalled how grand her friend had looked at her wedding earlier that summer. They'd scarcely had a chance to do more than nod at each other amid the festivities at Oakshire. What if she had changed?

But even as she wondered whether it was too late to call the footman back, a knock came at the door and a moment later she heard Pearl's own voice in the hall, demanding to see her. Rowena sprang to her feet and hurried out to greet her friend.

"Rowena!" Pearl exclaimed before she could speak. "You've come at last. I must say it's about time. Oh, I've missed you so!"

Laughing with relief and delight, Rowena returned her embrace, then ushered her into the parlor and called for more tea. "Surely with a new husband you haven't had much time to miss old friends?" she asked with a grin.

Pearl blushed slightly. "Well, perhaps not . . ." Then she smiled again, and she was the same Pearl as always.

"But what has brought you to Town?" she asked. "Never tell me it's simply to sightsee, or even to make your come-out during the autumn Season, for I won't believe it. Knowing you, there must be some ulterior motive."

Rowena had to chuckle. Pearl knew her so well. "I thought it was time I saw something of the world beyond Oakshire," she explained. "You above all should understand that all of one's education can't come from books."

"Very true. And I *am* delighted you are here. You can't imagine how insipid the conversation of most Society ladies is. Clothes, gossip, which entertainments to attend—never a word on serious topics. And heaven forbid I should introduce them myself. I'm considered enough of an oddity already."

Rowena gazed at her friend's violet-blue eyes, golden ringlets and classically beautiful face, such a contrast to her own bespectacled gray eyes, straight, coppery tresses, and unremarkable features. Pearl, an oddity? "Then I fear I'll never manage to fit in at all."

"Fitting in is overrated," Pearl declared. "Why, if I

hadn't been willing to ignore Society's rules, I'd never have met Luke, or found out—But that's a story for another time. Please tell me you'll stay at Hardwyck Hall. Luke is so busy lately, it would be wonderful to have someone around I can talk to—really talk to."

Though she had hoped for the invitation, Rowena hesitated. Her own life seemed so far removed from Pearl's now. But at her friend's pleading look, she nodded. She had never been able to deny Pearl anything.

"I'd love to. Will tomorrow be all right?"

"Certainly—as early as you can come. Luke has meetings all day, I believe, and this will give me the perfect excuse to avoid taking tea at Lady Mountheath's."

"If you're sure . . ."

Pearl rose to embrace her. "I'm absolutely determined on it, and you know how stubborn I can be. I'm due for a fitting, so I must run, but we'll talk more tomorrow. And welcome to London, Rowena. Trust me, you're going to love it here."

A moment later Pearl was gone, and Rowena was left to consider the likelihood of that parting prediction. While Pearl had been a zealous reformer in her own right before her marriage, Rowena had been the one to bring issues to her attention. More than once, Pearl had talked her out of taking radical steps to further their aims—steps that Rowena had to admit could have landed them both in serious trouble.

What would Pearl say if she knew about Rowena's political essays and the comments they occasioned? she wondered with a smile. Though she'd told her brother she had changed, she knew she hadn't. It only seemed that way because she had lately diverted her reformist energies into her writings.

Again seating herself at the writing desk, she began to jot down the thoughts that had occurred to her during her journey, for inclusion in her next essay for the *Political Register.*

At the appointed time, Noel knocked at the imposing front door of Hardwyck Hall. While Lord Marcus had been relatively easy to talk to, Lord Hardwyck had proved more elusive—due, no doubt, to the constant demands on a man of his wealth and importance. Noel had had to arrange an appointment through Hardwyck's secretary for an interview.

If he ever took up the title of Earl Ellsdon, for which he was heir presumptive, he would not be so self-important, Noel promised himself.

The door was opened by Hardwyck's surprisingly young butler. "Ah, Mr. Paxton. His lordship awaits you in the library."

Just as in his previous two meetings with Lord Hardwyck, Noel felt slightly defensive—as though he had kept the man waiting, when in fact he was a minute or two early. No doubt just what Hardwyck intended.

The earl rose to greet him as he entered the large, well-stocked library. "Good afternoon, Mr. Paxton. I must say, I was surprised to hear you wished for yet another interview. At our last, you implied you had put the case of the Saint behind you."

Noel seated himself on an expensively upholstered chair as the butler retreated and closed the door behind him. "I've given up trying to put a stop to his activities, yes," he said carefully.

"As they appear to have stopped of their own accord, that would seem a reasonable course." As before, Lord Hardwyck admitted nothing, though Noel knew full well he had been the original Saint—and Hardwyck knew that he knew it.

"So, your interest now is purely academic?" Hardwyck prompted, when Noel remained silent, trying to diplomatically phrase his first question.

"Not purely, no. One might say that it's of a more—practical nature." When Lord Hardwyck did not respond, Noel went straight to the point. "I'm looking for the sort of information a man might need to carry on as Saint of Seven Dials."

His host's brows rose. "Indeed. You have a candidate for the post, then?"

Noel met Lord Hardwyck's gaze squarely. "I do. Myself."

"Why?"

Having already decided that only the truth would do, Noel recounted the details of his own career as a spy during the war—first unofficial, then, once he had proved himself, under the direction of the Foreign Office. His work had necessitated constant and numerous disguises, as well as a fair amount of breaking and entering, to obtain the information the Foreign Office required to counter Napoleon's plans.

"So you are the fabled Puss in Boots," said Lord Hardwyck wonderingly, shaking his head with a smile. "You are well qualified, then, but I still do not understand your motive for wishing to become the next Saint."

Grimly, Noel explained about the Black Bishop—how he had pursued the murderous traitor in France until it was believed he was dead, and that he had now resumed that pursuit on English soil. To underscore the importance of his quest, he told Lord Hardwyck about his cohorts who had met their deaths at the hands of the Bishop, including the latest, right here in London.

"So while I do intend to carry on the Saint's work of providing for the poor, I also mean to use that guise to gather the information I need to bring the Bishop to justice—much as Lord Marcus gathered the information on those crimps," he finally concluded. "Will you help me?"

There was a long, tense silence, during which the earl stared at Noel, dark eyes narrowed, as though he would bore a hole in his brain. Finally, he leaned back in his chair and smiled.

"Call me Luke," he said. "It appears we are destined to get to know each other quite well, so we may as well begin on a first-name basis."

Chapter 2

"Are you certain you won't let Francesca attempt something with your hair?" Pearl asked, as she and Rowena prepared to go downstairs for dinner. "And I know you've never cared two pins for fashion, but a new gown or two wouldn't hurt."

Rowena smiled, but shook her head at her friend. "Would that not be hypocritical of me, after all the lectures I've given you over the years about conforming yourself to the expectations of a patriarchal Society?"

"You make me seem so frivolous. But we'll see if you feel the same after a few days in Town."

Rowena smiled again, but doubted she would change her mind—or that it would make any difference if she did. She was no beauty, after all.

"Oh, I forgot to mention, Luke sent up word that we are to have another guest for dinner tonight," Pearl said as they approached the dining room. "Some official acquaintance or other, I believe."

The ladies entered the long, elegantly appointed

room, where Lord Hardwyck and another gentleman awaited them. Rowena gazed about in appreciation at the rich but tasteful decor. Though her own home was far more simply furnished, she had spent enough time at the duke's manor in Oakshire to become accustomed to—and to appreciate—such surroundings.

"My dear, you have heard me mention Mr. Paxton, I believe. Noel, this is my wife, Lady Hardwyck," said Lord Hardwyck, by way of introduction. "And Miss Riverstone, who is staying with my wife," he added, almost as an afterthought. Rowena suspected he had momentarily forgotten her name.

"Lady Hardwyck, Miss Riverstone," Mr. Paxton murmured. He barely glanced at Rowena, before turning his attention to his hostess—not that Rowena could blame him. Pearl looked particularly beautiful tonight in lilac satin, while she herself all but faded into the woodwork in her plain brown cambric.

"I hear you are quite the philanthropist, my lady," said Mr. Paxton as they took their seats. "I would love to hear about some of your projects."

Rowena's attention was caught, and though he continued to ignore her, she examined Mr. Paxton with interest. Physically, at least, he certainly merited a closer look. He was tall, broad-shouldered and most definitely handsome, with curling chestnut hair and classic features. But it was the intelligence in his hazel eyes that gave him a deeper appeal for her.

Suddenly embarrassed, she looked away before anyone realized she was staring at the man and tried to pick up the thread of conversation.

". . . conditions at Newgate and other prisons," Pearl was saying.

"There is considerable room for improvement," Mr. Paxton agreed. Rowena couldn't help noticing that his voice was deep, firm, and rather pleasant. "If you'd like, I can pass along your concerns to my superiors at Bow Street."

"Bow Street? You are a Runner then, Mr. Paxton?" Rowena asked, startled. He didn't seem to fit what she had read of that elite group of law enforcers.

But he shook his head. "Not a Runner, no. I'm acting in a semi-official capacity, at the behest of Sir Nathaniel Conant, chief magistrate at Bow Street."

"Yes," added Lord Hardwyck with a curious smile. "He's to catch the Saint of Seven Dials for them, as he has managed to elude the regular Runners thus far."

Rowena stared, dismayed. She had read enough about the Saint to have developed a great admiration for the anonymous thief, and had praised his work in more than one of her essays.

"That seems an unworthy goal, sir," she said, "given how few true champions the common people can claim in these difficult times."

Noel had already turned to his host again, but now he looked back across the table at Miss Riverstone, really seeing her for the first time. Drab, old-fashioned gown, brownish hair scraped into a tight bun, spectacles—she appeared to be acting in the capacity of companion to Lady Hardwyck, and he had therefore dismissed her. Unworthily, it appeared.

"Surely a true champion should not find it necessary to break the laws of the land?" he said, repeating what he'd told more than one lady who had tried to talk him out of his pursuit of the legendary thief. "I would prefer to rely on Parliament to give relief to the deserving poor rather than the whims of some mysterious house-breaker."

"Parliament!" Clearly, Miss Riverstone did not hold that august body in great esteem. "Why, even now they are discussing yet more oppressive corn laws. Unless wages are raised to compensate, we shall soon have even more starving and homeless people to consider."

"Therefore we should give free reign to a thief like the Saint of Seven Dials to alleviate their problems—no doubt while lining his own pockets in the process?" Noel had all he could do not to chuckle at her outraged expression.

"At least he is doing *something*," she responded, waving her fork for emphasis. "Legislation, even if introduced, moves so slowly that people will starve waiting for it. In fact—"

She broke off, setting down her fork and glancing guiltily at Lady Hardwyck, but Noel was intrigued. Miss Riverstone clearly stayed abreast of political issues and held strong opinions on them. This did not seem the proper forum to pursue them, however, as he did not wish to get her into trouble with her mistress.

"Doubtless such matters are under discussion by Parliament," he said mildly. Despite her spectacles, severe hairstyle, and the scatter of freckles across her nose, Miss Riverstone was not unattractive, he suddenly realized. "Lady Hardwyck, you were discussing your ideas for prison reform, I believe?"

With a glance at her companion which, to Noel's relief, held more amusement than condemnation, Lady Hardwyck turned back to him. "Yes. If the overcrowding could be alleviated, several other problems would be solved as well."

As she continued to expound on her ideas, Noel's attention strayed back to Miss Riverstone, who now ate in silence. Though she appeared subdued, he suspected this was not her normal aspect. Her gray eyes had sparkled with spirit and intelligence when she had spoken before. What might she look like when she smiled?

He realized he very much wished to find out.

Rowena's pride was still smarting when she and Pearl left the gentlemen to their brandy and retired to the parlor. "I can't say I care much for Mr. Paxton," she said as soon as they were out of earshot. "Self-righteous, legalistic, toadying—"

"What?" Pearl cut her off laughingly. "I found him none of those things, though I confess I rather expected to." She paused while a maid brought tea, watching Rowena's face closely.

"Oh, I see," Pearl continued as soon as they were alone again. "You're irked that he didn't wish to discuss corn laws and Parliamentary reform with you."

"No, it's just—" Rowena broke off with a sigh. "Oh, Nelson was right. I can't spend half an hour in Society without spouting off my political opinions. I'm sorry if I embarrassed you, Pearl."

But her friend only smiled. "I thought you knew me better than that. I'll allow it was a bit rude of Mr. Paxton to change the subject so abruptly, but perhaps he didn't feel he could hold his own in such a discussion. He's not a member of Parliament, after all, and may not follow such issues closely."

"Perhaps." But Rowena didn't believe it. He had quite pointedly turned the conversation back to Pearl, whose views on reform had seemed to hold his attention quite well. But why should that surprise—or bother—her? Men had always behaved thus.

"What say you to a game of chess to pass the time?" she asked, to distract herself.

Pearl grimaced. "You're sure to win as you always do, but very well. The practice will be good for me." She rang for the chess set, and by the time the gentlemen joined them, they were well into their second game.

Rowena barely glanced up when Lord Hardwyck and Mr. Paxton entered, her mind filled with strategy for several moves to come. She had beaten Pearl handily the first game, but the second was proving more of a challenge—perhaps because her thoughts persisted in wandering far from the chessmen before her.

"Shall I call for another board, or would cards suit you better?" Lord Hardwyck asked his guest after the two of them had watched the game in silence for some minutes.

"I was going to offer to play the winner," Mr. Paxton replied. "Unless you would care for cards yourself?"

"Not at all. I quite enjoy watching a good game of chess."

Rowena felt a distinct thrill of anticipation mingled with alarm, though she was careful to let neither show in her expression. She expected to beat Pearl in four more moves and it might be interesting to discover whether the handsome Mr. Paxton was a worthy opponent.

"Checkmate," she said a few minutes later.

Pearl shook her head and rose. "I never even saw that coming. You're every bit as good as I remember. Mr. Paxton, you wish to try your luck? I warn you, Rowena is quite adept."

Rowena dared a glance at the gentleman, to find him regarding her appraisingly. Their eyes met for a long moment and she felt a quiver in her midsection that was unlike anything she had experienced before.

"With two skilled opponents, there is no luck involved," he said, taking the chair Pearl had vacated.

Refusing to let him fluster her, Rowena began placing the pieces back into position for another game, glad of the excuse to break away from his oddly intent gaze. Was this part of his strategy? If so, it certainly wouldn't work on *her.*

"I was going to offer to play black," he continued, "but if you feel I need an advantage, I am willing to take it, after Lady Hardwyck's warning."

Rowena had unthinkingly set up the board as it had been before, as by tacit agreement she always gave Pearl the first move. Traditionally, of course, a lady played white against a gentleman.

"I have no idea whether you need an advantage or not, sir," she said stiffly, to hide her embarrassment. "We can reverse the board if you prefer."

In response, he moved a pawn forward two spaces. "At the risk of taking unfair advantage of a lady, I will leave it as it is."

She regarded him uncertainly. Was he . . . he couldn't be *flirting* with her? No, doubtless he was simply smoothing over an awkward moment—an awkwardness of her own making. She moved a pawn herself, then watched the board as he made his next move, trying to concentrate on the pieces rather than the long, strong fingers manipulating them.

An hour later, Rowena realized she was pitted against the best opponent she had ever faced. After watching for some time, Pearl and Lord Hardwyck had retired to conversation in another corner while Rowena and Mr. Paxton continued to focus on the game.

Few words had been exchanged between them thus far, but now he said, "I've only seen that defense deployed once before, in Austria. However did you learn of it, Miss Riverstone?"

Rowena shook free of her strategizing for a moment. "I, ah, I have read about many famous matches over the years. You have been to Austria then, Mr. Paxton?"

The game had distracted her for a time from his unsettling effect upon her, but the warm timbre of his voice, so deep, so masculine, caused a renewal of that delicious quiver in her midsection.

"Yes, briefly, a year and a half ago." He moved a knight, blocking the line between her bishop and his queen.

"Were you involved in the Congress of Vienna, then?" she asked with sudden interest. She had assumed his background was in local law enforcement.

"Not directly involved, no. I had a small role to play, winter before last." He smiled into her eyes, making her breath unaccountably quicken. "Your move, Miss Riverstone."

With a start, Rowena looked down to discover she

had lost the thread of the game. What had she planned to do after circumventing his knight? Frowning, she moved her bishop two squares, hoping the next two obvious moves would nudge her memory for the third.

"And what of you?" he asked then, surprising her by moving his knight again instead of the pawn she had expected. "Have you been in London long, or did you become so adept at chess elsewhere?"

Revising her strategy, she took the unmoved pawn with her remaining rook, flattered in spite of herself by his words. "I arrived but yesterday. This is the first time I've left Oakshire, actually."

"Oakshire?" He regarded her keenly. "Then you are a . . . relative of Lady Hardwyck's?"

She wondered what he'd almost said. "No, a neighbor. I live next to the main Oakshire estate. Pearl, er, Lady Hardwyck and I have known each other all our lives."

"Ah." His tone implied he had solved some mystery, but she couldn't imagine what it might be.

Before she could ask, he reached forward to take her rook with his knight. *Blast!* How had she missed that? She stared at the board, her strategy in shambles. He had left his queen open, however. Seeing little else to do, she took it.

"You sound as though my history explained something to you, sir. How so?" She was still scanning the board as she spoke, and saw too late the trap into which she had just fallen.

"I was wondering how such an intelligent and obviously well-educated woman came to be hired as

Lady Hardwyck's companion," he replied, moving his knight again. "Checkmate."

Rowena wasn't sure whether she was more stunned by his assumption that she was a servant, or by losing so abruptly and disastrously. She stared at the board, then at him, totally at a loss for words. His eyebrows rose questioningly.

"Congratulations," she said, belatedly gathering her wits.

"Another game?"

Shaken by her first loss in years—since old Mr. Winston, the vicar, had died, in fact—she shook her head. "I believe Lord Hardwyck expressed an interest in playing the winner."

She knew she should correct his misconception about her place in the Hardwyck household but couldn't think how, without being rude. *How dare you assume I'm merely Pearl's companion?* No. *Do you assume any plain woman must be a servant?* Still worse.

Seeing the game was at an end, Pearl and Lord Hardwyck came forward. "Never say you beat her, Mr. Paxton?" Pearl exclaimed. "You must tell me how you managed it, for I never have."

"I fear I distracted her with personal questions," Mr. Paxton confessed with a smile. "Unsporting of me, but I was growing desperate."

"Do not discredit yourself, sir," said Rowena, stung. "Nor need you patronize me. I am not so easily flustered, I assure you, and know when I have been fairly beaten."

Even as she spoke, however, she knew her words

were false. He *had* distracted her, not only with conversation but with his very presence. She would far rather proclaim him a superior player than admit to such weakness, however. Especially since it now seemed clear he was merely being kind to Pearl's poor "companion."

"As you wish, Miss Riverstone." The glint in his hazel eyes told her he understood all too well.

Hastily, she turned away. "I believe I will go up to bed, if you will all excuse me. I have not yet become accustomed to Town hours."

"Of course, dear," said Pearl. "I will see you upstairs and make certain you do not lack for anything. Gentlemen, if you will excuse us? I will return in a moment."

Lord Hardwyck and Mr. Paxton bid Rowena good night, then settled down to the chessboard as the ladies left the parlor.

"Poor Luke doesn't stand a chance," Pearl confided as they climbed the staircase. "I have beaten him the few times we have played. He didn't have many chances to—that is—" She broke off.

Rowena scarcely noticed, her mind still on the scene below. "Did you know that Mr. Paxton thinks I am your companion? Your *paid* companion?" She was still outraged.

"No, really? How absurd!" Pearl exclaimed with a laugh. "What did he say when you corrected him?"

"I, er, didn't," Rowena confessed. "I didn't wish to seem rude, you see—"

"So instead you accused him of patronizing you." Pearl still seemed amused. "Really, dear, his mistake was understandable, seeing how you are dressed. Perhaps now you'll be willing to take my advice and buy a few new gowns?"

For the first time, Rowena considered Pearl's question seriously. She had always maintained that men who focused on such externals—nearly all men, in her experience—were not worth regretting. Now, however, she realized that there might be a more important issue at stake.

Men, after all, were the shapers of England's laws, much as she might wish otherwise. To influence those laws, she would have to influence those men. Pearl, clearly, was able to do so more effectively than she herself, no doubt due partly to her appearance. Could she, just possibly, increase her own influence by taking a page from Pearl's book?

Rowena nodded. "Yes, I believe I will."

"Splendid! We'll go shopping tomorrow," Pearl promised as they reached the upper hallway.

For a moment Rowena allowed herself to imagine Mr. Paxton's expression should he see her again, dressed as Pearl was. In such a guise, would she be able to distract him into losing a game of chess? She almost grinned at the thought, but then the pleasant fantasy dissipated.

A new gown and hairstyle would never turn her into a beauty, and there were still her spectacles. All she could really hope to do was fit in, so that she could meet men of influence—and perhaps become a person of some small influence herself.

"I shall rely on your guidance to help me look my best," she told Pearl as they reached her room.

Her friend seemed so delighted at the prospect that

Rowena wasn't sure whether to be pleased or concerned—or even insulted. Pearl directed a maid to see to Rowena's comfort, then kissed her cheek. "Good night, dear. I *am* so glad you're here, and I'm quite looking forward to tomorrow."

"So am I," Rowena echoed, and realized to her surprise that it was true.

As Pearl had predicted, Noel was finding Luke a far less challenging opponent than Miss Riverstone. By the time Lady Hardwyck returned to the parlor, the outcome was assured. Five minutes later, Luke conceded the game.

"Perhaps you can tutor me in chess while I tutor you in larceny," Luke suggested without rancor as he stood.

Noel glanced at Lady Hardwyck in alarm, but she appeared merely surprised, not shocked. She regarded her husband with an upraised brow.

"You've told him, then?"

Luke shrugged. "He already knew. We were both merely pretending otherwise. Now that Marcus has retired, Noel is interested in taking over himself—for various reasons."

"And you've agreed to help him." The look she sent Noel was less than approving.

"Only with advice, my lady," he assured her. "Lord Hardwyck will be in no danger from the law."

She glanced at her husband, seeking reassurance, and apparently received it, for her expression softened to a smile. "As you *are* the law in this case, Mr. Paxton, I suppose you can be trusted to know."

"The irony has not escaped me," he said with an

answering smile. "I suppose, in conscience, I should turn the investigation over to someone else to avoid a conflict of interest, but as that investigation is my ostensible reason for being in Town, I'll simply have to work very hard at catching myself."

They all laughed, but then Noel became serious. "You said there are people I will need to meet, if I am to take up the Saint's mantle," he reminded Luke.

The earl nodded. "You've already met one of them—the young footman who refilled the glasses at dinner. He used to go by the name of Squint when he lived on the streets, though now we call him Steven."

"Then he was one of the youths who used to help the Saint?" During his investigation, Noel had been thwarted more than once by that loyal regiment of street urchins.

"It would be fairer to say that the Saint helped him," Lady Hardwyck said, putting a hand on her husband's shoulder. "Most of our servants have been rescued from the streets."

Noel nodded, beginning to understand. "So your goals never changed—merely your methods. I salute you, my lord, my lady. However, your former methods are what I need to master now."

"And for that you will need the trust of those you would help," Luke said. "Where are you staying?"

"I have lodgings on Long Acre, near Bow Street."

"Convenient placement—only two streets away from Seven Dials. But for the next few days, I'd like to invite you to stay here as my guest. It will . . . simplify things."

This caught Noel by surprise, though it made sense. Frequent visits here might be noticed, while an extended visit would require but one explanation. "What will we give out as the reason for my stay?" he asked, suspecting Lord Hardwyck had already concocted one.

"My wife and I have decided to have a house party before everyone returns to their country seats. Have we not, my love?"

Though it was clear that this was the first Lady Hardwyck had heard of such a scheme, her eyes lit at once. "Indeed we have. We may even induce some of those who have already left Town to return for a week or two. It will be just the thing for Rowena, now that I think on it."

Confused, Noel asked, "Miss Riverstone, you mean? Your companion?" He wondered how he would keep his secret from that very intelligent lady while under this roof.

To his surprise, Lady Hardwyck laughed. "She is my friend, Mr. Paxton, not my companion. Her brother keeps a house on Hay Street, but I induced her to stay with me so that we could spend more time together."

With a start, Noel realized that Miss Riverstone's brother must be Sir Nelson Riverstone, a senior clerk at the Home Office and son of the late Sir Nelson, who had been a powerful political figure before his death. No wonder she'd been upset when he had all but called her a servant to her face. He'd thought she was merely irritated at losing a hard-fought game of chess.

"Pray convey my apologies to Miss Riverstone," he said to Lady Hardwyck. "I fear I implied—"

"An understandable mistake. I've told her for years

she should pay more attention to her appearance. But I'll tell her."

"I presume you'll want to send for a few things?" Luke asked Noel then. "You may as well stay the night, so that we can get started first thing tomorrow. Once other guests arrive, we may find it more difficult to be private."

Noel blinked, pulling his thoughts away from the intriguing Miss Riverstone. "Yes, of course. I'll have Kemp, my manservant, bring what I'll need." He quickly scrawled a note and sent it with a footman—the one Luke had called Squint, in fact.

"Now then," said Luke once that was done. "How are you at picking locks?"

Even as Noel explained his experience in that area, acquired during his years spying on some of Napoleon's highest officials, his thoughts strayed again to Miss Riverstone.

She might be the very link he needed to the Home Office. The Bishop was obtaining information from someone there, he was certain. Perhaps her brother, Sir Nelson Riverstone . . .

Sudden excitement gripped him. *Mr. R?* He couldn't go about suspecting every man with a surname beginning with that letter, of course, but Riverstone's estate was in Oakshire—Miss Riverstone had said so. Oakshire, where at least one of those mysterious essays had originated. And he worked at the Home Office, from which certain documents had been stolen—

"Mr. Paxton?" Lady Hardwyck recalled him to his surroundings.

"I'm sorry, my lady. I was recalling a particularly harrowing experience on the outskirts of Paris." He told of the time he had nearly been caught meeting his contact, during the months he had spent disguised as a servant in Fouché's own household.

Not until Lord and Lady Hardwyck began speaking again did he pursue this new train of thought.

He must get to know Miss Riverstone better, he decided—much better. If he could win her trust and liking, she might be able to tell him all he needed to know about her brother, and perhaps even introduce him to his newest suspect. As a potential suitor?

Noel smiled to himself. He rather doubted Miss Riverstone had had many suitors. It should not be difficult to turn her head with compliments and discover everything he needed to know.

Though deadly serious, this investigation might prove to have its charms. Along the way, he could look forward to many more stimulating chess matches, at the very least. And perhaps to other, even more enjoyable diversions—all in the name of duty.

Chapter 3

Rowena was surprised to hear male voices in the dining room when she descended to breakfast the next morning—and even more surprised to discover Mr. Paxton helping himself from the sideboard.

"Good morning, Rowena," Pearl said brightly from the table, before she could speak. "I expected you to be up before any of us, but then I remembered that you would still be tired from your two-day journey. I hope you slept well?"

Flustered by being the focus of three pairs of eyes—and particularly by one intense pair of hazel eyes—Rowena nodded. "Yes, I, ah, slept perfectly well, thank you."

"Good, because you'll need your energy for our shopping expedition today. I've decided to throw a house party, so I'll want to buy a few things for myself, as well."

Rowena regarded Pearl suspiciously. "A house

party? In London? I thought those were country affairs."

"I've never been one to bow to convention, you know that. We haven't had so much as a real dinner party since our return to Town, so this will be a way to welcome all of our acquaintances to Hardwyck Hall and chase away old ghosts, as it were." She and Lord Hardwyck exchanged amused glances.

Mr. Paxton had finished filling his plate, so Rowena moved to the sideboard as he took his place at the table. "I see," she said, though she did not really see at all. "Shall I return to my brother's house? You will be terribly crowded here."

"Certainly not. I'm counting on you to help me. I will send out invitations today for a ball Friday, which will open the party. Most of the guests will undoubtedly prefer to sleep at their own houses and come only for the activities, so I don't foresee a shortage of rooms."

"Activities?" Rowena asked weakly.

"She's been planning since daybreak," Lord Hardwyck said with a chuckle. "Picnics, group excursions to the 'Change, whist tournaments—what else, my dear?"

Pearl cheerfully listed off half a dozen other amusements while Rowena listened in dismay, forgetting the fragrant sausages and pastries before her. So many opportunities for her to embarrass herself—and Pearl as well.

During the litany she glanced over at Mr. Paxton and saw that he looked nearly as bemused as she felt. It heartened her a bit, especially when he caught her eye and sent her a rueful grin and slight shrug.

"I told you, did I not, that I intended to make sure you enjoy your stay in London," Pearl concluded. "This way, you'll see everything it has to offer, over the course of a week or two."

It seemed last night's resolve to enter Society was to be put to an immediate test.

"Yes, I . . . suppose I will. Thank you." She would not appear ungrateful, not when Pearl was going to so much trouble. She only hoped that both of them would not live to regret it.

Belatedly remembering her breakfast, she filled a plate and took the same seat she had occupied at dinner, across from Mr. Paxton. Their earlier shared glance of sympathy made it less awkward than she had expected, though her pulse still quickened.

He looked up from his plate as she sat down, his expression now serious. "Miss Riverstone, pray allow me to apologize. It appears I did you a disservice last night."

Rowena shot a quick glance at Pearl, who must have set him straight, but she was speaking with her husband. "A simple misunderstanding, sir. Pray think no more of it." His mistaking her for a paid companion still rankled somewhat, however.

He appeared to realize it. "I leaped to an assumption based on mere appearances—something I learned long ago is a dangerous thing to do."

Was this meant for her? She'd made her own assumptions about Mr. Paxton, she realized, while in truth knowing little about him. "I must agree, sir, though I fear it is a common human failing, from my own experience." Certainly she herself had been judged by her appearance for as long as she could remember.

His eyes were disconcertingly knowing, seeming to probe her very thoughts. "And from my own, as well—though I confess that I have used that failing to my advantage on occasion. Still, I apologize for falling victim to it myself, in your case."

"You are forgiven, Mr. Paxton." What else could she say? And in truth, she no longer felt any anger toward him. There was something about those eyes, that deep, warm voice . . .

"Thank you." He sounded sincere, still holding her gaze with his own. "I hope that we can start over and, in time, become friends."

"Of . . . of course," she responded, even more flustered than she'd been last night.

The idea of becoming friends with this handsome, intelligent man held an undeniable appeal, even though what little she knew of him was hardly to his credit. A supporter of Parliament, employed by Bow Street to catch the heroic Saint of Seven Dials—but he had played some role in Vienna, as well. Who *was* this man, really?

Besides the best chess player she had ever met.

Though she very much wanted to dig beneath the surface, to avoid judging by externals as he admitted he had done, she couldn't think how to ask questions without sounding impertinent. Wordplay with handsome men was something entirely outside her experience, alas.

As she was still trying to frame her next comment, Lord Hardwyck and Mr. Paxton rose. "We have business to attend, my dear," said her host, "but we will see you at dinner."

"If not before," Mr. Paxton added, his eyes still on Rowena.

All she could do was nod like a simpleton as they took their leave. Later, Rowena promised herself. Perhaps the transformation Pearl promised would give her the courage she lacked.

"Let me do the talking at first," Luke advised as he and Noel approached a crumbling three-story building in Seven Dials.

Noel nodded. Both gentlemen had changed into nondescript fustian coats in the coach. He was reminded of Miss Riverstone and her drab clothing, and wondered again about the woman beneath. She was undoubtedly more than she appeared, just as he and Luke were now. Perhaps even—

"Ah, we're in luck," Luke said, breaking into his thoughts as a tall, thin boy peered out of the doorway they were nearing. "Stilt—a word with you, lad."

Though he frowned suspiciously from Luke to Noel and back, the boy came forward. "Can't say I expected to see you in these parts, milord," he said as he reached them. "Thought you'd given up all to do with Seven Dials."

"I may not be playing the Saint anymore," Luke said, "but I've not given up my interest in those who live here."

"Aye, and your gifts have been much appreciated, milord." Again, the boy glanced frowningly at Noel.

"This is Mr. Paxton," Luke said, putting a hand on Noel's shoulder. "He's interested in helping, and I'm here to introduce him to some of the lads. You can trust him, Stilt—he's a friend of mine."

The boy relaxed visibly. "Then he's a friend of ours. But there ain't that many lads left from the group you knew, milord. You took in Flute and Squint, then his other lordship hired away Gobby and his sister, along with Renny. Tig wouldn't go, though—he's still hereabouts, and me and Skeet."

"Still working for Twitchell, are you?" Luke was frowning now, and Noel couldn't blame him. During his investigation of the Saint, he'd discovered how vicious Twitchell and his rival thief-masters could be to their young apprentices.

Stilt shrugged. "It's a living. And if we'd all gone to work in fine houses, who'd be left to help the Saint and his friends?" He flashed a sudden grin that lit up his lean face.

Luke laughed. "A hit, indeed. Now, take us to Tig, Skeet and any others you think trustworthy enough to help in our cause. If all goes well, it won't be long before the Saint of Seven Dials is back in business."

Bond Street, the heart of London's shopping district, was a novel experience for Rowena. She looked about with interest at the deep, narrow shops selling every conceivable ware, the raucous street vendors, and the bustling crowds of shoppers. Poor Matthilda was terrified.

"There must be cutthroats and pickpockets everywhere in a mob like this, miss!" she exclaimed as they descended from Pearl's opulent coach. "Can't we have the goods sent 'round instead?"

"And miss all this? Of course not. Buck up,

Matthilda," Rowena told her. "I'm sure it's not nearly as dangerous as all that." She turned to Pearl, who nodded.

"It's not dangerous at all. At this hour, it's mostly ladies and their maids and escorts. Hettie, reassure her, won't you?"

Pearl's own maid set about soothing Matthilda, pointing out objects of interest—*safe* objects of interest—as they proceeded to Madame Fanchot's establishment.

"The finest modiste in London, my dear," Pearl assured Rowena as they entered the shop. At once the proprietress hurried forward to greet them.

"Lady Hardwyck! How delightful to see you again." She turned shrewd eyes on Rowena. "A young friend from the country to outfit? Ah, great potential here, I think."

Rowena found herself warming to the modiste. At least *she* didn't assume she was Pearl's companion. That thought brought Mr. Paxton forcibly to mind, of course—not that he had been far from her thoughts all morning.

Pearl stepped forward with a smile. "I have in mind a complete makeover, Madame Fanchot. Once we've ordered a few suitable gowns, we'll discuss accessories and hairstyles. Francesca is itching to unpin that bun, as you may imagine."

"An excellent plan, my lady. This way, if you please." The modiste led them into her inner sanctum, a display room draped with swaths of beautiful fabrics, fashion magazines piled on elegant little tables.

"I've always detested pastels," Pearl confided, "but as a seventeen-year-old debutante, they were *de rigeur*. You, however, are old enough—and independent enough—to dispense with them. Nor are you an insipid blonde like me, lucky girl."

Madame Fanchot nodded vigorously. "Yes, your coloring demands stronger hues. That copper hair—rich greens, blues and yellows will set it off to admiration." So saying, she unrolled bolts of vibrant-hued silks, satins and muslins.

Rowena, who had always secretly envied Pearl her golden tresses, listened to them in amazement. No one had ever implied that her reddish-brown hair was an *asset* before. "If you're sure. It all seems so frivolous."

"But fun, you must admit," said Pearl with a wink.

And it was. Though a part of her recoiled at the cost of new gowns, another part reveled in pure, feminine pleasure. The money she was spending could feed a small village for months—but any guilt could wait until later, she decided, fingering a bolt of luscious turquoise blue satin.

An hour later they left the shop with the promise that the first gown would be delivered in two days.

"She must have an army of seamstresses," Rowena exclaimed.

Pearl nodded. "She can afford to, believe me—the very best seamstresses. Now, we must find gloves, stockings, slippers and ribbons to match those gowns."

When they finally left Bond Street, the carriage crammed with parcels, the number of ladies on the walkways had thinned considerably, to be replaced by gentlemen in top hats and tails.

"If we think of anything else, we can come back tomorrow," Pearl said, though Rowena couldn't imagine a single item they could have possibly forgotten. Guilt returned in full force when she mentally tallied up all of her purchases.

So much money, simply so that she could flutter along with the other Society butterflies, something she had always disdained. Was her goal of social reform really worth it? But then she thought of Mr. Paxton and felt it might just possibly be worthwhile after all.

On their return to Hardwyck Hall, they were informed that the gentlemen were not expected to return until evening.

"Just as well," Pearl said. "That gives us time to plan your transformation. This is Francesca's day off, so your hair, I fear, will have to wait."

Rowena stifled her disappointment. She had hoped to achieve that step, at least, before facing Mr. Paxton at dinner tonight.

Still, she thought with a spurt of amusement, it might be diverting to solidify Mr. Paxton's opinion of her as a drab nonentity before appearing in her new guise, that she might the better enjoy his surprise at her transformation.

"We'll have you ready by Friday's ball," Pearl promised, echoing her thoughts. "Then you can burst upon the scene in full splendor. In the meantime, we can work on other things."

"Other things?" Rowena asked almost fearfully.

Pearl frowned thoughtfully at her. "Just how badly do you really need those spectacles?"

Rowena put an involuntary hand to her face. "I'm quite nearsighted—you know that. You used to hide them from me for a prank when we were young."

"Oh yes, I remember. Without them you squint." Pearl sighed.

Nettled by her friend's obvious disappointment, Rowena said, "Anyone who can't see past my spectacles is not likely to be someone I care to impress. I know the *ton* tends to focus on the externals, but are they really so superficial as that?"

"Not all of them. In fact, you'll be pleased to know that I have invited a number of London's leading literary lights to my little party. Robert Southey, Leigh Hunt, and a few others you'll be interested to meet."

"Indeed I will," Rowena agreed, suddenly feeling a flutter of enthusiasm for the coming ordeal. "Who else?"

But Pearl shook her head. "I don't wish to raise your hopes too high. Most of these men eschew such things as balls and card parties, and some are doubtless gone from Town by now. However, if any do attend, I will be certain to introduce you."

So the very men she would most like to meet were the ones least likely to come—not that she could blame them, as she shared their aversion to such frivolous pursuits. Some might attend, however, giving her the chance to implement her plan.

Meanwhile, another game or two of chess with Mr. Paxton might serve to sharpen her wits for the challenges ahead.

When the ladies entered the dining room that evening, Noel's gaze went at once to Miss Riverstone, despite his hostess's blond beauty. As before, she was dressed almost as a servant, this time in puritanical gray and white. The lack of color in her dress only served to emphasize the bright shimmer of her hair, however. At least, what little he could see of it, in that bun.

It was as though she used her severe appearance as armor, keeping any man from seeing the woman within, he mused. Perhaps it had worked on the country gents she'd encountered thus far, but he prided himself on digging beneath the surface. That thought brought forth a fascinating—and distinctly inappropriate—image, so he quickly turned his attention to his host.

"You were going to tell me more about the concerns some in Parliament have expressed on the relief efforts," he reminded Luke as they took their seats. Out of the corner of his eye he saw Miss Riverstone's head turn toward him, her interest evidently caught—as he had hoped.

Luke nodded. "Yes, there are those who fear nothing less than the disintegration of the social order, should commoners be given control of even the smallest pieces of land. Absurd, of course, but the notion of land ownership and power going hand in hand is very deeply entrenched."

"And power in the hands of commoners is anathema, my lord?" Miss Riverstone interjected before Noel could respond.

Luke appeared startled, but answered readily enough. "To some, certainly, though not to all."

Her intelligent gaze swung from Luke to Noel and back. "And to those present?"

"Anathema would be too strong a word in my

case," Luke said rather evasively, motioning for the hovering footman to commence serving the soup.

"And in mine," Noel echoed. "I can understand the concerns of those who worry that sudden acquisition of land by those not trained to the management of it might result in abuses. However, a gradual, reasoned approach that includes the requisite training would seem to be a viable solution."

Miss Riverstone fixed clear gray eyes upon him. Lovely eyes, really, beneath the spectacles, fringed with thick, dark lashes. "So if change is inevitable, it should be embraced as slowly as possible?"

Noel pulled himself from contemplation of her eyes to respond. "Abrupt change without thoughtful preparation rarely serves anyone well."

"An excuse all too easily taken to extremes, precluding any change at all," she pointed out.

He tended to agree, but was enjoying their sparring too much to say so. "Better that than a headlong rush into changes that could prove disastrous for all sides, taking years or even generations to repair."

"I perceive you must have a vested interest in the status quo, Mr. Paxton," she said, finally picking up her spoon. "Who, pray, are your antecedents?"

The question bordered on rude, but it did not occur to Noel to take offense. Distracted by the motion of her spoon to her nicely shaped lips, he debated how much to tell her. "My father was a younger son to an earl, it is true," he confessed, "though his own estate was quite modest."

"An estate that is now yours, I presume?"

He nodded. "In Derbyshire."

"Not so very far from Oakshire," she commented. "And have you a mother? Siblings?" She seemed to suddenly realize she was watching him intently and turned her attention back to her soup dish.

"A mother and two sisters," he said, smiling at her confusion. "The eldest lives with my mother in Derbyshire. The younger is married, and currently in Yorkshire with her husband."

She seemed disinclined for more questions, apparently perceiving that she had overstepped the bounds of politeness. Noel was just as glad. Telling her that his twin sister's husband was in line to be the next Duke of Wickburn would do his case no good at all, he suspected.

Lord and Lady Hardwyck took over the conversation at that point, discussing plans for their coming house party. Noel found himself paying closer attention to what Miss Riverstone ate than to what his hosts said, however. Behind those lovely lips lay white, even teeth and a darting pink tongue that made him think of things she might do with it beyond talking and eating.

All too soon, the ladies excused themselves to the parlor. Eager for another chess match, Noel waved away the offer of a cigar and accepted only a small measure of brandy.

"You seem rather taken with Miss Riverstone," Luke observed with a grin once the footman had left them alone.

Oops. Noel hadn't meant to be so obvious. "Intrigued, at least. She seems quite an original." Though the word was generally not used as a compliment, Noel considered it as such.

"She is that," Luke agreed with a chuckle. "Not that I'd expect anything less of a girl my wife claims as a lifelong friend. But tell me, have you thought further about your plans, now that you've met some of the lads you'd be working with?"

They fell then to discussing the denizens of Seven Dials and the smoothest way to effect a transition to Noel as the next Saint. Lord Marcus would have to be advised, they both agreed.

"We'll be inviting him and his new bride to our house party, of course, but I'll try to have a private word with him beforehand," Luke said. "Now, what say you we join the ladies in the parlor?"

Noel was startled by the sudden lift in his spirits at these words. He had always enjoyed a challenging game of chess, he reminded himself. And Miss Riverstone was proving a challenge of a different sort, as well.

He could not afford any sort of emotional entanglement, of course, but winning her confidence was essential to his mission. Sheltered as she'd apparently been, she would no doubt be susceptible to a flirtation. At any rate, he would enjoy trying.

He and Luke entered the parlor to find the two women deep in conversation—a conversation that broke off abruptly at their appearance. Lady Hardwyck rose.

"Chess again, or would you prefer cards tonight, Mr. Paxton?"

Glancing at Miss Riverstone, Noel found her gaze averted, whether from confusion or some other reason, he couldn't say. As she offered no input, he made the decision himself.

"I confess I've quite looked forward to another match with Miss Riverstone. Besides, I owe her a chance to revenge herself for my win last night."

The lady in question did meet his eye then, and there was nothing of confusion in her bright gaze. "That's very sporting of you, sir. I accept the challenge."

Two boards were produced, and a few moments later he and Miss Riverstone faced each other across one while Lord and Lady Hardwyck matched their respective skills at the other.

"Given my pitiful performance last night, I'll not accuse you of arrogance for adhering to tradition this time," Miss Riverstone remarked when he set up the board so that she had the white pieces and subsequent first move.

"Pitiful? Hardly that," he replied with perfect honesty. "You're the best opponent I've faced in some time. I was quite sincere when I said I've looked forward to another match."

She smiled then, for the first time since he'd met her, and it transformed her face into something sweet and distinctly pretty, the impact hitting him like a blow. Had he actually thought her plain before? The smile was all too brief, but its effect on him lingered as she spoke.

"I can say the same for you, Mr. Paxton, though I've undoubtedly had far fewer opponents for comparison, which makes your compliment the greater. I thank you." Then, turning her gaze to the board, she moved her king's pawn two spaces forward.

For several minutes they played in silence, while Noel tried to rein in the effect her combined intelligence and attractiveness had upon him. He was contemplating how best to broach the subject of her brother when Miss Riverstone spoke again.

"You mentioned last night that you had played some small role at the Congress of Vienna, Mr. Paxton. I would be interested to hear what it was."

He glanced up, but her attention remained on the board between them. "I was merely a minor aide of sorts to Wellington," he said carefully. In fact, he had been the duke's eyes and ears in places a more prominent man could not venture without danger and suspicion.

Miss Riverstone did look up now. "You actually met the Duke of Wellington? Worked with him? What is he like?" Her face was alight, eager, and disturbingly alluring.

Noel forced himself to study the board for a moment, making his next move before replying.

"Physically, he is an imposing man, though perhaps not classically handsome. Mentally, he is even more impressive. He has an awesome intellect, particularly in matters of strategy. You would enjoy engaging him in chess, I assure you."

As he'd hoped, she smiled again. Though he might have expected a less dramatic effect upon him this time, the opposite was the case.

"I'm certain I would. I had hoped to meet him while in London, but I understand his visit here is to be a brief one, and that he returns soon to Paris."

"He might possibly accept Lady Hardwyck's invitation before leaving," Noel replied, startled to discover he didn't share her hope. Wellington was a notorious womanizer—not that Miss Riverstone was at all in his usual style, of course. Still . . .

"May I trouble you for an introduction, then, should he attend?" Even as she spoke, she took his rook with her knight. Damn! That hadn't been part of his strategy.

"Of course," he said vaguely, trying to concentrate on the game again. He'd planned to use that rook to draw out her queen. Now he'd have to extricate his other rook for that maneuver. Would Wellington be as intrigued by Miss Riverstone's intelligence as he was? Dash it all, he mustn't let it matter.

Shaking his head slightly, he moved the pawn that blocked the path of his remaining rook. He barely knew this girl, after all. Certainly, he had no business becoming protective of her. She had a brother for that. His goal was simply to win her confidence and liking so that he could learn more about that brother.

"What did you do before you went to Austria?" she asked then, taking his pawn just as he'd intended. "Were you in the army?"

"I, ah, worked *with* the army, in a civilian capacity." He knew it sounded evasive, but he could hardly tell her he'd spent nearly three years as a spy in France.

She blocked his rook with a bishop. "What sort of capacity?"

"I was a courier of sorts," he said, using the cover story he'd maintained for years. "First in Upper Canada, during the second war with America, and later traveling to various parts of the Continent."

"Canada?" The chessboard apparently forgotten for the moment, her eyes shone. "Is it as wild and expansive as I've read? Did you meet any savages there?"

In truth, Noel had never set foot in Canada, but he'd made a point of learning about it so that he could answer just such questions as these.

"The forests are so thick one can scarcely see through them, and extend for hundreds of miles, interrupted only by pristine, frigid lakes. A beautiful, if rugged, country. There were no savages near our outpost, however, so I know only what I was told of them."

"And what of the Continent? Where did you travel?"

Her expression was rapt as she soaked up every bit of information he revealed. The girl definitely had the mind of a scholar. And the face and body of . . . With an effort, he pulled his gaze away, to focus again on the board. His inattention had taken its toll, forcing him to again modify his strategy.

"Germany, Prussia, Italy—wherever messages were being sent," he replied absently, moving his rook three spaces to the left to circumvent her bishop. He could only hope she had been equally distracted from the game.

Apparently not. Her next move revealed that he had fallen into a carefully prepared trap from which he could see no easy escape.

"How I should like to travel," she said as he moved his rook back to its starting point. "That has long been one of my dreams."

"What other dreams do you have, Miss Riverstone?" he asked in an unworthy attempt to rattle her.

He had clearly managed it the night before, but now she seemed more resistant.

She moved her queen one space to the right before responding, tightening the noose around his remaining pieces. "To set the world to rights, of course. To effect justice for all, rich and poor, titled and base."

"A humble goal." He laughed, despite his dire position in the game. "So you would wipe out all crime and poverty—and war as well, no doubt?" He took her bishop with his rook.

"Of course, had I the means to do so. I have long maintained that if women ruled the world, it would be a far more peaceful and prosperous place." She slid her remaining bishop to the opposite corner of the board, exposing his king to her queen while blocking its escape. "Checkmate."

He'd seen it coming, of course, but losing was still a shock. "Well played, Miss Riverstone," he said sincerely, though he was hard pressed not to frown.

What on earth was the matter with him? He had played—and beaten—some of the best, most devious minds of Europe, while simutaneously ferreting out their deepest secrets. It was precisely what he'd planned to do tonight, but instead she had managed to distract him. He must be losing his edge.

Noel forced a smile. "Another match? I'm willing to play white this time, as it appears I need the advantage."

That elicited another smile, one that set his heart pounding. Merely pretty, he had thought her? He realized now that she was in fact one of the loveliest women he'd met, her beauty uncluttered by frivolous ringlets or fancy clothes, the pure curves of her face only slightly concealed by her spectacles, with no artful tresses to obscure them.

"I'm far less tired than I was last night," she said, her voice flowing over him like fine wine. "I'd enjoy another game, yes."

Taking white as promised, he began with a gambit he'd used successfully on many occasions. It appeared to be one with which she was unfamiliar, to judge by her level of concentration. He was just as glad to be spared more probing questions. It felt more wrong somehow to lie to Miss Riverstone than to all of the exalted dignitaries and officials he had deceived over the years.

Determined not to let his focus waver, Noel spoke not a word for half an hour. Then, feeling he had established a sufficient advantage, he launched another attempt at flirtation, aiming his flattery at her skill rather than her appearance. She would suspect the latter as flummery, he was certain.

"You are an audacious and unconventional player, Miss Riverstone. I continue to be amazed that you have achieved this level of skill immured in the country."

"I subscribe to a wide variety of newspapers and periodicals, some of which recount famous matches in great detail. In addition, I had the advantage of an accomplished master in our late vicar, Mr. Winston, a man whose intellect I fear few besides myself appreciated during his lifetime."

Again, Noel felt himself becoming caught up in curiosity about Miss Riverstone, to the detriment of his attention to the game. What was his next move to be?

She reached forward to counter his move with her

knight, and he noticed how long and slender her fingers were. He'd thought her plump on first meeting her last night, but now realized she was almost perfectly proportioned, though her frumpy dresses obscured her figure.

Sternly, he recalled his thoughts and made his next move, which should force her to withdraw her knight so that he could advance on her queen. Instead, she surprised him by taking his white bishop, sacrificing said knight.

"I've never been able to bear being funneled into a particular course of action," she commented, a twinkle in her gray eyes. "My tendency to rebel cost me more than one match with Mr. Winston, but he rarely beat me in the same method as he had planned, which I regarded as a sort of victory."

And so it transpired. Though Noel was eventually able to win the game, he was forced to alter his strategy numerous times in order to do so.

"Again, my compliments, Miss Riverstone," he said when he had finally checkmated her. "You kept me on my toes the entire time. I must say, you are a formidable opponent."

He realized his words were true in more ways than one.

Chapter 4

Rowena smiled sunnily, aware that she had acquitted herself well and feeling that she fully merited Mr. Paxton's praise. She had been determined not to let her ridiculous attraction to the man distract her tonight and was pleased by her success, though it had taken a surprising degree of concentration.

"I thank you, sir. I would suggest yet another match, but I perceive that it is nearly midnight."

Indeed, Pearl and her husband had long ago given up their own play, and were all but dozing on the sofa, leaning cozily against each other. They stood now and came forward to inquire about the match just ended.

"I fear I lack the patience for so long a game myself," Pearl confessed. "So you beat him tonight, did you, Rowena? Brava! A point for the so-called weaker sex."

Rowena glanced at Mr. Paxton and thought he looked slightly nettled. "I was able to rally for our second match," he said. "I won't deny, however, that your Miss Riverstone plays far better than I'd have believed a woman could. I flatter myself that she is far from typical of your sex."

Rowena wasn't certain whether he meant that as a compliment or an insult, but could not prevent herself from retorting, "I suspect I am more typical than you imagine, sir—simply less practiced than most at concealing my abilities."

Mr. Paxton's brows rose, but it was Lord Hardwyck who spoke first. "What a terrifying thought," he exclaimed. Then, to Pearl, "Never say you possess talents you have not yet revealed, my dear?"

"I can only hope so," Pearl replied with a grin. "But now, I think we terrifying creatures must bid you good night."

After taking polite leave of the gentlemen, Rowena accompanied Pearl out of the room, still irked by Mr. Paxton's remark. Not that she *wanted* to be thought typical, of course . . .

"Now I'll have to reassure Luke that I haven't been keeping secrets," Pearl said laughingly as they climbed the stairs. "Luckily for me, he seems to find my intelligence attractive rather than intimidating."

Rowena thought she understood the underlying message. "But most men are not so enlightened?"

"You scarcely need me to tell you that, after all of your study on such matters."

"Surely you are not suggesting that I should have let him win that first match?" Rowena asked in surprise.

"No, no, of course not." But Pearl's voice lacked conviction.

Mr. Paxton had seemed rather distracted, Rowena

recalled. It would have been an easy thing to play a shade below her best—but that would be a species of dishonesty she despised. She admitted that she had hoped for his friendship, but what sort of friendship would it be, if she could not be herself?

"Would you have done so?" she challenged her friend.

Pearl thought for a moment, then smiled ruefully. "No, I confess I would not have let him win either. After all, I do not let Luke beat me, and he would not wish me to. But he is a gem, in that way as in so many others."

Pearl's obvious adoration of her husband, clearly reciprocated, created a small ache somewhere in the vicinity of Rowena's heart. What must it be like to experience such love, such trust? It seemed unlikely that she, plain and too intelligent for a "proper" woman, would ever know.

"Your Miss Riverstone is rather a quiz, my dear," Luke said as he and Pearl prepared for bed. "Are you certain attempting to launch her into Society is a good idea?"

Pearl laughed. "You sound like her father used to. Rowena is my oldest, dearest friend, and has helped me through more than one rough spot in the past. I feel I owe her this much. Never say you are afraid she'll embarrass us?"

"Us? No. Perhaps herself. She seems to speak without thinking, for all she appears uncommonly intelligent."

"Uncommon indeed. I consider myself one of the best educated women in England, but Rowena casts me in the shade when it comes to intellectual pursuits. I doubt there is a book on her brother's estate—or my father's for that matter—that she hasn't read. Newspapers and magazines, as well."

Pulling Pearl down onto the bed next to him, Luke nodded. "I surmised that. She seems exceptionally well informed on current events."

"Indeed, if she weren't a woman, I've no doubt she'd stand for Parliament—not that we haven't had more than one discussion on the unfairness of a system that prevents women from doing just that," Pearl said with a chuckle.

Luke raised his hands in mock horror. "We men must preserve some small portion of leadership to ourselves, or your sex would ride roughshod over us all. No doubt she'll manage to scrape along in Society if she is so well informed as that, however."

Pearl frowned. "I hope so. But for all her reading, she's had precious little experience with the real world. I fear she may be . . . susceptible."

"To men, do you mean? She's hardly likely to draw the sort of masculine attention you do, my dear," he said teasingly.

Pearl grinned, but regarded him speculatively. "Do you think her so plain, then? I believe she merely hides her light under a bushel. I'd say something disparaging about male observational powers if I hadn't noticed the way your Mr. Paxton was watching her tonight."

Luke's brows rose. "Not matchmaking, are you, love?"

"Certainly not. In fact, I'd thought to warn her

away from him, as his prospects seem rather poor. Besides, will he not disappear once he's caught this spy you say he is after? I'd not have Rowena's heart broken over him."

Rather than reply, Luke gathered his wife to him for a kiss. Noel's prospects were far better than Pearl knew, but that was not Luke's confidence to divulge. And whatever might spark between Noel and Miss Riverstone was best left to burn or fizzle without Pearl's interference.

"With your shepherding, I'm sure your friend will do quite well," he murmured into her hair. "I have no doubt you can make her ready for Society in two days' time. I only hope Society is ready for Miss Riverstone."

The next morning Rowena was the first downstairs for breakfast. The *Times* and *Morning Chronicle* had been placed on the sideboard to await Lord and Lady Hardwyck's pleasure, along with that week's *Political Register*, which Rowena had not yet read.

She rather doubted that most of the great houses in Mayfair received that publication, but it didn't surprise her that Pearl's would. Surely her friend wouldn't mind if she took a peek.

Rowena was deep in her reading, coffee and toast having been supplied by an unobtrusive footman, when Mr. Paxton appeared. Flustered, she put down the *Register,* tucking it facedown under her saucer to hide the name of the controversial circular.

"Good morning, Miss Riverstone," he greeted her cheerfully. "I see Lady Hardwyck was right about your usual habits."

"I—I beg your pardon?" Rowena shot a guilty glance at the folded paper at her elbow.

"Rising early," he clarified. "I tend to keep country hours myself, being a relative newcomer to London."

She looked at him in surprise. "You do not strike me as a rustic, sir. In fact, quite the opposite." For a moment, her gaze became tangled with his and she was struck again by the perceptiveness of his complex hazel eyes.

"I've traveled a bit, yes," he conceded. "But until a few weeks ago I was buried in Derbyshire."

"On your estate." She knew her tone was disapproving, and regretted it at once. He could not help having inherited, after all.

His smile held a trace of mockery. "While you have lived . . . in the cottage of your brother's poorest tenant?"

She could feel the color rising to her cheeks. "No, of course not—and I apologize. I have grown up privileged as well." Then, lifting her chin, she met his eyes again. "However, I *am* trying to make some reparation for that."

"By stirring up sympathy for the common man—or by criticizing every landowner you meet?"

He had scored another hit but Rowena refused to acknowledge it, nettled by his obvious amusement. "The former, of course."

"How admirable." His expression softened to something she could not decipher, though it quickened her heartbeat. "And how—"

"Good morning, early risers!" exclaimed Pearl, breezing into the dining room and interrupting whatever Mr. Paxton had been about to say. She looked fresh and vibrant in blue-sprigged muslin, making Rowena feel dowdier than ever.

Mr. Paxton rose to bow in greeting. "Good morning, my lady. May I say that you look lovely today."

Rowena stifled a sigh. He had directed no such compliments her way—not that she merited them, of course. Still—

"I'm glad to find you both here," Pearl continued after thanking him. "I have realized that as this is Rowena's first visit to Town, she may need a few pointers in order to feel comfortable at her first Society function. I'd like to enlist your aid, Mr. Paxton."

"Honored to oblige, of course," he responded politely, but Rowena thought she detected a flicker of alarm in his eyes.

As for herself, she wished she could disappear through the floor. Pearl made her sound like a charity case, a poor country bumpkin with no idea of how to go on in civilized society.

Turning, Pearl caught her reproachful glance and came forward to hug her. "I'm sorry, dear, I shouldn't have phrased it so. I only meant that you've had few opportunities to practice your social skills in Oakshire. How long has it been since you danced, for instance?"

Rowena fought down a sudden stab of panic. "Ah, quite some time, actually." Not since her last lesson with the dancing master, some four years since, in fact. "But surely there will be no need for me to do so?"

"No need to dance—at a ball?" Pearl's delicate eyebrows arched in amusement. "It is the whole point. I won't have you playing the wallflower or disappearing into a corner to discuss politics. Not at your very first ball."

Swallowing, Rowena nodded, though she had hoped to do just that. "Then I suppose you are right that I will need a bit of practice first. I don't wish to embarrass you, after all." She was acutely aware of Mr. Paxton witnessing this humiliating exchange.

"I have no fear of that whatsoever," Pearl assured her warmly. "It's settled, then. We'll start directly after breakfast. I believe we should run over some of the more popular card games as well, as I've planned a card party for Saturday."

Lord Hardwyck joined them then, and Rowena was glad to no longer be the focus of attention. As the others talked, she was aware of a rebellious thrill at the thought of Mr. Paxton standing up to dance with her. His hand would touch hers, she would look into his eyes . . .

And then step on his foot. Oh, this was going to be terrible! She sat in barely concealed agitation while Lord Hardwyck and Mr. Paxton discussed the unusually cool weather.

As soon as all had eaten, Pearl directed them to the ballroom. Servants were already polishing sconces and hanging brackets for the flowers for tomorrow night's event.

"We will make do with humming for music for now," Pearl said after a quick check of the preparations. "If you will oblige me, my lord, I thought we might model a waltz."

"Very well, my love, one waltz," Lord Hardwyck replied. "But then I must leave you to your protégée's lessons. I have several appointments today."

Pearl pouted prettily, but nodded. "All right,

Rowena, watch how I place my hands. The style has changed slightly since last year."

"Not that that matters, as I never learned to waltz at all," Rowena muttered to herself, watching the effortless way Pearl and her husband moved about the floor.

"It's not as hard as it looks," came an answering murmur from just behind her. She hadn't realized Mr. Paxton was standing so close. "We'll have you waltzing beautifully in no time."

She half turned, to look up at him gratefully. "I'm sure this wasn't what you had planned for this morning, sir. I appreciate your sacrificing your time on my behalf. And I do hope you're right, though I take leave to doubt it."

"You've clearly spent your time on more useful pursuits than dancing and flirting. You shouldn't be penalized for that," he responded with a warmth that startled her. "My plans were not so urgent that they can't wait for such a cause."

He understood! Rowena started to thank him again, but found herself caught in his gaze, his eyes darkening to a deep green as they seemed to probe hers for secrets.

"Rowena, you're not watching!" came Pearl's admonishing voice, snapping her back to her surroundings.

Embarrassed by the direction her thoughts had been tending, she quickly swung back around. "I . . . I have been," she stammered. "But I fear I'll have to begin at a more basic level. You've committed to more than you know, Pearl, with your insistence on making me fit for a ball by tomorrow night."

Though Rowena was quite serious, Pearl only laughed. "You know how I love a challenge, dear. But I'm convinced you only need some pointers. I know from experience what a quick study you are."

Rowena was spared from replying by Lord Hardwyck, who took his leave of them then. With a glance at Mr. Paxton that might have been pitying, he said, "I'll see you this afternoon at White's, as we discussed?"

Mr. Paxton nodded. "I'm quite looking forward to it."

"Don't plan on us for dinner then, my love," Lord Hardwyck said to Pearl. He gave her a quick but undeniably passionate kiss, then was gone.

Pearl turned back to the others, her cheeks a bit pink. "Now, where were we? Mr. Paxton, if you are willing, I will play a simple waltz on the pianoforte and you may partner Rowena. Half-time, to start."

Accordingly, she moved to the instrument in the corner of the large room and struck up a tune at a dirgelike pace. Rowena, her heart hammering wildly, turned to face Mr. Paxton.

"You really don't have to—"

"Nonsense. We have our instructions." With a smile that soothed one set of fears while creating another, he held out his hand.

Tentatively, she placed her own in it, while he set his other hand at her waist. He was even taller than she'd realized, her face on a level with his shirtfront. "I . . . I'll try not to tread on your feet," she promised breathlessly.

"No matter if you do. My shoes are quite sturdy. Now." Slowly, in time with the music, he moved her across the floor. "A waltz is simply a count of three, repeated. *One*, two, three, *one*, two, three. No, the other foot. That's right."

Though his touch was hugely distracting, Rowena concentrated with all her might on his words and his feet, trying to match her steps to his. All the while he spoke calmly, patiently, correcting her in gentle, matter-of-fact tones whenever she made a mistake.

Gradually, she was able to relax. As she became less stiff, her mistakes grew fewer, and by the end of the piece, she felt she had the basic movements fairly well mastered. Her partner reinforced her satisfaction.

"I told you it wasn't hard," he said. "You're doing excellently. Another, I think, Lady Hardwyck, this time at full tempo."

Pearl began another waltz at twice the speed as the last, and Rowena had to concentrate all over again. This time her progress was faster, partly because Mr. Paxton seemed adept at anticipating her errors and correcting them in advance.

The music ended with a flourish and Rowena, flush with her success, tried a small flourish of her own. Unfortunately, her left foot came down squarely on Mr. Paxton's right.

"Oops!" she exclaimed, quickly taking her weight off that foot. Too quickly. She lost her balance, and was saved from falling only by his superior reflexes.

"I'm . . . I'm terribly sorry." The feel of his arms around her, like warm, supple steel bands, made it hard to think. She hadn't realized he would be so strong.

Gently, he set her upright. "No harm done. Shall we try the minuet? Balls traditionally open with that one."

Rowena nodded mutely, still exceedingly flustered.

Pearl obliged with a sprightly minuet. Without the disturbing distraction of constant contact, Rowena was able to think again. Automatically, she went through the motions of the familiar, old-fashioned dance—not perfectly, but at least no one's feet were endangered by her occasional missteps.

She had already recognized Mr. Paxton's superior intelligence, but now she had to credit him with an unusual degree of kindness, as well. She repeatedly caught herself staring at him as they danced, the line of his jaw fascinating her with its masculine strength.

"Without more people, we cannot attempt any of the country dances or the quadrille," Pearl commented at the close of the minuet. "You know enough of those to get by, do you not, Rowena?"

"I hope so," she replied doubtfully. She now regretted never practicing once her dancing lessons had ended when she was seventeen. At the time, she had seen it as a blessed release from weekly hours of torture.

"We will watch out for you, Miss Riverstone, and come to your rescue should you find yourself out of your depth," Mr. Paxton said with a smile that served to make him even more handsome.

Though she felt herself pinkening with embarrassment that such measures should be necessary, she thanked him. "I fear I shall never be proficient, but I do feel less nervous now than I did when we began."

"Good!" Pearl's tone was bracing. "I have no doubt you will do quite well. You need not dance every dance, after all. And you, sir," she said to Mr. Paxton, her eyes twinkling, "had best not promise her too many dances yourself, or it will give rise to expectations among those assembled."

Rowena turned away quickly to hide her mortification, but not before she saw the startled look in Mr. Paxton's eyes. Why must Pearl tease so? She was greatly relieved when the butler chose that moment to interrupt them to announce morning callers.

Noel watched Miss Riverstone as he followed the two ladies to the parlor where the visitors awaited. Not only did the girl have one of the sharpest minds he'd encountered, she possessed a humorous awareness of her own limitations that he found quite appealing. Too appealing.

There was courage there as well, for it was clear she was dreading tomorrow night's ball but meant to see it through anyway. He presumed an unwillingness to disappoint Pearl was her primary motivation, and that spoke well of her loyalty, too.

That same loyalty would likely make it more difficult to get to her brother through her, but he had no choice. He'd noticed her choice of reading material at breakfast, though he hadn't let on. That she read the *Political Register* was one more bit of evidence that her brother might be the mysterious essayist.

At first opportunity, he would have to deftly question her about her brother, to see if he fit the profile of the Black Bishop. He would create such an opportunity soon—for of course that must be his only real interest in Miss Riverstone.

"Lady Mountheath, how good to see you," Pearl exclaimed as she entered the parlor. "I apologize again that I was unable to come for tea on Tuesday.

This is Miss Riverstone, the friend I mentioned. Rowena, Mr. Paxton, may I present Lady Mountheath and her daughters, Miss Lucy Mountheath and Miss Fanny Mountheath."

All of the proper greetings were exchanged. Noel moved to sit next to Miss Riverstone, thinking to put his plan into effect at once, but was forestalled by the younger Miss Mountheath, who beckoned him to sit by her.

"Lucy and I met you at Lady Jeller's Venetian breakfast two weeks ago," she reminded him with a giggle. "I'm delighted to find you are still in Town, Mr. Paxton, it has become so thin of late." She giggled again.

Noel smiled blandly, remembering all too well the tedious half hour he had spent with the sisters on that occasion. Again he was trapped, listening to their fatuous chatter while his hope of more interesting conversation, Miss Riverstone, was out of reach on the far side of their gimlet-eyed mother.

It was a distinct relief when more callers were announced. He rose and greeted Mr. Galloway, Mr. Orrin and Lady Minerva Chatham with enthusiasm. The newcomers dispersed themselves about the room and he took that opportunity to move closer to Miss Riverstone.

"I just received the invitation to your house party, and I am so distraught," Lady Minerva was saying to Lady Hardwyck. "Mother and I leave tomorrow to join Father in the country, so we will not be able to attend. It sounds like such fun."

"I'm sorry to give so little notice, Minnie. It was one of my starts, thrown together at the last moment.

You've heard me mention my friend, Rowena Riverstone?" Lady Hardwyck made the introductions.

While Lady Minerva greeted Miss Riverstone pleasantly, Noel noticed that the two gentlemen gave her only the most cursory nod before turning their attention back to the other ladies present. He frowned at their rudeness, surprised that Lady Hardwyck did not call them to task for it—then realized he had reacted precisely the same way on first meeting Miss Riverstone.

What a difference a few hours in her company had made! Now he scarcely noticed her nondescript attire and unfashionable hairstyle, knowing the keen intelligence and wry humor that lurked beneath.

"So you are Bow Street's new hope to catch the Saint, are you, Mr. Paxton?" Lady Minerva interrupted his thoughts. "I can't say I wish you success, but I should love to hear any stories you know of our local hero."

Noel had to smile at her eagerness. "Most of what there is to tell has already found its way into the papers. It seems he is a master of disguise, able to act the nobleman as easily as the servant, making him quite difficult to track."

Miss Riverstone turned to listen, as did Lady Mountheath. The latter said, "I do hope you will manage it, however, Mr. Paxton. The villain stole jewels and plate from my home some months since, and they were never recovered. The Runners surmised that he masqueraded as a footman, hired on for the evening."

"A risky practice, hiring men off the street, Lady Mountheath," Lady Minerva commented. "I should be afraid to do so myself, much as I might like to have the Saint in my own house." She winked at the other ladies, drawing a general chuckle.

Miss Riverstone spoke for the first time since entering the parlor. "If everyone shared your caution, Lady Minerva, think how much harder it would be for those in difficult straits to earn enough to feed their families."

Lady Mountheath sniffed audibly, cutting off any reply Lady Minerva might have made. "Such men work cheaply, so will always find those willing to hire them. For my part, I now make certain that any chance hires are closely supervised, and carefully searched before leaving my employ."

Miss Riverstone frowned and opened her mouth, no doubt to protest such demeaning treatment.

"A wise precaution, my lady," said Noel quickly, before Miss Riverstone could draw the censure of the others. "I'd recommend requesting references as well, whenever possible."

All but Miss Riverstone murmured their agreement. The conversation moved on to the topic of Lady Hardwyck's upcoming house party, the Misses Mountheath and the two gentlemen clearly looking forward to such a novel amusement so late in the Season.

Noel glanced at Miss Riverstone to find her frowning at him, no doubt irritated by his implicit agreement with Lady Mountheath's methods. Though he could not explain, he smiled and shrugged to show he understood. He could not afford to lose her good opinion—not yet.

She raised one brow, as though trying to decipher

his meaning, then looked away. Lady Hardwyck caught his eye then and smiled approvingly. She, at least, realized what he had done for her friend.

The Mountheath ladies took their leave and other callers arrived. Over the next hour, it seemed that half the important personages still in London stopped by to congratulate Lady Hardwyck on her clever idea.

Lady Hardwyck dutifully introduced Miss Riverstone to each visitor, and almost without exception they greeted, then ignored her. Miss Riverstone appeared not to care, but Noel couldn't quite suppress his own irritation, hypocritical though it was.

He made a point of exchanging a few words with each visitor, memorizing names and mentally placing each one in relation to those he wished to cultivate. The groundwork for his investigation was being laid nicely.

When the last callers finally took their leave, Lady Hardwyck rose with a sigh. "Dear me, what a lot of curious people remain in Town! But it bodes well for tomorrow night's attendance. Dare I hope you will remember any names, Rowena?"

Miss Riverstone nodded. "I made a point of it, as it seemed one of the few things that might help me show to advantage. People are flattered to be remembered."

"Very true," Lady Hardwyck agreed with a laugh. "I suppose if you can plan a chess strategy ten moves in advance, a few dozen names should present little challenge. But now, let us continue our lessons. I thought we would move on to card games, as few people are likely to want to play chess."

Accordingly, she rang for decks of cards and the

three of them sat down to go over the rules of whist, faro, piquet and *vingt-un*. Not at all to Noel's surprise, Miss Riverstone proved a quick study, particularly in those games involving more strategy than luck.

"You should have no trouble holding your own in this arena," Lady Hardwyck declared after less than an hour. "How are you with a fan?"

Miss Riverstone stared at her, reminding Noel forcibly of a deer cornered by a hound. "A fan? Gesturing or, ah, flirting with one, do you mean?" She shot a quick, alarmed glance at Noel, then quickly looked away, her cheeks pinkening.

He stifled a smile. "Will that really be necessary, Lady Hardwyck?" he asked.

Somehow he couldn't imagine direct, unadorned Miss Riverstone intentionally flirting, fan or no fan. Flirting smacked of intrigue—one reason he'd made a point of learning to do it well himself—and her honesty was one of her more attractive traits.

"Only the basics, for now," Lady Hardwyck assured them. "Let me ring for a fan."

Noel hastily stood. "I'm certain you won't need me for this enterprise. Surely these are mysteries of which my sex is supposed to remain ignorant? Besides, it's getting late and I did promise to meet Lord Hardwyck."

"Coward," Lady Hardwyck teased. "Very well, run along then. You've been most patient and helpful, and I do thank you."

"As do I," echoed Miss Riverstone. "Without your help—both of you—I'd have been sure to embarrass myself. Now, perhaps, there is less certainty of that."

Again, Noel was charmed by her subtle, self-deprecating humor. "Fitting in is simply a matter of following the lead of those around you, Miss Riverstone," he said with a reassuring smile. "I have no doubt you will do splendidly. Ladies."

Bowing, he took his leave of them, trying not to notice the lingering anxiety in Miss Riverstone's eyes, or the effect that anxiety had upon him. She was simply a means to an end. He had no business feeling protective of her.

Perhaps it was just as well other gentlemen tended to overlook her. He had a vague suspicion he might not react particularly well should they do otherwise. Thankfully, her unfashionable appearance made it unlikely he would be put to any such test.

Chapter 5

"Ringlets? Are you certain? They seem so . . . frivolous." Rowena frowned at the sketch Pearl's coiffeuse showed her.

After a disastrous hour playing with fans, Pearl had given up on teaching her that particular skill and had led her upstairs to begin her transformation.

Francesca nodded vigorously. "See how your hair wishes to curl of itself? A natural curl, when released from its bondage, one many women would envy. And the color, so rich, now that one can see it. You will wish for that richness about your face, no?"

Rowena glanced questioningly at Pearl, who echoed the woman's nod. "I've learned to trust Francesca in such matters," she said.

"Very well," Rowena agreed. "At least she's not proposing to cut too much of the length, so if I don't like it, I can still put it back into its bun." She was only half teasing, still determined to go through with it. What did she have to lose, after all?

Only her integrity, a small voice whispered.

"It's as well the men will not be here for dinner," Pearl was saying. "You must take breakfast in your room tomorrow as well. We will wait until your transformation is complete before springing you upon the world tomorrow night at the ball. I can scarcely wait to see Luke's face, or Mr. Paxton's."

Rowena had thought the same, but now her feelings swung from one extreme to the other. Suppose she looked ridiculous in her new trappings, like an ape playing dress up? She didn't think she could bear for Mr. Paxton to regard her as a figure of fun.

"Now then." Removing Rowena's spectacles, Francesca plied her scissors. At the first sound of her hair being shorn, Rowena closed her eyes. Pearl was her friend. She would never make her a laughingstock, she told herself desperately.

Still, she was just as glad she was unable to watch as the coiffeuse fluttered about her head with scissors, pins and hot tongs. Pearl made no sound at all, which Rowena considered ominous. Finally, Francesca removed the cloth she had draped about Rowena's shoulders and backed away.

"Voila!" she cried. "A glass, my lady, if you please."

Rowena opened her eyes to see Pearl approaching with a hand mirror and a smile. "See what you think," she said, handing her the mirror.

Hesitantly, she lifted the glass. And gasped. How could a mere hairstyle effect such a change? But it had. Framed by coppery ringlets, her face looked softer, more feminine. Prettier. She darted a questioning glance at Pearl.

"I always told you that you were not so plain as

you believed," her friend reminded her with a smug expression. "Now you must confess that I was right."

Rowena looked again at the image in the mirror, not quite able to believe what she saw there. "My spectacles?" Pearl handed them to her and she donned them for a better look.

Now she looked a bit more like herself, her eyes less pronounced, the curve of her cheek somewhat disguised.

"Are you sure you don't want to try doing without them?" Pearl asked. "You could carry them with you, of course, to use if absolutely necessary."

For a long moment, Rowena hesitated. Dispensing with her spectacles would be pure vanity, and would make her feel more vulnerable, besides. But if she kept them handy . . .

Her goal, she reminded herself, was to become the sort of woman who might influence those in power to bring about necessary change. Slowly, she took off her eyeglasses and looked again at the mirror. Perhaps it would not be so impossible as she had thought.

"Very well," she said. "I will try."

"You're certain the family is away?" Noel surveyed the rear of the fashionable town house on Mount Street, noting that every window on the main floors was dark.

Stilt, the tall urchin lad, nodded. "Aye, guv. Lots of swells and their families are gone this time o' year, off to the country for whatever it is they do there."

Noel smiled at the boy's baffled tone. Clearly he couldn't imagine anything that would lure someone away from London. For a moment, he thought longingly of Tidebourne, his small estate in Derbyshire. And the grander estate of Ellsdon Abbey, where he had spent a few summers as a boy, and which he seemed likely to inherit on his uncle's death.

"Good," he said. "I'll try not to give the servants any reason to leave the attics." He started across the alleyway leading from the mews.

Stilt followed him. "Nowt but two of 'em anyway, from what we've been able to tell. An old couple, housekeeper and butler, most like."

In other words, no one to pose any threat, Noel thought. Still, he would do his best to get in and out undetected.

His goal tonight was simply to acquire enough booty to feed and house three Seven Dials families—and to brush up his housebreaking skills. Luke had told him about those families at their meeting earlier, suggesting he use this free evening for his first foray as the Saint.

Moving to a good vantage point just outside the back gate, he waited until the attic went dark, then cautiously moved forward. The gate was locked, but it was the work of a moment to climb it. As he'd expected, the back door and windows were also fastened securely. This would be the first test of his skills.

Luke had offered him the use of his set of lock-picks, but Noel preferred to use his own. They had served him well during his career as Puss in Boots in France, getting him into various locked offices and desk drawers.

Sliding a thin, curved piece of metal into the keyhole, he expertly turned it until the latch released. Then, pulling a tiny bottle from his breast pocket, he oiled the hinges before pushing the door silently open.

"Wait here," he cautioned Stilt, who had stood watching with obvious approval. The one thing that had motivated him to continue pursuit of the Saint, once he'd learned the Black Bishop wasn't involved, was the mistaken belief that the Saint was recruiting boys to help in his housebreaking. Noel certainly wasn't going to involve them himself, any more than necessary.

The back hallway was almost entirely dark, the only light coming from a fanlight above the front door at the far end, which let in some faint illumination from a nearby street lamp. Noel moved in that direction, peering into each of the four doors on that level as he went.

With the owners away, the plate would be securely locked up, probably in a closet belowstairs. He decided to check the dining room first, pulling a large sack from his waistband as he entered to examine the sideboard. The only dishes appeared to be pewter in the feeble light from the long front window, and the pair of candlesticks on top were undoubtedly silver plate. Still, they'd fetch something. Wrapping them in the cloths he'd brought, he stuffed them into his sack.

On his way back to the stairs, he slipped into the study for a quick look around. An ornate clock on the mantelpiece joined the candlesticks, and then he turned his attention to the desk.

Sir Randolph Olney was known to have strong connections to the Sussex smugglers, though no charges had ever been brought against him. It was one of the reasons Noel had targeted this house. He felt few qualms about stealing from a man whose wealth was largely ill-gotten.

The desk at first revealed nothing beyond a few letters, impossible to read in the dark. Reaching to the back of the smallest drawer, however, Noel discovered a handful of coins that, by their size and heft, he deduced must be gold guineas. Smiling, he pocketed them. No trip to the plate closet would be necessary now.

From the same breast pocket where he kept his phial of oil and his lockpicks, he pulled one of the cards Luke had given him, etched with the Saint's trademark sign: a black numeral seven surmounted by a golden halo. He tucked the card into the drawer from which he'd removed the guineas, then, with a last glance about, left the room and, a moment later, the house.

Rejoining Stilt in the small garden, he felt his first foray as Saint of Seven Dials had been rather anticlimactic. But then, he'd expected it to be easy, compared to most of his exploits in France. Even if he were caught—an unlikely event, considering he himself was Bow Street's prime weapon against the Saint—he'd face a more merciful fate than the French would have granted him.

"Care to have another go, guv?" asked Stilt as they regained the alleyway behind the garden. "House two doors down is empty as well. Skeet checked it out."

But Noel shook his head. He didn't know who lived in the other house, and he was determined to steal only from those he felt deserved it in some way—or who might yield some information about the Black Bishop.

"Not tonight, Stilt, but thank Skeet for his intelligence. We may attempt that one a different time," he added, hoping thereby to prevent the boys from trying a housebreaking on their own.

Unwrapping the candlesticks, he handed them to Stilt, along with the guineas. "Here's tonight's haul. This should take care of the O'Malleys, the Fabrizios and old Mrs. Fenniwick, as well as your cut for Twitchell."

"Aye, this'll do 'em for a good bit," Stilt agreed, rewrapping the candlesticks and pocketing the coins.

"You know how to contact me, if something else arises?"

The lad nodded. "Tig'll slip a note to Squint, who'll see you gets it."

"Right. Now, you boys keep your noses clean, and your ears to the ground in the meantime. We'll meet again in a few days."

Though he'd have liked to bring all of the boys back with him that very night, Noel knew they wouldn't come. Besides, they were useful on the streets. In addition to keeping an eye on the poorest denizens of Seven Dials, he'd told Stilt just enough about the Black Bishop that he was confident the lad would notify him if he heard anything.

Returning to Hardwyck Hall half an hour later, he was glad he planned no similar excursions over the next few days. Already he found himself missing Miss Riverstone and her quick wits. Perhaps he could manage a chess game with her before Lady Hardwyck's ball. It would be a good way to keep his own wits sharpened, and might afford him the opportunity he needed to ask about her brother.

Whether he had any other motive, he refused to contemplate.

The next morning, Noel was up early, despite a poor night's sleep. Thoughts of the intriguing Miss Riverstone had repeatedly interfered with the plans he needed to make, plans for the eventual unmasking and capture of the Black Bishop.

He could no longer deny that he found Miss Riverstone dangerously attractive. Her intelligence, curiosity and innocence all combined to form a potent allure that threatened to distract him from his real goal—a vital goal, he reminded himself. One that would likely alienate her forever, should he achieve it.

"Your blue coat, sir?" Kemp asked, opening the carved oaken wardrobe.

Noel shook his head. "Too flashy. Save that for tonight. The brown today, I think. I've an early appointment at Bow Street that's likely to last some time, then I plan to spend the afternoon and evening catching up with the word on the streets in the usual haunts. I've been out of circulation too long."

And starting tonight, he was unlikely to have a chance to approach his usual informants for some days, trapped here by Lady Hardwyck's house party. He was determined to use that opportunity to gather a different sort of information, however. If his suspicions were correct, it would be the only information he would need.

"Thank you, Kemp," he said as his manservant helped him into the brown coat. "Nip down to the kitchens and bring up a roll or two and some coffee, and then we'll be off."

Not knowing what stratum of Society the Black Bishop inhabited in England, Noel had begun with the lowest and worked his way up. Only in the past few weeks had he made real forays into the upper echelons of Society, and he had spent most of that time pursuing the false lead of the Saint.

He wondered if he should publicize the fact that his sister was so highly placed in Society, play up his grandfather's title. Neither fact would remain secret for long, anyway. But then Miss Riverstone's face rose before him.

No, he would wait. For the moment, he preferred she think him a mere son of a younger son. It would make her more likely to tell him what he needed to know.

"Luncheon as well?" Rowena asked in dismay when Pearl appeared in her bedchamber at two o'clock, followed by a maid bearing a covered tray. She had spent the morning writing a draft of her new essay for the *Political Register*. Now she had nothing to do—or even to read.

"I told you, I don't want anyone to see you before our grand unveiling tonight. Guests will begin arriving around six," Pearl continued, joining Rowena at a small table to partake of the tea and sandwiches. "Your gown should arrive by four. What fun it will be to put your toilette together!"

Rowena frowned at her friend. "I'm beginning to feel like a large doll, here for your amusement. I warn you, I won't go down at all if you make me ridiculous."

"Ridiculous?" Pearl's lovely eyes went wide and innocent, which Rowena found not at all reassuring. "Have you no more faith in me than that? You will be stunning, my dear—the belle of the evening. You must trust me."

Rowena nodded. Though she knew that her friend had unrealistic expectations, she could trust her to make certain Rowena's appearance would not be an embarrassment to either of them. It would be up to Rowena to make certain the same was true of her behavior.

Rowena's dress arrived on schedule. Matthilda lifted the emerald silk ballgown from the elegant box and gasped with delight. "Oh, miss!" she exclaimed in hushed tones. "The drawing at the modiste's didn't do it justice."

"No. No, it didn't." Rowena gazed at the shimmering gown in mingled awe and delight.

"Let's see how it looks on, shall we?" Pearl suggested.

Matthilda laced her into her best corset and dropped the silken folds over Rowena's head.

"Oh, Rowena, it's simply scrumptious," Pearl declared. "I wish I could wear such a color. No, don't turn around. Not yet."

Feeling more than ever like a large doll, Rowena stood passively while Matthilda and Pearl fussed about her, her frustration at not being able to see the result growing by the minute. Pins and ribbons were placed just so, with twitches at shoulders and waist to improve the fit of the gown.

"Now the hair. No, not yet, Rowena!" Pearl admonished as she tried to peek over her shoulder at the pier glass. "Francesca must put the finishing touches to you first. Promise not to look." She sent Matthilda to fetch her coiffeuse and a pot of tea.

The moment she arrived, Francesca set to work, murmuring to herself in French and English. "This curl, so. *Ceci aussi.* A ribbon through the top cluster. *Et voila!*" After what seemed an eternity, she stepped back, beaming at her handiwork.

Rowena glanced questioningly at Pearl, who was smiling as broadly as her hairdresser was. "Yes, you can look now."

Almost fearfully, Rowena turned around to see the stranger in the glass—for stranger it certainly appeared to be. Surely, this vision could not be herself?

The emerald green silk brightened the copper of her hair until it nearly glowed. Tied tight under her ample breasts with a darker green ribbon, cut low, but not too low, the gown emphasized her curves, skimming her narrow waist and the generous flare of her hips, making her look voluptuous rather than simply plump.

"Your spectacles, remember?" Pearl prompted as Rowena stared transfixed at her image. She handed her the green silk reticule that had come with the gown.

"Yes. Yes, of course." Still unable to look away from her reflection, Rowena removed her spectacles—and the reflection blurred.

"No squinting," Pearl reminded her as Rowena instinctively squeezed her eyes into better focus. "Here's your reticule. You can keep your spectacles there—in case of emergency."

Rowena glanced at Pearl in vague alarm, but even without seeing her expression clearly, she could tell that her friend was teasing. "Yes, we wouldn't want me to pick up a candlestick instead of a glass of ratafia, or a carnation instead of a canape, would we?"

"Now, now. I know you're not as blind as all that and it's not as though you'll do any reading at a ball. Have you a fan?"

"Yes, right here." Rowena displayed the green silk fan figured in gold that she'd purchased to go with the dress.

Pearl stepped back to take one more good look—an ability Rowena now envied—and nodded her approval. "Excellent. Now, wait here while I get ready myself—it won't take me more than half an hour, I promise."

She bustled off, Francesca in tow, and Rowena sighed. If only she shared Pearl's confidence. Now that her first evening in Society was less than an hour away, she realized afresh how unprepared she really was.

Oh, she looked well enough—far better than she'd ever imagined she could, in fact—but what of the woman beneath the trappings? She had no gift for small talk, for conversing upon trivialities while ignoring the larger issues.

And what would she do, she wondered in sudden panic, if some gentleman were to *flirt* with her? She would be completely out of her element. She'd do far better to remain in her room, where she would be unable to embarrass either Pearl or herself.

Matthilda, returning just then with the tea tray, gasped with delight. "Oh, miss, who'd have ever thought it? You're as beautiful as any fine lady ever was, and that's the truth."

Rowena shook her head, both irritated and flattered by her maid's overblown admiration. "Hardly that, but I do confess the gown suits me well. Have I not taught you by now not to focus on appearances, however?"

"I already know what's underneath," Matthilda replied saucily, setting down the tray. "And that won't have changed, will it? Where's the harm in saying how well you look?"

More than a bit shaken at her maid's so closely echoing her own thoughts, Rowena didn't answer, but moved to pour out the tea instead. She was relieved to discover she could do so without the benefit of her spectacles. Perhaps she could manage this after all, she thought, taking a fortifying sip of the hot liquid.

True to her word, Pearl reappeared not twenty minutes later, resplendent in pale blue satin and snowy Mechlin lace. "Ah, pour me a cup as well, Rowena, do. We still have a few minutes before we need to go down."

This time, conscious of her friend's watchful eye, Rowena spilled a few drops while pouring. Though it was surely due to nervousness rather than nearsightedness, she said, "See what comes of taking away my spectacles? You are fortunate I've sullied only the tray and not your gown."

"Pish! I do that all the time, and my eyes are perfectly fine. You've promised me to go through with our experiment," Pearl, reminded her severely. "Don't you dare cry craven now."

Though she felt a strong inclination to do just that, Rowena shook her head. "No, I'll go through with it."

Pearl laughed. "You needn't make it sound as though you are going to your own execution. Please,

Rowena, do *try* to enjoy yourself tonight. I've invited only a small, select crowd, so you should not be overwhelmed. Let's go down, shall we? The guests will be arriving soon."

Trying her hardest to look cheerful for Pearl's sake, Rowena rose. "Very well. And I will do my best, I promise. It's the least I can do, after all your effort on my behalf."

"That's the spirit! Come, we'll treat it as a military campaign, with you well armed to breach the defenses of whatever forces you meet."

Despite herself, Rowena's spirits rose at the metaphor. Yes, she would pretend the evening was merely an elaborate chess match, where each move by her opponents—the other guests—must be matched by a strategic move of her own. Absurd, of course, but oddly comforting.

They descended the stairs together, to find Lord Hardwyck waiting for them at the bottom. His eyes widened when he caught sight of Rowena, and he glanced questioningly at Pearl, then back at Rowena with an amazement that might have been insulting if she had not reacted the same way to her own changed appearance.

"My dear, you have outdone yourself," he said to his wife. "Miss Riverstone, I scarcely recognized you. You are quite stunning."

Though it came from her friend's husband, it was the first compliment upon her appearance Rowena had received from a man and it flustered her badly. "I, er, thank you, my lord. The credit all goes to Pearl, however."

"I see we need to work on your response to compliments," Pearl admonished her. "You're sure to receive many, and you can't refer them all to me. A simple thank you will suffice, if you do not feel bold enough to return the compliment or playfully accuse the gentleman in question of flattery—also acceptable responses."

Rowena felt her color rising with embarrassment. "I told you I was not ready for this."

"All you need is a bit of practice," Pearl assured her. "That's what tonight is for. Come, you can help me look over the buffet tables to be certain all is as it should be."

Rowena followed obediently, wondering where Mr. Paxton might be. Would she dither as badly when he spoke to her? Undoubtedly. Much as she hoped to see admiration in his eyes, at the moment she felt she'd prefer not to see him at all.

Pearl had just declared adequate the assorted dainties that were to serve in lieu of dinner when the sound of the door knocker reached the ballroom.

"Ah! Our first guests. No, you come with me, Rowena. You needn't greet the guests as they come in, but I'm not giving you an opportunity to hide, either."

Again Rowena followed her friend, this time with gathering dread. *Treat it as a chess match,* she reminded herself firmly. Lifting her chin, she took a position just inside the ballroom, only a few yards from Pearl and her husband.

To her surprise, the first guest was her brother. She had not known Pearl had invited him, though of course it made sense that she had. He completed the pleasantries with his hosts, then turned to the ballroom, only to see Rowena standing there.

Sir Nelson stared, blinked, then stared again. "Gadslife! Ro?" he finally said.

Suddenly struck by the absurdity of the situation, Rowena dropped into a curtsey. "How pleasant to see you again, Nelson," she replied in well-modulated tones. "I'm glad you could come."

"So am I. You look a treat, Ro." Her brother still looked disbelieving. "Lady Hardwyck must be some sort of sorceress to have pulled off such a change."

Both touched and irritated, Rowena clung to her smile. "Merely a new gown and hairstyle—but Pearl can be quite determined when she sets her mind on a project."

As they talked, more guests filtered in and before Rowena knew it, the room was quite crowded. Her earlier panic revived. She glanced at Pearl to find her urgently beckoning to her.

"I want you to meet Lord and Lady Marcus Northrup," Pearl said as Rowena came forward. "Lord Marcus is one of Luke's oldest friends, and his wife is also relatively new to London. You two should get along famously."

The couple greeted Rowena cordially, and she realized that it was easier to meet people who had no idea of the change that had been wrought in her. "Pearl tells me you two were but recently married?" she asked after greetings were exchanged.

"Yes, scarcely three weeks since," replied the diminutive Lady Marcus in a distinctly American accent. "And please, call me Quinn. I'm still not used to my new designation, and am determined to dispense with it when among friends."

Rowena warmed to the young woman at once, put

at ease by her casual air. She was quite different from the simpering, gossiping ladies Rowena met yesterday. They chatted about their impressions of London, while Lord Marcus moved away to speak to two other gentlemen.

"Were you as afraid of breaking some unwritten Society rule as I am?" Rowena asked the charming American.

"Oh, gracious, yes!" Quinn exclaimed. "I still am, in fact. Perhaps we should compare notes and combine our knowledge, to our mutual benefit."

Rowena laughingly agreed that this was a good scheme. Glancing at Pearl again, she saw her greeting an imposing man with a large, hooked nose who looked vaguely familiar. Squinting slightly in an effort to determine where she'd seen him before, she brought someone else into focus, someone who made her heart do a funny little flip.

Mr. Paxton, staring at her in blank astonishment.

Chapter 6

With an effort, Noel pulled his gaze away from Miss Riverstone to answer Luke's question. "No great successes today, but some small progress, or so I hope."

He had already related last night's events to Luke. He had spent the morning at Bow Street, and the afternoon visiting certain taverns and gaming hells, casting for information that might lead to the Bishop. He intended to follow up one lead about a group of radicals said to meet at the Crown and Horn.

"Good, good. We'll talk later," said Luke. "Go on and enjoy yourself. The crab puffs are excellent, I hear."

Noel nodded absently, his attention straying to Miss Riverstone again. What on earth had she done to herself? Her hair . . . that gown . . . and where were her spectacles? Slowly moving in her direction, he was almost surprised he had recognized her so quickly. She looked so different from the mousy chess master he knew and liked.

Before he could reach her side, he was accosted by Lord Marcus.

"Evening, Paxton," he said. "Luke mentioned you were to attend tonight. We'll have to talk later." His expression made it clear that Luke had explained Noel's new mission to Lord Marcus, the last Saint of Seven Dials. "You've met my brother, Lord Peter, and Mr. Thatcher, haven't you?"

Noel greeted all three gentlemen. "Yes, we all met in Vienna, winter before last," he said, regarding the yellow-waistcoated Lord Peter a bit warily. At that time, Lord Marcus's elder brother had considered Noel a bad influence on his friend, laughable as that was considering Harry Thatcher's own propensity for debauchery.

Lord Peter smiled cordially enough now, though his gaze was piercing. "Good to see you again, Paxton. Harry told me you were in Town. Something to do with thief-catching?"

"Yes, I've been working with Bow Street, helping them to run the Saint of Seven Dials to ground. Damnably elusive fellow, I must say," he added with a perfectly straight face. He found it hard to concentrate on the conversation with Miss Riverstone standing only a few feet away, just beyond Lord Peter's shoulder.

The change in her was both startling and disturbing: frilled, flounced and ringleted like every other lady present. Such fripperies seemed out of character. And her spectacles—how well could she see without them? Had she noticed him yet?

"—connection to Lord Ellsdon?" Lord Peter was

saying, snapping Noel's attention back. "In fact, it occurs to me—"

"Yes, you're right," Noel cut him off. Moving a step or two further from Miss Riverstone and Lady Marcus, he continued softly, "As you are no doubt about to surmise, the fact that my aging uncle has only daughters makes me his heir presumptive—something I've been careful not to publicize."

Peter's brows rose, while Marcus and Harry stared at him in evident surprise. "Indeed? The better to move unnoticed among the criminal class, I presume?"

As he had in Vienna, Noel marveled that someone of such dandified appearance as Lord Peter could possess such rapier intellect. "Precisely. If anonymity can help me to track down the slippery Saint—" He broke off. Did Peter know about his brother's involvement?

If so, he gave no sign of it. "Of course. Society won't learn the truth from me—or from any of us. Right, Harry? Marcus?"

The others nodded. "Can't say I blame you," Harry remarked, reaching for a glass of wine with his remaining arm. His left had been lost in the recent war. "Bloody nuisances, titles, from all I've seen. Even courtesy ones." He grinned at Lord Marcus. "Make you do idiot things like get married."

"The title had nothing—" Marcus began, then broke off with a shake of his head, perceiving that Harry was bamming him. "I'd say Peter had better watch out, then."

Lord Peter shrugged. "I'm willing enough, should the proper lady come along. Now Harry, here—if ever a man could benefit by matrimony—"

Harry Thatcher snorted and made an extremely rude reply, but Noel's attention had wandered back to Miss Riverstone, who now seemed to have attracted several male admirers. Damn it.

"If you'll excuse me?" he murmured to the arguing trio and moved away without waiting for a reply. Innocent as she was, someone should definitely warn Miss Riverstone away from such questionable personages as Mr. Galloway, a known fortune hunter, and Lord Fernworth, a complete fribble—both of whom appeared to be ogling her in a most improper manner.

"Well met, Miss Riverstone," he greeted her with forced heartiness, making the whole group around her swing around to face him. "Dare I hope to engage you in another chess match later?"

Galloway's brows rose and he regarded Miss Riverstone curiously, while Fernworth actually took a step away from her. Noel took advantage of the opportunity to move closer.

"This scarcely seems the setting, Mr. Paxton," she replied with a look he couldn't quite decipher.

Rowena had been achingly aware of Mr. Paxton's slow approach, but now that he had reached her, she felt more irritated than pleased. Beyond that first surprised glance, he showed no indication he even noticed the dramatic change in her appearance—not that she wanted his flattery, of course. Still . . .

"So you play chess, Miss Riverstone?" asked Mr. Galloway. "I'd like a match as well, sometime. I'm quite fond of the game."

She regarded the too-charming redheaded man with some amusement. When he had called on Pearl yesterday, he'd completely ignored her, but now he was overflowing with compliments.

Five minutes' conversation with him had only reinforced her low opinion of gentlemen's perceptiveness—though he did seem more intelligent than Lord Fernworth.

"Certainly, sir, should the opportunity arise."

Mr. Paxton had the effrontery to chuckle. "I should like to watch that match, I think. Shall I ask Lady Hardwyck to provide a board and a suitable corner somewhere?"

"Now?" Rowena asked in surprise. Not that she wasn't sorely tempted to retreat from this alien milieu to a more familiar one—

"Don't be absurd, Paxton," Lord Fernworth exclaimed. "Chess at a ball? You may be the biggest stick-in-the-mud in London, but there's no need to drag Miss Riverstone into your dull pursuits when so many more amusing ones offer."

Lady Marcus nodded. "I fear he's right, Mr. Paxton. This is Miss Riverstone's first Society function, after all. It would be a shame for her to miss any of it."

Rowena stifled a sigh. They were right, of course. And much as she enjoyed chess, she had to admit the experience of being admired by handsome gentlemen was a rather enjoyable novelty.

"Indeed, Lady Hardwyck gave me strict orders to meet as many people as possible tonight," she said. "As kind as she has been, I wish to be obedient."

"I was jesting, of course," Mr. Paxton said with a smile she thought looked rather forced. "I believe Lady Hardwyck said something about a card party tomorrow. That will be a far more suitable venue."

Was the man so determined to prove her win two nights since had been an anomaly? It was unlikely he simply wished to spend time with her, oblivious as he seemed to her appearance tonight. More nettled than she cared to admit by his indifference, she turned to Mr. Galloway with a smile.

"Will you be attending tomorrow as well, sir?"

He bowed gallantly. "I wouldn't miss another evening in your company for the world, Miss Riverstone."

Lord Fernworth snorted. "Won't miss a chance at cards, he means. If you can lure him away from *vingt-un* I'll be amazed."

"Prepare to be amazed, then," Mr. Galloway retorted, with a wink at Rowena. Flustered, she made no response.

"I'll stick to cards myself," Lord Fernworth said, missing the byplay. "Never been much for chess."

Mr. Paxton watched her rather knowingly. "I'm sure Miss Riverstone will oblige you both with a hand or two of whist."

That was the card game Rowena found to rely most on skill—and therefore the one at which she most excelled. Mr. Paxton must dislike these two gentlemen intensely to be so eager to see her best them at something.

"Or perhaps I'll try my hand at *vingt-un,*" she said with a warning glance at Mr. Paxton. She would not be a tool for any male posturing.

Vingt-un relied far more on luck than did whist, but Pearl had warned her that most gentlemen were put off by a lady who exceeded their own skills. If she wished to make her mark in Society, she must strive to suppress her competitive tendencies—at least until she was established.

"Dare I hope you still have a dance or two free?" Mr. Paxton asked then, obediently dropping the topic of cards.

The question revived all of Rowena's earlier nervousness. "Mr. Galloway has asked for the first set, but I am free after that."

"The second set, then? And perhaps a waltz?" Those penetrating hazel eyes soothed her with unspoken reassurance.

She relaxed marginally, though her senses tingled with his nearness. "Very well, sir." She didn't dare waltz with anyone else, in fact, as unschooled as she yet was at the new dance. But she could trust Mr. Paxton to overlook her inevitable errors.

"Third set to me, then?" Lord Fernworth asked.

As Rowena assented, Lord Marcus approached to introduce his brother and Mr. Thatcher, each of whom also claimed a dance. More people joined their circle, and soon Rowena was bespoken for most of the evening.

Amazement warred with both fear and delight. Pearl had been quite correct, it seemed. She only hoped she could get through the evening without committing any monumental gaffes.

While guests continued to stream into Pearl's "select" gathering, the orchestra started tuning its instruments.

"The dancing will begin in a few minutes," Mr. Paxton commented. "Would you care to visit the buffet tables beforehand?"

Suppressing a small thrill at his attentiveness, Rowena agreed, gingerly placing a hand on the crooked arm he held out to her. He looked far more handsome in his formal attire than she'd expected, making her nervous in his presence despite the rapport they'd achieved previously.

"See that man there, between the pillar and the potted palm?" He pointed. "That's the Duke of Wellington. I'll introduce you to him later."

Rowena looked eagerly in the indicated direction, but saw only a blurred figure of a tall man on the opposite side of the ballroom. With an impatient exclamation, she opened her reticule to retrieve her spectacles, but then noticed Mr. Galloway on her other side, watching her.

Guiltily, she dropped the reticule, mentally chiding herself for vanity. "Thank you," she said to Mr. Paxton. "I will look forward to that."

He rather transparently smothered a grin, letting her know that he'd noticed her dilemma. "Up close, you'll understand how he acquired the affectionate nickname of Old Nosey among his men."

"Up close?" Mr. Galloway laughed. "Why, you can see the fellow's proboscis from here."

Rowena realized he must be the man she had noticed earlier, greeting Pearl. She looked his way again and nodded, ignoring Mr. Paxton's amusement at her plight. She had promised Pearl to do without her spectacles as much as possible. This was not vanity—she was merely keeping her word.

"The duke's abilities must surely make up for any deficiencies of appearance," she said. "By all accounts, he is a brilliant military strategist."

Both gentlemen agreed, and fell to discussing one of his more famous campaigns. Rowena refrained from asking questions about the specifics, though she listened avidly.

"I am reliably informed that the crab puffs are excellent," said Mr. Paxton, dropping the military topic as they reached the buffet tables. "Perhaps some orgeat to drink as well?"

Rowena scanned the table, remembering not to squint, but before she could identify the crab puffs, Mr. Galloway had placed two upon a plate and handed them to her.

"Thank you." Relief gave her words added warmth, which he appeared to misinterpret, judging by his wide smile and the sudden sparkle in his blue eyes.

"Anything for a lovely lady," he said, and there was no denying the suggestiveness in his tone.

Suddenly uncomfortable, Rowena took a bite of crab puff, coughing when she swallowed too quickly. Her eyes watered and she tried desperately to get her breath back.

"Your orgeat." Mr. Paxton was at her elbow, offering a glass, concern in his eyes.

Rowena gulped gratefully, her eyes conveying her thanks until she could speak. "I—I didn't realize the puffs would be so flaky," she finally said by way of explanation. "I've never tasted one before."

"Really?" asked Mr. Galloway in evident surprise. "They're a staple at such dos here in Town. Do they not serve them at country balls?"

"Perhaps Miss Riverstone has had better things to do in the country than attend balls," Mr. Paxton suggested before she could answer.

Though he was perfectly right, she shot him an annoyed glance. Did he *want* her to appear a bookish rustic? She was likely enough to do so without his help. Just then, the orchestra struck up the opening chords to a minuet.

"This is our dance, is it not, Mr. Galloway?" she said sweetly, handing plate and empty glass to Mr. Paxton. She barely had time to see him raise one brow as she turned away.

Mr. Galloway led her to the floor with alacrity and she took her place opposite him. He bowed, she curtsied, and the dance began. For the first few minutes Rowena concentrated on her steps but it was a dance she'd known since childhood, and soon she felt secure enough to pay attention to those around her.

"I confess, I'm racking my brains to think what you might have done in the country that could be more enjoyable than a ball," Mr. Galloway said when the movement of the dance brought them together again.

Rowena decided it was safest to blend truth with convention. "I have been in charge of my brother's household for the past few years," she said, "and I see to the needs of our tenants. Not more enjoyable, perhaps, but necessary."

"But surely that leaves you some time for more pleasurable pursuits?" He waggled his sandy eyebrows. "Lusty country squires? Novels, perhaps?"

"I do read, yes," she admitted. Luckily, the dance moved them apart before she could add that her reading choices rarely encompassed anything so light as novels. No, better not to elaborate on that, or on her lack of beaux in the country.

When next they came together, her partner related tidbits of gossip about two or three of their fellow guests, identifying them with nods as he spoke. Rowena smiled and obediently looked in the indicated directions, though none were close enough to see clearly.

Just as well. She did not care to have her opinions clouded by such trivialities.

By the end of the dance, she had regretfully concluded that Mr. Galloway had no depth to his personality, flattering as his compliments might be. She hoped all of her partners would not prove the same.

"I thank you for an enjoyable dance, Miss Riverstone," he said, bowing gallantly. "Dare I hope you will favor me with another later on?"

She smiled politely, but noncommittally. "Perhaps. Thank you, Mr. Galloway."

It occurred to her that at least *one* of her partners promised interesting conversation. Her spirits rose, recalling that she was promised to Mr. Paxton for the next set. She was easily able to pick him out of the crowd as he approached.

When he was close enough for her to decipher the expression on his face, she was reminded that she had all but snubbed him at the buffet tables—even though he had been perfectly correct.

"Are you still willing to partner me?" she asked as soon as Mr. Galloway moved out of earshot. "I was rather rude to you, I fear."

To her relief, he grinned. "And I was baiting you, so I certainly deserved it. Unworthy of me, I know."

The orchestra struck up a waltz then, and his grin turned to mock dismay. "Unfair!" he exclaimed. "I had hoped for this dance *and* a waltz, and now I find the two are one."

Rowena felt a distinct surge of pleasure at this evidence that he enjoyed her company. He was, after all, the handsomest man she had seen here tonight, and could presumably claim dances with any lady present.

"Suppose I promise you the next waltz as well, should there be another?" she asked shyly as he took her gloved hand in his. "*You* already know how little I excel at this dance, but I would prefer that not become common knowledge."

She realized too late that her words might be construed as either flirtation or an insult, but he appeared to take them as neither, smiling warmly down at her. "Your secret is safe with me," he promised.

Where Mr. Galloway's closeness had made her uncomfortable, Mr. Paxton's caused tendrils of pleasure to curl through her midsection. Still, remembering what he'd said earlier, she felt obliged to ask, "And what of my other secrets?"

"I do apologize," he said, only the tiniest flicker of amusement in his eyes. "It is simply that I find the real you more interesting than this pattern card of propriety you are attempting to emulate tonight. I hate seeing you hide your light under a bushel—even such an exceedingly attractive bushel."

She felt herself blushing. Pearl had said something similar, but with far different meaning, regarding her usual plain appearance as the disguise. No wonder she felt so comfortable with this man—if "comfortable" was the right word.

The dance began and she followed his lead, belatedly grateful for her practice session yesterday. Without it, she'd have been forced to sit out any waltzes tonight. Earlier she had thought dancing would be torture, but now she was quite—pleased—to be able to participate in this particular dance.

"You are doing splendidly," Mr. Paxton commented after giving her a few moments to settle into the movements of the waltz. "I must be a better teacher than I realized."

Rowena smiled up at him, trying to ignore her pleasure at his words. "How like a man, to take the credit for a woman's achievement."

His brows rose, acknowledging the hit, but then she missed her step and he quickly adjusted his own to compensate before anyone watching could have noticed her mistake.

"Very well, I'll give you credit for that one," she said.

He laughed aloud, drawing glances from those around them. Quickly, he lowered his voice, though his eyes still danced. "You are a true original, Miss Riverstone. And I mean that as a compliment of the highest order."

Rowena refrained from pointing out that he'd become more liberal with his compliments since her appearance had improved. Certainly he was not so shallow as Mr. Galloway and his ilk, but she could not deny that his attitude toward her had changed subtly since seeing her in her new guise.

"Is your brother, Sir Nelson, to attend tonight?" he asked, when she made no reply.

She glanced at him in surprise. "Have you been making inquiries about my family, sir? Yes, Nelson is here. He was one of the first to arrive."

"Indeed? I should rather like to meet him. If you are any indication, he's likely to be an interesting man to talk to."

She felt flattered both by his compliment and this evidence of interest—wishing to meet her brother must indicate interest in her, mustn't it? Glancing up at him, however, she caught something in his expression that reminded her of the one he wore while playing chess.

"I'll introduce you at first opportunity," she told him, wondering if she had imagined it. What sort of strategizing could he be doing in a ballroom, after all?

"Thank you." He still looked somber, but before she could think how to ask about it, he smiled. "Care to attempt a twirl?"

Sudden panic drove all thoughts of Mr. Paxton's preoccupation from her mind. "A twirl? Do you think that's wise?" she whispered, as though he had suggested she petition Parliament to restructure the entire government.

"I believe you are up to the challenge," he responded with an encouraging wink that only flustered her further. "Take your hand from my shoulder, and turn to your right."

He removed his own hand from her back, lifting their joined hands higher, and she awkwardly followed his direction, turning about completely until she faced him again. She stumbled at the end of her twirl, but he quickly placed his hand at her back again, and she clutched at his shoulder for balance.

"Right," he said in apparent satisfaction, despite her clumsiness. "Now back to the steps: *one*, two, three, *one*, two, three." He counted until her steps were in time with his.

Relieved, she managed a shaky laugh. "At least I did not fall on my face. I think I would prefer not to attempt any more twirls at present, however." Indeed, her heart was hammering so quickly that it was all she could do to keep to the rhythm of the dance.

"Coward," he teased, just as Pearl had chided him yesterday. "I thought you more adventurous than that."

She raised her chin, spurred by his jibe to tell him she would attempt any maneuver he suggested, but fortunately the waltz came to an end just then. Casting about for something to say that would prove she was not afraid to try new things, she saw her brother approaching.

"Here comes Nelson," she said, abandoning her unladylike desire to have the last word. "Shall I introduce you?"

Mr. Paxton followed her gaze, successfully diverted. "Please," he replied, belatedly releasing his hold on her.

Rowena suppressed a small sigh as his hand left hers. For a short while, it had almost seemed—

"Ro, may I have a word with you?" her brother said the moment he reached them. He appeared vaguely troubled, she thought.

"Certainly. But first I'd like to introduce Mr. Paxton, a friend of Lord Hardwyck's. Mr. Paxton, my brother, Sir Nelson Riverstone."

The gentlemen shook hands. "Pleased to meet you,"

Nelson said distractedly. Rowena wondered what could have him so agitated.

"Likewise," Mr. Paxton responded. "I have heard your work at the Home Office spoken of highly."

Now Nelson's attention was caught. "Have you, then? That's nice to hear, I must say. We'll talk later, shall we? Need to have a quick word with my sister first."

"Certainly, certainly." Mr. Paxton bowed to them both and moved away.

Rowena frowned uncertainly at her brother. "I am engaged for the next dance with Lord Fernworth."

"Really? Making quite a splash tonight, I see. Good for you. But you can make it up to him later. I've just realized you're my best hope for dealing with a rather sticky situation." To her surprise, he actually flushed. "Ro, I have a problem, and I need your help."

Chapter 7

"Problem?" Rowena asked her brother in surprise. "What sort of problem?"

Before he could answer, Lord Fernworth appeared to remind her of their dance. Judging by his slurred speech and silly grin, he had clearly had too much to drink already. Rowena was just as glad to have an excuse to put him off.

"Would you mind terribly if we had our dance another time?" she asked, trying not to let her distaste show. "My brother had a prior claim, which I had forgotten."

Lord Fernworth waved one hand grandly. "Of course, of course. Not much of a dancer anyway."

Shocked, Rowena wondered frantically if the whole room had noticed her inexperience. Surely, if the inebriated Lord Fernworth had been able to tell—

"Prefer to spend my time at the card tables, you see," he continued. "Takes practice to be a good dancer, and I've not had enough. Was hoping to convince you to sit it out, actually."

"I've had little practice myself, Lord Fernworth," she confessed in her relief. "I'll be happy to sit out a dance with you later."

"Certainly, certainly." His voice was too loud, his gestures too broad, but at least he was affable about it. With a final wave, he wandered away.

At once, Rowena turned back to Nelson. "Now, what is this problem you need me to help you with?"

"Let's get out of the crowd first," he suggested, indicating a pair of chairs in a corner, well away from both the dance floor and those milling about the edges.

Growing increasingly curious, Rowena accompanied him, waiting until they were seated to say, "Well?"

He ran a finger between his neck and cravat before answering. "It's, ah, rather embarrassing, actually. A problem of a, er, financial nature. Now that you've access to your inheritance, it occurs to me that you may be able to help. You see, I, ah . . ." He trailed off, clearly debating how much to tell her.

Striving to hide her astonishment that Nelson was actually asking for her help, Rowena touched his hand. "Come, you know you can trust me. Is it gaming debts?" Nelson had always had a weakness for cards.

He nodded, dropping his gaze from her direct one. "Aye, you've hit it. I'm in pretty deep—too deep, in fact."

Rowena felt her first real flicker of alarm. "What do you mean? Is the estate at risk?"

"No, of course not," Nelson said quickly, looking

up. "It's entailed. But I never should have . . ." Again he hesitated.

"Have what? What have you done, Nelson?"

"I've . . . I've pawned some of Mother's jewelry, for a start," he said.

She stared, anger beginning to stir. "Do you mean you brought it to Town with you?" That jewelry was among the few things they had to remember their mother by. "Which pieces?" she asked then. "Not the—"

He nodded miserably. "The diamond and emerald set—necklace, earrings and brooch."

Rowena jumped to her feet. "We must redeem them at once, then. Where is the pawnshop?"

Nelson pulled her back down beside him. "Shh! Don't make a scene, Ro. And it's no use—they'll have been sold by now."

"Sold? How long ago did you pawn them?"

"Back in June."

She stared at him in dismay. "And you've only become concerned now? Why? Because I'm in Town?"

He shrugged. "It's not the first time—that is . . ."

"You've done this before?" She'd suspected once or twice over the past year that Nelson was engaging in high play, but never had she suspected he had actually run into debt.

"Only things of my own, one or two smaller bits of jewelry Father left me, when I was badly dipped," he said, as though that excused his actions.

"But the diamonds weren't your own."

Nelson didn't meet her eyes. "Yes I know. They were yours. But I thought they would bring enough to finally satisfy him, and it didn't seem likely you would ever wear them."

She ignored the subtle insult. "But you still owe money, even after selling the diamonds?"

"He offered me another game, to wipe out my debts if I won. But I lost. And now . . . now he's threatening to bruit it about that I'm in dun territory if—"

"And who is 'he?' " she interrupted. "Who is this man who cheats men at cards, then extorts them?"

Nelson glanced about them in alarm, then shook his head. "Never said he cheated. I wouldn't dare, even if I believed it, which I don't. He'd likely kill me for it. A crack shot, everyone says. And very highly regarded among the intellectual set. Moves in higher circles than I do, anyway."

"Nelson!" exclaimed Rowena in exasperation. "Who *is* he?"

"Lester Richards."

"Lester Richards?" she repeated, stunned. "Mr. Lester Richards, the Spencean reformer?"

Her brother shrugged. "I don't follow such things, but yes, I'm sure it's the same man. He attends salons at Holland House, that sort of thing."

"But—I don't understand," she said lamely, seeing no point in telling Nelson that she positively idolized Mr. Richards. She had done so for nearly a year, ever since reading a persuasive essay he'd written promoting some of the very causes she herself espoused. How could he possibly be victimizing her brother?

"Nor do I, precisely," Nelson admitted. "He seems a likeable chap, if rather intense. Always asking questions about my work at Whitehall, that sort of thing."

Rowena was thinking hard. Mr. Richards, champion of the common man, must need the money for his cause—in which case she couldn't really blame him. "If you can't afford to pay, you must tell him so."

"Now why didn't I think of that?" asked Nelson sarcastically. "And then Mr. Richards can simply make certain no one will accept my vouchers again."

"Perhaps that would be for the best," Rowena told him bluntly. "In fact, I'm certain Mr. Richards would do so for your own good." That fit more with her idea of her hero.

Nelson seemed unmoved by such a charitable motive for his own ruin. "You don't know, Ro. You've no idea what it would be like: unwelcome at any of the clubs, merchants unwilling to extend credit—I'd be humiliated. I have a reputation to maintain, you know. Not to mention my position at the Home Office."

After a few more moments of thought, a bold solution presented itself. "Suppose I speak with Mr. Richards? I'm certain he will be perfectly reasonable, once he knows how you are placed." It would be the perfect excuse to finally meet her idol.

Though he looked skeptical, Nelson nodded. "I'm willing for you to try, anyway. Tell him I'll pay him the rest of what I owe him when I get the next quarter's rents."

"And we must look into getting Mother's jewelry back, as well. Find out what it will cost, if the pieces are still at the pawnshop, and I will give you the money." Rowena now regretted spending so much on clothing for herself.

Instantly brightening, he nodded. "I'll check, and let you know. You're the best of sisters, Ro. I should have known you'd come through." He leaned down to kiss her cheek. She accepted the caress guiltily, knowing she had another motive.

"And you *must* not gamble any more, Nelson," she added. "Promise me."

"Of course, of course." He flipped open a snuffbox and took a pinch. "I've learned my lesson."

She rose. "I should hope so. Now, I must find Lord Peter Northrup—I promised him the next dance." She couldn't help enjoying the surprise on her brother's face at this evidence of her popularity. "If you think of anything else I should know, you can send word to me here at Hardwyck Hall."

Nelson cheerfully waved her on her way. Too cheerfully, she feared, but she considered her promise to meet with Mr. Richards with growing enthusiasm. She'd dreamed of that meeting since first deciding to come to London. He was surely a man worth knowing—intelligent, committed to a worthy cause, and with the connections to enforce changes.

For a moment, the memory of Mr. Paxton's face distracted her. But handsome and intelligent though he might be, he did not seem to share her ideals for reform. Quite the opposite, in fact. How might he react to her future friendship with Mr. Richards?

Noel watched from the edge of the floor as Miss Riverstone made her apologies to Lord Fernworth, then accompanied her brother, who seemed agitated about something. But what?

Could Riverstone possibly suspect that Noel was on to him? No, most likely it was some personal matter completely unrelated to his mission. Still, he couldn't afford to let his best lead escape. He moved along the edge of the dance floor so that he could observe them from a distance.

As her brother spoke, Miss Riverstone herself became visibly upset, first seeming to accuse, and then to reassure him. So, big brother found himself in some sort of scrape, and little sister was promising to help him out of it? That was Noel's guess—and experience had proved his guesses accurate more often than not.

From the look on Sir Nelson's face as his sister left him, he clearly believed she could help him. She was intelligent, and her brother appeared to trust her. Might she possess the information Noel needed to solve his case? If Sir Nelson was the essayist, she would surely know it. Might she be aware of his treasonous activities as well? Surely she couldn't condone—

She was coming his way. Not wishing to be caught staring, he quickly turned to find himself facing Lord Peter Northrup and Harry Thatcher, who had been in conversation just behind him.

"—last night. Or so the servants claimed, according to the paper," Lord Peter was saying. "If they're right, it appears the Saint is still quite active among us."

Noel hid a smile. "So you're among the group that believes that the Saint of Seven Dials is a member of the *ton*?" he asked.

"He'd almost have to be, wouldn't he?" asked Harry, gesturing with a half-empty wineglass. "Not for a job like last night's—any street thief could have broken into an empty house, after all. But some of his more legendary heists have occurred in the middle of Society dos, where no one but high sticklers were present."

"Except servants," Noel pointed out. "He could simply be an enterprising footman."

Lord Peter nodded. "Just what I've said myself. No need for the Upper Ten Thousand to go about suspecting each other—though I'll admit it's possible he's one of us. Easier for a gentleman to ape a servant than—Ah, Miss Riverstone!" he exclaimed then, looking over Noel's shoulder.

Noel forced himself not to look around, though the temptation was strong. He could feel his body responding to her presence.

"Pray forgive me for not seeking you out sooner," Lord Peter continued. "This is our dance, is it not? Come, I'll tell you the latest news." He led her to the floor, chattering about the Saint's latest caper, while she listened with apparent eagerness.

Once her back was to him, Noel turned to watch her, his eyes enjoying her progress while his brain dissected the conversation just past. He hadn't expected the servants to find his card so quickly. Still, that might work to his advantage.

"Pretty thing, isn't she?" Harry said, breaking into his thoughts. "At least, if you like that bookish type. Can't say that's my usual style, but I'd not say no to a tumble with her."

Noel rounded on him, a swift, unreasonable anger nearly stealing his control. "I can't think Miss Riverstone is the sort to offer you one," he said coldly, fighting down an irrational urge to plant the fellow a facer.

"No, probably not, more's the pity," Harry responded, oblivious to Noel's sudden fury.

With an effort, Noel brought his emotions into check. He couldn't help thinking of some of the women Harry had seduced in Vienna. The very idea of Miss Riverstone being numbered among such ill-bred, willing wenches—Mentally, he shook himself. What was wrong with him? Harry always talked like this.

"So, what was this story you and Peter were discussing, about the Saint?" he asked, as much to change the subject as to learn what was being said about his adventure last night.

But as Harry related the details—accurate for the most part, but with some embellishments on the part of the servants—Noel found his attention drifting again to the dance floor, where Miss Riverstone was dancing the Boulanger.

She smiled up at Lord Peter as their hands touched. He spoke a few words and she laughed, then the movements of the dance parted them. But now she was facing Mr. Galloway again, and the fellow was leering at her even more offensively than he had during the minuet.

Clearly, Noel hadn't managed to discourage the fellow by drawing Miss Riverstone into talk of chess and politics. He would have to risk her ire by broaching those topics again, he supposed. Better that than she fall victim to a rogue like Galloway.

Because that would undermine his goal, of course. He needed to reach a level of intimacy with her where she would not hesitate to tell him everything she knew. Therefore, he must make certain she cared more about him than about any other man.

It made perfect sense.

* * *

By midnight, Rowena was ready to drop with weariness. She had now danced at least twice as long as the longest lesson she'd ever had. How on earth did Society ladies hold up, dancing for hours on end, night after night—in corsets? She wouldn't be plump for long, if she kept this up.

"Thank you, Lord Marcus," she said as an unnecessarily vigorous country dance ended. Clearly these Society types carried on until all hours on a regular basis—so she must learn to do likewise, if she was to fit in.

"The honor was mine, Miss Riverstone. Ah! That would be the supper dance," he said then, as the orchestra began a waltz. "If you will excuse me, I am promised to my wife for this one." He bowed over her hand and made a quick departure.

Rowena smiled after him, thinking how lucky his wife was to have such a devoted husband—as lucky as Pearl. Perhaps happiness in marriage for an intelligent woman was not so impossible as she had always—

"My dance, I believe?" came a familiar voice at her elbow.

Turning, Rowena fought down the blush that threatened at Mr. Paxton's appearance on the heels of her foolish fancy. He could have no notion of her thoughts, after all. She summoned a smile and a careless air.

"Thank you, sir. I am yet nervous of attempting a waltz with anyone else," she said, placing her hand in his outstretched one, determinedly ignoring the effect the contact had on totally unrelated parts of her body.

He placed his other hand at her back, intensifying

the effect. "You needn't be, from what I have observed tonight. You are extremely quick at covering any small errors you make while dancing."

Mortified that he had noticed such errors—and she knew there had been dozens—she averted her gaze as he moved her into the dance. "Thank you . . . I think."

He didn't respond for so long that she finally glanced up at him again, to find him looking sheepish. "That was a clumsy thing to say," he responded to her questioning look. "I'm not particularly gifted at compliments, am I? For that's what I meant that to be."

"And I should have taken it as such," she replied, her earlier embarrassment evaporating. "I've made no secret to you that I am unused to dancing. I only hope to keep some portion of the room relatively ignorant of that fact."

"I'm quite certain they have no suspicion," he assured her with a smile that set her nerves tingling again.

She wasn't sure whether she believed him, but was grateful for his reassurance nonetheless.

"I owe you another apology," he continued before she could respond.

"You . . . you do?" She'd have liked to blame her concentration on the steps of the dance for her conversational shortcomings, but she feared that was not the true culprit.

He nodded. "I had promised to introduce you to General Wellington. He left early, however, and heads back to Paris tomorrow."

Sudden disappointment stole a measure of Rowena's pleasure in dancing with Mr. Paxton. "I am sorry to hear that—but it is scarcely your fault, sir."

"No, I suppose not. And I did try to catch your attention earlier, while I was talking with him, but you were quite absorbed in the dance, and your partners, at the time."

Did she detect a faint trace of disapproval—even jealousy? Surely not, but it was pleasant to imagine. "I would far rather have spoken with the Duke, had I known," she said with perfect truth. He could be reassured or not.

"In recompense, suppose I repeat to you everything he said, over supper?" Mr. Paxton offered. "Mind you, I only spoke with him briefly."

"I—I should like that." She hoped he interpreted her response as pertaining to talk of the duke, not to the prospect of having supper together. That *was* what she meant, of course.

The dance ended, and he led her to one of the small tables set up near the buffet and held out a chair. "Do you suppose your brother would care to join us?" he asked, glancing about the room.

Again, Rowena couldn't help feeling a bit flattered that he wished to make her brother's acquaintance, but she had to shake her head regretfully. "I fear he has already gone. He . . . was not feeling well."

"Nothing serious, I hope." Did she imagine that glimmer of knowingness in his eyes? "Perhaps you can tell me a bit about him as we eat—after I tell you about Wellington, of course."

"Er, certainly," she replied, though of course she could not tell him about Nelson's dilemma.

"Would you like me to get a plate for you, or would you prefer to make your own selections?" he asked then.

"I will trust your judgment." She didn't relish the idea of choosing foods she could not see clearly. Tired as she was, she was sure to squint.

While Rowena waited for him to return, Pearl stopped at the table. "How are you holding up, Rowena? You've been every bit the success I predicted, you must admit."

Rowena returned her smile. "I won't deny I'm exhausted, but I have enjoyed myself for the most part. Thank you, Pearl."

"I'm sorry that I've been unable to introduce you to any of the intellectual set, as I'd hoped. Even the Duke of Wellington left before I could bring you to his notice. However, there is one gentleman—"

Mr. Paxton returned just then with two heaped plates, a footman with glasses hovering behind him. "Will you be joining us, Lady Hardwyck?" he asked pleasantly.

Pearl shook her head. "Luke is waiting for me over there, once I've had a chance to make certain everyone is well situated for supper. I hope you are finding everything to your liking."

He and Rowena both assured her that they were. She moved on to speak with Lord and Lady Mountheath and their daughters, leaving Rowena to wonder who she had been about to mention before Mr. Paxton had interrupted them.

"Wellington is pleased with the peacetime progress in Paris, but finds administrative duties terribly dull," Mr. Paxton said as he seated himself across from her.

"Indeed? What of the rumors that Napoleon may attempt another escape?" she asked, Pearl's unfinished sentence forgotten.

They talked of Wellington and the politics of war and peace as they ate, Rowena eagerly adding specifics to her more general knowledge of recent and current events. Mr. Paxton seemed remarkably well informed.

Every now and then something in his expression would recall her to the present. Was he amused by her interest in such things? But amusement did not seem to be the precise emotion behind the occasional unsettling intensity of his gaze. She tried to remind herself that such a thirst for knowledge was unconventional, even unladylike, but as long as he was willing to supply so much information, she was more than willing to absorb it.

"I'm now giving you more surmise than fact," he said at last. "As I said, I only spoke with Wellington for a few minutes. But you were going to tell me a bit about your brother, were you not?" Again, there was a certain acuteness to his gaze.

Suddenly self-conscious, Rowena glanced down and was surprised to see that she had eaten everything on her plate. So much dancing had given her quite an appetite.

"Yes, of course. What did you wish to know?"

"What sort of man he is, what sort of work he does. Are the two of you very close? Is he . . . protective of you?"

Rowena's breath caught. Was he asking whether he would need Nelson's permission to . . . to court her? No, of course he wasn't.

"I can't say we've been particularly close in recent years," she confessed. "Once he went off to Cambridge, I rarely saw him. From there, he went to the

Home Office, where Father obtained a position for him. Since Father's death, he has taken on more important duties there."

"What sort of duties?"

Rowena shrugged. "He's never discussed them with me, to be honest. I know more about his work from what I read in the papers than from anything he has said to me."

"The papers?"

"Well, nothing specifically about Nelson, of course, but occasional news items mention John Addington, under whom he works. They seem primarily concerned with implementing Parliament's charges for peacetime defense and the rebuilding of the economy."

She thought Mr. Paxton looked vaguely disappointed, but couldn't imagine why.

"Surely, now that you are in Town, you will be seeing more of him?" he asked. "He must have wished that, to send for you."

"Oh, he did not send for me," she exclaimed without thinking. "That is, he was pleased to see me, of course." That was stretching the truth a bit, but he would not know that. "But I decided to come on my own."

"Did you? Why?"

Rowena hesitated, trying to formulate an answer that would be both truthful and vague. But before she could manage it, she felt a touch on her shoulder. Glancing up, she saw Pearl and an unfamiliar gentlemen.

"Rowena, I promised to introduce to you the more interesting of my guests," Pearl said with a smile toward her companion. The wiry, dark-haired man returned it briefly, though his angular face, more interesting than handsome, remained somber.

"Mr. Richards, let me make known to you Miss Riverstone, my oldest, dearest friend. I can't help but think you will find her opinions both well-informed and interesting. Rowena, Mr. Paxton, may I present Mr. Lester Richards."

Rowena stared up at her idol, the chandelier behind him casting a halo of light about his head that blurred and exalted his features. Struck speechless, Rowena could only offer him her hand, scarcely noticing Pearl's departure. He bowed, never taking his piercing dark eyes—his most attractive feature—from hers.

"I am charmed to make your acquaintance, Miss Riverstone," the older man said in a deep, cultured voice. "Lady Hardwyck speaks highly of your . . . abilities."

Fighting down a blush, Rowena wondered whether he remembered the two rather gushing letters she'd written him. "Pearl is exceedingly kind. I am pleased to meet you, Mr. Richards. I would love to discuss Spencean philosophy with you sometime."

"I am at your disposal, of course." There was no denying the amusement in his eyes. No doubt he thought she was merely flattered to be meeting someone of his stature and speaking of things she didn't understand.

"Tell me, what think you of Mr. Spence's later treatises, where he elaborated on the natural law he first proposed in *The Real Rights of Man?*" she asked, both because she was interested and to show him she knew the subject well.

His brows rose, and she was gratified to see a dawning respect in his eyes. "I think—" he began, but was interrupted by a throat-clearing behind Rowena.

Guiltily, she turned. "Oh! Mr. Richards, Mr. Paxton is a friend of Lord Hardwyck's. He is in Town to catch the Saint of Seven Dials, among other things."

Mr. Richards inclined his head toward the younger man. "Honored, of course, Mr. Paxton. I have . . . heard of your work." His smooth voice dripped disapproval.

"And I have heard of yours, such as it is," Mr. Paxton replied, his tone no more cordial.

Frowning, Rowena glanced from one gentleman to the other. Clearly they had not met before, but their instant antagonism was unmistakable.

"I take it you do not approve of my efforts to correct an inequitable system of government." Mr. Richards' words echoed Rowena's thoughts.

But Mr. Paxton did not rise to the bait, as she had expected him to. "Your efforts to influence Parliament are of little consequence," he replied with a smile that did not reach his eyes. "It is your impact on impressionable young minds that I find cause for concern."

Unwilling to witness an argument between two men she would prefer to have as friends, Rowena spoke up. "Suppose you join us, Mr. Richards, so that we can all debate our varying views on the subject."

Rowena belatedly remembered that she had promised Nelson to plead his case with Mr. Richards—

though now she had met him, she found it even harder to believe he was pressuring her brother for money. This was clearly not the time, in any event.

"You are kindness itself, Miss Riverstone, as well as a born diplomat," he said. "Perhaps another time." With a bow, pointedly in her direction rather than Mr. Paxton's, he took his leave of them.

Chapter 8

Noel watched Mr. Richards' retreating back with a frown. He knew little of the man beyond the fact that he was a proponent of the so-called Spencean philanthropists. John Stafford, chief clerk at Bow Street, suspected that group of sedition, and Noel was inclined to agree.

Richards, if he recalled correctly, was actively recruiting more adherents to that cause. Surely, that was enough to explain his instant dislike of the man.

"Mr. Paxton?" Miss Riverstone recalled him.

Turning, he saw both concern and curiosity in her expressive gray eyes. Feeling compelled to reassure her, he managed a smile. "I'm sorry. You were about to tell me your reasons for coming to London, were you not?"

But she would not be so easily put off. "You clearly do not care for Mr. Richards. Why?"

"Some of his ideas are dangerous," he said carefully, not wanting to antagonize Miss Riverstone. He still had much to discover about her brother.

"Then so are my own, for I agree with most of what he stands for," she retorted. "I had thought you somewhat sympathetic to the plight of the common man when last we spoke on the topic."

"Sympathetic, yes." If only she knew. "But not to the point of overthrowing what has proved a stable and relatively just system of government. Anarchy is not the answer."

Miss Riverstone frowned. "I don't believe Mr. Richards advocates any such thing. Like me, he simply wishes for reform that will enable families who have farmed the same patch of land for generations to own that land."

"But if Parliament will not act, is the common man justified in taking up arms against his own government?" he asked, irked at her defense of the man. "Such ideas may sound good on paper, but in practice they are likely to lead to bloodshed and suffering."

"Of course I don't advocate armed rebellion," she exclaimed. "What makes you think Mr. Richards would?"

Noel started to reply, then realized he had no actual evidence—and would not be authorized to share it if he did. "I've seen his sort before," he said vaguely. "Professional agitators."

"So you don't actually *know,*" she said in evident satisfaction. "I suspected as much. I won't have my good opinion of Mr. Richards swayed by mere speculation."

"Your good opinion—!" Noel was startled by a strong desire to shake her. Why should her opinion of Richards matter to him? But it did. It mattered quite a lot.

Abruptly, belatedly, it struck him that he was jealous—jealous!—of another man's influence over Miss Riverstone. And that, of course, was absurd. He needed to win her confidence and liking, but he could not allow *his* emotions to become involved.

"You're right, of course," he said with an effort. "While I won't deny I enjoy debating such matters with you, I have no real reason to slander Mr. Richards. My apologies."

Her expression softened, and Noel felt his pulse quicken. He felt the strongest urge to lean toward her, to . . .

"It is not I to whom you should apologize," she pointed out with a smile that forgave him.

Noel swallowed, thoroughly alarmed by her effect on him. It was just as well he was not required to stand at the moment, for that effect would be evident to the entire room. He had seen others brought low, even destroyed, by the allure of a woman. Then, he had not been able to understand such weakness. But now—

"If I should see Mr. Richards again, I will be more conciliatory," he said, hoping he would not be called upon to fulfill that promise. "Would you care for some sweetmeats?"

She shook her head—rather to his relief, since his body's response to her had not yet subsided. "I have eaten enough already to make me sleepy. When do you suppose I can escape without giving Pearl offense?"

"Some guests will undoubtedly leave after supper, though others will continue dancing for two or three more hours."

Her eyes widened with amazement. "More dancing? To think that I always regarded those in Society as lazy and useless."

"Useless some may be," he agreed with a grin, "but the social whirl can be gruelling for those determined to keep up with it."

"So I begin to perceive." Her voice held a hint of regret, and more than a hint of weariness.

Though aware of the danger, he could not help reassuring her. "You have used your energies far more productively, Miss Riverstone. Do not fault yourself for that."

She smiled gratefully at him. "Thank you. But now, I do believe I will attempt an escape, so that I may save a modicum of energy for tomorrow's activities."

Noel stood, finally able to do so without embarrassment. "Come. We'll stroll onto the terrace as we talk. We can make our way toward the garden door, and as soon as no one is looking, you may disappear inside that way. I can make your apologies to Lady Hardwyck once you are upstairs."

"You are very good to me, sir," she said, rising to place a hand on his outstretched arm.

He felt a ridiculous urge to confess to her his true motive in being kind, and squelched it at once. The mission was the thing, after all.

"Common courtesy is the mark of a gentleman, or so I have always heard," he said instead. "It is a designation I strive to merit."

"I too believe that a gentleman is evidenced by his behavior rather than the accident of his birth," she said as they moved toward the open French doors along the side of the ballroom. "As is a lady. I should wish to do as well in meriting that designation as you do that of gentleman, Mr. Paxton. But of that, I despair."

He glanced at her to find her gray eyes twinkling. "Why, Miss Riverstone, I do believe you are fishing for compliments. Far be it from me to refuse to rise to the bait."

They had reached the terrace now. A quick glance about showed no one observing them, so he led her down the broad stone steps into the gardens.

"Allow me to say that the world would be a better place were more ladies like yourself," he said as they moved along the graveled path toward the back door, between fragrant blooming rosebushes. "You have made the evening thoroughly enjoyable, and interesting as well."

Her eyes widened at his serious tone and he thought he could discern a blush by the light of the three-quarter moon. "Thank you. I . . . I must say the same for you."

They stopped near the door and Noel moved closer, probing her eyes with his own, trying to divine her secrets—for secrets he was certain she had. At the same time, her gray eyes searched his, threatening to unravel his own secrets. He felt another, stronger compulsion to tell her everything.

"Miss Riverstone—Rowena," he murmured.

She swayed toward him, almost imperceptibly, clearly eager to hear whatever he might say. Trapped between warring temptations, he gave in to the less dangerous of the two. Holding her gaze, he leaned down, resting one hand lightly on the nape of her neck. Her thick-lashed eyes drifted closed as he covered her mouth with his.

Noel thought to just brush her lips—a quick kiss to confuse her senses and keep her off balance. Instead, her sweet softness captivated him, demanding that he taste what she had to offer, to explore, to claim—

With a tiny sigh, she lifted her arms to his shoulders, clinging to him as though for support. Her answering kiss was innocent, inexperienced, but that made it all the sweeter. He found himself exulting that he was the first man to awaken this side of the serious Miss Riverstone.

Splaying one hand against her back, he drew her closer, intensifying the kiss, teasing at her lips with his tongue, coaxing them apart. Who could have guessed she would taste so good? He wanted—

Abruptly, she pulled away, staring up at him in near panic. "Oh! I—I— Good night, sir." Not quite meeting his eye, she turned and fled to the garden door, disappearing inside.

Noel stood watching after her, reflecting that it was just as well she had broken off that remarkable kiss. If she had not, he would almost certainly have accompanied her upstairs—and that was a commitment he was by no means ready to make.

Rowena ran up the back stairs and straight to her room, refusing to look back, refusing even to think, until she had barricaded herself inside. Was Mr. Paxton mad? Was she? What on earth had just happened?

"Miss? Is something wrong?" Matthilda emerged from the dressing room, her eyes wide with concern.

Managing a shaky laugh, Rowena shook her head.

"No, of course not. I am tired, that is all, and ran up here to escape before Lady Hardwyck could tease me into staying below. If you will unhook my gown, I can do everything else myself. I'm sure you want your bed as much as I do."

While the maid helped her to undress, Rowena tried to reel in her imagination. It was just a kiss, after all. Had she not read that men set little store by such things? It would not do to weave romantic fantasies about one single occurrence. No doubt she had said or done something to make Mr. Paxton think she was inviting such an attention, and he had felt it was only polite to comply.

That had not felt like a "polite" kiss, however.

"Thank you, Matthilda. Good night."

Slipping out of her shift and into her nightrail, Rowena shook her head. She would not know a polite kiss from a passionate one, never having experienced either. Perhaps he had meant it as a polite one and she had tried to turn it into something else. What must he think of her? Her cheeks burned with sudden embarrassment. Her inexperience must have been crystal clear to him. Was he even now chuckling at her expense?

She didn't know what to think, and her brain seemed too fuzzy to sort things out. She had not been exaggerating her weariness, but now her whole body tingled with newly awakened longings. Slowly, she climbed into bed, guiltily reliving every delicious sensation until she drifted off to sleep.

The day was well advanced when Rowena awoke, fully refreshed, if a trifle stiff from the unaccustomed exercise of the night before.

"Good morning, miss," Matthilda greeted her, bustling in as Rowena stretched the kinks from her joints. "Or good day, more like. It's nigh noon, but I dursen't wake you, late as you went to bed."

"And I thank you for that. I presume I've missed breakfast?"

The maid shrugged. "I wouldn't know, miss, but I can have a tray sent up if you'd like."

"No, I'll go down." She was eager to see Mr. Paxton again, though shy as well. Would he act differently toward her now? Should she act differently toward him?

Two new day dresses and another evening gown had been delivered while she slept, so Rowena donned a flattering yellow round dress with moss-green ruching about the neck and wrists. Not wishing to wait for Francesca, she had Matthilda pin her hair into a knot in back while allowing the rest to fall past her shoulders.

"You look a treat, miss," the maid assured her, and Rowena had to agree. Why had she eschewed bright colors all her life? As no guests were likely to be below so early in the day, she donned her spectacles and went in search of sustenance.

Pearl and Mr. Paxton were just leaving the dining room when she arrived.

"Good afternoon, sleepyhead," Pearl greeted her with a smile. "It seems Mr. Paxton was not bamming me when he said you were tired last night. In truth, I think you did splendidly for your first ball. I recall I slept until two the day following mine."

Rowena, acutely aware of Mr. Paxton's regard, returned Pearl's smile. "Then, as you were a mere sixteen while I am of a far more advanced age, I must credit myself with unusual stamina."

"You make it sound as though you are in your dotage," Pearl said with a laugh. "As we are of an age, I should take insult."

"No one could ever think either of you anything but young and vibrant," Mr. Paxton said gallantly. "Are you recovered from last night's exertions, Miss Riverstone?"

Something in his tone, and in his eyes, made Rowena blush, though it was a perfectly innocent question. "Yes, thank you. Or I will be, once I've had a bite to eat. Dare I hope—?"

"Yes, there's still plenty on the sideboard," Pearl assured her. "I expected you would be hungry when you finally emerged. But now you must excuse me. I need to speak with the housekeeper about arrangements for this evening's card party."

"And I must go out, I fear." Mr. Paxton sounded genuinely regretful, but Rowena tried not to read too much into that.

"How progresses your pursuit of the Saint?" she asked, more to remind herself of how divergent their ideals were than because she wanted to know.

He had started to turn away, but now faced her again, his gaze surprisingly sharp. "Slowly. Why? Have you heard anything?"

"I? Of course not," she said quickly, then immediately wondered if her vehemence might make it sound as though she were hiding something. Which she was, she realized, but it was of an emotional rather than a factual nature. She schooled her features to an expression of innocent interest.

He continued to regard her speculatively for a long moment, then gave a barely perceptible shrug. "I know you do not approve of my task, Miss Riverstone, but I hope that if you hear of anything . . . irregular, you will tell me."

Rowena would not promise anything that might lead to the capture of the Saint, but she could not quite hold out against the plea in those intense hazel eyes.

"I truly have heard nothing, Mr. Paxton, and can't imagine that I will. But if anything happens that causes me concern, I will let you know."

"Thank you. That is what I had hoped."

Again, his expression gave his words added meaning, and she realized that her promise could pertain to much more than news of the Saint. Still, she found she did not wish to retract it. Something about Mr. Paxton compelled trust, whether she agreed with his principles or not.

"You two are free to make moon eyes all afternoon, but I really must leave you," Pearl said then.

Belatedly aware that she had been staring, Rowena dropped her gaze.

"A dozen or more people will be here at two for a trip to see the tigers at the Exchange," Pearl continued. "We will return in time to change for dinner and the card party. You will both come, will you not?"

Rowena nodded, but to her distinct disappointment, Mr. Paxton demurred.

"My business is likely to take longer than that, my lady, though I will be here this evening, of course. And if I finish sooner than expected, perhaps I may join you at the 'Change."

He took his leave then, and Pearl bustled off as well, leaving Rowena to a solitary breakfast and some much-needed thought. Any eagerness she had felt for the afternoon's excursion was dimmed by the news that Mr. Paxton would not be one of the party—and that was absurd.

To distract herself, she picked up the copy of the *Political Register*, which had been left in the dining room, as she had not been able to finish it the other morning. She was deep in an editorial on the injustices endured by factory workers in the north, when a noise behind her made her turn to find Mr. Paxton reentering the dining room.

"I felt the need for another cup of coffee," Noel explained, nodding to the footman to bring him one. "What have you there?" He had returned in the hope of speaking privately with her, and was delighted at his good fortune in finding her holding that particular paper.

She made a motion as if to hide it again, then lifted her chin and met his eyes squarely. "The *Political Register*. Are you familiar with it?"

"Indeed I am. I can't say I always agree with the views expressed therein, but it makes for interesting reading." He seated himself across from her. By unspoken agreement, neither referred with so much as a look to that remarkable kiss they had shared last night.

Some of the tension left her shoulders, as though his response reassured her. "I agree. Mr. Cobbett and his contributors have a way of cutting to the heart of the injustice and hypocrisy infecting England."

"And yet," he said, taking a sip from the cup just handed him by the footman, "some of those contributors hide behind false names or initials. Is that not a brand of hypocrisy in itself?"

Sudden alarm flared in her eyes. So, she *did* know something! "Can you really blame them, sir, when Cobbett himself was once charged with sedition, along with such luminaries as Leigh Hunt?"

"The Hunt brothers were merely unwise enough to openly criticize the Prince Regent. I tend to agree that imprisoning them was an overreaction on the Regent's part, and only served to make him look foolish. Cobbett and some of the others, however—"

"Exposing injustice is *not* sedition," she insisted passionately. "If anonymity allows the truth to reach the public, I cannot help but think it justified."

Surely, this was the fervor of a sister defending a brother? His pulse quickened as he sensed his quarry almost in his grasp.

"One would almost think you had a personal stake in protecting the identity of these anonymous writers," he said, watching her closely.

There was no mistaking her alarm this time. "Why do you say that?"

"You seem so passionate in their defense," he explained. Unbidden came a vision of how passionate she had been last night—how passionate she might prove in other endeavors as well. Hastily, he thrust it away.

"I, ah, share the opinions of some of those writers, so in that sense I suppose I feel a personal concern."

She still appeared more agitated than the discussion would seem to warrant, but he realized that she, too, might be remembering that kiss. He needed clearer proof.

"Have you no suspicion, then, as to who any of those writers might be? There is one in particular—" Reaching across the table, he twitched the paper from her grasp, his hand grazing hers in the process.

They were both ungloved, and he was startled at the impact of that brief contact. That she noticed it too was evident in her quick, indrawn breath and the widening of her eyes.

Steeling his emotions against such weakness, Noel quickly scanned through the pages. "No, he appears not to have an essay in this issue. If you are a regular reader, however, you are doubtless familiar with the author I mean. He signs his pieces 'Mr. R.' "

She swallowed convulsively, but then took a deep breath and met his eye. To his surprise, something like amusement flitted across her face. "I fear I pay little attention to the initials following the essays, Mr. Paxton. Do you recall the topics this particular writer addresses?"

"Oh, the usual rants about the evils of the landed class, the plight of the poor farmer, the conditions of the poorhouses. You know." He spoke disparagingly, hoping to goad her into defending the writer—and perhaps giving something away.

"Rants? Those essays are well researched, and quite logical in presentation—or so I have thought."

Noel couldn't suppress a triumphant grin. "Ah, then you *do* know which essayist I mean?"

Caught, she flushed scarlet. Still, he couldn't help but admire the way she lifted her chin and tried to brazen it through. "I find that true of virtually all of the essayists, with one or two exceptions."

"Of course." He let her see that he wasn't fooled in the least. "To be more specific, one such essay a month or two ago was emphatic in its defense of the Saint of Seven Dials as a champion of the common man. As you may imagine, that caught my attention."

In fact, that was the essay which had convinced Noel that the author and the Saint might be the same.

"He spoke of the necessity of the redistribution of wealth," he continued, "insisting that if Parliament would not see to it, the public should support the efforts of vigilante reformers like the Saint. He was rather persuasive, alas, which has not made my job any easier—nor more popular."

She shrugged slightly, taking a bite of shirred eggs that must be stone cold by now. "You already know my own views on the subject, Mr. Paxton. Is it any wonder I should be sympathetic to that essayist?"

He frowned, nettled that he'd given her a plausible counterargument. "I still find hiding behind initials cowardly," he said, and was rewarded by seeing her flinch. "If convictions are firmly held, should they not be stated openly?"

"Perhaps some writers have other reasons for disguising their identities," she suggested, her color still high. "A . . . man in the public sphere may hope to effect change through conventional channels even while he persuades the public through others." She motioned at the paper Noel held. "Were it known the two were one, it might make both avenues less effective."

"But when a man's public politics are at odds with his personal opinions—and writings—what then? Surely you cannot absolve such a man of hypocrisy." Sir Nelson was publicly allied with the conservative Tories, as his father had been. Else he would not hold a position of such importance in the Home Office.

She raised a skeptical brow above the rim of her spectacles. "Yes, I suppose that *would* smack of hypocrisy, but I cannot say that I know of any such man."

She was proving a tougher nut to crack than he'd anticipated, particularly after last night. Abandoning the matter of the mysterious essayist, he tried a different approach. "Tell me, Miss Riverstone, did your brother fight in the war?"

"Nelson?" She appeared genuinely surprised by the question, or perhaps she was merely startled by the abrupt change of subject. "Perhaps 'fight' is too strong a word, but he served briefly in the army, yes. Why?"

He ignored the question. "In what capacity? To what unit was he assigned?"

"To the Fifty-second Light Infantry, but he was injured in a minor skirmish shortly after his arrival in France. After spending several months in a field hospital, he was eventually sent home."

"And when might that have been?" he asked, abandoning subtlety in his eagerness.

"He returned in the spring of 1814, a few months before Father died."

So Sir Nelson *had* been in France when the Bishop had been passing information to Napoleon. He could not have been at Waterloo, but perhaps a confederate had planted evidence—

"Mr. Paxton?" He looked up to find her frowning anxiously.

And well she might feel anxious. He was more certain than ever that the Bishop and Sir Nelson were one and the same. Still, he felt compelled to somehow reassure her, to erase the worry from her eyes—if only temporarily.

"I simply meant to make the point that a man who went voluntarily into the army would be guilty of hypocrisy if he were to criticize the war effort. Not that I'm claiming your brother has done so, of course."

She still looked dubious, and no wonder. His explanation sounded extremely feeble even to his own ears. Quickly, he gulped down his cooling coffee and stood.

"I really must go now, but I thank you for yet another stimulating conversation, Miss Riverstone."

"Um, yes, of course." She nodded to him almost absently, apparently lost in her own thoughts now.

As he hurried out of the room, for a moment it occurred to him that he had perhaps been unwise to tip his hand so soon. She was exceptionally intelligent, and even if she had not yet pieced together his disjointed questions, she would likely do so soon. He would have to keep her off balance, keep her wondering about his motives.

Otherwise, his very life might be forfeit.

He didn't want to believe that Miss Riverstone would intentionally put him at risk. But presuming she did not know of her brother's treasonous activities, nor how dangerous the man could be, she would have no compunction about warning him. She would not know that Noel's life would be at stake.

And if she did know . . . ?

Putting Miss Riverstone firmly from his mind, he left the house, hoping the inquiries he was about to make might solidify his case beyond doubt.

Rowena stared after Mr. Paxton, her mind in turmoil. What on earth had that been about? It was patently obvious that he was fishing for information of some sort, but what it might be, she had no idea.

For a few heart-stopping minutes she'd been convinced he'd identified her as MRR, but as he continued it seemed clear he believed her essays were written by a man. And he had called her arguments "persuasive," she recalled with a spurt of pride.

Then she frowned. What of that odd tangent about Nelson's army service? Mr. Paxton's "explanation" hadn't explained at all. Could he conceivably think that Nelson—or MRR—was the Saint of Seven Dials? Perhaps that all three were one? It was the only explanation she could fathom, but it made little sense.

She remembered the halfhearted promise he had extracted from her as he had left the dining room the first time. Yes, he must think she had information about the Saint, which must mean he at least suspected Nelson.

The very idea of Nelson writing her essays—or acting as the Saint—was so absurd she nearly laughed aloud.

Of course, he would find out soon enough that Nelson had been in the country while the Saint was active in London last winter. But she saw no need to disabuse Mr. Paxton of his amusing notion. While he pursued Nelson, he would not be pursuing the *real* Saint, whoever he was.

Still she could not ignore a small ache in the vicinity of her heart. Though she had tried not to, she had briefly allowed herself to believe that kiss last night had meant something to him. Now it seemed clear that he merely considered her a means to an end.

A spurt of anger abolished melancholy. Did he really think, if Nelson *were* the Saint, that she would betray her own brother? What kind of person would be capable of such a double betrayal, of both principles and blood—for a mere kiss?

No, she would think no more about the matter—or the man.

She had a mission in London, and any feelings she might have developed for Mr. Paxton would only interfere with that mission. Just as well she now saw him for what he was, and could nip such fledgling feelings in the bud.

She would use today and tonight strictly as the opportunities they were, to speak with men of political influence and to learn more about the undercurrents that bound or separated such men. Last night had been all but wasted in that sense.

But not completely wasted, she reminded herself. She *had* met Mr. Richards, and could look forward to future conversations with that most intelligent man. If he were not so much older than she—

No! She would certainly not entertain any romantic notions about Mr. Richards. Or Mr. Paxton, for that matter.

She signaled for a fresh pot of coffee, deliberately concentrating on what she would say to Mr. Richards about Nelson as soon as she had a chance for private conversation with him. The awkwardness of such a petition successfully distracted her for the remainder of her meal.

Chapter 9

To Rowena's surprise, nearly as many people arrived for the card party as had attended Pearl's ball the night before. Though the ball hadn't been quite the ordeal she had feared, she had hopes of feeling less out of her element tonight. At least with cards she need not fear treading on anyone's toes.

The trip to the Exeter 'Change had been rather disappointing, though she told herself that was because of the condition of the poor tigers. She had taken it upon herself to speak to the keeper, to the amazement of the other ladies present.

Mr. Paxton had not joined them, but after their conversation this morning she hadn't wanted him to. No, the real source of her disappointment was the absence of any men of influence she might cultivate. The party had consisted primarily of ladies, along with two or three young bucks who had only come along to spend time with said ladies. A pointless enterprise altogether.

"Well met, Miss Riverstone!" Mr. Galloway broke into her musings. Turning, she saw that he was again accompanied by Lord Fernworth and his cousin, Mr. Orrin.

"Good evening, sirs, my lord," she said with a smile, though these men would not serve her purpose either. "It is pleasant to see you again. I believe we will be breaking into various tables shortly."

"And Mr. Galloway promised you a chess match, if I recall," said Mr. Paxton, coming up just then to stand at her elbow. "I've already spoken with Lady Hardwyck to make certain a board is available."

Rowena fought to subdue the instinctive thrill that assailed her nerves at his nearness, sternly reminding herself of his true motive in befriending her.

"I had thought to play cards," she said, though in truth she would far prefer chess. She would do nothing to gratify Mr. Paxton, however.

"Come, there are four of us, not counting Stick-in-the-mud Paxton," Lord Fernworth exclaimed. "What say you all to a few hands of whist?"

He moved toward the nearest card table as he spoke, Mr. Galloway and Mr. Orrin following readily enough. Rowena glanced involuntarily at Mr. Paxton, who was frowning. That was enough to decide her. She joined the others.

"You'll partner me, will you not, Miss Riverstone?" Mr. Galloway accompanied his request with a charming smile and a pleading look that was undeniably flattering.

Pointedly ignoring Mr. Paxton, she assented, taking the indicated seat at the table. The cards were dealt and the play commenced.

At first, Rowena found it hard to concentrate, so conscious was she of Mr. Paxton hovering just behind her. After a few minutes, however, he wandered off and she was better able to focus on the game.

Focus, in fact, was her main concern. She had to continually remind herself not to bring the cards ridiculously close to her face, that she might better see the pips. Nor would she squint. Therefore, it was a fairly easy matter to play less than her best, which no doubt pleased the gentlemen.

"Oh, dear, silly me," she said when she played a club instead of a spade for the second time. "I told you I was new to the game, did I not?"

Her poor play cost the first hand, but after that she paid closer attention—and held the cards just a tiny bit closer—and she and Mr. Galloway rallied to win the rubber, just as Mr. Paxton returned.

"Change partners for another rubber?" Mr. Orrin suggested.

But Mr. Galloway shook his head. "First, that chess match Miss Riverstone promised me. If you're still willing, that is?"

"Of course." Rowena thought he looked rather smug at the prospect, and was torn between wanting to put him in his place and wanting to frustrate Mr. Paxton's evident desire to see her do just that.

They passed Lord and Lady Hardwyck as they crossed the room to where the chessboard was set up, and Pearl pulled Rowena aside for a quick word.

"Remember, dear," she said softly. "Most men are not like Luke, or your Mr. Paxton—they like to win."

Rowena nodded, though she nearly lost the sense of what Pearl said. *Her* Mr. Paxton? She opened her mouth to protest the designation, but the others were watching now, so she turned and followed them.

Of course he was not *her* Mr. Paxton. How absurd. Surely Pearl couldn't know—?

"Here we are," Mr. Galloway exclaimed gleefully as they reached the chessboard. "I'll take black, of course."

Even without spectacles, Rowena's eyesight was sufficient for this game she knew so well—as long as she paid attention. Still, she was determined not to afford the hovering Mr. Paxton the satisfaction of seeing Mr. Galloway soundly trounced, much as that might gratify her own ego.

She made her first move, the perfectly conventional king's pawn opening. Unfortunately, within five minutes it was clear that Mr. Galloway was a far poorer player than even Pearl. Losing to him would be all but impossible.

The only thing that kept her from ending it sooner was the obvious disapproval radiating from Mr. Paxton. Rowena did her best to delay the inevitable, sitting back to make it harder to focus on the pieces, ignoring several obvious openings and even allowing Mr. Galloway to take her queen. She could almost feel Mr. Paxton stiffening with outrage, and had to hide a grin.

Finally, however, she had little choice but to checkmate the black king and win the game. To her amazement, Mr. Galloway seemed genuinely surprised to have lost.

"It seems Mr. Paxton was not exaggerating, Miss Riverstone," he exclaimed. "You are a formidable opponent indeed. My congratulations."

Rowena glanced about and realized with some dismay that a fair number of guests had gathered to watch the conclusion of the match—including Lester Richards. Mr. Paxton was frowning at her, which bothered her not at all, of course, but Mr. Richards' opinion was another matter.

It was all she could do to accept Mr. Galloway's congratulations graciously, as poorly as she had played. She prayed he would not suggest another match.

In fact, Mr. Galloway appeared more than satisfied to return to the card tables. "Now that I need not have *all* my wits about me, I'll try some of the claret," he said, plucking a glass from a tray carried by a passing footman. "Perhaps one of you gents would care to try your skill against our clever Miss Riverstone?"

But most of the other gentlemen and one or two ladies merely regarded her quizzically before beginning to disperse. She shot a defiant glance at Mr. Paxton, but then turned to find Mr. Richards watching her. She flushed, wondering how much of the game he had seen.

"I'd enjoy a match, if you would oblige me," he said, a smile making his face almost handsome. Well, not handsome, exactly, but . . . magnetic.

"Certainly, sir. I am pleased to see you again so soon," Rowena replied, fighting down sudden nervousness. Much as she would prefer not to, she really must mention Nelson to him tonight. She had promised.

"And I, you, Miss Riverstone. Shall we?" Deftly, he began resetting the board.

Though most of the spectators had drifted away, Mr. Paxton remained. Irritated, Rowena turned to him. "Surely you have better things to do than to watch me play again?"

Her words were rude and she regretted them at once, but he only smiled. "I find it quite an enjoyable pastime, actually. I'd like to play the winner if she—or he—doesn't mind."

"I've no objection, Paxton," Mr. Richards said. Rowena thought she caught a hint of eagerness in his dark eyes.

"Nor I," she echoed. Then, turning resolutely back to the board, she opened with the same move as before. How could she bring up Nelson's delicate problem with Mr. Paxton within earshot?

A few minutes' play proved Mr. Richards a vastly superior player to Mr. Galloway, though not of Mr. Paxton's caliber. Rowena concentrated, unsure whether she wanted to best her idol or not. She very much wanted to win his respect, but she feared alienating him. After all, there was the matter of Nelson's—

"Gadslife, Ro! Trust you to find a chessboard at a card party." Her brother's voice at just that moment made her start.

"Good evening, Nelson. You know Mr. Richards, I believe? And Mr. Paxton—you wished for a word with my brother, did you not?"

To her relief, Mr. Paxton took the cue.

"Indeed. Do you have a few moments, Sir Nelson?"

"Anything beats watching a chess match," Nelson agreed readily. "May as well watch paint dry, I say."

The two men moved away, and Rowena relaxed

marginally—though what she had feared, she was not sure. Seizing her opportunity before she could lose her courage, she said, "I understand my brother has been—unwise—in his gaming, Mr. Richards."

Her opponent was frowning at her last move, but at this he lifted his eyes to hers and smiled slightly. "I suppose one might say that. Sir Nelson's luck is such that he would do better to avoid games of chance."

"I agree. However—" But just then, two couples wandered over to watch the match, and Rowena was forced to drop the subject. "Perhaps we might talk of this later?"

"As you wish," said Mr. Richards mildly, his attention again on the board.

Noel wasn't sure whether to bless or curse his luck. He had wanted a conversation with Sir Nelson, but he very much preferred not to leave Miss Riverstone alone with Mr. Richards. There was something about the man—

"What did you have in mind to talk about, Paxton?" Sir Nelson asked, reminding him of his mission—the only thing that should matter now.

Besides, Miss Riverstone was scarcely alone. The table she shared with Mr. Richards was in full view of half the room.

"Your sister tells me you served in the army, Sir Nelson. I was wondering if we might have an acquaintance or two in common."

"Oh? Army man yourself, are you?" The stocky young man puffed out his chest a bit. "My time under Wellington was the most memorable of my life, I must say."

Noel was experienced in sifting men's words and expressions, but could detect no false note in Sir Nelson—not yet. "I'm a great admirer of Wellington myself," he said, "though I never held a commission under him. I did some courier work during the recent wars, however."

The Black Bishop would know what that really meant. But though he watched Sir Nelson's expression carefully, it showed not the slighted flicker of comprehension—merely mild curiosity.

"Courier? Delivering messages and such, you mean? Not a fighting man, then, eh? Though I suppose you must have ventured into danger now and again." He said it kindly, as though offering a sop to Noel's pride.

"Now and again, yes." Noel smiled, pretending gratitude while actually recalling the dozens of life-or-death situations he'd faced—more than many soldiers had faced, in fact. "I take it you saw your share of the fighting, then?"

Sir Nelson's fair skin pinkened slightly. "Not as much as I'd hoped, truth to tell. Took a bullet in the leg at Bayonne and though I wanted to get back into the fray, the surgeon wouldn't let me. Got to hear many a rare tale, though, let me tell you."

This echoed Miss Riverstone's account, though of course it would, if it were the cover story her brother had been using. Noel had serious doubts now, however. Unless the man was a superb actor, he was nowhere near clever enough to be the elusive Black Bishop.

"You spent some months in France, did you not? That must have been—interesting."

Sir Nelson shrugged. "Maybe if I'd been nearer

Paris, instead of trapped in a minuscule hamlet miles from anywhere. Since I speak only the sketchiest French, my only news came from fellow soldiers, wounded more recently than I. And, of course, from Captain Steen, who came to visit us when he could."

Noel's attention sharpened. "Captain Emory Steen?"

"Yes, of course. I was in his company, you know. Never progressed beyond ensign myself, thanks to that bullet."

"Of course." Noel was acquainted with Captain Steen. It would be an easy matter to verify Sir Nelson's story. If it checked out—which he unfortunately feared it would—that would rule him out as a suspect. Still, there were those essays, and his sister must have picked up her revolutionary ideas somewhere . . .

Noel glanced across the room, reassuring himself that Miss Riverstone was still engaged in her chess match—and nothing else. "Tell me, Sir Nelson, do you ever read the *Political Register?*" he asked in as offhand a manner as he could manage.

His companion frowned. "What, Cobbett's twopenny trash? My sister may believe the tripe he prints, but I've never wasted my time on it. Seditious drivel, if you ask me. Ro been spouting her theories to you or something?"

Again, though he tried, Noel could detect no trace of guile in the man. He seemed genuinely contemptuous. "Your sister and I have had some . . . interesting . . . discussions, yes."

"Told her she ought to keep her opinions to herself." Sir Nelson snorted. "Not that she'd listen to me, any more than she did to our father. Warned her she'd never catch a husband with that tongue of hers."

Noel had an intriguing vision of Miss Riverstone's sweet, pink tongue, darting between those perfectly shaped lips, touching, teasing—

"Er, yes, I see your point," he said before his distraction could be noticed. Then, feeling obliged to defend her, he added, "There are some who might appreciate her intelligence, however."

Sir Nelson grinned. "Like you, Paxton? Or maybe Lester Richards there—he's the intellectual sort."

Following his glance to the chess match still underway, Noel frowned. "A bit old for her, I'd say."

"Ro needs a firm hand," her brother said with a shrug. "A man closer to our father's age might be just the thing. Besides—" But then he broke off and shrugged again. "Think I'll find a baccarat table if you don't mind, Paxton. Care to join me?"

"Thank you, no." Positive now that Sir Nelson was not the man he sought, Noel was anxious to return to Miss Riverstone's side.

She knew the identity of that essayist, he was certain. If it was not her brother, it might be someone else she knew from Oakshire, which meant she was still his best lead—reason enough to stay close to her. If there was another reason, he chose to ignore it.

Rowena moved her knight back to the same square it had occupied three moves ago, trying to prolong the game until another chance for private talk presented itself. That effort had been aided by her eyesight.

Twice, she had mistaken a bishop for a pawn, to her detriment. Still, she had made steady inroads and now held a clear advantage on the board.

To her relief, Lord and Lady Norville finally moved away. She glanced up at Mr. Richards, ready to reopen the topic of Nelson's debts—only to see Mr. Paxton returning.

"Still at it, I see," he commented with a smile.

"The lady is quite skilled." Mr. Richards' voice held an edge Rowena had not noticed earlier. "Her primary fault seems to be indecisiveness."

Rowena managed a thin smile. His words stung, even though she had to admit that her attempts to delay winning made her seem to merit his criticism. Boldly, she pushed her black bishop from one corner of the board to the other.

"Caution is scarcely a fault," Mr. Paxton said. "She appears to have the upper hand, in any event." There was no mistaking the satisfaction in his voice—a satisfaction that nettled Rowena more than it flattered her.

"Appearances can be deceiving," Mr. Richards retorted, blocking the line between her bishop and the rook it threatened with a pawn.

She could now checkmate him in two moves, a fact Mr. Richards seemed unaware of. First the knight, then the bishop, and she would have him. But did she want to?

"So you have noticed that too, Mr. Richards? A perceptive man." Rowena suspected Mr. Paxton was referring to herself more than to the game. "For example, I'd have guessed, based solely on appearances, that you would not be a complacent loser."

So he was prepared to gloat the moment she won, was he? Unwilling to afford him the satisfaction, Rowena moved her queen instead of the knight. She didn't know what Mr. Paxton's game was, with kisses he refused to acknowledge and barbed comments to a man he scarcely knew, but she refused to play along with it.

"Nor am I a complacent loser," Mr. Richards admitted, moving his king out of danger and threatening her queen with his now-exposed rook. "It's as well that I rarely lose."

"Then I must count myself fortunate to witness such a rare event," responded Mr. Paxton. The smile he sent Rowena was both intimate and possessive, she thought.

Though her heart quickened its beat, she sent him a warning look. She would *not* be manipulated like some brainless miss, swooning after any man who flirted with her. Especially now that she knew his flirting disguised another purpose.

"How daunting to think your fortunes rely on my actions, Mr. Paxton," she said lightly, holding his eye for a long moment. Then, deliberately, she moved her black bishop back a single space, removing the last threat to Mr. Richards' king.

Instantly, her opponent took advantage of the opening. "Checkmate!" he cried triumphantly, taking her queen with his rook and pinning her king.

Rowena regarded the board in mock surprise. "Why, so it is. Mr. Paxton, did you not wish to play the winner?" She rose smoothly.

The look Mr. Paxton gave her said clearly that he knew exactly what she was about. "I did, though I confess I was hoping it would be you, Miss Riverstone. I have quite enjoyed our previous games . . . all of them." He gazed pointedly at her lips.

Feeling the color surging to her cheeks, Rowena turned hastily away. Clearly, she was not so sophisticated as she had hoped. "Thank you, sir. And thank you for the game, Mr. Richards. I—I need to speak with Lady Hardwyck, but will return to watch your play."

Quickly, she walked away from the two men, not caring at the moment whether they laughed at her or engaged in fisticuffs. She wished only to be away from both of them and their smug maleness.

It occurred to her then to wonder what Mr. Paxton and Nelson had talked about. Nothing very involved, judging by how quickly Mr. Paxton had returned. She went in search of her brother, only to find him deep in a game of baccarat with several other men. For a moment, she tried to catch his eye to remind him of his promise not to gamble, but he refused to look her way. With a sigh, she left to find Pearl.

"What's this I hear about you playing nothing but chess at my card party?" her friend greeted her laughingly, beckoning for Rowena to join Lady Marcus and two other ladies with whom she stood chatting. "I thought you wanted to meet people."

"I started the evening with a few hands of whist," Rowena said defensively, not that Pearl seemed particularly upset. "The chess was primarily Mr. Paxton's idea."

Pearl's glance was rather too perceptive for Rowena's taste. "I see. His way of having you to himself at a crowded party?"

The two Melks sisters tittered. "I'd learn to play chess myself," said Miss Augusta Melks, "to spend time with that handsome Mr. Paxton."

"I haven't actually played with him tonight," Rowena said hastily, wanting to quash any speculation along those lines. It came too close to the truth for her liking. "Only with Mr. Galloway and Mr. Richards."

Again, Pearl seemed to be watching her closely. "Yes, I noticed. Did you—?"

"I managed to defeat Mr. Galloway after a hard-fought match, but I fear Mr. Richards bested me." Rowena answered the question her friend had been about to ask with a perfectly straight face, then turned to Lady Marcus. "Do you not play cards, Quinn?"

The diminutive brunette nodded. "I was doing so until a few moments ago, in fact. My husband made certain to teach me the more popular games. Still, it's pleasant to take a break from the competition and just chat for a bit."

Accordingly, the ladies did just that for a few minutes, though Rowena found her attention frequently wandering back to the ongoing match between Mr. Paxton and Mr. Richards. No, she would not look—not yet.

Her resolve lasted until Lord Marcus and Lord Hardwyck approached to claim their wives for new games just beginning. For a moment she wavered, knowing she would be wiser to accompany the others and distract herself with cards, but then curiosity won out. Excusing herself, she made her way back across the room, suddenly anxious to see how the chess match might be going.

Not until she was only a pace or two from the table could she see well enough to analyze the game, but it was instantly apparent that Mr. Paxton had played his best, unlike herself. In fact, she had scarcely reached the combatants when he made his final move.

"Checkmate," he declared. He accepted his opponent's grudging congratulations, then glanced up at Rowena with a smile that held more than a trace of mockery.

Though she knew the mockery was directed at her rather than Mr. Richards, she frowned. "Surely it is unsporting to gloat, Mr. Paxton?"

"Unsporting or not, he has earned it," responded Mr. Richards before he could answer. "I'd do the same in his position."

The two men stood, and Rowena glanced uncertainly from one to the other, struck again by how very handsome Mr. Paxton was. If only he shared the other man's sensibilities . . .

"Oh, surely not, sir," she protested. Mr. Richards wasn't the gloating sort—was he? She felt certain he would be above such pettiness.

He smiled at her. "Perhaps not. We'll have to play again sometime, Paxton. I find myself distracted in such a setting."

Did Rowena imagine it, or was Mr. Richards actually flirting with her? It seemed inconceivable—but heady. A great thinker and mover of events, attracted to her? She was suddenly more glad than ever that she had taken Pearl's advice and allowed him to beat her at chess. She returned his smile shyly.

"Would you care for some refreshment, Miss Riverstone?" Mr. Paxton asked then, his voice just a shade too loud. "Of course, you are welcome to accompany us, Richards."

"Yes, I believe I will."

Rowena looked uncertainly from one to the other. The animosity she had noted between them last night was more pronounced than ever. Understandable, perhaps, in Mr. Richards' case, as he had just lost at chess. But surely Mr. Paxton—

With a spurt of pleasure, she suddenly realized that she herself was the cause. He was at least a little bit jealous. This, surely, must be how Pearl and other popular ladies felt all the time. Fleeting as it surely must be, Rowena could not help but savor the feeling of pure feminine power.

Turning with a flirtatious smile on her lips, she suddenly froze. There, just behind the two men who so improbably seemed to be vying for her attention stood Lady Mountheath, with a disapproving frown.

It was not the frown that startled Rowena out of her brief moment of triumph, however. It was the fact that Lady Mountheath was wearing the emerald and diamond necklace and earrings that had belonged to Rowena's own mother.

Chapter 10

"Miss Riverstone," exclaimed Lady Mountheath, coming forward with a smile as false as it was broad. "When I saw you last night, I assumed Lady Hardwyck had indulged you for the evening, but now it appears her kindness may have gone to your head."

Rowena blinked, tearing her gaze away from the woman's jewels to focus on her face. "I beg your pardon, my lady?"

"Just a kindly word of advice, my dear," the older woman said airily. "A companion who forgets her station may find herself disappointed when she discovers others are all too aware of her proper sphere, much as they may pretend otherwise for the course of an evening." She looked significantly at the two gentlemen flanking Rowena.

Taken aback as she was by the unexpected attack, Rowena realized what must be at the root of it. Lady Mountheath's two daughters had both been without partners for much of the ball last night. It must gall their mother to see Rowena—who she clearly regarded as their inferior—with two eligible gentlemen dancing attendance on her.

"I fear you are laboring under a misapprehension, my lady," she said as evenly as she could manage. "I am Lady Hardwyck's friend and neighbor, not her paid companion. Therefore, you need not fear for the social order on my account."

Now it was Lady Mountheath's turn to blink, as she absorbed this new, and clearly unwelcome, information. "My apologies," she finally murmured ungraciously. "I was merely attempting to save you from folly." Her expression implied that Rowena was still on the path to ruin. She started to turn away.

"And I thank you, my lady," Rowena said, quickly adding, "Those . . . are lovely jewels you are wearing tonight. You have exquisite taste."

Her words had the desired effect, for Lady Mountheath turned again to face her, her smile now appearing quite genuine. "Why thank you, my dear. They were a gift from my husband only last week. So extravagant of him, but he knows how well emeralds become me." She patted her lilac turban complacently and Rowena noticed the wispy strands of faded red peeking from beneath it.

"Yes, very flattering," Rowena forced herself to say, hoping for more detail.

"I wouldn't be surprised to learn he had them commissioned specially," Lady Mountheath continued. "He wouldn't tell me from which jeweler he purchased them, doubtless because he knew I'd be cross if I discovered how much he spent on me." She then fixed Rowena with a stern eye. "A just reward for conventional behavior, Miss Riverstone. See that you remember that lesson."

With a sententious nod of her turban, she sashayed off, clearly satisfied that she had prevailed in the encounter.

"Hmph. I'm not surprised her husband wouldn't say where he bought those jewels, considering that it was a pawn shop," Rowena muttered to her retreating back. "Extravagant, indeed."

"A pawn shop?" Mr. Paxton asked in obvious amusement. "What makes you think so?"

Rowena flushed, embarrassed that her companions had heard her words. There was nothing for it now but to explain—or be thought intolerably petty. "Those jewels were my mother's. I discovered only last night that my brother sold them to . . . to meet an obligation." She glanced significantly at Mr. Richards, who had the grace to frown.

Mr. Paxton chuckled. "And that dragon flaunts them as proof of her husband's devotion. If she only knew!"

"Please, you won't say anything?" Rowena turned pleading eyes first on Mr. Paxton, then Mr. Richards.

Both gentlemen shook their heads. "You may depend upon my silence," Mr. Richards said gallantly. "I would not wish your brother—or you—embarrassed in any way."

Was he trying to tell her that he would forgive the remainder of Nelson's gaming debts? But of course she could not ask him in front of Mr. Paxton. She didn't wish to lower his opinion of Mr. Richards any further than it was already.

"Nor I," Mr. Paxton echoed after a pause. "Now, shall we continue to the buffet tables?"

Much of Noel's pleasure at beating the arrogant Mr. Richards at chess had been lost when Miss Riverstone had smiled so sweetly at the fellow, and now she was doing it again. Couldn't she see that he was nowhere near as clever as she'd believed? Hadn't her own match against the man taught her that?

In addition, there was something less than candid about the fellow, though he couldn't quite put his finger on it. Something about the way his eyes failed to reflect his expressions, perhaps. He'd learned over the years to trust his instinctive response to people, and his instincts told him not to trust Mr. Richards.

Or perhaps it was merely jealousy telling him that.

"The company is beginning to thin," he commented. "Between chess and conversation, the evening has passed remarkably quickly." Perhaps Richards would take the hint.

Miss Riverstone set down her empty ratafia glass and glanced about the ballroom. "It certainly has. I hope Pearl won't scold me for playing but one card game, after all of her coaching—and yours, sir."

"Surely you don't allow yourself to be *scolded*, Miss Riverstone?" Mr. Richards said, raising one brow. "You acquitted yourself quite well against that harridan, Lady Mountheath, earlier."

She dimpled up at him in a way that made Noel grit his teeth. "Thank you, Mr. Richards. Perhaps we should have quizzed her on the treatment of her servants, for Pearl hinted to me that it is abominable. As for scolding, Pearl is a good friend and means it in the nicest possible way."

"I am reassured. A woman of your intelligence need apologize to no one, you know."

Miss Riverstone pinkened slightly at Richards' intimate tone, and Noel cleared his throat loudly to remind them both of his presence. "I'm glad to see, Miss Riverstone, that you are not so tired this evening as you were last night."

She turned to him and he held her gaze, smiling down into her eyes until she could see what kindled in his own. Her eyes widened and she pinkened further—clearly remembering as vividly as he how last night had ended.

"That's scarcely surprising." Mr. Richards' scornful voice broke into the private moment. "Chess and cards are hardly as strenuous as dancing—frivolous pursuit that it is."

"Very true," Noel agreed, still not taking his eyes from Miss Riverstone's. Her lashes were remarkably dark and thick, he noticed. Beautifully so. "Dancing was not quite the ordeal you expected, however, was it?"

She parted her lips to answer, and Noel found himself mesmerized by the shape of those lips, the memory of—

"There you are, Rowena." Lady Hardwyck's voice came from behind him, before a word escaped the exquisite lips he was watching. "I'd like to introduce Mr. Robert Southey."

Miss Riverstone blinked and turned, the spell broken. She greeted Mr. Southey eagerly, but Noel tried not to take offense. Southey was a celebrated essayist, poet and biographer—someone bound to appeal to anyone of Miss Riverstone's intellect and sensibility.

"Charmed, Miss Riverstone," the newcomer said, bowing over her hand. Lady Hardwyck then introduced Noel and Mr. Richards, though it was clear at once that the latter was already acquainted with Mr. Southey—and that the two were not on the best of terms.

"I'll speak with you later, Miss Riverstone," Richards said after the most formal of greetings and an awkward pause.

She nodded, but scarcely seemed to notice his defection, so interested was she in hearing Mr. Southey's critique of a new play he had seen the week before. Noel could not regard Mr. Southey as a threat, given the man's age and marital status, so allowed himself to relax—only then realizing how tense he had been.

"Might I prevail upon you to make a fourth at whist?" Lady Hardwyck asked Noel then, and he hesitated only the barest moment before assenting. He could not afford to have his interest in Miss Riverstone marked again by his hostess. Miss Riverstone's continued conversation with Mr. Southey meant that she was safe for the moment from Mr. Richards' return.

Noel couldn't claim to play his best, distracted as he was by discreetly watching Miss Riverstone. She and Mr. Southey moved to another table to play at piquet, where they were soon surrounded by several others of the literary set.

Determinedly, Noel turned his attention back to his own game. What did he hope to gain from his observation of Miss Riverstone, anyway? Now that he'd ruled out her brother as a likely suspect, she had little bearing on his case.

Or did she?

"Mr. Paxton?" Miss Cheevers, his partner, recalled him to the game.

"Sorry." He played a card almost at random.

There was still the matter of those essays which, according to the clerk he'd questioned at the *Political Register*, had been posted from Oakshire. He glanced in her direction again—to see her rising from the piquet table.

"Your game again," Miss Cheevers said to Lord and Lady Hardwyck, with understandable irritation. "Mr. Paxton, will you deal?"

But Noel rose. "I beg you will excuse me. I seem to be too tired to concentrate properly." He beckoned to Harry Thatcher, just passing with a group of other men. "Take my place, won't you, Harry?"

With a shrug, Mr. Thatcher assented, freeing Noel to follow Miss Riverstone, who had just disappeared in the direction of the back staircase. Quickening his pace, acknowledging greetings from the two Mountheath sisters with only a nod, he reached the landing just as Miss Riverstone began to mount the stairs.

"Escaping again?"

She turned with a gasp. "You startled me, sir. But yes, I had thought to retire. It is well past midnight, after all."

"I've also had enough of games and chatter for one evening," Noel confessed. "May I escort you upstairs?"

She frowned, her cheeks brightening. "Surely that wouldn't be proper?"

"Who is to know?" he asked reasonably, though she was perfectly correct. "Besides, is not propriety one of those social constructs you despise?"

One corner of her mouth quirked up, fascinating him. "So I have always claimed. Come, then. We will escort each other."

Now that was a fascinating concept.

"It appears your brother does not share your political views," Noel commented casually as they mounted the stairs together.

"Nelson?" She chuckled—a low, erotic sound. *Erotic?* "Rather the opposite, I should say. It's why he—and my father—never wished me to come to Town. I fear I've been rather an embarrassment to them."

Noel didn't see how this intelligent woman could be an embarrassment to anyone. "Someone must have shaped your views," he persisted. "An uncle? A neighbor?" Perhaps whoever was writing those essays?

"My mother was rather a free thinker for a woman but she died when I was fourteen. I have shaped my own views, after reading widely. I need no man's sanction to form opinions." She spoke archly, daring him to doubt her.

And indeed, he could not. In fact, he could scarcely think, with her gazing up at him like that.

They had reached the upper hallway, where the bedrooms were situated. He wondered which was hers.

"You are unique, Miss Riverstone," he said warmly. "Or—may I call you Rowena? I feel I know you quite well, for all we've only been acquainted a few days."

"I . . . I was thinking the same," she said in a voice that was almost a sigh. "Still, Mr. Paxton—"

"Noel," he corrected her gently.

She smiled, a small, shy smile. "Noel, then. But I was going to say, as well as we understand each other, we seem to disagree about a great many issues."

He moved closer to her. "But that is what makes things so interesting."

"Yes," she agreed, her wide gray gaze probing his own.

As before, he could not seem to stop himself. As he lowered his head, she parted her lips slightly, her tongue flicking out to moisten them. That tiny motion undid him. With a guttural moan, he pulled her against him, claiming her mouth with a fierce kiss.

At once, her arms went about him, urging him closer, even as her lips responded eagerly to his claim. Somehow he had known, had known from the first, that she was capable of such passion, that a fire was concealed beneath her prim exterior—not so prim anymore.

His hands roved up and down her back, exulting in her lush curves, the way her small waist flared to generous hips. She twined her fingers through the hair at the sensitive nape of his neck, slid one hand across the breadth of his shoulders, his back.

Noel felt his breath coming in quick, shallow gasps. Never could he remember wanting a woman so desperately as he wanted Rowena. He tried to remind himself that she was a means to an end, but the feather-light explorations of her fingers, now stroking his ears, drove him past rational thought. Teasing her lips apart with his tongue, he tasted all her kiss had to offer, demanding that she do the same.

Nor did she hesitate. She twined her tongue with his, a joining that went beyond the mere physical. It was as though their very souls touched.

It was that sense of connection, of vulnerability, that recalled him to his senses—the knowledge that he danced on the edge of a precipice that he longed to plunge over until he lost himself in her entirely.

"I—we—" he murmured into her hair.

"Yes?" she breathed, then, "Oh!" much more distinctly. Taking a quick step backward, she stared at him, clearly aghast. "Oh, my."

"Indeed. I had no—That is, I suppose I should apologize, but—"

"No, don't. Unless . . . you are sorry?"

Slowly, he shook his head. "Not in the least, unless I've distressed you."

Again, that half-smile that made him want to kiss her again. "Confused, perhaps. But distressed? No."

"I'm glad. I never want to be a source of pain to you, Rowena." He realized he meant it—which presented him with a problem.

"Thank you. That is—this morning I thought—"

"Yes, I know," he said before she could say too much, tempt him to promise things he was not ready to promise. "I handled that clumsily, and for that I *do* apologize."

She smiled her acceptance of his apology and suddenly she was in his arms again, though he couldn't have said who moved first. Only that it seemed the most natural thing in the world.

Again he felt as though he were falling as desire swept away reason. Her tentative touch revealed her innocence, unleashing a fierce need in him to show her new delights, to be the one who led her through the maze of adult pleasures.

Dimly, in some far-off corner of his mind that still clung to the capacity for reason, he registered the fact that they were exposed here in the hallway. A servant might appear at any moment.

"Which is your room?" he murmured against her lips.

He felt rather than saw her swallow. "Here." She half turned, taking a step toward the next door on the left. "But my maid—"

Abruptly, reason returned. What on earth had he been contemplating? Had she been ready to allow—?

"Your maid. Yes, of course. I do apologize. I've overstepped—that is—Good night, Miss Riverstone."

Though his body protested, he turned from her and strode down the hall to his own room only two doors away. Not trusting himself to so much as glance back, he shut himself inside and leaned against the door, gulping great draughts of air in an effort to calm himself.

"Sir?"

Damn. "I'm fine, Kemp. I just need to think."

His manservant took the hint at once and withdrew without another word.

Was he mad? More than one French beauty had attempted to cloud his mind during the war. Always, he had been able to take his pleasure while keeping his mind, his mission, perfectly clear. Why should this be any different?

Perhaps he was simply out of practice. Still, did he dare risk his investigation—and perhaps men's lives—on the assumption that he would be able to rein in his emotions where Rowena Riverstone was concerned?

"Kemp?"

"Sir?" The man emerged from the dressing room.

"Pack my things. We're returning to our lodgings tonight."

He needed to put some distance between himself and Rowena Riverstone, so temptingly situated only two rooms away. Then, perhaps, he'd be able to recall just how vital his mission was.

Rowena stared, openmouthed, as Mr. Paxton—Noel—disappeared into his room without a backward glance. How could he have altered so abruptly? A moment ago, he had clearly wanted her, wanted—

She put her hands to her flaming cheeks. He'd wanted what she had wanted—what she'd actually been prepared to allow. Was she mad? If her bedchamber had been empty, with no maid to concern them, she had little doubt she and Noel would be in there now, and her virtue on its way to becoming a mere memory.

Thank heaven he had come to his senses, she thought with a discontented sigh. Turning the handle, she entered her room—only to find it empty after all.

"Matthilda?" Though the small fire had been recently tended, there was no answer.

In sudden frustration, Rowena snatched up her hairbrush from the dressing table and flung it across the room. They could have been alone after all! Why, oh why, had she mentioned her maid? She half turned back toward the door, thinking to somehow recall Noel, to let him know, but caught herself before she'd taken a step.

Really, she *must* be mad. Matthilda had likely gone down to the kitchens, and would be back at any moment. And even if she weren't, did she, Rowena, really hold her virtue so cheaply? Could she seriously contemplate destroying her reputation for a fleeting moment of passion?

Yes, she realized, she quite definitely could. She could imagine doing so all too vividly. Not that it meant she *would*, of course . . .

With another sigh, she crossed the room to retrieve her hairbrush, then seated herself at the dressing table to unpin her hair and brush it out with vigorous strokes. The rhythmic action calmed her, and gradually the jangling of her nerves, sensitized to a screaming pitch by Noel Paxton's kisses, quieted. When Matthilda entered a few minutes later, she was able to greet the maid with reasonable equanimity.

"Miss! I did not expect you so early. I'd have come up sooner, if—"

"It's no matter, Matthilda. I've only been here a moment. Run back downstairs and see if a bath might be possible, then come back to help me out of my gown."

A few minutes later, a tub and steaming kettles were brought. While the tub was filled, Matthilda undid the row of hooks down Rowena's back, then lifted the blue gown over her head. Not until she was alone again, lowering herself into the bath, did Rowena allow her thoughts to return to Noel Paxton.

What might he be doing, two rooms away? Was he,

perhaps, thinking of her? Would he have heard the servants bringing her bath water, know that she was now in here completely unclothed?

"Oh, stop it," she said aloud to the empty room.

She had read widely enough to know that men rarely set as much store by kisses, or even lovemaking, as women did. History was littered with stories of women who had foolishly given themselves to undeserving men, only to find themselves ruined and alone.

Of course, there were other stories that ended quite differently, and it had certainly *seemed* as though—

No. She could not count on that. He might have been merely dallying with her. Still, why could she not dally as well? Rowena had never entertained romantic expectations of marriage and family. Her dreams had run rather to ambition and influence, as a man's might. So why could she not take her pleasure as men did?

The novel notion intrigued her.

She would not discourage Noel, she decided. If he wished to pursue a dalliance, she would indulge him and take what enjoyment she might from it, without expecting anything more. That would leave her heart and her mind free for more important things.

If men could separate their emotions from their physical pleasures, then so could she.

But as she drifted off to sleep an hour later, her dreams inexplicably involved Noel Paxton not only kissing her, but declaring his undying love—a love she professed to return.

Chapter 11

"Gone?"

Rowena had dressed with extra care for breakfast, even leaving her spectacles upstairs, only to have Pearl inform her that Mr. Paxton had packed his things and left late last night.

"He said he had things to attend to at his lodgings—that he would be working more closely with Bow Street for a few days, which made staying nearby more convenient," Pearl explained. "I daresay we shall still see something of him, however, as the investigation cannot take up all of his time."

"I daresay," Rowena echoed hollowly. He had said nothing last night about his investigation, nor about leaving. She suspected his decision had been made after the passionate moment they had shared in the upstairs hallway.

But what did it mean?

"You sound tired, dear." Pearl peered at her in evident concern. "It's as well that it is Sunday, and that we have no particular plans for the day. I recommend you take the opportunity to rest."

Rowena nodded, then turned away to fill a plate from the sideboard before Pearl could read her expression. "Yes, I'm sure that would be best. Then I will be fresh for whatever you have planned for tomorrow."

"A picnic in Green Park, to be sure. If the fine weather holds, it will be perfect for a day out of doors. You'll want to choose a dress with a matching parasol, of course, to keep your freckles to a minimum."

While Pearl elaborated on her plans, Rowena's thoughts returned to Noel, though she tried to appear interested in both her breakfast and Pearl's words. *Had* he run away from her? Why? Was she really so threatening—or so distasteful?

But he had not seemed to find her distasteful last night.

Though she tried to distract herself with both reading and writing, by the end of the day Rowena had examined every conceivable explanation for Mr. Paxton's removal, finding none of them satisfactory. The one she wished most to believe—that he had felt honor bound to remove himself from the temptation to sully her virtue—seemed the least likely of all.

Nor was she satisfied with a second draft of the essay she had written for the *Political Register*. Reading it over, she saw that the opinions of both Mr. Richards and Mr. Southey had crept in, along with the mitigating influence of Noel Paxton's views. Had she always parroted the opinions of others like this, with no original thoughts of her own?

Pulling out copies of her previous essays, she realized that, to some extent, she had. In fact, her first two essays had been drawn almost entirely from Mr. Richards' letters. She had even used his handwriting as a model, to disguise her own as a masculine hand.

Surely she was capable of more independent thought—and expression—than she had shown so far. Picking up her pen, she began the essay afresh. Finally, after much work, she was satisfied that the opinions in the essay she would post in the morning were her own and no one else's.

Still, she went to bed that night in a far less complacent frame of mind than she had done the night before. Her life seemed to be teetering on the verge of some change—but whether for better or worse, she could not at all determine.

Noel also spent much of Sunday reading through all of Mr. R's essays, but with a far different purpose. A previous visit to the office of the *Political Register* had yielded the original of one of those essays. Now he carefully reexamined both the hand and the content, again comparing both to letters given him by the Foreign Office—letters known to have been sent by the Black Bishop.

While the writing had clearly been disguised in both cases, there were enough similarities to make it likely that the same hand had penned both, allowing for differences in pens and circumstances. And the similarity of expression struck him even more forcefully than before.

That one phrase, "the sacrifice of men as beasts," while perhaps not unique, was unusual enough to stand out when it appeared in both Mr. R's work and a letter from the Bishop.

He paused then, struck. Had not Lester Richards said something similar last night, while talking with Rowena? At the time, Noel had been watching the lady's face, trying to convince himself that she felt no more than intellectual interest in the other man. Now he recalled some of the actual words that had been spoken.

Mr. Richards? Surely it could not be so easy as that? Nor could he quite trust himself to be objective, given how much he resented the fellow's influence over Rowena. Still, he was duty bound to follow any lead—and he now had an idea of how to do so.

Early Monday morning, Noel again presented himself at the *Political Register*, pleased to discover the clerk who had helped him before, a Mr. Bell, was there. Noel waited until the other clerk was busy on the other side of the small, paper-filled room to put forth his plan.

"Those letters you mentioned before, the ones that have accumulated for the anonymous essayist Mr. R over the past few months," he said softly. "I've an idea how they might be delivered."

The bespectacled young man looked both pleased and surprised. "Do you, sir? Mr. Cobbett would be pleased to do so, I know. He's been so concerned some might be important, or of a timely nature, that he talked about opening them, but felt it would be a breach of privacy to do so."

"He never tried to trace those essays back to their source in Oakshire for that purpose?"

The clerk shrugged. "He would have, I'm sure, had any of them been delivered other than by post. There's another anonymous writer, an LB, who has his pieces delivered by a footman. That made it easy enough to figure out who he was—and to send on any letters he receives, the same way. He doesn't get nearly so many as this Mr. R, though."

"A popular and controversial writer, I perceive." Noel was not surprised, as the essays were both thoughtful and articulate, forcing one to reexamine long-held beliefs. That would draw both support and condemnation, both no doubt equally vehement.

"Oh, aye, he is that. Do you have an address we can send the letters, then?"

Noel shook his head, to Mr. Bell's obvious disappointment. "Not an address. A plan. How if you were to print a notice in this week's *Register*, saying that Mr. R could retrieve his letters himself?"

"I can't imagine he'd come here and risk anyone knowing who he is," said the young man skeptically.

"No, of course not. That's why the notice will specify a different location—one that he will choose himself. He can post a note to you, saying where the letters are to be left, and he can then retrieve them at his convenience. That should preserve his anonymity."

The clerk's brows rose with respect. "It's a good plan, sir. I'm sure Mr. Cobbett will approve. Am I right, however, in thinking that you will wish to know the location, once we receive his reply?"

There was no denying the young man was intelligent. But then, Cobbett would never have fools working for him.

"Yes, but no one else. I won't publicize his identity, I promise you."

"You said before that you're concerned with a matter of national security. I assume you don't want me to tell Mr. Cobbett about that part?"

Noel handed the clerk a few gold coins. "Not just yet. But if I am right, you will have done a very patriotic thing, Mr. Bell, believe me."

"I admit I'm a bit more conservative than some of our contributors," the young man confessed. "Certainly, I wouldn't want to see England go the way of France."

"That's precisely what we may be preventing."

Seating himself at the desk, Noel jotted down the wording for the notice, subject to Mr. Cobbett's approval. While he wrote, the morning's post came, diverting the clerk's attention until Noel handed him the notice.

He glanced up to take it, then back at the letters in his hand. "Sir!" he exclaimed, just as Noel was turning to go. "You may wish to see this." He held out a sealed envelope.

Curious, Noel took it. Even had it not been addressed in the distinctive disguised hand he had spent yesterday examining, the scrawled "Mr. R" on the corner of the envelope declared its source. And it had been posted this very morning, right here in London.

"Interesting," he said, handing it back to the clerk. "This makes me even more hopeful that this fellow will have his letters by the end of the week."

He would make certain inquiries into Richards' activities and try to discover his whereabouts during the war. If that did not rule him out as a suspect, this trap with the letters should prove that he was indeed the mysterious essayist—and the traitor Noel sought.

Lady Hardwyck had planned an excursion to

Green Park this afternoon, he recalled. Though he had intended to keep his distance from Rowena for a few days, he could not afford to ignore an opportunity to observe Mr. Richards more closely, nor an obligation to protect others from a possible traitor.

If he should be thrown into Rowena's company in the course of his investigation, it was simply the price of duty—a price he was more than willing to pay.

The lovely weather, particularly after the unusually dull summer that had cast a pall over England, drew a considerable crowd to assemble in Green Park for the day.

Rowena felt she looked her best in her green-sprigged white muslin with matching parasol—fresh, summery, and ready to captivate any man who looked her way. If Noel Paxton was frightened away by the idea of a dalliance, she would simply find her diversions elsewhere.

The rainy summer had rendered the triangular park as green as its name. Situated directly across Picadilly from Hardwyck Hall, it had been easy for Pearl to arrange to have vast quantities of refreshments carted over in baskets and barrows. Chairs were set up and cloths spread on the grass for the comfort of the guests.

Rowena settled herself on a white, lacy coverlet that complemented her gown and gazed about. Though people at any distance faded into a colorful blur, she did not *think* Noel was in attendance. Mr. Galloway was near enough to identify, however, as were Lord Peter and Mr. Thatcher, all potential "diversions."

Unfortunately, the first man to come her way happened to be her brother.

"Should you not be at the Home Office?" she greeted Nelson as he approached. It did not suit her purposes at all for him to attach himself to her for the day.

He shrugged. "A man must eat. Here, at least, I needn't pay for my food. I'll return to the Office in an hour or so." Dropping down on the cloth beside her, he added, "I needed to speak with you, as there was no opportunity last night. Have you talked with Richards?"

Though she did not feel at all like discussing Nelson's problems on such a lovely day, she nodded. "Briefly, but we were interrupted before I could ask him to forgive your debt. I did think he seemed sympathetic, however, and—oh! I know where Mother's jewels are."

"Do you?" he said eagerly, then frowned. "You haven't been visiting pawn shops unaccompanied, have you, Ro?"

"Of course not. As you said, the jewels would have been sold by now—and so they were. To Lord Mountheath, who gave them to his wife. She was wearing them last night."

Nelson puckered his brow. "They're well and truly gone, then, for there is no way to buy them back without an explanation—and we can trust Lady Mountheath to spread the story far and wide, should she get wind of it."

"Yes, I know," Rowena said with a sigh. "Still, I feel better knowing where the pieces are. And it's rather amusing to think of Lady Mountheath flaunting our mother's baubles with no notion that her husband redeemed them from a pawn shop."

"I suppose that's true," Nelson agreed with a chuckle. "But that don't help with the larger problem of the five hundred pounds I still owe Richards."

Rowena gasped. "Five hundred pounds? I had no idea it was so much. How could you possibly—" She broke off. "That is quite a sum to ask Mr. Richards to forgive. No doubt he has plans for it already."

Nelson nodded glumly. "No doubt. Though he's hinted he'd be willing to accept information in exchange for a portion of it."

"Information? What sort of information?"

"From the Home Office. Details about old spy cases, mostly."

Rowena frowned. "But the war is over. What would anyone want with such information?"

"I have no idea. Far as I can tell, what he wants isn't even secret, though it's not something anyone outside the Home Office would be likely to know about."

"He actually asked you for such information? And you're considering giving it to him?" She was struggling to understand both her brother's reasoning and Mr. Richards' motives.

Nelson shrugged. "As I said, it isn't sensitive or secret. Mostly cases that were closed by the Foreign Office and turned over to us. Can't imagine why he might want such stuff, to be honest."

Rowena was thinking hard. If Mr. Richards needed information or even money for his cause, could she really fault him? "Perhaps he intends to write a treatise, or even a book, on such things," she suggested.

"Perhaps. Anyway, what can I do? It's either tell him what he wants to know or pay him money I don't have."

"No," Rowena said firmly. "Let me speak with him again. Today should provide an opportunity. It would be far worse for your superiors to discover you passing along information—even information that seems perfectly innocent—than for Mr. Richards to publicize your debts."

Nelson was clearly skeptical. "I'd prefer neither occur, but perhaps you are right. I'll give you your chance before I tell him anything. Let me know how it falls out."

"Yes, I'll send word, or tell you the next time I see you."

He clambered to his feet. "You *are* a good sister, Ro! Now, I'm going to go see what it is they're putting out on those tables, before I have to return to Whitehall."

Rowena watched him go with mingled affection and exasperation, wondering if she were really doing him a favor by allowing him to avoid the consequences of his poor judgment. He was her brother, however, so she would do what she could for him.

Half rising, she looked to see whether Mr. Richards had arrived, only to discover him approaching her, along with Lucinda and Augusta Melks and Mr. Galloway.

"Miss Riverstone," he greeted her. "I thought you might like some refreshment, as your brother did not think to provide you with a plate." He handed her an assortment of small sandwiches and a glass of lemonade before taking his place beside her.

The others arranged themselves about the white cloth with their own plates and glasses in hand. Rowena glanced at Mr. Richards, then away, wishing he were as young and handsome as Noel Paxton—then immediately despising herself for such a wish.

"Mr. Richards tells me he succeeded where I failed last night," Mr. Galloway commented.

The ladies, Rowena included, regarded him questioningly.

"At the chessboard," he clarified. "Miss Riverstone is quite the whiz at chess, you must know."

"Indeed?" Miss Augusta regarded Rowena quizzically. "You must be very clever, then—but I suppose that is to be expected in Lady Hardwyck's good friend, as she is so clever herself."

Rowena was uncertain that the comment was meant as a compliment, but smiled her thanks. "Mr. Richards defeated me, however," she said to deflect attention.

"Miss Riverstone plays very well," he said in a manner some might have called condescending. "She needs to learn more focus, and to restrain her emotions from interfering with her reason. I have hopes of schooling her into a truly superior player one day."

Her pride severely stung, Rowena had to make an effort to keep her expression pleasant. "I am unused to playing amidst a crowd. I assure you that in quieter surroundings, I am able to focus quite well." *And would have beaten you last night, crowd or no, had I chosen to do so*, she added silently.

"No doubt, no doubt," he replied placatingly—which only served to irritate her further.

"I should like a chance to prove it to you sometime, sir."

He actually looked surprised—though still complacent. "Of course, my dear. Of course."

"It is a lovely day, is it not?" Miss Melks asked then, in an obvious attempt to change the subject. Her sister quickly agreed.

The others took the hint and conversed on more general topics while enjoying their sandwiches and other dainties. After half an hour, Miss Melks held out her hand to Mr. Galloway. "Sir, you promised to show Augusta and me the swans, did you not?"

"I did indeed." Leaping to his feet, he helped first Lucinda, then Augusta to rise. "Would you care to join us, Miss Riverstone?"

"Perhaps in a few moments," she replied. This might be her best chance to have a private word with Mr. Richards, though in truth she had little desire just now to ask favors of him.

Surprisingly, he broached the subject before she could. "You seemed in rather deep conversation with your brother earlier," he commented as soon as the others were out of earshot.

"Yes, Nelson is concerned about his debt to you," she admitted candidly. "He was asking my advice on the matter."

Mr. Richards frowned. "I am sorry to hear that he has troubled you. I would not have expected a gentleman to run to a lady with his problems, even an exceptional lady like yourself." He did not, Rowena noted, offer to solve the problem himself.

After a slight pause, she said, "Nelson has faith in my intelligence, Mr. Richards—more faith than you seem to show. You have put forth persuasive arguments for the equality of men. Do you not feel women should be accorded the same rights and respect?"

Though he appeared startled, he answered readily enough. "Men have a duty to protect the women under their care. While some, like yourself, possess abilities beyond the norm, you must admit that there are many things women are ill suited for."

"Like chess?" she asked, the stirrings of a plan beginning to form. Perhaps she would not have to beg after all.

He smiled. "Like chess—though you do show great potential."

"I am happy to hear it. I was quite serious when I said I should like another chance to demonstrate it. I might surprise you."

"I am at your disposal, of course. You have merely to name the day." The complacency on his face made it perfectly clear he expected no different outcome.

Time to put her plan to the test. "How if we play for stakes next time?" she asked. "That might help me to—focus."

He raised a thin brow. "What stakes did you have in mind?"

"My brother's debt," she responded. "If I win, you will agree to forgive the remainder. If you win, I will see that you are paid twice what he still owes you."

"I see that recklessness runs in your family, Miss Riverstone. How can I, in conscience, accept such stakes, knowing that I am the superior player? I was distressed enough to discover jewelry of undoubted sentimental value to you had been sacrificed to this debt already."

His concern softened her pride enough to allow a genuine smile. "As it was my suggestion, your conscience is clear. I told you I was not at my best last night. I wish an opportunity to show you I can do better."

He sighed, though she imagined that she caught a glint of eagerness in his eyes. "Very well, if you insist—and if your brother agrees. I would prefer not to have a lady indebted to me."

"I will speak to him, of course." Rowena fought to hide the triumph she felt. "Any debt will be in his name, not mine."

Mr. Richards rose. "I have a previous engagement tonight. A . . . personal matter. Perhaps tomorrow evening? What does Lady Hardwyck have planned?"

"A musicale, I believe. But it may be possible to find a quiet corner for a game, away from the crowd."

"I will look forward to it, Miss Riverstone. Now, if you will excuse me, I need to make certain preparations before this evening." He bowed and left her.

Rowena wondered what he might have planned—for he had seemed almost deliberately mysterious. Something to do with his efforts at reform, perhaps? The Spencean societies were under close surveillance by the authorities, she knew. If he were involved with them, it would make sense that he would not broadcast it.

For a moment, she almost regretted what she would do tomorrow night, but then she remembered his patronizing attitude and smiled. It seemed that even a forward thinker like Mr. Richards had a thing or two to learn.

Noel stood at the edge of Green Park, watching as Mr. Richards took his leave of Rowena. They had spent nearly fifteen minutes *tête-à-tête*, though of course they were in plain view of the rest of Lady Hardwyck's guests. Still, he could not quite suppress an instinctive urge to protect her.

Though he had promised himself he would keep his distance, as soon as Rowena was alone he found himself moving forward. He had a few moments to observe her closely before she saw him—to notice how lovely she looked in her fresh white dress, her coppery curls pulled back with a fetching green ribbon.

"Good afternoon, Rowena." He kept his voice low, not certain whether she would want anyone else to know she had given him permission to use her name.

She turned quickly, a smile lighting her face for an instant before her expression turned guarded. "Mr. Paxton. I had understood you would not be able to come today."

He shrugged. "I was able to conclude my business early." Though she did not invite him to sit, he lowered himself onto the cloth beside her.

"And what business might that have been?" Her gray gaze was as direct as her question, seeming to see right through him. He found himself oddly distracted by the attractive pattern of freckles dusting her nose.

"My investigation into the Saint of Seven Dials, of course."

He was not surprised when she looked doubtful.

"And that necessitated you leaving Hardwyck Hall like a thief in the night?"

Her phrase startled him. Surely, she couldn't suspect—?

"I did feel I could more effectively follow some new leads from my own lodgings near Bow Street, but—no. I admit my precipitousness was prompted by other concerns." Even now, when he should be planning his next move after this morning's inquiries, he found her nearness thoroughly—and pleasantly—distracting.

She lowered her voice. "Last night, I told you not to apologize unless you were truly sorry—and yet you did apologize. I am sorry if I have been a cause for regrets, Mr. Paxton."

"Noel," he reminded her, even though a more formal footing would be wiser. "And my only regret is that I may have distressed you by my actions."

"Yes, I was distressed." Still, she regarded him with that clear, gray gaze. "To learn that you had fled in the night was quite distressing—for a moment or two. I realized, however, that it would be foolish to allow your actions to affect me so."

"I did not *flee*, precisely," he felt obliged to protest. Then, leaning forward to add weight to his words, he added, "I must confess that your actions affect me, whether the reverse is true or not."

Though her color rose, she did not drop her gaze. "My effect upon you seems inconsistent at best, sir. How am I to interpret that?"

He had no idea how to answer her, so instead he rose and extended his hand. "Would you care to walk with me for a bit?"

"Very well." She allowed him to help her to her feet, her small hand warm beneath the thin lace glove she wore. "You did not answer my question," she reminded him as they turned toward the small pond in the center of the park.

"Because I'm not certain of the answer myself," he confessed truthfully. "I can't deny that I am drawn to you. I've never met another woman of your intelligence and candor—and loveliness. But my investigation is at a critical juncture, and I fear I cannot afford the level of distraction you afford."

This was also true, though his investigation was not the one she believed it to be.

"I, ah, never intended to *distract* you, of course," Rowena said after a pause. "Or, at least, perhaps I did—but I never expected it to work."

He glanced down at her in surprise, but she was gazing off into the distance, her cheeks still pink despite the parasol that shaded them from the August sunshine.

"I am flattered that you wished it—and I can assure you that it did indeed . . . work." He did not bother to hide his smile, as she was not watching him.

"So what shall we do about it?" she asked then, finally turning to meet his eyes.

Again startled—and charmed—by her directness, he quickly schooled his expression to one of proper seriousness. "I am open to suggestions. What should you prefer?"

She frowned, apparently not seeing the humor in this unconventional conversation. "I suppose it would make the most sense for us to avoid each other. While I would prefer to, ah, distract you from your investigation of the Saint of Seven Dials, it seems unsporting of me."

"That's unusually gallant of you, Rowena, presuming that avoiding me entails any sacrifice on your part. I would have thought your championship of the Saint would take precedence over the demands of sportsmanship."

She regarded him uncertainly. "Are you poking fun at me? However, I do see your point. Perhaps my priorities are askew."

"I would be surprised to find your priorities anything other than well thought out."

Finally, she smiled, an arch smile that only made her more fetching. "I'm pleased that my lack of social experience is a source of amusement to you, sir. On further thought, however, I see little point in our continued association."

"Oh?" Every statement she made seemed more surprising than the last. Noel was enjoying this conversation immensely.

"We have so little in common," she explained. "You are a proponent of the status quo, putting man-made laws above essential justice, while I am an unrepentant idealist."

He nodded. "I see. But what of chess? We have that in common, as well as a mutual enjoyment in arguing our differing views."

Her glance slid away from his again. "That . . . that is true. But scarcely enough to base a lasting—friendship—upon."

Noel abruptly realized that he wanted Rowena Riverstone for much more than a passing dalliance. He wanted to explore every facet of her mind as well as her body, to take his time getting to know her better than she even knew herself. He wanted her for life.

That shattering discovery sobered him as nothing else could have done. How could he have allowed this to happen, particularly now? But the fact was undeniable.

"Perhaps," he finally admitted, bringing his attention back to her words with an effort. "But friendships have flourished on far less, from my observation. Nor am I convinced that our ideals are so divergent as you seem to believe."

"Then—do you not wish to avoid me after all, despite the danger you claim I present to your pursuit of the Saint?" The look she sent him from under her lowered lashes was positively flirtatious, both out of character and exceedingly alluring.

Though still shaken by his discovery, Noel couldn't help grinning. "So you have decided to do your part to save the rogue, have you? But no—I cannot honestly claim that I wish to avoid you. Quite the opposite, in fact."

"Does that mean you will be returning to Hardwyck Hall?"

Noel considered. He still had numerous inquiries to make, and likely numerous forays as the Saint, to discover what he needed to know about Mr. Richards. In addition, there was his plan to positively identify the mysterious Mr. R once and for all.

"In a day or two, perhaps," he replied. "I do have certain responsibilities that I cannot ignore, much as I might like to. Once I have discharged them, I hope to have opportunity to turn my attention to more pleasant pursuits."

"Once you have captured the Saint, do you mean? Do you believe you are only days from doing so?" There was no mistaking her alarm. Noel rather enjoyed her concern for the Saint, construing it as concern for himself even though she could not know that.

He shrugged. "I dare not be so specific, but my investigation is progressing. I begin to understand the Saint quite well, in fact."

"Yet you still wish to put a stop to his work? You disappoint me, sir." Her eyes reproached him even more strongly than her words.

Noel wished, more than ever, that he could tell her the whole, not only about being the Saint, but about his suspicion that Mr. Richards was the traitorous spy he sought.

It was too soon, however. Too many pieces of the puzzle were yet missing. If he believed she was in any danger that would change things, but that seemed unlikely. She posed no threat to the Black Bishop, after all.

"Perhaps when you come to know me better, you will feel differently." It was all he dared to say, and it was not enough to erase the censure from her eyes.

He felt a strong desire to please her, to give her some tangible evidence of the feelings he finally admitted to himself. The perfect compliment, the perfect gift—

Her mother's jewels? He recalled how upset she had been Saturday night to see them upon Lady Mountheath's arrogant neck. Surely it would please her to have them back.

While he, Noel Paxton, could not approach Lady Mountheath about them without giving rise to dangerous speculation, the Saint was under no such constraint. The Saint worked anonymously.

And tonight, in keeping with his legendary *modus operandi*, the Saint would restore those jewels to their rightful owner.

Chapter 12

Rowena released Noel's arm as they reached the pond. He had that look again, the one he wore during chess matches—and this time she feared it boded ill for the Saint of Seven Dials. She had let his flattery distract her, even as he claimed she distracted him, but she saw now that they were as much at odds as ever on this one point.

"Do you know—or think you know—who the Saint really is?" she couldn't help asking, though she doubted he would tell her.

Nor did he. "See, here is the risk I spoke of. I find myself sorely tempted to tell you all I know, but that would be most unwise. Let us say that I suspect the Saint may reveal himself soon—perhaps to you as well."

Now *that* was an intriguing notion. But she saw from his expression that he would say no more on the subject. Had he meant it when he said she was lovely? No, she could not ask him that, either, without sounding both foolish and insecure.

"Will you be at the literary gathering Lady Hardwyck has planned for tonight?" she asked instead.

To her disappointment, he shook his head. "I am otherwise engaged. It sounds like something you will thoroughly enjoy, however. I daresay you will scarcely miss me."

In truth, she was looking forward to this gathering more than any other event Pearl had scheduled.

"Of course I will miss you," she replied automatically, then wondered if she should have been so honest. He said he admired her candor, but all too often it was simple lack of forethought. Why could she not treat conversation more like chess?

He smiled. "I must comfort myself with that, while I conduct my dull, official business tonight." Pulling out his pocket watch, he frowned. "I must go. I have been here longer than I had planned."

Though he sounded genuinely regretful, Rowena gathered what was left of her dignity. She did not wish him—or anyone—to think she could not enjoy herself without him. "Of course. It was pleasant to see you again."

The glimmer in his hazel eyes told her he knew that she had deliberately refrained from calling him by name, thereby not committing herself to intimate—or formal—appellation. "The pleasure was all mine, Rowena."

To her surprise, he raised her hand to his lips, his thumb stroking her wrist as he held it for a long moment. Unbidden, all of the feelings he had aroused in her two nights before came flooding back—as he no doubt intended.

"Until we meet again," he said softly, his eyes

probing hers, reading her emotions. Then he released her and turned away. As he had done Saturday night, he left her without a backward glance.

Rowena stifled a sigh, but not an unhappy one. This time, he had left her with an unmistakable promise to meet again—and to pursue their friendship, or whatever it was that was growing between them.

"Sir Nelson Riverstone? Are you sure?"

Noel had spent the afternoon and evening tracing Mr. Richards' movements over the past few weeks. That the man was fond of gaming and generally won did not surprise him. Discovering that Rowena's brother had lost heavily to him did, however.

"Aye, fair dipped he must be by now," said Willie, the proprietor of a popular gaming hell on Jermyn Street. He had acted as Noel's eyes and ears before—for a fee. "Last time they played, it was for double or nothing."

"And I take it Sir Nelson lost again."

The other man nodded. "Always loses, far as I can tell. Dunno why gents like that keep playing, though it keeps me in business. Must be a sickness, I'm thinking."

If Sir Nelson's luck was that bad, it seemed unlikely Richards was cheating him, as Noel had first hoped. Still—"Who else is deeply in debt to Mr. Richards?"

But Willie shrugged. "There was another government chap—Grant? Something like that. He lost a good bit of blunt, but was able to pay. Haven't seen him in here lately, though."

"Geraint?"

"Aye, that was it. Know him, do you?"

"I did." Roger Geraint was the agent who had been in London investigating the Black Bishop until his untimely death a few weeks since. It had appeared he had been murdered by footpads, but those at the Foreign Office suspected otherwise—and so did Noel.

"Richards suckers them in the usual way," Willie volunteered. "Loses a game or two, till they get cocky, then cleans 'em out."

Noel nodded. It was a familiar tactic. "You've been helpful, as always, Willie." He slipped the man a five-pound note.

"Always willing to do my part to keep London safe," he said, tucking the note into his breast pocket with a grin. "Just you let the chaps at Bow Street know how cooperative I've been—and that I run an honest house."

Noel clasped the man's grubby hand in his own. "Of course. May you have a profitable evening."

Walking back to his lodgings, he considered what he had learned today. It was little enough, really. Richards had lived in London for the past year or so, but where he had been before that, no one seemed to know. France was a possibility, of course, but he had no proof of that. That he could have been at Waterloo seemed unlikely, in any event.

Though he mingled with the intellectual set, he seemed to have formed no real friendships. His entrée to that circle was primarily by way of two treatises he had written last autumn on the Spencean ideal of the rights of the common man—the same treatises that had recommended him to Rowena Riverstone.

He appeared to have no family in Town, though Lord Peter Northrup had said something about his father having worked at Whitehall some years ago. Noel would have to follow up on that. Nor did he seem to have any noticeable means of support, beyond his skill at the card table.

Having supported himself in the same way for a time, Noel could not condemn the man for that. But he wondered now whether Richards' gaming concealed a darker purpose. Blackmail, perhaps? Geraint had been privvy to all of the information the Foreign Office had accumulated about the Black Bishop, and Sir Nelson had access to data that might be useful to a traitor as well.

Geraint would have refused to tell him anything, which might explain Geraint's murder. But what of Sir Nelson? Rowena said her brother had sold those jewels, presumably to pay a gaming debt—to Richards? He remembered now the look Rowena had directed at Richards after divulging her secret.

He remembered also how agitated Sir Nelson had been that first night, at the ball. What was Richards demanding from him? He meant to find out.

Now, however, he had other business to attend to. A change of clothes, a bite to eat, and then a clandestine visit to the Mountheath house. The Saint of Seven Dials had an interesting evening ahead of him.

Rowena was enjoying herself even more than she had expected. Never before in her sheltered existence had she had such a wonderful opportunity to exchange views with so varied a group of well-read, intelligent people. It was an exhilarating experience.

At the moment, she found herself in animated conversation with Leigh Hunt, Robert Southey and Lord and Lady Holland, of the vaunted Holland House circle. Talk of poetry had given over to politics, Rowena's particular interest.

"Then you feel the Luddites were justified?" she asked Lady Holland. "I read Lord Byron's opinion on the subject some years ago, and thought them well reasoned, though I felt the weavers should have done more to prevent violence against persons."

"Violence will undermine any cause," said Southey, "though I know not all agree with me."

This sparked another lively discussion, to which Rowena listened avidly, occasionally offering an opinion of her own. Indeed, this was the very sort of thing she had hoped to find in London.

At one point, Lester Richards was mentioned, with Mr. Hunt expressing some surprise at his absence, "—for he generally shines in a milieu such as this," he said.

"He mentioned a personal engagement of some sort," Rowena offered. "And indeed, he did express his regrets."

Mr. Southey snorted. "One of his damned Spencean meetings, I'll warrant. Stirring up the very kind of violence we discussed earlier. Of course, like Byron, Richards believes I traded my principles for position when I became poet laureate. But with age comes perspective, leading, I believe, to reason."

"So you feel Mr. Richards has not yet attained that degree of perspective, or reason?" Rowena had noticed the constraint between the two men Saturday evening. This helped to explain it.

"He seems the sort who would go to any lengths to further his ends—legal or illegal, peaceful or violent,"

Mr. Southey said with a shrug. "I have come to believe that the end does not in all cases justify certain means."

Rowena nodded noncommittally, but she was then struck by a sudden thought. Might Mr. Richards' principles lead him even to theft for a good cause—as the Saint of Seven Dials? The more she considered it, the likelier it seemed.

Stealing Rowena's jewels was going to be harder than Noel had anticipated. The Mountheaths were dining at home tonight, with another couple he had identified as Lord and Lady Plumfield. Shouldn't all of these people have retired to their country estates by now? he wondered irritably as he watched the dining room from atop the garden wall, using a small spyglass.

Lady Mountheath was wearing the jewels in question: diamond earrings, necklace and brooch with emeralds interspersed. Which meant he wouldn't be able to act until the Plumfields left. He would watch to see where Lady Mountheath placed the jewels before going to bed—and pray it would not be in her own bedchamber. He settled himself more comfortably on the wall to wait.

Presently, the ladies went into the parlor while Lord Mountheath, Lord Plumfield and a young man Noel presumed was Plumfield's son remained in the dining room over brandy and cigars. He couldn't see the parlor from this vantage point, but that scarcely mattered.

Noel was considering leaving and coming back later when the gentlemen rose and left the dining room. He jumped from the wall, making little noise in his thin-soled shoes, though his toes stung at the impact. Cautiously, he circled around to the other side of the garden, where he might have a clear view of the parlor.

Applying his spyglass again, he watched the two Mountheath girls flirt shamelessly with young Plumfield while their parents discoursed on undoubtedly boring topics. Fairly adept at lip-reading, a skill he had developed during his Puss in Boots days, he identified such words as "drainage," "imports," and "sleeves."

Eventually, they ran out of conversation—or perhaps were as overcome by boredom as Noel was—and the Plumfields took their leave. Lord and Lady Mountheath appeared to have little to say to each other once they were gone, though Fanny and Lucy giggled together as they left the room—no doubt comparing notes on the young man.

Again Noel crept through the garden, trying to keep Lady Mountheath in his sights. The angle was wrong for viewing the upper floor, where the bedchambers would be—all he could see were ceilings. No one lingered below, however, which meant the jewels had likely not been put into a safe or strong box there.

He sighed, settling in for another tedious wait until at last all lights in the house were extinguished. Now, finally, he could make his move. All doors and windows were locked, of course, but that was small deterrent. Plying his lock picks, he soon had the back door open and was creeping up the stairs in search of his goal.

Reaching the upper hallway, he was able to identify Lord Mountheath's chamber by the loud snores resonating behind the door. The next one along was likely to be his wife's. Slowly, he turned the door handle, only to find it locked as well. What the devil did the woman fear in her own house?

With an inaudible sigh, he again pulled out his picks, and in a moment was able to push the door open. One hinge protested, and he froze, listening for any movement from the direction of the bed. None came, so he moved forward—only to see the bristling whiskers of Lord Mountheath, the lone figure in the bed.

Noel backed out of the room as softly as he had entered, closing the door behind him after oiling the offending hinge. Was Lady Mountheath the snorer, then?

He went back to the first door, unlocking it as he had the other. The resonant snorting and wheezing doubled in volume, nearly rattling his teeth from his head. The faint light from the window revealed a frilly nightcap on the occupant of the bed, however. He was in the right room.

Turning his attention to the dressing table, he silently examined the assorted boxes and jars cluttering its surface. Opening first one, then another, he reflected that he was unlikely to be heard over the fearful din of Lady Mountheath's snoring. No wonder her husband slept in a separate room.

He had gone through almost every receptacle and drawer and was regretfully coming to the conclusion that the jewels must be elsewhere, when his fingers contacted something cold and hard at the bottom of a box of ribbons. One by one he extracted a brooch, necklace and earrings. Success!

After verifying that these were indeed Rowena's jewels, Noel pocketed them, then hesitated. Should he—? He glanced over his shoulder at the raucous sleeper, then grinned. Quickly, he pulled a card from the pocket where he'd stowed the jewels, placed it beneath the ribbons, closed the box, and left.

Rowena stifled a yawn. Fascinating as the conversation had been all evening, she couldn't deny that she was beyond tired. As the last of the guests took their leave, a glance at the clock on the drawing room mantelpiece showed it to be past two.

"Goodness, do they always stay so late?" she asked Pearl once the door had closed on Lord and Lady Holland, the last to leave.

"Not always, but frequently. I thought you were beginning to get used to Town hours?" her friend chided her.

Rowena smiled, despite her weariness. "Beginning, yes, but I fear it will take time. Thank you for a most fascinating evening."

"I knew you would enjoy it. Now, don't you wish you had come to London long before? I told you how many interesting people you would meet here."

"Yes, of course you were right—aren't you always?" Rowena did not point out that she could scarcely have come on her own over her father's or brother's protests before coming into her inheritance. "Now, can't we please go up to bed?"

By the time Rowena reached her chamber, she was

half prepared to go to bed fully clothed, she was so tired. However, one look at Matthilda's frightened face roused her to alertness.

"What is it?" she asked, instantly concerned.

The maid held out a small, wrapped package with trembling hands. "Oh, miss! I only stepped out for a few moments—down to the kitchens to fetch hot water for your washing up—and when I came back, this was on your pillow."

Rowena took the package with a frown. "Did you ask Molly if she knew anything about it?" The chambermaid occasionally entered the room to change linens and dust.

"Yes, miss, it was the first thing I thought to do. She has no more idea than I how it came there. Do you think it was housebreakers?" Matthilda twisted her hands together.

"A housebreaker who leaves gifts instead of stealing? Unlikely, I should think. Well, let's see what it is, shall we?" Rowena proceeded to untie the jaunty bow and unwrap the parcel.

When her fingers touched something hard within, she felt a sudden prickling of foreboding. Quickly, she tore away the rest of the paper, only to gasp at what lay revealed. Her mother's jewels, all of them.

"How—? You are certain you saw no one, Matthilda?"

"No, miss, on my oath." She leaned forward to look at what Rowena held. "Oh! Were those not Lady Riverstone's?"

Rowena nodded, still staring at the diamond and emerald set in puzzlement.

"Likely you left them somewhere, and they was returned." Matthilda was clearly relieved, the mystery solved in her mind.

But not in Rowena's. "Yes, I'm sure that was it. Doubtless tomorrow we'll find out who left them."

She thought that unlikely, however. Whoever had returned the jewels had either redeemed them or, more likely, stolen them from Lady Mountheath. Just now, though, she was too tired to puzzle out the possibilities.

"We're clearly in no danger, in any event. Help me get ready for bed, Matthilda."

It was as well Pearl had planned nothing before the evening's musicale, for Rowena did not rise until well past noon the next day. Almost the first thing she saw upon waking were her mother's jewels, lying where she had left them on her dressing table.

This was a mystery she was determined to solve—but if the jewels *had* been stolen, she'd best keep them hidden for now. She wrapped the jewels in a handkerchief, tucked them in the back of the drawer of the writing desk, then rang for her maid.

"You have just missed our first callers," Pearl greeted her when she came downstairs half an hour later. "Mr. Richards particularly asked for you, and left these." She indicated a small but lovely arrangement of carnations and sweetpeas.

Rowena felt absurdly flattered. No gentleman had ever sent her flowers before. "That was most kind of him."

"He apologized for his absence last night, but said that you would understand that some business is more important than socializing." Pearl's expression was frankly curious, but Rowena could not answer her unspoken question.

"He did not tell me where he would be—" she began, then stopped, struck by a wild suspicion. The jewels—could that be what Mr. Richards had been doing last night? He had expressed regret for involving her in Nelson's debt to him. Was this his way of repaying her?

"Rowena?"

Shaking her head, she managed a smile. "I was trying to remember just what he said yesterday, but it was nothing to the point. I have no idea what business he meant. Perhaps he will explain later."

Pearl looked as though she meant to ask more questions, but just then another caller was announced—Noel Paxton.

"Good day, ladies," he said with a bow. Rowena could not help noticing how exceedingly handsome he looked in his well-cut riding coat and top boots. "I trust I find you both well."

"Quite well, thank you, Mr. Paxton," Pearl replied. "We missed you last night."

"Duty does not always allow me to follow the dictates of my . . . wishes," he replied with a glance at Rowena that made her pulse quicken. Had he almost said "heart"?

Pearl was clearly not oblivious to the unspoken exchange. Rising, she said, "I must go speak with the housekeeper for a moment. Pray excuse me, Mr. Paxton. I won't be long." With a sunny smile, she left the parlor, though of course she did not close the door behind her.

"How went your 'dull, official business?'" Rowena asked, more for the sake of saying something than because she wished to hear the details. He was unlikely to give them to her anyway.

Nor did he. "Parts of it were dull indeed, but rewarding nonetheless. I hope your evening was more interesting, and equally rewarding?" He moved to sit across the tea table from her.

"Oh, quite." She proceeded to relate some of the more fascinating discussions, watching his expression as she mentioned one or two controversial points. "Mr. Southey is more conservative than I had expected, but Mr. Hunt was all fire and enthusiasm."

"I can see I would have been entirely out of my element, then," he said with a smile. Then, with a studied casualness that Rowena found rather amusing, "I presume Lester Richards made one of the company?"

"No, he was unable to attend." At the flash of satisfaction in his eyes, she could not help adding, "But he sent those flowers by way of apology."

Noel frowned at the arrangement she indicated. "Did he indeed?" He seemed to struggle with some decision, then moved his chair closer to hers. "Rowena, I hope you will not put too much trust in Richards. I have reason to believe he may not be as he appears."

So he *did* suspect Mr. Richards was the Saint. Rowena felt some satisfaction that she had come to the same conclusion on her own. "I imagine most men are not quite what they seem," she replied. Somehow, she must deflect Noel's suspicions.

He leaned forward, placing one hand over hers. "Perhaps you are right. I wish—" He broke off whatever he had been about to say, his gaze locked with hers. Slowly, he closed the short distance between them.

Rowena felt her heart thundering as his lips touched hers. Vainly, she tried to remind herself that she could not put her trust in this man, either—that he represented all she felt obliged to oppose. But her brain was rapidly giving way to her body and emotions, which pled Noel's case most forcefully.

For a blissful moment, she allowed sensation to take over, parting her lips to allow him to deepen the kiss. Their hands clasped between them, and again he stroked her wrist above her glove, sending spirals of delight up her arm and into her vitals. His kiss was tender rather than demanding, but still she felt an irresistible urge to give herself up to him, body, soul and mind.

"Rowena," he whispered against her lips, the vibration cascading through her body, making her very nipples taut. "I—"

Footsteps sounded in the hallway, and they abruptly broke apart. For a moment they stared at each other, Rowena noting with both satisfaction and alarm that his color was as heightened as hers must be. Then they both swung around to face the door with polite, social smiles.

"That is settled," Pearl declared as she entered. "I feared we would not be able to get enough fish for tonight's dinner, but Mrs. Potts assures me—" She broke off, her brows rising as she looked from Rowena to Noel and back. "You two haven't been arguing again, have you?"

Rowena felt her lips twitch and beside her, Noel's

cough sounded suspiciously like it had been converted from a laugh.

"Not about anything of importance," Rowena managed to say with a straight face. "Don't worry, Pearl. Both of us quite enjoy—arguing. Do we not, Mr. Paxton?"

"We do indeed," he asserted. "Now, what were you saying about the fish?"

Chapter 13

"Have you no leads at all?" Sir Nathaniel Conant, chief magistrate of the Bow Street Runners, ran a hand through his hair in evident frustration.

Noel looked the older man in the eye and shook his head. He hated to deceive Sir Nathaniel, but his true superiors were at the Foreign Office, and they had approved this course. No Saint of Seven Dials had ever killed or even harmed anyone, after all, while the Black Bishop was a genuine danger.

"As you know, I felt I had good evidence against Lord Hardwyck, but further investigation proved me wrong."

"Thank heaven for that, at least!" Sir Nathaniel exclaimed. "I don't like to think of the repercussions were we to attempt to arrest a peer of the realm on less than complete proof of guilt. But I'm under quite a lot of pressure now, what with this latest robbery at the Mountheath house."

Keeping his expression carefully neutral, Noel said, "It does seem strange that the Saint would target a household he had stolen from already. Has he ever hit the same place twice before?"

"No. And why it had to be Mountheath—! You can't imagine what it was like last spring, after the first theft from that house. Lady Mountheath sent a footman round every day—twice, some days—to ask about our progress. Had her husband stir up sentiment to launch a parliamentary investigation into our workings. I'm still dealing with the consequences of that."

Noel hadn't known the Mountheaths were behind that, but doubted he'd have acted differently if he had. Rowena deserved to have those jewels back, and Lady Mountheath deserved whatever came her way, as many young reputations as she had shredded over the years. Even his own sister Holly had not escaped the harridan's barbed tongue in the early days of her marriage.

"Perhaps that is why the Saint seems bent on harrassing the Mountheath household?" Noel suggested. "If he follows such things, he may fear that their interference will make his task harder."

"Damned foolish of him, if so," Sir Nathaniel declared. "This is only bound to redouble their efforts. Ah, well." He heaved a heavy sigh. "What comes, comes. Perhaps he's becoming careless and we can use that to finally rid London of the scoundrel."

Noel nodded. "Perhaps. I'll redouble my own efforts, sir, and report any progress."

"You do that, Paxton. And see you *do* have progress to report by the next time we meet."

Noel was still reflecting on his interview with Sir Nathaniel when he arrived at Hardwyck Hall that evening for the musicale. He'd been in some interesting situations over the course of his undercover career, but never had he been cast as his own quarry. While he couldn't deny the humor of his predicament, the moral implications were a bit bothersome.

If he could finally bring the Black Bishop to justice, however, it would all even out. More than one battle had been lost due to his duplicity, not to mention the men he'd had murdered or executed. As soon as he'd paid his respects to his hosts, Noel went in search of the one person he believed might help him to balance the scales.

"Ah, Miss Riverstone. You are lovely this evening, as always." And she was, arrayed in turquoise satin and pristine white lace. Surrounded as she was by other guests, he was forced to greet Rowena more formally than he'd have preferred.

Even so, her cheeks pinkened at his words. "Good evening, Mr. Paxton. I am pleased to see that your duties allowed you to attend."

"I made a particular effort to conclude my business early today."

"Music lover, are you, Paxton?" Harry Thatcher asked, coming up just then. "I seem to remember you saying so in Vienna. Charmed to see you again, Miss Riverstone."

She bobbed a quick curtsey. "The pleasure is mine, Mr. Thatcher. So you were at the Congress of Vienna as well? Perhaps you can tell me more about what it was like there than Mr. Paxton has been willing to do."

He bowed over her hand with the slow smile Noel

had seen him use all too effectively on other ladies. "It would be my extreme pleasure, Miss Riverstone. Would you care to retire to a private corner somewhere so that I may regale you with my stories?"

"I'm sure Miss Riverstone is too well versed in the proprieties to consent to being alone with you, Harry." Noel tried to keep the edge from his voice. "There's no reason you can't tell about what little you did there that is fit for a lady's ears in a more public forum."

The laughter in Harry's eyes showed that his flirtation had been designed to get just such a reaction from Noel. "I suppose you're right, Paxton—more's the pity. Do seek me out later, Miss Riverstone, won't you?" With a jaunty wink at Noel, he sauntered off.

"You do not approve of Mr. Thatcher?" Rowena asked, watching Harry disappear into the passage leading to the smoking room.

"Oh, he's an amiable enough rogue," Noel admitted, "but more used to dealing with high flyers and serving wenches than ladies of quality like yourself."

Rowena regarded him quizzically. "It's very touching that you feel obliged to protect me from various gentlemen, but I can't think it's necessary."

"I'm not—," he began, then realized that was precisely what he'd been doing, both yesterday afternoon with Mr. Richards and now with Harry. "I don't wish to see you hurt," he concluded, holding her gaze to prove his sincerity.

Her eyes widened at what she saw in his. "Oh." The word was almost a sigh.

Again, he was seized by a desire to take her in his arms, to prove with his lips, his body, just how strongly he felt. But of course that was impossible in this setting. In fact, Lady Marcus was approaching them just now.

"Rowena! Just the person I was looking for. You'll appreciate the humor in my latest blunder without making fun of me." She paused, glancing at Noel uncertainly.

He took the hint at once. "I believe I will visit the buffet tables before the entertainment begins. May I bring you ladies anything?"

They declined, and he moved away, scanning the room as he went. There was Richards, just entering. Noel was determined to keep a close eye on him, watch who he spoke to, how he conducted himself. Particularly around Rowena.

In fact, Richards was already heading her way, a certain intensity in his eyes that Noel found disturbing. Snatching up a canape to preserve his pretense of wanting food, he turned to follow his quarry at a discreet distance.

Deep in animated conversation with Lady Marcus, Rowena did not notice Richards until he spoke to her—perhaps because she was again without her spectacles. Though she smiled most pleasantly, Noel was pleased to note that her color did not change, as it had when she greeted himself.

Moving closer, Noel was able to hear snatches of their conversation.

"—my friend, Lady Marcus," Rowena was saying.

Richards bowed. "Charmed, my lady. Any friend of Miss Riverstone's must be worth cultivating, from my limited experience."

What might be the man's motive for ingratiating

himself with Rowena? If he were extorting her brother for information, as Noel suspected, perhaps he merely hoped to allay suspicion by also befriending the sister. Or did he perceive in her a kindred spirit who might be induced to help him in whatever seditious plans he was now formulating?

Either way, Noel felt duty bound to interfere.

"I believe the first performance will begin shortly," he said, rejoining the group. "We may wish to move into the gallery and take our seats."

Richards shot him a look of barely concealed dislike, quickly schooled to one of cool politeness before the ladies could note it. Lady Marcus excused herself to go in search of her husband, and the remaining three turned toward the archway leading to the gallery, where the first performance was to be held according to the programs Lady Hardwyck had provided.

They had taken only a step or two, however, before they were accosted by Miss Fanny Mountheath. "Miss Riverstone, how nice to see you again," she said with a falsely bright smile. "And you, too, Mr. Paxton. I trust you have all heard the news? My poor mother."

"Yes, I read of it in the afternoon papers," Rowena replied. "Is it certain that the Saint of Seven Dials was the culprit?"

"Oh, yes—he left one of his calling cards in my mother's very bedchamber! I declare, I shall be afraid to sleep for weeks now. It is most oversetting, as you can imagine. Mr. Paxton, perhaps you should call on us to allay my mother's—and my—fears." She batted her eyelashes at Noel.

Trapped, he forced a smile. "Certainly, if you feel it

would help. Remember, however, that the Saint has never yet harmed anyone, according to all I have been able to learn of his activities. You are doubtless quite safe from physical danger."

Clearly, this was not the level of sympathy she had hoped for. "You are the expert, of course," she said with an unattractive pout. "I do hope you will catch him soon, however. Oh, mother is beckoning to me. Good evening."

She hurried off and the trio resumed their progress toward the gallery. Rowena, to Noel's irritation, took Mr. Richards' arm rather than his own.

"I have reason to thank you, I believe," she said to Richards as they walked, in an undertone that Noel had to strain to hear. He managed to appear oblivious and disinterested, hiding his shock at what must surely be her meaning.

There was a pause, then Richards replied, "My goal was to please you, Miss Riverstone."

"You most definitely succeeded. And you may trust—" With the corner of his eye, Noel saw her looking over at him. "Thank you," she finished in a whisper, clearly not wishing to say more in Noel's hearing.

The long gallery, hung with dozens of portraits of Hardwyck ancestors, had been converted for the evening into a performance hall, with a small dais erected at one end and chairs placed for the convenience of listeners. Rowena selected a seat near the dais, and Richards and Noel sat on either side of her.

Noel was quite aware that Rowena wished to have a private word with Richards after their brief exchange, but he was determined to prevent it. Clearly, she had been referring to the return of her mother's jewels—the jewels he himself had procured for her, at great risk.

After their conversation this morning, it had occurred to him that she might interpret his warning against Richards as evidence that Noel suspected him as the Saint of Seven Dials—a result he had not considered at the time. It seemed he was right.

The music began, a haunting air by one of Europe's most accomplished flutists, but Noel scarcely heard it. He was overcome instead by the irony of his situation. Not only could he not claim credit for the favor he had done her, he must sit idly by while she showered his enemy with gratitude—a gratitude Richards was all too likely to exploit.

It was more imperative than ever that he not allow Rowena and Richards a moment alone, he realized. If he did, she would doubtless use that opportunity to warn Richards against him.

At best, Richards might inform her that he was not, in fact, the Saint. While Noel did not like giving Rowena one more reason to admire the man, her assumption did offer Noel himself extra protection from her perceptiveness. At worst, Richards might guess Noel's true intent, which could have disastrous consequences.

He would simply have to stick as close to Rowena Riverstone as her own corset.

And *that* intriguing image served to divert his mind for the remainder of the performance.

"What are you about tonight?" Rowena hissed as Noel accompanied her to the buffet tables between performances. "I am quite capable of filling a plate on my own, you know."

She realized she was being rude to him—again—but she was becoming concerned that she would never get a chance to arrange that most necessary chess match with Mr. Richards with Noel hovering this way.

"Of course," he replied, appearing not the least put off by her rudeness. "I simply enjoy your company, and the opportunity to be of use to you. The meat pies and the fruit tarts look remarkably similar, and I would not wish you to choose the wrong one by mistake."

He was referring, she knew, to her poor eyesight, but at least he did so subtly. Nor was the potential blunder he mentioned particularly unlikely.

"Very well, sir, if you insist," she said with a reluctant grin. "You may select a light repast for me—more fruit than meat, I think."

Mr. Richards had moved further down the table, making it impossible for her to broach the subject of the chess match just then. She wondered if he had reconsidered. After all, why should he risk losing what Nelson owed him for the chance at doubling an amount Nelson already could not pay? He might consider her assurances of payment worthless.

She moved in his direction, Noel close behind her as he filled two plates with select dainties. With sudden inspiration, she turned. "I believe I should like one of those . . . things . . . at the far end of the table," she said, pointing at an item she could not identify at that distance.

He looked. "A jug of cream?"

"No, next to that." She ignored his obvious amusement.

"Ah. The bowl of sugar lumps."

She glared at him. "Yes. The sugar lumps. I should like one."

Though his lips twitched, he went to do her bidding. Quickly, she moved forward to take advantage of the brief respite. "Mr. Richards," she said softly. "Are you still willing to allow me the rematch we discussed yesterday?"

He turned in evident surprise. "Of course, Miss Riverstone." Then, glancing behind her, "If you think you can shed your shadow for an hour."

Rowena was about to warn him about Noel's suspicions—fear that she might do so must explain his refusal to leave her alone with Mr. Richards—but it was already too late.

"Your plate, Miss Riverstone, complete with the sugar lump you requested," Noel said, rejoining her.

Earlier, when he had looked into her eyes while assuring her that he wished to keep her from harm, she had felt as strongly drawn to him as she had this afternoon in Pearl's drawing room. Now, as frustration warred with attraction, she thought how perverse it was that this particular man should have such an unsettling effect on her.

"Thank you, Mr. Paxton," she said, willing her color to remain neutral. "Mr. Richards and I were just discussing the possibility of another chess match later, when the guests disperse to hear some of the lesser performances."

There. If he would not leave her side, she would simply have to carry out her plans for the evening with him in attendance. He need not know about the stakes.

"Splendid. Much as I enjoy music, I enjoy watching skilled chess players matching wits more. And I imagine we shall still be able to hear some of the performances from whatever location we find for a table and board."

"Perhaps you would be so kind as to find Lady Hardwyck and ask her when and where we might play?" That would give her the chance she needed to warn Mr. Richards.

"No need. Here comes Lady Hardwyck now." If he knew what Rowena intended, he hid it admirably under a serene smile. "My lady, a word with you?"

At his behest, Pearl joined them. "There is no problem with the food, I hope? After the dust-up about the fish this morning—"

"No, no, everything is perfection," he assured her. "A credit to your organization and generosity. We were merely hoping you might do us a favor."

Unwilling to let Noel arrange everything, Rowena spoke up. "Mr. Richards and I were hoping to play a game of chess during the course of the evening, once the lead performers had concluded. Would it be terribly unsocial of us to do so?"

As she had feared, Pearl frowned. "Mr. Richards, you must know that this is Rowena's first visit to Town. You mustn't encourage her to act the hermit here, as she has done all her life in the country. I wish her to enjoy what Society has to offer."

"Oh, but—" Rowena began to protest, but Mr. Richards cut her off with a bow.

"Surely, Lady Hardwyck, it is possible for her to

enjoy both Society and her favorite pursuits? I had no mind to closet her away in a private room, I assure you. Merely some out-of-the-way corner, where we can still hear and see what is going forth."

Though she still shook her head at Rowena, Pearl smiled. "Of course I will not *forbid* it. I'll speak to one of the footmen and see that a board is set up. Would that alcove be acceptable?" She pointed to a recessed archway along the side of the ballroom.

"Thank you, Pearl. That would be perfect," Rowena said gratefully. Perhaps too gratefully, for Pearl shot her another keen glance.

"You are not finding so much activity upsetting after the quiet life you have led, are you, Rowena? My intent was to stimulate, not to overwhelm."

Suddenly self-conscious in front of these two gentlemen she wanted to impress, Rowena shook her head. "Not at all. I merely wished a chance to revenge myself for Mr. Richards' win the other night, and this seemed a good opportunity."

Pearl gave her a long look, which Rowena knew was an unspoken reminder that gentlemen preferred to win. This time, however, she could not oblige. Nelson's future was at stake. She met Pearl's gaze steadily and her friend gave it up with a slight shrug.

"Very well. But mind your competitive nature does not get you into trouble one day, dear."

Pearl left them to signal to a passing footman, and Rowena turned her attention to her well-filled plate, preferring not to comment upon Pearl's last remark.

Noel, however, seemed unwilling to let her ignore it. "I have never considered a competitive nature to be a flaw. Have you, Mr. Richards?"

"Certainly not in a man," Mr. Richards agreed. "However, it is far more—unusual—in a woman, and perhaps less useful for the role she typically fills in our society."

"Do you think so, sir?" asked Rowena. "In my few days in Society, I have noted many instances of competitiveness among women, though what they frequently compete for is attention and status, rather than victory in games or war."

"They compete for husbands, you mean—husbands that will provide them status, safety and respectability. Once married, however, they have little to strive for—which is no doubt as it should be."

"I must disagree," Noel said before Rowena could respond to this attack upon her sex. "Lady Hardwyck still works to better the lot of the poor and oppressed, nor is she the only married lady I can point to who continues to put her abilities to good use. My own sister—"

"Hardly typical examples," Mr. Richards pointed out. "Lady Hardwyck is wife to one of the richest men in England, while your sister, Lady Vandover, is in training to become Duchess of Wickburn one day. More is expected of women in such positions."

Rowena had been about to mention the accomplishments of women of lesser status, even commoners, who had set up orphanages and hospitals, but Mr. Richards' words sent such arguments out of her head. Noel Paxton's sister was to become a duchess? Why had he never mentioned such a thing to her?

She stared at him accusingly and he turned, as though feeling her eyes upon him. He gave her a rueful smile and a slight shrug before turning back to Mr.

Richards with examples of his own that showed women quite capable of accomplishing worthy goals, regardless of their positions in Society.

Gathering her wits, Rowena reentered the discussion, but she was torn. Lester Richards in person was proving rather different from what she had expected of the man she had idolized. He clearly held women in generally low regard, and then there was the matter of his gaming for high stakes and pressing Nelson for information from the Home Office, which seemed underhanded if not treasonous.

Was it possible she was wrong about him being the Saint of Seven Dials? But no, he had all but admitted it when she had thanked him for retrieving her jewels.

And then there was Noel Paxton, who derided views she held dear—including those she herself had expressed as MRR—and whose stated goal was to put an end to the noble Saint's career. Yet here he was championing the contributions of women, just as he had more than once shown admiration for her own abilities. Not to mention the sheer physical attractiveness of the man . . .

Was she really so shallow as to allow *that* to color her perceptions of the two? True, Noel Paxton fit the physical image of a hero better than Mr. Richards did, but one could never judge by appearances.

Could one?

"The next performance is beginning," she said to the two men, as much to distract herself from her disturbing ruminations as to quiet their argument, an argument that put her preconceptions about both at risk.

The singer and her accompanying pianist were both exquisitely skilled, and for a brief time Rowena was able to concentrate on the music rather than her jumbled emotions. At the conclusion of the performance, she excused herself to go to the ladies' withdrawing room, feeling strongly that she needed a respite from both gentlemen.

Once there, however, she discovered that the conversation of the ladies who had retreated to adjust the pins in their dresses or to avail themselves of the necessary was all about the Saint of Seven Dials and his latest daring exploit.

"—from her very bedchamber while she slept, can you imagine?" Miss Augusta Melks was saying.

"Had it been my bedchamber, I might have invited him to stay," responded Miss Stuckton with a giggle. "Oh, to discover who the Saint really is!"

Rowena left the room more disturbed than before. It occurred to her that she would never be able to wear her mother's jewels again—at least, not in public. To do so would be to advertise her connection to the Saint. Oh, this was becoming far too complicated!

Returning to her pair of self-appointed escorts, she noticed that the chess board she had requested had been placed in the alcove. Mr. Richards had noticed it as well, for he pointed it out the moment she rejoined them.

"Yes, let us play," she said at once.

Much as she had looked forward to this game, she was now only anxious to have it over. At least then she would have one less thing to worry about, and could perhaps devote her mind to untangling her conflicting emotions.

Chapter 14

Lester Richards carefully concealed his eagerness as he followed Miss Riverstone to the alcove where the chessboard had been set up for their match. A few inquiries had revealed that she did indeed have the means to make good on twice her brother's debt. One thousand pounds would be almost as useful to him as the information he had hoped to extract from Sir Nelson.

With that kind of money, he'd be able to buy the allegiance of a Home Office clerk lower in status but more willing to snoop. He'd also be able to ensure the privacy of his next meeting, as well as the critical one planned for next week—the one that should finally start the wheels turning for the downfall of England's damned aristocratic class.

For Lester Richards was a republican in the truest sense of the word. He had been fired with enthusiasm for the French Revolution as a lad of fourteen, when first hearing about it from his French mother, exiled by his autocratic father to chilly Cumberland. No excesses could be too great if they brought about the ideals of liberty and equality for all men.

Later, he had done his part to keep King Louis XVIII from the throne. Though he had failed at that, he was determined to bring about a new order here in his native England. At present, the radical Spenceans seemed his best means to achieving that end.

Therefore, he had insinuated himself into their midst until he became a leader of sorts, at the same time ferreting out and destroying all evidence—and men—that could link him to his former identity as the Black Bishop, one of Napoleon's staunchest, most useful supporters. For both enterprises, however, he needed information—and money.

"Shall I take white again?" Miss Riverstone asked when they reached the table.

"Of course," he said, moving to the side where the black pieces were arrayed.

Why the silly chit wanted a rematch, and for such enormous stakes, he had no idea. She seemed reasonably intelligent for a woman, so she must know she was incapable of besting him. Perhaps this was a way for her to contribute to his cause—a cause she seemed to approve—without publicly declaring her sympathy?

Whatever her reasons, he was more than willing to take her money.

Miss Riverstone took her chair, which that irritating legalist Paxton held out for her. The man had stuck to them both like glue all evening, and Richards did not believe admiration for Miss Riverstone was his sole reason.

One of his confederates had informed him earlier today that Paxton had been snooping about the gaming hells, asking questions about him. He had apparently been an acquaintance of Geraint's, the fellow Richards had had to dispatch when he grew too inquisitive. It appeared Paxton might have to follow his friend—a prospect Richards found not the least bit distasteful.

"I trust these surroundings are less distracting than those of the card party?" he asked as Miss Riverstone opened the game with her king's pawn.

"Yes, I believe I will be able to concentrate properly this time."

There was something almost smug in her expression, and he realized in sudden alarm that no one had witnessed their wager yesterday. Suppose, after losing, she planned to deny it had taken place? It was the only thing he could think of to account for her complacency, given his superiority as a player.

"Perhaps we should restate our terms, for the record," he said before making his first move. Paxton might be an enemy, but he was one of those honorable sorts and well regarded, which made him an adequate witness.

Miss Riverstone was clearly startled—and displeased. "Our terms?"

"Double or nothing for your brother's debt," he stated clearly, enjoying her anxious glance at Mr. Paxton. "He owes me nothing if you win, but one thousand pounds if you lose."

She glared at him, which must mean he had been right about her intention. "Yes, of course," she said stiffly. "It is your move, sir."

Paxton, he noted, looked interested but not particularly surprised at the stakes. If anything, he appeared amused. No doubt he would enjoy seeing the chit get her comeuppance after the merry chase she had led him all evening.

Richards moved his own king's pawn ahead two spaces and the game was underway.

Perhaps Miss Riverstone really had been distracted Saturday night, he thought several moves later. Certainly, she seemed far more competent this evening—or, perhaps, the stakes really did give her more focus. Not that it would matter, of course. He took one of her pawns with his white bishop.

She frowned, then murmured, "One moment." Opening her reticule, she pulled out a pair of spectacles and perched them on her nose. "Now, then."

Ah, so the lady was nearsighted, was she? No wonder she had played so inconsistently before. Still, he was not worried. The spectacles might give her confidence, but they could scarcely improve her strategy.

Miss Riverstone moved a knight, simultaneously threatening his queen and his white bishop, and it was his turn to frown.

Ten minutes later, Richards stared at the board in stunned silence. She had beaten him. The bespectacled bitch had beaten him—and in fewer than twenty moves!

"Checkmate," she said unnecessarily. "Mr. Paxton, you witnessed the terms of our wager. My brother's debt is now discharged. I thank you, Mr. Richards."

Disbelievingly, Richards raised his eyes to hers, to find her smiling—a smile he felt a violent urge to wipe from her face. He wanted to deny the terms, but it was too late. He himself had stupidly insisted on a witness, and now he was stuck for it.

"Yes, of course," he grated, pulling Sir Nelson's vouchers from his pocket. With an effort, he managed to refrain from flinging them in her face, instead depositing them in the center of the chessboard. "Here. You may inform him yourself. If you will excuse me?"

He stood, bowed, and strode quickly away, before his temper could betray him. How in hell could the chit have beaten him? She had played him for a fool, for it was clear she must have lost intentionally before. Never would he have believed a female brain capable of that level of play.

Obviously Miss Riverstone was a freak of nature, possessing a man's brain in a woman's body. Because of her, he had lost not only the money, but his only hold on her brother.

With a curt nod to his hosts, he retrieved his hat and coat and left Hardwyck Hall. Clearly, something would have to be done about Miss Riverstone. She was too clever by half, and no doubt deep in her brother's confidence, and perhaps Paxton's, as well.

It appeared Paxton was not the only person who would need to be eliminated to safeguard his plans.

"Well done," Noel declared the moment Richards was out of earshot. "Now don't tell me you didn't enjoy giving the fellow his comeuppance, apart from the money."

Rowena's smile was slightly sheepish. "I confess that his arrogance made it far easier to beat him with a clear conscience. But—I hadn't intended anyone else to know about my brother's poor judgment."

So that was why she had appeared so distressed when Richards called Noel to witness the wager. He had to laugh. "I suspect had Richards known how the match would fall out, he would have been perfectly happy to keep Sir Nelson's secret."

She stared at him. "Surely you do not believe he would have reneged on the wager?"

Noel shrugged. "I believe he was concerned that you might do so. It's the only conceivable reason for him to have made the terms public as he did."

Rowena's eyes narrowed in outrage. "How despicable! But you are only surmising, of course. We don't *know* that was his design."

"No, no, of course not." Noel reminded himself that Rowena had long been an admirer of Richards, however mistakenly. Her opinion would not be overthrown in an instant. "Do you feel up to another game?"

"Oh!" She glanced down at the board in surprise. "I hadn't really considered it, but I'm willing if you are."

"More than willing," he assured her with a warmth that made her color rise. Deftly, he reset the board, black toward himself. "This will make it easier for you to compare my play to Richards'," he explained with a grin.

She smiled back, having apparently regained her composure. "There *is* no comparison—you know that. Much as I might admire his opinions on social issues, yours is the superior mind." She colored slightly again, and Noel wondered what other comparisons she might be making.

Concealing a smile, he said, "I'm glad to hear you say so."

For a long moment she regarded him uncertainly, then moved a pawn to open the game. "It's been clear from the first that you do not care for Mr. Richards, and now I believe I understand the reason."

"Do you indeed?" He moved a pawn of his own. "Perhaps you will enlighten me, for I am having some difficulty narrowing my reasons down to only one."

She raised her chin to regard him squarely. "Now that you have undoubtedly realized my brother cannot possibly be the Saint of Seven Dials, you have turned your suspicions upon Mr. Richards. I assure you, however, that you are mistaken."

"Am I?" Noel asked, not bothering to hide his amusement. "How can you be so sure?"

"He, ah, told me where he was last night, and it had nothing to do with Lady Mountheath."

She was clearly lying, for Noel had made certain she had no opportunity for private conversation with Richards all evening. Was it really Richards himself she was trying to protect, or the Saint of Seven Dials?

"It is your move," he pointed out.

With an impatient frown, she looked at the board and moved another pawn, seemingly at random. "Well?" she challenged him.

"I don't find myself at an impasse just yet." He shot her a grin and brought a knight out onto the board, leaving her to wonder whether his words referred to the game or the Saint.

For half a dozen moves, they played in silence. Then, casually, Noel remarked, "My inquiries indicate that the jewelry stolen last night from Lady

Mountheath just happened to be that which you identified as your late mother's—and that nothing else was taken. Don't you find that intriguing?"

"Really? How . . . how curious." Though she tried for an air of surprised curiosity, her color betrayed her.

Noel managed not to smile. "I thought so. You'll let me know, of course, if those jewels should mysteriously turn up."

She swallowed. "Of—of course." Barely glancing at the board, she reached for her black bishop. Before she could touch it, however, Noel covered her hand with his own. Her eyes flew to his face in sudden alarm.

"It's my move," he said gently.

She snatched back her hand as though he had burned her. "My apologies. I am not usually so inattentive."

"Yes, I know. Not unless you are letting other gentlemen win, at any rate."

A reluctant smile tugged at her lips. "You are not going to let me live that down, are you?"

He shrugged. "I was never one for holding grudges." That was not quite true, he realized. He'd held one against the Black Bishop for years—but that was different.

"I'm happy to hear that," she said softly, almost wistfully.

Though her hand now rested on the table beside the board, he again covered it with his own. "We are not really on opposite sides, Rowena. I wish you would trust me."

This time she did not pull her hand away. "As you trust me?" she asked with a raised brow. "When did you mean to tell me that your sister was married to the heir to a dukedom?"

"I didn't think—that is, it never seemed something I could introduce into a conversation without sounding pompous. Why should it matter, anyway?" They both knew, though, that it did.

Instead of answering, she asked another question—a more difficult one. "Tell me, what evidence do you have against Mr. Richards?"

"I cannot do that," he replied, though in truth he wished he could. Surely, if she knew what atrocities the man had committed, she would never want to see Richards again.

"Because you do not trust me not to warn him?"

"Would you?" he asked, trying to read her expression. To his disappointment, she would not meet his eyes.

"Perhaps you are wise after all not to trust me," she confessed after a long pause. "It is still your move."

Frustrated that she had shut him out, and equally frustrated that he could not tell her the truth—all of the truth—Noel removed his hand from hers and turned his attention back to the game. Or, at least, he tried to.

Separated only by the small table, he found Rowena's nearness thoroughly intoxicating—the curve of her face, the shimmer of her hair, the smoothness of her skin, her faint, feminine scent. He thought back to the first night he had met her and found it incomprehensible that he had not known at once that she was unique, the missing piece of his own soul.

Wanting to hear her voice again, he finally broke

the silence with a topic sure to interest her. "The new *Political Register* is out today. Have you seen it?"

"I, ah, was able to glance at it this afternoon, though I have not read it thoroughly yet," she replied. "Mr. Cobbett's essay on the weavers was most interesting, I thought."

"Yes, most interesting," he agreed. But not disturbing, particularly—and Rowena suddenly seemed quite disturbed. "I was more taken by the anonymous Mr. R's latest offering, however," he said, watching her.

Her eyes were on the board, so he was still unable to divine her emotions. "Were you?" she asked with careful indifference, as she took his remaining bishop with a knight. "In what way?"

"I thought he pilloried the aristocratic class quite effectively, using both humor and truth to point up the hypocrisy one often sees at gatherings such as these. I believe it may be his best essay yet. Not, of course, that I agree with his premise that the lower classes are more honest."

"Do you not think so? I have never heard my maid, for example, speak in such a two-faced manner as some of the high-born ladies I have met since coming to Town."

He surveyed the board, carefully positioning a rook to defend his queen before replying. "Your maid no doubt has learned her values primarily from you, so that does not surprise me."

She blushed charmingly at the implied compliment. "You do not think her typical, then?"

"I imagine that I have had more opportunity than you have to observe the lower classes in their more depraved moments," he said. "Believe me, there is dishonesty enough to go around for all classes. If anything, the aristocracy is frequently constrained by Society's expectations from descending to true viciousness."

"That all depends on how one defines viciousness," she argued. "Not many dukes resort to highway robbery, I'll grant you, but is that not because they have no need to do so? Is it any less vicious to tax a man to the point of destitution than to take valuables from a wealthy man to supplement an inadequate income?"

Though she attracted him more than ever in her passionate defense of the downtrodden, her championing of this particular essay nettled him—particularly since he suspected she knew that Richards had written it.

"The former, at least, is less likely to result in loss of life or limb for either party." His voice was perhaps sharper than he had intended.

"So you do support theft by the government? That strikes me as the very height of hypocrisy." She made a sweeping movement with her hand to underscore her point, accidentally knocking a few pieces from the board to the floor. "Oh! I did not mean—"

Noel retrieved the pieces, but did not set them back in their places. "Neither of us seem to be playing at our best just now anyway. What say we postpone this match until another time?"

"Very well," she agreed with a rueful nod. But then she glanced up at him mischievously. "Do you also concede the point I was making?"

"You vixen," he said with a chuckle. "I concede neither the game nor the argument. I perceive, however, that most of the guests appear to have left. Perhaps we might continue the latter in more private surroundings?"

She regarded him uncertainly. "Private?"

"Nothing scandalous," he assured her, though his thoughts were definitely tending that way. "I had in mind the parlor." The parlor where he had stolen an extremely sweet kiss that afternoon.

That she also was remembering was evidenced by her agitation. "I—that is—do you not wish to return to your lodgings soon?"

He shook his head. "I am staying here again. I realized that where I am lodged makes little difference in how I carry out my investigation, so it seemed churlish to spurn the Hardwycks' hospitality."

In fact, Luke's expression had been far too knowing when Noel had requested his room back, using the same excuse. His true motive was to keep a closer eye on Rowena, to prevent Richards from somehow using her, and to prevent her from telling Richards too much. At least, he was fairly sure that was his true motive.

"Oh," she said faintly. "I see. Yes, I suppose we can repair to the parlor—but only briefly, as it is growing quite late." She nodded in the direction of a tall clock in the corner of the ballroom.

"I know I teased you earlier for leaving off your spectacles," Noel said, "but now I rather regret you wearing them, for now I cannot pretend it is earlier than it is."

"Why?" Rowena asked as they rose. "I mean, why do you tease me when I don't wear my spectacles?"

He took her hand and placed it on his arm so that

he could escort her to the parlor and was pleased when she did not resist. "Because I prefer you to wear them in public."

"Why?" she asked again. "Why should it matter to you?"

They moved out of the ballroom and down the passage to the parlor, which was still lit by numerous candles, though it was empty. Just inside the doorway, he stopped to look down at her, his expression serious.

"Because I don't want other men realizing how lovely you are, Rowena. I had hoped to keep that knowledge to myself."

Rowena stared up at him, her heart pounding in slow, heavy strokes. "Do you really think I'm pretty?" she asked, then immediately wished she could snatch the question back, lest he think she was fishing for compliments when it wasn't that at all.

"Don't sound so disbelieving," he chided her gently. "Your own glass must tell you that—assuming you can see it clearly enough." A wink took any insult from his words.

"But I recognized your beauty even before you turned yourself into a Society miss," he continued, to her amazement. "I rather enjoyed thinking I was the only one to perceive it, beneath your severe gowns and hairstyle—and your spectacles. But now it is revealed for all the world to see."

Rowena felt as though she would melt on the spot, but made an effort to rally herself. "You fear the competition, do you?" She forced herself to speak lightly, though she very much wanted to hear his answer.

"Craven as it sounds, I believe I do," he replied.

"The thought of you becoming as—friendly—with another man as you've been with me is almost unsupportable."

"It is?" The words escaped her like a sigh.

He nodded, gazing deep into her eyes, and then she was in his arms, as easily and naturally as though she belonged there. When his lips touched hers, she knew she had been waiting for this moment all evening—ever since their last kiss, in this very room. Rather than satisfy, his kisses seemed to create in her a hunger for more—and more.

His hands roamed up and down her back as he explored her mouth, her throat, her ears, with his lips. Incapable of thought, Rowena gave herself up to his caresses, reveling in the sensations he produced in her. Tentatively, she ran her fingers along his jaw, rough now with a day's growth of beard. Why that should excite her, she had no idea.

Finally, he lifted his head to gaze down at her again. "This wasn't supposed to happen, you know."

"Kissing me again?" She hadn't intended it either.

"Falling"—he cleared his throat—"under your spell. I've come to care very deeply for you, Rowena."

Her breath caught, and she stared up at him, unable to speak. Surely he hadn't been about to say—? But his eyes told her that he had. She felt something inside her unfolding, expanding, like a rose bursting into bloom from the sunshine of his regard.

Was this love? She rather suspected it was, though until this moment she had never quite believed in the romantic emotion. Should she tell him? If she said the words, would he? She found her courage not quite equal to that test.

Watching her face, his eyes suddenly grew guarded. "I'm sorry. I should not have—"

She interrupted him with a kiss, afraid to hear a retraction of what he had so nearly said, but almost equally afraid that he would speak more plainly. She felt as though they both teetered on the edge of a precipice, from which there would be no returning once the words were clearly spoken.

Though his lips made it all but impossible to think, she tried, while there was yet time, to remind herself of the differences that divided them. Noel still pursued the Saint of Seven Dials, something she could not possibly condone. Could she?

No, no, she mustn't do that, no matter how desperately she wanted to confess her own feelings, and to hear his in return. Before she could give her whole heart to him, she must somehow try to persuade him to her own views, convince him to give up the hunt. She could think of only one way to do so.

"Let's go upstairs," she whispered against his lips.

Chapter 15

At first Noel felt sure he was hearing what he wanted to hear instead of what Rowena had really said, there was so much unspoken between them already. Surely, she couldn't mean—? But already she was urging him toward the door of the parlor.

As though in a dream, he went with her, his senses overwhelmed by her taste, her scent, the silky softness of her hair and skin. Taking him by the hand, she headed for the stairs and he followed, unable—or unwilling—to resist.

A murmur of voices warned them a moment before Lord and Lady Hardwyck appeared on the landing before them, having just bidden the last guests farewell. Rowena released Noel's hand and he followed her lead by focusing on his hosts rather than this girl who had quite definitely cast a spell over him, even if he had chosen those words to mask what he had nearly said instead.

"Another success, my lord, my lady," Noel said, his voice sounding odd and stilted to his own ears.

"I thought so," Lady Hardwyck agreed with a smile that showed no trace of suspicion.

Luke's glance, however, was more perceptive. "Ready to retire, are you? It is growing rather late. Your man should have your previous chamber ready for you, I should think."

"I'm more than ready for my own bed," Lady Hardwyck declared. "Come, let's all go upstairs. We can discuss the relative merits of the evening's performers tomorrow."

A glance at Rowena showed her clinging to a polite smile with evident effort, making Noel wonder if she was as frustrated by the interruption as he was. Surely, though, it was just as well?

Though he had all but declared his love, he had made her no offer—nor had she indicated that she expected one. In fact, he recalled, now that the capacity for thought was returning, she had not mentioned her own feelings at all—not in words, anyway. He had no doubt read far too much into her seeming invitation. It would be madness to assume otherwise.

Madness seemed to be the order of the evening, however. As they reached the upper hallway and bid each other good night, Rowena held his glance while he bent over her extended hand, and mouthed the words, "Later. Join me."

Noel nodded slightly, then turned to bid his hosts good night, assuring himself that they had not witnessed the silent exchange. Rowena entered her chamber, then Noel entered his, while Lord and Lady

Hardwyck proceeded to their corner suite at the end.

Kemp awaited him, of course. "Would you care for a brandy before bed, sir?" he asked as he helped Noel out of his tailored coat.

Noel's only desire was to have the chamber to himself, so that he could think things through. Rowena knew who Mr. R was, of that he was certain. If he went to her now, could he persuade her to share that knowledge with him? Or was that a despicable motive for something he very much wanted to do anyway?

"No, thank you, Kemp. I'll sleep well enough without any brandy tonight, I believe."

The manservant bowed and left Noel to snort at his own words. Whatever he decided to do now, he would not be sleeping anytime soon, of that he was certain.

"That will do, Matthilda. Thank you." Rowena had never been so nervous in her life. But whether she was more terrified that Noel would come to her chamber before she could rid herself of her maid, or that he would not come at all, she could not say.

His nod had implied that he would come—hadn't it? Would he reconsider, now that he was away from her "distracting" influence? She found it hard to believe she could have such an effect on a man of Noel Paxton's intellect and resolve, but his actions and words seemed to prove that she did.

Matthilda was still puttering about the room, hanging Rowena's gown in the clothespress, tidying the dressing table and turning down the oil lamp on the bedside table. Rowena's agitation increased to unbearable levels.

"I said that would do," she said, more sharply than she intended. "Good night, Matthilda."

The maid sent her a startled glance but asked no questions, merely bobbing a curtsey. "Good night, miss. Sleep well."

Rowena knew there was little chance of that.

She listened as Matthilda's light footsteps receded down the hall toward the servants' stairs. And kept listening, for any other sound in the hallway. Would he come? Could she really go through with her outrageous plan if he did?

As the silence lengthened, she began to relax. Of course he would not come. Noel Paxton was a gentleman, with a high regard for the law and the proprieties. And she was a lady, who had no business attempting a seduction, not even for the noble purpose of keeping the Saint of Seven Dials safe from the law.

That *was* her purpose, wasn't it?

Not that it mattered now, anyway. She had no doubt read too much into what Noel had almost said—or what she *thought* he had almost said. With a sigh of mingled disappointment and relief, she turned toward her bed, then froze. Was that a step in the hall? No, she was imagining things. But then came another sound, a soft scratching at her chamber door.

Her heart pounding frantically, Rowena moved to open it. Noel stood there, more handsome than she'd ever seen him, wearing only shirt and breeches, his collar open to reveal a disturbing triangle of throat and chest. His curly hair was disordered and damp, as though he had already washed for bed. For a moment she thought she might swoon, then chided herself for such foolishness.

"I—I hoped you would come," she whispered, standing aside to let him enter. She needed to maintain complete control of her emotions if she was to put this opportunity to proper use.

He stepped past her, softly closing the door behind him without taking his eyes from her face. "I nearly convinced myself I had imagined—or at least misunderstood—your invitation." His voice held a question.

"No, you did not misunderstand," she said, hoping he would not notice the trembling that had begun in her midsection and now spread to her extremities. She wanted to ask a similar question of her own, but feared her voice might fail her—and feared his answer, as well. Instead, she smiled what she hoped was a seductive smile.

His gaze dropped to her lips, then returned to her eyes. He took a step nearer and she could feel the warmth emanating from his body, though he did not touch her.

"Are you certain that *you* understand what you are asking?"

She wasn't certain of that at all, but she nodded firmly. "Of course. I am . . . very well read, you know."

One corner of his mouth quirked up in a half-smile that sent odd sensations through her chest. "I'm aware of that. But there are some things one really cannot learn from books."

He was giving her a chance to reconsider and, cravenly, she was tempted to take it. For all of her studies of political intrigue, she actually knew very little of what went on between a man and a woman. For the first time, she regretted that she had not included romantic novels in her extensive reading.

"Then it is time I supplemented theory with practical application, is it not?" she forced herself to say, lifting her chin to look him full in the eyes—eyes that had darkened from hazel to dusky brown.

"Ever the academic," he murmured, moving even closer, until the fabric of his fine lawn shirt brushed against the thin cotton of her summer nightrail.

She tilted her face up for his kiss and he obliged her, his warm, firm lips taking possession of her own. His arms went around her, and her trembling subsided, to be replaced by a swirling need for something she could not define. Her noble plan forgotten, she clutched at him, pulling him closer, wanting more contact, more of . . . everything.

Noel's low, throaty growl inflamed her further with the evidence that he desired her as much as she desired him. He deepened the kiss, stroking her tongue with a rhythm that pushed her need to new levels. She heard another growl, and realized with a start that it had come from her own throat.

Pressing the length of her body against his, she reveled in the hardness of his chest, the strength of his arms around her—and in his insistent maleness, straining against his breeches, against her belly, proving just how much he wanted her.

Her body clamored for more, but she had no idea how to satisfy that longing. What should she do next?

He did it for her. Still kissing her deeply, he slid one hand to her shoulder, then her throat, deftly untying the ribbon that closed the neck of her nightgown. His lips followed his fingers, trailing kisses from her mouth to her shoulder, then to the hollow at the base of her throat, even as he undid the next fastening of her gown.

Swallowing convulsively, Rowena tilted her head back, giving him free rein to do what he would. Never had she imagined the sensations that swirled through her at his touch, and now she could imagine nothing worse than a cessation of his exquisite attentions.

Dimly, in the back of that tiny part of her brain that still clung to the capacity for thought, she remembered that she was supposed to be doing the seducing. Her hands clutched at his shoulders to keep her upright, but now she let go with one hand to fumble with the fastenings of his shirt. The angle was quite different from undoing her own buttons. That and the sweet distraction of his fingers against her flesh made her clumsy.

"I rather like this shirt," he said against her ear, a hint of a chuckle in his voice. "Let me help you, before my buttons are scattered about the room."

She knew she should be embarrassed, but somehow she was not. She was only anxious to proceed, to feel more of him against more of her. Judging by the speed at which he undid his buttons, he shared her eagerness. They embraced again, this time with much of her upper body exposed to his now bare chest, his shirt hanging completely open.

Though her breasts were still covered by thin cotton, the space above and between them was not, and the soft roughness of the hair on his chest stimulated her sensitive flesh to new heights of desire.

She could not bare more of herself to him without breaking contact, however. Her nightrail opened only to breast level. To remove it, she would have to take it over her head—an irrevocable step. Did she dare? Could she not?

Noel's hands were at her back now, massaging her spine between her shoulder blades, at her waist, lower. Sliding her own hands up to his shoulders again, she pushed his open shirt back, revealing more of his chest. He took his hands from her for an instant, but even that brief loss of contact made her whimper.

"Sshh," he whispered against her lips. Quickly, he shrugged out of his shirt, letting it fall to a heap on the floor, then his arms were around her again.

Now her hands had free access to the whole of his upper torso, and she made good use of that freedom, exploring his sides, his chest, the firm planes of his back, where she felt faint ridges that might be scars. His body was so different from her own, so beautifully *male*. She wanted to know it better.

Meanwhile, his hands were doing their own exploring, through the fabric of her nightrail. They spanned her narrow waist, then slid lower to cup her bottom and pull her tighter against him. He bunched up the thin cotton, and she could feel the hem moving up her calves, then her thighs.

In a moment he had it about her waist, and she was acutely aware that she had nothing beneath it, that nothing now stood between her lower body and his hands, his eyes. Her own eyes were tightly closed, but when he gently broke their kiss, she opened them to find him gazing earnestly at her.

"May I?" he asked softly.

She knew he was asking her permission to divest

her completely of her nightrail—to remove her last shred of defense against his touch. She nodded silently, not trusting her voice.

With a swift, fluid movement, he lifted the sheer fabric up and over her head, tossing it behind her. Then, gently clasping her shoulders, he smiled. "You are even more beautiful than I imagined."

Beautiful. No one, not even her mother, had ever called her beautiful before. But he seemed to mean it, his eyes admiring, even reverent. Still, Rowena had to fight an urge to cover herself, to shield her body from his eyes. Though she hadn't summoned it, sanity began to return. What was she doing?

Oh, yes. She was going to convince him to leave the Saint alone. Then she could be done with intrigue, admit her feelings for him, be his in every possible way. Was this the right time to ask? If she allowed him to take her, to compromise her, would it be too late? But what if she spoke too soon? Her desire to do nothing to stop him warred with her weakening resolve to appease her conscience.

He leaned forward to kiss her again, one hand coming up to cup her breast, and thought left her again, replaced by pure sensation. Again, she clutched at his shoulders, his back, pulling him against her so that her breasts rubbed against the firm roughness of his chest. It was an exquisite feeling.

Taking a step backward without releasing her hold on him, she guided him toward the bed. She had no idea what she would do once they reached it, but trusted that he would. A tendril of fear snaked through her—fear of the unknown—but she ignored it. She craved, and she must be satisfied.

He resisted her, however. "Rowena, you must be very sure," he murmured. "In a moment, I fear I won't be able to stop myself."

"I'm sure," she said, but then glanced up, into his burning eyes. Surely, his desire for her was at fever pitch now, as hers was for him. She *must* take this chance. "First, though," she forced herself to say, "won't you please promise me that you'll give up your investigation of the Saint of Seven Dials?"

Noel felt as though she had dashed cold water on him, chilling the blaze that had been consuming him an instant before.

"Is that what this is about?" he demanded, sick disappointment coiling in his stomach. "You are willing to—to trade yourself for my promise?" He wasn't sure whether he was angrier at her or himself. Certainly, he had known better than to come here.

Her gray eyes flew open, revealing dismay, fear, and desire. It was the desire that almost undid him again, but he made himself hold her at arm's length, trying to ignore the way her nude body enticed his own.

"No! That is, I hoped that . . . that if you cared for me, you might be willing to change your mind. To . . . to please me." She made a motion as though to cover her nakedness, and he released her.

Her words only confirmed his accusation. "Perhaps you would consider another sort of trade," he said, his ego still smarting. "Tell me who Mr. R is, and I'll consider leaving off my pursuit of the Saint."

She stared at him for a long moment, then knelt quickly to retrieve her nightrail and clutch it to her chest, concealing her charms. Though that should have made it easier to bring his desire for her under control, it did not.

"You—you say that very glibly," she finally said. "Was that *your* design in coming here, to get that information from me? Not that I know the answer, of course."

He hesitated, for that *had* been the reason he'd used to justify his presence here—though he knew it was not the real one. At his hesitation, as good as a confession, hurt flared in her eyes. Hurt, followed almost immediately by anger.

"So, you meant to use me—to seduce me for information? Is that why you said . . . what you did, downstairs?" The glitter in her eyes was more than anger. She was dangerously close to tears, and Noel was not sure what he would do if she cried.

"No! I meant—that is—" Why was he on the defensive? He should be doubly glad now that he had stopped short of a declaration. "You are a fine one to talk. It appears that neither of us had completely pure motives for this . . . rendezvous."

"Pure—!" She whirled from him, affording him an excellent view of her shapely bottom before she moved behind a chair. Hastily, clumsily, she pulled her nightrail back on, then folded her arms across her breasts as she faced him again.

For a long moment she stared at him across the dim room, as though trying to decipher his thoughts from his expression. He doubted she would have much success, as he could not decipher them himself. Regret, anger, guilt—and a substantial amount of lingering desire—warred within him.

"I . . . I thought—" she began, one hand fluttering free to reach tentatively in his direction.

"Yes, so did I," he responded. "Perhaps we were both mistaken. In any event, I must apologize, for I had no business coming here in the first place, whatever my motives. You are an innocent, but I am wise in the ways of the world. Just as well we stopped when we did."

Rowena swallowed visibly, her eyes so bereft that he longed to comfort her. But he dared not move closer, knowing how strongly she affected him, how easily he could lose his hard-won control.

"Do you really think so?" she whispered.

She really was an innocent. "Had we not, you would have found yourself bound to me for life, willing or no," he explained. "Is that what you would have wanted?"

She looked away, and even in the dim light of the oil lamp he could see her cheeks darken. "I would not have expected you to marry me, of course. I can't imagine that we would suit, as different as our views are."

"Had we finished what we began, I would have married you, nonetheless," he told her, knowing it was true—and now regretting that they had stopped for a whole new reason. "I would not have been able to live with myself otherwise. In fact, I should offer for you even now, considering how far things have gone."

"You needn't worry for my reputation," she said, still not meeting his eye. "No one knows you are here, so it is in no danger. And even if it were, I could simply return to River Chase. You are under no . . . obligation to me, sir."

The "sir" chilled him, but he could in honor do

nothing now but leave. She had made her feelings clear. "Very well, Rowena, I will not press you. But we must be very discreet, to be certain no hint of this becomes known."

"I think that will not be difficult."

Perhaps it would not be difficult for her—though he would swear she had desired him nearly as much as he had desired her just a few minutes earlier. Clearly, though, however passionate she might be, her heart was not touched.

"No. No, I suppose not. Good night, Rowena." He waited for a moment, hoping she would look at him, that he might divine something of what she felt. When she did not, he scooped up his shirt and left the chamber.

Rowena remained where she was, one hand tightly gripping the chair back for support, until his steps receded down the hall. Then she collapsed into the chair, buried her face in her hands and sobbed.

Waking late the next morning after only a few hours' fitful sleep, Rowena took breakfast in her room. She could not bear to see Noel across the dining room table downstairs. In fact, she was not sure she could ever bear to face him again. What a horrible mess she had made of everything last night!

She should never have invited Noel to her room, she realized that now. Her plan to convince him to leave the Saint alone had been merely an excuse, a salve to her conscience. The truth was, she had wanted his kisses, his touch, and more—something she would never have now. If she had only remained quiet . . .

But no. Then she would be ruined, and by Noel's own admission would have essentially trapped him into a marriage he had never actually said he wanted. Nor did she want it herself—did she?

Of course she didn't. Neither of them would be happy. She was too independent and he was too rigid. It would never work.

Tonight was to be another ball, but she intended to stay in her room, perhaps pleading illness. Certainly, she was mortally tired. She was just considering returning to bed when a tap on the door heralded the appearance of Pearl herself, who appeared depressingly cheerful and fresh to Rowena's scratchy eyes.

"Here you are, sleepyhead," she cried. "There are callers below already, and more than one has asked specifically for you—and you not even dressed to go down yet."

"I . . . did not sleep well," Rowena responded with perfect truth. "Perhaps you can make my apologies?"

Pearl regarded her closely—so closely that she was sure her friend would somehow divine what she had done—no, nearly done—last night. But Pearl only said, "You do look rather pulled. However, I have just the thing to cheer you. Wait here."

She hurried out, and returned a moment later with a small parcel. "It arrived less than an hour ago. I was worried it would not be here in time for tonight's ball, as it was to have been delivered yesterday." As she spoke, she pulled away the paper, then held up the most exquisite reticule Rowena had ever seen.

"Why, it is in the shape of a book," she exclaimed.

"Yes. I thought of you at once when I saw it at Mellon's on Friday. I'd hoped to give it to you for that ball, but the last one had been sold. But see? The colors match the dress you plan to wear tonight, so this is even better."

Indeed, the diminutive book-shaped purse was the same blue as Rowena's new ballgown. Charmed, she opened and closed it, smiling her thanks at Pearl. "It's perfect," she said, realizing that there could be no question of crying off attending tonight's affair now.

"There, did I not say it would cheer you up? Get dressed, do, and come downstairs. I must hurry back myself, as more callers will doubtless have arrived by now."

Pearl rushed off, leaving Rowena to toy with her gift. Interesting that Pearl should want her to carry this, when she had earlier tried to disguise Rowena's bookishness. Not that it had done much good, of course. She knew full well that by now she had been branded a bluestocking by nearly everyone who had met her.

And so what if she was? If Noel had done nothing else for her, he had shown her how much happier she could be when she was herself—playing chess, arguing politics . . . kissing him.

No! That part was not her. It couldn't be. Studious Rowena Riverstone, a wanton? Absurd. It was simply an error in judgment, nothing more.

But he *had* praised her latest essay—even if he had no idea she had written it. She picked up the *Political Register*, which she'd had Matthilda bring up with her breakfast tray, though the meal was still untouched.

Noel had said this was MRR's best essay yet, she remembered with a reluctant smile. Reading over it, she had to agree. She must work harder in future to convey her own opinions, as they could clearly hold their own against those of the other contributors, learned men all.

Turning the page, her eye fell on a small, boxed notice at the bottom that she had not noticed in yesterday's quick perusal.

To MRR: The PR has 16 letters to forward. Please advise where we may send or deposit them for your convenient retrieval.—WC

Rowena frowned. Sixteen letters, for her? It had never occurred to her that people might write to MRR—though it should have, since she had written to Mr. Richards after reading his treatise. Sixteen letters! What might they say? And how could she obtain them without disclosing her identity?

She read the notice again. *Send or deposit.* Presumably she could choose a location, they could leave the letters there, and she could retrieve them later, with no one the wiser. But what location?

Green Park was just across Picadilly from Hardwyck Hall. She recalled a large, lichen-covered rock near the entrance, with a small stand of trees nearby. Perhaps the letters could be left behind that rock? They would be at the mercy of the elements, but the weather was fine just now. If she retrieved them soon after they were left, they should not be damaged.

Her decision made, she went to the writing desk for paper and pen and wrote a quick letter requesting that the letters be deposited by that rock by noon tomorrow. She folded it, addressed it as she did her essays, then rang for Matthilda.

"Help me into the yellow round dress, please," she said when the maid appeared. "It's time I went downstairs."

Once she was dressed, she picked up the letter she'd just written and handed it to Matthilda. "Post this for me as soon as possible. Do as you did Monday—tell no one what you are doing, and return as quickly as possible."

"Yes, miss." Though Matthilda looked curious, just as she had on Monday, she asked no questions. She took the letter and left.

That brief flurry of excitement over, Rowena returned to her earlier brooding, but found she did not feel so hopeless as she had before. The thought of those letters and what might be in them lifted her spirits somewhat. Perhaps it was even possible that she and Noel could come to some sort of understanding.

Still, the idea of facing him after last night made her flush with anticipated embarrassment. What could she possibly say to him? What might he say to her? Aside from the way they had parted, he had seen her *naked.*

Before leaving the room, she donned her spectacles. Pearl should not mind, since her gift underscored her bookishness. Besides, being unable to see clearly made her feel vulnerable, and she already felt quite vulnerable enough.

Chapter 16

Lester Richards summoned a smile for Miss Riverstone when she entered the parlor. Last night he had let his temper get the better of his judgment, but once it cooled he realized that he could still make use of the girl, oddity that she was.

She was already sympathetic to the Spencean cause. With some flattery, she might be induced to get the information he needed from her brother. Or, he might convince her to give him specifics on Paxton's movements and motives, should she discover them.

For either purpose, he needed her trust.

"Miss Riverstone," he exclaimed, rising as she entered. "You look particularly lovely today." She did not, of course, wearing those damned spectacles again, not to mention the freckles marring her face. "I hope you will forgive my churlishness last night."

As he'd hoped, she moved at once to sit by him, ignoring Paxton, who had also risen at her entrance.

"Thank you, Mr. Richards. But I thought you remarkably polite, given the circumstances."

He must have hid his anger better than he'd realized. Habit was a useful thing, he reflected.

"I am relieved to hear it," he said with perfect truth. "Dare I hope you will allow me a dance this evening, in that case?" A plain, bookish sort like Miss Riverstone should be absurdly easy to charm.

"Certainly," she responded with a smile.

Lady Hardwyck then called her attention to the other callers, including that insufferable pup Galloway who persisted in pursuing her. When she finally met Paxton's eye, Richards noticed that her color rose and that she quickly glanced away. Paxton seemed similarly affected, though he concealed it better.

So the wind lay that way, did it? So much the better. It would make the chit excellent bait to lure Paxton to his doom, once Richards had what he needed from her. Then, he could rid himself of two problems with one stroke.

Noel kept his expression rigidly neutral. He would have avoided this encounter entirely if he did not feel an obligation to keep both Richards and Rowena under observation. Facing enemy fire would have been preferable, however.

He had watched as Rowena accepted compliments from Richards, fighting down a ridiculous urge to call the man out on the spot. Not only had he said nothing to reasonably provoke such a response, but any openly hostile action toward Richards on his part would certainly endanger his mission.

He could not see Rowena again without remembering—all too vividly!—how she had felt in his arms last night, how lovely she looked unclothed. It was all he could do to disguise his physical reaction to that memory.

When she spoke with Galloway and his cousin, it did not cause Noel the same pang of jealousy—probably because she had not been protecting either of them when she pretended to want him last night. If she had been pretending. Surely such an innocent could not counterfeit her body's responses so convincingly?

When she finally turned toward Noel, her reluctance was obvious. "Mr. Paxton." She coolly inclined her head, though her heightened color revealed her disquiet.

"Miss Riverstone," he responded just as coolly. When he tried to hold her gaze she flinched away, turning back to Richards at her side.

Damn him.

He did not, of course, believe that Rowena had any *romantic* inclinations toward Richards. She simply admired his mind—and, if he was who Noel thought he was, he was certainly crafty enough. Soon, he hoped to have the necessary proof . . .

Smiling fixedly at Lady Hardwyck as she chatted with the others, Noel felt sudden doubt. Was it possible that he was blinding himself to evidence that might point to other suspects simply because he so badly wanted Richards to be a villain? Surely not. Surely he was more objective, more professional, than that.

Now, however, he wondered. Rowena Riverstone clouded his thinking. She had done so almost from the first evening he met her. What if he were now pursing phantasms because of it?

All he had on Richards so far was an unusual turn of phrase and the circumstantial evidence of his gaming with certain men. Suppose his trap for the essayist did not work? He would be no further ahead than he was now. He needed more.

It was sheer torture pretending interest in the chatter around him as he waited for Richards to take his leave. When he finally did, Noel waited only a moment or two before rising himself.

"Pray excuse me, Lady Hardwyck," he said, resolutely refusing to glance Rowena's way. "I have business to attend."

"Of course," his hostess responded. She cast a curious look at Rowena, but Noel would not follow her gaze. "We will see you tonight, then."

He bowed his assent and headed up to his chamber to retrieve his hat and inform Kemp of his plans. There was one person who must have information on Richards' whereabouts during the war, solidifying his case against the man—or destroying it. He would discover where Richards' father might be and arrange an interview.

Rowena was finding this ball to be a vastly different experience from her first, the week before. This time she knew well over half of the attendees—and could recognize them, as she was wearing her spectacles.

Pearl had frowned when she'd come down for dinner with her eyeglasses on, but then had shrugged. "I suppose you've made most of the first impressions you're likely to by now, and I couldn't very well expect you to go about half-blind indefinitely. You've been a good sport, Rowena."

"Could I do less, after all you've done for me?" she had responded.

At the moment, however, Rowena wondered whether introducing her to Noel Paxton counterbalanced all the good Pearl had done. Judging by the wretched feeling in the pit of her stomach when he entered the ballroom, she thought perhaps it did.

Meeting his eyes across the room for only the briefest instant brought all the wanton feelings from last night flooding back, just as seeing him in the parlor this afternoon had done. Now, though she refused to look his way again, her whole being was focused on Noel, half a room away. She felt his eyes upon her like a physical caress—or was she only imagining that?

Her dance card was nearly full, but she had left the waltzes open, using the excuse that she was yet too unskilled at that dance. She knew, however, that she was secretly hoping Noel might claim those dances as he had before.

"Good evening, Rowena," Lady Marcus greeted her just then, giving her a welcome excuse to turn her back to Noel, who was moving slowly in her direction. "Are those spectacles new? They're really quite becoming."

Rowena had to laugh at Quinn's diplomacy. "Thank you, but no. I've worn them most of my life, and only left them off earlier at Pearl's insistence. It's much nicer to be able to see, however."

"My, that was courageous of you, I must say. I imagine it was rather distressing not to be able to see things clearly, especially with so many strangers about."

"Yes, it was, rather. But a novel experience nonetheless. If nothing else, it forced me to give my full attention to whoever I happened to be speaking with, as I could not recognize anyone more than a few paces away."

Now, however, she could see people all too clearly—including Noel, who had just moved past them to exchange greetings with her brother. Rowena's heart did an odd little flip at the sight of his handsome profile.

Quinn was chuckling. "That explains why the gentlemen were all so taken with you. They love nothing more than a woman who will give them her undivided attention, I have noticed."

"A lesson I will try to remember," Rowena said lightly. "I see my brother over there. If you will excuse me, I need to speak with him before the dancing begins."

By the time she reached Nelson, Noel had moved on, to her relief—and disappointment. "There you are, Ro. Any progress?" Nelson greeted her eagerly.

Hastily, she pulled her attention back to her brother. Noel's movements were nothing to her, after all.

"Yes indeed. Substantial progress," she replied. "You are no longer in debt to Mr. Richards." She pulled his vouchers from her book-shaped reticule and handed them to him.

He took them, his mouth dropping open in surprise. "How the devil did you persuade him?" His eyes widened in alarm. "You didn't do anything—improper, did you, Ro? I told you Richards is a crack shot. I'd as soon not be obliged to call him out to defend your honor."

Rowena choked on a laugh that was almost a sob, remembering just how improper she'd been—though not with Lester Richards. "Of course not, Nelson. How can you ask?" She would *not* blush. "I wiped out your debt with a wager of my own, if you must know."

His eyes widened even further. "You played Richards at cards—and won?"

"Not cards. Chess." *That* memory still had the power to make her smile.

Nelson stared at her a moment longer, then began to laugh. "And I always said you were wasting your time at that game. Damned if you didn't find a way to make it pay off!" He clapped her on the shoulder as he might a man. "You're too clever by half, Ro, but for once I'm dashed grateful for it."

"Clever. Yes." She had apparently exhausted her cleverness on that chess match with Richards, judging by her behavior for the remainder of last evening. "At any rate, you need not worry now about passing along any information to Richards and endangering your position at the Home Office." Curiosity about that still nagged at her.

Her brother gave her an awkward hug, then quickly released her, glancing about in some embarrassment. "You're the best sister a fellow could want, Ro. I'm glad you're here in London—and glad you've become such a success. I expect I'll have some buck calling on me one day soon, asking for your hand. Who'd have thought it?"

"I don't think you need worry about that just yet," she said, coloring despite her best efforts.

"Won't be long, mark my words. And don't sell yourself short, Ro. You deserve all the happiness a woman can have."

He left her then, to go in search of a card game at one of the tables set up in the alcoves. Rowena stared after him sadly. Whether she deserved happiness or not, she had ruined her best chance at it with her actions last night.

Again, she involuntarily picked Noel Paxton out of the crowd. She might have been truly happy with him, she realized, despite their differences. Ironic that she had not seen it until now, when she had given him a thorough disgust for her.

"The dancing is about to begin." Mr. Richards' voice snapped her out of her mournful reverie. "I believe the first is mine?"

She turned, forcing a smile to her lips. "I am flattered you remembered," she said. Then, realizing this might be her best opportunity for a private word with him, she lowered her voice. "Before we are separated by the dance, there is something I must tell you, Mr. Richards."

All day she had wavered between her duty to the common man and what Noel might see as a betrayal. But had he not betrayed her already? He had claimed to care for her, but today he had demonstrated his indifference. Painful as it was to contemplate, it appeared that he really had only hoped to learn the identity of the essayist from her.

Suddenly she remembered those sixteen letters she

hoped to retrieve tomorrow. What might be in them? Was it possible one would be from Noel? If so, would she dare to somehow reply?

Mr. Richards was watching her expectantly, so she put that matter from her mind for the moment. Taking a deep breath, she continued.

"I know who you really are—but I fear Mr. Paxton suspects you as well. You must be on your guard against him."

"Who I really am?" His dark brown eyes bored into hers with an intensity that made her shiver. Almost, she would have called it sinister—but that was absurd, of course. "And how came you by this knowledge, Miss Riverstone?"

"It was a matter of deduction," she explained. "Your convictions, with which I am well acquainted through your writings, as well as something Mr. Paxton said. And, of course, there was the matter of the jewels."

He blinked, breaking the intensity of his gaze. "Of course," he said slowly. "Your mother's jewels . . . stolen from Lady Mountheath. You will want them back, of course."

Rowena frowned uncertainly. "Yes, as I said last night, I appreciated—"

"The music is beginning. Later we shall discuss their return, shall we? It occurs to me that you may have something I want as well." With that cryptic comment, he led her into the opening dance.

Mechanically going through the movements of the minuet, Rowena's mind worked furiously. Mr. Richards spoke as though the jewels were still in his possession, when they had been returned to her the very night they were taken from the Mountheath house. Could she have been mistaken? But he had admitted just now that he was the Saint, hadn't he?

Glancing down the line of dancers, she saw Noel partnering Augusta Melks. He turned his head just then and their eyes met before she could look away. She felt an instant connection, a communion, mind to mind—and then it was gone as another dancer blocked her line of sight. When she could see him again, he was not looking her way.

Shaken, she had to concentrate to avoid losing her place in the dance. Surely she had imagined that link between them? A few kisses and one evening of wanton caressing could not forge such a thing—could it?

But no, it was more than that. She remembered their chess games, their conversations, both of them taking enjoyment in disputing each other's views. They had far more in common than she had been willing to admit, despite their differing opinions on certain issues.

She turned to face Mr. Richards again, and his gaze was overtly admiring. Rowena knew she should be flattered—the man was her longtime idol, after all—but instead she felt uncomfortable, even vaguely repelled. He was almost old enough to be her father, and she couldn't help remembering his patronizing comments at yesterday's picnic.

No, she did not feel the rapport with Mr. Richards that she felt with Noel Paxton, despite her endorsement of his opinions. Most of his opinions. Not the ones pertaining to women, of course.

"Shall we go to the refreshment table?" he suggested at the close of the dance. "That will give us an opportunity for conversation."

"I fear I am already engaged for the next dance with Mr. Thatcher," she said with feigned regret. In fact, she felt more relief than regret—and chided herself for it. Surely she did not think Noel was right, that Mr. Richards was somehow dangerous?

Mr. Thatcher appeared at her elbow then, and Mr. Richards bowed. "Of course. Later, then."

"Odd fellow, Richards," Mr. Thatcher said as he led her back to the floor. "Radical sort. Did he say anything to upset you, Miss Riverstone?"

She realized she must have let some part of her sudden distaste for her erstwhile idol show in her expression and quickly summoned a smile. "No, of course not. He merely wished me to sit out a dance with him."

"His loss, my gain," her partner said with a roguish smile. "Never thought I'd seek out a lady in spectacles—intimidating, don't you know—but I'm willing to risk having my egotism deflated for a dance with you, Miss Riverstone."

Rowena had to laugh at his outrageous flattery. "Intimidating? I find that hard to believe, Mr. Thatcher." Harry Thatcher was a longtime acquaintance of Noel's, she recalled. Did she dare question him about his friend?

The country dance began, and Rowena was again impressed at how well Mr. Thatcher compensated for his missing left arm. One scarcely even noticed it, as he seemed not to.

"How well do you know Mr. Paxton?" she asked

with all the nonchalance she could muster, when the movements of the dance brought them back together for a time.

"Noel?" He glanced across the room, where the gentleman in question was one of another set of dancers. "Haven't seen too much of him since his return to London, but we had some good times in Vienna. Bang-up sort. He can carouse—and fight—with the best of 'em, and match me bottle for bottle at the table."

This was a picture of Noel she would never have suspected. She had assumed his duties in Vienna had entailed delivering messages and attending meetings, interesting in its way, but involving little risk or adventure. Before she could request more details, however, the dance separated them again.

"I've noticed Noel watching you," Mr. Thatcher commented when they were able to speak again. "You could do worse, Miss Riverstone, if you'll excuse my impudence in saying so. Of course, you could also do better." He winked suggestively.

Again she had to laugh, despite the jumble of emotions that assailed her at his endorsement of Noel. "You do not seem the sort to be hanging out for a wife." But then, neither did Noel.

"Gad, no!" he exclaimed, and his horror seemed only partially feigned. "Just innocent flirtation, don't you know. Not looking for a straitjacket, not at this stage of my life."

Rowena suspected that a good woman might do wonders for Mr. Thatcher, but he was not the one she was interested in at the moment. "Pray do not panic, sir. You have raised no expectations. But what makes you think Mr. Paxton feels any differently?"

She had to wait for his answer, as they were temporarily separated again, which gave her time to regret her bold question. What if he repeated it to Noel? She would die of embarrassment.

When he took her hand again, he appeared more thoughtful, less the devil-may-care rake that he usually projected. "Don't tell Noel I said so, but he has the look of a man ready to settle down. 'Course, I could be wrong. I'd never want to be instrumental in leg-shackling a friend."

At least it appeared he was unlikely to share their conversation with Noel, she thought with relief. "I suspect you may be mistaken, Mr. Thatcher. Mr. Paxton seems quite single-minded in his pursuit of the Saint of Seven Dials. I'm sure no other thoughts have room in his head at the moment."

"Yes, Noel's become rather a stick-in-the-mud of late," Mr. Thatcher agreed. "Seems he's forgotten how to have fun. I'll have to see what I can do about that. I owe him a favor, after all—maybe even my life."

The dance ended then, and he bowed and left her before she could ask him to explain that remarkable comment. Frowning, she turned—to find herself face to face with Noel himself.

"Dare I hope you have a waltz yet open?" he asked, his voice raising all of the tiny hairs on Rowena's body as the orchestra played the opening strains of just that dance.

She opened her mouth, but no sound came out. Clearing her throat, she tried again. "As it happens, I have." Her voice sounded high and breathy, totally unlike her.

"Good." Smiling down into her eyes, holding her gaze with the question in his own, he took her hand and led her into the dance.

For several long moments, Rowena could not bring herself to speak, so distracted was she by the sensation of his hand against her back and the memories—and desire—that sensation aroused. The silence between them lengthened to awkwardness, and finally she forced herself to say what she knew must be said.

"I . . . I must apologize for my behavior last night. It was forward, and unladylike, and completely improper."

She waited for the disgust he must feel to show in his expression at the reminder, but instead his grip on her hand tightened and his eyes seemed to grow warmer. She felt her breath quickening, despite their surroundings.

"I cannot deny that however improper it might have been, I found your behavior more than enjoyable," he said softly, ensuring that no one around them could possibly overhear. "I am more concerned about the motives for it than the behavior itself."

Impossible to tell him what she now knew was the truth—that she had simply wanted him. That she wanted him even now. It would only confirm her as a wanton, not to mention opening her to humiliation, should he feel differently. At the same time, she did not want to anger him as she had last night.

Instead, she tried to skirt a line between the noble reasoning she had used to convince herself last night, and today's realization. "I seem not to have been thinking entirely clearly last night." That was true enough! "I thought I could both follow my inclinations and justify my indiscretion by attempting to dissuade you from a course you already knew me to oppose."

"I see." Though his grip did not loosen, there was an indefinable withdrawal in his eyes. "Tell me, what were you speaking about with Richards, earlier?"

Completely unprepared for the question, Rowena missed her step and came down hard on his foot. "Oh! I beg your pardon."

Deftly, he guided her back into the motion of the waltz. "I'm not so easily distracted, you know. Will you answer my question?"

"I did not tread on your foot intentionally," she protested, as much to give herself time as because it was true.

Noel would surely be angry if she told him she had warned Richards against him. He would see it as a betrayal—which, she admitted, it was, but one she felt justified in, given the good the Saint was doing for the poor of London.

He did not argue her defense but merely waited, watching her with that intensity that both excited and disturbed her. With an effort, she pulled her glance away to look over his shoulder.

"I, ah, attempted to verify a theory about Mr. Richards," she finally said evasively.

"That he is the Saint of Seven Dials." It was not a question.

Her gaze snapped back to him, to find him regarding her with that analytical expression he sometimes wore. "I knew you suspected him," she admitted, though clearly he was already aware of that.

"And now Richards knows it too?" There was no expression in his voice, but still he accused her.

Unfortunately, she could not deny it, much as she wanted to. She simply could not lie to this man. It appeared she would not make a good politician after all. "Yes," she whispered, not meeting his eye.

"You seem to have chosen your loyalties, though I fear you may find them misplaced. You are meddling in things you do not understand, Rowena."

Her pride stung, she lifted her chin. "How do you know what I understand? I have read"—she almost added "and written," but caught herself in time—"extensively about the Saint. I daresay I understand him as well as you do."

"I rather doubt that." Surely, that was not amusement she heard in his voice? "In any event—"

"It appears you have as low an opinion of a woman's intelligence as Mr. Richards does," she snapped, angry herself now. "I do seem to have faltered in my judgment—of you."

He smiled, but it was a mirthless smile. "Anyone can make an error in judgment when lacking relevant information. I have certainly done so myself, on more than one occasion."

What was he saying? That there was more to himself than met the eye, or was he referring to Mr. Richards—or to her? Not that it mattered. "One must make decisions based on the information available, mustn't one?" she challenged him.

"But one must also be careful not to ignore the facts, seeing only what one wishes to see."

The dance ended, and he released her at once,

though still he held her eyes with his own, daring her to look away. Clearly, he thought she was granting Mr. Richards additional virtues because of her prior admiration of the man—but that was absurd. Both men had strongly implied that Richards was the Saint. It was not some foolish fantasy she had invented.

"I pride myself on my objectivity," she told him. "I always consider all options before making a move, as you have seen at the chessboard."

"Always?" He raised a skeptical brow.

Last night she had not followed that maxim—quite the opposite, in fact. She knew he was reminding her of that, and she felt her color rising against her will. "Almost always," she amended, refusing to look away this time.

The first real smile she had seen on him today briefly lightened his features. "I've said before that I admire your honesty. Perhaps we can continue this discussion over supper, if you still have that dance free?"

Before she could answer, a soft throat-clearing sounded at her elbow. "Miss Riverstone?" It was young Lord Roland, to whom she had promised the next dance.

She smiled at the newcomer, then turned back to Noel. "Supper, then," she said, though she suspected she might be making yet another error in judgment by agreeing. He bowed, and she took Lord Roland's arm so that he could lead her to the quadrille just forming.

Noel watched Rowena take her place in the set, then turned away with a frown. He'd expected that she would warn Richards given an opportunity, but he wondered very much what she had actually said—

and how he had responded. Would he interpret her warning as pertaining only to the Saint, or would he guess that Noel suspected him of something far more sinister?

If the former, Rowena's assumption no doubt amused him mightily. If the latter, he might become desperate. Either way, Rowena herself might now be in danger. But how could Noel possibly convince her of that without telling her the truth, not only about Richards, but about the Saint?

He reminded himself that he still had no clear proof that Richards was the man he sought, though he hoped to within days. For the first time since suspecting him, Noel hoped he was wrong—but his instincts claimed otherwise. Until he knew for certain, he had to somehow protect Rowena, with or without her consent.

With that goal in mind, he kept a discreet watch on her for the next two hours, even as he danced with other ladies. Twice Richards approached her, but both times she smilingly rebuffed him to dance with her next promised partner. It was difficult from a distance to read the nuances of her expression, but Noel felt almost certain that she wished to avoid Richards.

Perhaps his words had not been entirely without effect, then. He could only hope so, for her sake.

And his own.

Chapter 17

Rowena was more than ready for this interminable evening to end. She felt as though her emotions had been put through a wash wringer, twisted and distorted until she no longer knew how she felt or what she believed. All she had felt sure of had been called into question, and she didn't much care for the sensation.

"I thank you for the honor, Miss Riverstone," said Mr. Orrin with a bow as their cotillion ended.

She smiled in response, her nerves stretched to a screaming point in painful anticipation. The supper dance was next, but she did not see Noel. Would he appear to claim her as promised? Did she want him to? What could she possibly say to him after their last exchange?

"Miss Riverstone," came a voice from behind her—a voice she was almost beginning to dread this evening, contrary as that seemed. "You mentioned earlier that you don't waltz. Might that mean we can finally talk during this dance?"

Summoning a bright smile, she turned to face Mr. Richards, nearly ready to agree. Perhaps it would allow her to figure out *one* of the conundrums besetting her. "I take it you do not waltz either, sir?" she asked, stalling for time until she could decide what to do.

"Dancing is a foolish pastime, in my opinion, intended to make the mating ritual easier for those who lack the address to go about it in a more direct and rational way."

His dark eyes held hers as he spoke and a shiver went up her back at his apparent meaning. Not a particularly pleasant shiver, unfortunately.

"Of course," she said in automatic agreement, but then realized that she was again parroting his opinion rather than proclaiming her own. "But I believe there is more to dancing than that. I find it a metaphor for the strictures of Society—some foolish, certainly, but some quite sensible."

"Do you indeed?" he asked in apparent surprise, but then smiled suggestively again. "But surely you don't believe those strictures apply—"

"My apologies, Miss Riverstone," Noel interrupted him, appearing without warning from behind a pillar. "Our dance, I believe?"

Rowena turned with a relief she feared she did not completely conceal. "Mr. Paxton! I assumed you were otherwise engaged."

"Never." Though his smile was as suggestive as Mr. Richards' had been, it warmed Rowena rather than chilling her. "Shall we?"

"The lady does not waltz," said Mr. Richards, an edge to his voice. "She prefers to sit this dance out, Paxton—with me."

Noel turned to the man, his brows raised. "The lady waltzes beautifully, with the right partner. You do not give her enough credit—still."

Mr. Richards' complexion darkened at this oblique reference to last night's chess match. "And you seem to have a habit of putting your nose where it doesn't belong," he snapped. "The lady and I were conversing."

"I find that I can learn quite a lot by putting my nose where others would prefer I did not," Noel responded with an enigmatic half-smile. "In any event, Miss Riverstone promised this dance to me earlier, did you not?" He turned to her for verification.

Embarrassed in the extreme, Rowena nodded. "He is right, Mr. Richards, I did. I . . . I am improving slightly at the waltz, with practice, though I am by no means proficient."

"Practice improves all skills," Noel said, his eyes giving his words an added meaning that embarrassed her further. "Shall we?" he said again.

This time, she put her hand in his. "My apologies, Mr. Richards. I did promise."

"Then you surely realize now that one should not make promises lightly, or without proper forethought," Mr. Richards said with a darkling glance at Noel. Then, he seemed to recover himself. "No matter. We will continue our conversation later."

As Noel led her to the dance already in progress, Rowena decided that "later" would not be tonight. She would retire immediately after supper, as she had before. She'd had enough emotional turmoil for one evening.

"Now then," said Noel, placing his hand at her

back to guide her into the movements of the dance. "Am I mistaken, or were you just as glad of an excuse to break off that talk with Richards?"

She looked up at him in surprise, trying vainly to ignore the sensations—and emotions—that rippled through her at his touch. "How could you—That is, he has seemed unusually determined to speak with me alone this evening, since our earlier conversation."

"And that makes you uncomfortable."

She nodded. Now, why had she admitted that to a man who was certainly Mr. Richards' enemy? "I don't really know him that well, after all," she temporized.

"Precisely the point I tried to make earlier," he said. "I know you think his motives are entirely noble, but I have reason to believe otherwise. I wish you would trust me, Rowena." The warmth in his eyes nearly made her melt, right there on the dance floor.

Valiantly, she tried to rally her reason. "How can I, when we are so ideologically opposed?" she made herself say. "Would you have me sacrifice my principles on the altar of that trust?"

To her surprise, he smiled. "I think we are not so opposed as you believe, Rowena. As I said, you have based some of your opinions on insufficient information."

"And will you supply the information I lack?" It was both a challenge and a plea, but he shook his head with apparent regret.

"I can't—not yet. That is why I want you to trust me, until I am able to do just that."

He seemed to be speaking in riddles, and it frustrated her that she could not decipher them. Normally, she was quite good at riddles. She made one more attempt. "Are you trying to tell me that Mr. Richards is *not* the Saint of Seven Dials?"

"Please, Rowena, do not press me for information I cannot safely give you just now. If all goes as I hope, my mission will be accomplished within days. Then, I will tell you everything."

Within days? He expected to have the Saint arrested within days? Or did he mean something else entirely? Though she asked no more questions, Rowena by no means intended to give up trying to figure out what was going on. To do so would be to betray who she was and all she believed in.

She thought back over the recent exchange between Noel and Mr. Richards. The older man seemed to be subtly threatening Noel, a threat that Noel had turned back upon him. They had all but openly acknowledged themselves as opponents—and not, she thought, simply for her affections.

Clearly, she would have to choose her loyalties, and choose soon, if she was to have any hope of affecting their contest.

The dance ended, and Noel led her in to supper. As before, he attempted to find a table where they might be private, but unfortunately they were joined almost at once by Lord and Lady Marcus.

"I see that your spectacles have in no way diminished your popularity," Lady Marcus remarked, seating herself next to Rowena.

Noel glanced at Rowena in surprise, drawing a confused look from her in return.

"Why do you look at me like that?" she asked him.

He smiled sheepishly. "I, ah, hadn't noticed that you

were wearing your spectacles tonight," he confessed.

"Knowing how observant you generally are, sir, I believe I will take that as a compliment," she said.

The other couple chuckled, and Noel joined in, still feeling foolish. It was true, however. Her eyeglasses were so much a part of her that he *hadn't* noticed. Certainly, they did not diminish her attractiveness. He wanted her more than ever.

He and Lord Marcus excused themselves to fetch plates of food for themselves and the ladies. Footmen were circulating with trays of drinks ranging from champagne to lemonade.

"Glad of this chance for a word," Lord Marcus said as soon as they were out of earshot. "I'm hoping you can meet with Luke and me later this evening. We're wanting to finally do something about Twitchell, who's become even more abusive of late."

"Certainly," Noel agreed. The vicious thief-master was a problem he'd been hoping to solve himself.

Other gentlemen joined them then, so the subject was dropped. When they returned to the table, the ladies were deep in conversation, but turned to greet them with smiles. The four of them talked primarily about the deplorable conditions of London's workhouses during supper.

Rowena was animated on the topic, and Noel enjoyed watching and listening to her, though he took a smaller part in the conversation than the others. He also noticed the overt affection between Lord Marcus and his wife, a rarity among their class that they shared with Lord and Lady Hardwyck.

It was what he wanted for himself, Noel realized, his gaze again going to Rowena. She glanced his way just then, and for a long moment their eyes locked. Hers still held a certain reserve, as well as a question—a question he dared not answer yet.

"Goodness, was the supper break so short at the last ball, or is it merely the company that has made the time pass so quickly?" Lady Marcus exclaimed as the orchestra began the next dance number.

"The latter, I'm sure," Rowena replied. "I have enjoyed our conversation immensely. Now, though, I pray you will all excuse me. I made a point of committing to no dances after supper, knowing how tired I was likely to be—and so I am."

Noel and Lord Marcus rose to help the ladies to their feet. "You plan to escape yet again, then?" Noel said to Rowena in an undertone. "Would you care for an escort?"

"Marcus wishes to talk to Lord Hardwyck later, so we will enjoy another dance or two," Lady Marcus said. "Sleep well, Rowena. Perhaps we can go shopping together later this week."

Rowena agreed that she would like that, then turned back to Noel. "I am quite capable of finding my room unassisted," she told him archly. Then, glancing over his shoulder, her expression changed. "However, if you would care to accompany me as far as the stairway . . ."

He extended his arm and she took it. As they walked, he cast a quick look behind him to see Richards watching them with a frown. So, she was still eager to avoid the man. Good.

"You do not seem so tired as you did at Friday night's ball," he commented. "Are you beginning to adjust to Town hours?"

Her expression had been solemn, but now she smiled. "Yes, I believe I am. Still, I don't really feel equal to more dancing tonight."

He suspected it was not the dancing she wished to avoid, however. "A ballroom can be much like a battlefield—or a chess board—I find. Campaigns are waged by matchmaking mamas and determined bachelors, by fortune hunters and aspiring peeresses, each with their own distinctive strategies."

"Precisely," she agreed. "As well as some campaigns far more subtle than those you have listed. The strategizing can be as wearying as the dancing, I find."

They were nearly to the stairway now, and she paused to look earnestly up at him. "I fear I may make a false move, as some of the pieces appear to be hidden. It is worse than when I played without my spectacles."

Her wide gray eyes pleaded with him for information—and for something else. Or was he imagining that? He led her toward a small alcove near the foot of the stairs, where they would be less likely to be seen by any chance passerby.

"Please believe that I don't wish to hide anything from you, Rowena, and would not if I did not have to. Soon—"

"Yes, so you said. Perhaps within days. But meanwhile . . ." Her voice trailed off with a sigh and he felt something inside him give way.

Reaching the alcove, he covered the small hand that rested on his arm with his own, and turned to face her. "Rowena, I—"

He could not even wait to finish his thought,

wasn't even certain what that thought was. Her nearness overwhelmed his reason, his senses, and he found himself kissing her—and found her responding eagerly.

With stunning force, the feelings he had experienced last night came rushing back and it was as though she were naked in his arms again, ready for the taking he so desperately wanted. Noel, who had always prided himself on his ability to sublimate emotion to cool reason, felt like a ravening beast with only one way to feed his hunger.

Rowena seemed to sense his urgency, his need—perhaps even to share it. Her arms came about him, pulling him more tightly against her until his arousal pressed against the firm softness of her belly.

Summoning his last vestige of reason and every ounce of his self-control, he broke away from her to stare, panting, into her eyes. She appeared as shocked as he, her soft lips parted, swollen with the ferocity of that kiss. Her breasts rose and fell rapidly as she stared at him, one hand to her flushed cheek.

"I—I didn't think—"

"Nor did I," he said, managing a half-smile. Raw passion still simmered just beneath the surface. "In fact, I have a difficult time thinking at all when I'm with you, Rowena."

Her helpless nod told him he affected her similarly. She reached toward him with one small hand, and he took it instinctively, though he now knew the risk he ran in doing so.

If he went up those stairs with her tonight, they would not stop until she was his completely, and he hers. He knew it with the same certainty that he knew the sun would rise tomorrow. His whole body tightened in anticipation and he took a step forward.

"There you are!" Lady Hardwyck's voice shattered the private world of passion they had woven together. As one, they swung around to face her.

Her eyebrows rose as she looked from Rowena to Noel. "Well. It appears I may have found you just in time, from the look of things. Rowena, I believe you'd best go up to bed. We'll talk later."

Noel tried to convey both apology and longing in his glance, but Rowena only met his eyes for an instant before turning away—too brief an instant for him to decipher the mix of emotions he saw there. "Good night, Miss Riverstone," he said softly.

She paused, but did not turn around. "Good night," she whispered. He watched her mount the stairs, unable to take his eyes from her, memorizing the curve of her shoulder, her waist, one glimpse of ankle—remembering what lay beneath those skirts.

"Mr. Paxton."

With a start, he remembered Lady Hardwyck's presence. "My lady?"

"Perhaps I should talk with you, as well as with Rowena. However, it is my husband who wishes to speak with you now. He and Lord Marcus are in the library."

Her blue eyes were filled with concern for her friend. He wished he could reassure her, tell her that he meant to make Rowena an offer in form, but until this business with the Black Bishop was concluded, he dared not—any more than he dared tell Rowena plainly that he loved her.

The next few days would be as dangerous as any he

had faced, and it would be wrong to bind Rowena to him unless he could promise her a future together. But had Lady Hardwyck not arrived when she did, he realized, he would have done just that.

"Thank you," he said, meaning more than her message. He suspected, from the look she gave him before turning back to the ballroom, that she understood.

Luke and Marcus both turned to greet him when he entered the study a moment later.

"I thought it was time all three Saints put our heads together to solve a persistent problem," Luke said. "You've both mentioned wanting to do something about that blackguard Twitchell. Earlier today a lad from his flash house was found, beaten unconscious. If Stilt hadn't found him, he'd no doubt be dead now."

"Twitchell beat him?" Noel asked.

At the same moment, Marcus said, "Who was it?"

"Tig," Luke replied, nodding in response to Noel's question. "He roused enough to tell Stilt that Twitchell caught him holding back part of his takings—money that I, in fact, had given him so that he wouldn't have to steal."

Noel felt a cold rage edging out his earlier, warmer feelings. Tig was the lad who had been his go-between, bringing messages from Stilt via Squint, the footman. A plucky, cocky lad with delusions of grandeur—and no more than ten years old.

"That bastard!" Marcus exclaimed, his voice low with a similar rage. "Where is Tig now?"

"Here in this house, in the servants' wing. I've already had a physician attend him, and it appears he will recover." Luke looked at each of them. "Then we are in agreement that it's time Twitchell was removed?"

They both nodded, but Noel said, "Or perhaps replaced? With Twitchell gone, will not the remaining lads simply move to Ickle's flash house—or an even worse one?"

He had recruited a lad or two from Ickle's group when trailing Lord Marcus as Saint earlier this summer, and knew those boys received their share of hard knocks from their master as well.

"My thought exactly, Noel," Luke said with an approving nod. "And I believe I have just the fellow. You may remember Flute, my erstwhile valet? I believe you were rather anxious to have a word with him at one time."

Noel chuckled. He'd been certain that young man would be the key to proving Luke was the Saint—and he might well have been, had Noel's own agenda not changed drastically upon learning that Luke was not the traitor he really sought. "He should be safe enough in Town now," Noel agreed.

"Which is why I've sent for him from Knoll Grange, one of my smaller properties, not far from London. He should arrive tomorrow. I'll brief him on the situation, and assuming Flute is willing to shepherd the boys, I'll confront Twitchell and give him a choice—between the gibbet and the colonies."

"And you'll want us to watch your back, I presume?" Marcus asked.

Luke nodded. "It seems prudent. And Noel, perhaps you can convince someone at Bow Street to ensure for us that he takes ship."

"That should present no problem." Noel thought

for a moment, weighing his other plans, then said, "I have a favor to ask of you, as well."

"Of course." Luke waited for him to proceed, which he did after another long pause.

"I will be engaged tomorrow, and perhaps the next day, conducting some necessary research on that matter I told you about."

"And what matter is this?" Marcus asked curiously.

Noel had not previously mentioned the Bishop to Marcus, on the theory that the fewer people who knew, the fewer would be at risk. Now, however, he quickly outlined the traitor's career, then added his suspicion that Mr. Richards might be the man he sought.

"I need proof, however. I discovered today that Richards' father lives in the country a few hours from Town, an invalid. I plan to question him as soon as possible."

"So you want us to keep an eye on Richards while you are away?" Luke asked.

Noel nodded. "If he suspects that I am on to him, he may attempt to leave Town—or do something desperate. I, ah, would particularly like you to keep him away from Miss Riverstone, if possible. She may be at some risk from him."

Both men stared, and Noel felt his neck heating with embarrassment. "It's not what you think," he explained. "Yes, he has behaved as though he has a romantic interest in her, and I won't deny that I do myself. But certain things he has said, and done, indicate a darker purpose. Already she is dazzled by his highflown revolutionary rhetoric and . . . she believes he is the Saint of Seven Dials."

At this, both men started to laugh. "How that must rankle!" Marcus said with a grin. "To have her admiring another man for *your* daring exploits. I believe I can sympathize."

"If Richards is the traitor you seek, he may attempt to inveigle Miss Riverstone into some scheme, or use her as a hostage against your moving against him," Luke said, sobering. "As she is a guest in my home, I feel honor-bound to prevent him doing so."

"Thank you." And Noel meant it from the bottom of his heart. Without that assurance, he would have to remain close enough to protect her himself—something he recognized as a risky proposition after tonight. It might be said that he himself posed a substantial risk to Rowena's future, if not her life. He *had* to conclude this case, and quickly.

"What explanation do you intend to give Miss Riverstone for your absence?" Marcus asked then. "We would not want to inadvertently contradict it."

Noel frowned. He knew it would be safest not to see her again—not yet. "Can you simply tell her that my duties require me elsewhere?" he asked Luke. "I hope to be able to explain everything soon enough."

"Everything?" both men asked together.

"Your wives both know, do they not?" They nodded. "As it is my hope that once this business is settled I can persuade Miss Riverstone to marry me, it seems only fitting that she know all."

"Then London will need a new Saint—again," Luke commented with a wry grin. "But time enough to think on that later. I recommend an early night, gentlemen. We all have a big day ahead of us tomorrow."

* * *

Rowena stared into the dark, sleep as far away as ever. Noel would not come to her tonight, she knew, not after Pearl had discovered them. He would consider the risk to her reputation too great—though she cared not a fig for that.

She did care about Pearl's good opinion, however. Unwilling to face her best friend's censure until she had sorted out her wildly conflicting feelings, she had feigned sleep when Pearl had peeked into her room half an hour since. There would be time enough for a scold in the morning.

Perhaps she should simply tell Pearl everything, and ask for her advice. From occasional comments between Pearl and Lord Hardwyck, she had the impression that their own courtship had been a rather bumpy one. The need to unburden herself, to get a more objective opinion, was strong.

Not nearly as strong as her need for Noel, however. He was all she really wanted at this moment—his voice, his face, his kisses . . . his body. Was this obsession?

No, she realized, this was love.

Though she had resisted both her feelings and the admission of those feelings to herself, she could no longer deny either. Not only was this love, it was the sort of love that drove the poets to ruin. An all-encompassing and all-too-likely tragic love, given their differences and her betrayal of Noel's mission.

All her life she had both doubted the existence and fantasized about the possible reality of love. Secretly, she had always hoped to find it for herself—to find that one man who would fill the empty spaces in her heart, who was her other half, who could make her whole, even as she made him whole. Now, she knew beyond doubt she had finally found that man.

Rowena cried herself to sleep.

Chapter 18

Noel was up at daybreak, determined to accomplish all that was necessary in time to be in the country by noon. His first order of business was at Bow Street, where he arranged for one of the Runners to make certain Mr. Twitchell boarded a ship for the New World within the week, with orders to arrest the thief-master if he did not leave London in that time.

Sir Nathaniel arrived while Noel was there, so he requested a private conference to explain his own proposed absence over the next day or two, implying that he was close to capturing the Saint but hinting that even more important matters were at stake. It was a measure of Sir Nathaniel's trust in him that he did not require more information than Noel was prepared to share.

By this time, he knew that the office of the *Political Register* would be open, so he went there next, to discover whether any response had yet been received from Mr. R.

"I was hoping you'd be by," the sympathetic clerk greeted him, nervously pushing up his spectacles. The motion reminded Noel sharply of Rowena.

"You have something, then?" he asked, firmly putting such distracting thoughts from his mind.

The clerk nodded. "Came yesterday." He held up a sheet of paper. "He wants us to leave the letters in Green Park, behind a specific rock near the entrance."

"When?"

"Today. He plans to retrieve them this afternoon, he says. I was planning to wrap them in oilskin and put them there myself, later this morning." He handed the note to Noel.

Reading through it, Noel fought to tamp down his sudden excitement. Today! He had not expected results so quickly. The Black Bishop was nearly in his grasp! His trip to question Richards' father would have to wait. In fact, if all went as he hoped, it wouldn't be necessary to go into the country at all.

"Yes, that sounds like a good plan." He handed back the letter. "And thank you. You have done England a great service, Mr. Bell. If all goes well, I'll see that you are recognized for it."

But the clerk shook his head. "I'd just as soon not, thanks, given Mr. Cobbett's politics. Being a hero might be nice, but I'd rather keep my job."

Noel chuckled, his spirits irrepressibly high. "Your choice, of course. But you have my gratitude, nonetheless."

Whistling, he headed for Seven Dials, where he was to meet Luke and Lord Marcus for the bearding of Mr. Twitchell.

* * *

Sunshine often serves to chase away mental as well as physical darkness, as Rowena discovered for herself the next morning. What had seemed hopeless in the dark watches of the night now seemed less so.

Noel had told her he cared for her, and he was nothing if not an honorable man. Now that their indiscretion was no longer secret, he would likely make an offer in form.

And she was very nearly resolved to accept him.

"The periwinkle cambric, Matthilda," she told her maid once she had washed. It was her most flattering day dress, brightening her hair and eyes. She wished to look her best for what might prove to be the most important day of her life.

Marrying Noel Paxton might well mean abandoning active pursuit of her more radical goals, but surely what she would gain in exchange would be worth it. Leisurely discussions of every topic imaginable, long walks, games of chess . . . and the promise of physical pleasures she could scarcely even imagine.

The very thought brought becoming color to her cheeks. She smiled a secret smile at herself in the looking-glass, then turned to allow Matthilda to help her into the gown.

Once married, surely she would be able to persuade Noel more to her way of thinking, she reasoned. He was always willing to listen to her arguments, to give her credit when she was right, though he might dispute her conclusions. Given unlimited time to explain her views, she was sure to bring him around in some areas.

Perhaps this was mere rationalization, making her natural inclination easier to accept, but she didn't care. After a miserable night, she was determined to be happy on this auspiciously sunny day.

"Thank you, Matthilda," she said as the maid put the finishing touches to her hair. Head high, she sailed out of her room and down the stairs, ready to face Pearl's lectures, confident that she could also expect Noel's addresses.

As she had expected, Pearl awaited her in the dining room. Noel was absent, perhaps by Pearl's request. "Rowena, I believe we need to talk," came the anticipated preamble.

"Yes, I suppose we do," Rowena agreed, smiling at her friend's evident surprise at her own cheerfulness. "I'll just get some breakfast and coffee first." She then proceeded to do just that, filling a plate from the sideboard while a footman poured her a steaming cup. "Now," she said, sitting to face Pearl expectantly.

"I'm not certain you are aware of the gravity of your situation," Pearl began once the footman had gone. "It is extremely fortunate that only I saw you and Mr. Paxton last night, in what looked suspiciously like a tryst."

Rowena considered. "Not a tryst, no. He merely escorted me to the stairs, as I was ready to go up to bed. I can't deny that we kissed, however. He is quite good at it." As well as other things, she added to herself.

"Rowena!" Pearl's eyes were wide with shock, though the corners of her lips twitched. "I must say, I never expected—That is, you seem to be treating this very lightly. And just how would you know how Mr. Paxton's kisses compare to any other man's?"

"Well, I don't, actually," Rowena confessed, though for the fun of scandalizing Pearl she was tempted to claim otherwise. "Oh, Pearl, you know I have never been missish. If I enjoy Noel's kisses and he enjoys mine, why should we not please ourselves?"

"So it is Noel now, is it? I suppose that is as well, considering. But I thought you were always opposed to the idea of marriage, likening it to slavery for a woman. Following this course with a man like Mr. Paxton is likely to end in a wedding. You must know that."

Rowena nodded, but slowly. Having Pearl put it into words like that was sobering, despite her earlier resolve. "I have thought of that, yes. But Noel respects my intelligence as no other man ever has. If I am to marry at all, I doubt I could do better."

"But—" Pearl waved a helpless hand.

Rowena looked her friend in the eye, all amusement gone. "Besides," she said simply, "I love him."

Pearl sighed. "I feared it might be so. I have watched how your eyes follow him—and how he watches you, as well."

"Why 'feared'?" Rowena asked in surprise. "I thought you would be pleased."

Her friend looked at her with a sympathy that set off warnings in Rowena's head.

"Where *is* Noel?" she demanded, feeling a sudden dark premonition despite the bright sunshine.

"He is gone," Pearl said. "I don't know where. He left very early this morning."

Rowena half-rose from her chair. "You sent him away, because of what you saw last night? But I told you—"

But Pearl was shaking her head. "No, I did not

send him away, nor did Luke. It was his own decision to leave."

"He has gone back to his lodgings, then?" That's what he'd done before, when he didn't trust himself to be near her. A prudent course, perhaps, but frustrating.

Pearl shook her head again, however. "I fear not. Luke tells me he is gone into the country, and may not return for some days."

Swallowing painfully around the lump that had suddenly appeared in her throat, Rowena stared at her friend. "But why?" she whispered. "Where has he gone?"

"I . . . I do not know. Luke seemed disinclined to discuss it, so I did not press for details."

Rowena's earlier euphoria turned to ashes and dread. He had implied that he was very close to catching the Saint. Might his absence be connected to that? But the Saint operated here in London. Was Noel so eager to avoid her that he had abandoned his quest and returned to his estate—perhaps never to return?

"A few days, did you say?" she asked, grasping at straws.

"Luke did not actually say how long he would be gone," Pearl confessed, "just that he had business to attend to in the country. Perhaps he will return tomorrow."

Rowena averted her gaze from her friend's pitying expression, which told her far more than her words did. *Had* she read more into Noel's words and actions than he had intended? But he had told her he cared for her, and she believed him to be honest, even if she frequently disagreed with him.

"I suppose I will simply have to wait until he returns, then," she said with an effort, pinning a smile back to her lips. Though her appetite had fled, she forced herself to take a bite of smoked ham.

"Of course." Pearl spoke bracingly, which was nearly as hard to take as her pity. "That's the spirit. Now eat up, do, before our morning callers arrive. You have more admirers than Mr. Paxton, after all."

But none who made her heart race and her insides turn to jelly, thought Rowena despondently. If Noel did not return, she saw little point to remaining in London. She thought of her causes, of the plight of the common man, of the heroic charity of the Saint of Seven Dials, but even those could not fire her now.

It was as though Noel had taken the fire that fueled her passions with him.

"Then it's settled," Luke was saying to a sullen Mr. Twitchell. "You can make a fresh start in New York—unless you would prefer Botany Bay, in Australia?"

The burly thief-master glared at him. "Nay, New York'll do. Haven't you growed all high and mighty, now you're a lord and all? I recollect when you wasn't no better'n Skeet, here. Quite the pickpocket you were, once upon a time."

Luke smiled. "I like to think any of these boys has the ability to rise above his circumstances, just as I have. With you gone, they'll have a better chance to do so."

Twitchell snorted his disbelief. "Half these lads would be dead now without me. Gave 'em a trade, didn't I?"

"Thieving is scarcely a trade. In any event, now they'll have a choice."

Noel watched the exchange from the shadows of a nearby alley, his pistol at the ready. He and Lord Marcus were to show themselves only if the situation grew dangerous—which it now appeared it would not. Luke had been adamant that Twitchell have no opportunity to link either of them to the Saint of Seven Dials.

In a few moments the business was concluded and Twitchell on his way to the docks, shadowed by the Runner Noel had engaged earlier that day. He and Marcus retreated to the prearranged meeting spot, two streets away.

"That went more smoothly than I expected it to," Luke said when he joined them. "I suspect Twitchell has more laid by than he's admitting to, and expects to set himself up nicely on the other side of the Atlantic."

"Where he'll be the Americans' problem and not ours," said Marcus with a grin. "I'd say this calls for a small celebration."

"It does," Noel agreed, "but I fear you'll have to count me out. I need to attend to that other matter I mentioned." He saw no point in explaining his change of plans, as he'd be heading to the country soon enough if his quarry didn't show this afternoon.

Noel left them then, stopping at the coaching inn where Kemp awaited him to delay their departure, but cautioning him to be ready to leave on short notice later on. He would go to Green Park alone, the better to stay concealed while he watched for the mysterious Mr. R.

With Richards safely in custody, Noel would be free to court Rowena properly. The thought of retiring to Tidebourne with her as his bride had him smiling again as he headed for Green Park, despite the dark clouds gathering on the western horizon.

Rowena had managed to cling to her smile through nearly two hours of callers, and even to enter into their conversations of gossip and flirtation, but it was most wearisome. All she really wanted to do right now was escape to her chamber until it was time to slip across the street to Green Park and her letters.

Those, she reasoned, should do nicely to help her pass the time until Noel returned.

For he *would* return. Even when they had been so at odds that they were scarcely speaking, knowing that he was hearing the same silly conversations and sharing her opinion of them had helped her to endure the shallow prattle of people like Fanny Mountheath. Now, however . . .

"Yes, if Lord Edgemont is wealthier than Lord Harrowby, that might make him seem a better catch, to some," she said, stifling a yawn. Miss Mountheath had been comparing the relative fortunes of every bachelor in England, it seemed, for the past twenty minutes. "Surely other factors should be considered, however."

"Oh, of course," her tormentor agreed. "I would never want to marry a man who was truly ill-favored, or older than Papa. I am only discussing *eligible* gentlemen. Don't you agree, Lucy?" She and her sister tittered together, while Rowena racked her brain for some plausible excuse to leave the parlor.

To her relief, the butler chose that moment to announce Mr. Richards. Finally, a chance for some rational conversation! So eager was she to escape the Mountheath sisters that she greeted him more effusively than she might otherwise have done.

"How delightful to see you again so soon, Mr. Richards," she exclaimed.

He moved at once to sit by her, after only the briefest acknowledgment of the other ladies present. "I am happy to hear you say so," he said. "Especially as I was able to spend so little time in your presence last night."

"Yes, Mama was saying earlier how amazed she was that you have become so popular so quickly, Miss Riverstone," Lucy Mountheath volunteered. "But of course, being Lady Hardwyck's friend and protégée must have its benefits."

Rowena did not allow the young lady's spiteful comment to sting. She knew by now that neither of the Mountheath sisters—nor their mother—ever had a kind word to say for anyone unless it served their own interests, and seldom even then.

"Pearl has been very kind to me," she replied blandly. Miss Mountheath only sniffed and turned to her sister, freeing Rowena to speak privately with Mr. Richards. "I do apologize for leaving the ball so early last night. I was quite tired by suppertime, however."

"Quite understandable," he said with a most flattering smile. "All of your admirers kept you dancing constantly, to my loss."

She recalled what he had said about dancing last night, but had no wish to argue with him now. "It is more exercise than I have been accustomed to, certainly. And enjoyable as it can be, I confess I prefer chess and conversation to galloping about a ballroom."

For the barest instant a frown crossed his brow—perhaps at her mention of chess, which she instantly regretted. Now, however, he smiled again. "That goes to prove your intelligence—as do the opinions you have shared with me on certain matters. Mr. Spence's proposals, for example."

Rowena's interest quickened and she was pleased to discover that she did still care about such issues after all. "I believe that some of his ideas might be quite workable," she said earnestly. "Certainly, I agree that land should benefit those who work it."

Mr. Richards leaned closer to her and lowered his voice. "Would you care to learn what some of his adherents hope to do, to help bring such a change about?"

Her eyes widened. "Certainly. I had feared Mr. Spence's plans might have died with him, kept alive only in writings. Do you mean that there are yet people actively working toward his ideals?"

"Not so loud," he said, even more softly. "There are those in government who believe anything which might threaten the current system of power to be seditious. But yes, a group of forward-thinking men carry on Spence's dream of a utopia where men are no longer sacrificed as beasts."

The Mountheath sisters rose to take their leave just then, requiring Rowena's response to their farewells. Pearl then asked her a question pertaining to her conversation with Lady Norville on the changes on the Continent since the Congress of Vienna. As Rowena had read extensively on the issue, she spent some time discussing it with them. By the time she was able to turn her attention back to Mr. Richards, he was rising to leave.

"I have exceeded my quarter hour," he said, taking her hand, "and don't wish to outstay my welcome. Before I go, however, I'd like to extend you an invitation."

Rowena looked up at him in surprise, to find him watching her intently, his expression serious. It occurred to her that she had never heard Mr. Richards laugh. "An invitation, sir?"

He bent over her hand, bringing his lips close to her ear. "Come driving with me tomorrow, and I will tell you about those forward-thinking men I mentioned. I believe you will learn much that will interest you."

Though she was undeniably curious, something about his manner bothered her. "I'll have to ask Lady Hardwyck—" she began, glancing over at Pearl, who was still talking with Lady Norville.

"I thought you were your own person, needing no one's permission for your actions?" he reminded her softly.

"Of . . . of course." She had been looking for ways to fill her thoughts and time until Noel returned, had she not? Along with her letters, discovering all there was to know about the Spenceans should fill that role admirably. "What time?"

He smiled, but it was a humorless smile, she thought with a tiny shiver. "I will call for you by five o'clock, the fashionable hour for a drive in the park."

Though an uneasy instinct warned her that she might be agreeing to more than a simple drive, she nodded. "As long as I can be back here by six, that should be fine."

"Of course," he said smoothly. "We can return whenever you wish. Until tomorrow, then." Releasing her hand, he turned to make his farewells to Pearl, and then left the parlor.

Rowena frowned after him, but then shrugged. How much trouble could she possibly get into in an hour? It would give her excellent material for future essays—and for future arguments with Noel. This would be one topic on which he could scarcely claim to be more expert than she was!

When the last callers left a few minutes later, Rowena headed upstairs. She would change into one of her nondescript gowns and conceal her hair before making her foray to Green Park, to reduce the risk that she might be recognized.

Who would have guessed that life would suddenly become so interesting? she wondered with a spurt of amusement. She, who had led such a completely dull existence for twenty-one years. It appeared she was now making up for it with a vengeance.

The most exciting adventure of all, though, was the one she had found in Noel's arms. She only hoped that he would return soon, so that she could experience his kisses and caresses again.

Noel shifted his weight from his right leg to his left, trying to keep his limbs from going numb after standing motionless for so long. Though he was fairly well concealed behind a pair of birch trees, any movement might serve to warn his quarry—not that he'd seen any sign of him yet.

Green Park had been fairly active earlier, with young families and a few couples strolling the paths, enjoying the balmy sunshine. Now that clouds had rolled in and a fresh breeze had sprung up, however, the park was nearly deserted. With a careful glance around, Noel pulled out his pocket watch. He'd been here almost two hours.

And he would wait past midnight and into tomorrow, if necessary, to finally catch the elusive traitor.

He could see the oilskin packet from here, nestled at the base of the black and gray mottled rock. Might he have been spotted? Could one of the apparently innocent pedestrians actually have been a confederate of the Black Bishop—or even the Bishop himself, if Noel were mistaken about Richards?

A few large drops of rain rattled the leaves around him, and he shifted his weight again. All he could do was wait.

The last few stragglers now hurried toward the park gates, clearly anxious to get indoors before the rain began in earnest. A low roll of thunder sounded in the distance. Noel cursed silently and turned up the collar of his coat, then stilled abruptly as a cloaked and hooded figure entered the gates, in defiance of the threatening weather.

Noel narrowed his eyes as the figure approached. Too short and slight to be Richards. Had the man hired a boy off the streets for this errand? All too likely. If so, Noel would have to somehow induce the lad to lead him to whoever had paid him—a gold sovereign should do it.

Now the figure slowed, glancing about as he approached the rock. Yes, he was clearly here for the letters, whoever he was. The hood was pulled close about the face against the intensifying storm—and against detection—but Noel caught a quick glimpse of a small hand and an almost girlish nose. Definitely not a grown man, he thought, not even a short one.

Could it possibly be a woman? That would be awkward, but it would not dissuade him from his goal. Not when he was this close.

Whoever it was had now reached the rock. Stooping, he—or she—groped about the base, found the packet of letters, and tucked it inside the cloak. It was time for Noel to make his move.

He waited just long enough for the person—he was almost sure it was female now—to turn back toward the gates, then followed, quickly but quietly, the now heavy rain masking his footfalls. Even before his quarry had reached the path, he closed the gap between them.

Noel realized now that he was a full head taller than his opponent. Subduing her—him?—should be no problem. When he grasped a cloaked shoulder, the figure gasped, flinched violently, then spun to face him.

His heart seemed to stop as he found himself staring down into Rowena Riverstone's terrified face.

Chapter 19

Rowena turned, one hand upraised, ready in her panic to fight off her attacker, only to find herself face to face with the last person she expected to see. Her heart was already pounding from being so badly startled, but now it began a happier staccato—until Noel's shocked frown penetrated her sudden euphoria.

"Rowena! How—What are you doing here?" he demanded. He sounded angry rather than pleased to see her.

It took her a moment to summon enough breath for a reply after her fright. "Me? What are *you* doing here?" Her voice sounded high and breathless to her own ears. Forcing herself to look him directly in the eye, deliberately strengthening her voice, she asked, "Have you been following me?"

His eyes widened, then narrowed, taking on his strategizing expression. "Rowena, listen to me. This is important. Who sent you here to retrieve those letters?"

He knew! That's why he was here. Still she tried to delay the inevitable. Shrugging, evading his eye, she said, "Letters? What letters?"

"The letters you have inside your cloak." Roughly, he jerked open her gray cloak and grabbed the packet she had tucked into an inside pocket. The back of his hand brushed her breast in the process, but he seemed not to notice the contact.

"Give me those!" she exclaimed, genuinely alarmed now. "They're mine." Vainly, she tried to snatch the letters back, but he held the oilskin package out of her reach.

"Yours?" he asked mockingly. "Do you even know what these letters are, or anything about the person they are addressed to? What were you promised as a reward for fetching them?"

Keeping an iron grip on her upper arm, he opened the packet with his teeth and free hand while she struggled against him, still trying to reach the letters. It was no use. His reach, his strength, far exceeded hers. She gave it up.

"Of course I know what they are," she said, her voice flat with defeat. "They are letters sent to the *Political Register* for the essayist MRR. And I think I can safely say that I know everything there is to know about that essayist. Now give them to me."

"You haven't told me what Richards promised you," he said harshly, a flash of pain in his eyes. That pain startled her again.

"Richards? Lester Richards?" she asked, now thoroughly confused. "What has he to do with anything?"

Noel's grip on her arm loosened somewhat, and he

suddenly looked as startled as she felt. "You were fetching these letters for him, were you not?"

She shook her head. "I told you, they're mine." Was it possible he really hadn't figured it out yet?

"If not Richards, then who?" he asked. "Your brother, perhaps?"

"Nelson has no more to do with this than Mr. Richards." No matter how it might risk her reputation, risk any hope of a future with Noel, she would not implicate anyone else to shield herself.

Noel stared at her, and she could almost see his mind working, trying to make sense of all the evidence. She couldn't suppress a slight smile.

"I thought you more intelligent than this, given your skill at the chessboard," she said patiently, anticipation of his surprise the only thing keeping worry at bay. "The answer should be obvious by now, though I still don't know why it is so important to you."

"And the answer is?" he ground out, clearly stung by her amusement.

Prolonging this was only making things worse. "MRR stands for Miss Rowena Riverstone," she explained, watching as understanding broke across his face. "*I* am the anonymous essayist you've been so curious about."

Noel had felt his heart die within him when faced with what seemed conclusive proof that Rowena was in league with Richards. It presented him with a terrible choice, for if Rowena was helping a traitor, she would share his fate, were she arrested. But now she said Richards was not involved at all. Surely *she* could not be the traitor he sought?

"You?" he asked, still stunned and confused. She must still be trying to protect Richards, as she'd done when she invited Noel to her room—to her bed—two nights since. Now she was claiming authorship of those essays rather than let him be brought to justice.

"How can it be you?" he asked again, more harshly, when she did not respond. "The handwriting, the turns of phrase—it can't be you, Rowena."

"I disguised my handwriting, of course," she told him matter-of-factly. "I knew the essays would never be printed if they were written in a feminine hand."

He continued to stare at her, trying to read her emotions, to detect any trace of a lie, but he saw none. What he did notice was that her cloak was wet through, making her shiver.

"Perhaps we can continue this inquisition indoors?" she suggested through chattering teeth.

He blinked, trying to disentangle his thoughts from the convoluted paths they'd been following. "Of course. My apologies." He spoke automatically, still unable to process this new information. "Shall I return you to Hardwyck Hall?"

Rowena glanced at the mansion across the street. "I suppose so, but we'll need to go in through the back. That's how I left, and no one knows I'm gone, or so I hope. This has taken a bit longer than I'd planned, thanks to you."

Unwilling to let her guess the depth of his conflict, he nodded curtly and extended an arm for her. The letters, at least, were still safe inside his coat.

"Will you not tell me why you were so determined

to discover MRR's identity?" she asked as they exited Green Park. "I assumed before that you believed MRR and the Saint to be one, but I don't know why you came to that conclusion."

So she knew nothing of Richards' treason, after all. Was it really possible she *had* written those essays? Certainly, that would explain her agitation when he had brought up the subject shortly after meeting her. He had assumed at the time that Mr. R—or, rather, MRR—must be her brother, for her to react so strongly—so personally.

With growing relief, he recalled that she had met Richards for the first time only the night before that discussion, and in his presence. She and Richards hadn't had so much as a private conversation at that point. Though she clearly admired the man's writings, she would have had no personal stake in those essays, had he written them.

She must be telling the truth, then. Which meant he was no closer to catching the Black Bishop than he had been weeks ago. Or was he? She was better acquainted with Richards now. Perhaps she could still help him.

He glanced at her to find her staring up at him quizzically. He had never answered her question.

"Why are you so disappointed to discover that I wrote those essays?" she asked now. "What do they mean to you?"

He made a sudden decision—one his superiors would no doubt condemn. "I've been investigating something far more important—and dangerous—than the Saint of Seven Dials," he told her. "MRR was my best lead, but now it appears to have been a false one."

She frowned into the rain as they started across the street. "So you didn't believe Mr. Richards was the Saint after all? You suspected him of something else? Something . . . worse?"

He didn't answer until they gained the other side of Picadilly. After helping her over the swirling mud in the gutter, he turned her to face him, gripping her by both shoulders. He held her eyes with his own and when he spoke, his voice was low and fierce, to underscore the importance of what he would ask.

"Will you promise to say nothing, not even the merest hint, to anyone—especially to Richards?"

Despite her confusion, despite the way he'd frightened her, she couldn't help trusting this man. The driving rain had turned his auburn curls dark, plastering them against his head, making him look oddly vulnerable, though his hazel eyes bored into her own as though he would read her very thoughts.

Mutely, she nodded.

"I have reason to believe Richards is a traitor," he said. "If I am right, he is a very dangerous man, one who has killed more than once over the years to keep his identity secret."

"Over the years?" she echoed faintly. Mr. Richards, a traitor? A killer? "During . . . during the war, do you mean?"

He nodded. "He acted as a double agent, betraying British secrets to the French. Though I know of only three men he deliberately had murdered, his actions indirectly caused the deaths of countless more. Until recently, we believed the traitor had died at Waterloo. Now we know that was not the case, that he is operating here in London."

She couldn't seem to grasp what he was saying. *We?* What had Noel really done during the war? What had he really been doing here in London? Clearly not pursuing the Saint of Seven Dials, as she had believed.

"But what has this to do with my essays? Why did you think MRR might be the traitor? My writings may be controversial, but they are hardly treasonous."

"Let's get indoors, and I'll try to explain." He took her hand, to lead her around to the back of Hardwyck Hall.

Though her world had been tilted on its axis, Rowena could not ignore the thrill that went through her at his touch. She threaded her fingers through his, and felt his grip tighten. Together, they skirted the side garden and took the gravel path to the garden door, to the very spot where he had first kissed her.

"No one saw me leave," she said as they approached, pushing away that memory. "I'd just as soon no one saw me return. Pearl would ask dozens of questions, and I'd be hard pressed to answer without betraying your confidence—or my identity as MRR."

Noel nodded. Holding a finger to his lips, he stepped to the door and pressed an ear against it. "I hear voices. If we enter here, we'll certainly be seen. Perhaps the terrace doors."

She followed him up the broad stairs to the double French doors that led into the ballroom. He tried the handle, but found it locked. Rowena bit her lip in disappointment, glancing about for another way of entry, but he released her hand and knelt in front of the doors.

As she watched in growing amazement, he pulled a wire of some sort from inside his coat and fitted it into the lock, turned the handle, and opened the door easily. "Quietly, now," he whispered.

She stared, but said nothing, following him across the wide ballroom. Someone was bound to notice the wet trail they were leaving, but there seemed nothing they could do about that just now. At the far side of the ballroom, he paused to listen, then led her out into the hallway, toward the main staircase.

This was the riskiest part, she knew, when they were most likely to be discovered by a passing servant or even Pearl herself. Their luck held, however, and they gained the upper hallway without encountering anyone.

"Your room or mine?" he asked softly, his eyes holding the first hint of softness she had seen since that unexpected meeting in the park.

She swallowed. "I, ah, sent my maid out earlier, but she may be back at any time, if she has not returned already."

"You need dry clothing, in any event. If your maid is there, she can help you to change and we can talk afterward. If not—"

"Just a moment," she whispered, suddenly nervous. She went to the door of her chamber, and he retreated further down the hall without finishing his sentence.

Her room was empty, so she removed her cloak, hanging it to dry, then gathered up a complete change of clothing. Afraid that he might disappear if she tarried, she stepped back into the hallway, telling herself that she didn't want to give him a chance to avoid telling her how MRR fit into his investigation.

He was still standing outside his own chamber door. "She's still gone," she said softly.

"But might return momentarily?"

She nodded.

"Then I suggest we talk in my room, as Kemp will be out until this evening." He opened the door as he spoke.

Rowena hesitated, glancing down at the gown and underthings in her arms.

"You can change behind the screen," he said, apparently divining her thoughts. "I promise not to peek."

Feeling foolish for her sudden attack of missishness, Rowena preceded him into the room. It was nearly identical to her own, though decorated in beige and brown, while hers was in green and white. The screen shielding the dressing area from the rest of the room was in the same corner. Before retreating behind it, however, she turned again to face him.

"Tell me, do others believe my essays to be the work of a traitor?" Noel had said "we" earlier, so others must be involved in his investigation.

He shook his head, smiling reassuringly. "I have spoken of that suspicion only to one other person, my superior at the Foreign Office, and he was skeptical. You need not fear you will be in trouble with the authorities for your writings."

"But why—?" she began.

"You should change first," he said, taking her hand in his again. "Your fingers are like ice."

"So are yours," she pointed out, staring down at their joined hands. "You must have been out in the rain longer than I was, if you were lying in wait for your traitor." She covered his fingers with her other hand, gently chafing them.

In response, he brought his other hand up to encase hers. "We could warm each other," he murmured, his voice suddenly low and rough.

Glancing up in surprise, she found his eyes smoldering, his expression hungry. It awakened an answering hunger within her, the one she had tried to keep at bay for two long days. "Yes," she whispered, "I suppose we could."

The knowledge that he hadn't truly been trying to deprive London's poor of the Saint of Seven Dials stripped away the last of her defenses against this man who already affected her so profoundly. She tilted her face up for his kiss, needing that reassurance that he still found her desirable.

He gave it to her, covering her lips with his own, first gently, then urgently. Releasing her hands, he gathered her to him, but their clothing squelched between them.

"We still need to change," she said with a shaky laugh. "I, ah, may need help with the hooks in the back of this gown."

"Of course." His eyes still burning into hers, he smiled—a smile that held a promise that took her breath away. "Turn around."

As though in a daze, she did so. Gently but deftly, he undid the row of tiny hooks fastening her dress, starting at the nape of her neck and working his way down. The air caressing her damp skin made her shiver, and he pulled her against him to kiss the back of her neck.

"I said I would warm you, didn't I?" he asked softly.

The warmth of his kiss, his touch, chased away the chill most effectively. She turned in his arms so that he could capture her lips again. He did so tenderly, his hands moving inexorably down her back as he continued to unfasten her dress.

This time, she could not fool herself that she was in his arms for some noble purpose, to save the Saint or the poor. No, she was here because she wanted him, needed him, to fill that aching void she had never known she possessed before meeting him.

She stroked his wet curls, then tried to remove his sodden coat, even as he was removing her gown. The soaked wool resisted her efforts, clinging heavily until he released her long enough to divest himself of it.

Her eyes widened at the unmistakable sight of a pistol tucked into his waistband. Instead of commenting, however, she turned away, taking the opportunity to strip off her dress, letting it fall to the floor in a soggy gray heap.

Now clad only in her damp chemise and stockings, she shivered again. At once, his arms surrounded her, enfolding her against the warmth of his body, only separated from hers by the thin cotton of his shirt and her chemise. The pistol, she noted, had disappeared.

"Would you prefer a blanket?" he murmured, his lips against her temple.

"No," she whispered, nuzzling his throat. "I trust you to keep me warm."

He leaned his head back far enough to look at her. "Only to keep you warm?"

She shook her head. "I trust you completely." As she said it, she realized it was true, and how important it was that he know that. "You are the only one in the world who knows my secret."

"I will guard it with my life." His eyes, his voice, made it a vow. "As I will guard you with my life."

Rowena's thrill of pleasure was marred by a tiny thread of fear. "Am I in danger, then?" If Noel was willing to risk himself to safeguard her . . . "Are you?" she added, before he could answer. She would rather die herself than have him die protecting her.

He rubbed his hands up and down her bare arms, warming them, before answering. "I have trusted you with my secret as well, Rowena—a dangerous secret. As long as no one knows that you are in my confidence, you should be safe enough."

"You didn't answer my second question." She reached up to caress the clean line of his jaw, enjoying the roughness of his faint shadow of beard.

"I don't know. I hope not," he replied, but now his expression was guarded.

"The truth. You said that you trusted me," she reminded him.

He nodded, meeting her eyes again. "I can't deny that I'm pursuing a very dangerous man, one who won't hesitate to kill me if he thinks that will help him escape justice. I simply have to make certain not to give him that opportunity."

Though it chilled her heart, she preferred knowing. It firmed her resolve to have all of him she could have now, that she might at least have that memory, that part of him to keep, should the unthinkable happen.

"Thank you," she said. "Now that I know what is at stake, I will be that much more careful." Her voice caught. "I . . . I would not put you at risk for the world."

It was almost a declaration of her feelings, and when his hands stilled their rubbing, she wondered if she had been too bold. Perhaps—

But then he crushed her against him, burying his face in her hair. "Rowena, my sweet. You can't imagine how much that means to me." His voice was muffled, the emotion in it warming her even more than his embrace.

Noel felt that if the Black Bishop burst upon them right then and struck him dead, he would die the happiest of men. Rowena cared for him, trusted him completely. He knew now that he loved her more deeply than he had known it was possible to love. The very thought of putting her in danger was insupportable.

That she felt the same both elated and humbled him. He kissed her again, trying to convey all he felt with his lips, his hands, skimming down her back and up again. She was still chilled—he could feel the gooseflesh on her arms.

"Just a moment." Releasing her, he pulled a blanket from the foot of the bed and threw it around her shoulders, pulling her to him again with the ends. "That's better. I'd be a poor sort of protector to betray your trust already."

Sliding her arms around him, she seized the ends of the blanket and wrapped them around his back until they were both covered. "I've made a commitment here as well," she said lightly, but with an undertone of meaning.

"Have you, Rowena?" He gazed into her eyes, trying to divine the depth of that meaning.

Though she blushed, she did not look away as she nodded.

Noel felt an urgent, overwhelming need to make her his completely, to forge a bond with her that nothing, not even death, could break. "I love you, Rowena. Will you be mine?" he asked, startled by the ragged edge to his voice. "Completely mine?"

"Yes," she whispered, gazing up at him with such trust and adoration that he felt suddenly invincible—and thoroughly aroused. "Please."

"How can I deny such a courteous request?" He tried to speak lightly, if only to disguise the depth of his feeling, which almost frightened him. Keeping the blanket about both of their shoulders, he led her to the bed. "First, let's get rid of the rest of these wet things."

Sitting on the edge of the bed, he yanked off his ruined boots, glad that Kemp was not one of those fastidious valets who would fly into the boughs over them. Then he turned back to Rowena, sitting beside him.

"Your shoes are wet as well—and your stockings," he pointed out. "Allow me."

He knelt at her feet to pull off first one shoe, then the other—sturdy walking shoes rather than thin ballroom slippers, but wet through nonetheless. He cradled one stockinged foot in his hands, marveling at how small and delicate it was—and how cold.

"Now your stockings," he said, his blood quickening in anticipation.

Her eyes widened, but she made no protest as he slid his hands up her calves, to find her garters just above her knees. Slowly, he peeled away the damp stockings, reveling in the smoothness of her flesh. Watching her face as he moved his hands over her legs, he saw her swallow, her breasts rising and falling with her quickened breathing.

Again he lifted one of her feet, now bare, and gently chafed her toes to warm them. She twitched and he grinned up at her. "Ticklish?"

"A little," she confessed, blushing, it appeared, even more deeply.

Releasing her foot without taking his eyes from her, he unbuttoned his shirt and then his trousers. Rising, he quickly stripped them off, then sat beside her on the bed again. She still had the blanket draped about her, so he reached beneath it to untie the ribbons of her chemise.

"I'm glad you're not wearing a corset," he commented, enjoying her softness beneath the thin cotton. He cupped one well-rounded breast, marveling at its perfection.

She gave a little gasp, then said, "I . . . I only thought to be wearing that gown for half an hour, so it seemed unnecessary. But . . . I'm glad, too." Her voice was breathless, but without fear or reserve.

He undid the last tie, then slid his hands up to her shoulders, to push the chemise down over her arms. She wriggled a bit to help him, and the small motion nearly drove him mad with desire. He wanted her now, this instant, but he knew he would have to control himself if he was not to frighten or hurt her. He had had women before, of course, but none had been virgin. This promised to be a very different—and very special—experience.

Finally her chemise joined all of their other wet garments on the floor. As he had done two nights ago, he feasted his eyes on her lovely, voluptuous body, still not quite believing that she was willing to share it with him. He felt honored and awed—and as eager as a ram in rutting season.

The blanket had fallen from her shoulders to the bed behind her, and now he gently pushed her down atop it. "I will try not to hurt you," he said, knowing that some pain might be inevitable.

"I trust you," she replied, her wide gray eyes as open to him as her body.

"And I trust you to tell me if you wish me to stop," he said, hoping he would not be put to that test.

She smiled, an incredibly seductive smile for one so innocent. "I won't, but I promise."

Determined to make this as special for her as he knew it would be for him, he set about pleasuring her. Stretching out beside her on the bed, he kissed her lingeringly on the lips while lightly running one hand from her shoulder, down her side, barely brushing her dark curls, then back up her belly and between her breasts.

She pressed her whole length against him, silently demanding more, and he gave it to her. He stroked her from collarbone to thigh, pausing only slightly at her cleft and breasts, teasing her, making her want him the way he so desperately wanted her. She clutched at him, pulling him closer, urging him on as she arched against him.

Now he brought his lips into play, trailing kisses down the side of her throat, down her chest, and finally capturing the tip of one breast to tease the nipple with his tongue. With a little squeak of pleasure she squirmed, and the feel of her softness against his arousal was almost more than he could bear.

Sliding one hand down her belly, he buried his fingers in her curls, finding and exploring her most sensitive spot until she gasped, pleading incoherently for the same release he craved. Shifting his weight to his arms, he moved above her, again capturing her lips with his as his straining arousal brushed the juncture of her thighs.

"I'm claiming you for my own, Rowena," he murmured. "My own forever. If you've any objection, now is the time to tell me."

Chapter 20

Rowena was sure that if he denied her the fulfillment she craved another moment, she would fly into pieces. She had never imagined such intense longing, such burning *need* was possible.

"No . . . no objections," she panted. "Oh, Noel, *please!*"

In response, he began to move above her, the length of his shaft stroking the spot that cried out most strongly for his touch. She arched her back, trying to increase the contact between them. Every place his body touched hers, chest against breasts, thighs against thighs, lips against lips, sizzled with sensation.

She wanted more.

Wrapping her arms around his back, she pulled him down until he lay atop her, reveling in the hard maleness of his body. His arousal had almost frightened her with its size at first sight, but now she wanted it against her—inside her. He moved again, brushing her thighs, brushing the sensitive juncture between them.

Instinctively, she spread her legs to give him access, then when he seemed to hesitate, she drew them up and around him, pulling him to her as she did with her arms. Her whole body seemed to throb with her need for him, for completion.

With a guttural groan, he slid the tip of his shaft inside her, then withdrew it. She heard herself whimper, then pressed him back down with her legs. This time he penetrated more deeply, but not deeply enough, before withdrawing again. Over and over, each time only an agonizingly tiny bit deeper, he moved into her, then away. She tried to hurry him, but he was stronger than she and took his time.

Her breathing, her heart accelerated, as though she were running a race, straining toward a finish line that hovered tantalizingly out of reach. "Now, Noel, now," she whispered against his lips.

"I don't want to hurt you," he replied with heart-wrenching tenderness. "I want this to be special for you."

She would have laughed if she hadn't been so desperate for him. Special? "What could possibly be more special than this?"

She felt his lips curve into a smile against hers. "I'll show you."

Sliding a hand between them, he stroked her even as he continued to enter her and withdraw, driving her desire higher yet, higher than seemed possible. She felt herself expanding, bursting into flame. Catching his rhythm, she rocked with him, each motion causing new buds of pleasure to bloom.

Just as she felt herself reaching a final crest, the one she was sure would kill her, he drove himself into her, filling her completely. She barely noticed the brief, stretching pain, for an instant later she raced over the top of the mountain of sensation she'd been climbing and exploded into a thousand pieces.

He stifled her cry of triumphant ecstasy with his kiss, absorbing it into himself. Again and again he thrust into her, prolonging her disintegration into pleasure. His arms trembling, he drove into her one last time, and this time she took his groan—almost a shout—into her mouth.

Slowly, slowly, she felt herself descending from the dizzying height she had achieved—that they had achieved together. She had never felt so complete, so satisfied. If this was what married couples did, it was no wonder Pearl always seemed so happy.

"I had no idea," she breathed, when she could speak again, gazing up at him—at her Noel—in wonder.

He smiled down at her with a tenderness that made her heart turn over. "Nor did I."

"You . . . you didn't?" His skill told her she couldn't have been his first. "But surely—"

As he did so often, he seemed to read her thoughts. "I've bedded women before, yes. But this is the first time I've made love to one—and had her make love to me. Believe me, it is an entirely different experience."

Hearing the word "love" on his lips made her almost giddy with delight. "I'm glad," she whispered.

"So am I," he said, then kissed her, a serious kiss that sealed the bond they had just forged between them.

The words "plighted troth" flashed into Rowena's mind. A week ago, the idea of binding herself to a man for life, putting her person and her future under his control, would have been anathema to her. Now it seemed the right and natural thing to do. Noel, she knew, would never abuse any privilege she gave him.

Still, there was much she didn't know about him. As passion ebbed, her natural curiosity reasserted itself. He seemed to sense the change, for he shifted his weight off of her, though he still gazed at her lovingly.

"There is more where that came from," he said teasingly, caressing her as he smiled.

Though his touch intoxicated her, Rowena kept enough of her reason to realize they could not remain undiscovered here forever. "My maid will have returned by now," she said with a sigh.

"Do you want to return to your room, then?"

Smiling, she shook her head. She never wanted to leave him again, though she knew she must. First, though, she needed to know more—enough to help him in any way she could. "You still haven't told me why you lay in wait for me in the park."

With obvious reluctance, he released her. "You're right. Come, let's get dressed, so we can talk without any other . . . distractions." His grin made her want to fling herself back into his arms, but she restrained herself.

While he pulled dry clothing from his clothespress, Rowena slipped her fresh chemise over her head, then pulled on dry stockings. They exchanged more than one heated glance while they dressed, but did not touch each other until Noel offered to do up the hooks of her fresh gown.

With a shiver of anticipation, Rowena turned her back to him.

"Not still cold, are you?" he asked softly, his fingers working quickly up the row of tiny fastenings.

"Not in the least," she assured him. "I don't think I could ever be cold when I'm with you."

His arms went around her to draw her close and he pressed a kiss to the sensitive skin below her ear. Rowena felt passion blossoming again, but forced herself to pull away.

"We need to talk, remember?"

He nodded, though his hazel eyes still smoldered and a smile played about his wonderful lips. "You're right. I'm sorry. Let's sit down."

They moved to the pair of chairs near his writing desk. Rowena clasped her hands in her lap to keep from reaching for him again. "Now, why did you believe the author of my essays was your traitor?"

He sighed. "I have read all of the letters in the possession of the Foreign Office that the Black Bishop sent during the war, as well as two that were intercepted once they knew he was helping the French. There were similarities in phrasing, sentiment, and even handwriting between some of those letters and those sent to the *Political Register* by MRR."

"You read my original, handwritten essays?" she asked. Though it had no real bearing on the matter, she was curious. "How?"

"I, ah, befriended one of the clerks there, once I suspected a link. What I can't understand is how I could have been so mistaken." His eyes were frankly questioning, though not condemning.

She thought hard, trying to piece together everything she knew as she would consider all of the pieces on a chessboard. "You said that you believe Mr. Richards to be this traitor, apart from the essays?"

He nodded. "Everything I have been able to discover about him fits: people he has been seen with, his political leanings, the recent death of a government official who had been linked to Richards—whom he might have been attempting to blackmail."

"Oh!" Rowena felt a sudden shock of fear as another piece of the puzzle fell into place. "Nelson," she said in answer to Noel's questioning glance. "Mr. Richards was demanding information from the Home Office in repayment of his debt."

"I suspected as much," Noel said. "He'll be looking for other sources now that you have settled that debt for your brother." He shot her a grin. "You did a service to more than Sir Nelson when you won that chess game, you realize."

She returned his grin, but quickly became serious again. "Will Nelson be in danger now, as that other man was?"

"It's possible, if he has any reason to believe your brother is suspicious of him."

"I doubt that he is, actually. Nelson is not the most perceptive of men," she admitted.

Noel smiled again. "I had gathered that. Let us hope Richards has, as well. It is your brother's only safeguard."

She nodded, then returned to her probing. "If you have so much evidence against Mr. Richards, why is he still free?"

"The evidence is purely circumstantial, thus far," he told her. "What I lack is any sort of proof that might hold up in a tribunal. I had hoped proving that he was MRR might provide that."

"But—" Similarity of phrasing, sentiments and handwriting, he had said. Suddenly embarrassed, Rowena bit her lip. "I, ah, think I understand now why you believed what you did."

Still there was no accusation in his expression, only curiosity—and tenderness. "Oh?"

"Last winter, after reading Mr. Richards' treatise on Spence's theory of natural law, I . . . wrote to him, expressing my appreciation of his views," she confessed, realizing now that she had acted like a moonstruck schoolgirl. "He responded, I wrote him again, and he sent another letter."

Noel frowned, now looking concerned. "So you have been corresponding with him for the better part of a year?"

"No, just those two letters," she hastened to assure him. "His second letter implied that he had more important things to do, so I dared not write again. However, I . . . I kept those two letters, rereading them frequently until I had all but committed them to memory."

"So your own writings drew heavily from his letters?"

She nodded. It was mortifying to admit to her hero-worship of Richards, and even more mortifying that she had sublimated her own opinions to his, but she was determined to help Noel in any way she could. "I fear I even used his handwriting as a sort of model when I began writing my essays."

"Ah." His brow cleared, though he still seemed

lost in thought. "Do you have his letters here, by any chance?"

"Why, yes. They are in my chamber," she said, blushing at this admission of how she'd cherished the things. "You may have them, of course."

He reached out and took her hand. "Thank you. And thank you for telling me this. Those letters may be even stronger proof than the essays could have been. He signed them, I presume?"

"Yes. So if they match those of the traitor, will that be enough to convict him?" She felt as though she should be worried about her longtime idol, but instead her only concern was for Noel.

"It might well be. That, plus certain information I'm hoping to obtain tonight or tomorrow." He stood. "I need to leave Town, Rowena, but only briefly. I should be back by tomorrow afternoon, and with luck this will all be behind us by the following day."

"Where are you going?" she asked, alarmed by the grim resolve on his face.

Though his smile was no doubt meant to reassure her, the very fact that he felt the need to do so only increased her fear. "I plan to pay a visit to Richards' father, in Hertfordshire. I'm hoping he can be induced to tell me about his son's whereabouts during the war—and perhaps more. The rumor is that they are not on good terms."

Abruptly, Rowena remembered her promise to go driving with Mr. Richards tomorrow. She opened her mouth to tell Noel, but then hesitated. Perhaps she would be able to learn something from Mr. Richards that would prove his guilt beyond doubt, lessening Noel's danger—as long as Noel did not forbid her to try.

"I will fetch you the letters now," she said instead, "so that you can return—safely—as soon as possible." She stood and turned toward the door, but he put a restraining hand on her arm.

"No, keep them for the moment. The letters must stay safe. I would rather leave them in your care until I can take them myself to the Foreign Office with what I hope will be additional evidence. If I should not return—"

"No! I won't even consider that," she said. "But should you somehow be . . . delayed, I will make certain the letters are delivered. Who is to receive them?"

He went to the writing desk and scribbled a name on a slip of paper, then handed it to her, along with the oilskin-wrapped package he had confiscated earlier.

"These are yours, I believe," he said with a smile.

She took it without replying, without glancing at it, her eyes only for Noel.

"You will see me again, Rowena. Nothing can keep me away," he assured her. "I love you. I have to return, to hold you to your commitment—to be my wife."

Though his words made her giddy, she searched his face, trying to divine any thoughts he might be keeping from her. He met her gaze frankly.

"I love you too, Noel. And . . . I believe you." Then, on sudden impulse, she threw her arms around him. "Oh, Noel, promise me you will be careful! Carry a pistol and keep an eye on the road behind you."

"I always do," he assured her, then gathered her in for a kiss.

Reassured, even, while she was startled to discover that the pistol he had carried today was no anomaly, Rowena returned his kiss, trying to put all that she had left unsaid into her embrace. Then, with a single, longing glance, she went to the door, listened for any sounds without, and stepped into the hallway.

When she opened her chamber door a moment later, Matthilda greeted her with wide eyes. "Oh, miss, you're back! I was beside myself, not knowing where you might be. Lady Hardwyck asked for you, and I told her you were having a lie-down."

"I'm fine," she said, keeping her packet of letters behind her. "I'll speak with Lady Hardwyck shortly."

Her maid's expression was still concerned. "Then it was not . . . not your voice I heard in another room a few minutes since?"

The wonder of her new understanding with Noel, temporarily overshadowed by the seriousness of his investigation, returned full force. "Matthilda, if I tell you something, will you promise to keep it a secret until I can inform my brother and Lady Hardwyck?"

The maid nodded, round-eyed.

"Mr. Paxton and I are to be married." Saying it aloud made it even more amazing.

"Oh, miss!" Matthilda ran forward to embrace her mistress. "I've been hoping for just that. A body with half an eye can see how he feels about you—and you, him."

That startled Rowena, but could not dim her happiness. "Then you approve?"

Matthilda nodded, fervently, her eyes shining. "I do love a happy ending," she exclaimed.

"So do I."

But Rowena knew that her happy ending had not yet come—and could not, until Noel succeeded in his quest. She prayed that he might do so quickly and, even more importantly, safely.

For a long moment, Noel stood watching the door through which Rowena had disappeared. This morning, he would never have imagined that his life could have been so completely changed over the course of a few hours. Rowena had given him a gift beyond anything he could possibly deserve—the gift of her love and trust.

Even the incredible experience of making love to her paled in comparison to the future she promised him. A smile still on his lips, he turned back to the writing desk to pen a note to Kemp, then rang for a footman to deliver it. It was absolutely imperative now that he put this business of the Black Bishop to rest once and for all. He would have to move carefully, however, despite his impatience.

Yesterday, he had believed that no sacrifice he could make would be too great if it brought the Bishop to justice. Today, he had much more to live for—and much more to lose.

Donning a cloak against the still-falling rain, he again tucked his pistol inside his coat. Picking up his hat, he headed out to meet Kemp at the coaching inn. There would have to be another slight change in plans.

"I want you to stay here in town." When Kemp would have protested, Noel raised a hand to silence him. "I have a task for you to do here—a vitally important task."

The two men sat at a small corner table in the

smoke-filled taproom of the Brindled Bull, a small coaching inn near Bow Street. The coach was horsed and ready for the journey to Hertfordshire, and Kemp already dressed in coachman's livery to drive it there.

"I can hire a coachman from the inn," Noel said. "If it weren't raining, I'd ride, but as it's a simple two-hour drive each way, anyone minimally skilled with the ribbons can handle it. I need your special talents here in London."

Kemp nodded reluctantly. "I was talking earlier with one of the drivers, a fellow name of Johnny. He'd do right enough. But what if something goes wrong? What if there's an ambush?"

Noel shook his head. "Unlikely in the extreme. No one knows where I'm going, save Lord Hardwyck and Lord Marcus." And Rowena, but he knew she would tell no one. "There's no reason my brief trip should arouse any suspicions."

"Then what is it you want me to do while you're away?"

"This has been a day of discoveries," Noel said with a wry smile at his confederate. "I now know who the mysterious Mr. R is."

Kemp's eyes widened. "I knew you'd catch him. But why do you even need to make this trip, then?"

"Because Mr. R is not the Bishop after all. It is Miss Riverstone."

"Never! That Quakerish girl at Hardwyck Hall?" Kemp was frankly disbelieving.

Noel couldn't help grinning. "You haven't seen her lately. There's nothing Quakerish about her now, I assure you. But yes, she was the one in Oakshire penning those essays."

"Then you're back where you started?"

"Not quite," Noel reassured him. "She has letters from Richards that I'm confident will provide the proof I need, even if this journey should prove fruitless. Still, the more evidence I can amass, the better. I refuse to allow him any leeway to wriggle off the hook, once I have him."

Kemp nodded. "Aye, it's time and more he was stopped. Myself, I won't be happy till I see him swinging at the end of a rope."

"That's my goal, as well. I want you to keep an eye on Richards while I'm gone. If he suspects anything, he may attempt to use Miss Riverstone to block my next move."

"I'll watch 'em both. You want I should stop him from going near her?" He patted the pocket where he kept his pistol.

"No, for he's likely to call on her even if he suspects nothing. We don't dare tip our hand too soon, or he may go into hiding. Just keep watch, and inform me of his movements when I return." With Kemp watching Richards while Luke and Marcus watched Rowena, Noel could feel confident she would be safe.

"Now, where is this Johnny you spoke of? I'll need to have a word with him."

Kemp went to fetch the driver, and Noel spoke briefly with him, explaining what he needed. He seemed an alert enough young man, but not particularly curious—which was just as well.

"I'll just nip around back to let the 'ostler know I'll be gone, and then we can be off," he said.

Noel nodded. He considered asking Johnny not to

tell the 'ostler their destination, then decided that would raise more suspicion than a simple trip to Hertfordshire would do.

"Very well, but don't be long. I'd like to be there by nightfall, if possible."

He would try to arrange an audience with the elder Mr. Richards this very night. Then he could be back in Town early enough tomorrow to prevent Richards from so much as calling on Rowena before he could be arrested.

Lester Richards dropped two gold coins into Johnny's outstretched hand. "Well done, my good chap. This man Paxton is dangerous, but by knowing where he is, I'll be able to prevent him causing any more harm."

"Dangerous?" The young man's eyes grew round. "Mayhap another driver—" He glanced around the stable yard at the bustling crowd of grooms, coaches and horseflesh.

"No, no, you should be at no risk," Richards assured him quickly. "He's a danger to the crown, not to you personally. With him out of Town, I can counteract his plans, and perhaps even prevent his return."

Though it was clear the fellow had no idea what Richards was talking about, he nodded. "My helping would make me a sort of hero, then, wouldn't it?"

"It would indeed. Now hurry on. You don't want him to become suspicious."

Richards watched as the man hurried away, a frown twisting his face. So, Paxton was going to visit his father, was he? There was no telling what the old fool might say to him. Nothing to Richards' benefit, that was certain.

His own investigations had pointed to a link between Paxton and the Foreign Office, though just what that link was, he wasn't yet sure. What was clear was that Paxton was digging for information about him—information that could conceivably identify him as the Black Bishop.

His first instinct was to leave Town before Paxton could return. But no—he had not come this far by letting emotion rule his head. His influence among the Spenceans in London had grown to the point that he was almost ready to fire them into action. They had the numbers and the drive to achieve what he could never do alone, now that France had lost the war. He couldn't abandon that plan now, when it was so close to succeeding.

No, what he needed was some sort of insurance against anything Paxton might attempt, or, better, a way to dispose of the man entirely.

Richards began to smile. The noose might seem to be closing about his neck, but he still had a valuable card or two to play and a few favors to call in. If all went well, Paxton would be in his power by this time tomorrow.

Rowena Riverstone would serve as both insurance and bait to lure Paxton to his doom should Richards' henchman fail. That way, he could rid himself of two problems at one blow, for it was clear Miss Riverstone was far too perceptive.

And she was expecting him to take her driving tomorrow.

Chapter 21

Rowena had never known time to pass so slowly. Dinner, and particularly the time afterward in the parlor, was a trial. She was dying to tell Pearl her happy news. She was certain her friend suspected something, for she kept sending her quizzical looks, but she was discreet enough not to pry, instead suggesting a game of chess.

Lord Hardwyck joined them only a few minutes into the game, and Rowena, anxious to be alone with her thoughts, quickly checkmated Pearl.

"I do believe that was a record," her friend said with a sigh. "However *do* you do it? Matching wits with Mr. Paxton appears to have improved your game—not that it needed improving."

"Can I interest you ladies in some three-handed whist?" Lord Hardwyck suggested, placing a sympathetic hand on his wife's shoulder.

Rowena stood. "Actually, I find myself unusually fatigued. I believe I will go up to bed."

Once upstairs, she waited with barely concealed impatience for Matthilda to finish her ministrations. The moment the maid left her, she pulled out her packet of letters and opened it. Perhaps they would serve to distract her from obsessing about Noel's dangerous mission.

One by one she opened and read them, both startled and amused by the variety of opinions they contained. Nearly all, even those which vehemently disagreed with her essays, praised her writing, which produced a glow of pride despite her gnawing worry.

Tomorrow she would answer every one, she decided, setting aside two, from well-known members of Parliament, for special attention. That project should occupy her until Noel's return.

As she climbed into bed, she sent up a small prayer for his safety, as well as a wish that he might return before five o'clock.

Earlier, when her courage had been high, she had felt more than willing to match wits with Mr. Richards, learning whatever she could for Noel's sake. The sooner he was brought to justice, the sooner Noel would be out of danger, after all.

With nightfall—and Noel's absence—her confidence wavered. Though she would never risk Noel's life or even his mission by refusing, she rather hoped she would not have to fulfill her promise to drive out with Mr. Richards after all.

"Mr. Richards will see you now."

Noel barely restrained himself from saying *finally* aloud.

Last night, he had been informed by the haughty butler that the elder Mr. Richards retired early and was already abed. Today, after returning at ten o'clock, as instructed, he had been kept cooling his heels in an anteroom of the crumbling country manor house for nearly two hours. His mood was definitely the worse for wear as he followed the butler through dim corridors to a cluttered study.

For a moment the room appeared to be empty, and he wondered if he would be expected to wait here for another interminable period. But then a movement caught his eye and he turned to see a slight, stooped man rising from an enormous wing-backed chair.

"So, my son sends his friends now rather than coming himself to demand money of me?" the old man asked querulously. "You can tell Lester to go to hell."

Noel stepped over a pile of books to extend his hand. "Thank you for seeing me, Mr. Richards. I fear you are under a misapprehension, however. Your son did not send me."

The old man snorted and sat back down, ignoring Noel's hand. "So you say. He's used every pretext you can imagine over the years, sirrah. None will work—not anymore. He won't have another groat from me before I die."

Though more encouraged than discouraged by the man's venom, Noel realized he would have to proceed carefully. "Perhaps, then, it will not surprise you to learn that your son may have run afoul of the law?"

The wheezing that emanated from the chair alarmed Noel until he realized it was laughter. "Surprise me? I'd be more surprised if he hadn't. Lester is a snake, never cared for anyone but himself—though to hear him talk, you'd think he was trying to save the world. Pah!" The old man spat.

"May I?" Noel gestured to a small, rickety chair next to the big wing-back. When the man made no objection, he seated himself and leaned forward, so that he had a good view of the man's face. "What do you know of your son's plans, sir?"

The old man fixed him with a keen glance from his watery blue eyes. "More than I'd like, though nothing recent. He hasn't been here in six months. So, are you here to help him, or to sink him?"

Noel hesitated, realizing his answer might well determine the outcome of this case. The man's animosity seemed sincere, so he gambled with the truth. "I'm hoping to prevent him from harming anyone else—ever."

"Found out what he did to me on his last visit, did you? Beat me so badly I couldn't walk for a week, when I refused him money. Surgeon blabbed, did he?"

"Something like that." It was news to Noel, and while it strengthened his position here, it also worried him. If Richards would abuse his own father, what might he do to Rowena if he suspected she was helping Noel?

"Mr. Richards, can you tell me where your son was during the war with France? Did he serve in the military?"

Another snort. "Military? Him? More like he was helping the Frenchies. Always did take their part. Too much like his mother, though I tried to beat that out of him."

"His mother was French?" That alone did not convict Richards, of course, as Noel's own mother was French. But this interview was proving far more valuable already than he had dared hope.

"Aye, pretty thing, before she turned shrewish. Lester blamed me for her death, but she was sickly for years, despite what the doctors did. Didn't have a sturdy English constitution, of course."

For the first time, Noel began to understand what might have originally turned Richards to his treasonous path—not that it excused him in any way. He still had no firm evidence, however.

"The war," he prompted. "Was your son here, or did he go abroad?"

"He left England after his mother died in '09," Mr. Richards said. "I didn't hear from him for three years, but then he showed up asking for money. I gave it to him. Thought he might stay, you see, and it was lonely here. Thought we could mend our fences. But as soon as he had the money and a good meal, he was off again."

"That would have been in 1812?" Noel asked. That fit perfectly with what he knew of the Bishop's movements. "Did you hear from him again after that?"

"Not until last summer. He showed up on my doorstep, again with no warning. He was injured, and all in rags. I took him in, called the surgeon, made sure he received the best care. But you already know how he repaid me, six months later."

Last summer. "When exactly did he arrive that time—when he was injured?"

"About mid-July it was, as I recall."

Shortly after Waterloo. "And that's when he started pressuring you for money again?"

The old man nodded. "Got more and more insistent with each passing month. Said he needed it to set England on the right path. Came himself up until that last time when he beat me. I had him thrown out of the house, and he's only written since then."

"But you gave him nothing?"

"Nay, I've no fault to find with England as it is. Corrupted by the Frenchies, Lester is, that's my thinking. He'd have another bloody terror here if he could. Used to read everything he could find about it, even though I thrashed him when I caught him at it. Got his mother to teach him French early on, behind my back—he can speak it like a frog, you know."

"Yes, I know." Noel had absolutely no doubt now that Richards was the Black Bishop. "Would you happen to have any of his letters? Might I see them?"

The old man rose with an effort. "I burned most of 'em, but I still have one or two from earlier on—before he turned vicious. But blood will out, they say."

Noel suspected Richards had learned his viciousness at his father's knee rather than inheriting it from his mother, but of course did not say so. He waited while the elder Mr. Richards rummaged through a large pile of papers on one of the desks. Finally, he found what he was seeking and shuffled back across the room.

"Here you are."

Taking the proferred letter, Noel scanned it carefully. Yes, the writing was identical to that of the Black Bishop's missives. Combined with what he now knew of Richards' whereabouts during the war, he had the proof he needed.

"You say he's written to you recently?"

"Got a letter from him just yesterday, but I've already burned it. Sounded more desperate for money than usual, but he always had a persuasive way with words. That's why I burn his letters."

Whereas Rowena had cherished them, Noel thought with a sudden pang. Not that she would anymore, of course.

"Did he say anything else in his last letter?" he asked. "Anything about what he might be planning to do?"

But the old man shook his head. "Just a lot of high-flown language about destiny and the future of England depending on him. Always did have an inflated sense of his own importance, no matter what I said or did to convince him otherwise."

Noel rose. "Thank you, Mr. Richards. You've been very helpful. I don't think your son will trouble you further. May I keep this letter?"

"You're welcome to anything that'll help give Lester what he deserves, the blackguard. Just make sure everyone knows his character flaws aren't my fault. It's all in the blood—that damned French blood."

"Of course." Noel was more than ready to take his leave of this bitter and bigoted old man. "Good day, sir."

Tucking the letter into his breast pocket, he retrieved his hat and went out to the waiting carriage.

"We'll make a quick stop at the inn for a bite, then be on our way," he told the young coachman. The lowering clouds promised more rain, which would slow his return, but he should still reach London early this evening.

With luck, the Black Bishop would be in custody by nightfall.

Answering her letters was not proving quite the distraction Rowena had hoped. For one thing, she was too tired to concentrate properly, having spent a nearly sleepless night imagining every possible thing that could go wrong for Noel. Suppose Mr. Richards had followed him, attacked him? Might he even now be lying in a ditch somewhere?

With daylight her fears had receded somewhat, but not her agitation. As he had described his mission, it should have taken little time. Shouldn't he be back by now? She set down her pen and glanced at the clock above the fireplace in her chamber. Four o'clock.

The rest of the letters could wait, she decided, rising. She would go downstairs and find Pearl. Perhaps she or Lord Hardwyck would have news of Noel.

As she neared the parlor, she heard voices and her heart quickened. She listened, hoping against hope to discern Noel's voice among them, but before she could do so, the door opened wide.

"Here you are, Rowena," Pearl exclaimed. "I was just going to send a maid upstairs for you. Won't you join us?"

"I'd love to. I was growing weary of my own company, I confess." Trying not to look too eager, she peered past Pearl to see who else was present. She saw three or four ladies she had previously met, but not Noel. Even as her heart sank with disappointment, a male figure moved into her line of sight.

Lester Richards.

"Well met, Miss Riverstone," he said, bowing

smoothly. "I know we agreed to drive out at five o'clock, but with the uncertain weather, I had hoped I might persuade you to leave early, while the rain is in abeyance."

Rowena struggled mightily to allow none of the sudden panic she felt to show in her expression. "Of . . . of course," she stammered, mentally chastising herself for such a show of nervousness. "Let me run up to my chamber to fetch my parasol."

He bowed again, and she fled—though she hoped it did not look like a flight to anyone else. She desperately needed a moment alone to think. Hurrying up the stairs and into her room, she shut the door behind her.

Whatever should she do? If she refused to go driving with Mr. Richards, he might well suspect that she knew the truth. He was a very clever man. He might even realize that Noel was the source of her new knowledge.

If he figured out that Noel was on to him, what then? He had murdered before, Noel had told her, though it had seemed incredible at the time. If he felt Noel was a danger to him, he might try to eliminate that danger.

No, she could not put Noel at such an additional risk.

But what of her? Sternly calming herself, she tried to think. They would go for a drive, and she would listen to all that he had to tell her of the Spenceans. She would ask questions, drawing him out. Perhaps he would slip and tell her more than he intended of his plans—plans she could share with Noel when he returned.

Yes, that would be best. Mr. Richards would

scarcely attempt to harm her in an open carriage—especially when it was known she had left with him.

And whether he would attempt it or not, she owed it to Noel to do all she could to avoid arousing his suspicions. If she was successful, she should be in no danger whatsoever. Her decision made, she picked up her parasol and left her room.

As she went down the stairs, her alarm began to subside. Whatever secrets he held, Mr. Richards was still the same man she had talked with and played chess with. As her rational mind took over, the idea of him doing her violence seemed unlikely in the extreme.

By the time she reached the parlor again, she was able to greet him with perfect calm. "I am ready, sir. Shall we go?"

As Noel had feared, so much rain had made the roads a morass of mud. The coach seemed to crawl toward London despite his eagerness to put this whole sordid business behind him and embark on his future with Rowena. Irritably, he shifted in his seat and pulled Richards' letters to his father out to read them through again.

Though he did not have any of the Black Bishop's letters here for comparison, he was certain the handwriting was the same. Surely his superiors—

A sudden sharp report interrupted his analysis—the all-too-familiar sound of a pistol shot. The coach swayed to a stop as the horses sidled in alarm. Highwaymen? Unlikely.

Swiftly, Noel tucked the letters back into his breast

pocket and checked his own pistols, tucking one into the pocket of his coat. Then he crouched on the floor of the coach, his other pistol leveled at the door. He heard shouting, and then the door was wrenched open to reveal a masked figure.

Noel did not hesitate for an instant, but discharged his pistol before his assailant could react. Impossible to miss at such close range, the man fell backward into the mud, a bloodstain spreading across his shoulder. He lay still, apparently unconscious.

Dropping his now useless pistol, Noel pulled the other from his pocket and listened for any other sounds outside the coach. When he heard none, he cautiously emerged.

" 'Ere, now!" came the coachman's voice. "What've you done?"

Though Noel suspected this was no random attack, he saw no point in alarming Johnny unduly. "I've shot a highwayman, of course," he said. "I'll search him for any clues to his identity, and then we can be on our way. We'll alert the authorities when we reach the next village."

He knelt to examine the unconscious man on the ground.

"Nay, I don't think so," Johnny said behind him. "Just get back in the coach calm like, and we'll wait here a bit."

Startled, Noel turned to find the young man pointing an ancient blunderbuss at him with shaking hands. "I allus keep this by me, just in case," he said, his voice now shaking as badly as his hands. "I'd rather not use it if I don't have to, though."

Noel's confusion lasted only an instant. "You are in Lester Richards' pay." It was a statement, not a question.

"He didn't tell me his name, but he paid me handsome. Said you were a traitor to the crown, but he could use this journey to keep you from doing whatever it is you plan. I mean to help him, money or no."

"Richards is the traitor, not I," Noel said, keeping his voice calm and rational, even while he marveled at Richards' cleverness. "You would serve England by helping me, not him, I promise you."

Now doubt clouded the young coachman's eyes. "That might be just what a traitor would say, begging your pardon, sir. How do I know which one of you is telling the truth?"

"I suppose you don't. Nor do I have time to debate the matter, if Richards knows of my errand. I'm sorry to do this, Johnny."

With a swift, fluid motion, he brought up his pistol and fired, knocking the blunderbuss out of the young man's hands but only grazing his arm. While Johnny clutched his arm and shook his head in dazed confusion, Noel leapt up to the box and pulled him down.

"I'll drive the rest of the way. You and Richards' other cohort can sit inside."

Noel picked up a coil of rope he had noted earlier without divining its intended purpose—which must have been to tie him up for delivery to Richards. He tied Johnny's hands behind him, pushed him into the coach, then bound his feet. He then bound the unconscious masked man hand and foot and heaved him into the coach as well.

Before closing the door of the coach, he pulled off his assailant's mask. He didn't know the man, but he looked vaguely familiar. Searching his memory, he realized he had been at the gaming hell on Jermyn Street when he was questioning Willie last week. Clearly, Richards had more spies than he had realized.

Which meant that he might know about Noel's meeting with Rowena in Green Park yesterday. Even if he didn't, he certainly knew of Noel's attraction to her, which made her a potential weapon—and put her in considerable danger.

Vaulting back onto the box, he picked up the reins and urged the horses forward through the thick mud, cursing the sticky miles that still lay between him and Rowena.

"Where are we going?" Rowena asked as Mr. Richards drove the slightly battered curricle past the gates of Hyde Park, heading north on Park Lane.

"You said yesterday that you wished to know more about current efforts to make Thomas Spence's dream come true. I am taking you to meet some of his adherents." His voice was calm and unruffled, but Rowena felt a flare of alarm.

"I see," she said, careful to keep her own voice light and unconcerned. "That should be most interesting. Where is the meeting to be?"

He slanted an enigmatic look at her and her apprehension increased. "A place we have secured for this purpose, a short distance east of Mayfair. Why?"

She shrugged, looking past him at the passing scenery, fearing what he might read in her eyes. "I was simply curious. I did tell Lady Hardwyck I would be gone only an hour."

"And she will—what? Send you to bed without supper, if you are late?"

Rowena managed a laugh, but it sounded forced to her own ears. "Of course not. I do not wish to worry her, however, or arouse her curiosity, since I presume you would not want me to tell her about this meeting."

"Of course." His voice was bland but pleasant, and she could tell nothing from it.

She summoned her courage with an effort. "You were going to tell me about the Spenceans and their plans, were you not?"

"I believe I will let you see for yourself, instead," he replied. "You will find it all most fascinating, I am certain."

They drove in silence then, turning east along Oxford Street, then continuing on for a mile or more, following the curve to High Holborn. Rowena was growing increasingly nervous, but dared not question him again, for fear of arousing his suspicions. She tried to convince herself that he could have nothing to gain by harming her, and much, possibly, to lose.

Finally, Mr. Richards turned the curricle north again, along a narrow street Rowena had never seen before, unfamiliar as she was with any of London outside of Mayfair. "We're almost there now," he said reassuringly.

But she felt anything but reassured. The street grew even narrower, and more and more dirty as they moved away from High Holborn. They passed a group of huddled children dressed in rags who pointed, laughed and scattered at their approach. A beggar in a doorway rattled a cup at them, his sightless eyes covered by a filthy strip of red cloth that matched his ragged uniform.

"Is . . . is this area entirely safe?" Rowena couldn't help asking, not much caring now how nervous she sounded. Any rational person would be nervous in such surroundings, she was sure.

"For those who know it well," Mr. Richards replied. "For those who don't belong here, however—" He pulled the curricle to a stop, leaving his unfinished sentence hanging ominously in the air between them. "Come, I'll escort you inside."

Rowena hesitated. "I . . . I'm not really sure—"

"It makes no difference whether you are sure or not." His voice was no longer bland, but hard and commanding. "Come."

When she still hung back, he seized her arm and roughly pulled her to her feet, forcing her out of the curricle. Thoroughly frightened now, Rowena cried out and tried to pull away from him, but he was far stronger than he looked. Inexorably, he led her to the door of one of the crumbling buildings that hung over the alleyway.

Taking a key from his pocket, he unlocked the door and pushed her inside. Releasing her, he then shut the door again, plunging them both into darkness.

"There is no meeting, is there?" she whispered.

"Not yet." She heard a scraping sound, and then a candle flared to life, lit by the tinderbox he held. "Others will join us shortly, however."

Why had she ever agreed to go with him, knowing what he was? *Because of Noel*, an inner voice reminded her. The thought strengthened her somewhat.

"What others?" she managed to ask. "The Spenceans?"

His face looked weirdly evil in the light of the candle he held between them. "One of them is a Spencean, yes. The others have helped my cause without knowing precisely what it is. I've found gold does an admirable job of silencing awkward questions."

Rowena swallowed. Was she to be silenced as well, in a far less pleasant manner? "What . . . what are you going to do with me?"

He smiled, a distinctly unpleasant smile. "That depends on what my informants tell me when they come. For now, we wait."

Chapter 22

It was past five when Noel finally reached London. His first stop was by necessity the Foreign Office, where he relieved himself of the two men in the coach.

"The younger one seems to have no real knowledge of this business," he told Under-Secretary Hamilton as the two men were conveyed to a secure room for questioning. "Richards paid and duped him. The other, however, may yield something useful."

"We'll have to have a surgeon take a look at that shoulder first," Hamilton replied with a stern glance at Noel. "You still believe Richards is the Bishop, then? Have you any more proof than you offered me before?"

"I have this." Noel pulled the letter Richards' father had given him from his breast pocket. "I have also discovered that Richards' movements during the war dovetail remarkably well with those of the Bishop."

"Then he is your mysterious essayist after all?"

Noel shook his head. "No, but following that trail led me to him anyway, via a more circuitous route."

"But—"

"Please, sir, I must go now, to see to the safety of someone who has helped me, and who may be in danger at Richards' hands. I will return as soon as possible."

The Under-Secretary sighed and nodded. "Very well, I won't detain you. Lord Castlereagh will expect a full accounting when you return, however."

"Of course." Noel hoped he could satisfy his superiors without bringing Rowena's name into the business. But more important was ensuring her physical safety.

Leaving the muddy, driverless coach at the Foreign Office, he hailed a hackney to take him from Whitehall to Hardwyck Hall.

He had barely given his name to the butler when Lady Hardwyck rushed down the stairs to greet him, her violet eyes wide with distress.

"Oh, Mr. Paxton, thank heaven you are here!" she exclaimed before he could utter a word. "I knew that note we received must be false. Luke is quite cross with me, but if he had only *explained* everything, I should never have let her leave with him."

Noel put up a hand to stem the outpouring, though what little he understood of her words caused him a deep foreboding. "Calmly, please, Lady Hardwyck. Do you mean to say that Miss Riverstone is gone?"

She nodded. "She went for a drive with Mr. Richards. They were to have returned within an hour, but it has been a good deal longer than that now. Then Luke returned home and said that Mr. Richards might be *dangerous*. If I had only known—"

"It is not your fault, my lady," Noel assured her, though his anxiety was increasing. "Is Lord Hardwyck here? Is there somewhere we may be private?" He glanced around at the alarmed faces of the footman and butler in the hall.

"Oh, of course. I'm so distracted I'm not thinking clearly. Poor Rowena! To think—But come, Luke is in the library."

Noel reached the door before she did and opened it for her. Luke was standing near the fireplace, talking to a pair of boys Noel recognized as Skeet and the footman Steven, formerly known as Squint.

"Then Stilt should be back soon with word?" Luke was asking the pair, who responded with nods.

"He took over at Oxford Street when I couldn't keep up," Skeet said. "Traffic was heavy, so he most likely won't have lost 'em."

Noel stepped forward. "What's this? Did Stilt follow Richards and Miss Riverstone?"

"Aye," said Steven. "Lord Hardwyck said as how I should keep an eye out for the rotter, 'specially if he came sniffing 'round Miss Riverstone, so when she left with him, I set Skeet after them and ran to get Stilt, as he's the biggest."

Lady Hardwyck rounded on her husband. "You told these boys, but didn't tell me?"

"I'm truly sorry, Pearl," he said, and looked it. "I thought I had. I've been so busy, it must have slipped my mind."

"What time did they leave?" Noel asked, pulling them back to the matter at hand.

Luke turned to him. "Don't look like that, man. I'm sure she will be all right."

Noel realized he must look as stricken as he felt, and made an effort to tame his features. "What time?" he repeated.

"Four o'clock, perhaps a bit later," Lady Hardwyck replied, her hands tightly clasped before her. "He said he was taking her driving in the park."

"Nay, drove right past it, he did," Skeet said. "She didn't look all that upset, neither, though I was a fair bit behind by then. It was a good job I saw Stilt when I did."

Noel frowned. "Then you think she never intended to go to the park either?"

The boy shrugged. "I can't rightly say. She was talkin' to him, but I couldn't hear nothing. She didn't seem put out, though."

Surely, Rowena couldn't have—"You mentioned a note?" Noel said abruptly to Lady Hardwyck.

"Yes. Yes, here." She handed him a folded slip of paper.

Dear Pearl, it read in a stilted feminine hand, *I have eloped with Noel Paxton, with the aid of Mr. Richards. Please do not be angry with me. Your friend, Rowena Riverstone.*

"It doesn't sound at all like her," Lady Hardwyck said as Noel frowned over the scrap. "Though it looks rather like her hand."

"Does it?" He had never seen Rowena's undisguised hand, he realized. This could well be Richards' writing, however, cleverly disguised. That would be ironic, considering how many times Rowena had disguised her own hand to look like Richards'. "When did you receive this?"

"I found it, actually, about half an hour since," Lady Hardwyck replied. "It was set at the base of the urn near the front door."

"To dissuade us from following, of course," Luke said brusquely, shooting a sympathetic glance at Noel. "I'm sure Richards planted it."

"Of course." Noel could not believe otherwise. He would not. "If you will excuse me a moment, I need to see whether my own man left any sort of message for me. I asked him to keep an eye on Mr. Richards as well."

Turning on his heel, he headed for the stairs. Surely, Kemp could not also have failed him? What he couldn't understand, the thing that gnawed at him most, was why Rowena had agreed to go with Richards in the first place. She couldn't possibly still have any sympathy for him, knowing what he was, what a risk he posed.

Could she?

What they had shared yesterday had been real, heart-wrenchingly real. He knew that with every instinct, every feeling, every bit of his reason. Emotion could never have clouded his judgment that completely.

He took the stairs two at a time and burst into his chamber—the chamber where he had shared such an incredible experience with Rowena only yesterday. It seemed eons ago, now. Scanning the room, his eyes lighted on a sheet of paper on the writing desk that he had not left there. He snatched it up and read what Kemp had written in a hasty scrawl.

Miss R gone in old brown curricle, chestnut pair, with BB. Following on horseback, will send word.

Thrusting the note into his pocket, Noel headed back downstairs. Kemp gave no clue as to whether Rowena had gone willingly or not, but at least she had someone beyond a street urchin watching out for her now.

"Has no other message come?" he asked the assembled group as he reentered the library. "My man followed them as well."

Four heads shook as one. "How—?" Lady Hardwyck began, when they were interrupted by a pounding on the front door. Disregarding all dignity, they hurried from the library *en masse* in time to see the butler, Woodruff, opening the door to a panting Stilt.

"Mr. . . . Mr. Paxton," he gasped, staggering into the hall when Woodruff, after a questioning look at Luke, let him past. "I have a . . . a message from . . . Mr. Kemp."

"What do you mean he never returned?"

Rowena, stiff from two hours on the one spindly chair her gloomy prison afforded, now listened to everything Mr. Richards and his unkempt confederate said, in hopes of learning something useful.

"Just what I said," the unsavory-looking older

man repeated. "Eddie never reported back, so I dunno if he done the job or not."

Mr. Richards cursed, first in English, then in fluent French. "I'll have to keep the girl until we know," he finally muttered. "If Paxton escaped, he'll be looking for her—and we can use her to lure him in."

It was all Rowena could do not to gasp aloud, but she dared not let Mr. Richards know she had heard. He had tried to have Noel killed—might even have succeeded! And her own life was apparently forfeit either way, though somehow she found herself worrying less about that than about Noel.

If he had survived, she would not allow herself to be used as bait to draw him to his doom, she was determined. She would contrive to kill herself first, if that was the only thing that could prevent it. Life would not be worth living without Noel, in any case. Living with the knowledge that she had caused his death would be far worse.

"We have lookouts posted about Lunnon. If Paxton returns to Town, we'll know it."

Mr. Richards snorted. "You and your cronies have not instilled in me a great faith in your abilities, Thirk. I should have handled the job myself."

The other man shrugged. "Mayhap you should. But mayhap you wouldn'ta had the stomach for it, neither."

"Fool!" Mr. Richards spat at him. "I've had more experience at—" He glanced at Rowena, who kept her eyes on the floor in apparent dejection, then lowered his voice so that she had to strain to hear it. "I've killed more men than you've picked pockets. One hundred times as many, if you count those the French managed for me during the war. Don't talk to me about 'stomach.' "

The ragged man Thirk backed away, apparently shaken. "Well, all ri' then. I'll, ah, just see if any of our lads have anything to report." He moved to the door.

Mr. Richards turned away from him with a sneer. "As you will. Miss Riverstone, why so glum? Did you not once express to me a desire for adventure?"

Rowena looked up, trying to keep both fear and loathing from her face. "I did, though I had hoped to be an active participant in it. Can I not help in whatever you are planning?"

He narrowed his eyes at her through the gloom. "Do you really have no idea? Has Paxton said nothing to you?"

"Paxton?" she repeated with what she thought credible-sounding surprise. "Noel Paxton? What has he to do with this?"

"What indeed." A grim smile twisted his mouth. "If I believed—" He broke off at the sound of voices at the door. "Yes, what is it?"

"Blind beggar says he's heard something," Thirk replied, coming back into the room. "Someone telling someone else to take a message to Mr. Paxton."

Mr. Richards rounded on the other man at the door, the beggar Rowena had noticed earlier, in his tattered infantry uniform and day's growth of beard, the dirty red cloth bound across his eyes. "What did they say?" he demanded. "Their exact words."

The blind man cringed away at Mr. Richards' tone, but Thirk seized his arm to prevent him from leaving. "Just you up and answer," he told him.

"It . . . it was a man and a lad," he finally said in a weak, quavering voice that spoke of long illness. "The man did most o' the talkin.' "

"And what did he say?" Mr. Richards bit out each word.

"Lessee . . . 'Get you to Hardwyck Hall,' he said, 'and tell Mr. Paxton where they are. I'll go meself to Bow Street.' I'm guessin' he means to fetch the Runners," the old man added.

Mr. Richards cursed. "How long ago was this?"

The beggar shrugged his stooped shoulders. "Mayhap an hour? Mebbe less."

"Then we don't have much time. Even if Paxton was dispatched, the Runners could arrive at any moment. Come along, Miss Riverstone."

Rowena had been watching the blind beggar closely as he gave his account. Something, she was not sure what, seemed slightly off about him. At Mr. Richards' command, she rose and moved closer, covertly studying the old man.

His hands she realized with a shock as she drew level with him. He twisted them together, and they were disguised by a thick layer of dirt, but they were not the wasted hands of an old man. Instead, they looked strong and smooth. She glanced up at his scruffy face and saw a wisp of chestnut hair peeping from beneath his knitted cap. Surely, it couldn't be—?

Quickly, she turned back to Mr. Richards. "Where will we go now? Have the Spenceans another meeting place, one the Runners won't find? We don't dare let them stop us now. Too many people stand to benefit by your success."

"Precisely," he agreed, giving her a speculative

glance and a slight smile. "If no one is here when they arrive, they will have no evidence beyond a serving man's word. Which means you'll have to come with us, old man," he said to the beggar.

The old man shuffled forward most convincingly, barking his toes on the door frame, even though Rowena was fairly certain he was no more blind than he was old. "But how will I find my way back?" he whined.

"That's none of my concern. Thirk, turn the horses around."

While the other man did as he was bid, Mr. Richards grasped Rowena's arm with one hand and the beggar's arm with the other and led them both from the room. Thirk made a difficult business of turning the curricle around in the narrow alley, while Mr. Richards looked on in growing impatience.

"Here, here, let me do it," he finally exclaimed. "You watch these two."

Thirk jumped down and Mr. Richards released his two prisoners. Rowena, alert for any move the false beggar might make, was ready when he acted. The moment his arm was released, he turned swiftly. Catching him totally by surprise, he knocked Mr. Richards to the ground. Rowena dove to the side, evading Thirk's lunge in her direction.

" 'Ere, now, none o' that!" Thirk cried, reaching inside his coat as Mr. Richards struggled to his feet. At the same time, the "beggar" tore the bandage from his eyes and pulled a pistol from beneath his rags.

Mr. Richards stared. "Paxton! How—?"

Before he could finish his question, Thirk pulled out his own pistol, leveling it at Noel—who fired without hesitation. Thirk crumpled to the ground. Richards lunged for Noel, but Rowena snapped out of her shock at the violence she had just witnessed and shoved him from behind.

"Good girl," said Noel in his normal voice, pulling a second pistol from his tattered coat. "You've just helped to apprehend the Black Bishop, one of the most dangerous men in Europe."

Mr. Richards glared up at him. "You've no proof. I made sure of that."

Noel raised a brow. "I believe I have more proof than I need, actually. Your man Eddie is in the custody of the Foreign Office even now, along with that poor coachman you duped. Unfortunately for you, he seems a patriotic sort. And then there are your letters, to your father and to Miss Riverstone. Remember, we have several you sent during the war, when you were pretending to work for England."

"And there was his plot to kill you, as well," Rowena added. "I heard him discussing it with Thirk, here."

Richards shot her a venomous glance. "I should have known better than to believe for a moment you were sympathetic to my cause. Women can't be trusted, especially women who fancy themselves clever."

"In Miss Riverstone's case, I'd say it's a good deal more than fancy," Noel said with a smile for her that set her heart racing, despite the grime and stubble marring his face. "She's the most intelligent woman I've ever known. Indeed, one of the most intelligent persons I've known, of either sex."

"There's plenty you don't know," Mr. Richards

spat. "I have friends, supporters. Your life won't be worth a fig if you kill me."

Noel shrugged. "Oh, I don't plan to kill you myself. Kemp should be arriving momentarily with a contingent from the Foreign Office. I rather doubt you'll escape the noose, however. As for friends, you've killed several of mine. I consider myself finally avenged."

"Several?" Mr. Richards looked genuinely curious, though not at all repentant. "I heard you knew Geraint—"

"And Burroughs and Thompson—perhaps better known to you as Graywolf and the Red Boar." Noel's expression was grimmer than Rowena had ever seen it, his eyes bleak with remembered grief.

Sudden understanding broke across Richards' face. "Puss in Boots!" he exclaimed. "I should have guessed it."

Noel sketched a cynical bow. "At your service. Or, rather, at my country's. Ah, here they come now." He turned to greet his manservant Kemp, who rounded the corner just then with six sturdy, uniformed men behind him.

"All's well," Noel told them. "Take these two in and I'll join you once I've had a chance to get Miss Riverstone safely home and clean myself up."

He supervised the binding and bundling of Richards and Thirk into the curricle, then turned to Rowena.

"Are you certain you are all right?"

"I'm fine," she replied, staring at him with wonder. "You . . . you were a spy during the war?"

He nodded, meeting her eyes with a crooked grin.

"And never set foot in Canada, I fear. I apologize for the falsehoods I told you."

"It seems they were justified." She could not stop staring at him as she fit all the pieces together in her mind. She remembered how deftly he had unlocked the ballroom door yesterday—was it only yesterday?—and another suspicion formed.

Lowering her voice, she asked, "Might you also be the Saint of Seven Dials?"

"I did say you were the most intelligent woman I've ever known." His grin widened.

Now it all made sense—his evasiveness about the investigation, the return of her mother's jewels, Noel's irritation when she had praised Mr. Richards for his daring as the Saint.

"So I can now give credit where credit is due," she said, smiling back at him. "It appears I have a debt of gratitude to repay."

He leaned down to brush her lips with his. "And I believe I know just what payment I will demand. But first, let's get you back to Hardwyck Hall. We both have some explaining to do—and an announcement to make."

Epilogue

Rowena wondered whether anyone had ever been happier than she was today—her wedding day. Noel's estate of Tidebourne was charming, similar in size to River Chase, but far more welcoming, in her opinion. When they had arrived at the rambling manor house yesterday, she had instantly fallen in love with it.

Now, less than an hour before the wedding, she was attempting to give a truncated version of the events of two weeks ago to Noel's twin sister Holly, who had traveled from Yorkshire with her husband, the Marquess of Vandover, to attend her brother's nuptials.

"So when Noel arrived, Kemp had already persuaded a blind beggar to exchange clothing with Noel. His impersonation was flawless—I did not recognize him myself for a full five minutes, though I was in the same room with him."

Holly, a handsome black-haired woman, laughed.

"Yes, Noel always loved disguises, even as a boy—we both did, actually. I believe it's the main reason he was so determined to become a spy during the war. So now this traitor is under arrest?"

Rowena nodded. "He will stand trial soon. Had I known the full measure of his crimes, I confess I would never have been so foolish to go driving with him that day—though I suppose that helped to speed his capture."

Just then a curly-headed toddler ran up. "Mama! Mama! Come see puppies!"

Holly knelt down with some difficulty, as she was in the latter stages of pregnancy. "Yes, Cliff, we'll go see them as soon as the wedding is over." She ruffled her son's hair.

Rowena watched with a lump—a happy lump!—in her throat. Three-year-old Clifton looked remarkably like his uncle Noel—like a child of her own might look one day. They had not yet spoken of children, but she was certain Noel would be a wonderful father, after seeing him play with his nephew last night.

Noel's mother and older sister, Blanche, bustled in then, along with Pearl, to help with Rowena's final preparations. Mrs. Paxton chattered in French-accented English with the occasional French phrase thrown in, while Blanche devoted herself to little Clifton, cuddling and cooing to him.

"You will wish to leave off the spectacles, *non*?" Mrs. Paxton asked as Pearl adjusted Rowena's veil.

She shook her head. "No, I promised Noel I would not. He says he likes them."

Mrs. Paxton clucked her tongue, but Pearl gave Rowena a quick hug. "You are a very lucky woman, you know," Pearl said. "You have found a man who loves you for yourself, and who will not attempt to change you into something you are not."

"Yes," Rowena said with a smile, "I know." Nor would she attempt to change Noel, as she had once thought to do.

It seemed but a moment later that she was entering the little village church where she and Noel were to be married by special license. He had not been willing to wait the extra week for banns to be read—and, in truth, neither had she.

Noel stood by the altar at the front, looking outrageously handsome in his tailored deep blue coat and breeches, his chestnut hair curling roguishly about his ears. His eyes met hers and he smiled, a smile of such infinite promise that it was all Rowena could do not to run down the aisle to him. Her stately procession seemed almost painfully slow, so eager was she to join him.

They repeated their vows steadily, gazing into each other's eyes throughout the brief service. The moment they were pronounced man and wife, Noel gathered her into his arms and kissed her, right there in the church, in full view of the assembly.

Rowena melted against him, but finally the tittering behind them pulled her to her senses. "Later," she whispered.

He answered with a suggestive wink. "I'll take that as a promise. You still owe me, you know."

"And I plan to pay you in full, in only a few hours." Anticipation made her giddy, and she knew she was smiling like a fool as she proceeded back down the aisle on his arm.

She didn't care. The one man whose opinion she valued considered her the most intelligent of women. What others thought of her mattered not at all.

Once out on the lawn under the warm September sunshine, they were surrounded by family and friends. Sir Nelson came forward to embrace his sister, while Noel was congratulated by Lord Hardwyck, Lord Marcus, Lord Peter and Harry Thatcher.

"You're a lucky man," Lord Peter said, clapping Noel on the shoulder. "Now it only remains for Harry and me to find our perfect mates."

Mr. Thatcher laughed. "You know my feelings about matrimony. I've no plans to marry, ever—whatever the inducement. And as for you, I can't imagine any woman living up to your exacting standards."

"Perfection or nothing," Lord Peter agreed with a grin.

"Then you're in no more danger than I."

"If you will excuse us, gentlemen?" Noel put an arm around Rowena's waist and led her away from the throng, toward the carriage waiting to take them back to Tidebourne. "Harry and Peter ought not to tempt fate like that," he said to her with a chuckle.

"Why?" she asked. "Did you once say something similar?"

He smiled down into her eyes and her heart turned over. "If I did, I was speaking from profound ignorance. Of course, how could I know I *would* meet the perfect woman, one who combines intelligence and passion in one beautiful package?"

"Passion?" she asked, grinning up at him.

"Mm. Were you not passionate about all of the causes you espoused? You certainly sounded so."

"Perhaps," she agreed. "But I was still very innocent then. Now I intend to turn my passions to other things."

"Dare I hope I might be one of those things?" he asked, his hazel eyes darkening with desire.

"Indeed," she said, letting all the love she felt for him shine from her own eyes. "I plan to adopt you as my pet cause."

"I believe I like the sound of that," he said, pulling her to him for a kiss that promised years of passion to come.

Winter snow is sure to melt with these hot romances from Avon Books

CONFESSIONS OF A SCOUNDREL by Karen Hawkins
An Avon Romantic Treasure

Legend says that whomever possesses the St. John talisman ring will find their one true love. With the ring in his pocket, renowned scoundrel Brandon St. John can't decide whether it is a blessing or a curse, for the delectable Lady Verena Westforth vows she will not be another of his "conquests" . . . even as she melts in his arms.

THE WAY YOU LOOK TONIGHT by MacKenzie Taylor
An Avon Contemporary Romance

A "do-gooder with a bad-girl streak," Jorie Morrison knows Simon Grant is all wrong for her. He's stuffy, serious, and to top it off, corporate! But sometimes, the wrong man couldn't be more right . . .

A NECESSARY BRIDE by Debra Mullins
An Avon Romance

Miss Margaret Stanton-Lynch intends to enjoy the Season without the hindrance of an unwanted romance. Though Meg refuses to be tied down before she fully explores what life has to offer, the dashing Earl of Rathmore has another idea—to tempt this spirited beauty to be his bride.

TO WED A STRANGER by Edith Layton
An Avon Romance

An *arranged* marriage for London's most desired lady? The *ton* is aghast! The exquisite Annabelle has been disillusioned by love, but she can't deny the unexpected passion discovered in the arms of her attractive new husband. Dare she trust her heart again?

Have you ever dreamed of writing a romance?

And have you ever wanted to get a romance published?

Perhaps you have always wondered how to become an Avon romance writer?
We are now seeking the best and brightest undiscovered voices. We invite you to send us your query letter to
avonromance@harpercollins.com

What do you need to do?

Please send no more than two pages telling us about your book. We'd like to know its setting—is it contemporary or historical—and a bit about the hero, heroine, and what happens to them.

Then, if it is right for Avon we'll ask to see part of the manuscript. Remember, it's important that you have material to send, in case we want to see your story quickly.

Of course, there are no guarantees of publication, but you never know unless you try!

We know there is new talent just waiting to be found! Don't hesitate . . . send us your query letter today.

The Editors
Avon Romance

MSR 0302

Avon Romances— the best in exceptional authors and unforgettable novels!

THE RAKE: LESSONS IN LOVE by Suzanne Enoch
0-380-82082-X/ $5.99 US/ $7.99 Can

THE MAIDEN WARRIOR by Mary Reed McCall
0-380-81787-X/ $5.99 US/ $7.99 Can

LONE ARROW'S PRIDE by Karen Kay
0-380-82066-8/ $5.99 US/ $7.99 Can

A GAME OF SCANDAL by Kathryn Smith
0-06-050226-6/ $5.99 US/ $7.99 Can

THE ROSE AND THE SHIELD by Sara Bennett
0-06-000270-0/ $5.99 US/ $7.99 Can

A CHANCE AT LOVE by Beverly Jenkins
0-06-050229-0/ $5.99 US/ $7.99 Can

ALL MY DESIRE by Margaret Moore
0-380-82053-6/ $5.99 US/ $7.99 Can

CHEROKEE WARRIORS: THE LOVER by Genell Dellin
0-06-000146-1/ $5.99 US/ $7.99 Can

HIGHLAND ROGUES: THE WARRIOR BRIDE by Lois Greiman
0-06-009218-1/ $5.99 US/ $7.99 Can

HIS BRIDE by Gayle Callen
0-380-82110-9/ $5.99 US/ $7.99 Can

THE MACKENZIES: COLE by Ana Leigh
0-380-82009-9/ $5.99 US/ $7.99 Can

HER SCANDALOUS INTENTIONS by Sari Robins
0-06-050353-X/ $5.99 US/ $7.99 Can

Available wherever books are sold or please call 1-800-331-3761 to order.

ROM 0902